I0806423

אורות
OROT

מגיד
MAGGID
אורות
OROT

אורות

א) אורות מאופל. ב) אורות התחיה.

מאת רבנו

אברהם יצחק הכהן קוק

הוצאת „דגל ירושלים"

(ע"י לשכת המרכז של ההסתדרות ירושלים)

ירושלים

התר"פ.

—בדפוס סלומון הי"ו.—

Title page of original 1920 edition of *Orot* (Jerusalem, 5680)

Rabbi Abraham Isaac Hakohen Kook

הרב אברהם יצחק הכהן קוק

אורות

OROT

The Original 1920 Version

INTRODUCTION, TRANSLATION AND NOTES

Bezalel Naor

Orot

Maggid Books

Orot
Rabbi Abraham Isaac Hakohen Kook

First Maggid Modern Classics Edition, bilingual edition 2022

Maggid Books
An imprint of Koren Publishers Jerusalem Ltd
POB 8531, New Milford, CT 06776-8531, USA
& POB 4044, Jerusalem 9104001, Israel
www.korenpub.com

Introduction, Translation and Notes © Bezalel Naor 2014

The publication of this book was made possible
through the generous support of *Torah Education in Israel* and *Orot*

All rights reserved. No part of this publication may be reproduced
stored in a retrieval system or transmitted in any form or by
any means, electronic, mechanical, photocopying or otherwise
without the prior permission of the publisher, except in the case
of brief quotations embedded in critical articles or reviews

ISBN 978-1-59264-718-7, *hardcover*

A CIP catalogue record for this title is
available from the British Library

Printed and bound in the United States

In memory of my dear father Samuel Nyer, a courageous fighter in the United States Army against the Nazis in France in World War II. As an advance scout behind enemy lines, he was offered by his commanding officer a fake "dog-tag" inscribed with "P" (for Protestant) to substitute for the true metal identity plate with the "H" (for Hebrew) and *mezuzah* that he wore around his neck. The thinking was that should he be captured by the Germans, his Jewish identity would surely sentence him to death, whereas feigning Protestant identity, he would survive the war in a Prisoner of War camp. Father's response, offered immediately and unflinchingly, was: "Thank you very much, Sir, for your kind offer. But I was born a Jew and will die a Jew!"

My father, my teacher, Shmuel ben Shaul, went to his eternity on the twentieth of Iyyar, 5771 [2011], with the setting of the sun.

May his soul be bound in the bond of eternal life.

נר זכרון

לנשמת אבי מורי

שמואל בן שאול

שהלך לעולמו ביום כ״ף לחודש אייר, שנת ה׳תשע״א.

שקעה נפשו עם דמדומי חמה.

תהי נפשו צרורה בצרור החיים.

Bezalel Naor

לזכר נשמת

ספרא וסייפא

הרב חיים אורי
בן הרב משה ליפשיץ

אדמו״ר מוויעליפאלי-פילדלפיה,

ולמעלה בקודש בן אחר בן עד

הרב אריה ליבוש ליפשיץ

בעל מחבר ספר **אריה דבי עילאה**,

חתן הגה״ק ר׳ משה טייטלבוים מאוהעל

בעל מחבר ספר **ישמח משה**,

זכר צדיקים לברכה.

בנעוריו שימש את הרב מטעפליק ר׳ שמשון אהרן פולונסקי

והוסמך להוראה על ידו, ועל ידי הרב איסר זלמן מלצר,

הרב יוסף גרשון הורוביץ והרב מיכל דיין, זצ״ל.

נולד בעיר הקודש בירושלים, כל ימיו ערגה אליה,

ושם מנוחתו כבוד.

נלב״ע א׳ דראש חדש כסלו (ל׳ חשון) ה׳תשס״ג

תהי נשמתו צרורה בצרור החיים

הונצח על-ידי צאצאיו

לעילו נשמת האישה החשובה

מרת שרה סטפנסקי ע"ה

אשת הרב אליעזר שליט"א
בת הרב חיים אורי זצ"ל
למשפחת ליפשיץ
נו"נ לבעל האריה דבי עילאי

ולמעלה בקודש
שמן תורק שמה
רואה בטוב עינה
תורה במסירות קיימה
שמחת חיים מהותה
רוח נשברה החזיקה
מקבל את כל אדם לימודה
שמרה לפיה כל ימיה
דבר אמת בלבבה
השתתפה בשמחת ובצרת זולתה

Dedicated by her children Estee & David
and grandchildren Ariella, Chaim Uri, Elianna & Lola Stefansky

Contents

Orot

Abbreviations

AT	*ʻArfilei Tohar*
IHR	*Iggerot ha-RAYaH*
KG	*Kol Gadol*
KS	*Kol Shofar*
LNY	*Li-Netivot Yisrael*
MBK	*Malki ba-Kodesh*
OHK	*Orot ha-Kodesh*
SK	*Shemonah Kevatsim*

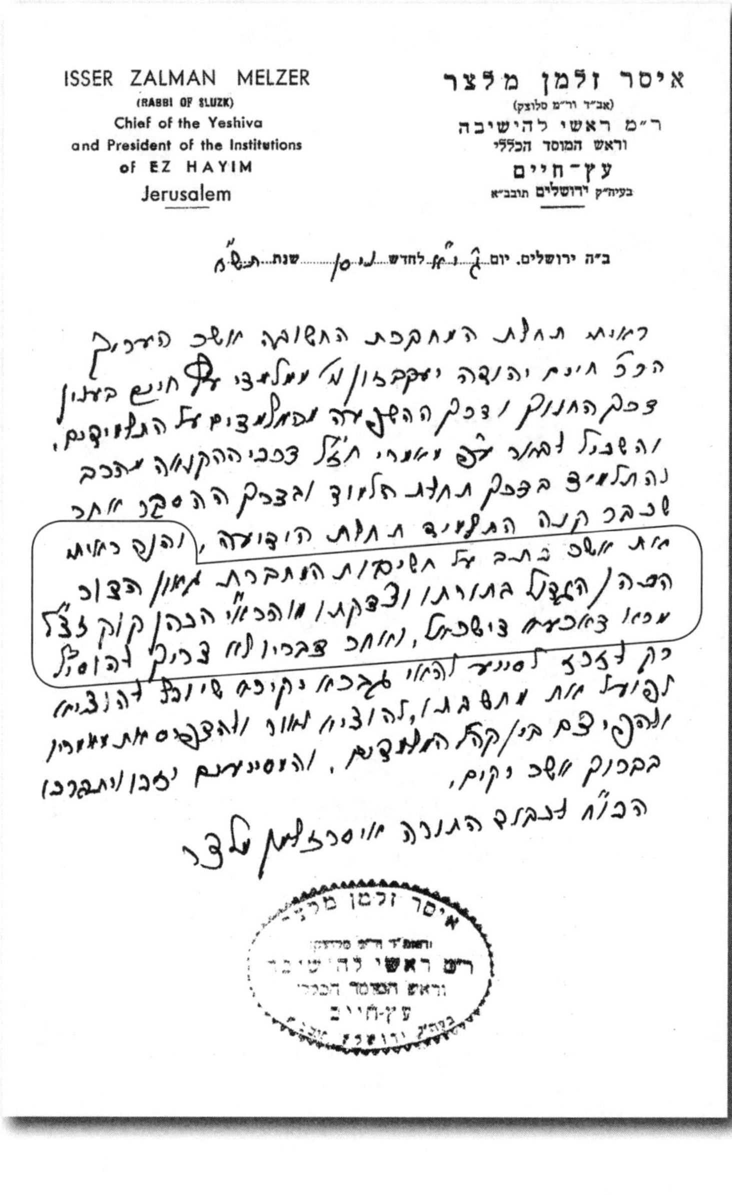

ISSER ZALMAN MELZER
(RABBI OF SLUZK)
Chief of the Yeshiva
and President of the Institutions
of EZ HAYIM
Jerusalem

איסר זלמן מלצר
(אב״ד ור״מ סלוצק)
ר״מ ראשי להישיבה
וראש המוסד הכללי
עץ־חיים
בעיה״ק ירושלים תובב״א

ב״ה ירושלים. יום ג׳ י״א לחדש ניסן שנת תש״ח

והנה ראיתי את
אשר כתב על
חשיבות המחברת
גאון הדור, הכהן
הגדול בתורתו
וצדקתו, מוהרא״י
הכהן קוק זצ״ל,
מרא דארעא
דישראל, ואחר
דבריו לא צריך
להוסיף

Formal endorsement (*haskamah*) of an educational manual in the hand of Rabbi Isser Zalman Meltzer (1870-1953), Rosh Yeshiva of Slutsk and Etz Ḥayim, Jerusalem. Rabbi Meltzer writes that his endorsement is superfluous as the booklet was already approved by "the genius of the generation, the high priest in his Torah and righteousness, our teacher R[av] A[vraham] Y[itsḥak] Hakohen Kook, of blessed memory, Master of the Land of Israel." The letter is dated "Tuesday, 11 Nissan, 5708 [1948]," thirteen years after Rav Kook's passing.

Orot

New Introduction

Twenty years, an entire generation, have passed since my English translation of Rav Kook's *Orot* appeared in print. Since then, interest in Rav Kook has grown exponentially. I would like to think that my own labors in disseminating Rav Kook's teachings have somehow contributed to this process. But I know that other, more powerful sociological factors were at work here. The laying of Islamist terror at the very doorstep of Western civilization has produced a growing anxiety, a feeling of malaise and foreboding of apocalyptic proportions. Within our own Jewish world, what some perceive as the failure of the traditional *Ḥaredi* lifestyle (in both its Ḥasidic and yeshivah varieties) to function as a viable system, has also contributed to producing an intellectual climate not radically dissimilar from that which prevailed in Rav Kook's time, and that engendered his epoch-making *Orot*.

The book emerged on the heels of World War One, a war that many viewed as the Apocalypse. Especially Jews, who suffered enormous loss of life and the uprooting of entire communities in Eastern Europe, viewed World War One as the "War of Gog and Magog." The air was rife with a sense of Messianic imminence.

Within the setting of *Erets Yisrael*, there was a feeling on the part of many—certainly the members of the New Yishuv centered in Jaffa (the precursor of Tel-Aviv), but also some of the most creative elements within the Old Yishuv of Jerusalem—that the traditional rabbinic establishment was morally (besides financially) bankrupt. In this time and place, Rav Kook emerged as a breath of fresh air and as a beacon of light, or perhaps better stated, a harbinger of Messianic light (*'oro shel mashi'aḥ*). His *Orot* offered a new synthesis, at terms with the latest developments and most pressing problems of the modern era, and suggesting the possibility of unprecedented spiritual heights culminating in *nevu'ah*, prophecy, no less!

Understandably, the attention of Israel's youth was grabbed by this small powder-keg of a book, while their elders (or at least some of them) viewed the book with consternation, typecasting its author as a modern-day Pied Piper, leading Israel's youth astray.

As we have said, historical conditions today are remarkably similar to those of the 1920s when *Orot* appeared on the scene. I have no doubt that its reissuing will bring light to many Jewish homes and hearts, now as then.

Since the first printing of my English version, I have had the opportunity to read several documents directly pertaining to the historical backdrop of *Orot*. I have seen a handwritten note that Rav Kook made available to the Rebbe of Gur, in which he expressed his regret if certain passages in his book *Orot*, due to their laconic style and brevity of language, were found objectionable by some.[1]

[1]Two versions of this note were offered at auction: one in the hand of the Gerrer Rebbe, Abraham Mordechai Alter; the other in Rav Kook's own hand. The facsimiles provided in the auction catalog have been blurred so that several words are illegible. According to the catalog description, the essential difference between the two versions is that in the Gerrer version, Rav Kook actually nullifies the offending passages in

---

his work ("הנני מבטל דברים ולשונות הללו"); in Rav Kook's version, he merely regrets that he did not make his meaning more comprehensible ("מצטער אני על קיצור הלשון באלו המקומות"), while maintaining the veracity and validity of the thoughts expressed there. See *Asufah* Catalog of December 2009, p. 107, Lot 518. (The sale took place on 3.12.2009 in Jerusalem.)

In the *Asufah* transcript, the Gerrer Rebbe's version reads:

"כאשר שמעתי שנמצאו בחיבורים שלי במקומות שונים אשר הגם שלפי דעתי כוונתי לשם שמים, אולם לפי דברי רבנים גדולים יש במקומות הנ"ל לשונות שיש בהם חו[ס] [ו]שלו[ם] חי[לול] הש[ם] ומיעוט כבוד שמים, לזאת למען כבוד שמים שיתרבה, **הנני מבטל דברים ולשונות הללו.**"

Par contre, Rav Kook's version reads:

"כאשר שמעתי שנמצאים בחבורים שלי במקומות שונים אשר הגם שידעתי שהם כולם דברי אמת וצדק לאמתה של תורה, אולם מפני קצור הלשון קמו עליהם מערערים, לומר שיש בהם לשונות שמביאים לידי חי[לול] הש[ם] ומיעוט כבוד שמים, לכן אני מודיע בזה למען כבוד שמים שיתרבה, כי **מצטער אני על קיצור הלשון באלו המקומות.**"

Of interest in this connection, is the New Year greeting in the Gerrer Rebbe's hand to Rabbi Ḥarlap (*Asufah* Catalog, p. 126, Lot 555), which evinces the Rebbe's sincere friendship for Rabbi Ḥarlap; and the letter of Rabbi Ḥanokh Tsevi Hakohen Levin, Rabbi of Bendin (and brother-in-law of the Gerrer Rebbe) to Rabbi Ḥarlap, dated 5681 [1921], requesting that Rabbi Ḥarlap prevail upon Rav Kook to retract (*Asufah* Catalog, p. 131, Lot 565).

A similar thread runs through the letter of Rabbi Menaḥem Mendel Alter of Pabianice (dated "*Tsom Gedalyah*, 5688," i.e., 1927) to Rabbi Ḥarlap, remonstrating with him to convince his soul-brother Rav Kook to nullify those expressions in his writings that have caused so much consternation to the pious ("הנהו מבטל בביטול גמור אותם הלשונות במאמריו"). Rabbi M.M. Alter was the brother of the Gerrer Rebbe. What prompted the Rabbi of Pabianice to write at this time was the humiliation caused his brother the Rebbe of Gur by the zealots of Jerusalem (*Sivan* 5687/1927) and in the aftermath, the umbrage taken by the Polish rabbinate. In order to defuse the potentially explosive situation and prevent further escalation of hostilities, the Rabbi of Pabianice suggested that Rav Kook issue a retraction of the objectionable passages in *Orot*, perhaps in the form of a personal letter to a friend in the Diaspora, such as himself. See *Eshel Avraham*: Memorial Volume for Rabbi Abraham Elkanah Kahana Shapira (Jerusalem 2010), pp. 740-741.

In this case, Rav Kook (once having been shown by Rabbi Ḥarlap the letter addressed to him) responded directly to the Rabbi of Pabianice:

> I almost never wrote things for publication. Rather, on occasion I put down in brief some of my *pensees*; afterward, if members of my household or those close to me desired to publish them, I saw no need to stop them. God knows that my entire intention is to benefit the public and to draw hearts close to their Father in Heaven. The thought never occurred to me that someone would bend my words and turn them destructive. Now that that which is improper was perpetrated by the other side, and the innocent have been snared by them in the trap of provocation, I certainly regret that my words did not come as explicit

I have also read a communiqué from the Sephardic Chief Rabbi (*Rishon le-Zion*) Jacob Meir to Rabbi Joseph Ḥayyim Sonnenfeld, Rabbi of the separatist *'Edah Ḥaredit*, reporting his conversation with his Ashkenazic counterpart, Chief Rabbi Kook, in which Rav Kook explained from where the funds for the release of Rabbis Meir Heller (Semnitzer) and Joseph Hoffman—two *kana'im* (zealots) jailed for their defamation of Rav Kook—could come.[2]

> as they are in the innermost heart, for they are all directed to the service of the Lord and His fear.
>
> I pray that we not err in our language, and that our mouths not utter something counter to its will, but rather that our expression be clear, to sanctify His great name and to enhance and strengthen Torah, as is the wish of all those who fear the Lord…
>
> I think that these words of mine will set at ease his pure mind, as well as the mind of all those who truly, sincerely seek the truth…
>
> Abraham Isaac Hakohen Kook
>
> (*Eshel Avraham* [Jerusalem 2010], pp. 741-742)

The letter is datelined "Jerusalem, 28 Kislev, 5688," i.e., 1927. What we have, in effect, is a reiteration of Rav Kook's earlier note of 1921 to the Gerrer Rebbe. Neither the position of the Gerrer contingent, nor that of Rav Kook had budged in six years.

[2]Datelined "Jerusalem, 20 Tishri 5683 [1922]," the letter addressed to Rabbi Joseph Hayyim Sonnenfeld reads:

> I approached my counterpart Rav Kook to wipe clean the amount of 420 g[rushim] that R. M[eir] Semnitzer and R. J[oseph] Hoffman yet owe the [British Mandatory] Court. He replied that he does not have on hand money to pay the above amount. However two or three days ago, he sent His Honor [i.e., Rabbi Sonnenfeld] the amount of 4 pounds that came to him in order that His Honor [i.e., Rabbi Sonnenfeld] disburse them as he sees fit. He [i.e., Rav Kook] thinks that from these monies it is possible to take out an amount such that the rabbis mentioned above no longer be detained in prison.
>
> With great respect and holiday blessings for good life and peace,
>
> Jacob Meir

(See the facsimile of the manuscript in the collection of Benzion Fishoff, *Mikhtavim ve-Igrot Kodesh* II, ed. David Abraham Mandelbaum [New York, 5770/2010], p. 114 [transcription on p. 115].)

From an unexpected source we have confirmation of the cordial relations between Rabbi Ḥayyim Sonnenfeld and Rav Kook's Sephardic counterpart in the Chief Rabbinate, the *"Rishon le-Zion"* Rabbi Jacob Meir. In a tape-recorded interview, Rabbi Amram Blau, founder of the Neturei Karta, revealed that at the funeral of Rabbi Sonnenfeld in 1932, the organizers, the leadership of the separatist *'Edah Ḥaredit,*

In my original introduction I made mention of the booklets *Kol Shofar* and *Kol Gadol* released by the *kana'im* or zealots of Jerusalem in the course of their unceasing campaign against Rav Kook. (It is now public knowledge that the earlier *Kol Shofar* was the work of Rabbi Akiva Porush, and the later *Kol Gadol* that of Rabbi Meir Heller [Semnitzer].) Recently, I came across a curiosity, a highly sophisticated diatribe against Rav Kook masquerading as a booklet in praise of the Rav! There appeared in Jerusalem in 1926 a twenty-page booklet by Ḥayyim Hakohen Horowitz entitled *Tosefot Ḥayyim* purporting to be a favorable summation of Rav Kook's philosophy. So insidious is the booklet that Rav Kook's biographer of late, Simḥa Raz, was evidently fooled by the contents, reproducing the title page of the booklet (which is quite laudatory) in his handsome, photographic work *Mal'akhim ki-Bnei Adam* (translated into English as *An Angel Among Men*)![3]

Over the past generation I have come to appreciate more the complexity of the controversy that engulfed Jerusalem during Rav Kook's tenure. In some cases, the testimony was presented to me orally by descendants of the rabbis who were involved in the controversy. In other cases, the testimony was written by the participants themselves. On the one hand, I learned that the esteem of Rabbi Pinḥas Epstein (member of the *Beit Din Tsedek* of the *'Edah Ḥaredit*) for Rav Ḥarlap ran so high that even

---

honored Rabbi Jacob Meir to eulogize the deceased, but he was prevented from doing so by the heckling of a solitary youthful individual (named by Blau). See *Mishnato shel Rabbi Amram*, ed. Krauss (Jerusalem, 2012), p. 130.

[3]See Ḥayyim Hakohen Horowitz (ed.), *Tosefot Ḥayyim* (alternate title *Viku'aḥ ve-ha-Shalom*) (Jerusalem: Rohald, Tammuz 5686/1926). One may view this parody at www.hebrewbooks.org. Evidently the bibliographer Ḥayyim Dov Friedberg was also unaware of the true contents of the booklet. See Ḥ.D. Friedberg, *Beit 'Eked Sefarim*, no. 498-ת, s.v. *Tosefot Ḥayyim*. Rivkah Schatz grasped the parodical nature of *Tosefot Ḥayyim* (aided by the fact that it is mentioned in Rabbi Meir Heller-Semnitzer's manuscript). See Rivkah Shatz, *"Reshit ha-massa' neged ha-rav kuk"* ["The Beginning of the Campaign Against Rav Kook"], *Molad*, Vol. VI (XXX), No. 32 (242), *Tevet* 5734/ December 1974, p. 261. See now Rabbi Yosef Leib Zussman, *Mi-Beḥirei Tsaddikaya* (Jerusalem, 5767/2007), p. 196.

after the terrible controversy, Rabbi Epstein would stand close enough to Rav Ḥarlap at the Western Wall (*Kotel ha-Ma'aravi*) that he could utter in the latter's ear: *"Shalom 'alekha mori ve-rabbi"* ("Peace be unto you, my rabbi and teacher").[4] A revelation concerning Rabbi Ḥayyim Mordechai ("Reb Mottel") of Slonim remains a riddle. The Rebbe of Slonim was one of Rav Kook's most outspoken critics. Yet it is known to the Rebbe's family that after Rav Kook's passing, the Rebbe foreswore eating meat for a period of time.[5] On the other hand, I discovered in the published letters of the *"Mal'akh"* (the "Angel") as he was referred to by his followers, i.e., Rabbi Abraham Dov Baer Hakohen Levin, that his opposition to Rav Kook was so intense that he wrote to his Jerusalem correspondent Rabbi Asher Zelig Margoliot that the *Beit Din* (Court) of Rabbi Sonnenfeld should decree upon Rav Kook…[6]

On April 1, 1925 Jerusalem was the scene of a gala ceremony upon the official opening of Hebrew University on Mount Scopus. In attendance were notables from around the globe, both Jewish and non-Jewish (including the esteemed Lord Balfour, Sir Herbert Samuel and Lord Allenby). Rav Kook spoke at length. The topic of his talk remains a sore point to this day. He concluded his lengthy address with the verse "For from Zion shall go forth Torah and the word of the Lord

---

[4]Heard from Rabbi Zevulun Charlop *shelit"a* (grandson of Rav Harlap).

[5]Heard from Rabbi Yosef Leib Hamburger *shelit"a*. Rabbi Hamburger's maternal grandfather, Rabbi David Werner, was the nephew of Rabbi Ḥayyim Mordechai of Slonim. Rabbi David Werner's mother, Dinah nee Kastelanets (wife of Rabbi Simḥa Bunem Werner, a prominent Jerusalem *dayyan*) was the elder sister of Rabbi Ḥayyim Mordechai Kastelanets, Rebbe of Slonim. Rabbi David Werner studied in Merkaz Harav and received rabbinic ordination from both Rabbis Kook and Sonnenfeld. Rabbi Werner went on to serve as Rabbi of Providence, Rhode Island.

[6]See *Otsar Igrot Kodesh* (Brooklyn, 5749 / 1989), Letter 85 (p. 86).

Rabbi Levin was a Ḥabad Ḥasid who attracted a following of disciples from Yeshiva Torah ve-Da'at in Brooklyn. These American youngsters venerated Rabbi Levin as a Rebbe in his own right. In his extreme views, Rabbi Levin interfaced with Rabbi Asher Zelig Margoliot of Jerusalem, who in turn served as "point man" of Rabbi Ḥayyim El'azar Spira, Rebbe of Munkacs (author Responsa *Minḥat El'azar*).

from Jerusalem." Those determined to calumniate Rav Kook took this concluding remark out of context, as if to say that Rav Kook saw in this secular institution fulfillment of the prophecy of Isaiah. The truth is quite the opposite. The full text of Rav Kook's address has been preserved for posterity and is open to analysis.[7] The gist of Rav Kook's message was that there is danger inherent in secular studies, which is cause for concern, and that alongside this institution of a secular nature there must arise in Jerusalem a world-class yeshivah consecrated to sacred studies. Finally, Rav Kook expressed the hope that the people merit to see the rebuilding of the Holy Temple, and in the latter regard uttered the prophecy "For from Zion shall go forth Torah and the word of the Lord from Jerusalem."

Regarding this event, something has come down to us from Rabbi Jacob Moses Ḥarlap, eminent disciple of Rav Kook and Rosh Yeshivah of Merkaz Harav.[8] The original plan was that Rav Kook would be flanked at the ceremony by his entire *Beit Din* or ecclesiastical court, including Rabbi Hirsch (Tsevi) Pesaḥ Frank, et al. However as Divine Providence would have it, the automobile conveying Rav Kook's court broke down *en route* to Mount Scopus. And thus it came about that Rav Kook, representing the Orthodox Jews of Jerusalem, was left a lone warrior to battle the winds of secularism, and to be singled out by the *kana'im* (zealots) for calumny.

~

I conclude on an autobiographical note. As a boy growing up in the small Jewish community of Bangor, Maine, I discovered the book *Massa' Yehudah* by Rabbi Judah Leib (Louis) Seltzer, who had once served as Rabbi of Bangor (but more significantly, later served as Rabbi of Safed, Israel). At the time, I had no idea how prominently this little-known work would one day figure in my work of contextualizing

[7]See *Ma'amrei ha-Rayah* II (Jerusalem, 1984), pp. 306-308.

[8]This anecdote was told to the present writer by Rabbi Zevulun Charlop as heard from his grandfather Rabbi Jacob Moses Ḥarlap.

historically the *maḥloket* (controversy) surrounding Rav Kook's Jerusalem rabbinate in general, and brought to a head by publication of his book *Orot*, in particular.[9] (Such are the mysterious ways of *hashgaḥa peratit* or divine supervision.)

Printed in Safed in 1914, *Massa' Yehudah* contains valuable correspondence between Rabbi Seltzer, (who assisted Rabbi Jacob Ridbaz, Rabbi of Safed), and Rabbi Kook, then Rabbi of Jaffa. [10] Rabbi Seltzer defends the intransigence of the rabbinic establishment, while Rabbi Kook is critical thereof and makes the case for spiritual renascence.

The exchange between Rabbis Kook and Seltzer is highly instructive. As opposed to Rabbi Kook, who believed that Orthodoxy would survive its confrontation with modernity only if the inwardness

---

[9]Concerning Rabbi Seltzer's *Massa' Yehudah* see Rivkah Shatz, *"Reshit ha-massa' neged ha-rav kuk,"* pp. 251-252.

[10]There is a suspicious discrepancy between the text of Rav Kook's letter (of 25 or 28 Tevet, 5673/1913) as printed in Rabbi Seltzer's *Massa' Yehudah*, and the version transcribed in Rav Kook's collected letters, *Igrot ha-Rayah*. In *Massa' Yehudah* the sentence reads: "Orthodoxy provisions itself with vanities and false illusions that life and reality destroy (*Massa' Yehudah*, p. 45). In *Igrot ha-Rayah* the statement has been modified to read: "Orthodoxy, *in its negative war at present* (*be-milḥamtah ha-shelilit ka'et*), provisions itself…" (*Igrot ha-Rayah*, Vol. II, p. 124).

If the words did not occur in the original, then where did they come from? In the second letter of Rav Kook addressed to Rabbi Seltzer (dated 28 Ellul, 5673/1913), we read: "As long as Orthodoxy, *in its negative war at present*, stubbornly says, 'No, only Talmud and Codes, not Agadah, not Mussar, not Kabbalah, not Philosophy, not worldly knowledge, and not Ḥasidism'…" (*Massa Yehudah*, p. 55). Strangely enough, these mitigating words are lacking from the version printed in Rav Kook's collected letters: "As long as Orthodoxy stubbornly says, 'No…" (*Igrot ha-Rayah*, Vol. II, p. 232).

How does one account for this discrepancy? Either Rabbi Seltzer deliberately deleted the words in the first letter, "in its negative war at present" ("*be-milḥamtah ha-shelilit ka'et*"), or the opposite scenario—Rav Kook's son, Rav Zevi Yehudah Hakohen Kook, editor of the collection *Igrot ha-Rayah*, sought to tone down this sentence which Jerusalem's zealots had seized upon to fan the fires of controversy and to denigrate Rav Kook. (See Rivkah Schatz, *loc. cit.*; Yosef Moshe Sofer and Menaḥem Mendel Gerlitz, *Mara de-Ara' Yisrael* [biography of Rabbi Joseph Ḥayyim Sonnenfeld] [Jerusalem, 2003], Appendix to Chap. VI, facsimile no. 19, *"Kol Kore me-Heikhal."*) Assuming that this conjecture is correct, the phrase "in its negative war at present" was cut from the second letter and pasted in the first letter.

of Judaism, namely its spiritual content, its "soul," were unleashed to the masses, Rabbi Seltzer's reading of the situation was that the *status quo ante*, which is to say, the definition of Judaism in terms of its halakhic edifice, should be maintained. Orthodoxy was not lacking in its content but rather in its presentation. What was called for according to Rabbi Seltzer, was a reformatting of the old content in an esthetic manner appealing to the modern palate. (Rabbis Kook and Seltzer shared a common ground in stressing the urgent need to produce Orthodox men of letters, capable of conveying traditional Judaism in works of belletristic note.)

The dialogue between Rabbis Seltzer and Kook is an echo of earlier exchanges between Rabbi Ḥayyim of Volozhin (author *Nefesh ha-Ḥayyim*) and Rabbi Shneur Zalman of Liadi (author *Tanya*); and between Rabbi Ḥayyim Soloveitchik (Rosh Yeshivah of Volozhin) and Rabbi Isaac Blaser (disciple of Rabbi Israel Salanter, founder of the Lithuanian Mussar movement). Their conversation would also prefigure the cross-currents of Rabbi Joseph Baer Soloveitchik and Rabbi Abraham Joshua Heschel, closer to our own day. In a word, it is the riposte of the Man of Halakha to the Man of Agadah, or vice versa. Unfortunately, oftentimes the two faces of Judaism, Halakha and Agadah, make themselves comprehensible to one another only with extreme difficulty.

Bezalel Naor

P.S. In the interim between the first edition of my translation and the present edition, there occurred within the world of Kookian scholarship a momentous event, namely the issuing of Rav Kook's journals from manuscript: *Shemonah Kevatsim* (*Eight Journals*). This revelation allows the student hitherto denied access to the *pensées* of Rav Kook in their original, unexpurgated form.

While there is no denying the contribution of *Shemonah Kevatsim* (*SK*) to our understanding of Rav Kook's writings, nonetheless, from a socio-historic perspective, one must not lose sight of the fact that it was the text of *Orot* and not that of *SK* that was read and judged by the rabbis of *Erets Yisrael*, as well as the Diaspora (thanks to the wide distribution given to the book by Rav Kook's opponents, intent on arousing rabbinic indignation the world over, from Louisville, Kentucky in the West to Baghdad in the East). Not once in the context of the ensuing controversy did Rav Kook breathe a word that the text of *Orot* might have differed from that of the original, which means that whatever editorial changes were made by his son Rav Zevi Yehudah, they did not influence negatively the rabbis' opinion. (On the contrary, as I pointed out in my Preface to the 1993 edition, Rav Zevi Yehudah's "censorship" may actually have softened somewhat the rabbinic judgment.)

In any event, whenever possible, I have indicated in recent notes where the text of *Orot* differs from that of *SK*. As for Rav Zevi Yehudah's method of rearranging words, resituating phrases and substituting one word for another—several learned papers have already been written in this regard. Whatever I might add to the scholars' findings would not alter significantly the conversation.

I wish to express my gratitude to the dedicated staff of Dynagrafik, Monsey, New York, for their excellent work and unstinting devotion.

I would also take this opportunity to thank the talented staff of Koren Jerusalem: Matthew Miller, Rabbi Reuven Ziegler and Tomi Mager.

B.N.

In honor of
a dear friend,
staunch supporter
and benefactor of Orot

Mr. Robert M. Schottenstein

ר׳ יהושע משולם הכהן
שוטנשטיין הי״ו

Translator's Preface

THE DIFFICULTIES OF TRANSLATING RAV KOOK

Translating Rav Kook is no easy task. There are several reasons for this.

Rav Kook's thought is intended to be the sum, the synthesis, of all Jewish thought preceding it. Beyond that, it attempts to provide the last, premessianic word on that entire tradition. As such, it expects the reader to be totally familiar with Bible, Talmud, Midrash, Philosophy, Mussar, Kabbalah, Ḥasidism, and Haskalah. Embedded in Rav Kook's writings are constant allusions to this vast, almost limitless literature. A phrase here, half a quotation there – these are key words for the initiate; to the uninitiated, they are more likely hieroglyphics. This is true not only of Rav Kook's works but of a great amount of rabbinic writing as well.

However, even by rabbinic standards, Rav Kook's writing proves an almost insurmountable difficulty. Rav Kook broke out of the traditional mold of communication. Rigid but predictable rabbinic structure has been replaced by Escherian staircases: sentences that – in the image of light that they constantly conjure up – move through curved space, trailing in the distance only to reappear when least expected. Most times, with great effort one can trace the elliptical noun that having appeared light-years ago is now the subject of seemingly endless modifications – but not always! The same generation that produced – *le-havdil* – Joyce's novels was the midwife to Rav Kook's monographs.

Rav Kook regarded himself as a human bridge between the Old and the New. While attempting to bridge the gap between these two worlds, in terms of readership, he may very well have lost both. The denizens of the Old World, who would have been equipped to follow speech peppered with classic erudition, were loath to cut loose from traditional linguistic moorings and follow Rav Kook into the unknown of experimental modern Hebrew literacy.[1] The avant-garde reader, on the other hand, while perhaps finding Rav Kook's cadence breathtaking and exhilarating,[2] would be hard pressed to identify the sundry sources that have subtly slipped by.

I am told that in Germany of late, students of Kant have taken to reading the master in translation, his German syntax being too difficult to follow. It is conceivable that native-born Israelis will want to read Rav Kook in translation. His Hebrew syntax is equally discouraging.

Besides the problems inherent in attempting to unravel Rav Kook's idiosyncratic diction, there is a universal dilemma involved here: the impossibility of translating poetry. Rav Kook, even when he attempts to write prose, is a poet.[3] In poetry, multiple levels of meaning are present. The translator may consider himself lucky to find a corresponding word that will convey more than just one of the meanings of the original. But a word that bears *all* the meanings of the text? That is asking too much![4] One arrives at a word that is the closest approximation possible and hopes that the reader will consult the notes for further *entendres*.

ABOUT THE TRANSLATION

Rav Zevi Yehudah Kook, only son of the author and the man responsible for compiling the text of *Orot*, did not exercise all the usual prerogatives of an editor. One has only to compare the finished product of *Orot* to that of *Orot ha-Kodesh* (*Light of Holiness*) by another of Rav Kook's "editors," his disciple Rav David Cohen, "the Nazirite," to see the difference. Both utilized essentially the same materials, the treasure trove of Rav Kook's spiritual diaries, but how different their presentations! The son feels constrained to present pieces in their original, sprawling, almost inchoate form, without superimposition of even so secondary an aid as a heading. On the other hand, the disciple has taken the editorial liberty of breaking up Rav Kook's notorious flow of consciousness into paragraphs, topically rearranging pieces in a more orderly and logical fashion by cutting lines that appear ancillary in the entry in which they occur and pasting them to pieces where they are of primary concern, and furthermore allowing himself and the reader the "luxury" of captions.[5] In so doing, the Nazirite has actually entered into the creative process.[6] Needles to say, a heading, while it may be helpful, may also prove a hindrance to understanding the true content of what follows, for we enter the situation deeply prejudiced by the Nazirite's logo. In this respect, Rav Zevi Yehudah was ever the purist.[7]

As translator, the decision of which model to opt for weighed very heavily on my conscience. On the one hand, it had already been decided for the sake of historical accuracy and exactitude to present the reader with the original 1920 edition of *Orot* published during the author's lifetime, over which a veritable "battle of the book" had been fought between the sages of Jerusalem and world-wide. On the other hand, it seemed grossly unfair to subject the reader to headingless, riderless, meandering "prophecies" where one could easily lose one's way, especially when the other option of headings did exist in a major work (perhaps the *magnum opus*) authorized by Rav Kook himself,[8] and when the representative of the purist school, Rav Zevi Yehudah, had sanctioned the use of secondary headings in the 1970 revised edition of *Orot ha-Teshuvah,* brought out under his supervision.[9] A compromise was struck. Within the Hebrew text of *Orot,* just as in the original, no chapter headings would occur, whereas in the English translation, chapters would be assigned titles[10] followed by brief summaries or extracts (as in the 1970 edition of *Orot ha-Teshuvah*).

'ARFILEI TOHAR AND *OROT*

Some of the material in the penultimate section of *Orot, Orot ha-Tehiyah/Lights of Renascence,* had already appeared in the curious work *'Arfilei Tohar* (*Clouds of Purity*) [Jaffa, 5674/1914]. This is the only one of Rav Kook's spiritual diaries ever to be published in its original form. (All other works we have from Rav Kook are actually selections from several such notebooks, arranged topically.) The book (for whatever reason)[11] never made it as far as the bindery, but a few unbound copies of *'Arfilei Tohar* did wind up in rare book collections. In examining the overlap of *AT* and *Orot*, I was fortunate to have before me just such an unbound copy of the 1914 edition, which differs in some instances from Rabbi Shilat's 1983 edition. Thus, I discovered that the twentieth chapter of *Orot ha-Teḥiyah* (which applies the story of King Solomon and the two harlots to contemporary society) had originally included such provocative phrases as, "the harlot who is to be spurned, who trumps up false accusations" and "the cruel surgeons" (old edition *AT*, page 71), which were emended in both *Orot* and the new edition of *AT* (p. 101) to "the one who is to be spurned" and "those who cruelly operate." Rewording comes not only to promote *lashon nekiyah* (euphemism) but also to cushion the shock of radical theology. Further in that same chapter, *AT*'s bold statement, "The foundation of the righteousness of the just in every generation is supported by the wickedness of the wicked, who in truth are not wicked at all, as long as they cling with their heart's desire to the collectivity of the Nation, *Your people are all righteous,*"[12] has been "lobotomized" to "The foundation of the righteousness of the just in every generation is supported by the wicked as well, who, with all their wickedness, as long as they cling with their heart's desire to the collectivity of the Nation are referred to (by the verse) *Your people are all righteous.*"

Comparative analysis revealed other indications of this tendency to tone down the language of the more outspoken *'Arfilei Tohar*. Whereas *AT* (Shilat edition, p. 96) has spoken of "the superficiality of admonitions and sayings which arouse anger and fraternal hatred," *Orot* (*Lights of Renascence,* chapter 24) hedges: "superficial understanding, which seizes upon isolated admonitions and sayings to arouse anger and fraternal hatred." Another example is chapter 22 of *Lights of Renascence*, which in *AT* (Shilat ed., p. 104) reads: "Secular nationalism is infected with the poison of misanthropy, under which lie hidden several evil spirits." The more subdued version of *Orot* reads: "Secular nationalism may be infected with much poison under which lie hidden several evil spirits."

SECONDARY LITERATURE

While preparing this edition of *Orot,* I had before me three commentaries: that of Rav Zevi Yehudah Hakohen Kook (of blessed memory), as reported in Ḥayyim A. Shvarts's *Mi-Tokh ha-Torah ha-Go'elet*, vol. 3 (Jerusalem, 5747);[13] Rabbi Moshe Yeḥiel Zuriel's notes in his *Ozerot ha-RAYaH*, vol. 1 (Tel Aviv, 5748), pp. 204-234; and the two volumes of Rabbi Moshe Ben-Zion Ushpizai's *Nitsnutsei Orot* (Ramat Gan, 5739, 5744).

The first commentary by Rav Zevi Yehudah is invaluable because it allows a glimpse into the editorial process itself, especially providing insight as to what is signified by the precise order of the book (see Shvarts, p. 195).

Rabbi Zuriel's telegraphic notes are especially helpful in shedding light on matters pertaining to kabbalistic sources, which are not generally known.

Rabbi Ushpizai has the distinction of having written the only full-fledged work devoted exclusively to *Orot.* His commentary is most unusual. Instead of the usual analysis, there is a running summary that is no less poetic than the original text. (It reminds me of Shem Tov's commentary to Maimonides' *Guide.*) In addition, Rabbi Ushpizai provides chunky quotations from traditional sources that he deems helpful in understanding Rav Kook. Perhaps it is one of the great ironies, or poetic justice, that Rabbi Ushpizai's maternal grandfather was Rabbi Menahem Mordechai Frankel-Thomim,[14] who served as Rabbi Y.Y. Diskin's secretary during the period of the terrible imbroglio between Rabbi Diskin and Rav Kook.

It is my pleasant duty to thank many dear friends and colleagues who helped both in terms of *Torah she-bi-khetav*, making available printed materials, and by way of *Torah she-be-'al-peh*, offering valuable insights and suggestions: Zalman Alpert, librarian of Yeshiva University's Mendel Gottesman Library and an associate editor of the *Orot Newsletter;* Rabbi Zevulun Charlop, dean of Yeshivat Rabbi Yitsḥak Elhanan (Rabbi Isaac Elchanan Theological Seminary), where I have had the privilege of teaching Rav Kook's writings, including *Orot*, to scholars both younger and older than myself; Rabbi Matis Greenblatt, literary editor of *Jewish Action*, the magazine of the Orthodox Union, where my review of *Mikhtevei Marom*, the collected letters of Rav Ḥarlap, appeared; Rabbi Yosef Leib Hamburger, who clarified many matters pertaining to the Old Yishuv of *Erets Yisrael*; Rabbi Joshua Hoffman, associate editor of the *Orot Newsletter;* and Rabbi Moshe Kolodny of the Orthodox Jewish Archives of Agudath Israel of America.

Above all, I am indebted to a "brother," Yehoshua Meshulam Hakohen (Robert M.) Schottenstein, who, working with me in Orot, an organization dedicated to the dissemination of Rav Kook's teachings, has made the publication of this book, and many other dreams tucked away in our souls, a reality. At times, when things have gotten rough, I have been blessed with the love and reassurance of my dear friend, saying to me, as did Rebbe Naḥman of Braslav: "*Zeit eikh nit meyya'esh*! Do not despair!"

Another man whom the Almighty ordained to be a partner in the spiritual enterprise of presenting Rav Kook's pure, unedited message to a broader, English-speaking audience is my editor, Avraham (Arthur) Kurzweil, of Jason Aronson Inc. I have been an inhabitant of "Bookland" for many years and can honestly say that rarely have I met an editor with such vision and commitment to spiritual ideals.

Last, but not least... No, let's express it the Hebrew way: *Aḥaron, aḥaron ḥaviv!* "The last are the most beloved." For my wife, Ruth and our children, Avraham Yitsḥak, Ilana, David Yehonatan and Avital Simḥa, who gave of themselves unstintingly so that this project might become a reality, I pray that the *Rav* be a *melits yosher* (an intercessor) – for us, for all Israel, and for the entire world – just as he was during his lifetime. Amen.

Introduction

The Historical Backdrop to *Orot*

RAV KOOK'S DREAM OF A WORLD MOVEMENT: *DEGEL YERUSHALAYIM*

Rav Kook, Rabbi of Jaffa for exactly a decade, weathered the war years 1914-1918 in European exile. After an initial brief internment in Germany, there followed two years of unemployment in St. Gallen, Switzerland, as the guest of an admirer (Mr. Abraham Kimḥi), and finally a stint as Rabbi of the prestigious Maḥzikei Ha-Dat Synagogue of London's East End. Setting sail for Europe in late summer of 1914 in order to attend the scheduled world convention of Agudat Yisrael, he had, in a sense, walked into a divinely preordained "trap," for within days of his arrival, World War broke out, making return to Palestine physically impossible. This was the first of two great traps upon which pivot Rav Kook's biography. The second trap, man-made, with lion's jaws, was the Jerusalem rabbinate – but we are getting ahead of ourselves.

As the bloody war drew to a close, Jewish nationalist – Zionist – ambitions reached a crescendo in the Balfour Declaration of 1917. It seems that divine supervision had maneuvered Rav Kook into London, so that he could be instrumental in procuring this historic assertion of Jewish rights to a homeland in "Palestine." However, whereas the secular, political vision of Herzl could presume to be solidly on the road to fulfillment with the creation of the British mandate, wheels of a much larger, spiritual, cosmic vision began to turn within Rav Kook's head. If it is at all fair to draw comparisons between the affairs of vastly different nations, we could say that Weizman would be the equivalent to Nehru in the annals of the Indian independence movement, while Rav Kook would be – forgive the comparison – the analog to Gandhi.[1] One man works solely within the political orbit, while his counterpart labors, as well, in the rarefied atmosphere of philosophy and even mysticism. We may extend the analogy further. Just as Gandhi's philosophy of nonviolence has had global impact (influencing among others, Martin Luther King), it is conceivable that Rav Kook's cosmic, holistic, messianic vision will one day influence men of different races and nationalities. But again we are jumping ahead.

While Rav Kook may not have been a very organized writer, he proved to be quite the programmatic leader. A well-formulated, if somewhat grandiose, plan of action began to congeal toward the end of the Rav's English interlude. Zionism was a body that needed a soul breathed into it. Rav Kook, together with his fellow rabbis and the Orthodox masses, would provide such a soul in the form of Jerusalemism, i.e., a worldwide movement to be known as *Degel Yerushalayim*, the Banner of Jerusalem (or alternately, *Histadrut Yerushalayim*, the Jerusalem Organization, to directly parallel the *Histadrut Ziyonit*, the Zionist Organization.) The platform of *Degel Yerushalayim* included plans for a universal *yeshivah* (rabbinical academy) and a supreme religious court (precursor of a Sanhedrin), both to be located in Jerusalem.

THE JERUSALEM RABBINATE: LIGHTS IN VESSELS

While Rav Kook, with the aid of his son, Rav Zevi Yehudah, began to attract their recent European acquaintances to membership in

Degel Yerushalayim, Rav Kook's closest disciple and "soul brother," Rav Ya'akov Moshe Ḥarlap, who had been physically (though not spiritually) separated from his beloved master for the duration of the war, began to set in motion difficult negotiations that would culminate in Rav Kook's return to *Erets Yisrael* as the Rav of Jerusalem.[2] The mystical reunion of the souls of master and disciple would also spell the incarnation of the "lights" of holiness in their proper "vessels," to employ Lurianic parlance. No longer would the lofty ideals of the movement for spiritual renascence wander naked in European capitals; they would have their rightful base of operations in Jerusalem once Rav Kook had been invested as Rav of Jerusalem. It was truly a plan of messianic proportions. However, there was one possible oversight or miscalculation in Rav Ḥarlap's purview of the situation. Whereas he and several of the other dynamic young luminaries of Jerusalem, such as Rabbis Zevi Pesaḥ Frank, the *dayyan* or halakhic judge; Yeḥiel Mikhel Tuckachinsky (married to the granddaughter of the previous Rav of Jerusalem, Samuel Salant); and Israel Porath,[3] to mention a few, viewed Rav Kook as a true godsend, a veritable saving angel to enhance Jerusalem's prestige with his charismatic, visionary, and unifying gifts, and to lead the city's religious institutions out of financial ruin – the elder rabbis of Jerusalem, Yitsḥak Yeruḥam Diskin and Yosef Ḥayyim Sonnenfeld, or at least their entourage, came more and more to regard Rav Kook as – excuse the language – Satan incarnate.

It is not our objective here to enter into all the complex political machinations that finally culminated in the worst-case scenario of there being *two* Rabbis of Jerusalem, Avraham Yitsḥak Hakohen Kook and Yosef Ḥayyim Sonnenfeld, each with his own *beit din* or ecclesiastical court. This is an entire chapter in modern Jewish history that requires protracted scrutiny and whose ramifications are felt even to this day in Israel's religious infrastructure. The primary texts where the inquiry must begin are the Agudah leader, Rabbi Moshe Blau's *'Al Ḥomotayikh Yerushalayim* (Tel Aviv, 1946), and the devastating rejoinder by Rav

Kook's faithful adherent,[4] Rabbi Menaḥem Mendel Porush, *Be-Tokh ha-Ḥomot* (Jerusalem, 1948).

Rabbi Porush's exposé is so devastating precisely because it reveals the *dramatis personae* as terribly miscast for the roles they were to play in this most decisive nexus of Jewish history. Rav Kook, far from being the "enlightened rabbi," was distinctly of the old mold: by outer appearance, dressed in traditional garb – fur hat, satin coat, long beard, and *payot* (side curls) – and inwardly, a man with distinctly ascetic and pietistic tendencies, to whom food was a distraction,[5] ablutions in *mikveh* (ritual bath) and visits to the *Kotel* (Western Wall) a daily, or rather, nocturnal ritual,[6] and having severe misgivings concerning women's suffrage[7] and other inroads into the time-honored pattern of Jewish life. Rabbi Yitsḥak Yeruḥam Diskin, on the other hand, at least in his European, pre-Jerusalem phase, was well groomed by conventional Western standards, a man at home in Russian, French and secular studies,[8] a recipient of correspondence from Dr. Herzl,[9] and married to a woman considered "modern" by Jerusalem standards of the day (she wore a wig and a hat).[10] The irony of ironies is that it was none other than Rav Kook's "point man" in Jerusalem, Rabbi Ya'akov Moshe Ḥarlap (a born and bred *Yerushalmi,* whose father, Rabbi Zevulun, had served as a *dayyan* in the elder Rabbi Yehoshua Leib Diskin's court), who was responsible for ingratiating the newly arrived Rabbi Yitsḥak Yeruḥam Diskin in circles where he was hitherto rejected as an intruder.[11]

Nonetheless, on one important point I must disagree with some of Rav Kook's staunchest defenders. It is too easy to dismiss the whole affair as either a socioeconomic clash between Jews of Hungarian versus Russian and Polish origins over control of the city coffers (as wrote Rav Zevi Pesaḥ Frank to his in-law Rabbi Ḥayyim Hirschensohn[12]), or to attribute it alternately to the instigation and agitation of hotheads such as the notorious R. Moshe Semnitzer,[13] or the overzealousness of Rebbetzin Yente Diskin in defending her husband's professional honor.[14] (There are chroniclers who attribute the Vilna Gaon's implacable opposition to the Ḥasidic movement – or at least, his unwillingness to meet with Ḥasidic representatives – to his mother's influence. The place of women in behind-the-scenes shaping of Jewish history should make for a fascinating study.) Between the lines of recorded history lie the spaces of metahistory, that which Jewish thought is made of. The combatants are fighting for high, ideological stakes. Such was the informed and also inspired judgment of an impartial commentator, Rabbi Ḥayyim Hirschensohn (one of the great, if unruly, minds of the generation, who was born in Jerusalem and after a brief sojourn in Constantinople came to the "New World," where as "Rabbi of Hoboken and West, the Hills of Jersey City, Union Hill and the Vicinity," he exchanged letters and confidences with the luminaries of his day).[15] This was also Rav Kook's own assessment of the matter after careful, painful reflection.[16] It was the philosophic issues underlying the *maḥloket* (controversy) that were to come to the fore in the battle surrounding a small powder keg entitled *Orot*.

ENTER A BOOK NAMED *OROT*

In 1920, Rav Zevi Yehudah Kook published a compilation of various manuscripts of his father, dating from the period immediately preceding and during the war (actually the brief stay in Switzerland where, it is assumed, the relaxation of communal duties allowed more time for creative writing).[17] This small, attractive booklet he entitled simply but elegantly, *Orot* (*Lights*). What prompted the publication of the book at this time?

Shmuel Hakohen Avidor in his somewhat fanciful biography of Rav Kook, *Ha-Ish Neged ha-Zerem* (*Man Against the Current*)[18] claims that publishing the book at this time was the son's way of lifting Rav Kook's spirits after the tragic death of his youngest daughter, fourteen-year-old Esther Yael, which occurred right after *Sukkot* 5680 (1919).[19] Rav Zevi Yehudah himself is reticent in this regard. In his brief preface to *Orot*, he says only that of certain writings of his father, whose publication had been postponed due to the war and that should shortly appear in print, he has culled passages – entitled *Orot ha-Teḥiyah* (*Lights of Renascence*) – to shed light on the process of national renascence and return to the Land.

Actually, the answer to our question is self-evident. One has only to scan the title page of *Orot* to learn that the book is a "*Degel Yerushalayim* publication," and if that is not enough, a line below, one reads: "By the Central Office of the Jerusalem Organization." Rav Kook's assumption of the office of Rav of Jerusalem in 1919[20] had not taken the wind out of the sails of *Degel Yerushalayim*. Quite the contrary, the vision he had brought back with him from exile was continuing full speed ahead, if anything, assisted by his high office.[21] Until this time, programs and manifestos of *Degel Yerushalayim* had been circulated.[22] Now, it was time to give the movement ideological moorings in the form of a full-length tract. The pragmatic work of *Degel Yerushalayim*, the preparations for the *Yeshivah* and the Chief Rabbinate, were but the tip of the proverbial iceberg. Now the titanic soul of the movement's founder would be revealed in all its psychic depth.

When exactly in the Hebrew year 5680 (Fall 1919 – Fall 1920) the book was brought out is difficult to ascertain. We first learn of the projected publication of *Orot me-Ofel* in a letter[23] of Rav Kook to his son Zevi Yehudah, dated "8 Adar, 5680." (Rav Kook's younger brother, Shmuel, is mentioned as the one to actually submit the manuscript to the printer.) This date would serve as the *terminus a quo*. The *terminus ad quem* would be the second week of Av. In a filial letter,[24] which though undated, has been pinned down by the editors of the collection in which it appears to the second week in Av, Rav Kook attempts to uplift the spirits of his aged parents, much upset by the detractors of *Orot*. Thus, publication of the book occurred between 8 Adar and the second week of Av, corresponding to spring or summer of 1920.

THE *OROT* CONTROVERSY: A LITTLE DARKNESS DISPELS MUCH LIGHT

After *Orot*'s publication, there followed a rapid succession of events. A certain Rabbi Eizik Ben-Tovim, a sympathizer of Rav Kook, finding a few of the passages in *Orot* seemingly questionable, but especially chapter 34, sought answers to his questions from Rav Kook. The latter not being found in Jerusalem (evidently having gone out of town to rest during the summer break), Rabbi Ben-Tovim turned to Rav Kook's intimate disciple, Rabbi Ya'akov Moshe Ḥarlap, for guidance. Rav Ḥarlap penned a lengthy response in defense of *Orot*, dated 2 Ellul, 5680, which Rabbi Ben-Tovim published as a fourteen-page booklet, entitled appropriately enough, *Tovim Me'orot* (*Good are the Lights*). (*Tovim* is a pun on the publisher's name, while *Me'orot* is reminiscent of *Orot*.)

At that point, Rav Kook's opponents in Jerusalem sounded a death knell in the form of a twelve-page *issur* or ban on *Orot*, bearing the title *Kol ha-Shofar* (*The Voice of the Shofar*).[25] (At a ceremony of excommunication, the *shofar* or ram's horn is traditionally sounded.) Affixed to the ban are the seals of the venerable sages, Rabbis Yitsḥak Yeruḥam Diskin and Yosef Ḥayyim Sonnenfeld. Thus, by Ellul 5680, just one year after his arrival in Jerusalem (on 3 Ellul, 5679), Rav Kook's philosophy was publicly pilloried by the two senior rabbis of Jerusalem. As if that were not enough, two pages of the remainder of *Kol Shofar* are devoted to *Tovim Me'orot* of Rabbi Ḥarlap, who in his attempt to justify his master, kindled the ire of the *kana'im* (zealots).

We reproduce here the original contents of the ban (in English translation):

> With the help of God, in the Month of Mercy [= Ellul] 5680
>
> Dear Rabbi …
>
> We are forced this time to depart from our wont of maintaining silence and let his honor know of our pain. There was brought

before us a recently published booklet by a local rabbi. We were astonished to see gross things foreign to the entire Torah of Israel. We see that that which we feared before his arrival here, that he would innovate corrupt ways unknown to our rabbis and fathers, has been substantiated, more than we ever imagined. There were also brought before us previous publications of his which we had never seen, in the spirit of the new age of heresy and "culture." But this latest one, called by its creator *Orot*, is too much. Deathly poison is in it.[26] There are contained therein many things which it is forbidden to hear, all the more so to write and to print. Unfortunately, they are read by the youth who do not know, nor do they desire to know, to distinguish between light and darkness, especially as the author is a rabbi. These words enter into them as poison, and in the wake of such words the destruction of Judaism is foreseeable in the spirit and education of the younger generation. If we were silent until now for fear of controversy, strife and desecration of the Name which could result thereby, they have already washed away the bounds of silence. Should we remain silent, we would be guilty of sin, God forbid. Attached is this booklet, of which several chapters sing the praises of the wicked. He has "converted darkness into light," "light into darkness," and proclaimed the wicked righteous (in chapters 43, 45, 20, and 16). Even those young men and women who engage in athletics and frivolity, known to us to be Sabbath-desecrators and immoral, he claims to be serving "holy service" (chapter 34). In his writings, he gives the sinners that which their souls crave. On the other hand, he stings the pious of Israel (chapter 20, "as the deed of Amalek, etc.") and maintains that the soul of sinners of Israel is more correct than that of the perfect believers of Israel (chapter 43). In several matters he interprets the Torah unlawfully. Therefore it is forbidden for us to keep silent so as not to be guilty of "shedding the blood" of the youth and students who will drink these evil waters. We have heard from reliable sources that this plague has already spread among innocent youth who invoke the rabbi's authority "to exercise" and that physical exercise raises up the *Shekhinah* as the reciting of King David's psalms .... This fire has already consumed several dear souls, delightful *yeshivah* students, and we must be quick to prevent it from devouring the entire vineyard of the Lord.

Let him arouse his acquaintances the *rabbanim ge'onim shelit"a* (great rabbis, may they live) to judge his books, if they are "works of charmers," and publicize that it is forbidden to study and rely upon his vanities and dreams. We have done our duty by revealing our pain to the rabbi. Now it is his responsibility to join together with us in publicizing this ban. Let him fulfill his holy duty and may the Lord be with us for His name's sake. "For the earth will be filled with knowledge of the Lord," and the spirit of impurity He will remove from the earth, and we will merit to see the coming of the Rightful Redeemer, speedily in our days, Amen.

Yitsḥak Yeruḥam
Son of the Gaon, the Ḥasid,
R. Moshe Yehoshua Yehudah
Leib Diskin
Elder Gaon,
President of Jerusalem
(Seal affixed)

Yosef Ḥayyim Sonnenfeld
RABaD,
Ashkenazic Community
Jerusalem
(Seal affixed)

Moshe Yosef Hoffman

RABaD, Papa

President, Agudat ha-Kodesh

Moshe Naḥum Wallenstein
RABaD, Jerusalem

Mordechai Leib Rubin
Dayyan

Yitsḥak Frenkel
(Seal of the BaDaTs of the
Ashkenazic Community
affixed)

With that, the two camps were pitched for battle. An impasse had been reached. No attempt on the part of Rav Kook or his disciples to explicate what had appeared in his printed work would clear him (or them) of the suspicion of heresy in the eyes of the extreme zealots of Jerusalem. The only possible recourse was to appeal for outside arbitration, the direction Rabbis Diskin and Sonnenfeld had already moved in, however clumsily and heavy-handedly. (Actually, the original draft of the elder sages' *letter* [not a ban] calling to specific rabbis in the Diaspora to serve as arbiters, was worded much more tactfully.[27] Its contents were tampered with and then leaked to the public[28] in the sensationalist *Kol ha-Shofar* by certain zealots whose credo was, "In a case of desecration of the Name, we do not pay honor to the Rav" – even their own Rav![29]) Finding an arbiter in the *Orot* controversy was easier said than done, for which rabbinical figure would enjoy the total confidence of both parties? The man who, so to speak, fit the bill, was Rabbi Avraham Mordechai Alter, Ḥasidic Rebbe of Gur (also referred to in Yiddish as *Ger*) or Gora Kalwaria, Poland, nowadays referred to as the *Imrei Emet* (after his book).

"AN ANGEL OF PEACE": THE REBBE OF GUR

There were a few factors that determined that the Gerrer Rebbe was suited for the role of arbiter. First, he was the spiritual leader and guiding light of the world Agudat Yisrael movement, especially the Polish Ḥasidic masses who in the interbellum period accounted numerically for most of the grassroots constituency of the movement. Besides the demographic consideration of being the *Rebbe* of the most numerous Ḥasidic dynasty in Poland, he was respected as a Torah scholar and saintly personality. There was one more element in his biography that recommended him as equal to this herculean, almost superhuman task of restoring peace to the City of Peace, and that was the fact that he was the son of and spiritual heir to the legendary Rabbi Yehudah Aryeh Leib, author of *Sefat Emet*. *Sefat Emet*, a classic Ḥasidic commentary to the Bible, was regarded as a hallmark of Jewish thought and one of the finest examples of the synthesis of Talmudic learning and mystical inspiration that is unique to Polish Ḥasidism. The son of the *Sefat Emet* could be expected to appreciate the subtleties of thought in the book *Orot.*[30]

At this point in the story, the name of one R. Zevi (Hirsch) David Hirschbein[31] gains prominence. This distinguished elder Gerrer *Hasid* and resident of Jerusalem for many years, who was the teacher of the young Avraham Mordechai Alter,[32] had since Rav Kook's arrival in Jerusalem simply fallen in love with the charismatic master and his Torah as heard at the third Sabbath meal and read in "sweet books which revived his soul."[33] It was R. Hirsch David who now revealed to Rav Ḥarlap a letter that he received from the Gerrer Rebbe's brother-in-law (married to R. Avraham Mordechai's sister), R. Ḥanokh Zevi[34] Hakohen Levin of Bendin, stating that the *gedolei ha-dor*, the great rabbis of the generation, were preparing to deliberate concerning Rav Kook's book. (But a few months earlier that same "diplomatic channel" had conveyed the blessings of R. Ḥanokh Zevi and his distinguished brother-in-law to Rav Kook,[35] to which Rav Kook responded in kind.)[36]

There ensued two lengthy epistles of Rav Ya'akov Moshe Ḥarlap to the Bendiner Rav (as he was known) requesting that he intercede with his brother-in-law, the Gerrer Rebbe, to give his master Rav Kook the fair hearing that he deserved. In the first letter[37] (dated 2 Rosh Hodesh Kislev, 5681), Rav Ḥarlap remonstrates how unfair it was for the signatories on the *Kol ha-Shofar* to judge Rav Kook and himself *in absentia*, as it were, without even bothering to receive their deposition and version of things.

He reveals to us some startling facts concerning the *Kol Shofar*:

> The truth is that some youngsters published the letter of the rabbis totally without their knowledge and added calumny and insult to our Master, may he live, and also to my humble self, may God forgive them. We here [= in Jerusalem] are fully

acquainted with the facts. There are found such persons who were given to wanton abuse even before they found anything wrong [in the book]. It is they who drew the rabbis too into the maelstrom. When they gathered the rabbis to judge concerning the book *Orot*, it was discussed not to mention in their letter even a word of insult and slander, but merely to present the question before some authorities in the Diaspora who would judge the book. They explicitly stipulated that the letter not be made public. Once they would receive answers from the Diaspora, they would certainly not have the audacity to print them without letting our Master know. Certainly they would request of him that he clarify his holy words. But these insolent youngsters know that if the elder *rabbanim ge'onim*, may they live, would question our Master, he has the ability to explain to them so that nothing remains difficult. Then they would be at a total loss: Not only would they not succeed in expanding the controversy – on the contrary, it would result in brotherhood and friendship [= between the elder rabbis and Rav Kook]. Therefore they went ahead and printed without the rabbis' knowledge. And when the rabbis confronted them, they responded: "In a case of *ḥillul ha-shem* (desecration of the Name) one does not pay respect to the rabbi." As is their wont to damage, they prevailed upon the *rabbanim ge'onim* to at least remain passive …

Our Master and my humble self upon learning of the dissemination of the *Kol Shofar*, accepted the tribulations with love, thinking that any upright person would realize that it was a forgery: They do not mention calling us to judgment or questioning us at all. Do we dwell across the sea that we are inaccessible? Is it suspected that we would refuse to respond to them? Certainly every intelligent person will recognize that all this was concocted strictly for the sake of controversy.

Rav Ḥarlap goes on to recount how in 1914, Rav Kook and Rav Sonnenfeld together traveled the land to return its inhabitants to Judaism and how impressed the latter was at that time with Rav Kook's ability to influence the younger generation through his visible love for them, though his methods were totally new to the older rabbi. Next, he tells of the real love that existed between Rabbis Diskin and Kook before the War,[38] a love that has now soured due to the rascality of the zealots. Rav Ḥarlap presents his teacher essentially as a Ḥasidic master searching out the hidden spark of holiness in every Jew, and it is in such a light, not that of a modernist reformer, that his writings must be viewed and interpreted. Rav Ḥarlap ends on a militant tone calling to the present leaders of the Ḥasidic movement to join Rav Kook in reviving the tenets of Ḥasidic faith, whereby Jews who have gone astray are brought back, rather than cast into purgatory.

Seeing from the Bendiner Rav's reply that his first letter had not hit the mark, Rav Ḥarlap sent off another equally long letter.[39] (The second letter is undated, but it must be later than 19 Adar Rishon, 5681, for it mentions in the past tense the proceedings to establish the chief rabbinate of *Erets Yisrael*, which were concluded by then.) In it, he reinforces the picture he drew earlier of Rav Kook as a staunch and eloquent defender of the faith.[40] He sketches Rav Kook's respectful attempts to placate Rabbis Diskin and Sonnenfeld regarding the rabbinic authority of Jerusalem. All attempts by Rabbis Kook, Ḥarlap, and Kliers of Tiberias to restore the peace had failed. Despite all this – even Rabbi Sonnenfeld's investiture as Rabbi of Jerusalem (on 25 Sivan, 5680) – Rav Kook continued to respectfully defer to the elder rabbis.

To the *Kol ha-Shofar's*[41] vicious insinuation that Rav Kook's way of fraternizing with the secularists must produce a forbidden mixture, *kil'ayim* or *sha'atnez*, Rav Ḥarlap retorts that saving Jews from total alienation results not in a forbidden mixture but rather in revealing the source of holiness in what outwardly appears as secular Israel. He explains the platform of Rav Kook's "Yerushalayim" movement: By endorsing the secularists' bid for Jewish independence in the Holy

Land, we in no way commend sacred affairs to their hands; instead, we reserve the right of men of holiness to adjudicate them.

Rav Ḥarlap concludes on a rather pathetic note:

> I am not a politician. I am alone in my house, bemoaning the terrible situation in which the Holy City is now found. Would that I had the ability to silence the quarrels, to remove some of the air of hostility which is choking!"

His eyes are trained on the Rebbe of Gur, whose coming to Jerusalem on a mission of peace would hopefully provide salvation. Rav Ḥarlap did not have to wait long. On Tuesday, the fourth of Nissan, 5681 (April 12, 1921), the motorcade of the Rebbe of Gur entered the portals of Jerusalem.[42]

As personal emissary of Rav Kook, Rav Ḥarlap lost no time in making advances to the Rebbe. Even before the visiting dignitary debarked in Jerusalem, Rav Ḥarlap – along with some forty other dignitaries representing the full political spectrum of Jerusalem's religious institutional life – was on hand to greet the Rebbe's train from Alexandria at the Lod station (the official arrival point in Palestine).[43] During his stay in Jerusalem, the Gerrer Rebbe was the house guest of R. David Leib Cohen[44] (who in the past, together with R. Zevi David Hirschbein, had been asked to convey blessings to Rav Kook).[45] This, the first visit of the leader of Polish Jewry to the Holy Land, held great promise for the future of the Jewish People. While from Rav Ḥarlap's point of view it symbolized primarily the hoped-for vindication of his master's philosophy and standing in the rabbinic world, from the Gerrer Rebbe's own perspective, the initiative of peacemaking between warring Jerusalem factions was part of a much larger process: massive immigration to *Erets Yisrael* by Orthodox Jewry and providing the infrastructure, spiritual and material, to cope with their needs upon arrival.[46] To this end, the visit served as a "fact-finding mission" or very deep probe into Palestinian society. During the visit, which lasted for almost a month, beginning slightly before and concluding slightly after the festival of Passover, the Rebbe had opportunity to meet with the different antagonists: Rav Kook's entourage, consisting of Rav Ḥarlap, Rav Zevi (or as he was commonly referred to in Jerusalem, "Hirsch") Pesaḥ Frank,[47] and others; and Rabbis Diskin and Sonnenfeld's following, which numbered several *kana'im* or extremists.

Shortly after his arrival in Jerusalem, the Gerrer Rebbe paid a "state visit" to Rav Kook,[48] Rav of Jerusalem (or, at least, one of two).[49] (The matter of protocol becomes very important here. Rabbi M.Z. Neriyah,[50] a disciple of Rav Kook, stresses that it was first the Rebbe who visited the Rav and not the other way around, as reported by other chroniclers.)[51] The encounter was mutually cordial and received much publicity in the press.[52] Of the exchanges between the Rebbe and the Rav, there survives from the period a halakhic discussion concerning reciting a blessing *She-heḥeyanu* upon tithing for the first time, where the Rebbe accepted Rav Kook's *pesak* (legal decision).[53]

For whatever reason, this initial visit of the Gerrer Rebbe with Rav Kook did not elicit the kind of vitriolic response from the extremists of Jerusalem that a later meeting did. Six years later, during another stay in *Erets Yisrael*, the Gerrer Rebbe would once again pay a visit to Rav Kook. Subsequent to this meeting, the inhabitants of Jerusalem found their billboards plastered with posters screaming:[54]

AVRAHAM = AVRAHAM

"Not for naught did the starling go to the raven – he's his type."

The first line was a pun on the names Avraham Kook and Avraham Alter. The second line drew on an old Talmudic adage[55] that corresponds to the English expression, "Birds of a feather flock together." The implication was clear: The Gerrer Rebbe was guilty by association. This manifestation of Jerusalem zealotry (whose brunt Rav Kook had borne for years) so outraged the Gerrer retinue that when subsequently Rabbis Sonnenfeld and Klatzkin tried to apologize for the undignified behavior of the zealots, the Rebbe's son, R. Simḥa Bunem (later known as "*Lev Simḥa*") refused them entry to his father.[56] But all this lay in the future.

At this time, Rav Ḥarlap, who, we can be sure, was privy to the inner transactions, both as an injured party and as Rav Kook's most trusted confidant, placed great hopes on the Gerrer Rebbe's abilities as arbiter. On Sunday, 9 Nissan, 5681, he wrote to his eldest son in America: "It seems that the Rebbe of Gur, may he live, has started to initiate the process of peacemaking. May God grant him success. All sides give great honor to the Rebbe of Gur, may he live."[57]

Though we have no exact minutes of the conversations between Rav Kook and the Gerrer Rebbe, Rav Kook's representations have come down to us in the form of a letter[58] addressed to the Rebbe, dated 11 Nissan, a week after the Rebbe's arrival in Jerusalem. He writes:

> I find myself obligated to offer my thanks to His Holiness for his effort and pure desire to bring the blessing of peace to the Holy City, may it be rebuilt, between scholars involved in Torah and fear of the Lord, who, due to our many sins, have been divided into camps, through the design of those who would stir up strife between brothers. Some of them made myself and my soul-friend the *Rav*, the *Gaon*, the *Tsaddik*, our master R. Y.M. Ḥarlap, may he live, their target, by latching onto words I had written, which are correct to the straight-minded.
>
> It is a necessity of the hour to bring into the hearts of the distant, thoughts of holiness by uplifting their soul to the source of life of the universal soul of Israel, and to influence those hearts with words of amity and pleasantness, by explaining the foundation of the unity of the people of God, the entire holy nation, and by illuminating the holiness of the Land of Eternal Delight and strident trust that the light of God will be revealed through all the causalities of time and the behavior of nations

and kingdoms, as we see the beginnings of the light, wonders of the Perfect of Intellect, with real eyes of flesh as well. In all those words there is no weakness or faltering, God forbid, from the observance of Torah and *Mitsvah* (Commandment) or the bond of Israel's sanctity or cleaving to the great sages and righteous of every generation, who are truly the pillars of life of the House of Israel. Now if in some places in my writings, there are brief remarks which require explanation, it is the obligation of every God-fearing person to give the benefit of the doubt and interpret those things as being consonant with truth and holiness, according to Torah and *Mitsvah*. How much has been said in this regard by the Rav [Yosef Albo] author of the *'Ikkarim* (in the comment to the second treatise).

I hope that merit will come through the meritorious, His Honor (may he live). Would that these important men whom I always respect, who, in our many sins, have risen against us, recognize that this is not the way, this is not the wish of God, to cause many to sin in the way of slandering and calumniating scholars, who are counted among the faithful of Israel in all their heart and soul, and strive always to sanctify the Name of Heaven. That he might bring upon Israel the blessing of peace and unity, and thus strengthen the foundation of the sanctity of Torah and faith, with the help of God, especially in *Erets Yisrael* at the time of its rebuilding.

Also, as concerns communal matters, isn't the surer way not to antagonize all who build and do good for Israel, even if it be only material good – but rather to unite all the religious, and to call to the entire holy nation to be strong in holiness, and to let the entire world, in Israel and among the nations, know that there is a general representative of the holy nation over all matters of religion and faith in *Erets Yisrael*? In my opinion, it should be called the Jerusalem Organization, which should have official standing no less than the Zionist Organization. …

It is my prayer that God put in the heart of all the great and holy of our generation to understand the correctness of my sayings in this holy matter. …

Avraham Yitsḥak Hakohen Kook

P.S. Let it be known that Agudat Yisrael is very close to my heart, and I desire to strengthen them, as far as my weak hand reaches. But we must be very, very careful not to weaken the right which the nations have granted us, with the help of God, according to the present situation, in any manner however remote, but rather strengthen the right of Israel to the Holy Land, from the source of holiness of the perfect, eternal Torah; strengthen the foundations of education in *Erets Yisrael* with *talmud torahs* and *yeshivot*, with the ancient sanctity of Torah and fear [of God].

Finally, the nearly month-long visit of the Gerrer Rebbe drew to a close. Before he set sail, Rav Kook sent him the following farewell note:

By the help of God, evening of 2 Iyyar, 5681

The blessing of God from the holy place to my glorious friend, the Rav, the Gaon, the famous *Tsaddik*, treasure of purity, rectitude and innocence, our Master R. A.M. Alter (may he live) of Gur and all his retinue … May His Holiness from Gur (may he live) please accept my written blessing hereby sent to him on his way, as he steps from the holy to the profane, with the intention of connecting to the Holy Land, the Land of Life, the delight of all Israel and delight of all the host upon hosts, above and below, the Land of Beauty, and Jerusalem. As God has granted him the privilege to see it and enjoy its holy pleasantness and be connected to its holiness, so His Holiness should be blessed to return to the holy place soon with the light of greatness and salvation … May God protect his going and coming, to life and to peace, with all good, Selah.

As his wish and the wish of his steadfast friend bound by the holiness of his friendship,

A. Y. Hakohen[59]

A LETTER FROM A SHIP AND THE SCROLL OF RABBI MEIR

Once aboard the ship back to Europe, the Rebbe dispatched the following letter[60] to his immediate family, which (having been reprinted innumerable times) has become, to this day, the authoritative "position paper" of certain segments of Orthodox Jewry vis-à-vis Rav Kook. As it is often quoted out of context,[61] I present the section of the letter salient to the Jerusalem rabbinate controversy in unabridged form:

> As I wanted to strengthen the Agudah, I observed that what prevents the consolidation and expansion of Agudat (Shalumei Emunei) Yisrael in Jerusalem, is the fact that the administrators of the Agudah there have been totally drawn into the controversy of the rabbis. Consequently, persons who do not want to enter into controversy cannot be counted among the members of the Agudah, all the more so, those persons who support the Rav, the Gaon R. Avraham Kook, may he live. And though the latter proposed to me that they form a separate Agudah – nevertheless, I could not give my approval that there be several Agudot within Jerusalem among the Orthodox, for I hope that it is necessary (and possible) for peace to reign in the city whose name is Peace.
>
> In ways which I deemed appropriate, I began to implement at least a partial peace, to begin with.
>
> In the Diaspora, there was a conception, a picture other than the reality. It was reported that the Rav, the Gaon R. Avraham Kook, may he live, is an "enlightened" rabbi and mercenary. They opposed him with bans and insults. The editorial boards

of *Der Jud* and *Ha-Derekh* at times carried one-sided reports. This is not the way, to hear only from one side – no matter who.

The Rav, the Gaon R. Avraham Kook, may he live, is a man of many-sided talents in Torah, and noble traits. Also, it is public knowledge that he loathes money. However, his love for Zion surpasses all limit and he "declares the impure pure and adduces proof to it," reminiscent of the one [= Rabbi Meir] who the Rabbis said in the first chapter of *'Eruvin* (13b) "had no equal in his generation" and therefore, "the final *halakha* did not follow his opinion." From this, came the strange things in his [= Rav Kook's] books. I argued much with him, that even though "his intention is good, his actions etc. [=are not good]," for he extends a hand to the sinners while they are yet in rebellion and desecrate all that is holy. He says he is emulating the ways of God, as it is written: "You extend a hand to sinners, etc." I say that on this account we confess, "Because of the hand which was sent against Your Temple." The building of "youths" is destruction, even concerning the construction of the Temple, as writes Rashi *(Nedarim* 40a).

True, in Vienna [= at the Agudah convention] too it was resolved not to vitiate the promise of rights granted to us in *Erets Yisrael*, or even to delay them, God forbid – for good can come from any place – but to glorify the athletics of sinners and to flatter them in such a shocking manner, to extend peace to them as if they were ministering angels – this outrages the pious beyond description. Also, his theory of uplifting the sparks is a dangerous road. As long as they do not return from sin, the sparks have no reality. Thus, he endangers pure, innocent souls who will connect in this way to the sinners, through the power of the beauty of Japheth. It is also dangerous for the one who delves in this, as our Rabbis, of blessed memory, taught us. Behold the wisest of all men [=Solomon] delved into this to uplift these sparks, as interpreted by our Sages. In this regard, it states, "Can a man stir a fire in his lap, and his clothes not be burned?" (Proverbs 6:27). Therefore our Rabbis said: "Wise men, be careful of your words!" (*Avot* 1:11). Concerning the wisest of all men [=Solomon], they said (*Shabbat* 30b) they attempted to suppress the Book of Ecclesiastes, even though later they retracted, stating that Solomon had written well. Why did they tell us that they had thought to suppress it? Only to teach us so concerning even a great man.

It is difficult for me to write at great length, so I will be brief. I initiated the peace and convinced the Rav, the Gaon R. Avraham Kook, may he live, and he gave me a written and signed assurance which states that even though his intention was for the sake of heaven, despite this, having heard that desecration of the Name and lessening of the honor of Heaven came about because of expressions in his books, for the sake of Heaven he nullifies those expressions and words.

Afterwards, I met with the elder rabbis, the Rav, the Gaon Rabbi Ḥayyim Sonnenfeld and the Rav, the Gaon Rabbi Yeruḥam Diskin, may they live, that they annul the *Kol Shofar,* the *ḥerem* (ban) and the insults. They are willing to sign on this, being as the Rav, the Gaon Rabbi Avraham Kook, may he live, wrote the above. However, they add that they only wrote letters to judge whether these expressions are *kosher*, but around them there was much tumult, and without their knowledge, surrounding their letter were published the *Kol Shofar* and the *ḥerem* (ban). However, they also did not want to protest to these individuals, as long as the strange, offending expressions remained. Among these zealots there are also many whose intentions are for the sake of Heaven, and with many I established a covenant of love, for their company is pleasant. But it is explained in *'Akedat Yitsḥak* [= by Rabbi Isaac 'Arama], section *Pinḥas,* on the verse, "Not in the noise is God," that such a way cannot be. If they would have gently approached R. Avraham Kook, may he live, in the beginning, they could have persuaded him to annul these expressions – without necessitating the shaming of a scholar and fanning the flame of controversy. For all sides, it is necessary now that the Orthodox come there [= to *Erets Yisrael*] to settle. It is understood that there is required a union of all the God-fearing there, in order that the settlers can concentrate properly and preserve Judaism without mixing with others. Therefore the bringing of peace is imperative and though I have not yet concluded it, I did initiate it. When, in the course of time, rabbis and *tsaddikim* arrive there – as promised at the meeting in Warsaw – they can work out the other details. For I heard from the Rav, the Gaon Rabbi Avraham Kook, may he live, that he is neither a Zionist nor a Mizraḥist, but being the rabbi of all, he must bring all close. He knows that one Orthodox Jew settling there is worth more than the settlement of a thousand secularists.

Even before a complete peace is concluded, if only the mutual mocking would stop, the Rav, the Gaon Rabbi Avraham Kook would recognize the *Beit Din* (Ecclesiastical Court) of the *Rabbanim*, the *Ge'onim* Rabbi Ḥayyim Sonnenfeld, may he live, and Rabbi Yeruḥam Diskin, may he live.[62] More so, Rav Kook even considers it beneficial. Since he is also in touch and contact with the secularists, in his capacity as Chief Rabbi, it is good that there be someone to arouse him on certain issues – of course, in a peaceful manner, without shaming and insulting.

Behold, from the above words of the Rav, the Gaon Rabbi Avraham Kook, may he live, you can tell his traits – for even though most of the inhabitants of the Holy City and many of the rabbis side with him, nevertheless, he gives respect to the older rabbis.

The Gerrer Rebbe clearly found Rav Kook's philosophy (or perhaps the right word is "mysticism") unacceptable as a *modus vivendi* for the Jewish People. What is most fascinating, though, is his likening of Rav Kook to Rabbi Meir, who while incomparable in his generation, could not be followed. Is some pun intended here on the names *Meir* (illuminator) and *Orot* (lights)? Also, that same mysticism of Rabbi Meir, so emphatically rejected by the school of Ger, was much appreciated within another Polish Ḥasidic tradition, Izbica-Radzyn-Lublin.[63]

Originally, the Gerrer Rebbe was to be accompanied to *Erets Yisrael* by the Rebbe of Radzyn, Rabbi Mordechai Yosef El'azar Leiner,[64] who at the time, occupied the number two position in the leadership of the Agudat Yisrael movement in Poland. There exists a letter[65] from this very period written by a Radzyner *ḥasid*, at the behest of his *rebbe*, to a fellow *ḥasid* residing in *Erets Yisrael*, demanding that besides detailed and comprehensive information regarding economic prospects in *Erets Yisrael*, all the works (or as many obtainable) of "Harav Avraham Yitsḥak HaKohen Kook, may he live," be sent immediately to the Rebbe of Radzyn. The letter is dated Thursday, *Kedoshim*, 19th day of the *'Omer*, 5681 (1921). This would mean that it was written at the onset of the Gerrer Rebbe's return voyage from *Erets Yisrael*. The two main themes that occupy the Radzyner Rebbe are: (1) pending massive settlement of *ḥasidim* in *Erets Yisrael*, and (2) the printed works of Rav Kook. These are the very themes that commanded the Gerrer Rebbe's attention at the time.

Was the aspect of Rav Kook's theology that so terrified the Gerrer Rebbe the very one that attracted the Radzyner Rebbe to his works? Did he hear in the teachings of *Orot* an echo of the "radical" theology of his great-grandfather, Rabbi Mordechai Yosef (Leiner) of Izbica; his grandfather's disciple, Rabbi Zadok Hakohen (Rabinowitz) of Lublin;[66] and his own father, Rabbi Gershon Ḥanokh (Leiner) of Radzyn?[67] If the Radzyner Rebbe had been on the boat back with the Gerrer Rebbe, would the latter's communique have taken the condemnatory tone it did? Looking over his shoulder would have been a scion of a most distinguished dynasty, who, as Rav Kook, had been committed to the terror-inspiring cause of King Solomon[68] and Rabbi Meir of old: to raise up the hidden, fallen "sparks."

Objectively, we have no way of knowing what the Radzyner's reaction to *Orot* was after presumably having received it in the mail. However, we do know of a most interesting exchange in Vienna between Rabbi Zevi Yehudah Kook and the famed Rebbe of Chortkov (Galicia), Rabbi Israel Friedman, one of the outstanding Ḥasidic leaders of the time. Their discussion revolved around the idea that the physicality and material aspect of *Kelal Yisrael* (the People of Israel) is holy, exactly the belief expounded in *Orot*.[69] It truly seems as if some of the ideas that the Gerrer Rebbe found most objectionable could dovetail with alternate Ḥasidic philosophies. Rav Kook should be situated within the tradition of mystic masters of sublimation, in whose *sefer*, as in the scroll of Rabbi Meir, "garments of flesh" are transcribed into "garments of light."[70]

After Rav Kook and Rav Ḥarlap's extended courtship of the Gerrer Rebbe, this was to be the latter's final verdict. (Though the relationship between Rav Kook and Rav Ḥarlap on the one hand, and the Gerrer Rebbe on the other, would blossom in the course of successive visits to *Erets Yisrael*,[71] and even continue into the next generation,[72] history – or, let us say, a certain history – would not record the many niceties and pleasantries, besides the real friendship that existed between these men, but only this shrill-noted document.) Could this have been the outcome Rav Ḥarlap had dreamed of? His master had been cleared of the terrible charge of heresy, but at what price? He had had to foreswear crucial passages in *Orot* that Rav Ḥarlap had striven to protect. Rav Kook, whom he revered as a near-messianic figure and saviour of the generation, was reckoned a man leading his people down a dangerous path. Though the Gerrer Rebbe had extolled Rav Kook as an *ish ha-eshkolot* (a man of universal talents), a concept that according to the Mishnah,[73] had died with Yosé ben Yo'ezer, Man of Tseredah, and Yosé ben Yoḥanan, Man of Jerusalem, the Rebbe had also consigned him to the role of a minority opinion, not to be followed.

Amazingly, there is no indication in Rav Ḥarlap's correspondence of any disappointment with the final results of the Gerrer *Tsaddik*'s visit.[74] On the contrary, in a letter written on the second day of Rosh Ḥodesh Tammuz, 5681, to his son in America, he observes:

> I hope that the coming of the Rebbe [of Gur] will bring much blessing, especially his devoted activity towards the blooming of the Holy Land, in terms of its construction and commerce. What is most amazing about the Rebbe is his alacrity; I have yet to see such a fast worker as he. In general, he is taciturn, but he listens and is attentive. When he has made up his mind to accomplish something, while others are yet deliberating, in his case it is already *fait accompli*. Thence the hope that on behalf of *Erets Yisrael* too he will achieve with feverish speed. I am sure that the positive actions to be started by all sides will bring the mutual understanding to inspire peace and tranquility on all sides.[75]

More crucial is how did the author of *Orot* himself feel after having signed away the "children of his spirit"? Was it for that reason that Rav Kook (on different occasions) compared himself to two tragic visionaries, the Italian Rabbi Moshe Ḥayyim Luzzatto[76] and the Ukrainian Rabbi Naḥman of Braslav?[77] Both had been forced by generations incapable of appreciating their gifts[78] to, by their own hand, commend their inspired writings to oblivion. Luzzatto agreed to have his vision locked away in a sealed chest, and the Braslaver ordered his very own disciples to set flame to the scroll of redemption.

From faraway America, Rabbi Ḥayyim Hirschensohn commiserated after a fashion. In his book *Malki ba-Kodesh*, he stormed:

> The opposition of the elder *ge'onim* of Jerusalem, may the Lord preserve and save them . . . reached such a state, that the Gaon Kook himself in his great humility signed, at the behest of the

> holy Rebbe of Gur (may his light shine) that he retracts the passages in the book *Orot* which caused the opposition, as the holy Rebbe attests in his letter written aboard ship. . . . On the one hand, I deem this weakness on the part of the Gaon Kook, a prince in Israel, to sign as if he recants his views, when he knows them to be proven true, as the incident in Petaḥ Tikvah will attest to the veracity of the light tucked away in the book *Orot* for the Future. Yet one must not grumble about the weakness of the Gaon, for it comes from an agitated state of mind: Assassins embittered and reviled him in *Kol Shofar*. . . . Especially when a *gedol ha-dor* (leader of the generation) such as the holy Rebbe of Gur (may his light shine) attempts to arbitrate between elders of Israel, one is allowed to change one's opinion for the sake of peace. [79]

Rav Kook forgave these "faithful wounds" of his friend Rabbi Hirschensohn. In reply to Rabbi Hirschensohn's letter apologizing for the use of such strong language, Rav Kook, who has been described as a genius at *shevirat ha-middot*[80] (literally, "breaking character traits," but which I would render as "self-reconstruction") reveals some of the topography of his soul during all this commotion, as well as the external outcome of the Rebbe of Gur's arbitration:

> I ask that his honor not be pained because of all he wrote regarding what transpired between me and the *Tsaddik* of Gur, may he live. Maybe I did give in too much for the sake of peace, but it did not affect, God forbid, the basic opinions, but rather the question was style of language. He said to me, in the name of these critics, that in their opinion, the brevity of language in certain places in *Orot* causes consternation. So I wrote a short note to the effect that if it is true that there are such expressions whose brevity brings pain to the simple of heart, I hereby regret that I did not make my intention clearer. Even this was on condition that the critics too, from their side, publicize some statement of regret, for having been party to

> maligning holy words and pure opinions stated in that book and other booklets published by me. However the condition was not kept. On their side, nothing was done to bring about peace, while the drift of my note was made public – I do not know whether verbatim or in some digest which probably is inaccurate. This is the whole matter, not worthy to deal with at all. His honor's intention is certainly for good, befitting his love for truth. Let him not think that I hold it against him – I know his pure, gentle spirit.[81]

Rather than agitation, there is evidenced in this letter a noble tranquility of spirit. As far as the externals, nothing came of the Gerrer arbitration because of the opponents of *Orot*'s failure to abide by the terms of the agreement. Rav Kook's critics claim that the reason for the noncompliance was the wording of Rav Kook's signed statement, which was found insubstantial.[82] The truce was terminated, or rather it had never begun.

THE LANGUISHING OF TWO WOULD-BE INQUISITORS

The real perpetrators of the infamous *Kol Shofar* (not Rabbis Diskin and Sonnenfeld but men who used their names for their own nefarious purposes) emerged from the negotiations unscathed and uncontrite.

In the summer of 1922, they launched a new offensive against Rav Kook, once again in pamphlet form, this one entitled *Kol Gadol* (basically more of the same diatribe, with some recent letters from rabbis attacking Rav Kook and his writings, added to the collection.)[83] However, this time the two individuals responsible for defaming Rav Kook's character were imprisoned by the British mandatory authorities. R. Meir Semnitzer (son of R. Moshe Semnitzer, after Semnitz, Hungary, where he had served as rabbi)[84] and R. [Moshe] Yosef Hoffman[85] (one will recall, formerly of Papa, Hungary, and president of the self-styled Agudat Ha-Kodesh) were sentenced to fifty days in jail, fines of twenty pounds each, and a bond of one hundred pounds that they not engage in propaganda for a period of two years. In addition, all the copies of *Kol Gadol* were seized by the government.[86] This action, in turn, stirred up a "hornet's nest."[87]

The zealots[88] accused the *Rav mi-Ta'am* (short for *rav mi-ta'am ha-memshalah,* the "Government's Rabbi," a derogatory term with negative associations going back to Tsarist Russia [in Russian, *kazyonniy ravvin*]) of the most despicable crime in Jewish life: *mesirah,* turning a fellow Jew over to non-Jewish authorities for judgment. It did not matter that the two rabbis had first been summoned to a duly convened *beit din* (rabbinic court). The two insisted that the case by decided in the court of R. Yosef Ḥayyim Sonnenfeld, invoking the dictum, "*ha-tove'a holekh ahar ha-nitba*'" ("the plaintiff must go to the place of the defendant"). In *Kol Yisrael,*[89] the paper of Agudat Yisrael in Jerusalem, R. Moshe Semnitzer, father of one of the jailed, writes that the two had alternatively requested that the case be heard before an impartial body of both parties' choosing (known in halakha as *zabla* [=*z*eh *b*orer *l*o *e*had]). He further deems unfair that the two were allegedly not warned that in the event of failure to appear before the *beit-din* they would be arraigned by the mandatory authorities. In the Jerusalem daily, *Do'ar ha-Yom,*[90] Rabbis Kook, Frank, and (Fishel) Bernstein, all three *dayyanim* (justices), maintained that they had not tried to coerce the two pamphleteers to be judged by the office of the Chief Rabbinate but rather they had been summoned to an impartial court of Sephardic rabbis. *Kol Yisrael*[91] retorted that Rabbis Semnitzer and Hoffman had no confidence in the impartiality of the said Sephardic court and therefore demanded that a team of three arbiters be arrived at by both parties (*zabla*). Furthermore, the Chief Rabbinate's assertion that it was out of the question to bring the case before Rabbi Sonnenfeld, for he had lent his aegis to the writers, was found wanting, "as neither he [Rabbi Sonnenfeld] nor the mighty Gaon Rabbi Y.Y. Diskin and the other members of the *BaDaTs* [Court of the separatist 'Edah Ḥaredit] knew anything of the publication of the booklet *Kol Gadol* until the local papers publicized the arrest of the authors."

Because Rabbis Semnitzer and Hoffman had failed to honor the Sephardic court's summons to appear, they were considered as having a status of *mesarevim.* Such being the circumstances, the rabbinic court allowed the case to be taken before the British mandatory court.[92] Halakhically, the *beit din* of a city, which finds an individual to be *mesarev* (refusing to appear in court), also has the power to declare a *ḥerem*, a ban on the individual.[93]

The tactics of the *kana'im*, the zealots, had not changed since the appearance of the *Kol Shofar,* but this time, the *kitvei plaster,* as they are referred to in Hebrew, or *paskevilin,* as they are known in Yiddish (defamatory literature), met with a different response. The Grand Inquisitor had been discomfited.

THE CONTENTS OF KOL *HA-SHOFAR*

The booklet entitled *Kol ha-Shofar* consists of the following:

1. The text of the *ḥerem* or ban on *Orot* (pp. 1-3).

2. Two decade-old letters from Rabbis Ḥayyim Berlin of Jerusalem and Ya'akov David Wilovsky (RIDBaZ) of Tsefat opposing Rav Kook on the issue of *Shemitah* (the Sabbatical year), as if that were somehow pertinent to the matter under consideration (pp. 4-5).

3. A reproduction of a year-old public proclamation signed "Agudat ha-Kodesh," targeting both Rav Kook and his disciple Rav Ḥarlap as spiritual enemies of the Jewish People who, it is feared, will create a new sect based on specious beliefs (pp. 5-6).

4. An independent *issur* dated "14 Ellul, 5679" and signed "Moshe Naḥum Wallenstein, RABaD (president of ecclesiastical court) Jerusalem," forbidding reading the works of Rav Kook and his disciple Rav Ḥarlap written in modern Hebrew and discussing novel philosophical issues (p. 7).

5. A sprawling lampoon of Rav Kook and Rav Ḥarlap written over the signature of the indignant "Agudat ha-Kodesh" (pp. 7-12).

THE GRIEVANCES IN THE *ḤEREM* ANALYZED

If we take the text of the ban proclaimed in *Kol Shofar* at face value, we find the opponents of *Orot* taking exception to chapters 34, 43, 45, 20, and 16. These criticisms form conceptual clusters.

The first line of criticism is leveled at Rav Kook's positive remarks concerning the wicked of Israel: his supposed placing of physical enthusiasts on a par with meditators and psalm-sayers (chapter 34); his attributing to the nationalist Zionists a dimension of soul impaired in the religious sector (chapter 43); and his justifying the existence of the wicked, deeming them indispensable to society, just as dregs are indispensable to wine (chapter 45).

Rav Kook's second offense was his denunciation of Orthodox separatism to the point of comparing it to the deed of Amalek who had singled out the (spiritual) stragglers at the end of the camp for extermination (chapter 20).

The third sore spot in Rav Kook's latest work was his call to the righteous "to discover a light of holiness in all the languages and wisdoms of the world" (chapter 16).

"CHAPTER THIRTY-FOUR": PHYSICAL EXERCISE ON TRIAL

The passage in *Orot* that has evoked more controversy and exegesis than any other is that contained in chapter 34 of *Orot ha-Teḥiyah*, where Rav Kook likens the merits of physical exercise by youngsters in *Erets Yisrael* to those accrued through the recitation of Psalms by King David and the mystical unifications *(yiḥudim)* of the Kabbalists. To the guardians of the Old Yishuv, the original settlement of pietists in

Erets Yisrael, needless to say, such a comparison aroused indescribable mortification. This group in many ways viewed itself as an "endangered species" struggling to preserve a distinct life-style, dedicated to prayer and sacred study, against the inroads of Western civilization with its essentially different values. To the *alter yishuvnik*, the sight of youths engaged in calisthenics rather than in the pursuit of God's Torah was a painful one indeed. Add to this the fact that oftentimes physical exercise brought with it mingling of the sexes and desecration of the Sabbath, and the outrage increases. But on top of that, the newly appointed Rav of Jerusalem draws comparisons between this profane activity and the most sacred activity of pious Jews, reciting psalms and kabbalistic meditation! Need we say more?[94]

The "fallout" from this passage began to be felt immediately. As early as 2 Tevet, 5680 (1920), Rav Ya'akov Moshe Ḥarlap, Rav Kook's ever-faithful disciple, was compelled by the sincere questioning of a sympathizer, Rabbi Eizik Ben-Tovim, to pen a fourteen-page pamphlet in defense of this radical theology. It came out under the title *Tovim Me'orot* (*Good are the Lights*).

In this essay, Rav Ḥarlap, for the most part, skirts the immediate issue at hand, launching instead into a broadsweep review of Rav Kook's theology in general. One recognizes many themes that are cornerstones of Rav Kook's teaching and that subsequently resurface in Rav Ḥarlap's own system: the volitional aspect of all – not only human – existence;[95] exposure of evil's illusory character as the most realistic approach to the problem of evil;[96] and finally, the unalterable chosenness of the Jewish People and their innate holiness.[97] Rav Ḥarlap attributes to the latter belief – the author's design to reveal the interior of a Jew – the perplexing saying in chapter 34. In fine, physical strength is a preamble to prophecy: "Prophecy descends only upon the strong, wise, humble and wealthy" (*Shabbat* 92a; *Nedarim* 38a). Rav Ḥarlap feels that both institutions, *tikkun ḥatsot* (the kabbalistic practice of rising at midnight to recite psalms) and physical brawn, are necessary for there to be *ru'aḥ ha-kodesh* (divine inspiration). His master, true to his overall philosophy, is seeing in the stirrings of physical prowess on the part of secular-minded Zionist youth an outward manifestation of a deep, positive psychic transformation to occur with the return from exile. A divine scheme is being played out here. Minds beset with anxiety and worry are incapable of proper concentration; the self-confidence of national resurgence can produce beneficial cognitive effects for those devoted to the pursuit of wisdom. Rav Ḥarlap concludes his short treatise with an exhortation to the *tsaddikei ha-dor,* the righteous of the generation, to reveal these divine processes at work and thus hasten the Redemption. The righteous must follow the example of Rabbi Akiva[98] who found the courage, based on a clear vision of the future, to laugh in the face of adversity. The *tsaddikim* must be able to see beyond the present tearing down of religion in *Erets Yisrael* to the Light that lies ahead. "If you see a generation belittling and insulting, look for the footsteps of Messiah."[99]

Not only did *Tovim Me'orot* not stem the tide of scorn for *Orot,* but its author was ridiculed for the attempt. In trying to extricate Rav Kook from the "mud," Rav Ḥarlap dug himself in. He provided fresh fuel for the fire of the zealots when he wrote in *Tovim Me'orot*[100] to the effect that the approach of battling evil as if it were a reality, was merely a *hora'at sha'ah,* a temporary measure in the Diaspora, but with the return of the People to its Land and the beginning of the Redemption, the ultimate solution, of revealing evil's illusoriness, must be opted for. This was all the publishers of the *Kol Shofar,* the self-styled *"Agudat ha-Kodesh,"* "presided" over by R. Moshe Yosef Hoffman of Papa, needed to hear! They devoted two whole pages of *Kol Shofar*[101] to lambasting Rav Ḥarlap's novel idea. They were not sure whether he had received this teaching from his master "who sees with his eyes the light of Elijah's life rising" (a parody on *Orot ha-Teḥiyah,* beginning chapter 30), or had himself been privileged to behold this vision "as the holy seraphs whisper in his ear that the ways of worship trodden by our fathers and rabbis until now were only a 'temporary measure'!" To employ a Yiddish expression, unwittingly Rav Ḥarlap had served up to them *mat'amim* (a savory dish): "Behold the *kohen,* A.Y.H. the 'Seer' and Y.M. the 'Visionary' are prophesying . . . saying: 'The Redemption has arrived!'"[102]

In the more subdued and respectful *Ha-Derekh,*[103] the official Hebrew organ of *Agudat Yisrael,* published in Vienna, the book reviewer had this to say of *Tovim Me'orot:* "The author strives to elucidate the words of the Rav, the Gaon R.A.Y. Kook in his book *Orot,* chapter 34, but even the words of the author require explanation."

This brief epitaph is preceded on the previous page by what one might consider a well-balanced critique of the "mother lode." The anonymous reviewer, who signs himself "Aleph,"[104] has this to say of the 123 pages of *Orot:*

> The spirit of love and affection for *Erets Yisrael* and the People of Israel pours over all the lofty articles and ideas in this booklet.
>
> It would be very good if the author, the Rav, the Gaon, would clarify more explicitly his deep thoughts, lest he present an opportunity for opponents. Especially now, when our new enlightened Jews of the type of the "*Tsaddik*" Martin Buber, are striving with all their strength to create a new species of mystery religion, it is very dangerous to write things which are misunderstood by the people, and which the new "mystics" can easily find – because the ideas are not sufficiently explained – proofs and endorsements.

There follow the inevitable references to the offending passages: chapter 34 regarding physical exercise; chapter 43 that gives the "sinners of Israel" a certain moral edge over *shalumei emunei yisrael,* the perfect believers of Israel; and chapter 45 that likens the wicked to the dregs necessary for the production of fine wine.

Concludes the anonymous Aleph:

> I do not permit myself to critique the words of the author, the Gaon whose "small finger is mightier than my hip." But as one of the people and as a student asking his teacher, I am permitted to comment on his words and request of him a proper, sufficient explanation so as to controvert those who err.

Today, several generations after it first appeared, the search for sources to validate the enigmatic chapter 34 continues.[105]

Interestingly, in this regard there has come down to us an oral exchange between Rav Kook and the Gerrer Rebbe. Rav Kook showed the Gerrer Rebbe a precedent for what he had written concerning physical exercise in Maimonides' *Guide of the Perplexed.*

Maimonides writes:

> For there are many things that are necessary or very useful according to some people, whereas according to others they are not at all needed; as is the case with regard to the different kinds of bodily exercise, which are necessary for the preservation of health according to the prescription of those who know the art of medicine. . . . Thus, those who accomplish acts exercising their body in the wish to be healthy, engaging in ball games, wrestling, boxing and suspension of breathing . . . are in the opinion of the ignorant, engaged in frivolous actions, whereas they are not frivolous according to the learned.[106]

To this, the Rebbe responded: "The *Guide* too we do not study."

Not to be deterred, Rav Kook then related to the Gerrer Rebbe the following anecdote. Rabbi Israel Salanter once sought medical advice from a certain professor. Afterward the professor told another patient that he never had such an obedient patient as Rabbi Lipkin (= Salanter). The professor had prescribed to Rabbi Salanter to play ball for a time. Of all the patients who received that advice, none was as meticulous in heeding it as the sexagenarian Rabbi Lipkin, who didn't miss a session of ballplaying.[107]

Recently, in an interview with Naomi Gutkind of *HaZofeh,*[108] Dr. Yehoshua Be'eri claimed to have made a great discovery; to have finally broken the "code" of chapter 34. It seems that in the Haganah, but even before that, in the "Ha-Shomer" movement, the Hebrew word for exercise, *hit'amlut,* cloaked the meaning of underground military (or paramilitary) training. Thus, Rav Kook was heaping praise not on sports enthusiasts but rather on young Jews who were covertly training for the defense of their land. This would explain the otherwise out-of-place allusion to the war games in the Book of Samuel, "Let the youths arise and sport before us" (II Samuel 2:14).

Dr. Be'eri takes this view so far as to say that Rav Kook's opponents also knew that "exercise" was a veiled reference to auto-defense but dogged him nonetheless because of their anti-Zionist stance. They relied on Rav Kook's character not to respond substantively to their attacks, which would have involved betraying the true meaning of the seemingly innocuous code word "exercise."

The problem with such an ingenious reading of chapter 34 is that it may be a classic example of "creative misprision" (misreading), for Be'eri himself acknowledges that none of those who were closest to Rav Kook and the text of *Orot,* including his son Rav Zevi Yehudah, who acted in an editorial capacity, ever revealed this as being the author's "true" intention, even years after the Union Jack, symbol of British dominion, had been lowered.

David Tamar rebutted Be'eri's thesis in a subsequent issue of *Ha-Zofeh,*[109] mustering as evidence to the contrary Rav Kook's own letter[110] of 12 Tevet, 5621 (1921) to the Sephardic Rabbi of Tiberias, the Gaon Rabbi Ya'akov Ḥai Zrihen:

Regarding physical strength in *Orot*. It is explained that according to the holiness of *Knesset Yisrael*, all is holy and immeasurably sublime. Samson, who excelled in bodily strength, is the holy of the Lord, judges Israel, and is called by God's name. Because of the great need for the strengthening of holiness in the world at the End of Days through *Knesset Yisrael*, bodily strength must also be aroused with great energy. Upon those who truly serve the Lord, devolves the responsibility to remember that the inner foundation of the strength is the ancient, spiritual strength. The lion whelp which Samson split apart, corresponds to the lion smitten by Benayahu ben Yehoyada', the "Living Man," whose entire service was an inner strength of holiness performed by very lofty and fearful holy *yiḥudim* (mystical unifications); who was incomparable in both First and Second Temples. Just as the inner service of the most holy of all the generations is drawn from the holy influence of Benayahu ben Yehoyada' (may he rest in peace),[111] so all the service of bodily strength by *Knesset Yisrael* in general, is drawn from the sanctity of the divine nazirite, the mighty Samson (may he rest in peace). And just as the roots of these souls are intertwined, so the branches are also intertwined. I hope that my words are sufficient for one as wise as His Honor. The descents and blocks are certainly much coarser in the exterior of the Strength which derives from the foundation of Samson's illumination, than they are in the interior from the illumination of Benayahu ben Yehoyada'. So proceeds the call; so branch the souls.

Tamar cites this letter as disproof of Be'eri's "discovery" but does not bother to explain to us how the letter clinches matters. Is there anything in the letter to Rabbi Zrihen truly incompatible with the assumption that the strength spoken of in chapter 34 is military strength?

As a postscript, *Yated Ne'eman,*[112] the official organ of the *Degel ha-Torah* party centered in B'nei Berak and opposed to Rav Kook's ideology, gave coverage to Tamar's demolition of Be'eri's "discovery." The columnist Y. Weiss's interest in the affair is most transparent: to preserve the *status quo* regarding *Orot.* He goes so far as to activate the entire slanderous file on chapter 34: the forged proclamation of "our Teacher, the Gaon Rabbi Yosef Ḥayyim Sonnenfeld, of blessed memory, and his *beit-din* (court)," and even a photographic reproduction of a slice of Rabbi Eliezer David Greenwald of Satu-Mare's ban[113] equating *hit'amlut* (exercise) with *"futbol,"* a word that neither occurs nor is implied in the original text of *Orot.*[114] Thus, many years later, the controversy surrounding chapter 34 continues to rage.

In summation, the fairest, most comprehensive treatment of the subject is Rav Kook's own, revealed in a letter[115] of 9 Tammuz 5686 (1926) to Rabbi Dr. H. Ansbacher of Wiesbaden, Germany. The letter demonstrates most adequately that Rav Kook clearly differentiated in thought and halakhic prescription between *"futbol"* and sports on the one hand, and physical exercise and bodybuilding on the other. After the usual amenities, Rav Kook writes:

> Concerning the view of the rabbis in his country to forbid ball playing, to which the youths have been excessively attracted, causing neglect of Torah study – of course, the leaders of the generation can erect a fence around the Torah and forbid anything which leads to the forbidden, or neglect of a *mitsvah* (commandment), and they will be blessed.
>
> As for the essence of the matter, it is known that the *Yam shel Shelomo* (*Massekhet Yom Tov* 1:34) remarked upon the words of *Tosafot* (ibid. 12a, s.v. *hakhi garsinan*) that we find ball-playing on *Yom Tov* (Festivals) in the public domain:
>
> "It is amazing to permit on Yom Tov playing ball, for it is not a necessity of the day at all, only a game of children who have

not yet reached majority, but for adults I view it as an evil custom, for this is not a stroll but childishness and frivolity . . ."

The words of the *Yam shel Shelomo* were cited by the TaZ and *Magen Avraham* in chapter 518. Nevertheless, the greatest *aḥaronim* (recent authorities) sided with the RaMA there and regarding *Shabbat* in chapter 308, paragraph 45, that some permit it and the custom is to be lenient.

So too in *Shulhan 'Arukh* of the GRShZ it is written that the permissive have on what to rely and are not to be upbraided. So, if we approach the matter strictly juridically, certainly it is impossible that we should censure that which was not censured by the holy rabbis of previous generations. But if sages come to prohibit ball-playing as an enactment to make a fence around the Torah – seeing that it causes ruination, lewdness and neglect of Torah study – certainly they are so empowered. Now on *Shabbat* and *Yom Tov*, we see that it brings about a great breach and shocking desecration of Sabbath and Festival, so we absolutely forbade the game on *Shabbat* and *Yom Tov*. Our words are addressed to the weekday.

As for myself here [= in *Erets Yisrael*], when the youths – those who do not study Torah – are carried away by this game – and of their number there are many who can see for themselves in the *Poskim* (halakhic authorities) the opinions of great rabbis who were lenient – certainly it was impossible for me to tell them that the thing is absolutely forbidden. That would have resulted in the ruin of other decisions; they would say that I pile upon them stringencies even when there is room for leniency. So I was forced to say to them, that if they would be heedful of the prohibition of transporting and all labor forbidden on the Sabbath, and the place would be paved so that it would not end in digging and making holes – in such a manner I cannot protest. Would that they heed my words and play in the permitted manner. I have no power here now to pass a new decree, for the youths who study Torah, if only at set times, do not play ball at all here; and those who play ball, are youths who usually are removed from Torah, so that it is not possible to decree on account of neglect of Torah study. It is also clear that they would not accept the decree, and it is better that they be unwitting rather than deliberate. But if in their land [= Germany], ball-playing has carried away even youths who could be drawn to the house-of-study, so that ball-playing is producing neglect of Torah study, once the rabbis know that the decree would be respected by them, then it is certainly proper to enact a decree as they see fit, all for the sake of Heaven.

Touching on the general striving, on the part of some of our youth in *Erets Yisrael,* towards exercise, to strengthen physical power – if its goal should be that the nation upon its return to the Land, should also be armed with physical strength – *this has no practical bearing, due to our many sins, in the state of holiness of our generation. The matter is but a looking to salvation, that God grant a new spirit in the heart of the generation, to understand the ways of God and to look to the true salvation which will come about through the steps of redemption that God arranges for Israel's return to the Holy Land, as a sprouting forth of salvation. These matters are connected to mysteries of Torah and very holy thoughts, which I was forced to reveal a bit for the correction of the generation* [italics – BN], to show the youths swept up in strengthening the body through exercise, who consider this a great perfection, and mock the students of Torah, thinking that they have no concept of strengthened vitality – that it is not so, that if only they would sanctify their ways and thoughts, there is a possibility of uplifting the concept of strengthening the body of *Kelal Yisrael* (the Jewish People) to the point that it would stand on a very holy and wonderful

> niveau. Then it would also provide power and strength to the *tsaddikim* (righteous) and *kedoshim* (saintly) in Israel, that they ascend in holiness, by virtue of the fact that there would be found in Israel a great reservoir of vital powers, to be used for holiness and purity, and the holy work of building the People, and instilling fear in the enemies of Israel, who insult its camps, which are the camps of the Living God. The might of our forefathers and the army of the House of David were of this type.
>
> But exercise which involves throwing off the yoke of Torah and *mitsvot* (commandments) – God forbid that there be attributed to it the dimensions of holy strength of Israel, with its intention of fundamental holiness.[116] If the thing reaches to neglect of Torah study, and the Sages of Israel find that they are able to fence in the breach caused thereby, God bless them, as I wrote above.

This then is the answer to all the questions surrounding chapter 34 of *Orot ha-Teḥiyah*. If Rav Kook was merely speaking to his generation, there could be but two plausible explanations, neither of which is very salubrious: Either the man had romanticized Zionist youth to the point where he was no longer in touch with the reality of their situation,[117] or he (for some unknown reason) was flattering them, playing on their sympathies. In either case, he was not really performing a service to the youth, for it is only when a person's situation is met honestly and squarely that he can be helped. It appeared to many at the time that Rav Kook was too caught up in his own starry-eyed vision of redemptive destiny, to deal effectively with the real spiritual problems confronting youths growing up in Palestine in the 1920s.

The truth is, as the epistle to Rabbi Dr. Ansbacher reveals, Rav Kook was and was not speaking to his generation. He was speaking to future generations, and to his own, only inasmuch as the present bears the gene of the future. In this way, he was the most noble of spiritual teachers. There are two types of *rof'ei ha-nefesh* (soul healers), two approaches to helping human beings grow. One therapist deals with the person as he is now, for better or for worse. This healer treats a very definable, tangible personality. There is another type of therapist who is more prophet than practitioner. He has a vision of human potential, of what this soul could become in the future, if only given a boost in the present. His theory of personality is extremely dynamic. Rav Kook is the second teacher. Having assumed the awesome responsibility of mentor, not only to individuals but also to an entire nation, he proceeded to set in motion a spiritual evolution, using some of the most advanced and esoteric techniques of the Kabbalah.[118] He would speak to future generations of Israelis through the living corporate entity of present "Palestinian" youth.[119] He knew that the present generation was hardly ripe to receive his words, but he also knew that the future starts in the present, that the seeds of future trends are even now being germinated, and that it is the task of the *tsaddikei ha-dor,* the righteous of the generation (to use the term he constantly reverted to), to be there at the accouchement, in order to shape on the most subliminal level the development of the *yeled ha-ge'ulah,* the Child of Redemption.[120] Yes, he was talking over his listeners' heads. As the Ḥasidic masters of old,[121] he was addressing the *Shekhinah* or *Knesset Yisrael* itself. But this lonely seer did not feel that his was a "voice crying in the wilderness," for he was addressing the oversoul of Israel.

THE MAN WHO WORE *TEFILLIN* ALL DAY – AND NIETZSCHE?

Out of the film archives that we call "memory," the following reel comes up:

A young man aged twenty-five, newly arrived in Jerusalem, makes a pilgrimage to the modest home of the venerable sage Rav Zevi Yehudah Hakohen Kook. The pilgrim has spent several years immersed in the study of the works of Rav Avraham Yitsḥak Hakohen Kook and now, on the second day since his *aliyah* to Israel, he is going to have the privilege of meeting the octogenarian son of the Rav, himself a national figure most recently cast into the political limelight because of the election of his protégé Menaḥem Begin. (With Begin's *volte-face* concerning the territories, this relationship will very soon sour.)

The pilgrim comes into the meeting not knowing what, if any, significance the encounter will have to the ancient scholar. Something must have clicked at the other end too, for at a certain point Rav Zevi Yehudah abruptly says, "I feel as if we have known each other for forty years!"

The young man has brought with him a paper[122] for the mentor's inspection. Coming to the part that discusses the relation of the elder Rav Kook's thoughts to Nietzsche, Rav Zevi Yehudah comments: "It is incongruous to lump a man who wore *tefillin* (phylacteries) all day,[123] together with – Nietzsche!"

End reel.

Another scene: I am sitting opposite Dr. Yisrael Eldad (Scheib) in his study in Reḥaviah (Jerusalem). Eldad is the Israeli counterpart to Walter Kaufmann of Princeton – the foremost authority on Nietzsche in the land. (Eldad, of Galician origin, was an important figure in LeḤI [the Stern Gang] during the underground resistance to the British, alongside Yitzhak Shamir. For this reason, he was barred by Ben-Gurion from teaching during the first years of the State, and to this day is referred to by certain left-wing elements as a "fascist.") I tell him of the Nietzschean influence I have discovered in Rav Kook's writings. Eldad replies that he always intuited as much but was never able to substantiate it. I show him the correspondence between passages in *Orot*[124] and *Genealogy of Morals.*[125] Eldad muses: If Nietzsche had only known the writings of certain Ḥasidic masters, such as Rabbi Naḥman of Braslav, he would have been impressed. . . .[126]

Eldad goes on to tell me of a curious visit he received very late one evening. Hearing a knock at the door, he opens it to find standing opposite him a caftaned figure with long beard and *payot*. The first thought that crosses the mind of the secularist professor with more than an average share of mortal enemies is: a "hit." The impromptu visitor turns out to be none other than Leibel Weissfish, of Neturei Karta infamy, come to discuss his hero – Nietzsche.

Dissolve.

It is 1985. The local bookstore in my neighborhood of Bayit ve-Gan, Jerusalem is selling a volume entitled *Orot he-Emunah* (*Lights of Faith*), which was compiled from Rav Kook's writings by a disciple, Rabbi Moshe Gurevitz, who after spending most of his days in Brooklyn, has just passed away there at a ripe old age. On page 21, I read:

> Sometimes a man may be ruined through books written by those of small faith whose souls have not the holy courage, the flame of holy fire; and books written by absolute atheists, drenched with a spirit of impure courage which comes from disbelief – will mend him, and arouse in him his slumbering soul. He will find himself full of life and vigor, flowing with lofty courage and a powerful faith in the Living God.

I think I know which books "written by an absolute atheist, drenched with a spirit of impure courage," the Rav has in mind.[127]

Fade out.

A final scene from this photo montage:

I am leafing through *Zemaḥ Zevi,* the first volume of collected letters of Rav Zevi Yehudah Hakohen Kook, of blessed memory. It is nine years since his passing. On page 181 my eyes spy a German word: *Sklavenmoral* (slave morality). In 1919, Rav Zevi Yehudah, aged twenty-eight, had written the following from St. Gallen:

> ... Friedrich Nietzsche and his battle against the *Sklavenmoral*, which is truly the main importance of his personality ...[128]

Tears well up in my eyes. We have come full circle.

A friend of mine who teaches philosophy at a state university tells me: "I can understand the positions of the Neturei Karta, on the one hand, and Rav Kook on the other. I have trouble relating to everyone in between." I wonder, is it coincidental that both the Neturei Karta and Rav Kook betray Nietzschean influence?

The man who wore *tefillin* all day was being charged thereby with added power: "The *tefillin* are electric batteries for the spirit of godly holiness, which is the power of Israel."[129] "*Tefillin* are the strength of Israel."[130] Samson's strength lay in his hair. Were the *tefillin* the secret source of Rav Kook's stoutheartedness that made him an admirer of Jewish gymnasts and a begrudging sympathizer of Nietzsche?

THE SOUL OF THE SINNERS OF ISRAEL

The other passage in *Orot* that most enraged the zealots is the one that occurs in *Orot ha-Teḥiyah* at the beginning of chapter 43:

> The *nefesh* [= the lower part of the soul in Kabbalistic tradition] of sinners of Israel in the "footsteps of Messiah" – those who join lovingly the causes of the Jewish People, *Erets Yisrael* and the national revival – is more corrected than the *nefesh* of the perfect believers of Israel who lack this advantage of the essential feeling for the good of the people and the building of the nation and land. But the *ru'aḥ* [= the higher part of the soul in Kabbalistic tradition] is much more corrected in the God-fearing and Torah observant, even though the essential feeling and arousal to Jewish activism are not yet firm in them ...

Note that in the tendentious *Kol Shofar*,[131] this bilateral passage is quoted unilaterally. While Rav Kook weighs the relative merits of the *nefesh* of the irreligious and the *ru'aḥ* of the religious sector of the population, the lampooner reads selectively: "the *nefesh* of sinners of Israel is more corrected than the *nefesh* of the perfect believers of Israel." Truncated and taken out of context,[132] the sentence appears as an outright denigration of the religious community, when in fact it is Rav Kook's intention in this and other passages of *Orot* to develop a theory of complementarity whereby from the diversity of strengths and talents of different orientations on the contemporary scene, results the overall wholeness of *Knesset Yisrael* (Ecclesia Israel). Just as body and soul, brawn and brain, *nefesh* and *ru'aḥ,* are inseparable aspects of an individual human being, so athletes and ascetics, laboring Zionists and learned Jerusalemites, are integral parts of an organic national unity.

A further instance of this theory of complementarity would be Chapter 45 of *Orot ha-Teḥiyah* where Rav Kook writes: "Just as wine cannot be without dregs, so the world cannot be without wicked people." As Rav Zevi Yehudah[133] pointed out, this thought was not wholly novel on his father's part, rather the Vilna Gaon had already observed in his commentary to Isaiah (5:6):

> The dregs are a good preservative for the wine. When the wine settles on its lees, the wine is clear above and the dregs are below, but if the dregs were to rise up they would mix with the wine and it would not be suitable for drink. So the evil inclination is a good preparation for the habitation of the world. When it is below the good inclination, the wine is pure; but if it rises up, the wine is ruined.

What might be considered novel here is the extrapolation from the "dregs" of an individual psyche to the dregs of Israelite society. It was Hillel Zeitlin's[134] perspicacious assessment that Rav Kook's lasting contribution to Kabbalah lay in his creation of a national-collective psychology of *Knesset Yisrael* (as opposed to *Ḥabad,* for instance, which had made Lurianic cosmology and metaphysics the model for individual psychodynamics and experience).

SEPARATISM VERSUS UNITY

Rav Kook's opposition to Orthodox insulation must be viewed in the broader perspective of Eastern (Russian and Polish) versus Western (German and Hungarian) traditions. A response of Torah-true Jews of Western and Central Europe to the danger of Reform had been the formation of separate Orthodox enclaves, first in Hungary under Rabbi Moses Schreiber, the great "Ḥatam Sofer," and later in Germany, where in a legal act of secession from the general Jewish community known as *"Austritt,"* Rabbi Samson Raphael Hirsch[135] founded his Frankfurt bastion of faith. Rav Kook's dim view of this isolationism was typical of Lithuanian rabbinical thinking. The founder of the Mussar movement, Rabbi Israel Lipkin (Salanter), is reputed to have said that in the Ḥatam Sofer's place, his response would have been to ensconce ten Torah scholars within the Reform Temple.[136] It was Rabbi Israel Salanter's firm belief that eventually the moral power of Torah learning would win out over Reform, making the surgeon's knife an unnecessary act of desperation. Likewise, Rav Kook's mentor in the Volozhin Yeshiva, Rabbi Naftali Zevi Yehuda Berlin (NeZIV), composed a lengthy responsum forbidding such a drastic measure as the atomization of Jewish society.[137] In all fairness, the Hungarian element of Jerusalem's population might have taken umbrage not so much at Rav Kook's antiseparatist stance, which one assumes was familiar to them from earlier encounters with East Europeans, but rather the militancy with which Rav Kook expressed it. The reference to Amalek at the end of the twentieth chapter of *Orot ha-Teḥiyah* resulted in "overkill."[138]

FOR SECULAR KNOWLEDGE

> "to discover a light of holiness in all the languages and wisdoms of the world"
> (*Orot ha-Teḥiyah*, chap. 16)

Only someone familiar with the early history of the *Yishuv* in *Erets Yisrael*, the existing ban on the study of foreign languages and secular sciences in the Jewish schools, a *ḥerem* that dated back to the mid-nineteenth century and still in force in Rav Kook's day, having been fought for by successive generations of Jerusalem rabbis, especially the fiery Rabbi Joshua Leib Diskin[139] (Rav of Brisk [Brest-Litovsk], b.1818 – d.1898), can fully appreciate how truly threatening to conservative-minded Jerusalemites was this seemingly innocuous platitude of Rav Kook. In fact, the inclusion of such a reverie in *Orot* was like opening an old wound, for Rav Kook had come under fire from Jerusalem zealots over just this issue in the early part of 1914.[140] At that time, he assumed spiritual responsibility for the Taḥkemoni school in Jaffa, where both languages and secular studies were taught to youngsters. (Ironically, on that occasion, Rav Kook received a letter of moral support – though not endorsement of the school – from none other than Rabbi Yitsḥak Yeruḥam Diskin!)[141] Immediately upon Rav Kook's reentry to *Erets Yisrael* in Ellul 5679 (1919), the issue of the "schools" came up. Rav Kook's acceptance by the zealots as Rav of Jerusalem would have required his buckling under on this point, which he considered unrealistic in a sociological setting that had changed dramatically since the great rabbis had issued the original *ḥerem* over fifty years earlier.[142]

CLEARING THE CHARGE OF CHRISTOPHILIA

One of the most vicious lies concerning Rav Kook was his alleged Christophilia. In *Derekh ha-Teḥiyah* (published in 1906 in *Ha-Nir*),[143] a fascinating essay outlining Jewish history as a seesaw between reason and charisma, Rav Kook had the misfortune of characterizing the Nazarene – along with Shabbetai Zevi and other false messiahs – as a man of great personal charisma. The fanatics never let Rav Kook live this down. They would always dredge up this early "indiscretion."

One pages 5 and 6 of *Kol Shofar* we find this biting satire: "After inquiring and investigating, we have arrived at his essential character and have been convinced that certainly *the power of his personality is wonderful, his personal charisma is great.* Rav Kook is bound to be the *founder* of a new cult." The italicized words occurred (roughly) in Rav Kook's typification of Jesus. And if *Kol Shofar* was restricted to allusion, its reincarnation, *Kol Gadol*[144] (1922), cited the entire excerpt from *Ha-Nir* verbatim:

> In this weakened state, Christianity arrived and wreaked havoc with the nation. Its founder possessed a wonderful personal power, his personal charisma was great, but he was not spared the pagan defect, which is the upsurge of personal charisma without ethical and intellectual training. He was so given to the current of his psychism, and so enveloped in it those who clung to him, that they lost the Israelite component and in deed and spirit became alienated from their source.

Nothing could be farther from the truth than the accusation that Rav Kook was fond of Christianity, or the man who inspired it. He refers to Jesus the Nazarene as, "that sinner of Israel *(poshe'a yisrael)* whom the gentiles made into an idol."[145] His aversion to that religion may be traced to childhood when, as a passerby, he would find the odor of churches – though externally quite aesthetic – to be offensive.[146] Our own text *Orot* bears eloquent testimony to the sustained intellectual battle Rav Kook does with Christianity, as he hammers away, piece after piece, at the moral turpitude, hypocrisy, and spiritual inadequacy of the Church.[147] Indicative of Rav Kook's outlook on Christianity is the fact that he refers to it by the name *Minut* (Heresy),[148] the classic term employed by the Rabbis of the Talmud.[149] If anything, "Christophobia" would more likely be the word to describe Rav Kook's attitude toward Christian civilization, both in the spiritual and temporal realms. (Of course, Rav Kook's historic critique of Christianity as a world religion in no way precludes fondness and real – not feigned – love for individual Christians.) Finally, as a halakhist, Rav Kook ruled, as did Maimonides,[150] that Christianity has the status of *'avodah zarah* (idolatry).[151]

THE DIALECTIC OF MONOTHEISM AND ATHEISM

Perhaps the most profound and innovative aspect of Rav Kook's thought is the notion that a dialectic exists between faith and disbelief, and that the challenge of atheism acts as a purifying agent to rid monotheism of the last, most rarefied vestiges of corporeality.[152] It is certainly the most radical of Rav Kook's theses, and while but a subdued expression of it showed up in the 1920 edition of *Orot*, the idea, which they considered arch-heresy, was already familiar to the Jerusalem pamphleteers, who as we have shown, had several old accounts to settle with the former Rav of Jaffa. Pages 9-10 of *Kol Shofar*, and pages 10-11 of *Kol Gadol*, were devoted to treating pages 16-18 of a lengthy essay entitled "*Zer'onim*" that Rav Kook had published before the First World War in the since defunct journal *Ha-Tarbut ha-Yisraelit*.[153] The lines the zealots found so provocative are the following:

> Disbelief has the right of temporary existence because it must digest the impurity which adhered to faith for lack of intellect and service.[154]
>
> . . . Disbelief must come out in the form of civilization to uproot the memory of God and all the institutions of divine worship . . . and upon the desolate ruins wrought by disbelief, will the exalted God-knowledge build its palace.[155]
>
> The destructive wind of disbelief will purify all the filth which gathered in the lower realm of the spirit of faith . . . [156]
>
> He who recognizes the interior of disbelief, as a result sucks its honey and returns it to the source of its holiness; he beholds in the majesty of the terrible ice – the frost of heaven.[157]
>
> Disbelief returns ... to the heights of the purest belief.[158]

En passant, *Kol Shofar*[159] further refers the reader to our own *Orot ha-Teḥiyah*, chapter 51. There we find the following *pensée*:

> As long as the nation has no need to correct in general its approach to life, the impurities in the understanding of divinity, awe, faith, and all connected with them, do no visible damage. However when the time arrives in which national renascence is necessary ... immediately these impurities impede. . . . This is the reason that a great negative power is aroused in the "footsteps of Messiah," with great impudence, and this negation will purge all that is indistinct in theological conceptions. . . . Even though it is terrible to see so many truthful things, good qualities, laws and customs swept away and seemingly uprooted by the flood of negativity – despite this, eventually all will grow in purity and strength, in supernal holiness, from the firm, pure exalted kernel, which no negativity can affect. Its light will shine as a new light on Zion, with a wondrous greatness that is above every conception that souls tired materially and spiritually by a long debilitating exile, could ever conceive.

Here too, while it is possible to find precedents for such radical theology in the writings of certain Ḥasidic masters – Rabbi Nahman of Braslav wrestles with the angel of atheism[160] and Rabbi Gershon Ḥanokh of Radzyn declares that God desires to be worshiped from a world of doubt and perplexity[161] (texts probably beyond the purview of the writers of *Kol Shofar* and *Kol Gadol*) – I think Hillel Zeitlin's[162] pronouncement is essentially correct: The collectivist interpretation of history as an ongoing catharsis of the human spirit, and more specifically, the view of contemporary sociological trends as being in some way the instrument of that unfolding, the maidservant doing the bidding of the *Matrona, Knesset Yisrael*, is uniquely Rav Kook, and it is unlikely that the above-named Ḥasidic masters could have followed his thinking.

If that is the case, would we then have to surrender Rav Kook to the "wolves" who have claimed all along that there are no *bona fide* Jewish sources for Rav Kook's novel approach? Must we content ourselves with the realization that the author of *Orot* is no more than a Jewish Hegelian[163] whose theology should logically have no more impact on Torah Judaism than, say, that of an earlier Hegelian, Naḥman Krochmal (the author of *Moreh Nevukhei ha-Zeman*)?

Not so quick! True, Hegel spoke of the role of the negative,[164] the antithesis in history, but hundreds of years before Hegel there erupted in Prague a volcano of Jewish thought in the person of Rabbi Judah Loewe, MaHaRaL. In the fifth chapter of his work, *Gevurot Hashem*, MaHaRaL treats us to a history lesson:

> It has been explained that Abraham and Israel were similar in the respect that their incubation was in a nation opposite to them. . . . It is possible to provide a single reason for both of them, namely that though opposites are essentially antithetical, nevertheless, inasmuch as the opposites together perfect the total, for this reason, they combine – to perfect the total. Therefore, though Israel and Egypt are essentially opposites, nevertheless, as the thing and its opposite perfect the total, they combine together. Therefore Israel dwelled in Egypt[165] and Abraham in Ur of the Chaldees because the two opposites together form the total. Do not fret that this phenomenon is restricted to opposites such as fire and water which are each considered existents, but in the case of opposites where one is considered good and the other evil, the concept does not apply – it is not so. Certainly, even though it is evil and not an existent, nevertheless the two of them perfect the total, for it [= evil] is also a requisite of creation.
>
> In the Midrash (*Numbers Rabbah* 19:1) it states: "*Who can produce the pure from the impure – not One?* For instance, Abraham from Teraḥ, Ḥezekiah from Aḥaz, Josiah from Amon, Israel from the Nations – who did this, who decreed this? Is it not the Only One of the World (*yeḥido shel 'olam*)?" Our Rabbis, of blessed memory, explained that logic dictates

> thus, that the pure should arise from the impure. Therefore the verse states, "Not One?" This means that because they are polarities they have one cause, for existence is not divided but rather has a single cause. This is the First Cause from whom came the opposites .... Therefore it says, "Not the Only One of the World?" who unites existence ... even evil existence He unites. This is a very deep matter. It has been explained that though Terah was an idolater, the side of holiness issued from him, being as the opposites proceed from one another. The main explanation is, as we said, that it is seemly that the opposites proceed one from the other, because of the relation and synthesis they have together. The two opposites perfect a total which lacks nothing; it is a thing and its opposite, so nothing could be lacking. This is the concept of unity, which by definition is the all, outside of which there is nothing. For this reason, one pole which is part of the total proceeds toward perfection, and there derives from it a second part, in order to complement, so that the action derived from the Actor – God – has all, just as the Actor has all, being as He is One. Therefore He who is One perfects the all: "Not One?" in the sense that He is All. The farther apart the poles, the more seemly that they derive one from the other, for in this way they are the whole. . . . This is the phenomenon of Abraham coming from Teraḥ, Ḥezekiah from Aḥaz.

Maharal of Prague is universally accepted by the Jewish People. Who would dare cast aspersions or mutter imprecations on his teaching?!

SHEER IGNORANCE

If one reads further in the *Kol Shofar*, beyond the actual "*ḥerem*" itself, other objections surface, one of which betrays real ignorance and paranoia. On page 10, Rav Kook was bludgeoned for having abbreviated (in *Orot ha-Teḥiyah*, chapter 53) the verse in Exodus 20:2

to read, "I am the Lord your God – from the land of Egypt," as if in the omission of the words "Who took you out" lurked some sinister Zionist plot! Actually Rav Kook was not guilty of omission at all but rather had quoted – in its entirety – a less-known verse in Hosea 13:4. (Subsequent editions of *Orot* clarified this by dissolving the dash, which could be misinterpreted as an ellipsis, and providing the letter *vav* [and] at the onset of the quote from Hosea.)

Equally preposterous is the charge on that page of *Kol Shofar* that Rav Kook has given credence to the gods of the nations by writing (in the first chapter of *Orot ha-Teḥiyah*), "The soulful, divine, national feeling blossoms," etc. True, in the Hebrew original no comma demarcates between the words *divine* and *national*, but neither are they hyphenated to indicate an equation.

ZIONISM: WHETHER IT IS BETTER TO FIGHT IT OR REVEAL ITS INNER LIGHT

On page 11 of *Kol Shofar*, the author takes exception to the passage at the end of the ninth chapter of *Orot ha-Teḥiyah*, where Rav Kook says:

> Now if at a certain time there should be found an arousal, whereby people will speak only of the spirit of the nation and will attempt to negate the spirit of God from all these assets and from their revealed source which is the national spirit – what should the righteous of the generation do? To rebel against the spirit of the nation, even verbally, and to reject its assets, this is something impossible: The spirit of the Lord and the spirit of Israel are one. Rather the righteous must work hard to reveal the light and the holiness in the national spirit, the light of God in all these . . .

For Rav Kook, outright rejection of Zionism with all that it entailed – love of the Land, agrarian sentiment, resurrection of the Hebrew language, aspirations to national and military independence

– was out of the question. "What should the righteous ... do? To rebel against the spirit of the nation . . . this is something impossible." But for many of the Jerusalem pietists this was the only realistic option. Writes the author of *Kol Shofar*:[166] "Eradicate the evil from your midst, etc."; "Happy is the man who went not in the counsel of the wicked and in the way of sinners, etc."; "There is no peace, said the Lord to the wicked"; "Do not unite with the wicked even to perform a *mitsvah*" (*Avot de-Rabbi Nathan*). Here it is not a case of badmouthing Rav Kook so much as a real ideological difference how the righteous are to approach the nascent Zionist movement.

'ARFILEI TOHAR: *CLOUDS OF PURITY* AND SINS FROM GOD

Rabbi Eliezer David Greenwald of Satu-Mare, Romania, in his 1926 ban on Rav Kook's writings,[167] cited as proof of deviance the following line from *'Arfilei Tohar*, page 11:[168]

> At times, when there is need to transgress the way of the Torah, and there is no one in the generation who can show the way, the thing comes about through breaching.

The rest of the piece, that Rabbi Greenwald did not cite, reads:

> Nevertheless it is better for the world that such a matter come about unintentionally. This is the fundamental, "Better that they be unwitting rather than deliberate sinners." Only when prophecy rests on Israel, is it possible to innovate such a matter as a "temporary measure." Then it is done with express permission. With the damming of the light of prophecy, the innovation comes about through a long-lasting breach, which saddens the heart with its externals, but gladdens it with its inner content.[169]

Actually, this very idea had already been enunciated by the Ḥasidic greats, Rabbi Aharon Halevi Horowitz of Starosselje (eminent disciple of Rabbi Shneur Zalman of Liadi, the famous *"Ba'al ha-Tanya"*) and Rabbi Zadok Hakohen Rabinowitz of Lublin.

Rabbi Aharon Halevi wrote:

> This concept is either through a "temporary measure," or a divine command, or done unwittingly and unintentionally, such as a *ba'al teshuvah* (returnee to Jewish observance) who, possessed by a spirit of folly, had committed sins.[170]

And the "Kohen" (as he was referred to in Ḥasidic circles) wrote:

> If he had already repeated the same sin, it becomes as if permitted in his eyes .... There is a great secret here. . . . It becomes as if permitted, for all is the thought of the Great of Counsel, may His name be blessed, to benefit a man, even a sinner and wicked man, to better his end, when he will return and correct that which he destroyed, precisely in this way. None will be lost from Him.[171]

But again, such treasures of Ḥasidic esoteric literature were probably beyond the ken of those bent on destroying Rav Kook. And even if they were familiar with such books, had not the Vilna Gaon banned the teachings of the *Tanya* (the classic of Ḥabad, written by Rabbi Shneur Zalman of Liadi), and had not the more conservative-minded Ḥasidic masters been at loggerheads with the school of Izbica (pronounced "Izhbitsa") to which Rabbi Zadok Hakohen of Lublin belonged?[172]

RAV KOOK ON *OROT*

Though Rav Kook suffered immensely on account of what he had written in *Orot*, in the letters at our disposal his tone never descends to the level of bitterness. The voice that he admirably maintains sounds a high note of transcendence and maturity.

In the summer of 1920, when the first ominous clouds begin to gather over the halcyon skies of Jerusalem, Rav Kook wrote a letter[173] of assuagement to his aged parents:

> Concerning those grumbling about *Orot*, pay no attention. This is the way of people accustomed not to study *hilkhot de'ot* (philosophic matters); they are incensed against any explanation or illumination which appears to them novel, even though the foundations of the things are truly ancient and issue from a holy source.[174] Men greater and holier than me throughout the generations suffered this pain. For me, it is enough that the understanding just men, whose treasure is true awe of heaven, will be invigorated by things which I consider generally beneficial and spiritually advantageous to publish at times.
>
> To explain the sources would be of no avail. Most of the time, the sources do not state explicitly my thought. Only after contemplation and deep feeling do they reveal this. These agitators, or even simple-minded people who are not accustomed to such concepts, will not accept the results even when shown the source from which the things flow.
>
> I implore my dear parents not to be pained by any of these things. This is the obligation of the holy work, the work of God, whose seal is truth, not to be afraid of agitation and insult. I do not complain about them at all, especially the innocent among them, in whose pain I share. However, I see that I am obligated to explain matters which will bring benefit and honor to the People of God and strength to Torah in the course of the days to come, with the help of God.
>
> Your dutiful son, respectfully,
>
> Avraham Yitsḥak Hakohen Kook

The contents of the letter are remarkable for their altruism. Not only is Rav Kook able to transcend his own predicament to comfort his parents,[175] but more startling is the compassion he feels toward uncomprehending Jews who are pained by his abstruse writings. He absorbs the arrows shot his way, confident in the knowledge that he is serving the Lord and His people Israel.

This document is invaluable to the study of Rav Kook's philosophy. One of the crucial questions that beleaguers scholars of his works is the problem of sources. There are those who would argue that Rav Kook's truly revolutionary thought is bereft of Jewish sources, if by "Jewish" we mean traditional sources of Torah. Gloats the *Kol Shofar*: "They [= Rabbis Kook and Ḥarlap] say, write and preach things without a reason – pure prattle – as the speakers on the stage at the Civic Center, without any source from our Rabbis, of blessed memory, because that is the truth: They have no valid source but are taken from a foreign well . . ."[176] On the other hand, there are those who contend quite the opposite, that a thoroughgoing search for duplication in the works of MaHaRaL, Rabbi Zadok Hakohen (of Lublin), et al, would leave to Rav Kook's *oeuvre* scant original motifs. For those of us who are uncomfortable with the glibness of both these extremes, formulation of an answer becomes difficult. Rav Kook, in this letter to his parents, could be the spokesman of just this middle-ground quandary. In general, originality is not something easily defined. There are schools of literary criticism[177] that suggest that originality is a phantom, that every text is to be sure an outgrowth of an earlier text. These attempt to develop a model adequate to the complexity and intricacy of the creative (or not so creative) process whereby the visible text is in some way a reaction to an invisible precursor.[178] In the specific case of Rav Kook's thought, there are three coordinates that the researcher must lock onto: Jewish sources, both traditional and modern; general, philosophic sources; and finally, the source of Rav Kook's own *ru'aḥ ha-kodesh* or divine inspiration (see below the letter he would write on the first day of Ḥanukkah, 5681).

Shortly after the appearance of *Kol Shofar*, on the fourteenth of Tishri 5681 (1920), Rav Kook writes to his son Rav Zevi Yehudah. His reaction to the diatribe is one of pity for the city of Jerusalem. Again, he is absolutely convinced he is in possession of some higher truth that he is morally bound to reveal.

> Here once again the indignation of our slanderers has been aroused concerning *Orot*. They are especially angered by the booklet *Tovim Me'orot* by our dear Rabbi Y.M. Ḥ[arlap] (may he live). In the name of the "Agudah," they issued very alarming libelous proclamations. I pity poor Jerusalem whose honor is sullied by such deeds, but what can we do? Do we have the right to bottle up the revealed truth?[179]

After some months of reflection, in a letter[180] dated 8 Kislev, 5621 (1920), Rav Kook confides to his son his belief that the differences in ideology between his own stance and that of the Agudat Yisrael movement are insurmountable. Rather than recrimination, we find resignation to the sincere difference in outlook:

> It seems that the lofty nationalist aspect expressed in *Orot*, as in all our inner aspirations, really runs counter to their spirit and soul-ability. Can we blame them for this?[181]

A couple of weeks later (on the first day of Ḥanukkah), again to Rav Zevi Yehudah,[182] Rav Kook's tone has become defensive as he chalks up an unnamed European rabbi's opposition to *Orot* to small-mindedness and fanaticism:

> I wonder upon what the respected rabbi[183] who opposes the opinions set forth in *Orot*, bases himself. You did not explain his opposition. If there would come to me well-reasoned comments, perhaps it would be worthwhile to elucidate the foundations of the matters, but I suspect that the entire source of the criticism is some basis of pettiness and anger, which generally are fed by poor understanding of holy concepts, in

> which case, great, lengthy explanations are required – and most of the time, it is difficult for me to explain the depth of thought in lucid language. Especially, after all the explanations, the essence of these matters stands beyond consciousness. They are dependent on the fount of poetry and supernal faith – the secret of the just, the fearers of God and respecters of His name, with true purity and hope of salvation.

In Rav Kook's own final analysis, no amount of rational explanation could do justice to concepts whose source was not conscious deliberation but streams of mystical, poetic, or prophetic inspiration.

In a practical vein, the lesson Rav Kook learned from the *Orot* incident was not to print ideas that were not fully elucidated. The publishing of his philosophic oeuvre would continue undaunted, but caution would not be thrown to the winds. Concerning the forthcoming publication of *Orot ha-Teshuvah* (1924), Rav Zevi Yehudah was advised: "For God's sake, be exacting that nothing is issued which is not thoroughly explained. Examine this with your straight intellect and consult with my intimate friend, the Gaon R. Ya'akov Moshe Ḥarlap (may he live)."[184]

THE METAHISTORY OF *OROT*

As we have seen, *Orot* is one of those rare books in history whose sociological impact is still felt years later. *Orot* introduced to the Jewish scene a new vision and movement that is referred to as the "*dati*" or "*dati-le'umi*" (national-religious) current in contemporary Israeli society. The opposition to the book should not be interpreted as restricted to isolated literary criticism; rather it is the clash of two worlds, the pitting against one another of two orientations within Orthodoxy, which would later come to be known as the "*ḥaredi*" (anti-Zionist) and "*dati*" sectors, peopled by the spiritual heirs of Rabbis Diskin and Sonnenfeld on the one hand, and Rabbi Kook on the other. In this respect, one might correctly compare the place of *Orot* in the *dati-ḥaredi* controversy to that of the *Tanya* (written by Rabbi Shneur Zalman of Liadi) in the Ḥasidic-Mitnagdic polemic in Lithuania at the end of the eighteenth century. The ban proclaimed against *Orot* is definitely on a par with the *ḥerem* pronounced by the Gaon of Vilna on the now classic Ḥasidic text, referred to by Ḥabad cognoscenti as the *torah she-bikhtav* (written Torah) of *Ḥasidut*. Today, this is hindsight, but there was one man living in the 1920s for whom all this and more was foresight. Reading the lines Rabbi Ḥayyim Hirschensohn penned in the immediate aftermath of the *Orot* controversy, we marvel at this view from above:

> Evidently it was this situation which the great intellect, Master of the Land of Israel, the Gaon Rav Avraham Yitsḥak Kook, saw when he thought to establish the Yeshivah "Merkaz Ha-Rav," whose studies will include all the branches of Jewish learning and all that is relevant to the life of the Nation. May the Lord His God be with him and may the will of the Lord through his hand succeed. However, every creation which begins from the center may hope to exist, to be strengthened and even expand to a degree, but not to broaden too much, because breadth depends on the amount of potential in the periphery for being drawn to the center. A small, mighty center was the company of the Ba'al Shem Tov and his disciples, of blessed memory. But there was great potential for Ḥasidism among all the Jews of Volhynia, the Ukraine and Romania, and they were immediately attracted to the center which broadened and expanded. There was great potential for Torah in Lithuania and they were drawn to the center of the Gaon of Vilna and his disciples, of blessed memory. Those who had certain potential for enlightenment were drawn at that time to the Berlin center. Thus, I do not know if there is enough raw material in our people for the Kabbalistic enlightenment which is in the girth of the understanding heart, the Gaon Kook (may his light shine) so that his center may widen to broader horizons. To

vivify the dry bones, in my opinion, a center is insufficient. Only a spirit which comes from the four qualitatively different directions can breathe life into the various bones and bring them together. Only then will they take on flesh, sinews and skin. Finally, the Torah of Rabbi Meir who enlightens the eyes of sages in the Law, will transform the skin (*'or*) into light (*'or*), and they will arise and live.

Nevertheless, it may be that there is in *Erets Yisrael* enough potential to broaden the center of this Gaon, and the indication of this, is the opposition which arose in Jerusalem to the original opinions which are in the book *Orot* by that Rabbi. Opposition to an idea is a sign of renascence. When an idea gives off signs of life and light, they penetrate to the hearts of opponents and generate in their blood "antibodies," which battle for the conservative existence to which their souls have become accustomed. I am not considering here the despicable opposition of the libelous broadsheet *Kol Shofar*, etc., for such things come only from the thorns which surround the supernal rose. They are not as a flashing sword to protect the rose from harm, but on the contrary, endanger the very rose which at the slightest movement could be pierced by the thorns which pretend to be her lovers. I am thinking of the opposition of the elder *ge'onim* of Jerusalem (may the Lord preserve and save them) which reached such a state that the Gaon Kook himself, in his great humility, signed at the behest of the holy Rebbe of Gur (may his light shine) that he retracts the passages in the book *Orot* which caused the opposition.... This opposition and the attempt by the greats of the generation to achieve reconciliation, demonstrates that there is enough potential in the Land for Merkaz Ha-Rav....

This is the truth. Polite opposition indicates the great value of the two sides, and that there is enough potential in both to attract and broaden to great centers – whether one side

> will overcome the other, or they remain on an even par. Lack of opposition to an original idea indicates brittleness of the People's bones . . . [185]

"HOLY OF HOLIES"

Rav Zevi Yehudah, paraphrasing Rabbi Akiva (who said, "All the Writings are holy, and the Song of Songs is holy of holies"[186]), used to say that all of his father's writings are holy, but *Orot* is holy of holies.[187] One struggles to understand what he meant by this ejaculation. Was it the fact that the holiness of *Orot* had been called into question that prompted a defensive, hyperbolic statement? (Just as Rabbi Akiva had been forced to defend the sanctity of the Song of Songs by those who viewed it as merely an early pastoral romance.) Or is it that *Orot* is in a very real sense Rav Kook's seminal work, the inner sanctum, the innermost spiritual laboratory, from which flow creative energy and inspiration to many other, perhaps more developed, works? Finally, and this is most likely, Rav Zevi Yehudah meant it literally: *Orot* is the holiest of his father's writings. Why is that?

We should look to the title itself for an answer. *Orot. Lights.* What sort of lights? Is it not the "Light of Messiah" (*'oro shel mashiaḥ*), a term that occurs with great frequency in this slim volume?[188] It is the Light of Messiah that informs Rav Kook's entire vision. It is this messianic light that makes *Orot* holy of holies.

We must yet define the term *kodesh ha-kodashim* (holy of holies) from within Rav Kook's own system. What is the precise meaning of the term in Rav Kook's lexicon? In *Orot ha-Kodesh* we read:

> There is a world of *ḥol*, the profane, and a world of *kodesh*, the holy; worlds of holiness and worlds of profanity. The worlds contradict one another. Of course, the contradiction is subjective. Man with his limited apprehension cannot reconcile the sacred and the secular; he cannot overcome their

contradictions. However, they are reconciled at the pinnacle of the world, in the foundation of the *kodesh ha-kodashim*, the holy of holies.[189]

In the *sanctum sanctorum*, the innermost chamber of the Temple, were contained the cherubim, angelic figures reminiscent of male and female locked in a loving embrace.[190] This was the mystery that the nations of the world could not fathom: How could the most human of activities, the relationship between male and female, be metaphoric of the most sublime divine dimensions?[191] It is this same conjugal symbolism that permeates *Shir ha-Shirim*, the Song of Songs. It is this reconciliation of the seemingly contradictory realms of the sacred and the profane by attainment to the level of *kodesh ha-kodashim* (holy-of-holies), which is the stuff of *Orot*, wherein physical exercise done to serve the Lord becomes an act of divine devotion.[192]

Contents

In exile, the universalist side gains prominence; in *Erets Yisrael* the universalism is expressed through the medium of particularism. Exile is a cleansing of the particularist phenomenon. Jewish history, which began on a universalist note, comes full circle.

4 Authentic and Distorted Jewish Vision

Exile distorts Judaic vision. The thoughts of a Jew regain authenticity to the degree that they are attached to the Land of Israel.

5 Land of Prophecy

Prophecy is a function of the imaginative faculty. Inasmuch as the imagination is warped in exile, prophecy is dependent on the Land of Israel. Intellect is also affected, as the two, imagination and intellect, are intertwined.

6 The Mission of a Jew from the Land Living Outside

The divine inspiration of the Land of Israel follows a Jew into exile. There it acts as a magnet to attract elements of holiness in the Diaspora. The feeling of spiritual alienation outside the Land is a barometer of inner attachment to the Land.

7 Torah Letters and Soul Letters

The correspondence of the "letters of the Torah" and the "letters of the soul." The "letters of the soul" thrive in the "air of the Land of Israel." The justice of Torah is the essence of the soul-letters of all Israel.

8 Land of Israel: Vessel to Jewish Lights

The lights within the Israelite soul seek the vessels for their full expression: the Land of Israel where all the commandments of the Torah may be fulfilled. This yearning fills even the emptiest of Jewish spirits.

Ha-Milḥamah (The War)

1 The Messianic Dimension of War

World conflagration has a messianic dimension. Such conflicts produce tangible results in the Land of Israel.

2 Reincarnations of Biblical Warriors in Our Day

The times determine the caliber of souls that appear. The battle for

Yisrael u-Teḥiyato (Israel and Its Renascence)

1 Israel, Narrator of God

Israel is a living narration of God's greatness.

2 The Causal and Ethical Approaches to Understanding Existence

Two approaches to understanding existence: the causal approach and the ethical approach. In Jewish history they are bound together.

3 The Legal System: Challenge to Spirituality

Unlike other nations, all Israel's values stem from holiness. The significance of the institution of *Semikhah* (Ordination). Jewish jurisprudence. The difference between the "religion of law" and the "religion of love."

4 The Christian Attempt to Supplant Judaism

Christian civilization effaces the specific Jewish content, replacing it with a shabby imitation that it stretches over the nations.

5 Judaism versus Christianity: Holism and Dualism

Judaism's holistic approach to spirituality versus the schizoid spirituality of Christianity.

6 The Return of Spiritual Plunder

Judaism retrieves from Christianity its spiritual plunder.

7 Tradition and Heresy

Jewish tradition is wary of heresy, i.e., Christianity.

8 The Divinity of the World

The divinity of this world. God's omnipresence. The revelation of this truth through Israel.

9 The Messianic Light of Panentheism

Christianity purports that the everlasting covenant between God and Israel is abrogated. Christianity's fallacy: Even evil is subject to divine authority. The "Light of Messiah" reveals the truth of panentheism.

10 *Tikkun 'Olam* (Cosmic Correction)

Beyond the correction of man's soul, Israel aspires to cosmic *tikkun*

20 The "Light of Messiah" within the Zionist Movement

Faith alone is not enough. Israel grounds faith in action. Even in the secular Jew the "Light of Messiah" shines. The "Light of Messiah" within the Zionist movement. Resurrection of the dead. The return of the Nations.

21 The Prophetic Character of the Different Jewish Ideologies

Hidden prophecy flows in every soul of Israel. The different Jewish ideologies are but branches of a single supernal root.

22 The Great Challenge of the Renascence: Synthesis

The unification of Kabbalah and Halakha. The creative forces that converge in the national renascence. The challenge to "students of the Lord": Synthesis.

23 The Chaos of the "Footsteps of Messiah": The New Universality

The search for discipline: intellectual and national. The chaos of the "Footsteps of Messiah" is the harbinger of a new universality.

24 The Poise of Pharisaic Judaism

Halakha: the base for Agadah. The dangers inherent in extreme agadism. The balance of Pharisaic Judaism as opposed to other currents within ancient Judaism.

25 The New Return: "We Never Left!"

The cosmic yearning for holiness. The New Return: realization that the world was never distanced from God. The "Fallen Booth of David" truly never fell.

26 The Role of Family in Cosmic Harmony

Emun and *Emunah* (Family and Faith). The waters of *Sotah,* the adulteress. The reparation of all human and domestic relations.

27 The Disappearance and Return of the Twelve Tribes

The dissolution of tribal divisions: in exile, a blessing in disguise. The significance and return of the twelve tribes of Israel.

28 Redemption: An Ongoing Process

The ongoing redemptive process: from Egypt to now.

Orot ha-Teḥiyah (Lights of Renascence)

true creativity and free inquiry follow. National defense against false creativity and scientism. The defensiveness is understandable, but "those who are truly full of courage" adopt another tack: explaining that Torah is the surest basis for free creativity and science.

3 Ethics: Imposed and Natural

European nationalist philosophy rejects foreign Judaic ethical influence. In Israel, ethics are natural. Exile purified this nature of Israel. Through the renascence, the disembodied natural spirit will concretize. The connection of past and future.

4 *Kehunah:* The Spiritual Elite

The existence of pietists allows the rest of the nation to focus on the material. Mediocre spirituality allows only halfhearted attention to the material; great spirituality permits concerted material effort. Great spiritual personalities are not depressed by the material achievement of the nation. The institution of priesthood *(kehunah).*

5 The Architecture of Future Judaism

The implications of recognizing ourselves as "the Chosen People." Israel, which bestowed ethics on the world, will now bestow enjoyment and vivacity as well. There must be an ideal higher than socialism. The Israelite collective gives vent to godliness. The commandments will be rekindled with life. The present is informed by past and future. Full-bodied Israelite life: Land, Temple, Kingdom, Prophecy. The relation between present and future. The commandments dependent on the Land: the sabbatical year and tithes. Their present observance is education for the future. The power of the *mitsvot* to move the People into the future. The experiential element of tithing: exposure to the priests *(kohanim)* and Levites. The longing for Kingdom and Temple, Priesthood and Prophecy. The phony sophistication of Western civilization is as nothing compared to the innocence of humanity's childhood – Israel.

6 Ideals into Action

The inviolability of the aspirations of the nation's soul. Those aspirations are contained in the Torah. The arduous task of translating

13 Setting God Free

The divine existential quest of the People. Its clouding over in exile. In exile, God shrinks the divine light of the cosmos to fit the People in their reduced state. Thus, the salvation becomes the salvation of God Himself, as it were.

14 Putting Together Pre-Torah and Torah

The "Light of Messiah" as the convergence of different periods of Jewish History – the period of the Patriarchs and the later chapter of Torah.

15 The Relation of Periphery to Center

When Israel is whole – embracing Temple and State, prophecy and wisdom – it has the ability to encompass the secular and worldly. In exile, this is not possible. Sabbath limits: two thousand cubits versus twelve *mil.*

16 Uplifting the Sparks within Labor, Languages, and Sciences

The righteous man's love of work. The union of the righteous of the generation with the common laborers. The conversion of the curse of work to blessing. The sanctification of all languages and wisdoms of the world. The influence of the Holy Tongue. Illuminating the embellishments of modern society.

17 Two Great Luminaries: Faith and Love

Two luminaries of life: faith and love. Contemporary civilization is predicated on disbelief and hatred. Torah is love, and *mitsvot,* faith. *Hitkashrut* – connecting to the righteous. "The civilized wicked" are incapable of cleaving. Living spiritual life to its fullest in the Land of Israel.

18 The Three Wrestlers – Orthodoxy, Nationalism, and Liberalism – and the Referee

Three forces wrestling in our camp: the Orthodox, the Nationalist, and the Humanist. Moving from divisiveness to unification. The positive aspect of the negation. *Kemitsah* (the handful of flour in the Temple). Holiness as one of three camps; supernal holiness that transcends the three camps.

29 The Israelite Poet

As Redemption beckons, the national poet of Israel becomes a poet of nature.

30 "I See with My Eyes the Light of Elijah's Life Rising"

Elijah heralds the holiness of Nature.

31 The Spiritual Forecast of the Emerging *Yishuv* (Settlement)

The People, once solidly rooted in the Land, will grow organically toward a life of observance of *mitsvot.* One needn't be overly alarmed by the outer husks of the nationalist movement that will naturally fall away.

32 A Yet Anonymous Redemption

At present, the Redemption is an anonymous work – God's name is not called upon it. Eventually the divine nature of the Redemption will be revealed. The interim, painful period is referred to as *ḥevlei mashiaḥ* (the Pangs of Messiah).

33 Rediscovering the Holiness of the Flesh

Part and parcel of *Teshuvah* is the return to the body, the rediscovery of the holiness of the flesh.

34 On Physical Exercise

Just as King David combined his ability as warrior with his sacred liturgical activity, so nowadays physical exercise done to provide the Nation with strength and the spiritual exercises of the mystics are mutually reinforcing.

35 Pitfalls and Purity of Flesh (and Imagination)

An historical survey of alternating periods of Intellect and Imagination: Ezra – Exile – Ḥasidism – National Renascence. Ritual purity as a demand of the in-body approach to spirituality.

36 On Modern Hebrew Literature

In attempting a renascence of Hebrew literature, writers must purify their souls to be worthy of the name *soferim.*

37 The Revolution in Hebrew Literature

The readers, who will be disgusted with the impurity of contemporary

46 The Holy in the Secular

Just as Man is higher than the angels, so the holy found in the lowly is higher than the undescended holy.

47 Atheism and the Higher Belief

Souls imprinted with a higher vision cannot be satisfied with mediocre religiosity and end up in disbelief. The cure is to prepare "vessels" for the higher "lights."

48 Torah from Heaven

In Exile, the Heavens were portrayed in a gross, corporeal manner. As the End approaches, the Heavens are revealed in their ethereal light and the concept of "Torah from *Heaven*" is upgraded accordingly.

49 Thank Offering for the Evil

The "Light of Messiah" will reveal that it is proper to thank the Lord for evil as well as good.

50 The Oral Torah: An Outcropping of Organic Jewish Life

In Exile, the Oral Torah receives ever-waning inspiration from the light of the Past, from the Written Torah; with the Redemption, the Oral Torah will once again receive inspiration directly from the People of Israel.

51 Atheism: Cleanser of Belief

In Exile, the Nation could make do with foggy notions of God. With the national renascence, the concept of God must be purified. This is the *raison d'etre* of the passing phenomenon of atheism.

52 Rejecting Questionable Means

The light of Redemption will reject all but the purest means, even though initially this will weaken the end.

53 Overviewing History

The divine inspiration that abounds in *Erets Yisrael* today allows an overview of the "hand of God" manipulating the entire history of mankind.

54 The Mistake of Emulating European Nihilism

Europe rightly rejects Judaic morality, which is beyond its spiritual

63 The Hidden Cruse of Oil

The Nations defiled only the outer trappings of Judaism; within, the soul of Israel – and each individual Jew – burns brightly.

64 The Mysteries of Torah Bring Redemption

The true arousal to return to the Land comes not through outer persecution but rather through the unleashing of the mysteries of Torah, which demand the Land of Israel.

65 The Light Grows Strong

The spiritual light begins to radiate out from the souls of the elite to encompass all aspects of life.

66 To the Wellspring of Prophecy

We aspire to what all nations aspire to, but more: prophecy. The fact that we have not yet reached it, does not cast us into skepticism.

67 The Laws of the Universe and the Laws of the Torah

The interconnection of the laws of the universe and the laws of Torah. The national renascence, by which the People returns to the Land and to Torah, rebounds throughout the cosmos.

68 Major *Teshuvah* and Minor *Teshuvah*

Two species of Return: fear of punishment/freedom born of the mysteries of Torah. Israel aspires to the latter.

69 The Great Return

Before full-fledged Prophecy, *ru'aḥ ha-kodesh* (divine inspiration). The Great Return that flows from *ru'aḥ ha-kodesh.*

70 Fallen Giants and the Flames of Inner Torah

Great masters effect the return of the fallen souls of Israel, not through externals but by putting people in touch with the inner Torah. In this way, the fallen messianic potential of the national revivalist movement will be repaired.

71 Soul: Body :: God: World

The soul, which is not bounded by space, works through the body. So

A Great Call (Jaffa, 1908)

אורות

Orot

מתוך כתבי קדש של מרן אבא הרב שליט״א. אשר הוצאתם לאור נתעכבה לרגלי המלחמה, ושעתידים לצאת לאור בקרוב בעזר השם. הוצאתי בזה את ״אורות-התחיה״ האלה, המאירים בדבריהם ערכי הרוח והמעשה של מהלך בנין בית ישראל בתחיתו ושיבתו בארץ קדשו.

יחד עם זה ראיתי לנכון, להקדים לפני הפרקים האלה - שנכתבו בערך שנתים לפני המלחמה - את פרקי ״אורות מאופל״ אלה בשלשת מחלקותיהם: ״ארץ-ישראל״ ״המלחמה״ ״ישראל ותחיתו״, אשר נכתבו במשך השנתים הראשונות של המלחמה, ששהה מרן אבא הרב שליט״א בשויציה.

צבי יהודה הכהן קוק

Preface

Out of the holy writings of our teacher, my father, the Rav (may he live long, good years, Amen) whose publication was delayed due to the war, and are due to appear shortly, with the help of God – I have taken these "Lights of Renascence," which illuminate by their words the values of spirit and action of the process of building the House of Israel through its renascence and return to its Holy Land.

At the same time, I have seen fit to precede these chapters – written approximately two years before the war – with the chapters of "Lights from Darkness," subdivided in three: "The Land of Israel," "The War," "Israel and Its Renascence." The latter were written during the first two years of the war, which our teacher, my father, the Rav (may he live long, good years, Amen) spent in Switzerland.

Zevi Yehudah Hakohen Kook

לדגל "ירושלים"

תחית גוי קדוש
על אדמת הקדש

אנו מדברים על דבר נשמת התחיה הלאמית שלנו, על דבר שורש החיים של שאיפת בנין הארץ, ארצנו הקדושה, בידי העם ההולך וחי, שהיא תחית הקדש.

אוצר החיים של הקודש, בכל לב בישראל הוא גנוז, בכללותה של האומה, כח זה הוא הרודה בכל הליכותיה ומהותה, עריגתה למחצבתה, לתחיתה, לארצה, רק בתכונת הקדש המיוחד לאופיה היא קימת; והאופי של התכונה אשר לתחית החול איננו כי־אם פרוזדור של הטרקלין, הצעדים הראשונים שהילד מתחיל ללכת, ואשר הם יביאוהו לרוץ אורח כגבור.

החול עם כל תפארתו המפורסמת לא תמלא הנפש ממנה, ואין הערך שלה נשלם, כי־אם כשיופיע אור הקודש העליון עליה, כל

Degel Yerushalayim
(The Banner of "Jerusalem")

RENASCENCE OF A HOLY NATION ON THE HOLY SOIL

We are speaking of the soul of our national renascence, the root-of-life of the aspiration to build the land, our holy land, by the living people – that is, the renascence of the holy.

The treasure-of-life of the holy is stored in every heart of Israel. In the nation as a whole, this is the power that controls all its ways and essence. The nation's longing for its origin, its renascence, its land, exists only in the quality of holiness that is peculiar to its character. The dimension of secular renascence is but a corridor before the banquet hall, the first steps that the child begins to walk, which will eventually bring him to run as a strong man.

The soul cannot be satisfied by the profane despite all its famous glory. Neither is the value of the secular complete until the sublime light of holiness has appeared over it. The vigor of life finds its solid base only through the light of holiness permeating national life and all

העז של החיים ימצא את בסיסו האמיץ, רק על-ידי אור הקודש שיתפלש בחיים הלאמיים וכל מעבדיהם, ולשם כך אנחנו צריכים לעבד את ההגדרה הברורה, מהו תכן הקדש, ומהו תכן החול, זהו אחד מיסודי העבודה הלאומית שלנו, שהזמן גרמה.

התחיה השלמה תחדש לנו לעיני כל חי: הארה מלאה הוד והדרת קודש בתפלה, בתורה, בדרכי המוסר, ובהקשבת האמונה, בכל הקפה הרעיוני והמעשי, בחיי היחיד ובחיי הציבור. התחיה תחדור בלבבות שהן נתונות למשא נפש רוחני כולו, לתקוות קדושות שמימיות אשר מתוך מרחקם מהעולם ויושביו אינם מתמזגים עם החיים הרגילים, מפני שהיא מוכרחת להיות תחיה שלמה.

לתחית הקדש אנו שואפים, להשלמתה של תחית החול אנו מצפים, להרשים את אור החיים של תנועת התחיה הלאמית שלנו ברושם המלא שלה, זאת היא מגמתנו.

ולשם זה הננו מעוררים או יותר טוב לומר הננו מגלים את מציאותה של התנועה הירושלמית. והננו קוראים בשם "ירושלים" וירושלמיות את צד הקדש שבתחיתנו הלאמית - כשם שהננו קוראים בשם ציון וציוניות את הצד החול שלה - ועם **דגל ירושלים** נרים את נס הקדש בתחית האומה, להראות לעין כל מהו הכח הצפון אשר בנשמת הגוי אשר עד כה לא הוכר, להראות את עז ד', את עז הקדש, להחיות את האומה בכל מובנה, להחיות את החול בתחית הקדש, להחיות את הקודש בהתגלות מפעליו בחיים, במעשה, ברגש, וברעיון, בכל ההיקף של החיים הלאומים שלנו.

תחיתנו הלאמית תקום לתחית עם גמורה, באותה המדה שההארה האלהית תתגלה בה, באותו הערך שהאפלה החמרית

its deeds. For this reason, we need to work out a clear definition. What is the content of the holy? What is the content of the secular? This is one of the foundations of our national work that the times necessitate.

The whole renascence will unfold before the eyes of all: an illumination full of majesty and holy beauty in prayer, Torah, ethics, and faith – in all its conceptual and practical scope – in the life of the individual and in the life of the community. Renascence will penetrate hearts that are given to spiritual vision, to holy, heavenly hopes that, due to their distance from the world and its inhabitants, do not mix with regular life – because it must be a complete renascence.

We aspire to the renascence of the holy. We look forward to the completion of the renascence of the mundane. Our objective is to produce the full impact of the light-of-life of our national movement of renascence.

Toward this objective, we arouse, or more correctly, reveal the existence of the Jerusalemite movement. By the name "Jerusalem" or "Jerusalemism," we refer to the holy side of our national renascence – just as we call its secular side "Zion" or "Zionism." With the "Banner of Jerusalem," we will raise the banner of holiness contained in the renascence of the people, to show everyone what is the power hidden in the soul of the nation, which until now was not recognized, to demonstrate the strength of the Lord, the strength of the holy, to revive the nation in all respects, to revive the mundane through the renascence of the sacred, to revive the sacred through manifesting its effects on life, action, emotion, thought, on the entire scope of our national life.

Our national renascence will result in total revival of the people to the degree that the divine illumination is revealed therein, to the extent that the materialistic darkness that shrinks life will not control our consciousness. With courageous spirit we will lift our hearts to recognize the great deed that God does with His people – and through

המקטינה את החיים, לא תהיה שולטת על הכרתנו, וברוח אמיץ נשא את לבבנו להכיר את מעשה ד׳ הגדול אשר הוא עושה עם עמו, ועל ידי עמו, ישובו לתחיתו על אדמת הקדש עם יצוריו כולם. וההכרה הבהירה הזאת וכל סדרי החיים, המעשיים, והרוחניים, היוצאים ממנה, היא יסודה של תחית האומה והמרכז המבסס את בנין הארץ והעם.

ואשים דברי בפיך ובצל ידי כסיתיך לנטע שמים וליסוד ארץ, ולאמר לציון עמי אתה.

His people coming back to life on the holy soil, with all His creatures. This clear consciousness and all the life-patterns – practical and spiritual – that derive from it, are the foundation of the renascence of the nation, the center that is the basis of the building of the land and the people.

I will put My word in your mouth and with the shadow of My hand I will cover you, to plant heaven and to establish earth, and to say to Zion, You are My people.[1]

אורות מאפל

Orot me-Ofel[1]
(Lights from Darkness)

ארץ ישראל

א

ארץ ישראל איננה דבר חיצוני, קנין חיצוני לאומה, רק בתור אמצעי למטרה של ההתאגדות הכללית והחזקת קיומה החמרי או אפילו הרוחני. ארץ ישראל היא חטיבה עצמותית קשורה בקשר חיים עם האומה, חבוקה בסגולות פנימיות עם מציאותה. ומתוך כך אי-אפשר לעמוד על התוכן של סגולת קדושת ארץ ישראל, ולהוציא לפועל את עומק חבתה, בשום השכלה רציונלית אנושית כי-אם ברוח ד' אשר על האומה בכללה, בהטבעה הטבעית הרוחנית אשר בנשמת ישראל, שהיא ששולחת את קויה בצבעים טבעיים בכל הארחות של ההרגשה הבריאה, ומזרחת היא את זריחתה העליונה על-פי אותה המדה של רוח הקדושה העליונה, הממלאת חיים ונעם עליון את לבב קדושי הרעיון ועמוקי המחשבה הישראלית. המחשבה על-דבר ארץ ישראל, שהיא רק ערך חיצוני כדי העמדת אגודת האומה, אפילו כשהיא באה כדי לבצר על-ידה את הרעיון היהודותי בגולה, כדי לשמור את צביונו ולאמץ את האמונה והיראה והחזוק של המצות המעשיות בצורה הגונה, אין לה הפרי הראוי לקיום, כי היסוד הזה הוא רעוע בערך איתן הקודש

Erets Yisrael (THE LAND OF ISRAEL)

1

The Spiritual Dimension of the Land

The Land of Israel is not a means to an end of collective solidarity but rather an end in itself. It defies rationalism; it is a mystical dimension. The hope of the Land of Israel is what gives the Diaspora the strength to continue to exist. The essential difference between the Judaism of the Diaspora and that of the Land of Israel.

The Land of Israel is not something external, not an external national asset, a means to an end of collective solidarity[2] and the strengthening of the nation's existence, physical or even spiritual. The Land of Israel is an essential unit bound by the bond-of-life with the Nation, united by inner characteristics with its existence. Therefore, it is impossible to appreciate the content of the sanctity of the Land of Israel and to actualize the depth of love for her by some rational human understanding[3] – only by the spirit of the Lord that is in the soul of Israel. This spirit radiates natural hues in all avenues of healthy feeling and shines according to the measure of supernal holy spirit, which fills with life and pleasantness the heart of the holy of thought and deep Jewish thinkers. The thought of the Land of Israel as only an external value serving as a cohesive force – even when it comes only to reinforce the Jewish idea in the Diaspora, to preserve its identity and to strengthen faith, awe (of the Lord) and observance of *mitsvot*

של ארץ ישראל. האמוץ האמתי של רעיון היהדות בגולה בא יבא רק מצד עמק שקועו בארץ ישראל, ומתקות ארץ ישראל יקבל תמיד את כל תכונותיו העצמיות. צפית ישועה היא כח המעמיד של היהדות הגלותית, והיהדות של ארץ ישראל היא הישועה עצמה.

ב

על-ידי התרחקות מהכרת הרזים באה ההכרה של קדושת ארץ ישראל בצורה מטושטשת. על-ידי ההתנכרות אל סוד ד׳ נעשות הסגולות העליונות של עמק החיים האלהיים לדברים טפלים שאינם נכנסים בעמק הנשמה, וממילא יחסר הכח היותר אדיר בנשמת האומה והיחיד, והגלות מוצאת היא חן מצד עצמותה; כי למשיג רק את השטח הגלוי לא יחסר שום דבר יסודי בחסרון הארץ והממלכה וכל תכני האומה בבנינה. יסוד צפית הישועה הוא אצלו כמו ענף צדדי שאיננו יכול להתקשר עם עומק הכרת היהדות, וזה בעצמו הוא הדבר המעיד על חסרון ההבנה שיש בשיטה מעטת הלשד כזאת. לא שוללים אנחנו כל מין ציור והבנה המיוסד על ישרות ורגשי דעה ויראת שמים באיזו צורה שהיא, רק את אותו הצד ששיטה כזאת תחפוץ לשלול את הרזים ואת השפעתם הגדולה על רוח האומה, כי זהו אסון שאנו חיבים ללחום אתו, בעצה ובתבונה, בקדושה ובגבורה.

(commandments) – bears no permanent fruit, for this foundation is shaky compared to the holy might of the Land of Israel.[4] The true strengthening of the Jewish idea in exile will come about only through the depth of its immersion in the Land of Israel, and from the hope of the Land of Israel it will receive always its essential characteristics. The expectation of salvation is the force that preserves exilic Judaism;[5] the Judaism of the Land of Israel is salvation itself.[6]

2

The Truth Concerning the Land Revealed in Kabbalah

Jewish Mysticism (Kabbalah) militates for life in the Land of Israel. Rationalist approaches to Judaism place no special value on the Land of Israel.

Distance from awareness of the mysteries[7] produces a distorted awareness of the sanctity of the Land of Israel. Due to alienation from the "secret of the Lord," the higher qualities of godly life are reduced to trivia that do not penetrate the depth of the soul. When this happens, the most mighty[8] force is missing from the soul of nation and individual, and *Galut* (Exile) finds favor essentially.[9] To one who grasps only the outer surface, nothing fundamental is lost with the loss of land, sovereignty, and all the ingredients of an intact nation. For such a person, the expectation of salvation[10] is but a side[11] branch that never connects to the depth of Jewish awareness. This itself attests to the lack of understanding in such a lifeless approach. We do not negate any conception based on rectitude and awe of heaven, of any form[12] – only the aspect of such an approach that desires to negate the mysteries and their great influence on the spirit of the nation. This is a tragedy that we must combat with counsel and understanding, with holiness and courage.

ג

יצירה עצמית ישראלית, במחשבה ובתקף החיים והמפעל, אי-אפשר לישראל אלא בארץ ישראל. לעומת זה, כל הנעשה מישראל בארץ ישראל מתבטלת הצורה הכללית שבו לגבי הצורה העצמית המיוחדה של ישראל, וזהו אושר גדול לישראל ולעולם. החטאים שגורמים גלות הם הם שמדלחים את המעין העצמי, והמקור מזיל הזלות טמאות, "את משכן ד׳ טמא". וכשהמקור העצמי המיוחד נשחת, מתעלה המקוריות היסודית לאותו החלק העליון התמציתי שיש לישראל בסגולת האדם, וזה נשאב דוקא בגלות, והארץ מתחרבת ומשתוממת וחרבנה מכפר עליה. המעין פוסק מלהזיל והוא מסתנן קמעא קמעא, וההופעות של החיים והמחשבה יוצאות דרך הצנור הכללי, שהוא פזור בכל העולם כלו, "כארבע רוחות השמים פרשתי אתכם", עד אשר ההזלות הטמאות הפרטיות מתפסקות וחוזר כח המקור לטהרתו. ואז נמאסת הגלות לגמרי והרי היא מיותרת, והאורה הכללית חוזרת היא להיות נובעת מהמעין העצמי הפרטי בכל חילו, ואורו של משיח המקבץ נדחים מתחיל להופיע, וקול בכי תמרורים של רחל המבכה על בניה מתמתק על-ידי שפעת תנחומים, של "מנעי קולך מבכי ועינך מדמעה, כי יש שכר לפעולתך, נאם ד׳, ושבו מארץ אויב, ויש תקוה לאחריתך, נאם ד׳, ושבו בנים לגבולם". ויצירת החיים המיוחדים, בכל מאורם והטיביותם המיוחדה, רוויה בטל העושר הכללי של האדם הגדול בענקים, ברכת אברהם, חוזרת היא דוקא על-ידי שיבה זו להתגלות. "והיה ברכה - בך חותמים".

3

Particularism and Universalism; Land and Exile

The two aspects of Jewish existence: particularism and universalism. In exile, the universalist side gains prominence; in Erets Yisrael *the universalism is expressed through the medium of particularism. Exile is a cleansing of the particularist phenomenon. Jewish history, which began on a universalist note, comes full circle.*

Independent Israelite creation, in thought and in life and action, is possible only in the Land of Israel. In everything produced by Israel in the Land, the universal form is subsumed[13] under the unique form of Israel, and this is a boon for Israel and the world. The sins that cause exile are the very ones that muddy the essential spring,[14] and the source emits impure issues. *The Tabernacle of the Lord he defiled.*[15] When the independent, particularist source is destroyed, originality rises to the supernal portion that Israel has in mankind. This is drawn upon in exile, and the Land is laid waste and desolate, and her destruction atones for her. The spring stops flowing and is filtered; manifestations of life and thought are emitted through the general conduit, which is spread throughout the globe. *As the four winds of heaven I have scattered you.*[16] Until the impure particularist issues stop and the source is restored to its purity. Then exile is detested and superfluous, and the universal light reverts to flowing[17] from the independent, particularist fount with full force. The Light of Messiah who ingathers exiles begins to appear, and the sound of the bitter crying of Rachel mourning her children is softened by this consolation: *Stop your voice from crying and your eyes from tears, for there is reward for your effort, says the Lord, and they shall return from an enemy land. There is hope toward your end, says the Lord, the children will return to their borders.*[18] Creation of distinctive life with all its light and particularity, drenched in the dew of the universal wealth of the *great man among giants,*[19] the blessing of Abraham, reappears through precisely this return.[20] "*Be a blessing* – with you they conclude."[21]

ד

אי-אפשר לאדם מישראל שיהיה מסור ונאמן למחשבותיו, הגיונותיו, רעיונותיו ודמיונותיו, בחוץ לארץ, כתכונת הנאמנות הזאת בארץ ישראל. הופעות הקדש, באיזו מדרגה שהן, נקיות הן בארץ ישראל לפי הערך, ובחוץ לארץ מעורבות הן בסיגים וקלפות מרובים. אמנם לפי גודל התשוקה והקשור של האדם לארץ ישראל, הרי רעיונותיו מזדככים מיסוד אוירא דארץ ישראל החופף על כל מי שמצפה לראותה. "שמחו את ירושלם וגילו בה כל אוהביה".

ה

הדמיון של ארץ ישראל הוא צלול וברור, נקי וטהור ומסוגל להופעת האמת האלהית, להלבשת החפץ הרומם והנשגב של המגמה האידיאלית אשר בעליונות הקדש, מוכן להסברת נבואה ואורותיה, להבהקת רוח הקדש וזהריו. והדמיון אשר בארץ העמים עכור הוא, מעורב במחשכים, בצללי טומאה וזיהום, לא יוכל להתנשא למרומי קודש ולא יוכל להיות בסיס לשפעת האורה האלהית המתעלה מכל שפלות העולמים ומצריהם. מתוך שהשכל והדמיון אחוזים זה בזה ופועלים ונפעלים זה על זה וזה מזה, לכן לא יוכל גם השכל שבחוץ לארץ להיות מאיר באורו שבארץ ישראל. "אוירא דארץ ישראל מחכים".

4
Authentic and Distorted Jewish Vision

Exile distorts Judaic vision. The thoughts of a Jew regain authenticity to the degree that they are attached to the Land of Israel.

It is impossible for a Jew to be faithful to his thoughts and visions outside of the Land[22] in the same way that he is faithful in the Land of Israel. Manifestations of holiness, of whatever level, tend to be pure in the Land, and outside the Land, mixed with dross. However, in relation to the longing and the attachment of a person to the Land of Israel, his thoughts become purified by virtue of the "air of the Land of Israel"[23] that hovers over all who long to see her.[24] *Gladden Jerusalem and rejoice in her all her lovers.*[25]

5
Land of Prophecy

Prophecy is a function of the imaginative faculty. Inasmuch as the imagination is warped in exile, prophecy is dependent on the Land of Israel. Intellect is also affected, as the two, imagination and intellect, are intertwined.

The imagination of the Land of Israel is pure and clear[26] and suited for the appearance of the divine truth, for garbing the lofty, exalted will of the ideal direction that is at the height of holiness; ready for the explication of prophecy[27] and its lights, for the shining of divine inspiration and its brightness. The imagination that is in the Lands of the Nations is murky, mixed with darkness, with shadows of impurity and pollution. It cannot ascend to the heights of holiness and cannot be the basis for the influx of divine light that transcends the lowness of the worlds and their straits. Since intellect and imagination are intertwined and interact,[28] even the intellect outside the Land cannot shine with the same light as in the Land. "The air of the Land of Israel makes wise."[29]

ו

פעולת רוח הקדושה הנקלטת בארץ ישראל פועלת היא תדיר, גם אם נזדמן הדבר ויצא האדם חוצה לארץ, על-ידי טעות או על-ידי איזו סבה מוכרחת. הרי גם הנבואה כשחלה כבר בארץ ישראל אינה פוסקת גם בחוץ לארץ. "היה היה דבר ד' אל יחזקאל בארץ כשדים - היה, מפני שהיה כבר". שפעת הקדש, שהותחלה בארץ ישראל, מלקטת היא את כל ברורי הקדש הנמצאים בחוץ לארץ בכל המעמקים, ומקרבתם בכחה המושך אליה. כל מה שקשה יותר לסבול את אויר חוץ לארץ, כל מה שמרגישים יותר את רוח הטומאה של אדמה טמאה, זהו סמן לקליטה יותר פנימית של קדושת ארץ ישראל, לחסד עליון, אשר לא יעזב ממנו מי שזכה להסתופף בצלצח של ארץ חיים, גם בהתרחקו ונודו, גם בגלותו וארץ נדידתו. הזרות שמרגישים בחוץ לארץ הרי היא מקשרת יותר את כל חשק הרוח הפנימי לארץ ישראל וקדושתה, הצפיה לראותה מתגברת וציור חקיקת תבנית הקדש של ארץ אשר עיני ד' בה תמיד, מראשית השנה ועד אחרית שנה, מתעמקת יותר ויותר, ועומק תשוקת הקדש של חבת ציון, של זכירת הארץ, שכל חמודות בה קשורות, כשהיא מתגברת בנשמה, אפילו יחידית, הרי היא עושה פעולת נביעה מעינית לכל הכלל, לרבבות נשמות הקשורות עמה, וקול שופר של קבוץ נדחים מתעורר ורחמים רבים מתגברים, ותקות חיים לישראל מתנוצצת, וצמח ד' הולך ופורח, ואור ישועה וגאולה מתפצל ומתפשט, כשחר פרוש על ההרים.

6

The Mission of a Jew from the Land Living Outside

The divine inspiration of the Land of Israel follows a Jew into exile. There it acts as a magnet to attract elements of holiness in the Diaspora. The feeling of spiritual alienation outside the Land is a barometer of inner attachment to the Land.

The effect of the holy spirit absorbed in the Land of Israel works constantly, even if it should happen that a person leave the Land by mistake or necessity. Even prophecy, once it had come to rest in the Land of Israel, did not cease outside the Land. *The word of God was to Ezekiel [son of Buzi, the priest] in the land of the Chaldeans.*[30] "Was, because it was already."[31] The flow of holiness, which began in the Land of Israel, gathers all the refined (sparks) of holiness found outside the Land in all the depths and attracts them by its magnetism.[32] The more difficult it is to endure the "air" outside the Land, the more one feels the spirit of impurity of an impure land – this is a sign of an inner absorption of the holiness of the Land of Israel; of a supernal (divine) love, which will not abandon one who has merited to find shelter in the pure shade of the Land of Life, even when one wanders far away, even in one's land of exile. The strangeness that one feels outside the Land binds all the inner spiritual desire to the Land of Israel and its holiness even more. The expectation to see her grows stronger and the mental picture of the holy structure of *a land which the eyes of the Lord are upon always, from the beginning of the year until the end of the year*[33] deepens. When the deep holy desire of love of Zion, of remembrance of the Land to which all delights are attached,[34] grows strong in the soul, even the individual soul, it opens up a fountain-flow for the entire community, for myriad souls attached to her, and the voice of the *shofar* (ram's horn) of the ingathering of exiles is aroused and great (divine) mercy prevails, the hope of life for Israel glitters, the sapling of the Lord flourishes, and the light of salvation and redemption breaks and spreads, as dawn spreading on the mountains.

ז

מלאה היא הנשמה אותיות מלאות אור חיים, מלאות דעה ורצון, מלאות רוח הבטה ומציאות מלאה. מזוהר האותיות החיות הללו מתמלאות זיו חיים כל יתר הדרגות אשר לבנין החיים, אשר לכל שדרות הרצון, הדעת והמפעל, לרוח ונשמה, בכל ערכיהם. כשנגשים למצוה, המצוה היא תמיד מלאה זיו חיים של כל עולמים, מלאה היא כל מצוה אותיות גדולות ונפלאות, מכל תרי״ג מצות התלויות בכל מצוה, מכל חיי העולמים שבסוד האמונה. זיו אור אלהים חיים, אור חי העולמים, חי בכל נעם בהוד כל מצוה. תיכף בגשתנו למצוה לעשותה מתגדלות כל האותיות החיות שבמהותנו, אנו מתגדלים ומתגברים, מתעצמים באור חיים והויה עליונה, מפוארה ועשירה עושר קדש עולמים ובאור תורה וזיו חכמה. נוהרות עלינו אותן האותיות של מקורות התורה ולעומתם מתנשאות אותיות החיים המלאות זיו ואור פנימי שבמהותנו, ותסיסה הרת עולמים מתהוה. עז חדות נעם, גבורות קודש וששון עדנים מתהוה ברוחנו פנימה, ובכל היקום מתחדש אור וחיים. העולם מוכרע על ידינו לזכות, על כל פנים מתוסף אור ויושר, רצון ושובע טוב פנימי. בארץ ישראל מתגדלות האותיות של נשמתנו, שם מחשיפות הן נהרה, יונקות חיים עצמיים מזיו החיים של כנסת ישראל, מושפעות הן מסוד יצירתם המקורית בדרך ישרה. אוירא דארץ ישראל ממציא את הגדול הרענן של אותיות החיים הללו, בזיו תפארה, בידידות נעימה ובגבורת רעם עליזה מלאה שפעת קודש, ״כל הכתוב לחיים בירושלם״. הצפיה לראות בהדר ארץ חמדה, השקיקה הפנימית לארץ ישראל מגדלת את אותיות הקודש, את אותיות החיים העצמיות הישראליות שבפנימיותנו ועצמיותנו, היא מגדלתם גדול

7

Torah Letters and Soul Letters

The correspondence of the "letters of the Torah" and the "letters of the soul." The "letters of the soul" thrive in the "air of the Land of Israel." The justice of Torah is the essence of the soul-letters of all Israel.

The soul is full of letters that abound with the light of life, knowledge and will, a spirit of vision,[35] and complete existence. From the glow of these living letters, all the other levels of the structure of life – all the avenues of will, intellect, action; of spirit and soul, of all varieties – fill with the splendor of life. When we approach a *mitsvah* (commandment), the *mitsvah* is always full of the splendor of life of all the worlds. Each *mitsvah* is replete with huge, wonderful letters, of the 613 *mitsvot* (commandments) that connect to every *mitsvah,*[36] of all the eternal life that is the secret of faith. The splendorous light of the Living God, the light of the Life-of-Worlds, lives in every *mitsvah.* Right before we commence doing a *mitsvah,* all the letters that live within us expand. We expand and grow stronger[37] in the light of life and supreme existence, rich in the holiness of eternity and in the light of Torah and the splendor of wisdom. The letters of the sources of Torah flow down on us, and the letters of life, full of splendor and the internal light that is within us, ascend to meet them, and a cosmic eruption occurs. The strength of a pleasant joy, holy power, and pleasurable rejoicing occur within our spirit, and throughout existence light and life are renewed. The world is saved on our behalf; at least light and rectitude increase, will and a good, inner satisfaction. In the Land of Israel the letters of our soul expand; there they expose the light,[38] draw nourishment from the splendor of life of *Knesset Yisrael* (Ecclesia Israel), [and] are influenced directly from the secret source of their formation. The "air of the Land of Israel" produces[39] the fresh growth of these living letters, with splendid beauty, with pleasant amicability, and with thunderous power full of a holy flow. *All who are written for life in Jerusalem.*[40] The expectation to see the beauty of the land of delight, the inner longing for the Land of Israel expands the letters of holiness, the essential

רוחני פנימי, "אחד הנולד בה ואחד המצפה לראותה", "ולציון יאמר איש ואיש יולד בה, והוא יכוננה עליון. ד' יספור בכתב עמים, זה יולד שם סלה". המשפט - העמוד האמצעי, שכל הטרקלין עליו נשען, "משל למטרונה ההולכת ושפוליה מכאן ומכאן. משפטים באמצעיתה של תורה", הם הם מהות החיים, "משפט בני ישראל", מהות החפץ הנשמתי הספוג בנשמת משיח רוח אפנו אשר יקראו לו ד' צדקנו, אשר יגלה אור משפט ד' בארץ בגבורה עליונה השוללת כל מלחמה וכל שפיכות דמים. משפט בני ישראל על לב אהרן - תמצית האותיות הנשמתיות של כל ישראל, מאירה באורים ותומים, "בולטות או מצטרפות".

ח

בתוך הלב פנימה, בחדרי טהרתו וקדושתו, מתגברת היא השלהבת הישראלית, הדורשת בחזקה את ההתקשרות האמיצה והתדירה של החיים אל מצות ד' כולן, לצקת את רוח ד', רוח ישראל המלא, הכללי, הממלא את כל חללה של הנשמה, בתוך כל הכלים הרבים המיוחדים לה, להביע את הבטוי הישראלי המלא בהבלטה גמורה, מעשית ואידיאלית. הרשפים מתגברים בלב הצדיקים, יקוד אש קודש יוקד ועולה, ובלב כל האומה הוא בוער מימים ימימה, "אש תמיד תוקד על המזבח לא תכבה", ובלב כל ריקנים שבישראל ובלב כל פושעי ישראל האש בוער ויוקד בפנימי פנימיות, ובכללות האומה כולה כל חפץ החירות וכל תשוקת החיים, כל תשוקת חיי הכלל והפרט, כל תקוה של גאולה, רק ממקור מעין חיים זה הם נובעים, כדי לחיות את החיים הישראליים במלואם בלא סתירה ובלא הגבלה. וזאת היא תשוקת ארץ ישראל, אדמת הקדש, ארץ ד'

Israelite letters of life that are within us. "One who is born there and one who expects to see her."[41] *But of Zion it will be said, "This and that man were born there," and the Most High Himself will establish her. The Lord will number when he writes down nations, "This one was born there." Selah.*[42] Justice – the middle column[43] on which the entire palace rests ("comparable to a noblewoman who walks, the folds of her dress here and there – justice is the middle of the Torah"),[44] is the essence of life, *the judgment of the Children of Israel,*[45] the essence of the soul-desire drenched with the soul of Messiah, *the breath of our nostrils,*[46] who will be called *the-Lord-is-our-Righteousness,*[47] who will reveal the light of divine justice in the land with supreme strength, which negates all war and bloodshed. *The judgment of the Children of Israel on the heart of Aaron.*[48] The essence of the soul-letters of all Israel shines in the *Urim and Tummim*, "protrude or cojoin."[49]

8

Land of Israel: Vessel to Jewish Lights

The lights within the Israelite soul seek the vessels for their full expression: the Land of Israel where all the commandments of the Torah may be fulfilled. This yearning fills even the emptiest of Jewish spirits.

Within the heart, in the chambers of its purity and holiness, grows stronger the Israelite flame, which seeks impassionedly the constant integral connection of life to all of God's *mitsvot* (commandments), to pour the spirit of God, the full universal spirit of Israel that fills all the chambers of the soul, into all the many vessels that were designed for it, to give full expression – practical and ideal – to the Israelite conception. The flames glow in the heart of the righteous, a holy flame ascends, and in the heart of the entire nation it burns constantly – *An eternal flame shall burn on the altar, it shall not be extinquished*[50] – and in the hearts of all the empty of Israel and the sinners of Israel it burns deep within, and in the nation at large, all desire of freedom and longing of life (the life of the individual and the community), all hope of redemption flows only from this spring of life, in order to live

שבה המצות כולן מתגלמות ומתבלטות בכל חטיביותן. והתשוקה הזאת של הוצאת צביון רוח ד׳, של נשיאת ראש ברוח ד׳ בעצם גדולתו, היא פועלת על הלבבות כולם והכל חפצים להתאחד עמו, לטעום נעימת חייו, ״על כן אהבתי מצותיך מזהב ומפז״. האמץ שבלב, המראה לעולם כולו את גבורת האומה בשמירת צביונה, שמה וערכה, אמונתה, ומשאת נפשה, כלול הוא בתשוקת חיי האמת, והחיים של המצות כולן, שיהל עליה אור התורה בכל מלואו וטובו. אם יפלא בעיני כל עומד מרחוק: איך אפשר שכל הרוחות, אשר לכאורה גם מאמונה הם רחוקים, יפעם בהם רוח החיים בכחו הפנימי לא לבד לקרבת אלהים כללית כי-אם לחיי ישראל האמתיים, להחטבתן של המצות בציור וברעיון, בשירה ובפועל - אל יפלא בעיני כל הקשור במעמקי רוחו בתוך עמקיה של כנסת ישראל ויודע את נפלאות סגולותיה. זהו רז הגבורה, רוממות החיים אשר לעד לא יתמו. ״ושמרתם את חקותי ואת משפטי אשר יעשה אותם האדם וחי בהם אני ד׳״. ״להתהלך לפני ד׳ בארצות החיים, זו ארץ ישראל״.

full Israelite life without contradiction and constriction. And this is the desire for the Land of Israel, the holy soil, the Land of the Lord, in which all the *mitsvot* (commandments) are actualized. This desire for the actualization of the spirit of the Lord, for uplifting the head in the greatness of the spirit of the Lord, works on all the hearts and all want to unite with it, to taste the pleasantness of its life. *Therefore I loved Your commandments more than gold.*[51] The fortitude in the heart that shows the entire world the strength of the nation in maintaining its character, name, values, faith, and vision, is included in the desire of the life of truth and the life of all the *mitsvot*, that the light of Torah in all its fullness and goodness should glow on it [i.e., the nation]. If someone who stands afar should be amazed: "How is it possible that within all of the spirits which are seemingly removed from faith, there should pound the spirit of life with its inner strength, not only for abstract closeness to God, bur for true Israelite life, for the expression of *mitsvot* in theory, poetry and practice?!" – this does not amaze one who is connected in the depths of his spirit to the depths of *Knesset Yisrael* (Ecclesia Israel) and knows her wonderful gifts.[52] This is the secret of strength, the height of life that will never end. *And you shall observe my laws and judgments, which if a man do them, he shall live thereby, I am the Lord.*[53] *To walk before the Lord in the land of life.*[54] "This is the Land of Israel."[55]

המלחמה

א

כשיש מלחמה גדולה בעולם מתעורר כח משיח. עת הזמיר הגיע, זמיר עריצים, הרשעים נכחדים מן העולם והעולם מתבסם, וקול התור נשמע בארצנו. היחידים הנספים בלא משפט, שבתוך המהפכה של שטף המלחמה, יש בה ממדת מיתת צדיקים המכפרת, עולים הם למעלה בשורש החיים ועצמות חייהם מביא ערך כללי לטובה ולברכה אל כלל בנין העולם בכל ערכיו ומובניו. ואחרי כן בתום המלחמה מתחדש העולם ברוח חדש ורגלי משיח מתגלים ביותר, ולפי ערכה של גודל המלחמה בכמותה ואיכותה ככה תגדל הצפיה לרגלי משיח שבה. מלחמת עולם של עכשיו צפיה נוראה גדולה ועמוקה יש בה, מצורף לכל גלגולי הזמנים והוראת קץ המגולה של התישבות ארץ ישראל. בדעה גדולה, בגבורה עצומה, ובהגיון עמוק וחודר, בתשוקת אמת וברעיון בהיר, צריכים לקבל את התוכן הנשא של אור ד׳ המתגלה בפעולה נפלאה בעלילות המלחמות הללו ביחוד, ״בעל מלחמות זורע צדקות, מצמיח ישועות, בורא רפואות, נורא תהלות, אדון הנפלאות, המחדש בטובו בכל יום תמיד מעשה בראשית, אור חדש על ציון תאיר ונזכה כולנו מהרה לאורו״.

HA-MILḤAMAH (THE WAR)

1

The Messianic Dimension of War

World conflagration has a messianic dimension.
Such conflicts produce tangible results in the Land of Israel.

When there is a great war in the world, the power of Messiah is aroused. *The time of song* (zamir) *has arrived,*[56] the scything *(zemir)* of tyrants,[57] the wicked perish from the world, and the world is invigorated *and the voice of the turtledove is heard in our land.*[58] The individuals who are killed unjustly in the revolution of the flood of the war participate in the concept, "the death of the righteous atones,"[59] they rise above in the root of life and the essence of their lives brings a general quality of good and blessing to the overall structure of the world in all its values and senses. Afterward, at the cessation of the war, the world is renewed in a new spirit and the feet of Messiah are revealed even more. According to the extent of the war in quantity and quality – so increases the expectation of the feet of Messiah through it.[60] The present world war is possessed of an awesome, great, and deep expectation attached to the changes of time and the visible sign of the End[61] in the settlement of the Land of Israel. With great intellect, powerful courage, and piercing logic, with true longing and clear thought, we must receive the lofty content of the light of the Lord that is revealed wondrously in the events of these wars especially. *Master of wars, sower of righteousness, producer of salvations,*[62] *creator of cures, awesome of praises, master of wonders, Who renews with His goodness daily the act of creation, let shine a new light on Zion and let us all merit quickly to its light.*[63]

ב

אנו מסתכלים בדורות הראשונים, המסופרים בתורה, בנביאים ובכתובים, אותם הדורות שהיו עסוקים במלחמה - והם הם הגדולים שאנו מתיחסים אליהם בידידות וגדולת קודש. הננו מבינים, שהזיק הנשמתי הוא היסוד: אותו מעמד העולם, שהלך במרוצתו אז, שהיתה המלחמה כל כך נחוצה בו, הוא גרם להופיע את אלה הנשמות, שהרגשתן הפנימית בתוכֶן שלם היתה. מלחמת קיומם, קיום האומה, מלחמה ד' היתה בהכרה פנימית. עזוזים היו ברוחם וידעו בעמק החשך לבחור בטוב ולסור מן הרע, "גם כי אלך בגיא צלמות לא אירא רע". כשאנו מתבוננים אליהם, הננו, בכל ההופעה הרוחנית שאנו כל כך שוקקים לה, משתוקקים לאמוצם, לכח החיים החטוב והגבוש, האיתן והמוצק, ששכן בקרבם, ומתוך תשוקה זו, כחנו הרוחני מתאמץ וכח גבורתנו מתעדן, ואותן הנשמות החזקות חוזרות לחיות בנו כימי עולם.

ג

עזבנו את הפוליטיקה העולמית מאונס שיש בו רצון פנימי, עד אשר תבא עת מאושרה, שיהיה אפשר לנהל ממלכה בלא רשעה וברבריות; זהו הזמן שאנו מקוים. מובן הדבר, שכדי להגשימו אנו צריכים להתעורר בכחותינו כולם, להשתמש בכל האמצעים שהזמן מביא: הכל יד אל בורא כל עולמים מנהלת. אבל האיחור הוא איחור מוכרח, בחלה נפשנו בחטאים האיומים של הנהגת ממלכה בעת רעה. והנה הגיע הזמן, קרוב מאד, העולם יתבסס ואנו נוכל כבר להכין עצמנו, כי לנו כבר אפשר יהיה לנהל ממלכתנו על

2

Reincarnations of Biblical Warriors in Our Day

The times determine the caliber of souls that appear. The battle for the Land of Israel conjures up a soul that is reminiscent of the biblical warriors of old.

We regard the early generations, recounted in Torah, Prophets, and Writings; those generations that were engaged in war – they are the great people that we cherish and glorify. We understand that the spark of soul is the determining factor: that state of the world that proceeded then, that necessitated war, caused these souls (whose inner feeling was whole) to appear. The battle for existence, for the existence of the nation, the War of the Lord, was with an inner consciousness. Mighty in spirit, they knew in the depth of darkness to choose good and eschew evil. *Yea though I go in the valley of the shadow of death I shall fear no evil.*[64] When we meditate on them, we, with all the spirituality that we so desire, long for their strength, for the solid life force that dwelled in their midst, and out of this longing our spiritual strength is fortified and our physical strength is refined,[65] and those strong souls return to live in us as ever.[66]

3

Jewish History and Politics: A Dialectic

Israel's stepping off the stage of history was only a temporary measure. The reappearance is imminent.

We left[67] world politics by force of circumstance that (nevertheless) contains an inner volition, until a fortunate time will come, when it will be possible to conduct a nation without wickedness and barbarism – this is the time we hope for. It is understood that in order to achieve this, we must awaken with all of our powers to use all the media that time makes available – all is conducted by the hand of God, Creator of all worlds. However, the delay is a necessary one; we were repulsed by the awful sins of conducting a nation in an evil time. Behold, the time is approaching, the world will be invigorated and we can already prepare

יסודות הטוב, החכמה, היושר וההארה האלהית הברורה. ״יעקב שלח לעשו את הפורפירא״: ״יעבר נא אדוני לפני עבדו״, אין הדבר כדאי ליעקב לעסוק בממלכה, בעת שהיא צריכה להיות דמים מלאה, בעת שתובעת כשרון של רשעה. אנו קבלנו רק את היסוד כפי ההכרח ליסד אומה, וכיון שנגמל הגזע הודחנו ממלוך, בגוים נתפזרנו, נזרענו במעמקי האדמה, אד אשר עת הזמיר תגיע וקול התור ישמע בארצנו.

ד

לולא חטא העגל היו האומות יושבות ארץ ישראל משלימות עם ישראל ומודות להם, כי שם ד׳ הנקרא עליהם היה מעורר בהן יראה הרוממות, ולא היתה שום שיטת מלחמה נוהגת, וההשפעה היתה הולכת בדרכי שלום כבימות המשיח. רק החטא גרם ונתאחר הדבר אלפי שנים, וכל מסבות העולם הנן אחוזות זו בזו להביא את אור ד׳ בעולם, וחטא העגל ימחה לגמרי וממילא כל רואיהם יכירום כי הם זרע ברך ד׳, והעולם יתוקן באורח שלום ורגשי אהבה, ונעם ה׳ יוחש בכל לבב, לענג רוח ולעדן נשמה ולכל בהם תחיה נפש כל חי.

ourselves, for it will already be possible for us to conduct our nation by principles of good, wisdom, rectitude, and clear divine enlightenment. *"Jacob sent to Esau the royal purple."*[68] *Let my master pass before his servant.*[69] It is not worthwhile for Jacob to engage in statecraft when it must be full of blood, when it requires an ability for wickedness. We received but the foundation, enough to found a people, but once the trunk was established, we were deposed, strewn among the nations, planted in the depths of the earth, until *the time of song arrives and the voice of the turtledove* will be heard *in our land.*[70]

4

The Need to Battle for the Land: Reduced Spiritual Stature

Were it not for the sin of the Golden Calf, Israel would not have had to fight for possession of the Land.

Were it not for the sin of the Golden Calf, the inhabitants of the Land of Israel would have been reconciled with the People of Israel,[71] for the name of God called upon them would have aroused awe. No war would have been necessary, and the influence would have proceeded peacefully as in the Days of Messiah. Only sin intervened and the thing has been delayed thousands of years. All the causes of the world are interlocked to bring the light of God into the world; the sin of the Calf will be totally erased, and thereby all will recognize the Jewish People as *seed blessed by God.*[72] The world will be perfected in a way of peace and feelings of love. The pleasantness of God will be felt in every heart as a spiritual pleasure and delight, and all in whom there is a soul will be revived.

ה

הכבישה המוסרית שעל-פי התרבות החולונית, ששלטה הרבה על העמים, העיקה על לבם, והרבה מדות רעות, חליים וקצפונות, נצברו במעמקי נשמותיהם. והם יוצאים מחרצבותיהם על-ידי המלחמות רבות הדמים וגדולות האכזריות, הנאותה יותר לטבעם הבלתי-מזוקק עדיין כעת.

ו

כל העמים מתפתחים, ויוצאים אל הפועל על-ידי תנועותיהם הטבעיות. המלחמות מעמיקות את הערך המיוחד של כל עם, עד שמתבלטת צורתו ויוצאת אל הפועל בהגמרה בכל פרטי עמקיה. ישראל הוא האספקלריא הכללית של כל העולם, וכל זמן שיש עם בעולם, שלא יצא אל הפועל הגמור בכל תכסיסיו, יש כֵּהוּת לעומת זה באור הספוג של כנסת ישראל. על-כן בכל זמן שמלכיות מתגרות זו בזו יוצאים אל הפועל ציורים מיוחדים להשלמתם של העמים וממילא יולד כח השלמה בכנסת ישראל והיא מצפה לרגלו של משיח שיבא ויופיע במהרה בימינו.

ז

מתגלה בכנסת ישראל צבעה העצמי. הולכים הכחות ומתפתחים, הולכת ושבה לה החכמה, הגבורה, היושר והטהרה הפנימית, הולכת האומה ונבנית, מתתקנת היא לגאולתה, גאולת עולמים, פורחת היא ביפעת תפארתה. מתוך המון גלי הצרות העוברים עליה, מכל הגוים, מכל הנפוצות, היא מכניסה הון רב דעה ומעוף

5

War: Collective Release for Repressed Drives

War is a collective release for drives pent up by Western civilization.

The ethical suppression by which secular civilization dominated peoples caused them anxiety,[73] and many evil traits, illnesses, and rages gathered in the depths of their souls. These are unfettered by the bloody, cruel wars, fitting their nature that is as yet unrefined.

6

War, Crystallization of National Character, and Messiah

In wars, national characters crystallize. Israel, as the universal reflection of mankind, benefits thereby. The heels of Messiah follow upon world conflagration.

All nations develop and are actualized by their natural movements. The wars deepen the specialty of each nation until its form reaches full expression of all its contents. Israel is the general speculum of all the world.[74] And as long as there is a people on earth that has not been fully actualized, there is correspondingly a dimness in the absorbed light of *Knesset Yisrael* (Ecclesia Israel). Therefore, whenever nations confront one another, special features of peoples are realized, and thereby there is born a power of wholeness in *Knesset Yisrael* (Ecclesia Israel) and she awaits the footsteps of Messiah,[75] who should appear speedily in our days.[76]

7

Nationalism, Supranationalism, and Godliness

The appearance of Jewish nationalism. Israel's ability to incorporate the nobler elements of other nations. Israel's mission as a godly people.

There is revealed in *Knesset Yisrael* (Ecclesia Israel) her very own hue. The energies develop gradually; her wisdom, power, rectitude, and inner purity return to her. The nation is rebuilt, she prepares for her

הבטה למרחקים ומוסיפה את הצדדים הטהורים שמבחוץ על רכושה העצמי. קנאת עם מתגברת, הכרת עצמותה מתגדלת. היא יודעת כבר שיש לה ארץ, שיש לה שפה, ספרות, שיש לה צבא - התחילה להכיר במלחמת עולם זו. ועל כולם יודעת היא, שיש לה אור חיים מיוחדים, שהם מעטרים אותה ומעטרים את העולם כולו על ידה, ועל-ידי כל זה יחד יודעת היא את חסנה כי עז לה באלהי אמת.

ח

בכתם עון שופכי הדמים, מלכי אדמה הזדים וכל מרגיזי ארץ. לא יכופר לארץ לדם אשר שופך בה כי-אם בדם שופכו, והכפרה מוכרחת לבא: בטול כללי לכל מכונות התרבות של עכשיו, עם כל שקרן ותרמיתן, עם כל זוהמתן הרעה וארסן הצפעוני. כל התרבות, המתהללת בצלצלי שקרים, מוכרחת להכחד מן העולם, ותחתיה תקום מלכות עליונין קדישין. אורם של ישראל יופיע, לכונן עולם בעמים בעלי רוח חדשה, בלאומים אשר לא יהגו ריק ולא ירגזו עוד על ד׳ ועל משיחו, על אור חיי העולם ועל התום והאמונה אשר לברית עולמים. וישראל יראה בעיניו שלומת רשעים, יצעוד על חרבנם של המתהללים באלילים החדשים כאשר צעד על חרבות בבל ואשור העתיקות. אז ידע ויוכח, כי אך בו אל אלהי ישראל מושיע. ותשועת ד׳ בא תבא. הנדפת הכח של הגוים, שקויי כוס התרעלה, מוכרחת היא לבא. פתח ד׳ את אוצרו ויוציא את כלי זעמו. אם עוד תתאמץ אירופא וכל גויה להחזיק מעמד בצביונה, לא באמת ולא בצדקה, את ד׳ לא ידעו ואת דרכיו לא יחפצו ללכת בהם. מצב זה הוא רגעיי ברגעי התולדה. אור התשובה

redemption, the redemption of worlds; she flourishes beautifully. Out of the multitudinous waves of troubles that roll over her, from all the nations, from all parts, she takes in wealth, brimming with knowledge and farsighted vision, and adds the pure aspects from without to her own property. Nationalism grows strong, self-awareness increases. She already knows that she has a land, a language, a literature – that she has an army, she began to learn in this world war.[77] But above all, she knows that she has a special light of life that adorns her and the entire world through her, and through all of this, together,[78] she knows her fortitude – the God of Truth.

8

The Unhinging of Contemporary Civilization

The dissolution of contemporary European civilization and the rise of a new divine world order.

The sin of the murderers – the wicked kings and all provocateurs – is indelible. The blood that was shed in the land will be atoned only by the blood of those who shed it, and the atonement must come: total dismantling of all the foundations of contemporary civilization,[79] with all of their falsity and deception, with all their poison and venom. The entire civilization that rings false must be effaced from the world, and in its stead will arise a kingdom of a holy elite.[80] The light of Israel will appear, to establish the world with peoples imbued with a new spirit,[81] nations that do not speak in vain and no longer rail against the Lord and His chosen, against the light of eternal life and the simplicity and faith of the eternal covenant. Israel will see with its own eyes the perfection of the wicked, will stride on the destruction of the new idolaters[82] as it strode on the ruins of ancient Assyria and Babylon. Then it will know for certain that only with it is God, the God of Israel, the Savior. The salvation of God will come. The dissipation of the strength of the nations, who have drunk the cup of poison,[83] must come. The Lord has opened His arsenal and brought out his instruments of wrath.[84] If Europe (and all her nations) yet strives to persist in her character (which is) other than truth and righteousness, ignoring the Lord and

יופיע בהכרח וישליך איש את אלילי כספו ואת אלילי זהבו. וישוב הכל אל טוב ד׳. אז תכחד התרבות ההוית בכל יסודותיה, ספריותיה, תיאטריה וכל מכונותיה, וכל החקים אשר בהבל ועול יסודם וכל נימוסי החיים הרעים והחטאים כליל יחלפו. ונשגב ד׳ לבדו ביום ההוא. הארג הרוחני והמעשי, אשר בצביונו ההוי לא היה יכול לעצור, עם כל תפארת חכמתו, בעד שפך דמים רבים ובעד חרבנו של עולם בצורה איומה כזאת, הרי הוא מוכיח על עצמו, שהוא פסול מעיקרו, ״זורו רשעים מרחם תעו מבטן דוברי כזב״, מראשית יסודו, וכל מהלכו כלו אינו כי־אם עצת שקר ונכלי רשעים מסובכים, שהם קשורים עם הנטיות הנפשיות והגופניות אשר נתעצמו בהאדריכליות של בנין הלאומים של זמננו, שכחי ד׳ בכליותם ונושאים את שמו על שפתם, בפיהם ובלשונם. על־כן חרב תחרב כל התרבות ההוית, ועל משואותיה יתכונן בנין העולם באמת ובדעת ד׳. ״והיה באחרית הימים נכון יהיה הר בית ד׳ בראש ההרים ונשא מגבעות ונהרו אליו כל הגוים״.

ט

בנין העולם, המתמוטט כעת לרגלי הסערות הנוראות של חרב מלאה דם, דורש הוא את בנין האומה הישראלית. בנין האומה והתגלות רוחה הוא ענין אחד וכולו הוא מאוחד עם בנין העולם, המתפורר ומצפה לכח מלא אחדות ועליוניות, וכל זה נמצא בנשמת כנסת ישראל. רוח ד׳ מלא בה, רוח שם מלא בקרבה, ואי־אפשר לרוח אדם, שהרגשת נשמתו פועמת בו, להיות שוקט בשעה גדולה זו, מבלי לקרא לכל הכחות הצפונים באומה: עורו וקומו על תפקידכם. קול ד׳ קורא בכח, ומתוכיות נשמתנו ומתנועות החיים

rejecting His ways – this situation is but a moment in history.[85] The light of Return must perforce[86] appear, *each man shall throw away his idols of silver and gold,*[87] and all will revert to the goodness of the Lord. Then the present civilization will disappear with all its foundations – literature and theater, and so forth; all the laws founded on inanity and iniquity, all evil etiquette will pass away. *And the Lord alone will be exalted on that day.*[88] The spiritual and practical fabric that in its present state could not prevent, despite all its glorious wisdom, wholesale slaughter and such fearful world-destruction, has proven itself invalid from its very inception [*The wicked are estranged from the womb; those who speak lies go astray from their very birth*[89]], and all its progress is not but false counsel and evil entrapment, connected to the psychic and physical tendencies that have become entrenched in the architecture of contemporary nations[90] forgetful of the Lord in reality but bearing His name on their lips. Therefore, the entire contemporary civilization is doomed, and on its ruins will be established a world order of truth and God-consciousness. *And it shall be at the end of days, the mountain of the house of the Lord will be established on the mountaintop, exalted above the hills, and all the nations will stream to it.*[91]

9

Israel and the New World Order

At the hour of the downfall of Western civilization, Israel is called upon to fulfill its divine mission by providing the spiritual basis for a new world order.

The world order that is now tottering due to the awesome storms of a sword covered with blood, demands the construction of the Israelite nation. The building of the nation and the discovery of its spirit are one concept, linked to the building of the world, which is disintegrating and longing for a force filled with unity and loftiness, and all of this is found in the soul of *Knesset Yisrael* (Ecclesia Israel). The spirit of the Lord pervades her. The spirit of a complete Name is in her midst, and it is impossible for a man whose soul pounds within him to be silent at this hour, without summoning all the powers that lie dormant in the

אנו מבחינים אותו. ישראל מוכרח לחשוף את מקור חייו, לעמוד הכן על רגלי אפיו הרוחני, "מי גוי גדול אשר לו אלהים קרובים אליו" - "אומה היודעת אפיה של אלהיה". התרבות העולמית מתנודדת, רוח האדם נחלש, מחשכים מכסים את כל העמים, "החשך יכסה ארץ וערפל לאומים". והשעה הגיעה, אור עולם, אור אלהים אמת, אור אלהי ישראל, המתגלה על-יד עמו, עם פלאים, צריך הוא להתגלות בהכרה, וההכרה צריכה לבא באומה פנימה, להכיר את האחדות של כחותיה היא, להכיר את ד' השוכן בה. ובהכירה כי יש אלהים בקרבה, תכיר איך לחשוף את מבוע חייה, תדע להעמיד חזון עמדתה על מקורה העצמי. לא לשאב מבארות זרים היא קרואה כי-אם לדלות ממעמקיה. תדלה רצון מעמק תפלתה, חיים מבאר תורתה, אומץ משורש אמונתה, סדור מיושר שכלה, גבורה מעז רוחה, וכל העולה על שפירירי שמיה, הכל מרוח אלהים המרחפת על מלא היקום מימי בראשית עד אחרית. "כי אני אתכם נאם ד' צבאות, את הדבר אשר כרתי אתכם בצאתכם ממצרים, ורוחי עומדת בתוככם, אל תיראו".

כל התרבויות שבעולם יתחדשו על-ידי חדוש רוחנו, כל הדעות יתישרו, כל החיים יאורו בשמחת לידה חדשה בהתקוממותנו, כל האמונות ילבשו בגדים חדשים, יסירו את הבגדים הצואים מעליהן ויתלבשו בלבושי יקר, יזניחו את כל פגול, כל טמא וכל תיעוב שבקרבם, ויתאחדו לינק מטללי אורות הקדש, אשר הוכנו מאז לכל גוי וכל אדם בבאר ישראל. ברכת אברהם לכל גויי הארץ תחל את פעולתה בתקף ובגלוי, ועל-פי יסודה יחל, מחדש, בנינו בארץ ישראל. החרבן העכשוי הוא הכנת תחיה חדשה, עמוקה ואופיית. אור חסד עליון מנתוצץ. שם ד' אהיה אשר אהיה הולך ומתגלה. הבו גדל לאלהינו.

nation: Awake, arise to your task! The voice of the Lord calls loudly, and from the interior of our soul and life's movements we distinguish it. Israel must uncover the source of its life to stand apprised of its spiritual character. *Who is a great nation to whom God is close?*[92] "A nation which knows the character of its God!"[93] World civilization totters, man's spirit is weakened, darkness covers all the peoples, *darkness will cover the earth and fog, the nations.*[94] The hour has arrived; the light of the wold, the light of the true God, the light of the God of Israel, revealed by His people, a wondrous people, must be revealed in consciousness, and the consciousness must be internalized within the nation, to recognize the unity of her talents, to recognize the Lord Who rests within her. When she will recognize that there is a God within her, she will understand how to tap the spring of her life, she will know how to establish her redemptive vision upon her essential source. She is not called to draw from foreign wells but rather to tap her depths. She will draw will from the depth of her prayer, life from the well of her Torah, strength from the root of her faith, organization from the straightness of her mind, courage from the fortitude of her spirit, and all that arises on her halcyon heavens, all is from the spirit of God that hovers over the fullness of existence, from the days of Beginning until the End. *For I am with you, says the Lord of Hosts, the thing that I promised you when you exited Egypt, and My spirit stands in your midst, do not fear.*[95]

All the world's civilizations will be renewed through renewal of our spirit, all opinions will be straightened, all life will glisten with the joy of rebirth at our emergence, all beliefs will don new clothes, will take off their dirty clothes and wear precious raiment, will abandon all the abominations in their midst, and unite to suckle from the dew of the lights of holiness, which were pre-established in the well of Israel for each nation and individual. The blessing of Abraham to all the nations of the Earth[96] will commence activity forcefully and visibly,[97] and based on it will recommence our building in the Land of Israel. The present destruction is the preparation of a profound renascence. The supernal light of grace twinkles. The name *Ehyeh Asher Ehyeh – I will be that I will be*[98] – is revealed. *Give praise to our God.*[99]

י

בגדולת העולם, בהופעת הזיו של קדושת ישראל ברוממותו, אין אחיזה לכל זונים, לכל העומדים מבחוץ, לבסס איזה מוסד הדוחק רגלי אור ישראל, לבצר איזו הארה מיסתית, מכונה אמונית, אשר תוכל עמוד חוץ ממציאות האומה, כבודה ושפעת יקרת קדשה. כי האור העליון וזיו היחוד המאוחד, שיסודו העליון, אור האמת בבהירותו, חי בו, הרי הוא קשור בסגולת ישראל, "ד' אלהיו עמו ותרועת מלך בו". מירידת העולם והשפלת הנשמה הישראלית נפרד היחוד העליון ממקור אחדותו ועלה למעלה להרקיע לשחקים. בעולם החיים לא יופיע כי אם נגהי הזהרורית של היחוד התחתון, הנשאב מהבורות השאובים ויד זרים בו נוגעת. וכנסת ישראל תחיל, תזעק בחבליה: אוי נא לי, כי עיפה נפשי. רזי תורה לחיצונים נמסרו. התורה נשרפת, גויליה נשרפים ואותיות פורחות, ולבני ציון היקרים אפר תחת פאר, הושם. קמים נבוני לבב בחצות לילה וידיהם על חלציהם כיולדה: על צרת העולם, צרת ישראל, צרת השכינה, צרת התורה, הם בוכים ומבכים. ויודעים הם ומכירים את עמק הצער במקורו ובתולדותיו, יודעים הם, שכל הצרות והמחשכים, כל נהרי נחלי הדמים הנשפכים, כל התלאות והנדודים, כל הבוז והמשטמה, כל הרשעה והזוהמא, אינם אלא תולדה קלושה מהד הקול של אותו הצער העליון, צער השמים, צער השכינה, צער האידיאליות המהותית בהפרדה ממקור תענוגיה, והאידיאליות העליונה ברוחם של הבריות ובחירת האדם, תשובת ישראל ורוממות אצילות הרוח הרציני, היא קשורה. והם קוראים לתשובה, ואנו ליה ועינינו ליה.

10

The Election of Israel

The election of Israel will be revealed at the maturity of the world. Christianity, which had expropriated certain Jewish mystical doctrines, will stand repudiated. In the meantime, the righteous experience the pain of the Shekhinah *(divine presence).*

At the maturity of the world, when the splendor of Israel's holiness is revealed, there is no room for strayers, for outsiders, to base an establishment that would repel the Light of Israel, to enforce some mystical enlightenment or faith[100] that would stand outside of the (Israelite) Nation's existence, honor and holy influence. For the supernal light and splendor of unity – whose highest fundamental, the light of truth in its clarity[101] lives in it – is connected to the unique quality of Israel. *The Lord his God is with him and the trumpet of the King is through him.*[102] Because of the descent of the world and the lowering of the Israelite soul, the higher unity is separated from its source of unity and ascends above to the heavens. In the world of the living there appears but the glow of the lower unity, drawn from secondary sources and subject to foreign domination. *Knesset Yisrael* (Ecclesia Israel) shudders, she shrieks in pain: Woe is to me, my soul is weary! Secrets of Torah are transmitted to outsiders.[103] The Torah is burnt, her scrolls fired and the letters fly, and for the dear children of Zion, ash *(efer)* has replaced glory *(pe'er).*[104] The understanding of heart arise at midnight, their hands on their loins as a woman in childbirth: on account of the suffering of the world, of Israel, of the *Shekhinah* (divine presence), of the Torah, they cry and mourn. They realize the depth of pain, its source and effects. They know that all the troubles and darkness, all the rivers of spilt blood, all the sufferings and wanderings, all the derision and hate, all the wickedness and pollution, are but a vague echo of the supernal pain, the pain of heaven, the pain of the *Shekhinah* (divine presence),[105] the pain of the essential ideal when sundered from the source of its joy,[106] and the supernal ideal is connected to the spirit of people and the choice of man, the Return of Israel and the exaltedness of the volitional spirit.[107] They [i.e., the understanding of heart] call for Return – *We are to Yah and our eyes are (turned) to Yah.*[108]

ישראל ותחיתו

א

ישראל מספרים תהלת ד׳, כח גבורה העליונה, במלא תפארת מעשיו בכל מקומות ממשלתו, מעולם ועד העולם, ומרומם על כל ברכה ותהלה, זהו גורל ישראל. ישראל מכיר הוא את כח מעשי ד׳, ישראל מכיר ומעיד עדות אל גבור יוצר כל לבדו, ״ואתם עדי נאם ד׳ ואני אל״. מלא הוא ישראל מאור הגבורה והתפארת העליונה שהכרתן מלאה חיי חכמת עולמים, חיי חסד ואהבת כל הבריות, חיי פאר מקדושים. ישראל עומד הוא בקרן אורה זו ברוחו, בחיי כל נשמה בפרטיות ובחיי האומה כולה, בבנינה, בדורותיה, בשאיפת שיגוב פאר זיו הדר כונניות מלכותה, בהיכל קדש מקדשה, בלהט אש חיי נעוריה, ״אשר בנינו כנטיעים מגודלים בנעוריהם, בנותינו כזויות מחוטבות תבנית היכל״, וחפץ רכושה ועשרה ״מזוינו מלאים מפיקים מזן אל זן, צאננו מאליפות מרובבות בחוצותינו, אלופינו מסובלים, אין פרץ ואין יוצאת ואין צוחה ברחובותינו, אשרי העם שככה לו, אשרי העם שד׳ אלהיו״. והעם אשר ד׳ אלהיו יודע לספר כח מעשי ד׳, יודע לספר, שאלהי ישראל אלהי עולם הוא, בורא שמים וארץ ושהכל ברא לכבודו, וכבודו כבוד כל עולמים, חיי כל עולמים, וחקר כבודו כבוד. וידיעתו זאת היא תכונת רוחו, מורשת אבותיו והכרתו הפנימית, חודרת בו בכל לב ובכל נשמה, אחוזה, קשורה ודבוקה בנעימת אמונתו, אמונת אומן, בבירור תולדתו,

ISRAEL AND ITS RENASCENCE

1

Israel, Narrator of God

Israel is a living narration of God's greatness.

Israel tell the praise of the Lord,[109] the supernal might, the glory of His deeds in all places of His realm, from eternity to eternity, exalted beyond all blessing and praise – this is the fate of Israel. Israel recognizes the strength of the Lord's deeds;[110] Israel attests for the Mighty God Who created all Himself. *And you are my witnesses, says the Lord, and I am God.*[111] Israel is full of[112] the light of the supernal strength and beauty; their consciousness is full of the life of the wisdom of worlds, the life of grace and love of all creatures, the life of holy beauty. Israel reflects this light in its spirit,[113] in the life of each individual soul and in the life of the entire nation, in its structure, its generations, in its aspiration to establish its kingdom, in its holy temple, in its fiery youth – *our sons as grown saplings in their youth; our daughters as corner-pillars, sculptured in the model of a palace,*[114] and her desire for property and wealth – *our garners full, furnishing all manner of store; our sheep bringing forth thousands and ten thousands in our open pastures; our oxen strong to labor; there is no breach and hue and cry in our streets; Happy is such a people, happy the people whose God is the Lord.*[115] The people whose God is the Lord knows (how) to tell the mighty deeds of the Lord, knows to tell that the God of Israel is the God of the world, Creator of heaven and earth, Who created all for His honor, and His honor is the honor of all worlds, the life of all worlds, and the investigation of His honor is an honor. This knowledge is the characteristic spirit (of

בנצחונותיו על כל, בסגולת קיומו ועמדתו נגד צריו הרבים, אשר המה כשלו ונפלו והוא קם והתעודד. ויותר מכל חרותה ידיעת קדש עולמי עולמים זו בנשמתו הפנימית, בתביעת רוחו, בזהר שירתו, בהתגלמות חייו, מותאמת לאפי מוסרו, לתכנית מדיניותו, והיא יסוד כל שאיפותיו. והאמת העליונה הזאת היא מקוממת את כל היקום, כל יציר נברא ממנה חי, הכל מכחה ישתלם, כל הנופלים יקומו על ידה, כל עשוקי כח, כל רצוצי משפט ישובו וינהרו מזיוה, כל טבועי שאול בחילה יעלו ויעמדו במרחב, כל זהומי כל תמונה סוררה, כל החשוכים על-ידי כל סכלות וכל תעוב - על-ידי אור עולמי אין קץ זה יביטו וינהרו. אור ישראל זורח והולך ואור, מפעם בקרב נשמתו את הלמות גאולתו. "כח מעשיו הגיד לעמו, לתת להם נחלת גוים. מעשי ידיו אמת ומשפט, נאמנים כל פקודיו. סמוכים לעד לעולם, עשוים באמת וישר. פדות שלח לעמו, צוה לעולם בריתו, קדוש ונורא שמו". וגבורת אלהי עולם אלהי ישראל, אדון כל העולמים, מתברכת ומתגברת בתועפות הופעותיה ברוממות קרנם של ישראל, ביסוד האומה היא זורחת ומופיעה, בתאות גאולתה היא חיה ומתעוררת - האל, הבורא, היוצר, הקורא כל יש מאין, הנוטה צפון על תהו, אשר בידו מחקרי ארץ ותועפות הרים לו, מעונה אלהי קדם. "מעון אתה היית לנו בכל דור ודור, בטרם הרים יולדו ותחולל ארץ ותבל, ומעולם ועד עולם אתה אל". ותפארת אל זאת, כתר מלכות אלהים חיים, בישראל היא שרויה. אין עם ולשון בעולם שיוכל להגות ברוחו אמת חודרת תבל ומלאה זאת. עד מתי עוזך בשבי ותפארתך ביד צר. עוררה גבורתך אל אלהים עליון. "לפני אפרים ובנימין ומנשה עוררה את גבורתך ולכה לישועתה לנו". הושיעה את עמך ופדה גוי ואלהיו, ופדה תפדה, כי גואל חזק אתה. "כי בכל חכמי הגוים ובכל מלכותם מאין כמוך", "מאין כמוך ד' גדול אתה וגדול שמך בגבורה". "מי כמוך חסין יה ואמונתך סביבותיך. אתה מושל בגאות הים, בשוא

Israel), the inheritance from its ancestors and its inner consciousness, penetrating each heart and soul, intertwined with its faith, its history, its overcoming all, its miraculous endurance against its many oppressors, who succumbed and fell while it rose and was encouraged.[116] More than anything (else), this holy, eternal knowledge is engraved within the interior of its soul, in its incessant longing, in its shining song, in the embodiment of its life; it conforms to its ethical character, to its political project and is the foundation of all its aspirations. This higher truth is (what) gives existence, every creature lives thereby, all are perfected by virtue of it, all who are falling rise through it, all the oppressed and downtrodden will shine by its splendor, all sunken in the underworld will rise up, all polluted by a rebellious picture,[117] all darkened by folly and abomination – through this eternal light will see and radiate. The light of Israel shines on, pounding in its soul the beat of redemption.[118] *The power of His deeds He told His people, to give them the portion of nations. The works of His hands are truth and justice; faultless are all His precepts. They are well supported for ever and eternally; they are framed in truth and uprightness. Redemption He sent to His people; He has commanded His covenant forever; holy and fearful is His name.*[119] The strength of the God of the world, the God of Israel, Master of all worlds, is increased and manifested by the uplifting of Israel, in the foundation of the nation it shines, in the desire for its redemption it lives and is wakened – God, Creator, Maker, Who called forth something from nothing, *Who fixed North on the abyss,*[120] *in Whose hand are the deep places of the earth, and Whose are the heights of mountains,*[121] *your refuge is the Eternal God.*[122] *A place of refuge You have been for us in each generation. Before the mountains were brought forth or You had produced the earth and the world, from eternity to eternity You are God.*[123] This glory of God, the royal crown of the Living God, rests in Israel. There is no (other) nation in the world that can conceive in its spirit this earth-shattering truth. *How long will Your strength be in captivity and Your glory in the hand of an oppressor?! Arouse Your might,*[124] *Most High God. Before Ephraim and Benjamin and Menasseh awaken Your might and go for our salvation.*[125] *Save Your*

גליו אתה תשבחם. אתה דכית כחלל רהב, בזרוע עזך פזרת אויביך. לך שמים אף לך ארץ, תבל ומלאה אתה יסדתם. צפון וימין אתה בראתם, תבור וחרמון בשמך ירננו". "כי לד' מגננו, ולקדוש ישראל מלכנו". "כי כל אלהי העמים אלילים וד' שמים עשה".

ב

שתי הבנות כלליות הן, המקיפות את ההויה ואת התורה, את כל ההסתכלות בכל שנויי דרכיה: ההבנה המוסרית וההבנה הסבתית. בתוך ההבנה הסבתית, הקדומה בזמן לגבי רוח האדם, כלולה היא, בתור נשמה עליונה המחיה אותה, ההבנה המוסרית. ההבנה הסבתית מציעה חקים אחוזים זה בזה על כל מרחב היש. מתחיל בעולם החמרי וכוחותיו והולך ומקיף, מטפס ועולה עד רוממות העולמים הרוחניים ומנתח את סעיפיהם, כפי עשר הרוח הגדול אשר לאדם, שצד גדלותו מתעלה ומתבלט בהיותו אחוז בחופש ציורו, עם כל קטנו להחליט דבר ודאי במה שנעשה מחוצה לחוג פנימיותו. בשלשלת הסבתית מונחה איזו העקה כללית, איזו מניעה, המעצרת את החקים ותכנם שלא ילכו בדרכים אחרים כי־אם באותם הדרכים שהשלשלת הסבתית מקשרת אותם להם. העקה זו עצמה חידה נעלמה היא, ומכל מקום, עם כל המניעה שיש בתכונת שכלנו מלחדור לעמקיה של חדת עולם זו, אין זה חוסם לפנינו את דרך ההסתעפות השכלית לכל אותו הבנין הגדול של ההבנה החקית. אבל בעת אשר אנו עולים למעלה יותר עליונה של חירות נשגבה, אז אנחנו משתחררים מכל אותה המועקה הסבתית, וכל הבנין החקי מצטיר לפנינו בתור קשרים מוסריים אחוזים זה בזה, שההידוק והאמץ שבהם הוא לא פחות חזק ואמיץ, ועוד יותר מחוטב, מאותו של התכן אשר להבנה הסבתית, וערכו הכללי הוא נשגב ונעלה ממנו באין

people and redeem a nation and its God.[126] And You shall redeem, for You are a strong savior. *Among all the wise men of the nations and in all their kingdom there is none like You.*[127] *There is none like You, You are great and mighty is Your name.*[128] *Who is powerful like You, Yah, and Your faithfulness is round about You. You rule over the pride of the sea; when its waves are lifted up, You assuage them. You crushed Rahab as one that is slain; with Your strong arm You scattered Your enemies. Yours are the heavens, also the earth; the world and its fill, You founded them. North and south You created them; Tabor and Hermon will rejoice in Your name.*[129] *For the Lord is our shield, and the Holy One of Israel is our King.*[130] *For all the gods of the peoples are idols, but the Lord has made the heavens.*[131]

2

The Causal and Ethical Approaches to Understanding Existence

Two approaches to understanding existence: the causal approach and the ethical approach. In Jewish history they are bound together.

There are two general understandings that encompass existence and Torah, all the varied aspects of perception: the ethical approach and the causal approach.[132] Within the causal approach, which chronologically preceded the human spirit, is subsumed the ethical approach that acts as an oversoul vivifying it. The causal perpective presents laws that ripple throughout existence. It proceeds from the material world and scales the spiritual heights as it examines their details. This in proportion to the wealth of the human spirit, which is great when given freedom of conception, though puny when it comes to deciding something outside of its inner realm. In the chain of causality there is contained a general restriction, a constriction that constrains laws to those pathways. This restriction itself is a mystery, but yet, given our minds' inability to penetrate this world mystery, this does not obstruct our cognition of the magnificent edifice of the laws (of the universe.) However, when we ascend to a higher plane of freedom, we are freed

ערוך. אז אנו עומדים בעולם של חופש. כשהעולם המוסרי מתגלה לפנינו, מרומם הוא את העולם החקי, הסבתי כולו ומושכו אליו, משפיע עליו מאורו ונמצא שהוא כולו טבוע בים של אור חיים זה של החקים המוסריים, שהם הרבה עליונים ונשגבים מהחקים הסבתיים. וכשאנו מעמיקים בדבר הרינו מוצאים אחר כך גם את כל הפרטים של העולם הסבתי, כולם עומדים בתבניתם המעולה בעולם המוסרי המלא זיו, המתנשא ממעל להם.

כשאנו מסתכלים בקשר התורה עם האומה, ברית כרותה לארץ ולעם, כשדבקים בד׳ אלהיהם הרי הם מצליחים, עולים ומתפתחים, משתרשים בארצם ועושים חיל, כשזונים אחרי אלהי נכר הארץ הרי הם מתדלדלים ונופלים, חרבן האומה והארץ בא וצרות וכליונות הולכות ובאות. כשאנו מחפשים את הפתרון בעולם הסבתי הרינו מוצאים שרוח ישראל אחוז הוא בשלשלת אורגנית חזקה. דעותיו, מהלכי חייו, מגמת פניו בתעופת רוחו הכללית, האמת העליונה המתגלה בו ועל ידו, תכונת ארצו וברכותיה, התאמצות הנשמות היחידיות, המשכת ברכותיהן, לשדי חייהן, החן המשוך על הכלל ועל הפרט, העצות והנטיות הבונות את הבנין הכללי ומבועיהן, בהירות הסקירות, המנוחה הפנימית, חזוק הרוח ושלות החיים - הכל אחוז זה בזה. באותה ההבטאה הנפשית של הדבקות בד׳ אלהיו, אלהי אבותיו הראשונים, המעלה אותו מארץ מצרים מבית עבדים, המביאהו אל ארץ הברית והשבועה, המורהו דרכי חיים ונתיבות עולמים, אחוזים הם זה בזה הקישורים; והיא משאבת אל תוכו את כל אוצר החיים והתנובה. ובהפרדו ממקור חייו, הרוח מתחלחל. שפעת החיים הכלליים, האחוזים ברתוקות הגוי והארץ, המורשה והמקדש, המוסר והאמונה, מתחלשת. רוח זר בא ומפעם, והוא צמח לא יעשה קמח, לא יקלט ולא יצמיח. והננו רואים את המארה באה ועושה שמות, עד אשר ישוב העם אל אל חייו, אל מקור ישעו, ישיב אליו את

of this causal restriction, and the entire structure of laws appears to us as being held together by ethical bonds that are no weaker and are even stronger than those of the causal explanation, and whose total value is infinitely more exalted. Then we stand in a world of freedom.[133] When the ethical universe is revealed to us, it uplifts the causal universe, attracts it and enlightens it, flooding it in a sea of living light of ethical laws that far surpass the causal laws. Were we to delve into the matter, we would subsequently rediscover the details of the causal universe residing intact within the splendorous ethical world.

When we regard the connection of Torah to the nation, a covenant was made with the Land and the People that when they cling to the Lord their God, they succeed and develop, sink roots in the Land and prosper; when they stray after foreign gods they are impoverished and fall, the People and the Land are destroyed, and troubles and annihilation follow. When we seek an explanation in the causal world, we find that the spirit of Israel is connected to a strong organic chain. Its opinions, its life-directions, its national spirit, the truth revealed through it, its geography and its blessings, the striving of individual souls, their blessings, their vitality, the charm of nation and individuals, the schemes that contribute to the general building, the clarity of perspective, the inner peace, the fortitude of spirit and the prosperity – all are intertwined. By that soul-utterance of cleaving to the Lord its God, God of its ancestors, Who raised it from Egypt, house of bondage, brought it to the Promised, Covenanted Land, teaches it ways of life and eternal paths – the bonds are interconnected. (This utterance) brings to Israel the entire storehouse of life. When Israel is detached from its source of vitality, the spirit swoons. The flow of universal life, which hinges on the nation and the land, the (spiritual) legacy and the Temple, morals and faith, is weakened.[134] A foreign wind blows, which produces no crop and brings no flour. We see the curse coming, ravaging, until the people will return to its Living God, to its source of salvation. Its spirit will return to Him, will be bound tight by a spirit of understanding to the name of the Lord, God of Israel, and from

רוחו, יִקָשר באמץ לבב וברוח בינה אל שם ד׳ אלהי ישראל, ומגולי פלגיו של הרעיון הכללי, העמוק והחסון, המותאם לרוח עולמים ולחטיביות המיוחדה של ישראל, ישועה חוזרת ומוארה. - כל זאת היא בינה גלויה, הכרה מעשית המחיה ומשיבה רוח. אבל מיד אנו באים להתרומם בחדירה יותר פנימית, שממעל לכל הארג החקי הזה ארג מוסרי נתון. במוסריות הרעננה, המחיה את השלשלת הסבתית הגדולה הזאת, שם שם מונח כל האמץ, כל הזיו של החיים האלה המתגלים בהופעותיהם בעזיזות כל כך גדולה, בדיקנות כל כך אדירה. ההופעה המוסרית מגלה בנו צביון של אמרה, ״שכך ראוי להיות״, ״כך צריך להיות״, לא רק ״כך הוא״ ו״ככה נהיה״. ומההכרה ש״כך צריך להיות״ בהתגלותה של הבינה המוסרית אנו חוזרים אחר כך להכיר את השלשלת החקית-המוסרית בכל פרטיה, בכל עמקה וגבהה, רחבה והקפה, פנימיותה וחיצוניותה. השתגבות כפולה, חיה ורעננה, מתעוררת אז בקרבנו פנימה, ומעינות של עצה ותבונה, צביונים חיים ותחבולות ישרות, הולכים ומתגלים בקרב כל כליות ולב. רוח האומה מתעורר לתחיה, ובמחבא החיים אור קדושה וטהרה זורח - אורו של משיח.

ג

מרכז החיים של נשמת ישראל במקור הקדש הוא. דרך אמת ואמונה נולדנו ובה אנחנו מתגדלים. אין בנו ערכים פרודים, האחדות שוכנת בנו ואור ד׳ אחד חי בקרבנו. הדינים, דיני תורת אלהים חיים, מציינים אותנו מכל עם ולשון. הקדש הוא פועל בקרבנו פנימה, שאיפות חיינו הכלליות אליו הן הולכות. יש נטיפות של קדש בכל עם ולשון, אבל ערכי החיים כולם אינם צומחים מזה. לא כן בישראל. בכל דרכיך דעהו, שהיא פרשה קטנה שכוללת

the waves of the general conception, deep and mighty, attuned to the universe and the specific constitution of Israel, salvation returns and is rekindled. All of this is revealed understanding, a practical recognition that restores life and breath. But immediately we ascend and penetrate deeper: Beyond this fabric of laws there is an ethical fabric. In the refreshing ethic, which enlivens this grand causal chain, there is lodged all the strength, all the splendor of this life that is revealed so mightily and precisely. The revelation of ethics prompts us to say, "So it should be," "So it must be" – not just "So it is," "So it exists." From the awareness that "So it must be," revealed by ethical understanding, we return afterward to understand the causal-ethical chain in all of its details, depth and height, width and circumference, interiority and exteriority. A double elevation is aroused in our midst, and springs of counsel and understanding, living conceptions and straight thoughts, arise in every heart. The spirit of the nation is resurrected, and in the hidden place of life, a light of holiness and purity shines – the Light of Messiah.

3

The Legal System: Challenge to Spirituality

Unlike other nations, all Israel's values stem from holiness. The significance of the institution of Semikhah *(Ordination). Jewish jurisprudence. The difference between the "religion of law" and the "religion of love."*

The center of life of the soul of Israel is in the source of holiness. Through truth and faith we were born and thereby we grow. We do not have disparate values; unity rests in us and the light of the One Lord lives within us. The laws, laws of the Living God's Torah, distinguish us from every other nation.[135] Holiness is at work on us internally,[136] the great aspirations of our life are directed to it. There are inklings of holiness in every nation, but not all their life-values stem therefrom. This is not so in Israel. *In all of your ways know Him,*[137] that small passage that encompasses the entire corpus of Torah,[138] which is actualized by rare individuals, is actually the inheritance

כל גופי תורה, שיוצאת אל הפועל ביחידי סגולה, נחלת הכלל היא באמת. כל שאיפת החיים וכל חפץ החיים, הקנין ותשוקותיו, העשר והכבוד, הממשלה וההתרחבות בישראל, ממקור הקדש הם נובעים. על כן המשפטים הם קדש קדשים בישראל, ועל כן הסמיכה, שהיא נושאת שם אלהים עליה, היא כל כך נחוצה לנו, היא כל כך אופית לתכן לאומנו. והרשעה היונית-הסורית הרגישה בחוש העור שלה את ערך הסגולה הגדולה הזאת וגזרה על הסמיכה, ורבי יהודה בן בבא מסר את נפשו עליה. ופעולת מסירת הנפש הזאת נשארה, כי העמיקה את תכן החיים האופיים המיוחדים של קדש ישראל לד׳. משה רבנו, עליו השלום, בתפסו אתו את כח המשפט, בתחלת יסודו באומה, העלה את כל ערכי המשפט עד סוף כל הדורות לאותו התכן האלהי שמשפטי ישראל באים אליו, ודרישת אלהים באה יחדו עם המשפט הישראלי. ״כי יבא אלי העם לדרש את אלהים, כי יהיה להם דבר בא אלי ושפטתי בין איש ובין רעהו. והודעתי את חקי האלהים ואת תורותיו״. ודרישת אלהים של המשפט נשארה סגולה ישראלית, שהיא מתגלה באופי האלהי הכולל עולמי עד וזורח בארץ ישראל, בארץ חבל נחלתו, מקום האורה של סגולת הקדש.

המינות הפקירה את המשפט, תקעה עצמה במדת הרחמים והחסד המדומה הנוטלת את יסוד העולם והורסתו. ומתוך עקירת יסוד המשפט מתכנו האלהי תופסת אותה הרשעה היותר מגושמת, ובאה בזוהמא לחדור במשפט הפרטי של האישיות היחידית וחודרת היא בהתפשטות גדולה לנפשות העמים, ובזה מתיסד יסוד שנאת לאומים ועמק רעה של טומאת שפיכת דמים, מבלי להמיש את העול מעל צואר האדם. אמנם עיני כל מוכרחות להיות נשואות לאור עולם, אור ד׳, אשר יגלה על-ידי משיח אלהי יעקב. ״והוא ישפט תבל בצדק, ידין לאומים במישרים״.

of all (Israel). Every life's aspiration and life's desire – acquisition, wealth, honor, dominion, expansion – in Israel flow from the source of holiness. Therefore the laws are holy-of-holies in Israel, and therefore the *semikhah* (institution of rabbinic ordination) that bears the name of God[139] is so vital to us and typical of our national character. The evil Greek-Syrian government intuited the value of this great treasure and forebade the *semikhah,* and Rabbi Judah ben Bava gave his life to preserve it.[140] The effect of that martyrdom remains, for it deepened the special character of Israel, holy to the Lord. Moses our Teacher, of blessed memory, upon grasping the power of the law when it was first instituted in the nation,[141] uplifted all the values of law until the end of generations, to the divine content to which the laws of Israel reach,[142] and the search for God came together with Israelite jurisprudence.[143] *When the people will come to me to seek God, when they will have a matter come to me, I shall judge between a man and his neighbor. And I shall make known the laws of God and His precepts.*[144] The God-quest of Law has remained an Israelite treasure, which is manifest in the divine character that encompasses eternity, and shines forth in the Land of Israel,[145] the land of His portion, the place of light of the holy treasure.

Christianity[146] abandoned law, rooted herself in apparent mercy and love[147] that undermines the world and destroys it. By emptying law of its divine content, it becomes seized by the grossest wickedness. The poison invades the private law of the individual and spreads through the souls of nations, becoming the foundation of national hatred and the depth of evil of bloodshed, without removing the yoke from man's neck. The eyes of all must be lifted to the light of the world, the light of the Lord,[148] which will be revealed through the Messiah of the God of Jacob.[149] *And He shall judge earth righteously, nations justly.*[150]

ד

יש מין ארס רוחני כזה, שבטבעו הוא לטשטש את התכן הישראלי המיוחד, שהוא אור הקדש היותר מעומק שבעולם. החיים הקדושים, השופעים בפנימי פנימיות ההבהקה של אור אלהי אמת והולכים בדרך ישרה על כנסת ישראל ופתוח נשמתה, אחוזים בלשד החיים של קדושת אמונתה הטהורה בטהר עליון, שרק העולם העתיד להתחדש ברום טהרת קדשו יוכל לספגו ולהאיר את עלילות החיים על ידו. רוח עליון זה קובע בכחו, בחיים המעשיים שבישראל מעבר מזה ובחיי האמונה ותכן שפעת הלב והסתעפות הרוח מעבר מזה, את תביעתה הפנימית של האומה, גבורת עמדתה וחשק נצחונה, מעוז בטחת תקותה ואור עתידה. נגד זה, אותו הארס מגיע בפגמו אל תוכיות דם החיים של טהר האמונה, פסגת עז הקדש, ומרפף את יסוד המעמד האחדותי, האיתן של האומה, נוטל מן העולם את זיו החיים הפנימיים של הטהר האלהי ונותן במקומו נגה חיצוני, שאין בו כלום מאותו החידור, הדיוק, הנצחון, הבטחה ואור האמת המנצחת כל עדי עד. יונק הוא ארס זה משפעת הלח של רוח האמונה והמוסר, מתפשט הוא על המון עמים רבים ונאות הוא מאד ללאומי התבל בחוג רחב. עומד הוא על בסיס של הכרה מתדלדלת באופי המוסר והטעם של האמונה והדבקות האלהית, המובעה בחיי האומה הישראלית בכל חסן וטהר. לוחך הוא כלחוך השור, מכה כשאיה שער, חושק הוא לבלוע את פנים החיים, שוקק למחות את שם ישראל מעל פני האדמה, לאבד את הזהר הפנימי של העולם ולקבוע תכן חיצוני מגושם, מקיף בהכללה רפויה ומרופד בתוכיותו באויליות ורשעה של אליליות. ושליטתו מגעת עד עת בא דבר ד׳ להגלות וישועת ישראל מעמק נשמת חי העולמים להופיע, אז ינוסו הצללים ואור חדש על ציון יזרח.

4

The Christian Attempt to Supplant Judaism

Christian civilization effaces the specific Jewish content, replacing it with a shabby imitation that it stretches over the nations.

There is a certain type of spiritual poison, whose nature it is to rub out the special Jewish content,[151] which is the deepest light of holiness in the world. The holy life, which flows in the very interior of the shining light of the true God and proceeds directly to *Knesset Yisrael* (Ecclesia Israel) and the development of its soul, is bound with the sap-of-life of the sanctity of her pure faith, so pure that only the world that in futurity will be renewed in the height of its pure holiness, will be able to absorb it and illumine life's deeds thereby. This sublime spirit sets with its power – in the practical life of Israel on the one hand, and in the life of faith, the content of the heart's flux and the ramification of the spirit, on the other hand – the inner demand of the nation, the strength of its stand and the passion of its victory, the fortitude of its hope and the light of its future. Opposite this, that poison reaches with its impurity to the midst of the lifeblood of the purity of faith, the height of holy strength, and weakens the foundation of the mighty unitive state of the nation. It removes from the world the splendor of the inner life of the divine purity and replaces it with an outer shine, which has none of that penetration, precision, victory, certitude and light of truth that overcomes all forever and ever. This poison draws sustenance from the moist flow of the spirit of faith and ethics. It spreads over a multitude of nations and is very well suited to the outer orbit of the nations of the earth. It stands on the foundation of an impoverished consciousness of the character of ethics, the taste of faith and the divine rapture, which is expressed in the life of the Israelite nation in all strength and purity. It munches as an ox, totally destroying,[152] desiring to swallow the interior of life, thirsting to erase the name *Israel*[153] from off the face of the earth, to destroy the inner splendor of the world and set up an outer coarse content, which encompasses with a weak universality, and is accoutered on the inside with the folly and wickedness of paganism.

ה

העולם ומלאו לאור ישראל מחכים, לאור עליון של בהירות תהלת שם ד׳, של עם זו יצר לו אל לספר תהלתו, הידיעה המנוחלת מברכת אברהם, הברוך לאל עליון קונה שמים וארץ, לעם לבדד ישכון ובגוים לא יתחשב, לעם אשר ד׳ בדד ינחנו ואין עמו אל נכר, העם המטהר את העולם כלו מטומאתו ומכל מחשכיו, העם אשר נחל חמדה גנוזה, כלי חמדה, שבה נבראו שמים וארץ; לא חזיונות לב, לא מוסר אנוש, לא רק חפץ הגון וציור טוב, לא הפקרות העולם החמרי בכל ערכיו, לא עזיבת הגוף ביסוד ערלתו וטומאתו, ועזיבת החיים והחברה, הממלכה והמשטר, בשפלות זוהמתם, ולא עזיבת העולם וכחותיו הטבעיים אשר נפלו יחד עם חטאת האדם בשפלותם, כי־אם רוממות הכל, ״אור הלבנה כאור החמה ואור החמה שבעתים כאור שבעת הימים״. אין מוחם ולבם, אין נפשם ורוחם של כל עם ולשון יכולים עדיין להסתגל לקדושת עולמים, לחדות גאות ד׳, שליטת היצירה מעומק ראשיתה עד עומק סופה, החבוקה כולה באחדות האלהית בעמק טובה, ברעם גבורתה, בטהרתה וצחצוחה. ואנו מכירים את כל השפעותיהן השונות של כל ההדרכות של האומות כולן, את דרגותיהן לפי ערכן, את האור שבתוך החשך לכל מדותיו ואת עמק המחשכים לכל מיניהם ושאיפותיהם. נצחנו את העננים הכבדים והמגואלים אשר לממלכות האליל, והננו הולכים ומנצחים גם את ענני החשך הקלים מהם. בטול המצות המעשיות אשר יצא מהמינות וצדדי אליליותה, יחד עם התגברותה לקלוט לה מדתנו ערכי אמונה ומוסר בפום ממלל רברבן, לאמר הרבה ושלא לעשות גם מעט - מקושרים הם המאפלים הללו עם אותה ההתטמטמות הגויית, שלא תוכל

Its dominion extends until the time comes for the word of the Lord to be revealed and the salvation of Israel from the depth of the soul of the Life of Worlds to be manifest. Then the shadows will flee and a new light on Zion will shine.

5

Judaism versus Christianity: Holism and Dualism

Judaism's holistic approach to spirituality versus the schizoid spirituality of Christianity.

The entire world waits for Israel, for the sublime light of the clarity of the name of the Lord,[154] of this people that God created to recount His praise,[155] the knowledge bequeathed through the blessing of Abraham, blessed to the Most High God, Creator of heaven and earth,[156] to a people that dwells apart and is not reckoned among the nations,[157] a people whom God leads alone and has no foreign god,[158] the people that purifies the entire world from its impurity and all its obscurity, the people that received a hidden treasure,[159] a vessel of delight,[160] with which heavens and earth were created;[161] not fantasies of the heart, not human ethics, not just good intention and conception, not the wantonness of the material world with all its values, not the neglect of the uncircumcised body, its impurity, and the neglect of life and society, state and government, with their lowly pollution, and not the neglect of the world and its natural resources that fell with the sin of Adam, but rather the uplifting of all: *The light of the moon as the light of the sun, and the light of the sun sevenfold as the light of the seven days* (of Creation).[162] Neither the mind nor the heart, neither the soul nor the spirit of the nations, can yet adapt to the eternal holiness, to the joy of the pride of the Lord, ruler over the creation from the limit of its beginning to the limit of its end, totally enwrapped in the divine unity, in the depth of its goodness, the thunder of its strength, its purity, and cleanliness. We are aware of the different influences of all the orientations of the nations, their levels according to their value, the light within the darkness, in all its proportions, and the depth of darkness, all its species and ambitions: We triumphed over the heavy, filthy clouds

להכיל בלב הערל את השקפת העולם האלהית העליונה בכל זהרה, שהיא קושרת שמים וארץ, גוף ונשמה, אמונה ומעשה, ציור ומפעלים, אישיות וחברה, עולם הזה ועולם הבא, הוית העולמים בראשיתם וגורלם באחריתם, רוממות עולמי עד, שמחת שמים וארץ וכל צבאם, במחיית שם ושאר וכל צל אלילי, בהטהר גם שפל דרגת העולמים מזוהמותיו, בהתישר גם העקמומית היותר מעוותה ומלפפת יחד עם כל סילוף גם היותר קטן וקל, ואור יזרח לישרים. - והעולם הגויי ככה הוא, מורכב, מחולק, אין אחדות לגוף עם הנשמה, אין חבור והתמזגות פנימית לרוחניות העולם וגשמותו, אין קשר פנימי בין המעשים ורחשי הנפש. השתוף הוא להם לעת עתה תכלית העליה, לפני זריחת אורן של ישראל. אבל כמה אומלל הוא העולם, שהרשעה והחשכה הזאת מרימה בה [בו?] ראש והיא מתאמרת למבחר מאוייו. כמה אוצרות רשע כלולים תחת שקר נורא ואיום זה, שיש לו טלפי חזיר המתפשטות לעין כל עובר לאמר: ראו שאני טהור. וכמה אומללים הם הרעיונות השוטפים מתוך העולם הטהור והאמתי אל שפך זוהמא עכורה זו. כמה אור צריכים להרבות לגאול את האורות נפילי המחשכים! - והם יגאלו, גאולת עולמים, בגאולת גוי קדוש.

ו

ההפקר של העולם המעשי, הבא מתוך ההתפרצות אל העולם הרוחני בלא סדר ותקון של קודש, כשם שהוא מונע את אור הקודש מהתפשטותו במרחב ההויה, כך הוא מוריד את ערכו ומחשיך את יפעתו ברום עליון, ונשאר הציור האלהי, שאין קץ וסוף, ראשית ואחרית לרומו, מך ונשפל. "אויב חרף ד' ועם נבל נאצו

of the pagan kingdoms, and we are also going to vanquish the lighter clouds of darkness. The nullification of the practical commandments that issued from Christianity[163] and its pagan aspects, together with its gathering from our religion[164] values of faith and ethics, as it speaks loudly and does not even a little – these obscurities are connected to the gentile blockage, which cannot contain in the uncircumcised heart the sublime divine world-outlook in all its splendor, which connects heaven and earth,[165] body and soul, faith and deed, concept and event, personality and society, this world and the next, the beginning of the worlds' existence and their final fate, eternal sublimity, the joy of heaven and earth and all their hosts,[166] with the elimination of every last vestige of idolatry,[167] when even the lowest level of the worlds will be purified of its pollution, when the most perverse, most pervasive crookedness will be straightened together with the most minor, lightest distortion, and light will shine for the upright.[168] So is the Gentile world: complex, divided, without the unity of body and soul, without an inner joining and synthesis of the spirituality of the world and its corporeality, without an inner connection between deed and thought.[169] For the time being, for them, Christianity[170] is the height of ascent, before the shining of Israel's light. But how unfortunate is the world in which iniquity and darkness raises its head and boasts it is the choicest of its [= the world's] wants. How many deposits of evil are subsumed under this awful lie, which has the feet of a swine that are extended, as if to say to passersby: "See that I am pure!"[171] And how unfortunate are the conceptions that must flow from the real, pure world to this polluted spill. How much light must be generated to liberate the lights that have fallen into the darkness! They will be liberated, eternally, with the redemption of a holy nation!

6

The Return of Spiritual Plunder

Judaism retrieves from Christianity its spiritual plunder.

Just as the wantonness of the practical world, which results from storming the spiritual world without the order and preparation of

שמך". "תאות ענוים" היא גאולת ד', אורן של ישראל מודיע שם ד' במרומים ובמעמקים, וכל עומק השפלת ההשגחה והשליטה, ההויה והיצירה, מביאה רוממות השקפה והתעלות אין-סוף. אמנם יש אשר הרשעה מקבצת כח מפוזר בכל מרחבי העולם החיצוני, בכל חוג המעשה והמפעל, ומוסיפה ברק לההדלקה הרוחנית הציורית, ואף שהוא מקסם כזב ושקר שאין לו רגלים, מכל מקום הרי הוא נִטל מזיו הקודש בגנבה. והקדושה לוקחת בחזרה את כל האורות הגנובים הללו, ומעמקי האמונה הציורית והתארת אידיאלי המוסר מתגדלים ומתאמצים יותר ויותר על-ידי שבית האויב והחזרת כל הנפש והרכוש אשר לקח, בהעשותו כמצולה שאין בה דגים וכמצודה שאין בה דגן.

ז

כשם שמכירים תנאים אקלימים, מסוגלים לבעלי חיים ולצמחים שונים, ויותר מזה תנאים מובדלים לסוגים: הים והיבשה, העפיפה באויר וההליכה, ומי שמסוגל לאחד מהם, אם יחליף את תפקידו במה שמוזר לו, את נפשו הוא חובל - ככה הם גם החילופים הרוחניים, מצד פנימיות ערכי החיים שלהם. בכל ספירה רוחנית יש צביוני חיים מיוחדים. כל זמן שהדברים באים רק למגע של הכרה אין הדבר חודר כל כך עד עומק החיים, אמנם כיון שבאו לידי הרגשה, כבר החיים מתרשמים בו ביותר על-פי תנאיהם המיוחדים. וכשבא עד לידי אמונה ודבקות אז החיים מוטבעים במטבעתם המיוחדה, ואם הם נאותים לאותו המקצוע אז הם מתברכים ומתאדרים, ואם אינם נאותים לו, אז כפי מדת רחוקם ונגודם ולפי מדת שקועם בתוכו והשרשתם, ככה תהי מדת חרבנם

holiness, impedes the light of holiness from expanding through the breadth of existence, so it reduces its value and darkens its sublime beauty. Then the divine conception, to whose height[172] there is neither limit, beginning, or end, remains lowered and debased.[173] *An enemy blasphemed the Lord; a corrupt people insulted Your name.*[174] The "desire of the humble"[175] is the redemption of the Lord. The light of Israel publicizes the name of the Lord on high and in the depths; and the entire depth of the descent of the (divine) supervision and rule, creation and formation, brings sublime outlook and infinite ascent. However, it sometimes happens that iniquity gathers energy scattered throughout the expanses of the external world, in the entire orbit of action and deed, and adds glitter to the spiritual, conceptual fire. And even though it is a false enchantment that has no "feet,"[176] nevertheless, it was taken by stealth from the splendor of holiness. Holiness (now) takes back all these stolen lights,[177] and the depths of conceptual faith and the theorization of the ideals of ethics grow stronger and stronger through the plunder of the enemy and the recovery of all the souls and property that he took, as he becomes like a net without fish and a trap without grain.[178]

7

Tradition and Heresy

Jewish tradition is wary of heresy, i.e., Christianity.

Just as we recognize climatic conditions, conducive for various fauna and flora, and beyond that, abruptly different conditions: sea versus dry land, flight versus locomotion, and were one who fits in one environment to replace his *modus vivendi* with a foreign one, he would injure himself – so are spiritual changes, as a result of the inwardness of their life-values. In every spiritual sphere there are special life-characteristics. As long as things reach no further than (the stage of) consciousness, the matter does not penetrate so much the depth of life, but once things reach (the stage of) emotion, life becomes imprinted with those specific conditions. And when the matter progresses to faith and devotion, then

ואבודם. זאת היא התכונה העמוקה של ההשתמרות מאשה זרה במובן הרוחני, אשר "דרכי שאול ביתה ורגליה יורדות מות", וכמה גדולה היא מדת ההמשכה לרכי לב וקטני דעת, "הולך אחריה פתאום כשור אל טבח יבוא, וכעכס אל מוסר אויל". בית ישראל יודע בחוש קודש העמוק שלו איך להשמר מפח יוקשים ויודע הוא בבהירות להגן על עמדת קיומו הרוחני האיתן, גם נגד אותו כח המושך של הזרות, אשר נגוזה מבטן אמו אחרי שנתנכרה וקנתה לה תכונה זרה. ואת פרטי הזריות, איכות ההשתמרות ועמקי האבדון שבהם וכל הליכות היחש עמהם הוא סוקר, והם בספרתו בדיני תורה והכרות אמונה בדעה מבוססת ורוח אמיץ, כראוי לעם עז, אשר עז לו באלהים סלה.

ח

ד' צבאות הוא ד' אלהי ישראל, וצבאות ישראל צבאות ד' הם. ברוחנו ועצמות נשמתנו חרותים במכתב אלהים כחו וגבורתו של יוצר בראשית. העולם ומלאו מיד ד' נוצרו, נתהוו וקמו, מתהוים וקמים, חיים ומתקימים, מתפתחים ומתאזרים. הלאמתנו בנחלת ד' קשורה היא ביצירת מעשה בראשית. "כח מעשיו הגיד לעמו לתת להם נחלת גוים". הגבורה האלהית השרויה בעולם, שחדשה את העולם ומחדשתו בכל יום, היא היא שמפיה שמענו את התורה. מפי הגבורה שמענו "אנכי" ו"לא יהיה לך", וכל התורה כולה קבל משה מפי הגבורה. את הגוף אין אנחנו עוזבים, לא את הגוף הפרטי ולא את הגויה הלאומית, כי־אם אנחנו מנצחים אותו. יודעים אנחנו, שהיצר הרע והיצר הטוב יצירה אחת היא מידי אל עולם, וכמו כן עולם הזה ועולם הבא, העולם החברתי, המשטרי

life is stamped with their specific stamp: If life fits that profession, then life is blessed and strengthened; if not, then in relation to their distance and opposition, and in relation to life's immersion and rootedness in it, so will be life's destruction and loss. This is the deep quality of self-protection *from a foreign lady*[179] in the spiritual sense, whose *house is the way to perdition*[180] and whose *feet descend to death.*[181] And how enticing she is to the soft of heart and small of mind: *He goes after her suddenly as an ox to slaughter and as a snake to the counsel of a fool.*[182] The House of Israel knows by its deep holy instinct how to keep guard from the hunter's snare; it knows clearly to protect its strong spiritual existence, even against the allure of the foreign element that was cut from its mother's womb[183] by alienating itself and acquiring a foreign quality. The details of the foreignness, the how of the self-protection, the depths of the danger, and all the ways of relating to them – it [i.e., the House of Israel] reviews, and they are to be found in its literature, in laws of Torah and realizations of faith, in cogent intellect and courageous spirit, as befits a mighty nation, whose strength is in God, Selah.[184]

8

The Divinity of the World

The divinity of this world. God's omnipresence.
The revelation of this truth through Israel.

The Lord of Hosts is the Lord God of Israel, and the hosts of Israel are the hosts of the Lord. In our spirit and the essence of our soul are engraved with divine writing the strength and power of the Creator. The world and its full by the hand of the Lord were created, came, and come, into existence, live and endure, develop and are strengthened. Our emergence as a divine people is bound up with the creation of Genesis. *The power of His actions He told His people to give them the inheritance of nations.*[185] It is from the mouth of the divine power that rests in the world, that originated the world and continuously renews it every day, that we heard the Torah. From the mouth of the Power[186] we heard "I am"[187] and "You shall not have,"[188] and the entire Torah Moses received

והרוחני, התיאורי, המוסרי, האידיאלי והממשי, הכל חטיבה אחת היא והכל עולה במעלות הקדש ומשועבד לרצון גבוה, הכל הוא, "אמרתי ונעשה רצוני". גבורתנו עדינה היא, אי-אפשר שתהיה גבורת חרבן וכליון. הגבורה האלהית בעולם אינה נפגשת במה שחוץ להמצאתה, וקל וחומר שחוץ לשלטונה, אם כן היא בכל תכסיסיה מלאה עומק רחמים. המצאת הנגודים מרחיבה את גבול היש. הטוב מבחין את הרע והרע מעמיק את הטוב, מרשם ומאלם אותו. ספיגה כללית זו בהכרה עולמית אלהית, חדורה עד תהום הנשמה, משולבה במעמקי ההיסתוריה הלאומית, אחוזה במלא עולמים, חובקת באהבה את כל ומתנשאת בגבורה על כל, מלאה ענוה עם כל וחשוקת רחמים על כל, היא יסוד תפארת ישראל, המובעה באמת ליעקב, במטרת כסא ד׳ בעולם, שלא תפסק לעד, היא מקימת ומחיה אותנו. לא ברכב ולא בסוסים הוא יסוד גבורתנו, כי-אם "בשם ד׳ אלהינו נזכיר, המה כרעו ונפלו ואנחנו קמנו ונתעודד". ואם שטוחה היא הכרתנו את עצמנו, שטוחה היא הכרת העולם עת ערכנו, לקויה היא הבנת העמים את חשקנו ואת המעוף האלהי שבחיי נשמתנו, על כן מתמוזמים הנסיונות הראשונים שלנו, שקמו בלא העמקת היסוד, בלא חשיפת מעין החיים. ומזומז זה, רקב נורא וכאב חודר זה, עולם חדש יחדש, רוח חדש יבא בעמים, הכרה חודרת ופנימית בישראל. עז וגבורה, חשק ואבירות, אמונה ונצחון עז, התהפכות עמק היאוש למקור ישועה ופריחת חיים, רוממות קדש כימי עולם, והכל נוהר הופעת גאולה: התבונה, הברקת הבקורת, ההסדרה החברתית ועמק האמונה, חדוש הנשמות והרטבת הגויות, בדליגה ובסדור, ממקור הכרת האמת של גדולת שם ד׳ אלהי ישראל, אלהי כל עולמים יוצר כל העולמים ויוצר רוח האדם בקרבו, אשר ממקור חיים אשר

from the Power. We do not abandon the body,[189] neither the individual body nor the body politic, but rather we triumph over it. We know that the good inclination and evil inclination are one creation from the hands of Eternal God. So too this world and the next, the social world, the governmental, the spiritual, the theoretical, the ethical, the ideal, the real – all is one unit, and it all ascends the rungs of holiness and is subject to a higher authority. All is "I said and My will was done."[190] Our power is delicate; it is not possible that it should be a power of destruction and obliteration.[191] The divine power in the world meets nothing outside its invention, *a fortiori* outside its rule – therefore in all its trappings, it is full[192] of the depth of compassion. The arising of contradictions broadens the scope of existence. Good accentuates Evil and Evil deepens Good,[193] delineating and strengthening it. This total absorption in the divine cosmic consciousness, penetrating to the abyss of the soul, wrapped together with the depths of the national history, bound to the fullness of worlds, embracing all with love and transcending all with strength, humble and compassionate to all, is the foundation of the glory of Israel – expressed in the truth of Jacob, with the goal of the Throne of the Lord in the world, which will never end – that keeps us alive.[194] Neither with chariots, nor with horses, is the foundation of our strength, but rather, *We will utter the name of the Lord our God; they succumbed and fell, we rose and were heartened.*[195] If our self-awareness be superficial, the world's awareness of our value will be superficial. The nations' understanding of our passion and the divine flight of our soul-life is faulty. Therefore, our first attempts – which arose without the deepening of the foundation, without baring the spring of life – are ruined. This ruin, this terrible rotting, this penetrating pain, will eventuate a new world; a new spirit will circulate among nations, a penetrating, inward consciousness in Israel. Might and strength; passion and chivalry; faith and victory; transformation of the depth of resignation to a source of salvation and blossoming of life; sublime holiness as old; and all glows with the appearance of redemption:[196] the understanding, the critique,[197] the social order and depth of faith, the renewal of souls and freshness of bodies, through acceleration and progression, from the

עמו חי ישראל מעולם ועד עולמי עד. "והתגדלתי והתקדשתי, ונודעתי לעיני גוים רבים וידעו כי אני ד'", "כי ימין ושמאל תפרצי וזרעך גוים יירש וערים נשמות יושיבו. אל תיראי כי לא תבושי ואל תכלמי כי לא תחפירי, כי בשת עלומיך תשכחי וחרפת אלמנותיך לא תזכרי עוד, כי בעליך עשיך ד' צבאות שמו וגאלך קדוש ישראל אלהי כל הארץ יקרא".

ט

המינות מתוך שיצאה מהמחנה אל החוץ הרי היא נפרדת, מחרפת ומגדפת, אומרת: מי לי בשמים, אף על-פי שבפיה תדבר רמות ודבריה חלקו מחמאות. רפיון בטחונם של ישראל, שמתאמצת המינות להרחיב, אחרי כל ההבטחות ושבועות עליון ובחירה אלהית נצחית בהם להיות סגולה מכל העמים, הרי הוא סעיף מסורי הגפן נכריה של הפרדת רשות הגבוה, אותה הרשעה החושבת להפר ברית בשר וברית הארץ גם יחד, המדמה בחולשתה הפנימית כי הגוף וכחותיו והעולם החמרי והופעותיו, בחירת האדם ורצונו בכל ערכיו, הנם דברים מופרדים, שיכולים לסכל את עצת ד' העליונה, ותוכל לפי זה ברית עולמים להיות מופרת על-ידי סבות צדדיות כחטאות ישראל והתגברות הרשעה החמרית בעולם. ולא ידעו ולא יבינו בחשכה יתהלכו, כי אלהי עולם ד' עושה שלום ובורא רע והכל עבדיו, ולא כאלה חלק יעקב כי יוצר הכל הוא וישראל שבט נחלתו ד' צבאות שמו, והעולם הגשמי עם כל עומק הרשעה המקננת בבשר, הכל קשור בתנאים שחקק בהם צור עולמים בעולמו, שהוא רשות היחיד של יחידו של עולם, אין עוד מלבדו, "אפילו מעשה כשפים שמכחישים פמליא

source of the truthful recognition[198] of the greatness of the name of the Lord, God of Israel, God of all worlds, Creator of all worlds, and Creator of the spirit of man in his midst; from the source of life with which Israel lives forever and ever. *I will be magnified and sanctified, and manifest to the eyes of many nations, and they shall know that I am the Lord.*[199] *Left and right you shall expand, your seed will inherit nations and desolate cities will be inhabited. Do not fear nor be confounded, for the shame of your youth you will forget and the embarrassment of your widowhood you will no longer remember, for your lover is your Creator, the Lord of Hosts His name, and your redeemer the Holy One of Israel, Who will be called God of all the earth.*[200]

9

The Messianic Light of Panentheism

Christianity purports that the everlasting covenant between God and Israel is abrogated. Christianity's fallacy: Even evil is subject to divine authority. The "Light of Messiah" reveals the truth of panentheism.

Christianity, once having exited from the camp, is separate. Insultingly she says: *Who is there for me in heaven?*[201] even though with her mouth she speaks loftily and her words are slick as butter. The insecurity of Israel, which Christianity attempts to magnify, after all the divine promises and oaths[202] and Israel's divine eternal election as a chosen nation[203] – this is a branch of the corrupt shoot of separation of the higher authority. It is that wickedness that thinks to abolish the covenant of flesh[204] and the covenant of the Land[205] at once; which imagines, in its (state of) inner weakness, that the body and its powers and the material world with its manifestations, and the election of man and his will with all its values, are separate things; that they can frustrate the sublime counsel of the Lord, and that in this way the everlasting covenant may be abolished through incidental causes such as the sins of Israel and the rise of material iniquity in the world. They neither know nor understand, they walk in darkness, for God of the world, the Lord makes peace and creates evil[206] and all are his servants. *Not as these is the portion of Jacob, for He*

של מעלה". ונשמת ישראל באור עליון זה היא שרויה, ממקור חיים עליונים הללו היא מקבלת את שפעת חייה, על כן תורתו תורת עולמים, ברית עולם לא תשכח, ולא תוכל שום הגברה חצונית או רוחנית פנימית לעבור את פי ד' ולסור מחקותיו חקות עולמים, ומקור הגבורה והעז, גם זה שמתגלה בכבישת החיים, מתוך אוצר גבורת אל ד' יוצר עולמים היא לקוחה. ולהגשים ולגלות בחיים ובמעשה תוצאת תורה עליונה זו, קרואים אנו לאורו של משיח, שיתנוצץ מכל העברים, מכל מסבות החיים, מכל הבחירות, מכל העצות, מכל משטרי הטבע, מכל ההשכלות ומכל הקדושות, מכל הנסים ומכל הנפלאות, והעני הרוכב על החמור בעצמו עם ענני שמיא כבר-אנש אָתֵה.

י

כנסת ישראל שואפת לתקון העולם בכל מלואו, לסליחה מקורית מטהרת, שבאה לא רק מישועת נפש האדם והטבת רצונו מצד עצמו - שבזה צריכים להפגש בויתור ומדת חסד מיוחדה, בלא התכללות עם כל המדות כולן ובלא שקול של עז צדק ומשפט - כי-אם תקון כולל לסבת החטאים. חק הטהרה, העברת רוח הטומאה על-ידי שמו של משיח שקדם לעולם, "פרה אדומה מכפרת", והיא מטהרת מטומאת מת, נעוץ בסלוק המיתה מיסודה בהעלאת העולם מעמק חטאו, מחטא הארץ ומקטרוג הלבנה, מנפילת התיאוריה העולמית ביסוד מציאותה, מהנמכת האידיאל העולמי במציאות, מה שהכשיר את החטא האנושי וכל הצרות הרבות הבאות ממנו. הכל, הכל צריך להיות מתוקן, הכל צריך להיות מטוהר. שאיפת ישראל לבנין האומה, לשיבת הארץ, היא

is the creator of all, and Israel is the tribe of his inheritance, Lord of Hosts is His name.[207] The physical world with all the depth of evil that nests in the flesh – all is conditioned by the laws that the Source of Worlds established in His world, which is the private domain of the Only One in the world.[208] *There is none but Him*[209] – "even works of magic, which would deny the heavenly host."[210] The soul of Israel is drenched with this supernal light; from the source of this supreme life she receives her life-flow. Therefore His Torah is an eternal Torah, an eternal covenant that will not be forgotten, and no force, external or spiritual, internal,[211] can counter the mouth of the Lord and deviate from His eternal laws. The source of strength and might, even that which manifests in the conquest of life, is taken from the store of the might of God the Lord, Creator of worlds. In order to actualize and reveal in life and deed the effect of this sublime Torah, we are called to the Light of Messiah, which will sparkle from all sides, from all the causations of life, from all the elections, from all the counsels, from all the regimes of nature, from all the intellections and all the sanctities, from all the miracles and from all the wonders. And the "poor man riding on the donkey"[212] is himself "the man who descends with clouds of heaven."[213]

10

Tikkun 'Olam (Cosmic Correction)

Beyond the correction of man's soul, Israel aspires to cosmic tikkun *(correction): the phenomenon of death, the sin of the earth, the accusation of the moon.*

K*nesset Yisrael* (Ecclesia Israel) aspires to the correction *(tikkun)* of the world in all its fullness, to purifying, original forgiveness, which comes not merely from the salvation of man's soul and improvement of his will, as such – which requires compromise and a special attribute of kindness, irrespective of all the other attributes and regardless of the deliberation of rigorous righteousness and justice – but rather a comprehensive correction of the cause of sins. The law of purity, the elimination of the spirit of impurity through the name of Messiah that preceded the world[214] – "the red heifer atones,"[215] and cleanses from the impurity of death – is linked to the removal of death[216] from its very foundation, by

שאיפה של עומק הטוב החודר את כל היש בשרשו. לא זקיפת לבנה מאיזה בנין כי-אם פניה שלמה ועמוקה אל היסוד של כל הבנין, לכוננו בתקון. לא עצים אחדים וענפים מאילן החיים והטוב, אלא לחשוף את המקור, את מעין החיים שלשד עץ החיים, עם כל שרשיו, גזעיו, ענפיו, פארותיו ועליו, משם יונק, וממנו יבא רוח חיים, רוח חדש, ועולם חדש יבנה, "כי כאשר השמים החדשים והארץ החדשה אשר אני עושה עומדים לפני נאם ד׳ כן יעמוד זרעכם ושמכם".

יא

כל מה שנותן כח יותר גדול לעולם הבא הרי הוא יותר חי באומץ גם בעולם הזה. והדבר מתבחן בישראל לענין בנין האומה. כל המאמץ את חיי עולם הרי הוא בונה את האומה בפועל, כי חיותם הלאומית של ישראל המשך היא מהצלחת עולמים. וזהו הגודל של תורה שבעל-פה, שעמדה להשגיר את חיי העולמים במלא מובנם באומה ולהוציא מלבן של צדוקים, שהתלהבותם הלאומית דמתה ללהבת של תבן, שנשתלהבה ודעכה ואיננה, לומר: ברכו את ד׳ אלהי ישראל מן העולם ועד העולם. ומיסוד עולם זה יבנה ויכונן גם עכשיו עמק החיים הלאומיים בישראל ויתגדל בנין הארץ, וכל האמוצים הכלליים ההולכים לעומת התחיה, ההולכת ומתגלה במסבותיה הרבות, האחוזות זו בזו בתאר שלשלת גדולה, ארוכה, מסובכה ונפלאה, מפלאות תמים דעים.

uplifting the world from the depth of its sin, from the sin of the Earth[217] and the accusation of the Moon,[218] from the fall of the cosmic theory in the foundation of its existence, from the lowering of the world ideal in reality, which prepared the way for human sin and all the troubles that come from it. All, all must be fixed; all must be purified. The aspiration of Israel for building the nation, for return to the Land, is an aspiration of the depth of good that penetrates to the root of all existence. Not the "upraising of a brick"[219] of some structure but rather a whole, in-depth turning to the foundation of the entire structure, to establish it correctly. Not a few trees or branches of the Tree of Life and Good, but rather exposing the source, the spring of life from which is fed the sap of the Tree of Life, with all its roots, trunk and branches, trailers and leaves. From it will come a spirit of life, a new spirit, and a new world will be built. *For as the new heavens and the new earth which I am making, stand before me, says the Lord, so will stand your seed and your name.*[220]

11

Pharisees and Sadducees: Eternal versus Temporal Nationalism

Stress on eternal life is the key to temporal success as well, thus the advantage of Pharisaic over Sadducean nationalism.

Whatever gives greater power to the world-to-come lives more vigorously in this world as well. The thing may be analyzed in Israel regarding the building of the nation. Whatever strengthens eternal life, builds the nation in actuality, for the national vitality of Israel is a continuation of eternal success. This is the greatness of the Oral Torah, which arose to make the nation conversant with eternal life in its fullest meaning, and to remove the heresy of the Sadduccees,[221] whose national fervor was comparable to a flame of straw, which glowed and died down. The Oral Torah would proclaim: "Blessed is the Lord God of Israel from this world to the next!"[222] From this eternal foundation will be built and established now too the depth of national life in Israel. The building of the land will expand, and all the general strengthenings

יב

הסקירה הרואה את הכח האלהי החי ופועל בתועפות גבורותיו ורוממות קדשו בכל מסבות הטבע, בכל הליכות רוחות האדם, בכל סבוכי המלחמות, בכל תכני תעתועי האישים והעמים, היא מסדרת אור קדוש על מלא כל העולם. היא מחברת את הנפש העולמית עם רוחה ונשמתה, מאגדת את כל המפעל והמעשה המסותר בחגוי סלעים וסתרי מדרגות אל כל הגלוי והמופע בפליאות נוראות, ביד חזקה ובזרע נטויה, באותות ובמופתים, בגלוי שכינה ובנבואה מאירה. והחבור הזה, השכלי, מתמם את צביון האדם ומחיה את העולם, כשאור ישראל מתגלה על-ידי עמק הדעת ומעמקי האמונה לראות, איך כל העלילות מראש ועד סוף, מראש מקדמי תבל עד אחרית ימים אחרונים, מתועפות תנועות רוחניות אדירות, הופעות שכליות ומוסריות מלאות וטובות, חדושי חכמות ומדעים נשגבים ומשוכללים, כל הארות תוריות בכחות כלליים ופרטיים, כל זהרי רוח הקדש וכל השפעות צדיקים יסודי עולמים, הם וגורמיהם העליונים והתחתונים - הכל תנועת עולמים גדולה אחוזה בהם, תנועת הארת אורו של משיח, שנברא קודם שנברא העולם. בכל עת שמתגלים מקרים ומאורעות, רעיונות ומחשבות, להרים נס של קירוב גאולה וישועה, בין שהיא גשמית ובין שהיא רוחנית, הדעה מכרת את אור ד׳ החי המופיע בהם ואת קול ד׳ הדובר וקורא מתוכם, וכל אשר תיטיב הדעת להכירו ולהבינו כה תגלה את האורות של המסבות, כן תישרם אל מטרתם וכן יתחברו האורות העלומים עם הגלויים, יתאגד הטבע עם הנס אגד עליון וחזק, ״אז ירד שריד לאדירים עם, ד׳ ירד לי בגבורים״. כל ההשלמה השכלית הזאת, המתממת את האמונה ומאזרת כח

that advance toward the renascence, which is increasingly revealed in its many causations, which are intertwined as a great chain, long, complicated, and wonderful – *wonders of the Perfect Intelligence.*[223]

12

The Unity of Miracle and Nature

What is required is an overview that will reveal how all of history is an ongoing march to reveal the "Light of Messiah." This light is the true unitive vision.

The overview that sees the divine power as it lives and works with its might and exalted holiness in all the causations of nature, in all the ways of man's moods, in all the complexities of the wars, in all the cunning contents of personalities and peoples, arranges a holy light over the fullness of all the worlds. This overview connects the *nefesh* (lowest level of the soul) of the world with its *ru'aḥ* and *neshamah* (higher levels of the soul); binds all the deed that is hidden in the crevices of rocks and hidden steps, to all that is revealed and manifest in awesome wonders, with a strong hand and an outstretched arm, with signs and wonders, with the revelation of the *Shekhinah* (divine presence), and with illuminating prophecy. This intellectual connection perfects the character of man and vivifies the world, as the light of Israel is revealed through the depth of knowledge and profundities of faith, to see how all the events from beginning to end, from the origins of earth to the end of final days, from the might of powerful spiritual movements, intellectual and ethical manifestations full and good, innovations of wisdoms and sciences exalted and advanced, all Torah illuminations with powers general and specific, all the splendors of divine inspiration *(ru'aḥ ha-kodesh)* and all the influences of the righteous *(tsaddikim)*, foundations of worlds, they and their causes higher and lower – bound with all of them is a great cosmic movement, the movement of the illumination of the Light of Messiah, which was created before the world was created.[224] Whenever there are revealed incidents and events, concepts and thoughts, to raise the banner of hastening redemption and salvation, whether it be physical or spiritual, the intellect recognizes the light of the Living Lord manifest in them and

את החיים לפעול ולעשות, לתור ולדרוש, לצפות לישועה ולעבוד עבודת ד׳ וישראל עמו, עבודת שמים ועבודת ארץ, ליחדא שמיא וארעא, היא באה בהשתלמותה על-פי אותן המדרגות, שאורו של משיח זורח ומתגלה בהן, שהוא כולל ביחד את כל הרוחות: ״רוח ד׳, רוח חכמה ובינה, רוח עצה וגבורה, רוח דעת ויראת ד׳״. ואור התחיה הרוחנית הולך ומתגלה, וצץ ופורח הוא אור התחיה המשיחית העזיזה, הבאה לטהר את סרחון הבשר, את זוהמת הנחש ואת שורש כל חטא, לשמח את העולם ולמלאותו אהבה וחדוה, בהסרת העצבון הבשרי המקושר עם הסרחון התולדתי, הסותם כל הופעת רוח טוהר. ״והריחו ביראת ד׳ ולא למראה עיניו ישפט ולא למשמע אזניו יוכיח, ושפט בצדק דלים והוכיח במישור לענוי ארץ. והכה ארץ בשבט פיו וברוח שפתיו ימית רשע״; התחיה המוסיפה חיי דעת להכרת הנצח, להכרת עמדת מעז חיי הרוח, את הכרת שקרות המות, את הסרת כל פחד שוא וכל עצב נתעה, התחלת תקופת הזרחת אור תחית המתים בכל מלא חסנו.

אורות עולמים אלו כלולים הם בהופעת האחדות של הנס והטבע, אשר יאוחדו על-ידי משכילי טוהר, החוזים בבטחה ובגלוי גמור את יד ד׳ אלהי ישראל בכל חליפות העתים ומכירים את התסיסות ההיסתוריות, כמו הטבעיות והעולמיות, מראש קדמות היצירה, ״בטרם הרים יולדו ותחולל ארץ ותבל, ומעולם עד עולם אתה אל. תשב אנוש אד דכא ותאמר שובו בני אדם״. לא נעזבה היא הטבעיות במהלכה, לא אלמנה היא ההיסטוריה הסבוכה במסבותיה, בתוכה חי גואל חזק, צור ישראל וגואלו ד׳ צבאות שמו, אלהי כל בשר, אלהים לכל ממלכות הארץ, אדון כל המעשים, צור כל העולמים צדיק בכל הדורות. לא עשתה הנבואה שום

the voice of the Lord that speaks and calls through them. The better the intellect recognizes and understands it, so it will reveal the lights of the causations, so it will direct them to their goal, and so the hidden lights will connect to the revealed. The natural will be bound with the miraculous by a strong, supreme bond. *Then a remnant came down to the mighty of the people, then the Lord came down to me with warriors.*[225] All this intellectual wholeness, which perfects faith and girds life with strength to achieve and do, to inquire and seek, to hope for salvation and work in the service of the Lord and Israel his people,[226] the work of heaven and the work of earth, to unite heaven and earth – this reaches completion according to those levels in which the Light of Messiah is revealed, Messiah who includes at once all the spirits: *the spirit of God, the spirit of wisdom and understanding, the spirit of counsel and strength, the spirit of intellect and awe of the Lord.*[227] The light of the spiritual renascence continues to be revealed. There sprouts and blossoms the light of the strong Messianic renascence,[228] which comes to purify the rot of flesh, the pollution of the Serpent and the root of all sin, to gladden the world and fill it with love and joy, with the removal of the fleshly sadness that is linked to the stink of generation, which bars any appearance of a spirit of purity. *He shall be fragrant with fear of the Lord. Not by the sight of his eyes will he judge; nor by the sound of his ears will he rebuke. He will judge justly the poor and rebuke rightly the humble of the earth. He will smite earth with the staff of his mouth and with the spirit of his lips he will execute the wicked.*[229] The renascence, which adds a life of knowledge to the realization of eternity, to the recognition of the fortitude of the life of the spirit, the recognition of the falsity of death,[230] the removal of all vain fear and all deluded sadness, the beginning of the period of the shining of the light of the Resurrection of the Dead in all its impact.

These cosmic lights are included in the manifestation of the unity of the miraculous and the natural, which will be unified by pure intellectuals who witness confidently and openly the hand of the Lord God of Israel in all the changes of the times and recognize the historical fomentations, just as the natural and cosmic, from the origins

נס כי־אם כשקשרתו לאיזו טבעת טבעית, אפילו קלושה וקטנה. חשבו בזה חושבים סימבולנים מחשבות, שכצללים נהלכו, והאמת המסרתית תביע אמריה בכל הוד גבורתה: רכוס מהודק דרוש תמיד להיות מעולם העליון, מהופעת השליטה הנשמתית, אל העולם התחתיתי המוגבל ומצומצם בטבעיותו. גם שם גם פה המהלכים קבועים ומסודרים, בחכמה, בחפש, במלא קדש, והכל הולך הלוך ואור. כפי ההפריה של זיו ההכרה של חכמת ישראל העליונה, של עטרות הנבואה ואספקלריא המאירה הנותנת עליהן את זיון מהוד קרניה, ככה תזרח הדעת להכיר את המגמה של כל המון המסבות וללכת עם כולן ולברך את שם ד׳ המאיר ומחיה, מסדר ומטיב את כל, ״אברכה את ד׳ בכל עת, תמיד תהלתו בפי״. השם המשולב של הויה ואדנות מאיר ומופיע ביקר תפארתו בכל אורותיו, מקורותיו, מבועיו ומעיניו, בכל צירופיו ולבושיו, בכל טעמיו ונקודותיו, תגיו ואותיותיו, ובלב ישראל חרותה אש דת, מטרת עולמים לכל תנועת החיים, לכל היש בעבר, הוה ועתיד, ומבעד כל מפלשי העננים אור הקדש יחדור, ״הנה ד׳ אלהים בחזק יבוא וזרעו מושלה לו, הנה שכרו אתו ופעולתו לפניו״. הכל לפי רוב המעשה ולפי הרחבת ההקשבה, לפי הגדלת התורה ולפי הפצת המעינות אשר לתהומות הרוחניות, לפי השלטת הגאון של חכמת ישראל המנוחלת הדוברת רק אמת בשם ד׳ על כל מחשבות אדם אשר המה הבל. ״יבש חציר נבל ציץ ודבר אלהינו יקום לעולם״.

of creation. *Before mountains were born You established earth, for ever and ever You are God. You thrust man into depression and say, Return sons of man!*[231] Nature is not abandoned in its course, complex history is not a widow in its causations. Within it lives a strong redeemer, the Rock of Israel and its Redeemer,[232] Lord of Hosts is His name,[233] God of all flesh,[234] God to all the dominions of the earth,[235] Master of all deeds, Rock of all the worlds, Righteous in all the generations.[236] Prophecy did not perform any miracle unless it had connected it to some natural link,[237] even the most minute and weak. Symbolic thinkers proffered theories that are fleeting as shadows; the traditional truth expresses its statements with all its majestic power: There must always be a tight link from the higher world, from the manifestation of the soulful governance, to the lower world, limited as it is by its naturalness. There (above) as here (below) the processes are fixed and orderly, with wisdom, freedom, full sanctity, and all becomes increasingly bright. In proportion to the splendor of the recognition of the higher wisdom of Israel, of the crowns of prophecy and the shining speculum that bestows its rays upon them – so the intellect will be illumined to recognize the purpose of the multitude of causations, to go with them and bless the name of the Lord who illumines and vivifies, arranges and benefits all. *I will bless the Lord at all times, always His praise is in my mouth.*[238] The name YHVH/ADNY interpenetrated,[239] shines with its precious glory, with all its lights, sources, fountains and springs, with all its permutations and garments, with all its cantillations and vocalizations, its crownlets and letters. In the heart of Israel is engraved the Fire of the Law,[240] the purpose of the cosmos, for all the movement of life, for all existence, past, present, and future. Through all the tears in the clouds, a holy light will penetrate. *Behold the Lord God will come in strength, his arm ruling for Him. His reward is with him and his deed before him.*[241] All according to the amount of action and the expansion of listening; according to the increase of Torah and the spreading of the springs of the spiritual depths; according to the rule of the genius of the inherited wisdom of Israel – which speaks only truth in the name of the Lord – over all the thoughts of man that are nought.[242] *The hay dries, the grass withers, but the word of our God will stand forever.*[243]

יג

תכונת סוד ד׳ ליראיו היא היא המלמדת את הכבוד אשר ירחש האדם אל הטבע, ועל-ידי כבודה האמתי הרי הוא מעלה אותה, משגבה ומרוממה. כמו בהליכות המוסר של חיי האדם היחידי כן בהליכות עולמים. העליה המעולה בחיי המוסר היא ההתיצבות הישרה בכל הכחות, "רגלי עמדה במישור", ההתאמה המפוארה של כל נטיות החיים, עד שהשכל העליון נמצא בתור גלוי עליון של סכום החיים כולם, וכל אשר מתחת לו הרי הם ענפיו המתפשטים ממנו, שבים אליו ומתרפקים עליו, מוכנים לרצונו, ולעבודתו כסופה ירדופו, וכל המהלכים הטבעיים של הנפשיות והגופניות מוארים הם באור עליון ובמהות הקדש המנצח, המלא הוד ויפעת קדשים של זיו ההשכלה הטהורה המאירה באור חכמה ודעת יסודית. התוכן הזה עומד למעלה מהאופי המוסרי המוכרח לאסור מלחמות פנימיות, או להסיח דעה ורעיון ממהותו הטבעית ומכל תפקידיו, אשר אז המוסר מוסר צולע הוא, מוסר מסוכן לנפילה למהמורות. על כן האידיאליות של העין הצופיה של המוסר העליון, לפחות, היא העלאת כל התוכן, התגלות כל היש, הופעת החיים בפנימיותו וכל מקיפיו. היא אמנם כלולה בתוך המערכה העליונה, מערכת הקודש, שהיא באמת כבר עולה ממעל לכל ערכים מוסריים, והיא תוכן התֹּם, התמימות השלמה, שאין בה דופי, פיסוק וקיצוץ מכל ההופעות, יושר השכל, יושר הלב, יושר הרגש, יושר הרוח, יושר הטבע, יושר הבשר, יושר ההופעה, יושר ההקשבה. וקול אלהים חיים דובר אז מכל מרומים ומכל תחתיות, והעינים למישרים חוזות והמעוף מתחת לרום הוא תדירי, והחזרה חלילה בשביל הופעה והארה, בשביל העלאה והתממה, היא גם

13
The Higher Ethics

The higher ethics of sublimation. The unity of miracle and nature. The light of Israel is the soul of human history revealed. The higher Torah. The all-encompassing vision of history.

The quality of "the secret of the Lord to His fearers"[244] is what teaches the respect that a man should feel toward nature, and through its true honor, he uplifts it, ennobles and sublimates it. As in the ethical ways of the individual man's life, so in the ways of the cosmos.[245] The optimal ascent in the ethical life is standing straight with all one's powers – *My foot stood straight*[246] – the glorious coordination of all the tendencies of life, until the higher intellect has become a supreme revelation of the sum total of life, and whatever is below are branches extending from it, returning to it and longing for it, ready at its will, and running tempestuously to its service. All the natural courses of soulfulness and physicality are illumined by a sublime light and by the orchestrating essence of holiness, which is full of majesty and beautiful sanctity, the splendor of pure intellection shining with the light of wisdom and fundamental knowledge. This content stands so much higher than that ethical character that must wage internal wars or ignore its natural state and all its functions. Then ethics is a crippled ethics, and ethics prone to pitfalls. Therefore the ideality of the watchful eye of the higher ethic, at least, is the uplifting of all the content, the revelation of all being,[247] the manifestation of life in its inwardness and all its compass. This ideality is subsumed in the higher system, the system of the Holy,[248] which truly transcends all ethical values. It is the perfect content, complete perfection, which has no blemish, limitation or curtailment of all the manifestations. Straight intellect, straight heart, straight feeling, straight spirit, straight nature, straight flesh, straight appearance, straight attunement. Then the voice of the Living God speaks from all the heights and all the depths. The eyes see directly; the flight upward is constant, and the return – for revelation and illumination, for uplifting and perfecting – is also constant, easy,

כן תדירית, קלה ובטוחה. "הקדוש ברוך הוא עושה להם לצדיקים כנפים כנשרים והם שטים על פני המים, שנאמר וקוי ד' יחליפו כח יעלו אבר כנשרים, ירוצו ולא ייגעו, ילכו ולא ייעפו". בפרטיות מתגלה חזון העולמים בכל תקופה שהקדוש ברוך הוא מחדש בה את עולמו, שהכל לקוח הוא מאלף השנים של ההחרבה הכללית, שענפיה מתפשטים בכל עת אשר תחיל ארץ ותנוע, "יהמו יחמרו מימיו ירעשו הרים בגאותו סלה. נהר פלגיו ישמחו עיר אלהים קדוש משכני עליון, אלהים בקרבה בל תמוט, יעזרה אלהים לפנות בקר". ואור הבקר גם בראשית קדרותו מבהיק הוא מתוכו את האורה העליונה, שהמוסר העליון דורש מהפרטיות על כללות היש ושורש המציאות, הנהגת העולם ועז החיים, סבוב העמים ותהלוכות הממלכות, "אתה הוא האלהים לבדך לכל ממלכות הארץ", והנס והטבע מתאחדים באחדות מאירה. מאור הנס העליון מתגלה איך סעיפי הטבע כולם, הבלתי-מובנים מצד עצמם, הם הם ענפיו והתפשטות אורו, וכל הטבע כולו המתגלה בכל תפקידיו, בעולם ובאדם, בנפש היחיד ובנפש העמים, בדאגות החיים היומיים ובהתגדרות הלאומים והממלכות, בעליותיהם וירידותיהם, בנכלי הפוליטיקה, בשגעונות המשתגעים, בערמת הערומים ובישרת לבב הישרים, בחכמת החכמים, בבינת הנבונים, בגבורת הגבורים וברוח החלש של החלשים, בכל, רק יד האורה העליונה, אור חכמת כל עולמים, רוח ד' נשמת חיי העולם היא מופיעה. והיד נטויה, והזרוע מושלת, "למשפטיך עמדו היום, כי הכל עבדיך". וצפית הישועה חודרת היא אז ממעל לשחקים ועד עמקי תחתיות ארץ, עולה היא ממעמקים, וערבות היא רוכבת, ומכרת בסקירה אחת את כל הנפלאות ואת כל המפעלות, את כל האמת ואת כל השקר, את

and sure. "The Holy One makes for the righteous wings as eagles and they hover over the face of the water, as its says, *We will not fear when earth is turned, when mountains fall down into the heart of seas.*[249] You say they experience pain? Therefore it teaches, *Those who hope to the Lord will be refreshed, they will fly with wings, as eagles, they will run and not tire, walk and not be exhausted.*"[250] Specifically the cosmic vision[251] is revealed in every epoch that the Holy One renews His world, for all derives from the thousand years of general destruction,[252] whose branches extend into every age when the earth shakes and moves. *When its waters roar and foam, when mountains quake before His majesty, Selah. There is a river, its rivulets gladden the city of God, the sanctuary of the dwellings of the Most High. God is in her midst; she shall not be moved; God will help her at the dawning of morning.*[253] The light of morning, even in its initial blackness,[254] radiates the higher light; the higher ethic demands of the particular the universality of being and the root of existence, the conduct of the world and the strength of life,[255] the rotation of peoples and the course of kingdoms. *You are the God alone for all the kingdoms of the earth.*[256] The miraculous and the natural are united in a luminous unity. From the light of the sublime miracle is revealed how all the branches of nature, incomprehensible on their own, are its branches and the radiation of its light. All of nature, as it is revealed in all its capacities, in world and man, in the soul of the individual and in the soul of peoples, in the daily worries of life and in the territorialism[257] of nations and kingdoms, in their ascents and descents, in the plottings of politics, in the insanity of the crazed, in the cunning[258] of the deceitful and in the straightforwardness of the just, in the wisdom of the savants, in the understanding of the discerning, in the bravery of the courageous, and in the cowardice of the weak-kneed, in all, only the hand of the supernal light, the light of the wisdom of all the worlds, the spirit of the Lord, the soul of the Life of the World is apparent. The hand is outstretched, the arm rules. *For your judgment they stood today, for all are Your servants.*[259] The expectation of salvation penetrates from highest heaven to the depths of the earth; it rises from the depths and rides the

כל הצדק ואת כל הרשע, והנה הכל התיצב ומתיצב הכן לפקודת אור דבר אלהים חיים, והארת העולם באור ישראל, היא נשמת ההיסתוריה האנושית בגלוי, ונשמת כל היקום בחביון עוזו, "עד לא עשה ארץ וחוצות וראש עפרות תבל, בהכינו שמים שם אני, בחוקו חוג על פני תהום, באמצו שחקים ממעל בעזוז עינות תהום". ההכרה הזאת על-ידי אספקלרית הקודש מתהפכת היא לכח פועל, לכח סוקר, לכה מחיה, וכל המפעלות הסבוכות אשר בקרב כל משפחות העמים מתגלות בתור מערכה סדורית, אמנם מעורפלת ומאופלת, התובעת נהרה, והנהרה תבוא ממקום אשר האורה תצא לאור עולם - מציון מכלל יופי אלהים יופיע. ורוח אלהים אמת, המתפשט על כל מערכות האדם, הרי הוא מעלה את הטבע מתחתיותו אל מרומי הקודש, ומכשיר את כל הנִסיות להופיע ולהגלות, מתמם את חזון העבודה האלהית בכל הסתעפיותיה על הבסוס הריאלי של החיים, עולה ממעל לאספקלריא הבלתי מאירה, ומביט באור הקודש של אור התורה העליונה, תורת משה, "במראה ולא בחידות", המבססת את המוסר ואת הדעה על יסוד החיים והמעשה ועולה עם כולם יחד למרום הנצח והשלום, אל מקום התפארת ואמת העולמים, אל יסוד **החכמה** העליונה שתחיה את בעליה בכל הדרות חיים מלאים, המנצחים את כל התמותות, אל מקום גבורה העליונה שכל הנעימות וכל החסדים מסוכים בה. התנוצצות אורה זו בעקבות משיח היא מופעת ובצרות העולם האחרונות היא מוצצת. וכבירי כח נתבעים לברר ולהסביר, לאחוז בכל כח חוסן, בכל יפעה, בכל מפעל וכל תכונה, בכל אמצעי וכל יכולת, בכל התעודדות וכל התעוררות רוח, בכל עת כושר ובכל תכונה אפשרית, לתמם את החזון העליון ההולך ומתגלה, זה החזון

clouds, and recognizes with one look all the wonders and all the deeds, all the truth and all the falsehood, all the righteousness and all the wickedness, and behold all stood and stands ready for the command of the light of the word of the Living God. The illumination of the world with the light of Israel is the soul of human history revealed and the soul of all existence in its hidden might. *While as yet He had not made the land and open fields, nor the chief of the dust of the world. When he prepared the heavens, I was there; when He drew a circle over the face of the deep. When He fastened the skies above, when the springs of the deep became strong.*[260] This perception through the speculum of holiness is turned into an active force, a reviewing force, a vivifying force, and all the complicated events that are in the midst of all the families of the peoples are revealed as an orderly system, though foggy and mysterious, which demands light. The light will come from the place from whence light proceeds to the world – from Zion, perfect beauty,[261] God will appear. A spirit of the true God, which spreads over all the systems of man,[262] uplifts nature from its lowliness to heights of holiness, prepares for all the miraculousness to appear and be revealed, perfects the vision of divine service in all its branches, on the real basis[263] of life, rises beyond the dim speculum, and looks with the light of the holy, the light of the higher Torah, the Torah of Moses, *with vision and not with riddles,*[264] which bases ethics and knowledge[265] on the foundation[266] of life and action and rises with all of them[267] together to the height of eternity[268] and peace,[269] to the place of glory[270] and the truth of eternity, to the foundation of the supernal wisdom[271] that will enliven its masters with all the beauty[272] of full life, which vanquishes all deaths, to the place of supernal strength[273] wherein all pleasantness and kindness[274] are poured. The shining of this light appears in the [epoch of the] "footsteps of Messiah," and may be glimpsed in the latest world calamities. The mighty are enlisted to clarify and explicate, to grasp every strength, every beauty, every deed and every quality, every medium and every ability, every encouragement and every arousal, every opportunity and every possible dimension, to perfect the higher vision that is being revealed. This vision whose footsteps are thousands

אשר אלפי דור הם צעדיו, והקיפו הוא אותו הרום והשפל אשר לעולם ולאדם, האחוז בהרום והשפל אשר לסגולת האדם, לסגולת העמים, לאישון האדם, "כי לד׳ עין אדם וכל שבטי ישראל", ורוחב הדעת, מעמק דרך ארץ, התיצבות לפני מלכים, הבעת המבוקש האדיר בכל הבלטתו, שעבוד המחשבה לרום העליון, הבעת הבטחון האלהי בכל עוזו קדשו, הבִטחה שהופעת הממלכה העליונה של אמרת ד׳ לא תחסר את התגלותה ובכל עת שתדרש, הנִסיות כולה היא מוכנה על צדה - הם תכסיסיו. וקול אלהים חיים בהגלותו בלבבות הרי הוא עומד אחר כתלנו להגלות בעולם ובכל עולמים. שרעפים הללו מביאים אורו של משיח, וחכמת ישראל המנוחלת תנצח את העולם, תעטר את התורה בעטרות עליונות ותטהר את ערפלי האמונה הכללית והפרטית מכל סבוכיהם, כאש מטהר וכבורית מכבסים, אור השלום בישראל יופיע ואור התשובה יאיר את כל נאות יעקב, ו"מגדל עז שם ד׳ בו ירוץ צדיק ונשגב", "ונשגב ד׳ לבדו ביום ההוא". וקרוב הוא היום, ובידינו לקרבו, רק אם נטה אוזן לשמוע קול שיח קודש ואור תורת אמת וחכמת ישראל העליונה תהיה לנו למורשת פלטה.

יד

באחיזת הפשט והסוד זה בזה, יסוד אחדות תורה שבכתב עם תורה שבעל-פה, ההסתכלות היותר פנימית עם ההסתכלות החצונית בעולם, בחיים, במציאות, בסבות, בסגנון, באדם ובהויה, כן היא התאחדות הנס והטבע. בהנהגה וכמו כן באמונה. ההתעמקות החודרת מאחדת את הנפרדים, מה שהשביל הבינוני מפרידם. אורו של משיח, שיסודו רם ונשא וגבה מאד, מואר הוא מהתוכן

of generations,[275] whose compass is the sublimity and the lowliness of World and Man, which is bound to the height-and-lowliness of [Israel], the gift of Man, treasure of the peoples, the pupil of Man's eye.[276] *For to God is the eye of Man and all the tribes of Israel.*[277] Breadth of knowledge, depth of earthiness, standing before kings, expressing eloquently the mighty desire, subjecting thought to the highest sublimity,[278] expressing the divine certainty in all its mighty holiness, the certitude that the appearance of the supernal kingdom of God's word will not hold back its revelation and on every occasion that the miraculous is required, it is ready in waiting – are its stratagems.[279] The voice of the Living God as it is revealed in hearts, stands beyond our wall[280] to be revealed in the world and in all the worlds.[281] These thoughts bring the Light of Messiah, and the inherited wisdom of Israel will conquer the world, adorn the Torah with sublime crowns, and purify the obscurities of faith, general and specific, from all their complications, as a purifying fire and as a cleansing soap. The light of peace will appear in Israel and the light of Return will illuminate all the dwelling place of Jacob. *The name of the Lord is a tower of strength, in it will run the righteous and lofty.*[282] *On that day the Lord alone will be supreme.*[283] The day is close, and it is in our hands to bring it closer. If we only bend an ear to hear the sound of holy conversation, and the light of the Torah of truth and the supernal wisdom of Israel will be our surviving inheritance.

14

The Pangs of Messiah Himself

The unification of miracle and nature in the "Light of Messiah." Messiah's embryonic state. The interaction of positive and negative forces. The pangs of Messiah: the four forms of capital punishment.

As the interface of *peshat* (the simple meaning) and *sod* (the mystical meaning); the fundamental unity of the Written Torah together with the Oral Torah; the innermost regard together with the outermost view of the world, life, existence, causes, style, man, and being – so is the unification of miracle and nature[284] – in conduct and also in belief.

העליון שהנס והטבע מאוחדים שם וכל העלילות של הטבע מקטן ועד גדול פועלים בעדו ועמו, על ידו ובהשפעתו, כמו העלילות הנסיות. המעשים כולם עומדים בצורה עוברית, כל ההויה כולה נשמות אפרוחים או ביצים ורוח אלהים מרחפת עליהם, ומשיח גנוז הוא בקן צפור, זהו היכלו, והאפרוחים מתפתחים ומתגדלים והביצים מתחממים, והולכים ומתקרבים לצורת הוית החיים והמפעל, ובכללות-הכל הכל כלול, הכל פועל, לא יחסרו גם כל הכחות השוללים, שגם הם מצטרפים להוציא כלי למעשהו, כמו הכחות החיוביים. והכחות השוללים, שהם מצטרפים אל הכל לעשות את הצביון של המטרה העליונה, שם בעומק ירידתם אורה חיובית עליונה גנוזה. תחת העוני הנורא עושר עליון גנוז וחי, קודשא בריך הוא וחד מסכנא הם המה יושבים בהיכל קן צפור וטהורי לב היודעים רזא דמלה דשטותא, ואיך היא מצטרפת להאיר רזא דחכמתא, כרב המנונא סבא, הם דרים בהאי מגדלא ומסתכלים הם במפלאות תמים דעים באור ישועתו, וחבלי משיח הפנימיים, הם חבלי משיח עצמו: הירידה למעמקי הסבות של כל מוחין דקטנות הם הם יסורי חנק לרוחא דמלכא משיחא דבגלותא בתראה בסיפיה, המתקן את הצעדים האחרונים "אשר חרפו אויביך ד׳ אשר חרפו עקבות משיחך, ברוך ד׳ לעולם אמן ואמן"; יסורי סקילה היו בכל התקופה של עבודה זרה, וכל הרעות, הירידות והטמטומים, הפרעות הפנימיות והחיצוניות, שהם ענפיה; יסורי שרפה - החורבנות והגזירות המלכותיות על התורה, שרפות התורה והשמדות הנוראות שהיו מכוונות לעקירת הנשמה והפנימיות, שרפת נשמה וגוף קיים; יסורי הרג הם הם כל ההרגות, המיתות המשונות, וכל הרדיפות החיצוניות במעמד הכלכלה, "ואכל קצירך ולחמך יאכלו בניך ובנותיך". יסורי חנק הם

Deep penetration unifies the disparate; the mediocre approach rends them asunder. The Light of Messiah, whose foundation is mighty, exalted, and very high,[285] is illumined by the supernal content where miracle and nature are unified, and all the events of nature – from the smallest to the largest – work for it and with it, through it and its influence, just as the miraculous events. All acts yet exist in embryonic form; all of existence are souls of chicks or eggs, and the spirit of God hovers over them. Messiah is hidden in a bird's nest.[286] This is his chamber. The chicks develop and grow, and the eggs are warmed, and increasingly approach the form of existence of life and actuality. In this totality all is included, all works. Neither shall the forces of negation – which also contribute to the actualization of the vessel, just as the positive forces – be lacking.[287] These negative forces, which contribute to the total to effect the character of the higher goal – in the very depth of their descent is hidden a supernal positive light. Beneath the terrible poverty, a supreme wealth is hidden and lives; the Holy One and a poor man[288] dwell in the chamber of the bird's nest. The pure of heart, who know the mystery of the word of folly,[289] and how it contributes to illumine the mystery of wisdom, as did Rav Hamnuna Saba,[290] dwell in this tower and view the wonders of the Perfect Intelligence,[291] with His light of salvation. The inner pangs of Messiah are the pangs of Messiah himself:[292] The descent to the depths of the causes of all the small minds is the suffering of strangulation of the spirit of King Messiah at the end of the last exile, which prepares the last steps, *Your enemies, O Lord have blasphemed, they have blasphemed the steps of your Messiah, blessed is the Lord forever, Amen and Amen;*[293] the sufferings of stoning were throughout the period of idolatry, and all the evils, descents and blocks, the inner and outer disturbances, which are its ramifications; the sufferings of burning – the destructions, the imperial edicts against Torah, the burnings of Torah, and the terrible forced conversions that were directed to the uprooting of the soul and the inwardness, burning of the soul and preservation of the body; the sufferings of the sword – all the murders, the bizarre deaths, all the outer persecutions of an economic nature, *he will devour your harvest and bread, the food of*

הם היסורים האחרונים של ירידת האור למעמקים לחשוף סבות קטנות וקלות, לנעוץ תקוות במרחקים ומאורעות זמניות, בנטיות לב של מושלים, ובמהלכים של השתדליות פוליטיות, לעורר גם קטני רוח, שאין להם כי־אם מטרות קרובות מגושמות ומצומצמות, והקטנות מחוללת את החוצפא, וחבל המחנק אחוז על הצואר, מונע את הדבור וסותם את האויר. רק רוח ה׳ אשר על עמו, אור התורה הפנימית יופיע להשיב רוחא דמשיחא, ומתוך האפלה יביא אור גדול.

טו

דסוד הרשעה, שהיא מתפצלת לעבודה זרה ולמינות, הוא בא לבצר מקום לסיגי החיים, למותרות המציאותיות שבהויה ובאדם, במוסר ובחפץ, במפעל ובהנהגה, לתן להם גודל ושלטון בתוך הטוב והקודש; לא לטהר את הקודש, כי־אם לטמאו ולסאבו. אמנם מקומה של עבודה זרה הוא מבחוץ, עומדת היא במקום הזוהמא והמותרות המגושמות ומאופלות, ומבקשת את בצורם ואת שליטתם והתגברותם על כל תוכן קודש והתערבותם עמו בכל האפשרות. גדולה ממנה היא הרשעה הצפונה הארסית של המינות, שהיא מחפשת לה פינה בעצם הקודש, ״שממית בידיה תתפש והיא בהיכלי מלך״. מתאמצת היא להשאיר את כל זוהמת העולם, את כל הגסות הגופנית, ואת כל הנטיות הרשעיות האחוזות בגוף הגס, בפנימיות יסודיו החמריים, ולעלות עמו אל האושר של הקודש, שהוא מיד מתחלל ומסתאב בנגוע בו היד המסואבה. לא שעה ד׳ אל קין ואל מנחתו מפני הרשעה שהיתה בו אחוזה; אותו הרצח, שיצא אל הפועל אחר כך, היה גנוז וספון בכח גם בעת הבאת

your sons and daughters.[294] The sufferings of strangulation are the last tribulations: the descent of the light to the depths to expose small, minor causes, to insert hopes in distances[295] and current events, in the whims of rulers, in the course of political intercession, to arouse even the small of spirit, who have nought but immediate, material, narrow agendas.[296] The smallness produces impudence *(ḥutspah)*, and the rope of strangulation is placed around the neck, preventing speech and cutting off air. Only the spirit of the Lord that is upon His people, the light of the inner Torah, will appear to restore the breath of Messiah,[297] and from the pitch-dark will bring a great light.

15

Christianity: The New Koraḥism

Idolatry and heresy. Cainism, Korahism, and Christianity.
Israel – a beacon to the Nations.

The foundation of wickedness, which is subdivided into idolatry and heresy, comes[298] to set up a place for the dross of life, for the existential extravagances[299] that are in being and Man, in ethics and will, in action and behavior, to give them greatness and rule within the good and holy; not to purify the holy, but rather to defile and contaminate it. The place of idolatry is outside. It stands in the place of pollution and coarse, dark extravagances, and seeks their strengthening, their domination of the entire content of holiness and their comingling with it whenever possible. Greater yet is the hidden, poisonous wickedness of heresy, which seeks a corner in the very essence of holiness. *The spider you can catch with your hands, and yet it is in the palace of a king.*[300] Heresy strives to leave intact all the pollution of the world, all the coarseness of the flesh, and all the wicked inclinations that inhere in the coarse body, in the interior of its material elements, and rise with it to the happiness of the holy, which is immediately profaned and defiled by the impure hand. The Lord did not turn to Cain and his offering[301] because of the wickedness that inhered therein. That same murder, which later materialized, was already lurking in

הקרבן מפרי האדמה, וקרבן זה תועבה הוא, הוא הוא המגביר את כל כח רע, והחטאת הרובץ על הפתח הוא מתגבר ומתאמץ על-ידי ריח הקודש שהוא קולט אל קרבו ומהפכו לתכונתו. כה סובבת והולכת היא הקינות הרשעה, החפצה שתיטב בעיני ד׳, שד׳ ישעה אליה ואל מנחתה, ובחובה יודעת היא היטב, כי מאס ד׳ בה ופניה נופלים וחרה לה מאד וכעסה אגור בתוכה ובכל עת מצוא הנה יד הרוצח מתגלה, צביון החטאת, שאליה תשוקתו של האדם הקיני, מתראה בכל תועבתו. יסוד המינות, שלעגה על דברי חכמים ועשתה שמות בישראל פנימה, אשר אמנם מפני היד הגדולה מלאתי כח ד׳ אשר בחיי האומה לא הצליחה להרוס את השתות, בכֹל זאת הכינה לה קורים, אשר צלחו להיות לארג של מחסה כזב על פני עמים רבים. הוחלפה האלילות במינות. לא התוכן הפנימי הוטב, כי-אם העמדה. התואר החצוני גוהץ כמעט, אבל המטרה אחת היא, לא לקדש את הרצון, את החיים, את העולם הגס ואת הפנימיות המהותית על-ידי כל אותו הסדר המוכן לכך בעצת ד׳ הגדולה, שיסודה הוקבע בישראל, בגוי קדוש, ומהסתעפיותיה יוכלו עמים רבים לינק כל אומה לפי תכנה, לפי מוסרה והכנתה הטבעית, ההיסתורית והגזעית, לפי השכלתה ומצבה הגיאוגראפי והכלכלי, וכל התכנים החברתיים והאישיים שלה המצטרפים לזה - לא זאת היא מגמתה. הקינות עשתה באדם את מעשה המפעל הקרחי בישראל. הקריאה של ״כל העדה כולם קדושים ובתוכם ד׳״ היתה קריאה לועגת לכל תוכן הקודש ולכל הרוממות וההכנה התוכית, הדרושה להעשות עד שיהיה הקודש מבוסס בחיים באמת, שיהיה מובטח מכל פגם וסאוב, שלא יהפך לרועץ ולצרה היותר גדולה של העולם. על כן הוכרח הדבר שירד חיים שאולה, להאבד מתוך הקהל ולהיות לעולם לאות לבני מרי, שלא

potential at the very time the sacrifice was brought of the fruit of the earth. This sacrifice is an abomination. It is that which amplifies the power of evil; the sin that crouches at the door[302] is fortified by the fragrance of the holy that it absorbs into its midst and converts to its quality. So continues wicked Cainism, which would seek favor in the eyes of the Lord, that the Lord may turn to it and its offering, while inwardly it knows full well that the Lord has rejected it. Its face falls and it is extremely angry, and at every opportunity the hand of the murderer appears; the character of sin, which is the longing of Cainite man,[303] is visible in all of its abomination. The founding of Christianity, which ridiculed the words of the sages[304] and wreaked inner havoc in Israel – though unable to destroy the foundations, because of the great hand full of the power of the Lord which is in the life of the nation, nevertheless wove cobwebs, which succeeded in becoming a web of deceit over the faces of many peoples. Paganism was exchanged for heresy. The inner content did not improve, only the posture. The outer appearance was pretty much scrubbed up, but the goal is one: not to sanctify the will, life, the coarse world, and the essential inwardness through the entire order that has been prepared by the great plan of the Lord, whose foundation was established in Israel, a holy nation, and from whose branchings many nations can derive nourishment, each nation according to its content, its ethics, and its natural, historic, and racial disposition, according to its education, geography and economy, and all the social and personal factors that contribute to this – this is not its objective.[305] Cainism accomplished among mankind that which Koraḥism[306] perpetrated in Israel. The cry *All the congregation are holy and in their midst the Lord*[307] was a mocking of the entire content of holiness, and all the inner uplifting and preparation necessary so that holiness would be truly established in life, so that it would be protected against any defect and contamination, so that it would not become the world's greatest oppression. Therefore it was necessary that [Koraḥ's band][308] descend alive into the bowels of the earth, to disappear from the midst of the community,[309] and to be forever a sign to mutineers that they not emulate Koraḥ and his congregation.[310] The call to all the

יהיו עוד כקרח וכעדתו. הקריאה אל כל העמים, השקועים בכל רפש הטומאה, בכל מעמקי הרשע והבערות, בתהומות החשך היותר מחרידות: "הנכם כלכם קדושים, כלכם בנים לד', אין הפרש בין עם לעם, אין עם קדוש ונבחר בעולם, כל האדם הוא קדוש בשוה" - זאת היא הקרחות האנושית, שהיא הקינות החדשה שממנה סובל האדם, שממנה "נוע תנוע ארץ כשכור והתנודדה כמלונה, וכבד עליה פשעה ונפלה ולא תוסיף קום", עד אשר יפוח היום ויפקוד ד' על צבא המרום במרום ועל מלכי האדמה על האדמה. הבצור המרומי וההרקעה לשחקים, שהמינות מתימרת בהם, מוכרחים לפול ולהעקר מיסודם. העולם צריך שיכיר, כי לא בהגה אחד, באמרת אמונה מתוארה לבדה, די לאדם לעוף לגן עדן, וכל אוצר הרעה, הרצח והתעוב, הספון בכל חדרי רוחו, בדמו ובבשרו, יכול להשאר בעינו, וממילא הלא איננו צריך צרוף ולמוד, רכוז ועליה, "לית דעתיר מחזירא", מזונותיו, גם הרוחניים, מצוים לו בכל זמן ובכל מקום, "ודמיין מיעיה למעי דאנשא". קץ יושם לכל אותו החשך, יכיר האדם וידע, כי כל עמלו צריך שירוכז לטוהר הנפש, האפשרות של הטהר בתכונת העמים טעונה היא מילוי של רִכּוז, שהוכן כבר מאז על-ידי אותה ההכנה הגדולה, שהפליאה יד ד' לעשות על-ידי אותה האומה הנפלאה, "לבזה נפש, למתעב גוי, לעבד מושלים, מלכים יראו וקמו שרים וישתחוו, למען ד' אשר נאמן קדוש ישראל ויבחרך", "הן עד לאומים נתתיו נגיד ומצוה לאומים, הן גוי לא-תדע תקרא וגוי לא-ידעוך אליך ירוצו, למען ד' אלהיך ולקדוש ישראל כי פארך". החפץ של העמדת גוי אחד בעולם בתור ממלכת כהנים וגוי קדוש, שהוא צריך להיות למופת על האור העליון האלהי החודר בחיי העמים, שרק בהיותו מצוי ועומד, בהיותו חסון וחפשי, בהיותו שב לבנינו ולאשרו, אחרי כל

nations, who are sunken in all the mud of impurity, in the abyss of wickedness and ignorance, in the most frightening depths of darkness – "You are all holy, all sons of the Lord, there is no difference between peoples, there is no holy, chosen people in the world, all men are equally holy" – this is the Koraḥism of mankind,[311] the new Cainism from which man suffers, from which *the earth reels as a drunkard and totters as a hut, her sin is heavy upon her and she shall fall and not get up any more,*[312] until the day will expire[313] and the Lord will command the heavenly host on high and earthly kings below.[314] The lofty fortress and the flight to the heavens, of which Christianity[315] boasts, must fall and be fundamentally eradicated. The world must recognize that one syllable, a statement of theoretical belief, is insufficient for man to fly to Paradise, while the entire gamut of evil, murder, and abomination, which is tucked away in the chambers of his spirit, in his blood and flesh, is allowed to remain intact. Consequently he requires no purification or education, no concentration or upliftment. "There is none so rich as the swine":[316] His food, including the spiritual, is to be found always, everywhere. "The swine's stomach resembles that of a human."[317] An end will be put to all of that darkness.[318] Man will realize and know that all his toil must be concentrated on the purity of the soul. The possibility of purity as becomes the peoples, requires concentration, which was established of old in the way of the great preparation, which the hand of God wondrously accomplished through that wonderful nation. *To him who is despised by men, to him who is abhorred by nations, to the servant of rulers, Kings shall see it and rise up, princes, and they shall prostrate themselves, for the sake of the Lord, who is faithful, the Holy One of Israel, who has chosen you.*[319] *Behold, a witness to the nations I have appointed him, a prince and commander to the nations. Behold a nation you do not know, you will call, and a nation that did not know you, will run to you,*[320] *for the sake of the Lord your God and for the holy one of Israel, for He has glorified you.*[321] [This is] the desire to establish one nation on earth as a kingdom of priests and a holy nation, to be a demonstration of the supernal divine light that penetrates the lives of peoples. Only when found, strong and free,

הופעותיו המרובות בעבר, אחרי כל נסיונותיו הקשים, אחרי כל צרופיו ולבוניו, בשובו עם כל דעותיו ועם כל קניניו, עם כל רכוש נשמתו וכשרון חייו, עם כל טהרתו הגופנית, הגזעית והאמונית, עם כל תוכן ההופעה האלהית, שהיא לו למורשה ושסגולת ארצו מגדלתו ומרחבתו, אז על-ידי אותה הידידות הפנימית שהוא יכול להראות לאומות העולם תחת כל המשטמה והרדיפות אשר קבל מהם, על-ידי כל הכבוד וההשתוממות אשר כל הגוים כולם יוכלו להראות עליו תחת כל הבוז והחרפה אשר טפלו עליו, על-ידי כל אותה התשוקה של ההתחברות והרֵעות עם עם ד׳ אלה, עם נחלת ד׳, אשר סגולת הקודש בטהרתה לטהרת החיים ספונה בו, אשר רק על-ידי חקוי ארוך על-ידי הדרגה של העמקה דורית יכולה היא לצאת אל הפועל במדה הגונה גם בשאר העמים, בכל האדם אשר על פני האדמה - אז יבורר לכל, כי סגולת הקודש אינה סגולה זלה, שיכולה להנטל בכל ידים מסואבות, כי-אם סגולה העולה בעמל נורא, במסירת נפש קבועה, ועל-ידי זכות נחלת קודש של אבות לבנים נושאי עולם באהבה ושומרים דרך ד׳ בכל עז. אז יוסרו פני הלוט מעל כל העמים והמסכה הנסוכה על הגוים, ואותה הותרנות של המינות תוכר כמו שהיא בתור מטבע פסולה, המסמאה את העינים ומטמאה את הנפשות, מרבה רצח ודם וכל תועבה. ״ד׳ עוזי ומעוזי ומנוסי ביום צרה, אליך גוים יבואו מאפסי ארץ, ויאמרו: אך שקר נחלו אבותינו הבל ואין בו מועיל״. ״ונשגב ד׳ לבדו ביום ההוא, והאלילים כליל יחלוף״. ״ולא ירעו ולא ישחיתו בכל הר קדשי כי מלאה הארץ דעה את ד׳ כמים לים מכסים״.

having returned to its intact, fortunate state, after all its many manifestations in the past, after all its difficult tribulations, after all its catharses and refinements, returning with all its opinions and acquisitions, with all the wealth of its soul and talent of its life, with all its purity – of flesh, race, and belief, with all the content of the divine revelation, which is its inheritance and which is nurtured and broadened by the gift of its land – only then, through that inner friendship that it can show to the nations of the world despite all the hatred and persecutions that it received from them, through all the honor and amazement that the nations can show it instead of all the ignominy and shame heaped on it, through all that longing for relationship and companionship with this people of the Lord, the inheritance of the Lord, in which is hidden[322] the gift of holiness (in its purity) for pure living, that may be appreciably actualized by the other peoples, by all mankind on the face of the earth, only by a long, gradual imitation, through an internalization over generations – only then will it be apparent to all, that the gift for holiness is not a cheap trinket to be seized by any impure hands, but rather a treasure purchased with awesome toil, with constant self-sacrifice, and through the merit of the holy heritage of fathers to sons who bear their yoke with love and guard the way of the Lord with all might.[323] Then the fog, the mask, will be lifted off the face of all the peoples,[324] and the compromise of Christianity will be recognized for what it is: an invalid coin, which blinds the eyes and sullies the souls, which increases murder, bloodshed, and every abomination. *The Lord is my strength, fortress and refuge in a day of affliction. To You, nations will come from the ends of the earth, and will say, Our fathers inherited only falsehood, vanity and inefficacy.*[325] *The Lord alone will be exalted on that day, and the idols will totally disappear.*[326] *They will not harm nor destroy in all My holy mountain, for the earth will be full of the knowledge of the Lord as the waters cover the sea.*[327]

טז

הישרת העקמומיות בתכונות, בדעות, בהשקפת החיים, עד לעליות הקודש המעולות, זקוקה היא לחדור בשרשים התחתיים, ועמם לעלות לספירות הגבוהות. כשההתפצליות התחתיות שולטות לעצמן הן מעכירות ומחלחלות, מזהמות ומגשמות הגשמה גסה ומזוהמה את כל אויר החיים, וכשהן נאחזות ומתבטלות בתכנים שממעל להן ועולות בעליתם הרי הן המוסיפות אור וחיים, טוהר וקודש, אומץ ותפארת בכל. יסוד נצחי הוא "ואהבת את ד' אלהיך בכל לבבך - בשני יצריך: ביצר הטוב וביצר הרע". האהבה אינה שלמה ואינה נובעת יפה ממקור האחדות המטוהרה כי-אם כשכוללים את היצרים ביחד, והיצר הרע מתאגד עם היצר הטוב, וכל כחותיו הרעים הנם נאחזים בשורש הטוב ומתהפכים לטובה, לצחצח, להחיות, להבהיר ולזקק יותר את להט הטוב. דבר זה נוהג בדעות, בתכונות ובעצמיות החיים; בהבנת העולם, בהשכלת האמונה, בחנוך הכללי והפרטי, בשאיפות העדינות של החיים, של האנושיות, של הלאומיות ושל השלמת האדם באור תקות האושר המעולה. ולזה דרושים כל כחות הטוהר האדיר של גבורת החכמה העליונה, ומטרתו של סוד ד' אשר ליראיו ההולך ומתנוצץ בלבבות, המכבש לו את דרכיו על-ידי כל האמצעים הרבים והשונים, החוצב לו גולות עליות וגולות תחתיות, הבא דרך פתחים חרכים וחלונות, גם דרך פרצים והריסות, והכל אל מקומו שואף זורח הוא.

16

Holistic Love of God

Holistic love of God and its cosmic implications.

To achieve lofty spiritual ascents, straightening of perversities in characteristics, in opinions, in outlook on life, must penetrate the bottommost roots, and rise with them to the highest spheres. When schizoid states rule sovereign, they oppress and terrify, polluting and coarsening the entire atmosphere of life; when contained and subsumed in contents higher than themselves and rising with their ascent, they add to everything light and life, purity and holiness, vigor and pride. This is an eternal principle: "*You shall love the Lord your God with all your heart*[328] – with both your inclinations, with the good inclination and with the evil inclination."[329] Love is complete and flows well from the source of pure unity only when both the inclinations are integrated and the evil inclination bonds with the good inclination, all of its evil powers bound to the root of good and transformed to good – to refine, enliven, and clarify even more the ardor of Good. This approach applies to opinions, characteristics, and the essence of life; to the understanding of the universe, to the intellection of faith, to collective and individual education, to the genteel aspirations of life, of humanity, of nationalism, and of Man's perfection in the light of the hope for supreme happiness. To this end are required all the powers of mighty purity of supernal wisdom's courage and the objective of the Lord's secret, known to His fearers,[330] which increasingly sparkles in hearts, paving its way through all the sundry, different means, digging higher wells and lower wells,[331] coming through openings, vents, and windows, also through breaks and ruins. And all aspires to its place, shining.[332]

יז

כל התרבות הזמנית בנויה היא על יסוד כח המדמה. זוהי מורשת גורלם האלילי של עמי התרבות האחוזים בכח המדמה, שממנו באה התפתחות היופי הגופני בפועל ובציור מעשי. הולך ומשתכלל כח המדמה, ועמו משתכללים המדעים המעשיים והנסיוניים, ועל-פי עליתו של כח המדמה ותפיסתו את החיים מסתלק האור השכלי, מפני שחושב העולם כולו שכל האושר תלוי בפתוחו של כח המדמה. וכה הולכים הענינים בהדרגה, עד ששרידי השכל שברוח החכמה החולונית גם הם הולכים ונעתקים אל כח המדמה. המליצים והמספרים, הדרמתוריים וכל העוסקים באמניות היפות נוטלים מקום בראש התרבות, והפילוסופיה פוסחת וצולעת ואין לה מעמד מפני שהשכל הנקי הולך ומסתלק. כפי סלוקו של השכל ורוח החכמה כן חוצפא יסגי וחכמת סופרים תסרח, יראי חטא ימאסו והאמת תהא נעדרת ופני הדור כפני הכלב. אותה העדינות הפנימית, הבאה מרוח החכמה, הולכת ונמוגה, השאיפה לרוחניות ואצילות, לדבקות אלהית, לעולם העליון, לזוך המוסר, ברום טהרתו, לציורי המושכלות מצד עצמם ונצחיותם, נעשית חזון יקר, וכפי אותה המדה, הנוהגת בעולם בכללו, נוהג הדבר בישראל כלפי רוח הקודש ואהבת התורה ברוח פנימי ורעננות עצמית של היהדות הנאמנה. ובעולם שולט רוח מגושם. "אי לך ארץ שמלכך נער ושריך בבקר יאכלו". אמנם כל זה הוא יסוד עצה מרחוק, עצת ד׳ היא להשלים את כח המדמה, מפני שהוא בסיס בריא לרוח העליון שיופיע עליו, ומתוך העליונות של התפיסה הרוחנית שקדמה בישראל הוכרח כח המדמה להתמוגג, מה שגרם חלישות לאחיזת רוח הקדש העליון, שעתיד לבא על-ידי מלכא משיחא.

17

Modern Society and Prophecy

In modern society, hypertrophy of the imaginative faculty serves as a preparative to prophecy.

All of contemporary culture[333] is built on the foundation of the imaginative faculty. This is the pagan legacy of the civilized nations[334] caught up in the imaginative faculty, from which developed physical beauty, both in action and in representation. The imaginative faculty progresses, and with it, the applied and empirical sciences, and in proportion to the ascendance of the imaginative faculty and its hold upon life, the light of intellect recedes, because the entire world supposes that all happiness depends on the development of the imaginative faculty. So things continue gradually, until the remains of reason in the spirit of secular wisdom are also converted to the imaginative faculty. The speakers and raconteurs, the dramaturges[335] and all engaged in *les beaux arts,* assume prominence in society, while philosophy hobbles and totters because pure reason disappears. As much as reason recedes, so "impudence increases, and the wisdom of sages rots, the sin-fearing are reviled and truth is absent, and the face of the generation is as the face of a dog."[336] That inner gentleness, which comes from the spirit of wisdom, disappears. The longing for spirituality and transcendence, for divine communion, for the higher world, for the clarity of ethics in the apex of its purity, for the concepts of intellect in and of their eternal selves, becomes a rare spectacle. This global phenomenon is reflected proportionately in Israel *vis-á-vis* divine inspiration and love of Torah with an inner spirit and essential freshness of faithful Judaism. There rules in the world a material spirit. *Woe unto you, O land, when your king is a lad and your princes eat in the morning!*[337] But all of this is a far-reaching plan, the Lord's plan to perfect the imaginative faculty, for imagination is the healthy basis for the supernal spirit that will descend on it.[338] As a result of the ascendancy of the spiritual perception that came early in Israel, the imaginative faculty was forced to collapse,[339] weakening the position of the supreme divine spirit destined to come

על כן מתבסס כעת רוח המדמה עד שיגמר בכל תיאורו, ואז יהיה כסא נכון ושלם לרוח ד׳ העליון ויוכשר לקבל אור רוח הקודש עליו, שהוא רוח ד׳ ״רוח חכמה ובינה, רוח עצה וגבורה רוח דעת ויראת ד׳״.

יח

כח המדמה זה הוכרח להיות נדחה ונלקה קצת על-ידי שפעת רוח הדעת העליון של רוח הקודש הנשגב שבמקור ישראל, שהוכרח להקדים ולבא לעולם מפני שלא יוכל העולם להתקים עד אלף דור בלא אור תורה, שהיא אוצר כל הדעת. מכל מקום יסודו היסודי נשאר בישראל, והקורטוב הפנימי שלו הוא באמת יסוד כל היופי, ומתגלה על ידי חזיון הנבואה, שאור הקודש מתלבש בתוכו, ״וביד הנביאים אדמה״; ובכל זאת מונח גם בנבואה יסוד הצמצום של האספקלריא שאינה מצוחצחת, ומפני זה קרובים אומות העולם לקלוט קצת מן הארת הנבואה ורחוקות הן מן אור התורה. אבל ליסוד בסוסה הגשמי של האומה, ההתקשרות הארצית עם ארץ ישראל והתרתקות האומה אל עצמותה וצמצום כחה שלא יתפזר, כל זמן שאין העולם ראוי לאגד הכל בשכל העליון, מוכרחת היא חכמה תתאה למלא את המקום, אשר המדמה הוא מלבישה הרבה והיא מבצרת מדת הדין בעולם, על-ידי ההתקשרות אל הקנינים הזמניים בחיי כל יחיד וההתענינות העמוקה של הכלל לחיי הרכוש והמשטר הממשלתי מצד עצמם. כשלא הגיע עדיין הזמן של כל הטהר להופיע אל המרומים המגמתיים, נשלחו מאת יהושע שנים אנשים מרגלים חרש לרגל את הארץ ובאו לבית אשה זונה ושמה רחב, והכל נקשר בקדש ובטוב העליון, אבל מדת הדין

through King Messiah. Therefore, now the imaginative faculty is being firmly established. When it is completely finished, the seat will be ready and perfect for the supernal spirit of the Lord, fit to receive the light of the divine spirit, which is the spirit of the Lord, *a spirit of wisdom and understanding, a spirit of counsel and strength, a spirit of knowledge and awe of the Lord.*[340]

18

The Clarification of Imagination in History

The clarification of the imaginative faculty in the course of history: Joshua – Solomon – Men of the Great Assembly – End of Days.

This power of imagination had to be somewhat repressed and eclipsed by the influx of the spirit of the higher knowledge[341] of the lofty divine inspiration at the source of Israel, which had first to come to the world because the world could not exist a thousand generations without the light of Torah,[342] the repository of all knowledge. Nevertheless, the basic foundation of imagination remained in Israel; its inner ingredient is truly the source of all beauty and is revealed through prophetic vision, in which the light of holiness is garbed: *By means of the prophets I have spoken in images.*[343] Yet even in prophecy there inheres the basic restriction of the "unpolished speculum."[344] Therefore the nations of the world have some access to the illumination of prophecy while being distant from the light of Torah. But for laying the physical foundation of the nation, the telluric connection with the Land of Israel, the fastening of the nation to its essence, and the concentration of its power that it not scatter, as long as the world is not worthy of binding all together with the higher intellect, the lower wisdom *(ḥokhmah tata'ah*[345]*)* must fill its place.[346] The lower wisdom is greatly informed by imagination, and it enforces the attribute of judgment in the world,[347] through the attachment to temporal possessions in the life of every individual and the deep interest of the collective in the life of capitalism and the governmental regime as such. When the time had as yet not arrived for all the purity to appear at the final heights,[348] there were sent by

מתעוררת ויראת העונש האמתית נצרכת לפי ערך השלטת כח המדמה והתעמקותו. אבל בעצמיות החפץ האומתי לא נשלם אז עדיין הפרצוף הדמיוני, לאחיזת הדעת בהגלמתו מצד אחד והיופי בכל תיאוריו מצד השני, וזה הושלם בימי שלמה: "אז תבאנה שתים נשים זונות" לפני משפט מלך ישראל היושב על כסא ד׳. אמנם על-ידי ההתערבות של הנשים הנכריות, עם חולשת הכח לעכל דברים זרים, יצאה הרשעה שגרמה ליסוד כרך גדול של רומי, וסינוני היסודות הוצרכו להאריך עדן ועדנים, עד שנתגרש כח המדמה משליטה רחבה בגבול ישראל, ויצרא דעבודה זרה נעצר "בדודא דאברא" "ונכיס יצרא", ולעומת זה אין עוד נביא אתנו ולהבת אהבת האומה והארץ איננה מורגשת באותו הטעם העמוק של ימי הטובה. והדברים מקושרים עם צער העולם כולו, עד שבאחרית הימים עקבות כח המדמה מתגלים ואהבת הארץ מתעוררת. מתראה הדבר בשמריו, אבל עומד הוא להזדכך. "הקטן יהיה לאלף והצעיר לגוי עצום, אני ד׳ בעתה אחישנה".

יט

בכבד הוא הרצון הטוב הפונה לאלהים בעמק שאיפתו, אבל מה יעשה הרצון לבדו בחיים? על כן כל זמן שאינו מתנשא עד רוממות אור הדעה, להקשיב לחכמה עליונה, אינו יכול לפלס נתיבות החיים; רק לבנה עזובה ישבור לו, שלא תוכל להצטרף לבנין גדול. אם הרצון, המשולל מאור עליון יותר ממנו, מתגבר להרחיב צעדיו בצורה מתרחבת, עד שלא ישאיר מקום לאותה הדאגה המדיקת כל פעולה וכל נתוח של מחשבה והנהגה בארחות החיים, אז יונק הוא זה הרצון עצמו, עם כל נטיתו שבלעה ניצוצים טובים, מצנור

Joshua two spies to reconnoiter the land, and they came to the home of a harlot by the name of Raḥav.[349] All is tied together with holiness and the highest good, but the attribute of judgment is aroused and true[350] fear of punishment is required in proportion to the empowerment of the imagination and its deepening. But in the essence of the national will, the imaginative dimension – which entails the embodiment of knowledge on the one hand, and all description of beauty on the other – was still not completed at that time. This was brought to completion in the days of Solomon: *Then two harlots came*[351] before the judgment of the King of Israel, who sits on the throne of the Lord.[352] However, through the interference of the foreign women,[353] together with the inability to digest foreign things, there resulted the wickedness that caused the founding of the great city of Rome,[354] and the siftings of elements had to be stretched out for aeons, until the imagination was disempowered in Israel. The drive for idolatry was captured in a "lead pot"[355] and "slaughtered."[356] By the same token, *there is no more any prophet*[357] and the flame of love for nation and land is not felt in the same profound way as in the good days. This is related to the pain[358] of the entire world. Until at the End of Days, the traces of the power of imagination are revealed and the love of the Land is aroused. The thing appears with its dregs, but it is destined to be purified.[359] *The smallest will become a thousand, and the youngest, a powerful nation, I am the Lord, in its time I will hasten it.*[360]

19

The Relation of Will to Intellect, and the Law

The excellence of Judaism consists in its subjugation of will to intellect and the Law.

The good will that turns to God in its depth of aspiration is respected, but what can the will alone accomplish in life? Therefore, as long as will does not soar to the heights of the light of intellect, to hearken to a higher wisdom, it is unable to pave the paths of life; it will break off an abandoned brick,[361] which cannot join a great structure. If

בלתי-טהור שזוהמת הנחש יכולה להקלט בתוכו. ביחוד כל זמן שלא עלה הרצון הנטיתי ולא דבק בארח החיים, שמשם חקי החיים נחצבים, עלול הוא לכל שנוים. מעמק טוב יכול הוא להיות נדח לעמק רע. כנסת ישראל אשת חיל היא, נאמנה היא מעמק רצונה לאותה האורה האלהית, שממנה חקי החיים כולם נחצבים, ובדרך תורה תומכת היא אשוריה. מחזקת היא את עמדתה בידיעתה העליונה כי דבר ד׳ ברית עולמים לו ולא תטה אזן לכל חולם חלום, לכל מסית ומדיח, גם אם יתלבש בלבושים של תגבורת המית רצון לטוב ולדבקות אלהית, אם רק יגע בדרך ד׳ המסורה, אם יפגום באור תורת חיים; וכה הולכת היא בדרך נצחונה הפנימי. אמנם חלק העמים לא יוכל להיות יותר מרומם מהמית רצון בנטיה אלהית, אבל כמה מסתבכת היא הנטיה הזאת שם וכמה משתנה היא בערכיה, כמה פלגים עכורים של שטפי אליליות נשפכים בה וכמה חלש כחה של נטיה חלשה זו הנשענת על נטית לבב אנוש אנוש למלא את התפקיד העולמי הגדול של שפיטת עמים מישור. אמנם יצורפו לאומים ויזוקקו בכור עוני ובהמון מלחמות וצרות, יכותתו גוי בגוי וממלכה בממלכה, והנטיה הקטנה של עלית הרצון אל העריגה האלהית, הסתמית, הכלולה בנשמת האדם, תזדקק מסיגיה, והעינים יוארו לחזות מהו מקור ישראל, וכנסת ישראל תשא דעה למרחוק, תראה לדעת כי בשמרה את ערכה העליון, מבלי להשפל מטה, הביאה טובה ואורה לעולם, כי בעצרה את הזרם העכור והנשפל שלא יתפשט יותר מדאי, סגרה בעד אותה הזוהמא והריקניות של האליליות והרשעה המדותית וכל עיוותי החיים, שלא יחדרו עמוק בנפש האדם הכללי עד לאין מרפא. אז יכירו וידעו כל יושבי תבל, כי רוח ד׳ מרחף על עמו וכי לעדי עד תביא יונת אלם זו את האורה לכל העולם כולו וערכה העליון

the will, devoid of a light higher than itself, is determined to broaden its influence, so that it leaves no space for exacting concern for every action, analytical thought and living comportment, then this very will is nourished – despite all of its tendency that absorbed good sparks – from an impure conduit in which the pollution of the Serpent[362] can be absorbed.[363] Especially, as long as the tendentious will has not ascended and cleaved to the way of life, from whence the laws of life are hewed – it is prone to all mutations. From the depth of good it may be diverted to the depth of evil. *Knesset Yisrael (Ecclesia Israel)* is a woman of valor;[364] from the depth of her will she is faithful to that divine light from which all the laws of life are hewn, and she treads the way of Torah. She strengthens her position with her higher knowledge that the word of the Lord is an eternal covenant. She will not turn an ear to any dreamer, enticer, or deceiver,[365] even if he should be dressed in garments of enhanced longing, of will for good and divine ecstasy, if he but touch the traditional way of the Lord, if he mar the light of the Living Torah. So she goes on her way of inner victory. Surely the portion of the Nations cannot be more exalted than the longing of a willful divine orientation, but how this orientation becomes complicated there! How transvaluated it becomes; how many muddy currents, pagan flows, pour into it; and how powerless is this feeble orientation, resting on the whims of a human heart, to assume the great global role of judging peoples justly! However, nations will be purified and refined in the smeltery of poverty and by numerous wars and troubles; they will be ground up, nation by nation, state by state, and the small tendency of the ascent of will to the simple, divine longing, which is subsumed in the soul of man, will be refined of its impurities. The eyes will be enlightened to see what is the source of Israel, and *Knesset Yisrael (Ecclesia Israel)* will look to the distance and discover that by preserving her highest value, without stooping, she brought good and light to the world. By preventing the muddy, lowly current from spreading too much, she stopped the pollution and the emptiness of paganism, characteriological evil and all the perversions of life from penetrating deep into the collective human soul to the point of no return. Then all the inhabitants of earth will realize that

יעמד תמיד לנס עולמים. אז תברר לה האמונה את ערכה וחקות החיים יפלסו את דרכיהם על מלא רחב הארץ, יבררו הדעות והטוב האלהי הפנימי המקורי, עם כל ענפיו העליונים ועם עמקי שרשיו, יהיה לברכה לכל האדם, והמבוקש של אור תורה ונר מצוה, אשר שמר את הצביון הישראלי בתומו, ייקר בעולם מזהב ומפנינים. מושגי החיים יתחוורו וכל העולם יחפש את נתיבות השלום העליון לא רק על-ידי עריגה עורת כי-אם על-ידי הארה מלאה, שבקרבה אור תורה זורח, ומשפטי ד׳ ומשפטי האדם יאוגדו לאגודה אחת, אשר יאירו זה בזה מלא זהרם, "והיה ד׳ למלך על כל הארץ ביום ההוא יהיה ד׳ אחד ושמו אחד".

כ

כל נתיקה שבמערכי הלב מהקוים העליונים הארוכים, במרחקי אידיאליהם העליונים, כשהיא באה בין ביחיד ובין בצבור הרי היא מערערת את יסוד האושר והטוב כולו. גם בצורה כהה וזעירה, כשחל בה רוח העליון, המאוגד לאידיאליות המאושרה באושר בלא גבול, הרי יש בה מעין חיים ההולך ומתגבר, מחיה דורות, מאשר תקופות, ומישר דרך לעמים רבים, מדריך עולמים לחיי עולמי עד ומפנה להם את המכשולות שבארחות חייהם הקטנים והזמניים. אורו של משיח, האושר העליון בחיי החברה והכלל, בצרופו העמוק אל האושר הפרטי, מחובר הוא עם האושר וההצלה המוחלטה של כל היש בתחית המתים. לגודל העתיד הזה מוכרחת כל עין לצפות, הצפיה האידיאלית היא מְגַוֶנֶת את הגונים העליונים החיים, היא מקבעת את חותם ההויה בגודל מאורותיה. נתיקה כל-דהי מראשית הרום, מאחרית העדן המעולה, נפילה היא לעמקי שחת,

the spirit of the Lord hovers over His people, that forever this "silent dove"[366] will bring the light to the entire world, and her supreme value will stand always as an eternal banner. Then faith will clarify its value and the laws of life will pave their ways over the full breadth of earth. The opinions will be clarified and the inner, original divine Good, with all its lofty branches and deep roots, will be a blessing for all mankind. The desired light of Torah and candle of commandment, which preserved the Israelite character intact, will be more precious in the world than gold and pearls. The concepts of life will be crystallized and the entire world will seek the paths of the higher peace, not only through a blind longing but rather through a whole illumination, in whose midst the light of Torah shines; the laws of the Lord and the laws of man will form a single bond,[367] their lights will interpenetrate brilliantly. *The Lord will be king over all the earth; on that day the Lord will be one and His name one.*[368]

20

The "Light of Messiah" within the Zionist Movement

Faith alone is not enough. Israel grounds faith in action. Even in the secular Jew the "Light of Messiah" shines. The "Light of Messiah" within the Zionist movement. Resurrection of the dead. The return of the Nations.

When some sundering of the conceptions of the heart from the long, supernal lines – in the expanses of their lofty ideals – occurs in an individual or a collective, it undermines the entire foundation of happiness and good. When, even in a faint, minute fashion, there rests upon it a supernal spirit, bound to the fortunate ideality with infinite happiness, there is in it a living fount that surges, vivifying generations, strengthening epochs, forging a way for many peoples, steering worlds to eternal life and removing obstacles from the ways of their small, temporal lives. The Light of Messiah, the highest happiness in the life of the society and the collective, in its deep connection to the individual happiness, relates to the fortune and absolute salvation of all being through the Resurrection of the Dead. Every eye must look

ושעירים קמים ומשחקים במקום זמירות שרי קודש ונעם שיח סוד המוני מעלה. האמונה העליונה היא בעצמה המנהגת את החיים אל המרומים שהיא שרויה שמה. היא בעצמה, בחטיבותה העליונה, בצורתה המשוכללת באמונת ישראל, נותנת את האומץ ומפתחת את החוב העמוק לאשר את החיים כולם וכל הפרטים שבהם, מעומק ראשית עד עמק אחרית, לאותה השאיפה המאושרה, הבלתי-פוסקת מלפעום בלבבות הקדושים מאושרי אלהים חיים, ומהם הולכת היא הזליפה השירית ומתגברת על החיים כולם, וכל עדינות שבלב כל איש וכל בריה - מאושר העדן היא לוקחת את רכושה. כשמתגלמת שאיפה, כשמתקרבת אל המציאות, והמציאות מציאות קרובה היא ובאפלה היא שרויה, צריכה היא תמיד הגנה שלא תאבד את ברק עומק חייה. אורו של משיח באמונה נעוץ, והאמונה באור קדוש ישראל בחיים וחובותיהם היא מבוססת. האמונה לא בסגולה פורחת באויר לבד היא מביאה אל מרומות מציאיותיה את כל חוסי בה, כי-אם בהתוית הדרך לכל מערכי הלב, לכל משאות הנפש, לכל מפעלי כפים, על-פי עוזה וחסנה המרום וקדוש. לפעמים נופלים רבים מההתבססות המציאותית ונשארים תלוים ברפיון רק ב צ י ו ר האמונה. מדה זו היא של אומות העולם, שבאו רק להסתכל באיזה ציור אידיאלי ולא בוגרו עד לכדי הגשמתו בפועל, וממילא נדע שגם ההסתכלות לקויה ורפויה היא. ההסתכלות הבהירה שולטת על הכל, על כל סדרי החיים והחברה ועל כל האישיות היחידה, על כל מזג ותקופה, על כל חפץ ושאיפה. אבל תלויי הרפיון אשר ממקור ישראל יצאו ובאחדות האומה הם כלולים, יש בהם ברק אור קודש, ניצוץ שיוכל לעלות ולבא לידי לבת אש קודש: אור הצדק, האמת, החסד והמשפט בחיים החברתיים - אורו של משיח בגודל תעצומו

toward the magnitude of this future. The ideal seeing[369] provides the living, supernal hues; it sets the stamp of existence with the magnitude of its lights.[370] Any detachment whatsoever from the Beginning of the height, from the End of the sublime pleasure, spells a fall into the depths of depravity. Evil spirits rise up and sport instead of the songs of holy princes and the pleasant conversation of the angels above. It is lofty faith itself that directs life to the heights where it rests. Faith itself, in its highest distinctiveness, in the perfect form of the faith of Israel, provides the fortitude and develops the deep duty to steer all of life and all its specifics, from the depth of the Beginning to the depth of the End, toward that happy aspiration, which never ceases to pound in the hearts of the holy, made happy by the Living God. From these hearts proceeds the lyrical outpouring, surging over all of life, and all the delicacy in the heart of every man and every creature – takes its wealth from the happiness of this pleasure. When an aspiration is embodied, when it approaches reality, and the reality is immediate and rests in darkness, the aspiration must be protected that it not lose the sparkle of its living depth. The Light of Messiah hinges on faith, and the faith is based on the light of holy Israel in life and its obligations. Not by an ethereal quality alone does faith bring to the heights of its existences all those who trust in it, but rather by marking the way for all the reflections of the heart, for all the ideals of the soul, for all the labors of palms, according to its strength and lofty and holy might. Sometimes many fall from the realistic grounding and are left loosely connected by the mere concept of faith. This is the degree of the nations of the world, who only behold some ideal conception and have not matured to the point of its actual materialization, and thus we know that even the beholding is faulty and weak.[371] The clear beholding rules over all, over all the arrangements of life and society and over every individual personality, over every temperament and era, over every desire and aspiration. But those weakly connected, who stem from the source of Israel and are subsumed in the unity of the people, have in them a holy ray of light, a spark that may ascend and develop into a holy flame of fire: the light of righteousness, of truth, lovingkindness and justice in the societal life – the Light of Messiah with its great power heartens them. The secular

מלבבם. עיני החול של האדם כהות הנה, בשום אספקלריא חקרנית אי אפשר להגיע לרום רז חבוי דנא. אבל גם צל צלה של אורה צחצחה זו אורי אורים יש בו, והאורה האוירית משוטטת היא, נעה ונדה, מסוכנת היא שלא תפול ממדרגתה, שלא תטמע בין בשר חמורים ונפשות אשר עמק חפצם הוא דם ורצח ולעיטה של נזיד עדשים. אבל אורו של משיח אחוז הוא בישועת ישראל, באיתניותו של גוי איתן זה, חטיבה אחת בעולם, אשר בורא כל עולמים משתבח ביקרם "מי כעמך ישראל גוי אחד בארץ". אור עליון זה, שהוא כתגא על רישא דספר תורה, שלא נתן מרוב עוזו ופארו לשמוש ומפעל ידים, באחרית הימים ימצא לו שבילים ודרכים רחבים, נתיבות חדשות לבא אל תפקידו המפעלי, והגדל יתעלה על כל קטן, וכל המכשירים בו כלולים. קמה באחרית הימים תנועה חרישית מלאה אונים וחפצים, מלאה נגודים וסתירות, מלאה אורות ומחשכים, וחושבת לחתור אל החוף לישועת ישראל. אורו של משיח הַכֵּהֶה בה. רבים ממחזיקיה של אבוקת אודים קטנה זו בגדו לכאורה באותה האורה הגדולה, האחוזה בקו הארוך אשר לאור עולם, נמוטו הפעמים ממעמד הנבואה הצופיה צפית עולמים. אבל ישועתם של ישראל תמיד היא ישועת ד', "אני והו הושיעה נא", וכאשר "פדית ממצרים גוי ואלהיו" כן היא כל ישועה, גדולה שבגדולות וקטנה שבקטנות. העולם רועש, ההרים מתקלקלים, ארץ כשכור תנוע, עמים עפים בדי ריק, ישראל עומד בתָוך. בתוך סערת הגלים חותר הוא אל חופו, ושרי קדש באים ויבואו ואת הדגל העליון יחזיקו, למרחוק שְׁעות דעה, והשלום בא יבא מכל עברים, ממזרח וממערב, מצפון ומים, ובתוך החלקה המעשית העלובה, החרבה מכל לשד עליון, יפתחו נהרות רחבי ידים לאורו של משיח, לתקון עולם מלא ברעיונות נצחיים מובטחים מראש

eyes of man are dim; it is impossible from any speculative viewpoint to reach the apex of this hidden mystery. But even the shadow-of-the-shadow of this brilliant light contains lights upon lights. The ethereal light flutters about, moving, wandering, in jeopardy of falling from its level, of being assimilated among asinine flesh[372] and souls whose deepest desire is blood and murder and gulping down the proverbial potage of lentils.[373] But the Light of Messiah is bound to the salvation of Israel, to the firmness of this firm nation, unique in the world,[374] in whose honor the Creator of all worlds is praised, *Who is like unto Your people Israel, one nation on earth?!*[375] This lofty light, which, as the crown on top of the scroll of the Torah,[376] is not given to practical use due to its strength and glory – at the end of days will find paths and roads, new ways to implement its function, and the greatness will transcend all smallness, and all the means will be subsumed within it. There arises at the end of days a silent movement[377] full of prowess and wants, full of oppositions and contradictions, full of lights and darkness, and it plans to arrive at the shore of the salvation of Israel. The Light of Messiah is dim within it. Many of the holders of this small torch have seemingly betrayed that great light, bound to the long line of the eternal light; the feet have fallen from the prophetic stance that sees into eternity. But the salvation of Israel is always the salvation of the Lord – *Please save me and Him!*[378] Just as *You redeemed from Egypt a nation and its God,*[379] so is every salvation, the greatest and the smallest. The world is tumultuous, the mountains are ruined, earth spins as a drunkard,[380] peoples tire of emptiness,[381] Israel stands at the center. Within the storm of the waves, Israel seeks its shore, and holy princes are coming and will come, holding the lofty banner, seeking knowledge from afar.[382] Peace will come from all sides, from east and west, from north and south, and within the poor realm of the practical, dry of any sublime moisture, will open wide rivers for the Light of Messiah, for the perfection of a world full of eternal concepts, assured by an ancient divine assurance, written in iron and blood, in a covenant of flesh and a covenant of language,[383] in a covenant of land and a covenant of people, in a covenant of eternity and a covenant of eternal life. The line goes straight, meeting up with the vision that is beyond all visions: the eradication of death and its

אמנה הבטחה אלהית כתובה בברזל ודם, בברית בשר וברית לשון, בברית ארץ וברית עם, בברית עולם וברית חיי עולמים. הקו הולך ישר, אחד באחד מוגש עם הצפיה שממעל לכל צפיות, הסרת המות ומארתו; בראשית הצעדים, אותו המות המעשי שידי אדם יוצרות אותו באולת ורשעה, ואחריה המסלה ישרה היא להעמיד את הכל על עומק רום הטוב, רוח הטומאה יבוער מן הארץ ובלע המות לנצח. אם תדמה לנו הדרך דרך רחוקה, אל נבהל. רק היא קרובה היא. רק האחיזה באותו הקו הארוך מגבירה את הכל ומכשרת את הכל. ברכת הענוה תשוב אלינו, גודל העליון ממעל ומתחת יפרס עלינו את הודו ואת סוכת שלומו. כל המארות, כל הנגודים, לברכות ולעזרים יתהפכו, כל הרוחות אשר בלאומים וכל הנטיות הדתיות, אשר נחשבו לזועה, אשר אמרו: "לכו ונכחידם מגוי ולא יזכר שם ישראל עוד", הן הן עצמן אל מקורן ישובו, יבושו ואחרי כן ינהרו. האחדות הישראלית בכללותה וההתעלות של גרעיני החיים שבה, הרוממות של קשב קול תורה, ההגה העמוק של דורשי רשומות, של חכמי חידות, וחכמת החיים של יודעי בינה, הדם הרותח של בני נעורים רווי רגש ושירה עליזה, ועמק רוח של צופי קדש, דכאות פנימית של שבי פשע, וגבורת רעם של שמחי חיים, יצרי כל לב ומערכי רוחות של כל בשר - והכל יאגדו באגד הקו העליון, ששם אור קודש קדשים. ובתוך הפעולות הפעוטות אור משיח יזרח, ונהרת תחית עולמים ומחיית המות תסול מסלתה, "ויעבור מלכם לפניהם וד׳ בראשם".

bane[384] – in the initial steps, the death created by human hands[385] with stupidity and wickedness, and after the road is clear to erect all on the depth of supreme[386] good, the spirit of impurity will be eradicated from the earth[387] and death vanquished forever.[388] If the way should appear to us distant, let us not panic. It is really close. Only adherence to that long line strengthens all and prepares all. The blessing of humility will return to us; the supreme greatness from above and from below will spread over us its majesty[389] and booth of peace. All the curses, all the oppositions, will turn to blessings and aids. All the spirits of nations and all the religious tendencies, which were considering catastrophe, which said, *Let us exterminate them as a nation and no longer shall the name Israel be mentioned,*[390] will themselves return to their source, be ashamed and after stream [to Israel]. The unity of Israel in its totality and the ascent of its nuclei of life –

the sublimity of hearing the voice of Torah;

the deep meditation of interpreters of markings, of masters of mysteries;

the wisdom-of-life of the understanding;

the boiling blood of youths drenched with emotion and gay song;

the depth of spirit of holy seers;

the inner depression of those returning from sin;

the thunderous power of celebrants of life;

the inclinations of all hearts and the ruminations of all flesh –

all will be bound by the bond of the supernal line,[391] where there is light of the holy-of-holies. And within the petty acts the Light of Messiah will shine, and the illumination of eternal renascence and erasure of death will pave its route. *Their king will pass before them and the Lord at their head.*[392]

כא

ברכת ישראל היסודית היא תוספת הדעת העליונה שבה נטוע שורש הדעה המיוחדה לישראל, המרוממה מכל לשון, והיא הולכת בשטף של נבואה גנוזה וממלאה לשד טללי חיים את כל נשמה שבישראל, ועומק החיים העליונים של האומה דוקא ממקור הדעת העליונה הזאת הם יונקים. קוי הדעת חודרים ממקור האומה הכללי בכל דורותיה ומתפשטים ברז הידיעה ההכרית השרויה בכל אחד ואחד מישראל, שבשבילה חי הוא ודורותיו את החיים הישראליים בכללם ובפרטם, כל חד וחד לפי מעלתו. כל נתיבות העצות והמחשבות להנהגתם של ישראל, בעניני החיים והעולם ובעניני הקדושה והאמונה, בעניני המדע והרוח, בעניני הזמן והתדיריות, משפעת זו הדעה העליונה הם באים. כל חלוקי הדעות והמחשבות השונות - פלגים מחולקים וחדרים שונים הם של הדעת העליונה הזאת, אשר "אדרין ואכסדראין מתמלאין מינה", ובהתחלקותם הם מימין ומשמאל מתאחדים על-ידי שורש הדעת העליון, המתחלק באחדותו לשני הצדדים, "חולקין דדעת הם תצ"ט ופלגא מכאן ותצ"ט ופלגא מכאן". והם כולם כלולים בשורש הראשי האלהיי, הממלא באורו הרוחני את כל החדרים בהון יקר ונעים. גדולי וטהורי הדעת מתאמצים לאחוז בשורש הדעת העליון, שהוא באחדותו המקורית בלתי-מתחלק הוא ומשקה את הכל בשפעתו המיוחדה, וכל החדרים הפרטיים שמימין ומשמאל הם מסתגלים על-ידי זה בסגולותיו, וכל העצות העליונות והתחתונות המתהוות בעולם הנן הולכות ומתברכות בברכת השלום, וכל הנטיה העולמית בכל האנושיות ובכל היצורים הולכת ונוטה אל היושר ואל השלום הבא לרגליו. "ונתתי שלום בארץ ושכבתם ואין מחריד. והשבתי חיה רעה מן הארץ וחרב לא תעבור בארצכם".

21

The Prophetic Character of the Different Jewish Ideologies

Hidden prophecy flows in every soul of Israel.
The different Jewish ideologies are but branches of a single supernal root.

The fundamental blessing of Israel is the additional supernal knowledge in which is planted the root of the knowledge that is unique to Israel, exalted beyond all tongues. It proceeds in a flow of hidden prophecy and moistens with the dew of life every soul in Israel,[393] and the depth of the sublime life of the nation is nourished just from the source of this supernal knowledge. The lines of the knowledge penetrate from the general source of the nation in all its generations and spread by the mystery of the conscious knowledge that rests in every one of Israel. On account of this knowledge, each one and his progeny live the Israelite life in its entirety and its details, each person according to his level. The various approaches as to how to lead Israel – in worldly matters and concerns of holiness and faith, in affairs of science and spirit, in temporal and eternal concerns – come from the flow of this supernal knowledge. All the differing thoughts and opinions are rivulets and chambers of this supernal knowledge, "from which rooms and chambers are filled,"[394] and which divided right and left, are united at the root of the supernal knowledge. Yet retaining its unity, that root divides laterally, "four hundred, ninety-nine and a half on this side, and four hundred, ninety-nine and a half on this side."[395] They are all subsumed in the principal divine root, which by its spiritual light fills all the chambers with precious and pleasant riches. The great and pure of knowledge strive to grasp the supernal root of knowledge,[396] which in its original unity is indivisible and waters all with its special flow. Thus all the private chambers of the left and the right receive its qualities, and all the high and low ideas that come to be in the world are blessed with the blessing of peace. The entire cosmic orientation of all humanity and all creatures tends to rectitude and to peace, which follows upon its heels. *I shall give peace in the land; you shall sleep and none shall cause fright. I will arrest wild animals from the land and the sword shall not pass through your land.*[397]

כב

ההשכלה הנשאבת ממקור רוח הקדש היא תמיד מתאימה עם אותה ההפריה המפליאה שבטבעיות הנתוח ההלכותי, שהוא הוא התוכן הממלא את לבן של ישראל: הגבורה האיתנה, המושלת על החיים ומתוה להם את ארחם ואת צביונם, יחד עם אותה הטבעיות שבתוך ההשכלה הרזית העליונה הזאת, הנובעת ממקור החופש הישראלי. מהתגלות המוחלטה של נשמת ישראל נובע גם כן המעין החי והמפרה של הגות כבוד אין קץ ואהבה בלתי-גבולית לישראל. זאת היא הסקירה החודרת, היודעת לחשוף מצפוני החיים ויודעת להעריך את הערך של היקר הישראלי מצד חטיבותו הפנימית. באותם הפלגים, ששפעות החיים, המעשיים והעיוניים הללו, זורמות ביחד במרוץ עזוז ואדיר, שם רז החיים לישראל גנוז, שם סוד האמונה והבטחה העליונה מונח, ומשם ישראל עושה חיל לנצח כל אויביו ולקום לחיים חדשים בצמיחת קרן ישועה. הגבורה הלאומית, דקדוקי מצות בהשתלהבות של אהבה מקורית, הערצתה של האומה וכבודה, חיוב נצחונה ובטחון רוממותה להיות עליון על כל גויי הארץ במובן של עליוניות אמתית, מוסרית, רוחנית, אידיאלית, הדורה ובריאה, רוויה שובע של שלום, של ברכת החיים ושפעת היצירה והבנין - כל אלה כטל יזלו בהחשפת המבוע של המחשבה הישראלית המורשתית, מסרתה של חכמת ישראל המותאמה למסרתה האמונית הגלויה ביסודי האמונה ותורת המעשה. כל הכשרונות העולמיים אשר נספגו בישראל וכל התעוררות של חיים מסבת כל צרה ומדחיפת כל קו אורה - הכל יתקשר ביחד להוליד כחות חדשים ומחוזקים, העלולים לחדש את זיום, בכל עת, בכל תקופה ובכל מהלך חיים

22

The Great Challenge of the Renascence: Synthesis

The unification of Kabbalah and Halakha. The creative forces that converge in the national renascence. The challenge to "students of the Lord": Synthesis.

The enlightenment drawn from the source of divine inspiration always fits the wonderful[398] productivity that exists in the naturalness of halakhic analysis.[399] This is the content filling the heart of Israel: the tenacious courage that administers life, pointing its way and character, together with the naturalness within this lofty, mystical enlightenment that flows from the source of Israelite freedom. From the absolute revelation of the soul of Israel flows too the living, fertilizing wellspring of infinite esteem and unlimited love for Israel. This is the penetrating gaze, that knows to bare the hidden in life and to evaluate the worth of the preciousness of Israel from the vantage of its inner distinctiveness. In those currents, where the flows of the practical and contemplative[400] lives stream together in a mighty, powerful sluice, is hidden the mystery of Israelite life, the secret of sublime faith and trust. From there Israel is geared to vanquish all its enemies and rise to new life with the sprouting of salvation. National strength, punctilious observance of the commandments *(mitsvot)* with the ardor of original love, esteem for the nation, the inevitability of its victory and the certainty of its superiority over all the nations of the earth, in the sense of true superiority, moral, spiritual, ideal, comely, healthful, drenched with an abundance of peace, of the blessing of life and the flow of creativity and building – all these will run as dew with the baring of the fountain of inherited Israelite thought, the tradition of the wisdom of Israel coordinated with its faith tradition revealed in the fundamentals of faith and the Torah of action. All the worldly talents that have been absorbed in Israel, all the reawakenings to life, whether they be as a result of trouble or the prompting of a ray of light – all will interconnect to produce new, reinvigorated powers, bound to flash anew at any time, in every period and life-situation that erupts in the world. The watering of all these saplings, which are constantly branching,[401] will come about through those students of the Lord[402] who stand in the House of the

שיתפרץ בעולם. והרטבת כל אלה הנטיעות, המסתעפות תמיד, בא תבא על-ידי אותם למודי ד׳ העומדים בבית ד׳, האמונים על רוח האומה בכל צביונה, חכמי חידות ורבי תושיה, היודעים להתרומם בהכללה רבה, על כל ההסתעפות הרוחנית והמעשית האדירה, שתביא עמה ישועת עולמים.

כג

לפעמים מרגיש האדם, שאיזה חלק מן התורה והחכמה נדרש לו לפי תכונתו ותיקון נשמתו וכל מהותו, וכשהוא נוטה ממקצעו לדרך אחר מרגיש הוא עצבון ושברון פנימי בקרבו. וזהו עומק הרז של "וליוצא ולבא אין שלום, כיון שיוצא אדם מתלמוד לתלמוד אין שלום". מתוך גודל הכללות הנדרש להיות בעקבתא דמשיחא, יש שמתבלבל העולם עד שלא יוכל האדם למצא את בחינתו וערכו ויחוג וינוע מתלמוד אל תלמוד, ועמים רבים מתבלבלים ואינם יודעים גם הם את מקום אחיזתם ומטרת כונניותם, "נוע תנוע ארץ כשכור והתנודדה כמלונה, וכבד עליה פשעה ונפלה ולא תוסיף קום, והיה ביום ההוא יפקד ד׳ על צבא המרום במרום ועל מלכי האדמה על האדמה". הפקידה היא לא הכבדה וכליון כי-אם חלוף מעמדים ותכונות, ומתוך עמק החשך יתעודד ישראל לאחוז באור תורתו בכל כלליותה, ואז נתיבות עולם יאירו לפניו ויחזיק במעוזו ויעשה שלום לו, שלום יעשה לו ותורה חוזרת ללומדיה ובשובה ונחת יושעו.

Lord,[403] who are nurtured on the spirit of the nation in all its character; masters of mysteries and of practical counsel, who know how to rise to a synthesis of all the prodigious spiritual and practical branchings, which will bring with it eternal salvation.

23

The Chaos of the "Footsteps of Messiah": The New Universality

The search for discipline: intellectual and national. The chaos of the "Footsteps of Messiah" is the harbinger of a new universality.

At times a man feels that some portion of Torah and wisdom is required for him according to his condition and the perfection of his soul and his very essence,[404] and when he turns from his subject to another discipline, he experiences within sadness and inner breakdown. This is the depth of the mystery, "*For the one who exits and the one who comes there is no peace* – when a person goes from one study to another there is no peace."[405] Due to the great universality required in the epoch of "the footsteps of Messiah," the world is sometimes so confused that a person cannot find his niche and worth, and flits from one discipline to another. Whole peoples too are confounded and do not know their place or purpose. *The earth reels as a drunkard and totters as a hut, her sin is heavy upon her and she shall fall and not get up any more. And on that day the Lord will command the heavenly host on high and earthly kings below.*[406] The "command" is not oppression and destruction but rather switching states and features.[407] Out of the depth of darkness Israel will be heartened by grasping the light of its Torah in all its universality. Then the ways of the world will light up before Israel; it will hold on to His strength and make peace with Him, make peace with Him.[408] Torah returns to its students[409] and tranquilly they will be saved.[410]

כד

יש רוח ממוזג שמתערב יפה עם העולם והחיים, עם סדרי המעשים והנהגות המדות, איננו נִכָּר כל-כך בפעולתו לעצמו, אבל הוא מגלה את כחו הנאה והמסודר בכל עת שיגיע הדבר לידי תלמוד ולידי מעשה. זהו רוח ההלכה, רוח תורה שבעל-פה, המסדרת את הקדש בארח החיים. כשרוח זה מתוקן ומשוכלל כל צרכו הרי הוא נעשה כסא ובסיס לרוח עליון של האגדה העליונה, המשוטטת בגבהי מרומים ותופסת את המאויים הנצחיים. אמנם יש רוח סער, שאינו מתקשר עם הרוח הממוזג, פורץ הוא גדרים ואינו מחכה לסדור העולמי שיבוסס, לסדרי החיים ותיאוריהם שיתאחדו במזג הקדש והטוב, ומגבוה ידאה עד עמקי תחתית בלא סדור. לא יוכל להתערב עם חיי בני אדם המסודרים, מוכרח הוא לקחת לו לעזר את החוצפא, העזות ועוד מדות רעות כאלה. לצורך שעה, לעת מלחמה יש שרוח זה נחוץ הוא, אבל אם ירצה להקבע לסדר חיים קבועים לא יֵרָצה. פירות מסודרים וקבועים להיות ראוים למְחִית דור דורים לא יתן. יתגדר באגדה עליונה, בחכמות נסתרות, בהגיונות עליונים, במחזות גדולים, בפלאים ובמופתים, בתפלה של מסירות נפש, בסגולות של קשור נשמות ובפליאי פליאות של נהורים ושל מחשכים, אבל אותו היושר העליון, האור המתוק המתוקן והמקובל, מימי השלוח ההולכים לאט, זה יחסר לו. בישראל יגלה רק בצורה של סעד לעת רעה, לבצור חיל בעת זעם לעת קרב ומלחמה, והיא באה לתקונה השלם כשהיא מתחזקת ומשתרשת ביהדות העתיקה תורת הפרושים, לכל גדלה, ארכה, עמקה ורחבה, עם כל עמקיה והרריה, עם כל חילה, עזה ותקפה, שהיא כוללת את הכל, את המעלה ואת המטה, עלית ותחתית

24

The Poise of Pharisaic Judaism

Halakha: the base for Agadah. The dangers inherent in extreme agadism. The balance of Pharisaic Judaism as opposed to other currents within ancient Judaism.

There is a temperate spirit that mixes well with the world and life, with practical arrangements and ethical deportment. It is not so discernible in and of itself, but it reveals its aesthetic, orderly ability whenever it comes to study and action. This is the spirit of *Halakha*, the spirit of the Oral Torah, which fixes the sacred within the way of life. When this spirit is sufficiently developed and perfected, it becomes a seat and basis for the sublime spirit[411] of the lofty *Agadah*, which soars in the heights and grasps the eternal desires. However, there is a stormy spirit that does not connect with the temperate spirit. It breaks down fences and does not wait for the worldly order to become established, for structures of life to unite with the temperament of holiness and good. From the height it dives to the lowest depths without order. It cannot mix with the established lives of people. It must brace itself with impudence, haughtiness, and other such negative traits. Temporarily, in time of war, this spirit may be necessary,[412] but it is unwanted as a permanent pattern of life. It will not yield permanent fruits worthy of sustaining generation upon generation. It thrives on lofty *Agadah*, on mysticism, on elevated thoughts, on great visions, on wonders and signs, on soulful prayer, on telepathy, on wonders-of-wonders of light and darkness[413] – but that supreme rectitude, the sweet, adjusted, accepted light, *the waters of the Shilo'aḥ that go slowly*[414] – it is lacking. In Israel this spirit is manifested only as a support in rough times, to provide strength during battle and wartime. It attains perfection when strengthened and rooted in[415] the ancient Judaism, the Torah of the Pharisees, in all of its height, length, depth, and width, with all its valleys and hills, with all its strength, might, and toughness – the Torah that subsumes all, the above and the below. One who enters with her [i.e., the Torah's] authority and fortitude the supernal lofts, the hidden orchards, goes confidently in the tower of divine strength. The great multitude who follow the "Torah

כרוכים בה. הבא ברשותה ובכח עצמתה אל העליות העליונות, אל הפרדסים הגנוזים, הרי הוא הולך במגדל עז ד' מלא בטחה, וכל ההמון הגדול הנמשך על-פי תורת אם יוכל לבא לאור חיים נאמנים, מסוגלים לתחיה שלמה, בלא פרץ ובלא יוצאת, ומפנימיות רוחו יחזה חזות הכל ובשובה ונחת יושע.

כה

רוקק העולם ויואר, יתעלה ויונהר, יתודע ויתגלה, אחרי הסרת סיגיו וצירוף בדיליו, שכל מה שהוא שואף ושוקק אליו, כל מה שהוא מתגבר ומתאמץ להגיע לו, בכל הצדדים ובכל הדרכים, הכל דבר ד' הוא, הכל מנהרי נחלי עדני קדש העליון יוצא. יוחל הדבר בכנסת ישראל, המוגבלה בגבול נחלת ישראל, זאת האומה היחידה בעולם, אשר ד' הוא נחלתה מאז מעולם, ויורחב הדבר ויבורר על כל העולם וכל העולמים, שכל מה ששאפו ושואפים אליו, הכל עם אל פועלים, הכל פונה למגמה הרוממה הרצויה האידיאלית אשר בצל שדי תתלונן, הכל משכלל את העצה העמוקה אשר שועשעה על כפים מראש מקדם, "ואהיה אצלו אמון ואהיה שעשועים יום יום משחקת לפניו בכל עת, משחקת בתבל ארצו ושעשועי את בני אדם". לא כימים הראשונים שהציץ שביב אור ויעלם, לא העולם אל יוצרו ישוב, במחשבה כי רוחק ממנו; העולם כולו ימלא כבוד והכבוד יהיה מחוטב וגלוי, מלך עולמים יחזיק בידי מלכות שמים להקימה, עצות קדומים יופיעו בכל גוני אורותיהם, יגלו בשלל צבעיהם ופלגי חכמתם, בנעם שיחם ובשיא חוסן יקרתם, על כל מפעלי רוח העולמים, רוח כל היצורים ונשמת כל אדם וכל חי, כל לאום וכל ממלכה וכל מחנה וכל מערכה, בהגלות יקר מלך

of the mother"[416] can reach the light of faithful life, disposed to whole renascence,[417] without some breach. And from its inner spirit, it will behold all and tranquilly will be saved.[418]

25

The New Return: "We Never Left!"

The cosmic yearning for holiness. The New Return: realization that the world was never distanced from God. The "Fallen Booth of David" truly never fell.

The world will be refined and lit up, will be elevated and illuminated. It will be known and revealed, after the removal of its impurities, that all that it aspires to and longs for, all that it strives to attain, in all aspects and all ways – all is the word of the Lord, all goes out from streams of bliss of the sublimely holy. The thing will start with *Knesset Israel* (Ecclesia Israel), residing within the border of the inheritance of Israel. This is the only nation in the world whose inheritance from eternity has been the Lord. [After] the thing will expand to all the world and all the worlds: All they aspired, and continue to aspire to – all do God's bidding. Everything turns to the exalted, desired, ideal purpose that rests in the shadow of the Almighty; everything rounds out the profound plan that was entertained before the Beginning, *I was near Him as a nursling and I was day by day (His) delights, playing before Him at all times, playing in the world, His earth and having my delights with the sons of men.*[419] Not as the first days when a light sparked and disappeared; the world will not return to its Creator with the thought that it was distanced from Him.[420] The entire world will be full of *Kavod* (Glory) and the *Kavod* (Glory) will be distinct and revealed. The King of worlds will hold on to the kingdom of heaven to raise it.[421] Ancient projects will appear in all the hues of their lights, will be revealed in their full spectrum and streams of wisdom, in their pleasant conversation and in their utmost honor, over all the works of the spirit of worlds, the spirit of all creatures and soul of all mankind and all life, every nation, kingdom, camp, and party, when the glory of the King of worlds is revealed upon His world, when the beauty of the Source of Israel and its Redeemer[422] will show on the root of the soul of His people and His house of prayer. The fallen

עולמים על עולמו, בהראות יפעת צור ישראל וגואלו על שורש נשמת עמו ובית תפלתו. תקום סוכת דוד הנופלת, אך באמת לא תקום רק יראה לעין כל שמעולם לא נפלה, אור אמת זה כי יתגלה כבר יהיה ערובה בטוחה על עמדתה לנצח נצחים, ״אהל בל יצען, בל יסע יתדותיו לנצח וגם חבליו בל ינתקו, כי שם אדיר לנו ד׳ אדוננו מקום יאורים פלגים רחבי ידים, בל תלך בו אני שיט וצי בל יעברנהו, כי ד׳ שופטנו ד׳ מחוקקנו ד׳ מלכנו הוא יושיענו״. זאת היא הקימה הצפויה לכנסת ישראל, שהעולם ומלואו עסוק בהכנתה, ״מידי אביר יעקב משם רעה אבן ישראל״.

כו

האֵמון המשפחתי הוא תולדה והמשכה קַוית מאותה האמונה הגדולה השרויה בעומק האהבה, הפועלת ברוח חיים בשכל עליון ומפואר, בסדר והתאמה בכללות המון היצורים והעולמים כולם. המעילה המשפחתית היא מעילה מהרסת את האשיות המעמידות את היצירה וכחותיה בעולם הכללי, לשכלל את העולם המעשי הרוחני. האותיות המבטאות את שם ד׳ אלהי ישראל, הכוללות בקרבן את כל חיי העולמים כולם, עם מקוריותם ושרשם העליון, עם סדרם והרמוניותם, כוללות בקרבן את כל האמון היסודי, שהתוכן התאורי והמעשי של משפחת האדם המשוכללה נובע מהם. בלכתם בדרך ישרה, בהיות החיים מבונים כהוגן בתיקון ונמשכים בפנימיותם ברגשי האמון האידיאליים, המשוטטים בכל המון הבריאה ממעל ומתחת, הרי הם מפכים מעינות של ברכה, של אושר ושל הופעות נשמתיות עדינות לכל. בשבורם, בעכירתם, במרידת הסדר האידיאלי שלהם, הרי הם יסוד ההרוס, ההרוס העולמי, ההרוס האורגני,

booth of David will rise up,[423] but really it will not arise – rather, it will be visible that it never fell. When this true light appears, it will serve as a sure guarantee of its eternal standing. *A tent that shall not be struck for removal, its stakes shall never be moved, its chords shall never be torn loose. For there the Lord our master shows Himself mighty unto us, in a place of rivers and streams of ample breadth, wherein no oared galley shall go, and a ship shall not pass thereby. For the Lord is our judge, the Lord is our lawgiver, the Lord is our King. He will save us.*[424] This is the rise foreseen for *Knesset Israel* (Ecclesia Israel), with whose preparation the entire world is busy. *From the hands of the mighty God of Jacob, from there you became the shepherd, the stone of Israel.*[425]

26

The Role of Family in Cosmic Harmony

Emun *and* Emunah *(Family and Faith). The waters of* Sotah, *the adulteress. The reparation of all human and domestic relations.*

The familial upbringing *(emun*[426]) is a product and linear extension of that great faith *(emunah)* that rests in the depth of love, which works in a spirit of life, with glorious, sublime intelligence, in harmony and coordination in the totality of the multitude of creatures and worlds. Betrayal of the family is a betrayal that destroys the foundations of the creation and its powers in the general world, to perfect the practical and spiritual world. The letters that spell the name of the Lord God of Israel, which subsume all the life of the worlds, with their originality and supernal root, with their order and harmony – include the foundational nurturing, from which flows the theoretical and practical content of the perfected family of man.[427] When (the familial) life goes in a straight way, when it is properly constructed and inwardly draws on the ideal emotions of nurturing, which hover in the entire creation, above and below – life gushes forth wellsprings of blessing, of happiness and of gentle soulful manifestations, for all. When (familial life) disintegrates, when it is troubled, when its ideal order is disrupted – it is the very foundation of destruction – cosmic, organic, familial, soulful destruction, the troubling of life and its bane. The examining

ההרוס המשפחתי, ההרוס הנשמתי, עכירת החיים ומארתם. בדיקת מי סוטה, ממקור החיים העליונים היא לקוחה, מכל אשרה וברכתה של תורה אשר דרכיה דרכי נעם וכל נתיבותיה שלום. העולם הולך ותועה בנתיבותיו, אבל מבקש הוא את האמון האלהי, את הנתיב של אור החיים, ובא יבא האור, והתכן בבנין משפחתי בין ד' אל עולם ובין כל מעשיו יופיע על-ידי התגלות אמונת אמון, אשר בישראל מאז היא אצורה, "וארשתיך לי לעולם, וארשתיך לי בצדק ובמשפט, בחסד וברחמים, וארשתיך לי באמונה וידעת את ד'". האמון המשפחתי בהבנותו בשכלולו יסוב ויעבור את כל גבוליו וימצא את משקלו הנכון בכל הערכים היחושיים, ימצא את מעמדו הישר הבלתי-מעול בין איש לאיש בין שכיר לשוכרו, בין עובד לנותן עבודה, בין חכמי חידות לעמלי כפים, בין עמים רבים, בין יושבי אקלימים ומדינות שונות, בין התביעות הבשריות לתביעות הנשמתיות אשר לאדם, בין האדם ובין כל היצור, בין חיי שעה לחיי עולם, בין הכל אל הכל. האמונה הפנימית, היודעת את כבודה, את אשרה וגבורתה המדושנת עונג פנימי, המכירה שהיא בכל מושלת, שהיא מחלקת במדה ובמשקל של צדק ויושר, אור וחיים, לכל המון יצורים לאין תכלית, על-פי סדר וערך של יחושים נאמנים, דרוכים ברוח שלום ואמת, אמונת עולמים זו תהיה תפארת הכל, "עטרת תפארת ביד ד'", "אשת חיל עטרת בעלה".

כז

שכחת השבטים ליחוסם היא הכנה לאחדות האומה. על-ידי הזכרון של חלוק השבטים היתה הגלות גורמת, שכל שבט יחולק ויפרד לגמרי מכללות האומה, וארס הנכריות היה חודר בחלקים

waters of the suspected adulteress[428] are derived from the source of supernal life, from all the happiness and blessing of Torah whose ways are ways of pleasantness and all its paths peace. The world bumbles along, but it seeks the divine nurturing, the path of the light of life. The light *will* come, and the content of familial structure[429] between the Lord, God of the World and His creatures will become manifest through the revelation of nurturing-faith *(emunat-emun)*, which has ever been stored in Israel. *I betrothed you to me forever, I betrothed you to me with righteousness and justice, with loving-kindness and compassion. I betrothed you to me with faith, and you shall know the Lord.*[430] When the familial upbringing is built and perfected,[431] it will surpass its borders and find its proper measure in all relational values; it will find the straight, unbetrayed status between man and man, between employee and employer, between mystics and manual laborers, between peoples, between inhabitants of different climates and states, between the fleshly demands and the soulful demands of a human being, between man and every creature, between temporal life and eternal life, between everything. The inner faith, which knows its honor, its happiness, and its courage that is full of an inner joy, which recognizes that it rules all, that it apportions justice and rectitude, light and life, to an unending amount of creatures, according to the order and value of faithful relations, conducted[432] in a spirit of peace and truth – this eternal faith will be the glory of all. *A crown of glory in the hand of the Lord.*[433] *A woman of valor is the crown of her husband.*[434]

27

The Disappearance and Return of the Twelve Tribes

The dissolution of tribal divisions: in exile, a blessing in disguise.
The significance and return of the twelve tribes of Israel.

The forgetting of the tribal genealogy is a preparation for the unity of the nation. Through remembrance of the tribal divisions, the exile would have caused each tribe to be completely separated from the totality of the nation, and the poison of alienation would have penetrated the separate, isolated parts. True, through this forgetting

המיוחדים והבדודים. אמנם על-ידי השכחה הזאת של ההתפרטות נתרבה הבלבול והערבוב, לא רק התפלות המיוחדות וראויות לכל שבט ושבט בפני עצמו בתקון העולם נתבלבלו, כי-אם כל ערכי החיים, הפנימיים והחיצוניים, כל צביוניהם של ההרגשות, הלמודים, המנהגים וההדרכות, שכל אחד מהם במקומו הוא מוסיף תקון אור וחיים מתאים עם הלך הנפש השבטית ובונה את עולמו, והוא לפעמים מעכר וסותר בנין בהיותו מלופף בסדרים שאינם מענינו. אמנם כל זה מסבב רק צרה ויגון ארעי, אבל בפנימיות החיים חיה היא הנשמה הכללית שנתעוררה הרבה על-ידי מְחִיַּת הקוים הפרטיים, ואם הנעם והסדור נתמעט ומרירות ויסורין רוחניים וגשמיים מתחברים עם כל מעשינו, בכל זה "אף על-פי שמיצר ומימר לי דודי לי ובין שדי ילין". ומתוך האחדות הבלולה, המלאה ערבוב וחסרון סדור, יצא לאור תכן חיים מתוקן ומסודר, שיגלה ויראה בהופעת אור חיים של גאולה וישועה, וישראל ישוב על מכונו וכח שבטיו ישוב אליו באחדות הרמונית, "ועוד תעבורנה הצאן על ידי מונה". ומזבח ד' ההרוס יבנה עוד הפעם על-ידי שנים עשר אבנים "כשנים עשר שבטי בני יעקב אשר היה דבר ד' אליו לאמר ישראל יהיה שמך", על-ידי אליהו מלאך הברית, אשר מאז נקרא על-ידי קנאתו "ד' הוא האלהים", הולך הוא ועובד עבודת השלום להשיב לב אבות על בנים ולב בנים על אבותם, על-ידי אור רזי תורה העליונים ההולך ושוטף בכנסת ישראל ומתפלש בכל מעבדיה, עסקנותה, ספריותיה, תקוותיה ועבודותיה, המתראים בצורות שונות, מקדש ומחול, מבנין וגם מהירוס, אמנם כולם כאחד עסוקים בבנין הפנימי והחיצוני, הפרטי והכללי, למעלה למעלה מחוג הכרתם של כל הפועלים והעובדים עצמם וגבוה הרבה יותר מכל מטרותיהם המצומצמות, רק בעצת ד' אשר יעץ לתת לעמו אחרית ותקוה. "באחרית הימים תתבוננו בה בינה".

of specificity, confusion and mixing increased. Not only the special prayers reserved for each individual tribe[435] as its part in the restoration of the world *(tikkun ha-'olam),* were confounded, but rather all the internal and external life-values: the entire character of emotions, studies, customs, and guidelines, each of which in its place adds to the perfection of light and life convenient for the tribal temperament[436] and builds its world, and [contrariwise] sometimes undermines structure when it is surrounded by frameworks that are not its own. However, all this engenders only temporary trouble and agony, but in the interior of life, lives the universal soul that was much aroused by the dissolution of the individual lines. If pleasantness and organization suffered, and bitterness and suffering – spiritual and physical – accompany all our actions, nevertheless, "Though he afflicts and embitters me, *my Beloved is mine; between my breasts he will rest.*"[437] Out of the heterogeneous unity, full of mix-ups and disorganization, will come to light a perfected, organized life-content, which will be revealed with the manifestation of the light-of-life of redemption and salvation. Israel will return to its foundation and the power of its tribes will return[438] to it with harmonic unity. *The sheep will yet pass by a counter.*[439] The ruined altar of the Lord will be built once again of twelve stones, *As the twelve tribes of the sons of Jacob, to whom the word of the Lord came, saying, Israel will be your name.*[440] This, through Elijah, Angel of the Covenant, who, since having brought about through his zealousness the cry, *the Lord is God,*[441] continues the work of peace, to return the heart of the fathers to the sons and the heart of the sons to their fathers.[442] This, through the light of higher mysteries of Torah that flows in *Knesset Yisrael* (Ecclesia Israel) and permeates all its deeds, communal activity, literature, hopes, and actions, appearing in different forms, holy and profane, constructive and even destructive. However, all as one are involved in the internal and external, individual and collective building – so far beyond the orbit of consciousness of all the laborers and workers themselves, so much higher than all their limited goals. This is but the plan of the Lord who designed to give His people a future and hope.[443] *At the end of days you will understand it.*[444]

כח

הגאולה נמשכת היא והולכת. גאולת מצרים וגאולת העתיד השלמה היא פעולה אחת שאינה פוסקת, פעולת היד החזקה והזרוע הנטויה, אשר החלה במצרים והיא פועלת את פעולותיה בכל המסבות. משה ואליהו גואלים הם לגאולה אחת, המתחיל והגומר, הפותח והחותם הם יחד ממלאים את החטיבה. ורוח ישראל מקשיב הוא את קול התנועות של פעולות הגאולה ההולכות מכל המסבות עד מלא צמיחת קרן הישועה במלואה וטובה.

כט

הגאולה מוטבעת היא בטבע ישראל, היא חותם פנימי. "גם את בדם בריתך שלחתי אסיריך מבור אין מים בו". משה מאיר את אור התורה ואליהו את אור הטבע הישראלי הנקי, קדושת הברית, המקנא לברית, מלאך הברית. באבות מתגבר אור התורה, בבנים - אור הטבע הישראלי הקדוש, וזה יוצץ באחרית הימים בחבורם, "והשיב לב אבות על בנים ולב בנים על אבותם". ומשה ואליהו יתחברו יחד באומה ובכל אחד מישראל בפני עצמו, "מידי אביר יעקב משם רועה אבן ישראל" - "אב ובנין דבית ישראל".

28

Redemption: An Ongoing Process

The ongoing redemptive process: from Egypt to now.

The redemption continues. The redemption from Egypt and the complete redemption of the future are one unending action: the action of the strong hand and outstretched arm,[445] which began in Egypt and works through all eventualities. Moses and Elijah[446] are redeemers in a single redemption; the beginner and the ender, the opener and the closer together complete the unit. The spirit of Israel hears the sound of the movements, the redemptive actions, brought about through all eventualities until the sprouting of salvation will be complete, in all its plenitude and goodness.

29

Moses and Elijah: The Light of Torah and the Light of the Body

Moses and Elijah; the light of the Torah and the light of the holy Israelite body; fathers and sons.

Redemption is imprinted in the nature of Israel;[447] it is an inner seal. *You too, because of the blood of your covenant, I sent your prisoners out of the pit wherein there is no water.*[448] Moses illuminates the light of Torah, and Elijah – zealous of the covenant, Angel of the Covenant[449] – the light of the pure Israelite nature, the holiness of the covenant.[450] In the fathers, the light of Torah predominates; in the sons, the light of the holy Israelite nature. This will be visible at the end of days when they join together, *And he* [i.e., Elijah] *will return the heart of the fathers to the sons and the heart of the sons to their fathers.*[451] Moses and Elijah will join together in the nation and in every individual of Israel.[452] *From the hands of the mighty God of Jacob,*[453] *from there you became the shepherd, the stone* (even) *of Israel*[454] – "Father and sons of the House of Israel."[455]

ל

צריכים לעורר את תחית ישראל בכל הכחות המכונסים באומה, בכל תורתה, בכל אמונתה, בכל מדותיה, בכל טובה, בכל עשרה, בכל כחה, בכל הגיונותיה, בכל שירתה, בכל עצמה, בכל חום חייה, בכל שכלה והשכלתה, בכל מרצה ונצחון כשרונותיה. את כל האורות כולם שבקרבה צריכים להוציא מחביון הגניזה לאור החיים. החוש הרוחני רואה אבוקת ישראל עולה, מארץ ישראל פורח הכל. אוצר גרעיני הנשמות של כל ישראל שמה הוא, "מציון מכלל יופי". כל יחיד ויחיד שבישראל יש לו גרעינו בארץ ישראל, שהוא עצור בפנימיות רוחו בעוצם תשוקה ואהבה, אם היא גלויה או מסותרת זהו רק חלוק דרגאי, אבל הקישור הנשמתי ישנו, ושלהבת אש הקודש צריכה להתלהב מכל הכחות, מהכחות הפנימיים והחצוניים, מאותם העומדים בצביונם ולא פנו חוצה ומאותם אשר מעומק הגלות או מסיבות אחרות, קדומות או מאוחרות, נטשטש צביונם. ההכרזה הכללית תקח עמה את הכל, וביסוד החיים הכללים אשר לישראל עמק התשובה גנוז. הכרת הצדק הפנימי של האומה, המכירה את אמתה העליונה ואת ההשתרגות של כל חמדה וכל אושר עולמי לשם כל התשוקות היותר נצחיות והיותר נאדרות, לאגד כל הטוב וכל הנחמד, כל היושר וכל הצדק שבכל פנה, לקשר את כל טוב ונשגב, את כל הדור ומקודש המלא בכל, והכל יתרומם ברוממותם, ועם גדל תבערת להב הקדש לרוממות ולשגוב, כל תוכן וכל מבוקש ישר משמש לעזרה; הטבת מצב החיים בכל תיאור ובכל אופן, הוספת עז גופני ועזוז מוסרי, אמץ פנימי וגדולה של עדינות, הרחבת התורה ומלוי החכמה, הגברת הרוחניות והופעת הפועל, הבלטת צורת החיים והגברת האחוה

30

National Return: *Teshuvah*

Each Israelite soul's portion in the Land of Israel.
National return: Teshuvah.

We must arouse the renascence of Israel with all the faculties concentrated in the nation: with all her Torah, faith, traits, goodness, wealth, strength, thoughts, song, essence, life's passion, intellect and enlightenment, energy, and success. All these lights in her midst, we must bring out from the hidden store-place to the light of life. The spiritual sense sees the torch of Israel ascending; from the Land of Israel flowers all. There is the storehouse of souls of all Israel, *From Zion, perfection of beauty.*[456] Each and every individual of Israel[457] has his nucleus in the Land of Israel, which is stored in the interior of his spirit with enormous longing and love.[458] Whether the love be revealed or hidden is but a difference of degree, but the soul-connection is there, and a flame of holy fire must be fanned by all faculties: by inner and outer powers, by those who maintained their character without turning to the outside, and by those whose character was blurred, either by the depth of exile or other reasons, earlier or later. The general announcement will sweep all. Within the foundation of the universal life of Israel, the depth of return *(teshuvah)* is tucked away. Recognition of the inner righteousness of the nation, which takes into cognition its higher truth, and the intertwining of all delight and all worldly happiness[459] for the sake of all the most eternal and most mighty desires, to bind together all the good and pleasant, all the rectitude and righteousness that is in every quarter, to bind all the good and lofty, all the lovely and holy that permeates all, and all will be uplifted in their uplifting,[460] and with the great conflagration of the holy flame for loftiness and highness, every content, every just desire serves as an aid; improvement of the situation of life in every way and description – adding physical strength and moral might; internal fortitude and humble greatness; expansion of Torah and completion of wisdom;

הכללית, חשק השלום הכללי וחפץ האושר העולמי, חלוץ עצמות והברקת העין, התיצבות לפני מלכים והתערבות בין הבריות מכל השדרות, התבודדות עליונה בהתקשרות פנימית למגמת החיים והעולם, למטרת ההויה ברזי רזיה, וחריצות של תקונים והתעודדות רוח - הכל ביחד מוכרח להיות מוקף, והכל דורש את תפקידו וקורא בקול גדול: עורי, עורי!

לא

טעות גדולה היא ביד אותם שאינם מרגישים את האחדות הסגולית שבישראל, וחפצים הם בדמיונם להשוות את הענין האלהי הזה, המיוחד באופי הישראלי, לענין כל תוכן של עם ולשון אשר בכל משפחות האדמה, ומזה בא הרצון לפלג את הענין הלאומי ואת הענין הדתי לשתי פלוגות, ושתיהן יחד נחלו בזה שקר, כי כל עניני המחשבה, ההרגשה והאידיאליות, שהננו מוצאים באומה הישראלית, חטיבה אחת בלתי מחולקה היא, והכל ביחד עושה הוא את צורתו המיוחדה. אמנם כשם שטועים המתאמצים להפריד את החלקים הבלתי מתחלקים הללו, ככה יותר הם טועים אותם שהם סבורים שאפשר הדבר שהחלוק והפרוד יעלה בידם של כל המתאמצים להפריד את התיומת, ומזה בא שהם לוחמים נגד מחזיקי חלק אחד מהחטיבה הישראלית בחמה שפוכה, על הפרדתם המהבלת, מבלי לשים על לב איך צריכה המלחמה הזאת להתכונן. אם היה אפשר להפריד באמת את התכנים הרוחניים שבכנסת ישראל, אלא שהדבר מנוע מפני איזה חק תורי, אז היתה צריכה המלחמה להיות מכוונת נגד המחזיקים בחלק נפרד מיוחד, לבלע ולכלות את צביונם מעל שמי האומה. אבל כיון שמניעת

strengthening spirituality and manifesting action; accentuating the form of life and enhancing general brotherhood; passion for universal peace and desire for worldly happiness; invigorating bones and sharpening study; standing before kings and intermingling with people of all walks of life; sublime isolation while connecting inwardly to the orientation of life and the world, to the purpose of existence with its most recondite mysteries, and the alacrity of activism and upbeat disposition – all together must be encompassed,[461] and all demands its role and cries aloud: "Wake up! Wake up!"

31

The Inseparability of Jewish Nationhood and Religion

The inseparability of Jewish nationhood and religion. The posture adopted by "the sound of thought and Israelite will" should be to reveal that they are inseparable.

There is a great error on the part of those who do not feel the unique unity of Israel, and desire in their delusion to compare this God-thing,[462] which is specific to the Israelite makeup, to the content of any nation of the families of the earth – and from this comes the wish to separate nationality and religion into two divisions. In this both err, for all the matters of thought, feeling and idealism that we find in the Israelite nation are one indivisible unit, and all together bestow its unique form. As much as those who strive to separate these inseparable elements err, those who are convinced that it is possible for all who strive, to achieve this division and separation, err even more. Thus the latter combat furiously those who embrace but one half of Israelite identity for their would-be separatism,[463] without thinking as to how this war should be conducted.[464] If it were possible to truly separate the spiritual contents of *Knesset Yisrael* (Ecclesia Israel) – the only thing preventing that, being some Torah law – then the war would have to be directed against those attached to one separate part, to blast their character from out of the skies of the nation. But since the impossibility of separation is an

הפירוד היא מניעה מוחלטת, בטוחים אנחנו שהמפרידים, מחזיקי החלקים הבודדים, אינם טועים כי-אם בציור דמיונם ולא בפועל הויתם, כי באמת בזה החלק הפרטי, כיון שיסודו בחיי האומה בכללה, הרי הכל כבר נמצא בו, וצריכה המלחמה להיות מיוחדת רק לגלות להם את טעותם ולברר להם שכל מאמצי חילם להפריד את האחדות הישראלית העליונה לא יעלו בידם. וההסתגלות של שלמי המחשבה והרצון הישראלי בכל עמק טבעיותו, צריכה רק להיות לבקר את החזיון החלקי מכל עבריו, ולהראות בו בעצמו את כל סימני תמותו וכליליותו מכל הנושאים כולם, גם מאותם הרעיונות שבעלי הרוח רצו כבר להסיח מהם את דעתם ולעקרם מנפשותיהם. על-ידי בירור ענין אמתי זה יעמדו סוף סוף כל בעלי התפרדות על ההכרה, שדי להם לכלות לשוא את כחם, ותחת להחזיק בחלק נפרד מדומה, שכל השאיפות והתכנים הכלליים של כל האומה כולה, בכל ערכיה, כלולים בו, אלא שהם כהים ומטושטשים, ומתוך כך מונעים הם מהנפשות המחזיקות בו את שובעם הרוחני, מצמצמים את מרחב רוחם ומדריכים אותם בנתיבות מלאי חתחתים - יותר נח יהיה להם להכיר באמת את האמת המציאותית ולהחזיק בכל התוכן החי הקודש של אור ישראל השלם בכל הופעותיו בגלוי. בזה יושיעו את נפשם מכל צרה ומחשכים, ויביטו וינהרו אל ד׳ ואל טובו, ולא יצטרכו עוד לענות את נפשם בשברי רעיונות כהים ומטושטשים, אשר לא יוכלו מעבר מזה להפטר מהם לנצח, ומעבר אחר למצא להם ברור והארת רוח, כי הם תכנים אשר טובם ולשד חייהם הנלהב והעצום לא יתגלה כי-אם על הככר הרחב והשלם שכל החיים הישראלים, במהותם הכללית והשלמה, מתראים בו בכל מלא עזוזותם.

absolute impossibility, we are confident that the separatists, attached to isolated elements, are deluded only in their conception but not in the deeds of their being. Truly, in this particular element – being founded on the life of the nation as a whole – everything is already found. The war must be intended[465] only to reveal to them their error and clarify for them[466] that all their bold attempts to break down the sublime Israelite unity will not succeed. The posture adopted by the sound of thought and Israelite will, in all the depth of its naturalness, should be only to critique the partial vision from all its sides and to show in it all the signs of wholeness and inclusiveness of all subjects, even of those concepts that the fantasts[467] would rather ignore and eradicate from their souls. By elucidating this fact, eventually all separatists will arrive at the realization that they have wasted enough of their energy, and instead of fostering what is imagined to be a separate dimension, in which are contained all the ambitions and collective contents of the entire nation, with all her values, though they be dim and blurred, and therefore deprive the souls attached to it of their spiritual satisfaction, hem in their spirit, and lead them on rough roads – it would be more convenient to truly recognize the existential truth and embrace the entire living, holy content of the whole light of Israel in all its revealed manifestations. Thus they would save their souls from all affliction and obscurity, and look and stream to the Lord and His good,[468] and would no longer need to torture their souls with dull, blurry bits of thought from which, on the one hand, they can never be free, and on the other, can never provide them with clarity and spiritual illumination, for they are contents whose good and tremendous vitality cannot be revealed other than upon the broad, whole forum where Israelite life, in its whole, universal essence appears in full strength.

לב

הפלגים יבלי המים של החיים העליונים של הנשמה הטהורה, במעמקים הם זורמים, במעמקי הטבע הגופני ובתחתית הבשר והדם הנם הומים ורועשים, אמנם מתפרצים הם אל על, צועקים ובוכים, מתנודדים וקובלים, מתאמצים ומתפתלים הם באין הרף לעלות אל הרום, להגלות בצורה מאירה חיה חיים שלמים, מלאים זיו הוד ופאר הדרת גבורת קדשי קדשים. אשרי האיש, השומע את קול נשמתו מתוך מעמקיו, ואשרי העם המאזין את הד הקול של הנשמה הכללית שלו, איך היא מתגעשת מתוך מעמקיה, ואשרי המקשיב הטהור אשר יקשיב את בת הקול של כל היצור הקורא מתוך מעמקיו להתגלות בהירה עליונה, טהורה וקדושה. אורו של משיח נתון בכלאי היסורים של עמקי העמקים, ובעת קץ גאולה, בעת אשר רק קו אחד יגלה בתכונה של איזו זהרורית אורה להחיש ישועה כללית לבית ישראל, יגלו ויחשפו אלה הסמנים המורים על צעקת העומק, ומתוך כל התנועות הכלליות והפרטיות, הנפשיות והגופניות, יוקשב אותו הקול האדיר והחזק, "קול ברמה נשמע נהי בכי תמרורים רחל מבכה על בניה, מאנה להנחם כי איננו". והקול עולה ומתעלה בתכונות חיים ומעשה, בתכונות רעיון ומחשבה, בתכונות המון גוים ורוח עריצים, בתכונות נפשות כמהות, עורגות ומקוות, בתכונות חולמי חלומות כועסים ומתקצפים, בתכונות אנשי ישוב ומתינות, בונים ומשכללים, בתכונות אנשי קדש משקיפים ומקוים, פועלים וצופים ישועה וגאולה, ומכולם יעלו ויגלו זרמי אפיקי הנחלים של המעמקים, שכולם אומרים אותה התשועה המנחמת: "מנעי קולך מבכי ועיניך מדמעה, כי יש שכר לפעולתך, נאם ד', ושבו מארץ אויב, ויש תקוה לאחריתך, נאם ד', ושבו בנים לגבולם".

32

Messiah Bound and Rachel Comforted

Listening to the soul: individual – human – cosmic. The "Light of Messiah" imprisoned. The voice of Rachel; her consolation.

The rivulets of the supernal life of the pure soul run in the depths, in the depths of bodily nature; in the nethermost of flesh and blood they churn and roar. However they crash upward, shrieking and crying,[469] undulating and grumbling, striving, twisting ceaselessly to reach the height, that there be revealed in a luminous form whole life, full of splendor, majesty, and the glory, the beauty of the strength of the Holy of Holies. Happy is the man who hears the voice of his soul from his depths; happy is the people that hears the reverberation of its universal soul, how it erupts from its depths; happy is the pure listener who hears the echo of all creation calling from its depths for sublime, pure, holy revelation. The Light of Messiah is thrown into the prisons-of-pain[470] of the deepest depths, and at the time of the final redemption, at the time when only one ray will be revealed as some glimmering of light to bring total salvation for the House of Israel, there will be revealed and bared these signs that indicate the cry of the deep, and from all the movements, general and specific, soul and body, there will be heard that strong, mighty voice: *A voice is heard on high, bitter weeping, Rachel crying for her children, refusing to be comforted for her children are gone.*[471] The voice rises and ascends through preparations of life and deed; through preparations of idea and thought; through preparations of a multitude of nations and a tyrannical spirit; through preparations of souls thirsting, pining, and hoping; through preparations of enraged dreamers; through preparations of settled and deliberate men, building and perfecting; through preparations of holy men who observe and hope, effect and envision salvation and redemption. And from all of them will rise up and appear the currents of the underground streams, all of which will utter the same salvific consolation: *Stop your voice from crying, your eyes from tears, for there is reward for your work, says the Lord, they will return from enemy land; there is hope at your end, says the Lord, the children will return to their borders.*[472]

אורות התחיה

Orot ha-Teḥiyah

(Lights of Renascence)

א

הבינה היותר שלמה ומתוקה של דעת האלהות היא הכרת היחש האלהי אל העולם הכללי ואל כל פרט ופרט מפרטיו, החמריים והרוחניים, יחש הנשמה, הצד הרוחני המחיה והממלא אור קיום והפרחה, אל הגוף, אל הדבר הנדרש לחיים לאורה ולהפרחה. היחש הזה כשהוא מתמלא בלב ונפש, הוא ממלא אותם אהבה יותר מיראה, ונעימות הגיון ושלוה יותר ממרירות הזדעזעות. ההכרה התרבותית של ההשכלה היותר מתוקנת הולכת היא לשכלל יפה יפה הכרה מתוקה זאת.

בחיי היחיד קל הדבר לבוא לידי מדה זו, על-ידי הטבת המוסר המעשי והשכלי ועל-ידי העלאת אור הדעת בכלל. כשהאופי האנושי מתיחש בסימפתיה אל הנשגב, אל הטוב המוחלט, בשכל ובחיים, מיד ההכרה הזאת הנשמתית של האלהות מתאחזת בו יפה, נקלטת בכל רעיונותיו ומתמזגת עם כל חושיו ורגשותיו לעדנם. האורגן הקבוצי, שלו יש פסיכולוגיה מיוחדת, אם גם הוא יהיה בעמק עמקו נוטה לסימפתיה מוסרית עליונה, ואהבת הטוב האצילי תהיה חקוקה

1

Whole God-Knowledge

Whole God-knowledge entails the integration of soul and body. The application of this idea to national psychology. The unreadiness of the Nations for this approach. Israel as the paragon of this virtue. In the initial stage of the renascence, love for God is manifested negatively rather than positively – in intense antipathy to false piety or fanaticism. Eventually the positive – the love displayed by "the heads of the people, masters of the soul, of the world of transcendence" –will win out.

The most complete and sweet understanding of God-knowledge is the recognition of the divine relation to the general world and to all its specifics, material and spiritual; the relation of the soul – the spiritual side that vivifies and fills with the light of existence and blossoming – to the body, to the thing requiring life, light, and blossoming. When this relation fills the heart and soul, it fills them with love more than fear, and the pleasantness of thought and tranquility more than bitter shock. The civilized consciousness of the most refined enlightenment goes to complete beautifully this sweet recognition.

In the life of the individual it is easy to arrive at this state, through the improvement of ethics, practical and intellectual, and through the uplifting of the light of knowledge in general. When the personality

יפה בעצם טבעה, על-פי בחירתה או על כל פנים על-פי מורשת אבות שלה, אז תתפלש יפה בקרב האומה גם כן ההכרה הזאת הנשמתית, ויהיה הנועם של האהבה האלהית עם יראת רוממות מתוקה ומתוקנת שרוי בכללות האומה ומישר את כל דרכיה.

אבל לפי מדת רחוקה של הפסיכולוגיה האורגנית מהחבה הפנימית אל הטוב המוחלט, כן לא יוכל היחש הנשמתי לחדור בקרבה ביחש האלהי, ומוכרח קשר האלהות להיות בקרבה קשר נכרי, והאלהים יהיה בה אל נכר ואל זר, ואל זר זה יקנה לו תכונות משונות וקריקאטוריות, המעותות את החיים הרבה יותר ממה שהן יכולות לישר אותם. לעת עתה עוד לא באה התרבות למדה זו, להכין סמפתיה אלהית של הטוב המוחלט בעומק הנשמה של האורגנים הקבוצים, ועל כן הננו רואים בהם עדיין סמני רשע ועריצות ומהות המוסר הולכת ומתמסמסת ונעזבת מן הלב הכללי של הקבוצים.

אבל מורשת פלטה יש לה לאנושיות בכנסת ישראל, שהסמפתיה האלהית נמצאת בחוגה הפנימי. הרגש מעיד והבינה מבררת, שאלהי עולם היחיד והמיוחד הוא הטוב הגמור, החיים, האור, הכל, המרומם על כל ומרומם על כל רוממות, וטוב מכל טוב, טוב לכל ורחמיו על כל מעשיו, מחיה הכל ושומר הכל, מצמיח ישועה לכל, והסמפתיה הכוללת הזאת חודרת באומה זו לא רק בפרטיה, כי-אם דוקא בכללותה. אם נזדמן ששכחה את נשמתה, את מקור חייה, נסתגלה לה הנבואה להזכירה והוכנו לה הגליות לפשט את עקמומיותיה, עד שסוף כל סוף תנצח בקרבה הסמפתיה של הטוב המוחלט.

הצמאון החי, המוחש, הזה הממלא באורו ומהותיות גבורת הויתו את החיים המעשיים, גם החברתיים והלאומיים, כשם שהוא

relates sympathetically to the sublime, to the absolute good, in intellect and living, immediately this soulful consciousness of divinity settles in, is absorbed in all its conceptions, and mixes with all its senses and emotions to refine them. The collective organism, which has a special psychology – if it too in its depth will incline to a sublime ethical sympathy, and the love of the transcendent good will be well engraved in its essential nature, either by choice or at least by ancestral inheritance – then this soulful consciousness will pierce the midst of the nation as well, and the pleasantness of the divine love together with a sweet, refined awe *(yir'at ha-romemut)*, will be resting in the nation as a whole, straightening all her ways.

However, in proportion to the distance of the organismal psychology from the inner affection for the absolute good, the soulful relation will be incapable of penetrating it (the nation) with the divine relation, and perforce, the bond to divinity will be a foreign bond in its midst. In this nation, God will be a foreign god, a strange god, and this strange god will acquire odd, caricatural qualities that distort life much more than they can rectify it. For the time being, civilization has not yet reached this stage of preparing a divine sympathy[1] of the absolute good in the depth of the soul of the collective organisms. Therefore we still witness in them signs of wickedness and tyranny, while the essence of ethics dissolves, abandoning the general heart of the collectives.

Humanity has a surviving inheritance[2] in *Knesset Yisrael* (Ecclesia Israel), in whose inner orbit the divine sympathy is found. Feeling attests and understanding clarifies that the one and only God of the universe is the absolute good, the life, the light, the all, exalted beyond all and exalted beyond exaltedness, better than good, good to all and merciful to all His creations,[3] sustaining and preserving all, providing salvation to all. This universal sympathy penetrates this nation not only individually but precisely collectively. If it should happen that the nation forget its soul, the source of its life, it had the gift of prophecy to remind it, and the exiles were designed to straighten her crookedness

ממלא בהם את הכחות המיטאפיזיים והחזיוניים, הולך הוא ומפלש את נתיבו, וקורא לאומה בבא עתה להתעודד, להתרומם, להתנער מעפר השפלות, לנתק כבלי הגלות ולדרוש פריחה חדשה על הארץ אשר בה החלה התרבות הנשמתית האלהית, בעד האומה ובעד העולם כולו, להתרקם. והתביעה הסמפתית האלהית איננה מתגלה בכל אורה בהתחלתה, אדרבא, היא מתגלה מקודם באופן שלילי, בגרשה את ההרגשות האלהיות הזריות שאינן ממלאות את הנפש ביחש נשמתי כי-אם בשלטון של אדנות קשה וכח של אלימות, הבאים משמות הבעלים, מחוסרי האורה העדינה של יראת הרוממות והאהבה הטהורה והקדושה של קבלת מלכות שמים המוטבעת בישראל, "זרע אברהם אוהבי". ולפי תגבורת השלילה בידי המוכשרים לה, כן הולכת ובאה גבורת החיוב מהמחנה הגדול כמחנה אלהים, מראשי עם בעלי נשמה של עולם האצילות, והרגש הנשמתי, האלהי הלאומי, הולך ומפריח ומתחבר אל כל המאורות הגנוזים בהיסתוריה המוחשית, הבולטים בזהרם בנושא של ההיסתוריה ההיא, זאת היא ארץ הירושה, ארץ חמדה, ארץ קודש, ארץ צבי וארץ חיים. "גואלנו ד' צבאות שמו קדוש ישראל".

until eventually the sympathy of the absolute good would win out in her midst.

This living, tangible thirst that fills with its light and the essence of the strength of its being, practical life, both social and national – just as it fills with them the metaphysical and visionary faculties – goes on and paves its way. It calls to the nation when its time has come, to be encouraged, uplifted, to throw off the dust of lowliness, to break the fetters of exile, and seek a new blossoming in the land in which the soulful, divine civilization – for the nation and for the entire world – began to take shape. The demand of the divine sympathy is not revealed at the beginning in all its light. Quite the contrary, it manifests itself initially in a negative manner by driving out the bizarre divine feelings that do not fill the psyche with a soulful relation but rather with the rule of an imperious domination and a violent power, which come from the names of the Ba'alim,[4] devoid of the gentle light of awe *(yir'at ha-romemut)* and the pure, holy love of acceptance of the kingdom of heaven, implanted in Israel, *the seed of Abraham my lover.*[5] As the negativity on the part of those disposed to it grows stronger, so increases the power of the positive from the great camp, the camp of God, from the heads of the people, masters of the soul, of the world of transcendence. The soulful, divine, national feeling blossoms and bonds to all the lights hidden in the tangible history, which vibrate in the subject of that history, namely the Inherited Land, the Land of Delight, the Land of Holiness, the Land of Beauty, the Land of Life.[6] *Redeem us, Lord of Hosts is His name, Holy One of Israel.*[7]

ב

הטבע מוצא את רְדִיָתוֹ בקבוץ האנושי יותר מאשר בפרטיו. הפרטים הנם יותר חפשים, והטפוס של החופש המיוחד לאדם מתגלה בהם יותר. אבל החברה, האנושית והלאומית, עומדת ביותר תחת השפעת הטבע, וההופעה האינסטינקטיבית מתגלה בה יותר.

דרכי השמירה המכוונות לשמירת המין והאיש, המתראות בבעלי חיים הטבעיים יותר מבאדם התרבותי, הנן מתגלות בכלליות האנושיות באפנים יותר קרובים לטבע החי. ההכרה הפנימית, הכוללת בקרבה את הנטיות להשמר מכל מזיק ולהכיר את האויב, בלי כל צורך לחכמה ונסיון, מתגלית בחיי העמים ביחוסם זה לזה, עם לעם, דת לדת, גזע לגזע.

האלילות הרגישה בישראל, ביהדות, את אויבתה היותר גדולה, את הכח, אשר לפי מדת הגלותו יצר לה העולם, ותצא שנאה אינסטינקטיבית עזה לישראל מכל הגוים. המינות, אף על-פי שהשתדלה להנזר מן האליליות הרשמית, מכל מקום נוסדה על בסיסים קרובים לאליליים. לא היתה יכולה להתפלש בתוך אומות אליליות, אשר האליליות חדרה בתוכיות נשמתן, דמן ובשרן, כי-אם בקחתה לה סגנון אלילי לרפידתה והשטחת סגנונה. יודעת היא יפה, שאם באפס יד יתמסמס ויכלה הסגנון האלילי, הרפוד לה, לא תמצא עוד מעמד בחיים למטבעה המיוחדת ותוכרח להבלע בליעה רוחנית ביהדות, מקורה, על כן עומדת היא גם כן על נפשה, ותמלא שנאת מות ליהדות ולישראל מחזיקיה.

וכן הדבר הולך בכל השדרות ובכל המצבים. מלחמת הקיום עושה את דרכה כבעולם החמרי גם בעולם הרוחני, בעולם הדעות

2
Healthy National Instincts

In individual psychology, freedom is more evident; in collective psychology, the animal instinct of self-preservation prevails. Christianity took over paganism's paranoia of Judaism. Philosophers lay bare civilization's deepest instincts. National tendencies will not be dislodged by science. Judaism's natural instinct is godliness. Practical preparations provide the media for this national idea. The special "diet" of Israel. Only when this national spirit is hale and healthy do true creativity and free inquiry follow. National defense against false creativity and scientism. The defensiveness is understandable, but "those who are truly full of courage" adopt another tack: explaining that Torah is the surest basis for free creativity and science.

Nature finds its control in the human collective more than in individuals. Individuals are freer, and the type of freedom specific to man is more evident in them. But society, human and national, stands more under the influence of nature, and the manifestation of instinct is more evident in it.

The methods of preservation designed for preservation of the species and the individual, which are more visible in wild animals than in domestic man, are revealed in collective humanity in ways that are closer to animal nature.[8] The internal consciousness, which includes within it the tendencies to be preserved from danger and to recognize the enemy, without having need of wisdom and experience, is revealed in the life of nations in their relations to one another: people to people, religion to religion, race to race.

Paganism sensed in Israel, in Judaism, its greatest foe, the force, [from] which – in proportion to its revelation – paganism would suffer. Thus there issued a mighty instinctive hatred toward Israel from all the nations. Christianity, though it attempted to foreswear official paganism, nevertheless was founded on bases close to the pagan. It could not have penetrated pagan nations, whose souls, blood and flesh were permeated with paganism, other than by adopting for itself a pagan style as its accoutrement. Christianity knows full well

והרעיונות. בכל תוקף והכרה פנימית מלמדת היא קבוצים רבים, המון בלתי מלומד, לעמוד על נפשם בבחינתם הרוחנית, כשם שהיא מלמדת את התורה הזאת את פרטי בעלי החיים ואת הקבוצים האנושיים בבחינתם החמרית. רק אחרי אשר הנטיות הללו יוצאות אל החיים ומחוללות מעשים כבירים, באים פלוסופים, חוקרי הנפש וטבע העמים, ומגלים את חכמתה של ההכרה האינסטינקטיבית אשר הקדים ההמון, ההולך אחר רגשותיו, לדעתה, ולפלס על פיה את נתיב חייו.

המדע יבסס את הנטיות הטבעיות וכפי האפשרי יתן להן צורה תרבותית ומוסרית, אבל לא יעקרן ממקומן, כי עצומות הן ממנו, וגם המשפט והצדק על ימינן. כי הלא הן הן מעמידי החיים הקבוציים, וכל זמן שיש זכות קיום לקבוץ לאומי וחברתי באיזו צורה שתהיה, יש לו המשפט להגן על קיומו, מכל דבר אשר יבלעהו, ובתחבולות יעשה לו מלחמה.

היהדות מכרת את עצמה גם היא בהכרה טבעית - קודם שיבארו לה כל פלוסופיה וכל הגיון מה היא - לההארה של האלהות בצורה היותר טהורה ומאירה בקרבה פנימה ובעולם ובחיים בכלל, והשלמת טפוסה הלאומי הזה על-פי רוחה העצמי בארצה ההיסתורית, וזאת היא כל מגמתה. הכונניות המעשיות שלה באות למלאות את מלאכת הצנורות, שעל ידם ימלא דבר היחש של הזלת שפע טל החיים מהאידיאה האלהית הטהורה אל האידיאה הלאומית שלה, ברוח בשכל ובמעשה, לא רק בחיי כל יחיד כי-אם גם וביחוד בחיי הלאום כולו.

ישנם בעולם חסידים, פלוסופים, אנשי קודש ואנשי אלהים, אבל אין בעולם אומה, שנשמתה העצמית לא תוכל להשתלם כי-אם על-פי המגמה של האידיאה האלהית העליונה בעולם, כי-אם ישראל.

that if by neglect, the accoutrement of its pagan style should dissolve and disappear, it would no longer find standing in life for its peculiar formula, and it would be forced to be reabsorbed in Judaism, its source. Therefore Christianity too defends itself, and is filled with lethal hatred toward Judaism and toward Israel, its adherents.[9]

So goes it in all avenues and situations. The battle of existence makes its way in the material world as well as in the spiritual realm, the world of opinions and concepts. With might and inner consciousness, it teaches many collectives, the uneducated mass, to preserve their souls spiritually, just as it teaches this theory to individual living creatures and human collectives in regard to their material existence. Only after these tendencies are expressed in life and effect great deeds, come philosophers, researchers of the soul and the nature of peoples, and reveal the wisdom of the instinctive consciousness that the mass, which follows its feelings, already knew and forged thereby its way in life.

Science will sublimate the natural tendencies, and as much as possible, give them a civilized and ethical form, but will not dislodge them because they are more powerful than it [i.e., science]. Also justice and righteousness are on their side, for these natural tendencies are what preserve the collective life, and as long as the national and social collective has the right to exist in some form, it has the right to preserve its existence from whatever would engulf it, combating with wise counsel.[10]

Judaism too has a natural self-consciousness – before philosophy and logic explicate her to herself. Judaism's entire purpose is the illumination of godliness in the purest, brightest form, in its very midst and in the world and life at large, and the completion of this national character, according to its essential spirit, in its historic land. Its practical preparations provide the "pipelines" through which will flow the dew of life from the pure divine idea to its national idea, in

רוח שונה מרוחות כל העמים אשר תחת כל השמים מוכרח שתהיה לו, גם כן כלכלה מיוחדה הנאותה לו, המפרנסת אותו, מחזקת את כחו ונותנת לו את קיומו.

לא תוכל, לפי זה, היהדות לסמוך רק על המזון התרבותי הכללי, שאין בקרבו אותם החלקים שגופה הרוחני נבנה מהם. במה שבבחינה עיקרית הוא שונה מרוח כל העמים, לא נשלל בזה בשום אופן את אותו הצד האנושי, שבו הוא שוה לכל האדם, ומצדו היא זקוקה גם לכלכלה תרבותית לצדה הרוחני ככל המזון הרוחני אשר לכל האדם במקצוע זה. אבל כלכול זה לא יפטר אותה ממזונה המיוחד לה.

ואם תראה, שיבוא איזה רוח זר להעתיק אותה ממקור חייה המיוחדים ולהטותה לצד הספוק רק בכלכלה הכללית, ומכל שכן אם בשלילה תקיפה ומכרחת ישלול אותו הרוח את מזונה, המיוחד להחזיק את רוחה ולפרנס את יסוד קיומה, תדע כי אויב נצב לה, ובכל עז כחה הפנימי תעמוד על נפשה.

הטוב האלהי בקרבה ובעולם, שיגלה על-ידי ישיבתה השלמה בארצה, זאת היא תכונתה האידיאלית. היצירה החפשית והמדע ההולך ואור הנם לה סניפים נכבדים לתכונתה האידיאלית הזאת, אבל גם שני אלה לא יוכלו לבא בה למרומי גבהם כי-אם כשישתמר רוחה העליון בקרבה על-פי טבעה המיוחד, המרומם מכל יצירה אנושית ומכל מדע וחזון לב, כגבוה שמים מארץ וכגבוה מחשבות אלהים ודרכיו ממחשבות בני אדם ודרכיהם.

כשישתמר בקרבה התכסיס המביא את טבע הרוח להבריא על-פי תכונתה, שהם ארחות היהדות שבחיים, באומה בכללה

spirit, intellect, and action, not only in the life of every individual but also, and especially, in the life of the entire nation.

There are in the world pious men, philosophers, holy men, men of God, but in the world there is not a nation – besides Israel – whose essential soul cannot be whole other than by the purpose of the sublime divine idea in the world.

It must have a spirit different from the spirits of all the peoples under the skies – also a special nourishment, fitting for it, which supports it, enhances its strength, and grants its existence.

Therefore, Judaism cannot rely only on the general diet of civilization, which lacks those elements from which its spiritual body is built. By saying that in a major aspect Judaism is different from the spirit of all the nations, we do not negate in any way the human side, in which it is the same as all humanity, whereby it requires also the nourishment of civilization for its spiritual side, all the spiritual food of any human. But this nourishment will not exempt it of its special diet.

If Judaism should see that there comes along some foreign wind to remove her from her unique life-source and turn her exclusively to the general nourishment; all the more so, if with coercive force that wind negates her special diet necessary to sustain her spirit and support the foundation of her existence – she will know that an enemy has arisen against her, and with all the might of her inner strength she will defend herself.

The divine good in her midst and in the world, which will be revealed through her complete dwelling in her land, is her ideal character. Free creation and progressive science are worthy adjuncts to this ideal character, but both of these will be capable of reaching in her their heights only if her sublime spirit is preserved in her midst according to her unique nature, which is beyond any human creation, science, or vision – as heaven is loftier than earth, and the thoughts of God and His ways loftier than the thoughts of men and their ways.

באופן רשמי ובכל צביון של פומבי וביחידים לפי האופי היותר אפשרי להקלט בחנוכם ובדעותיהם אז ימצאו להם היצירה והמדע החפשי כר נרחב ובטוח בקרבה. וכל זמן שהיא בטוחה בכלכלתה המיוחדת תדע בטח כי תשוב לה לברכה גם הכלכלה הכללית, שהיא צריכה לה לא פחות מכל עם, ואולי עוד יותר לפי מדת עלויה הרוחני.

כשבאים נמהרי לב ומזלזלים ברוחה, ובועטים ברגל זדון בתכסיסי חייה, היא מתחלחלת ויודעת כי עת צרה היא לה.

השאלה על דבר המהות והערך של ההכרה הטבעית של נמוק הצער הזה, כמובן, לא תוכל להפתר מן ההמון המרגיש כי-אם מאנשי לב המבינים אל תכן החזון. היא עורגת למלוי אָפיה, המלוי הזה צריך הוא גם ליצירה חפשית ולמדע במובן היותר מלא, ועם זה היא רואה שהמהרסים הללו, שנעשו לה כזרים, גורמים לה, שהיא מוכרחת כדי להגן על רוחה המיוחד, לסתום חלונות נגד ההארה החיצונה של יצירה ומדע שאינה מיוחדת בבירור גמור לרוחה פנימה, מפני שבשם יצירה ומדע זה באים הלוחמים הללו למחוק את דמותה.

ואם גם נאמר שלא תוכל לנחול נצחון מוחלט בדרך זה של השמור המצומצם בלבדו, הלא "כל אשר לאיש יתן בעד נפשו". אך אותם שהם באמת מלאים רוח אמץ בעת משבר כזאת צריכים הם להכריז ולפרש, שתכסיסי החיים הקדושים, התורה והמצוה, שהם מלאים מרוח האומה ואוצרים בקרבם את כח חיה בצביונה המיוחד, הם הם הבסיס היותר מובטח גם לחופש היצירה והמדע וגם להפרחת האומה והכרת אידיאליה, תחיתה ובנינה.

If there will be preserved in her midst the system that promotes the health of her natural spirit, namely the ways of Judaism in life, in the nation at large, officially and publicly, and among individuals to the maximum that their education and psyches allow – then creativity and free science will find in her midst a broad and secure workspace. As long as she can be sure of her special nourishment, she rests assured that she will also derive blessing from the general nourishment, which she needs no less than any people, and maybe more, proportionate to her spiritual excellence.

When rash persons come and make light of her spirit, and maliciously kick her life-system, she shudders and knows that it is a time of trouble.

The question as to the essence and value of the natural consciousness of this source of pain understandably cannot be solved by the feeling mass but rather by men of heart who understand the content of this spectacle. The nation longs for the fulfillment of its character. This fulfillment requires also free creativity and science in its fullest sense. However, the nation sees that these destroyers, who have become strangers to her, force her to protect her unique spirit, to stop up windows against the outer illumination of creativity and science that is not thoroughly clarified for her inner spirit, for in the name of this creativity and science these fighters come to erase her image.

Even if we say that she cannot be totally victorious in this way of narrow guarding, "all that a man has he will give for his soul."[11] But those who are truly full of courage at this time of crisis must announce and explain that the system of holy living, the Torah and the Commandment, which are full of the spirit of the nation and store within them her unique life-force, are the surest basis for free creativity and science,[12] also for the blossoming of the nation and consciousness of her ideals, her renascence and upbuilding.

ג

כשהחיים פורחים, כשיש להם גלויי היצירה והמדע הראויים, אי-אפשר כלל שהדעות תהיינה קבועות רק על-פי מטבע אחת וסגנון אחד. סדורי הצביון שבהם הולכים תמיד ממטה למעלה, ממלוי של חיים במדה מועטת למלוי חיים במדה מרובה, מזהר קלוש לזהר עז ומקרין.

אבל כל זה הוא כשיש להם, עם היצירה והמדע החפשים, הבסיס היסודי של רוח האומה היחידי, של השאיפה אל הטוב האלהי המונח בטבע נשמתה.

אירופא נתיאשה בצדק מאלהים, אשר לא ידעתו מעולם. יחידי האנושיות הסתגלו אל הטוב העליון, אבל לא אומה שלמה. איך עורגים אל הטוב, אל הכל, לא תוכל כל אומה ולשון להבין, וקל-וחומר שלא תוכל להטביע בזה את החותם של יסוד קיומה. על כן כשגברה בימינו הלאומיות וחדרה אל תוך מערכת הפלוסופיה, הוכרחה האחרונה להעמיד סמן שאלה גדול על כל התוכן של המוסר המוחלט, הבא באמת לאירופא רק בשאלה מאת היהדות, וככל זמורת זר לא יוכל עדיין להקלט ברוחה. אותנו, אם נהיה מה שהננו, אם לא נתגבר להתעטף בשמלת זרים, אין שאלת המוסר דוקרת כלל. הננו חשים בקרבנו כולנו, כללות אומתנו, שהטוב המוחלט, הטוב אל הכל, לזאת ראוי לכסוף, ועל יסוד זה ראוי ליסד ממלכה ולהנהיג פוליטיקה, ואנו רואים מבשרנו שהטוב המוחלט הוא הטוב האלהי הנצחי שבמציאות כולה, והננו שואפים תמיד לצאת בעקבותיו במובן לאומי וכללי. על כן האהבה האלהית והדבקות באלהים היא לנו דבר עצמי אשר לא יוכל להמחק ולהשתנות.

3

Ethics: Imposed and Natural

European nationalist philosophy rejects foreign Judaic ethical influence. In Israel, ethics are natural. Exile purified this nature of Israel. Through the renascence, the disembodied natural spirit will concretize. The connection of past and future.

When life flourishes, when it has the worthy revelations of creation and science, it is totally impossible that opinions should be fixed according to a single stamp, a single style. The order of life's character always goes from lower to higher, from lesser life-content to higher life-content, from a weak glow to a powerful, brilliant glow.

But all this is when life has, together with free creativity and science, the basic foundation of the singular spirit of the nation, the aspiration to the divine good that is lodged in the nature of its soul.

Europe rightly gave up on God, Whom she never knew. Individual members of humanity adapted to the sublime good, but not an entire nation. No nation or tongue could understand how to aspire to the Good, the All, let alone how to impress this seal upon the foundation of its existence. Therefore, when in our day nationalism grew strong and penetrated the system of philosophy, the latter was forced to place a big question mark over all the content of absolute ethics, which truly came to Europe only on loan from Judaism, and as any foreign implant, still cannot be absorbed in its spirit.[13] The question of ethics does not prick us at all if we will be what we are, if we will not force ourselves[14] to be cloaked in foreign clothing. We feel within all of us, our total nation, that the absolute good, the good for all, is that for which we should yearn, and upon this foundation it is worthy to found a kingdom and conduct politics. We see from our flesh that the absolute good is the eternal, divine good that is in all of existence, and we yearn constantly to follow in its tracks in the national and universal sense. Therefore, love of God and cleaving to God is for us something essential that cannot be erased or altered.

לא היינו יכולים לעמוד נגד הזרמים הכלליים של העולם, שאין להם ביסודם כי־אם האהבה העצמית הגסה, וכאשר התהלכנו עם הלאומים שכנינו קלטנו אל קרבנו את רוחם הזר, אשר לא היה יכול להמזג בנו והיה בעוכרינו. והנה נצטרפנו בכור עוני, עברו עלינו שנות אלפים שלא היה לנו מצד כללות האומה עסק עם דברים חמריים, היינו אומה פורחת באויר וחלמנו רק על דבר מלכות שמים, על דבר הטוב האלהי המוחלט. מצב משונה זה היה לנו לרפואה יפה: הוקלטה בקרבנו פנימה השאיפה הטבעית לנו על דבר הטוב האלהי הכללי.

אבל עכשיו שוב אנו קרואים לגשמה בחיים - זהו דבר התחיה. אם חלקים רבים מהסתעפות חזיונותינו יתקטנו בכמותם בהפגשם עם המציאות, בראשית דרכנו, אין רע. המציאות אין לה כנפים מהירים כאלה אשר לחזיון.

התחיה צוברת את כל אידיאלינו הנצחיים וגונזתם בהתחלתה במעשים קטנים, בהשתדלות מתנחלת לדורות לשוב אל הארץ, אל המקום שזכיותינו וסגולותינו ממתינות לנו, בהתיחסות של כבוד לכל אוצרנו בעבר ורוח נשא לקראת התרוממות האומה בעתיד, ההולך ומתעלה על־פי חפצנו ועבודתנו. החבה ההסתורית לעם ולארץ מוכרחת להתפרנס מהאמונות והדעות של העבר, אמנם כל זמן שמתעלה שאיפת רוחנו מתגדל בנו אור העבר, וקל־וחומר שלא יתקטן, לא יסוף, ולעד לא תחזור בקרבנו הדעה האלהית למין מיכניקה טבעית עורת־חרשת, אסורה בדעות עקרות, שאין להן מה להפרות ומה להחיות, כי־אם "ילכו מחיל אל חיל יראה אל אלהים בציון". ואם גם נדמה בכהות עין שהעבר הוא, לפי עילוינו העתיד, מעורפל, יזרח עליו האור ויזהר ויוציא אל הפועל את גניזותיו. "אשים מחשך לפניהם לאור ומעקשים למישור, אלה

We could not stand up to the general currents of the world, which have as their basis naught but coarse self-love, and when we interacted with our neighboring nations, we absorbed into our midst their foreign spirit, which could not be assimilated in us and proved our adversary. Behold we have been purified in the smelting pot of poverty; there passed over us two thousand years during which, as a nation, we had no truck with material things; we were a nation floating in air, and we dreamt only of the kingdom of heaven, of the absolute, divine good. This strange situation was for us an elixir: Our natural longing for the overall, divine good was interiorized within us.

But now once again, we are called to materialize the longing in life – this is the word of the renascence. If many portions of the branching[15] of our visions will be quantitatively reduced upon encountering reality, at the beginning of our way, it is not bad. Reality does not have such fleet wings as vision.

The renascence accumulates all our eternal ideals and hides them at its beginning in small deeds, in the inherited attempt of generations to return to the Land, to the place where our rights and gifts await us; in a respectful relating to all our past heritage and a lofty spirit toward the elevation of the nation in the future, which ascends according to our desire and work. The historic love for People and Land must be nourished by the beliefs and opinions of the past. Truly, as long as our spiritual aspiration ascends, the light of the past waxes in us – certainly it will not be diminished or cease. Never will the knowledge of God become in our midst a sort of natural mechanism, blind and deaf, bound by sterile opinions, which can neither fructify nor vivify. Rather, *they will go from strength to strength, it will be seen to God in Zion.*[16] Even if it should appear superficially that the past is befogged, in relation to our future ascendance – the light will shine upon it so it will glow and actualize all its hidden treasures. *I will place darkness as light before them, and crookedness as straightness, these things I wrought and will not abandon.*[17] – "I wrought them already for Rabbi Akiva and his companions."[18] If the personal relation of every individual – in all the

הדברים עשיתים ולא עזבתים" - "עשיתים כבר לרבי עקיבא וחבריו". אם היחש האישי, של כל פרט בכל דרכי החיים, במלואם ובטובם, בכל עדינותם ומתקם, בכל חום עדנת אהבתם ורעם עז גבורתם, אל הרוח הלאומי הכללי, השואף רק אל הטוב האלהי בכלל, בכל ועל כל, ואתו אל כל ארחות חייו ותכסיסיהם, לא פותח עדיין - ילך הלוך והתפתח לפי תגבורת רוח עמנו, וכשיגיע בזה למדה זו שיהיה קולו נשמע בעולם המדיני, כשם שהוא נשמע בעולם המוסר והאלהות, אז יגלה את עצמו וכחו.

ד

הסבלנות, הנדרשת מאד לקבוץ אורגני אנושי, מדת החסד והענוה, הממתקת את כל הדינים ובונה את העולם בשכלולו, צריכה היא לטיפוחה למדת החסידות הגדולה, היוצאת מתוך בינה אלהית עליונה ותכופה. דוקה על-ידי מה שימצאו בקרב האומה חסידי עליון, חסידים עליונים מאד, שהבינה האלהית והחיים האלהיים ממלאים את כל הויתם, בטוחה היא אז האומה בכחה הרוחני האצור ביחידיה אלה, ועל סמך זה יכולה היא לשים עין פקוחה ולב נכון לכל צרכיה המעשיים, בלי כל חרדה פנימית, שמא יתיבש לשדה ויחרב מעין רוחניותה, הנותן לה את כח נשמתה והמהוה את אידיאליה, שעושים אותה לעם ולהטיבה מיוחדת.

ביחוד באומתנו, אשר הרוחניות העליונה של האידיאלוגיה שהיא הרבה הרבה למעלה מכל עולם ההוה הוא בסיס נשמתה, יש אשר מכל תנועה של חופש חמרי ושל התמכרות לעבודה בענינים חמריים, מעשיים וחברתיים, נכנס בה מיד רטט פנימי שמא הטרדה המעשית תמעט את מעינה, שמא "כל מה שיוסיף

ways of life, in their fullness and goodness, with all their delicacy and sweetness, all the warmth of their love and thunder of their strength – toward the general, national spirit, which aspires only to the general, divine good, in all and over all, and with it, to all the ways of its life and their trappings, has not developed yet – it will gradually develop in consonance with the reinforcement of our people's spirit, and when it reaches the degree that its voice will be heard in the diplomatic world, just as it is heard in the world of ethics and divinity, then it will reveal itself and its strength.

4

Kehunah: The Spiritual Elite

*The existence of pietists allows the rest of the nation to focus on the material. Mediocre spirituality allows only halfhearted attention to the material; great spirituality permits concerted material effort. Great spiritual personalities are not depressed by the material achievement of the nation. The institution of priesthood (*kehunah*).*

Tolerance, so necessary for an organic human collective, the attribute of kindness and humility, which sweetens all the judgments and builds the world in perfection – requires for its development great piety, derived from a constant, sublime, divine understanding. Specifically by the fact that there are found in the nation sublime pietists, very sublime indeed, whose entire existence is permeated by divine understanding and godly living, the nation is confident of its spiritual power stored in these individuals. Thus assured, she may attend to all her material needs, without any inner anxiety lest her sap dry up and the fount of her spirituality – which gives her the strength of soul and comprises her ideals, which in turn make her a people and a distinct unit – go dry.

Especially in our nation – where the sublime spirituality of the ideology that is so much higher than all the present world, is the basis of her soul – it may occur that from every movement of material freedom and of compulsion to work in material, practical and social

הישוב תקון, יוסיף השכל חורבן", ומתוך כך היא עושה את פעולותיה הכלליות המעשיות במחצית אנרגיה, והרי הרוחניות מתטרפת מפני הסבוך החמרי, והחמריות מתחלשת מפני העירוב הרוחני הנדחק אל תוכה. על כן היא צריכה להעמיד חסידים גדולים, המיוחדים בגדולת הדעה, המבצרים את המעמד הרוחני של כללות האומה בקרבם פנימה. הם, העליונים הללו, יודעים, שאוצר רוח האומה הוא בקרבם, על כן אינם חרדים כלל על מעוט המבוע הרוחני של כללות האומה מפני הטרדה של העבודות המעשיות. הרוחניות החיובית כבר היא מתפלשת באומה מאליה, על-פי סגולתה הפנימית, על-ידי הארת אלה היחידים, שהם שלוחי צבור, ונושאים הם בלבבם את אוצר הרוחניות המחיה של כל העם. הם מכירים כי סגולתם העליונה היא האוצר הקבוצי של כללות האומה, והאומה מכרת בהם את המקום המכובד לנכסיה היותר יקרים, ועל כן היא מכבדתם ומתיראה מהם יראת הרוממות. ברית אלהים בארץ היא גלויה דוקא על-ידי עבדי אלהים העליונים, והגבורה החמרית הולכת ועושה את דרכה ואת סדריה, בטוחה היא שלא תחלל את מעין קדשה, כי ישנם עמה שומרי חומתה העליונה. אז הסבלנות מתפתחת והחיים המעשיים פורחים. וגם הדבורים האחדים היוצאים לפעמים מפיות של קדושים, נותנים מזון בשפע רב יותר מהמון דרשות וספרים ארוכים בינונים. זהו המצב המאושר שעמנו צריך לשאוף אליו ולדאוג להקימו בתנועת תחיתו על אדמתו.

הכהונה, האמצעות בין האדם לאלהים על-ידי הבחירים היותר עליונים שבאדם, איננה אמצעות כי-אם תכיפה הגונה. כשהאדם הפרטי מתקרב לאלהים איננו מתקרב על-ידי כחותיו הפחותים, על-ידי נטיותיו השפלות, כי-אם על-ידי העליונות שבקרבו, והצד

affairs, there is triggered in her immediately an inner shudder lest the practical preoccupation lessen her fount, lest "the more the habitation becomes established, the mind is destroyed."[19] Therefore she performs her general, practical deeds with only half energy; the spirituality is disoriented as a result of the material complication, and the material is weakened because of the admixture of spirituality forced into it. Therefore, the nation must produce great saints, special in greatness of knowledge, who fortify within their midst the spiritual state of the total nation. They, these lofty ones, know that the treasure of the spirit of the nation is within them. Therefore, they are not at all anxious concerning the reduced spiritual fount of the total nation as a result of preoccupation with practical works. The necessary spirituality automatically penetrates the nation, according to its inner gift, through the illumination of these individuals, who are public servants, and carry in their hearts the treasure of spirituality that vivifies the entire people. They recognize that their sublime gift is the collective treasure of the total nation, and the nation recognizes in them the honored repository of its most precious assets, and therefore respects them and holds them in reverent awe. The covenant of God in the Land is revealed precisely through these sublime servants of God, and the material power makes its way and its arrangements, assured that it will not desecrate its fountain of holiness, for it has guardians of its supernal wall.[20] Then tolerance develops and material life blossoms. Even the few talks that issue at times from the mouths of the holy, provide more abundant food than a multitude of long, mediocre sermons and books. This is the fortunate state to which our people must aspire and be concerned to establish in its movement of renascence upon its soil.

The priesthood, the intermediary between man and God via the most elect of humanity, is not an intermediary but rather an immediacy. When the private man approaches God, he does not approach through his base drives, through his lowly inclinations, but rather through the highest ones in his midst, and his sublime side draws everything to the side of clear, godly life. So too the national and human organ is

העליון שבו ממשיך את הכל לצד החיים הבהירים האלהיים. כן גם האורגן הלאומי, וגם האנושי, איננו ראוי ואיננו יכול להתקרב אל האלהים בקטנו, בכחותיו הדלים, בהרגשותיו המהוממות ומטורפות בין גלי חיי החושים הטורפים אותו. אור האלהים של הקטנים מתקטן, ועל-ידי השפעתו החוזרת מתקטן העולם כולו ומתדלדל. לכן מאציל האדם חלק עליון מקרבו, מקרב קבוציו, לשם התקרבותו כולו לאלהים. הכהן החסיד העליוני, המלא חסד ודעה עליונה, הוא יודע את האלהים באמת, ועל סמך דעתו והרגשתו העליונה נסמך הוא העם כולו, בעתים שזרם החיים השלם מאחד את העם עם העליונים שבבניו. הוא נסמך אז בחילם ומאזין את שיחם, באמונה ברורה המתבררת לו בכח כללי, בהרגשה בהירה ובהכרה כוללת המתנשאת לפעמים עד כדי פתוח של חכמה, ספרות ושירה, הוא מתיחש אל גדוליו ומתגאה בגדלם, מתברך בברכתם ומתקדש בקדושתם, ומתמלא חיל לעבודתו החמרית, החברתית והמדינית, ומלא עוז ואומץ הולך הוא את דרכו, יודע הוא ברור שאלהי אמן עמו.

הנטיה ליסוד הכהונה היא נטיה קבועה באדם, נובעת היא ממעמקי הרגשתו הפנימית. רק על-ידי פתוח ארוך תגלה לפנינו בכל אורה, ואנחנו, כדרכנו שלא להתירא מדרך ארוכה, הננו הולכים וסוללים לאטנו את הדרך הזה אשר החלונו מימות עולם שלנו לסלול אותו. אין אנו עוזבים את זכר הכהונה, אין אנו חודלים מלצפות לשלמותה, אף על-פי שסבלנו הרבה ממנה קודם שבאה לידי ברורה הגמור, אבל ידענו שגם את הטוב קבלנו ממנה ועוד נקבל. לעשות את האומה כולה כהנת, בלא הדרגה, כולה חכמה, נזירה ויודעת אלהים, בפרטיה על דעת עצמם, זה אי אפשר כעת לפי עולם המבונה באותן התכונות שאנו מוצאים בהן את עולמנו. על כן לרוח אלהים הכללי אשר על כללות האומה עלינו לשאף

not worthy to, and cannot, draw close to God in its smallness, with its meager powers, with its emotions dulled and torn between the waves of sensate life. The light of God of the small becomes smaller, and through its refraction, the entire world grows small and impoverished. Therefore Man sets aside a sublime portion from his midst, from the midst of his collectives, so that all of him may approach God. The priest, the sublime saint, full of kindness and superb knowledge, truly knows God, and on his knowledge and lofty emotion, the entire people is based, at times when the whole current of life unites the people with the highest of its sons. The people is supported by their [i.e., the priests'] strength and listens to their conversation. With clear faith, clarified by a universal power, with clear emotion and universal consciousness that ascends at times to the point where it develops into wisdom, literature, and song, the people relates to its great men and is proud of their greatness, is blessed by their blessing and sanctified by their holiness, and fills with power for its [i.e., the people's] material, social, and political endeavor. Filled with strength and courage, the people goes on its way, knowing clearly that faithful God is with it.

The inclination for founding the priesthood is a set fixture in Man, flowing from the depths of his inner feeling. Only through a protracted development will it be revealed to us in all of its light, and we, accustomed not to fear a long road, gradually pave this way that we began to pave as of yore. We do not abandon the remembrance of the *kehunah* (priesthood); we do not cease to look forward to its completion. Even though we suffered much from it[21] before it reached its final clarification, we knew that the good too we received and shall yet receive from it. To make the nation entirely priestly, without gradation; entirely wise, ascetic, and God-conscious on the individual level – this is presently impossible in the characteriological state in which we find our world. Therefore, we must now aspire to the general spirit of God that is upon the total nation. This will be revealed in the nation's finest limbs, just as the most rarefied emotions of Man are revealed by the highest limbs of the individual organisms.

עתה, וזה יתגלה באבריה היותר מעולים, כמו שההרגשות היותר אציליות שבאדם מתגלות הן על-ידי האברים היותר עליונים שבאורגני היחידים.

הבו אומץ לדעה העליונה, לחסידות האלהית הרדיקלית הרוממה ותנו בזה יד לסבלנות ולענוה, לגבורה ולעבודה מעשית, חברתית, מדינית, חפשית, שתתהלך ברחבה בישראל ותתבלט יפה בכל צביוני חייה בארץ ישראל, ההולכת ופורחת ומצפה לתחיה מעשית ולישועה מורגשת קרובה.

ה

דרכנו בחיים הלאומיים וצדודם כלפי היחש האנושי הכללי ארוכה היא מאד. ארוכים הם חיינו וארוכים הם, על כן, דרכינו. גדולים אנחנו וגדולות הנה משוגותינו ובשביל כך גדולות הן צרותינו, וגדולים גם תנחומותינו.

טעות יסודית היא החזרה מכל היתרון שלנו, החדלון מההכרה של "אתה בחרתנו". לא רק משונים אנחנו מכל העמים, משונים ונבדלים בחיים הסתוריים מצוינים, שאין דוגמתם בכל עם ולשון, כי-אם גם מעולים וגדולים מאד מכל עם. אם נדע את גדולתנו אז יודעים אנו את עצמנו, ואם נשכח את גדלנו אנו שוכחים את עצמנו, ועם שישכח את עצמו בודאי הוא קטן ושפל. רק בשכחת עצמנו הננו נשארים קטנים ושפלים, ושכחת עצמנו היא שכחת גדולתנו. נשמתנו מקפת עולם ומלאו ומצגת אותו על בסיס אחדותו העליון, ומשום כך היא בקרבה תמה וכוללת, ואין בה כלל אותם הנגודים וההרכבות השונים, הרגילים בנשמות עם ולשון. גוי אחד אנחנו, אחד כיחידו של עולם. זהו עומק טבענו הרוחני שיש

Give strength to sublime knowledge, to exalted, radical,[22] godly saintliness, and thus give a hand to tolerance and humility, to strength and to practical, social, political, free work, which will fan out in Israel and be pronounced in all its living dimensions in the Land of Israel, which flourishes and awaits practical renascence and imminent, felt salvation.

5

The Architecture of Future Judaism

The implications of recognizing ourselves as "the Chosen People." Israel, which bestowed ethics on the world, will now bestow enjoyment and vivacity as well. There must be an ideal higher than socialism. The Israelite collective gives vent to godliness. The commandments will be rekindled with life. The present is informed by past and future. Full-bodied Israelite life: Land, Temple, Kingdom, Prophecy. The relation between present and future. The commandments dependent on the Land: the sabbatical year and tithes. Their present observance is education for the future. The power of the mitsvot *to move the People into the future. The experiential element of tithing: exposure to the priests* (kohanim) *and Levites. The longing for Kingdom and Temple, Priesthood and Prophecy. The phony sophistication of Western civilization is as nothing compared to the innocence of humanity's childhood – Israel.*

Our way in national life and its orientation vis-à-vis the general human relation is very long. Our life is long, and therefore, our ways are long. We are great and great are our mistakes and therefore great are our troubles, but great also are our comforts.

A fundamental error is the turning back from all of our advantage, the cessation of the recognition that "You have chosen us." Not only are we different from all the peoples, distinguished by historical life that has no comparison among other peoples and tongues, but we are also exalted and much greater than any people. If we know our greatness, then we know ourselves, and if we forget our greatness, then we forget ourselves, and a people that forgets itself, certainly is small and lowly. Only when we forget ourselves do we remain small and low, and the forgetting of ourselves is the forgetting of our greatness.

בנו בכח, והדרך ההיסתורי שלנו ההולך את מהלכו בדרכים שונים, בדרכי אורה העוברות בין הררי חושך וצלמות, הוא מדריך אותנו להוציא את עומק טבע הויתנו מן הכח אל הפועל. כל הדברים הקטנים, הנדרשים לכל עם ולשון בעצם ענינם, הנם טבועים בנו במטבע הגדולה של כללותנו. אי-אפשר הוא לנו לקצוץ ענף אחד מעץ חיינו הגדול והענף ולתת לו מהלך ויניקה בפני עצמו. כל היש שבנו יתעורר ויתנגד על זה במלא עז כחו הפנימי והרגשת עצמיותו. הדרך הארוכה שואפת להקמה גמורה לתחיה אותנו ואת כל אשר לנו, צרור לא יפול ארץ, קו אחד מקוי קלסתר פני לאומנו לא נתן למחוק. הננו חזקים מרוח הזמנים, איתנים מכל איתני תבל. הננו שואפים לקום לתחיה באותו הגודל של אבותינו, ולהיות עוד גדולים ונשאים מהם. מוסר השפענו רב בעולם, והננו נכונים להשפיע עמו גם כן עונג וחיים רעננים. את האנושיות כולה הננו מקפלים ברוחנו בגלוי, ואת כל המציאות כולה במצפוננו, וכל מה שיש עמנו, ושהיה חי מאז בקרבנו, הכל יהיה מלא וחי, דבר לא יעדר. רוחנו איננו ירא מפני הזמנים; הוא יוצר את הזמנים ומטביע עליהם את צורתו. כח היצירה שלנו מטביע את הרוחניות היותר עליונה, בחומר ריאלי מעשי, שכל מה שתגדל ההתפתחות יגדל כשרון היצירה והצד האומנתי הנפלא הנותן חיים לעולם, בהגלימו את כל העליוניות שבמחשבה ושאיפה - בפעולות מעשיות מוחשות ומוגלמות, שבהן הוא מחיה אותה ומשליטה במציאות. וזה יקום עוד לתחיה בכל מלואו בתחיתנו השלמה.

חיים וסואנים הם לשעתם החיים החברתיים, אבל מה חדל מה קטן ודל הוא חייהם, מה גדולה היא הרקניות הנשארת בלב אחרי כל ההתרגשות הרבה של המלחמות והמהומות, כשאין בהן תכלית נצחית כי-אם חיים עוברים של קבוצות יחידים. גם הערך של התעוררויות חברתיות כוללות, ביחוד כשבאות בשאון ובהתפעלות

Our soul encompasses the world and its fullness[23] and presents it on the foundation of its sublime unity, and therefore inwardly our soul is perfect and universal, and not fraught with the various conflicts and complexities usual in the souls of a people or tongue. We are one nation, one as the unity of the world.[24] This is the depth of our spiritual nature that we possess in potential, and our historic way – which proceeds in various ways, in ways of light passing through mountains of darkness and the shadow of death – guides us to actualize the depth of our existential nature. All the small things that every people and tongue require, are stamped in us with the great stamp of our totality. It is impossible for us to cut off one branch from our great, sprawling tree of life and give it separate nourishment. All of our existence would be aroused and opposed to this with the fullness of its inner strength and self-awareness. The long way aspires to full renascence of our selves and all that which is ours. Not a stone will fall to the ground, not one line of our national face can be erased. We are stronger than the spirit of the times, mightier than all the mighty of the earth. We aspire to be reborn with all the stature of our fathers, and to be even greater and higher than them. We bestowed much ethics on the world, and we are ready to bestow with it enjoyment and vivacity as well.[25] All of humanity we visibly enfold in our spirit and all of existence in our conscience, and all that we have, and which always lived in our midst, all will be full and live – nothing will be missing. Our spirit does not fear the times; it creates the times and impresses upon them its form. Our creative power imprints the highest spirituality in practical, real[26] matter. The more evolved it becomes, the greater will become the creative ability and the artistic side that gives life to the world, by embodying all the sublimity of thought and aspiration in sensate, concrete actions, whereby the sublimity is vivified and rules existence. This will be reborn in its fullness with our complete renascence.

Social life at the time is vibrant, but how puny and impoverished is this life, how great the vapidity that remains in the heart after all the emotionality of the wars and turmoil, when they have no eternal

המלהבת את הלב ומקדרת את הדעה, לא יגדל הרבה מזה. אם אין תכלית עצמית נצחית אידיאלית, שתוכל להעלות את הכל לכלל הצורות היותר חשובות שיש כח בהגיון ורגש עליון לתן להם, אז כל התנועות אינן חשובות כלום ואינן יכולות להחזיק מעמד לאורך ימים.

אבל אנחנו שבים אל המגמה האלהית, אל הטוב הכללי המקיף את כל ומתגלה בהשלמתו של כל פרט ושל כל קבוץ, אשר רק אותו הקבוץ האנושי שיוכל להביע את זאת ממלא הפה של כל פנות נשמתו, ביותר בליטה ופתות, הוא הוא היותר מתקרב אל השלמות והבטחה בהמשכת מציאותו והיכול לתן לעניניו צורה חשובה, שתשאר חשובה לעד, לא רק במעמד של תבערת ההרגשות. את אשר לא יוכל להאמר בכל שפה ולשון, יאמר ויובע בכל תקפו במשטר האלהי החובק כל והנצב לעד.

אמנם בשעת ירידתנו כהים הם נצוצי האורה החיים ביחוד בזכרונות המתגלמים בחיי האומה המסרתיים, בכל המצות וההלכות המסתעפות מהעבר ופונות אל העתיד. אבל כח חיים אדיר יש בהם, בתנועה חרוצה, ברוח התעוררות פנימית לחפץ חיים לאומיים מלאים שלנו, יתפזר מעליהם גל האפר של טמטום הלב הצבור עליהם מחמת כשלון רוחנו ויראו הזיקוקין די נור העומדים להעשות שלהבתיה מחממת עולם ומאירה אל כל פנות.

צללי הענינים שלנו העתקות הם מהעבר הגדול, ופונות הן תמיד אל העתיד הנשגב, שהוא כל כך נשגב עד שהוא מאיר את ההוה ועושה אותו להוה מעשי מצד גדל כחו, אף על-פי שאין בו בעצמותו כי-אם עריגה וצפיה לעתיד. אמנם הכל מדוד לפי ערכו, יש עתיד שיוכל לחמם ולהאיר רק את ההוה הקרוב והסמוך ביותר, וכל מה שיגדל כחו של העבר וערכו של העתיד, כך הם יכולים לעשות את ההוה, המזריח מכחם, להוה גמור המלא חיים ותנועה

goal but rather the ephemeral life of groups of individuals. Even the value of general social awakenings, especially when they come with the hoopla and excitement that inflame the heart and heat the mind, does not exceed this by much. If there is no essential, eternal, ideal purpose, which can uplift all to the most significant forms that sublime logic and emotion can give, then all the movements are worthless and cannot survive for long.

But we return to the godly destiny, to the universal good that encompasses all and is revealed in the perfection of every individual and collective. Only the human collective that can express this good from every nook of its soul, with full expression, is the closest to perfection and its assured continued existence, and able to give its affairs an important form, which will remain important forever – not only in the state of flaming passion. That which cannot be uttered in any language, this collective will utter, and it will be expressed in all its might, in the divine order that embraces all and stands forever.

However, in our hour of descent, the sparks of light – which live especially in memories embodied in the traditional life of the nation, in all the commandments and laws that derive from the past and face the future – are obscure. Yet there is within them tremendous *élan vital.* Given an energetic movement, a spirit of inner arousal to full national life, there will be blown away from these sparks the mound of ash of apathy that has collected over them due to the failure of our spirit, and there will be seen fireworks, soon to become a divine flame warming the world and illumining all corners of the globe.

The shadows of our affairs are transferences from the great past, and they forever face the lofty future, which is so lofty that it lights up the present, making it a practical present as a result of its great power, even though essentially it is but a longing and expectation of the future. However, all is measured according to its value. There is a future that can warm and enlighten only the closest, most immediate present. The greater the power of the past and the value of the future, so their

אמיצה. גדול הוא עברנו ויותר מזה גדול הוא עתידנו, שמתבאר יפה בחפצנו בצדקת האידיאלים הגנוזים בנשמותינו. בכח הגדול הזה חיים וקימים בקרבנו ברוח חיים מלא כל רגעי ההוה, וכל הזכרונות ממלאים הם בעוז כח חיים המון מעשים רבים, כח בינה מיוחדת, כח יצירה בצביון מיוחד, השקפת עולם מסומנת, מצות, מנהגים וסדרים, וכולם מלאים לקח ולבוב, אהבה ועדן, ומשוקים מטל של חיים ושל גבורה והוד, מעדן שלנו, מגבורה שלנו, מהודנו היחידי.

הצורה התמציתית של כל סדרי חיי החברה על-פי המטבע האלהית המתאמת אל החיים, המרחבת אותם, מטהרתם ומרוממתם אל החופש ואל הרכוז של כל האמצעים העושים את החופש למתנה טובה באמת, גנוזה היא במערכה של המצות התלויות בארץ, במקדש ובממלכה השלמה הישראלית, בהם ובסדריהם, בסגולת הנבואה המיוחדת לאומה במלוי צביונה, שהיא מצפה תמיד לשיבתה אליה בצורה מאירה, שתשפיע עליה את כל הטוב של העבר, עם חדוש כח גדול לפי העתיד וחדושיו הרבים בעולם ובחיים. העתיד איננו פוסק מלתבע את תפקידו מן ההוה וההוה מתמלא ענין כפי ידיעתו שהעתיד נזקק אליו, איננו נעשה בזה רק בטל אל העתיד, כי-אם הוא מתמלא על-ידי זה בכל צביונו ועצמו, וההכללה בתוך שאיפת העתיד ורום מעמדו מוסיפה לו עדנה וגבורה חיה.

לכן מלאי חיים הם לנו הזכרונות האצורים בזכר שאנו עושים, על-פי המסורת ועל-פי תקון סופרים, על-פי קבלת אבות מקדם או על-פי שריד מעיקר חיוב דין תורה, לפי התפצלות ההכרות המתפרדות בשיטות המעשיות של חכמת ההלכה לכל המצות התלויות בארץ. מצומקים נראים לנו עתה הדברים, צורה דלה יש להם מבחוץ, אבל חיים וענין רב הם מלאים בפנים. אנו מערימים

ability to make the present, shining through their power, into a whole present, full of life and vigorous movement. Great is our past and even greater is our future, which is clarified when we desire the righteous ideals hidden in our souls. With this great power all the moments of the present live and exist in our midst with a full spirit of life, and all the memories by their might fill a multitude of deeds with vitality; infuse *mitsvot* (commandments), customs, and orders with a special power of insight, a distinctive creative ability, an outstanding world-outlook. These are all full of meaning and romance, love and ecstasy, and drenched with the dew of life, of courage and majesty, from our ecstasy, from our courage, from our singular majesty.

The quintessential form of all the arrangements of the life of the society according to the divine formula that corresponds to life – broadening life, purifying and uplifting it to freedom and to the concentration of all the media that make freedom a truly good gift – is hidden in the system of the *mitsvot* (commandments) dependent on the Land, on the Temple, and on the full Israelite kingdom, on them and on their orders, on the gift of prophecy that is specific to the nation when its character is full-bodied. The nation always awaits prophecy's return in luminous form, which will bestow on her all the good of the past, along with the renewed strength of the future and its many innovations in the world and in life. The future does not desist from demanding of the present its role, and the present becomes interesting to the degree that it knows the future is in need of it. Thus the present is not inconsequential vis-à-vis the future but rather fills up thereby with all its character and essence, and its inclusion in the aspiration of the future and its exalted height adds to it pleasure and living strength.[27]

Therefore, full of life are the memories stored in the commemoration we perform – whether it be according to tradition; according to the enactment of scribes; according to an early acceptance of ancestors; or according to the remnant of a Torah obligation – subject to the split in understandings that separate into the practical methods of [applying] the wisdom of *Halakha* (Jewish Law) to all the commandments

על שמירת השמיטה במכירה לנכרי את הקרקעות, מקיימים את נתינת המעשרות לכהן וללוי על-ידי תקון שאין בו הפסד גדול לנותן, ולא ריוח גדול למקבל, מברכים ומפרישים, ופודין את המעשר השני הראוי להאכל בקדושה בעיר המרכזית הקדושה והחיה, המקום אשר בחר ד׳, לב האומה לכל זרמי חייה, משלמים פרים שפתינו, שפך שיח תחת סדרים חיים, במשטר חי וקים, המלא הוד ויפעה, שירה וזמרה, עז וחדוה. אבל אלה הגרגרים הזעירים כח צמיחה גדול גנוז בהם, אל כל מה שהם עורגים, מכל מה שהם צומחים בעבר, ואת כל מה שהם עתידים להצמיח להבא. כל זה כלול בהם באופן טפוסי, וכן הם פועלים בחשאי על הנשמה המקימת, פועלים להלהיב בהתמדה אש קודש לאהבת הארץ באלה המניות של קדושה, ביתרון האלהי, הדתי, הלאומי והמוסרי הכלול בכל המעשים הללו, ומחנכים את העם בימי שפלותו לרוח גדלו. זאת השכילה כנסת ישראל ובניה בוניה ולא חדלה להגשים את זכרונות חייה אלה בפועל, כמה שאפשר לה בארצות נודה, ובצורה יותר נכרת ומתפשטת בשובה באיזו צורה שהיא אל מקומה, אל חבל נחלתה.

ההוד וההדר והפאר המיוחד שיש במצות התלויות בארץ, כשהן מתקימות עכשיו בארץ ישראל על ידינו, על-ידי אותו החיל החלוץ ההולך ובונה את ארץ האבות ומכין אחרית ותקוה יותר חזקה ויותר בהירה לדור יבא, מתגלה הוא לנו מתוך עז חפצנו הפנימי המפעם בקרב נשמתנו, להעמיד את צביון אומתנו על ארץ אבותנו במלא תארה, בכל שרטוטיה וקויה המשלימים את תכונתה, המגלים ומבליטים שזאת היא אומתנו אנו בערכה הרם המקורי, בגויתה, בנפשה, ברוחה ונשמתה. לזאת אנחנו שואפים לחדש עלינו ימים קדמונים, כימי עולם וכשנים קדמוניות. הנה ישננו שנת תרדמה לאומית משך גלות ארוכה וקשה מאד. כחותינו הלאומיים נשארו

dependent on the Land.[28] The things look to us now shriveled, their outer appearance is meager, but inside they are full of life and content. We circumvent the observance of *shemitah* (the sabbatical year) by selling the lands to a non-Jew; we observe the giving of tithes to the *kohen* (priest) and to the Levite by a device that inflicts no great loss on the giver, nor brings great profit to the receiver; we bless and tithe, and redeem *ma'aser sheni*[29] (the second tithe) worthy of being eaten in sanctity in the central city, holy and living, the site chosen by the Lord, the heart of the nation with all the streams of its life. *Our lips make up for bullocks*[30] – an outpouring of speech instead of living orders, a living regimen full of majesty and beauty, song and music, strength and joy. But in these minute grains great potential for growth is contained, for all that they long, from all that has grown in the past, and all that they will eventually produce. All this is contained in them in a typical way, and they silently influence the observant soul, constantly fanning a holy fire of love of the land – through these shares[31] of holiness, through the divine, religious, national and ethical superiority of these actions. They educate the people in its days of lowliness to its spirit of greatness. *Knesset Israel* (Ecclesia Israel), its sons and builders, understood this and did not cease from actualizing these memoirs, as much as was possible in the lands of its wanderings,[32] but especially upon its return in any form to its place, its inheritance.

The majesty and beauty,[33] and the special glory that there is in the *mitsvot* (commandments) dependent on the Land – when observed now in the Land of Israel by us, by that pioneering (*ḥaluts*) force building the ancestral land and preparing a more certain, clearer prospect for the coming generation – is revealed to us from the strength of our inner desire that pounds within our soul, to assert the character of our nation in our ancestral land with its full countenance, with all the contours and lines that make up its character, which stress that this is *our* nation with its original, lofty value, with its body, spirit, and soul. For this, we aspire to renew upon us early days, *as in the days of old, and as in former years.*[34] Behold, we slept a national slumber

אז בלועים בקרבנו פנימה, מבחוץ הכל נעשה מקומט מזוקן, אבל מבפנים טל החיים הולך וזורם. כשם שהמצות המעשיות בכללן בכל מלואיהן הלכו עמנו בגולה ושמרו לנו בה את לח חיינו ואת חותם רוחנו על-פי עצמותנו הפנימית, הביאו אותנו לאלה ימי התחלת תקופת ההארה לחיים של חפץ תחית האומה בארצנו, כן יביאו אותנו המצות התלויות בארץ לידי רוממות החיים שעל-פי צורתם השלמה הן נקבעו. וכל אשר נוסיף להתבונן במהותן של המצות התלויות בארץ כולן ונראה כמה רחוקות הן מאתנו, כמה חיינו צריכים להיות בתנאים יותר בריאים וחזקים עד שיהיו אלו המצות מתקימות בהם, כן יגדל בנו החשק לקים באהבה וביקר את אותו החלק שאנו יכולים לקימו בתור זכר לדבר, זכר קודש, זכרון לחיים שלמים שיבאו לנו בבא תשועה שלמה לעמנו על אדמתנו לתשועת עולמים, ואשר בקימנו אותן עכשיו הננו מעשירים את נשמת אומתנו באותה אש הקדש אשר תהיה לשלהבת הקדש מלאת החיים לעת חיה.

כשאנו מקימים עתה מצות תרומה ומעשר, גם בשעה שאין לנו כל היסודות הממשיים שמצות אלו בנויות עליהן, "לא כהן בעבודתו ולא לוי בדוכנו", הנה החזון מתיצב לפנינו והננו מתמלאים רוח שירה רוממה בתעופת נשרים לעומת האורה של הימים המאושרים המחכים לאומתנו על אדמתנו הברוכה. הנה המקדש על מכונו לגאון ולכבוד לכל הגוים והממלכות, והנה אנו נושאים ברנה אלומות ארץ חמדתנו, באים ברוח מלא חפש אמתי ובטחה טהורה אל הגרן והיקב המלאים בר ויין ולבנו שמח על טוב ארץ חמדה, והנה לפנינו מופיעים כהנים אנשי קדש משרתי מקדש ד׳ אלהי ישראל, לבם מלא אהבה וחסד, רוח הקדש שפוך על פניהם וזוכרים אנו את כל רוממות רגשי הקדש אשר מלאנו בעת ראינו את פניהם בעלותנו לרגל, בראותנו אותם בעמדם

during a long and very difficult *galut* (exile). Our national energies remained absorbed within our midst. Outside all becomes atrophied and aged,[35] but inside the dew of life continuously streams. Just as the practical *mitsvot* (commandments) in general, in their fullness, went with us in exile and preserved for us in exile our vitality and our inner, essential spirit, bringing us to these days, the beginning of the period of the resurrection of the desire of national renascence in our land, so the *mitsvot* (commandments) dependent on the Land will bring us to the upliftment of life, as they [i.e., those *mitsvot*] were determined by life's full dimension. The more we contemplate the essence of all the *mitsvot* (commandments) dependent on the Land, seeing how far they are from us, how much healthier and stronger our lives must be in order for these *mitsvot* (commandments) to be observed by us, so will the ardor grow in us to observe with love and honor that portion that we *can* observe as a commemoration, a holy commemoration, a remembrance of whole life that will come to us when complete salvation will come to our people on our soil, an eternal salvation. When we observe those *mitsvot* (commandments) now, we enrich the soul of our nation with that holy fire that will become a holy flame full of life at the time of rebirth.

When we fulfill now the *mitsvah* (commandment) of tithes, even though we do not have all the concrete foundations upon which these *mitsvot* (commandments) are constructed, "neither a *kohen* (priest) at his service nor a Levite at his song"[36] – behold this vision appears before us and we are filled with a spirit of song exalted as the flight of eagles, in view of the light of the happy days that await our nation on our blessed soil: Here is the Temple on its foundation, a pride and honor for all the nations and kingdoms, and here we carry with joy sheaves of our Land of Delight. We come with a spirit full of true freedom and pure trust to the silo and winery, full of grain and wine, and our heart is gladdened by the abundance of a Land of Delight. There appear before us priests, holy men, servants of the Temple of the Lord, God of Israel. Their hearts are full of love and kindness, the holy spirit floods their faces, and we recall the crescendo of holy feelings that filled us at the time we

לשרת בקדש בתוך מקדשנו גאון עוזנו ומחמד עינינו. כמה נהדרים ונעימים הם לנו, ועתה הנה גרננו המלא ברכת ד׳ מארץ חמדה זאת אשר הנחילנו מאבותינו, וחלקי האנשים הללו, אנשי הרוח, אתנו הם. מאושרים אנו לתן להם את תרומתם בשמחה, מוצאים אנחנו בקרבנו רגש מרומם ועולים יחד עם התרומה אל אותו הגבה הרוחני ששם אנשי קדש הללו מתעלים, ונפשנו רוויה ממגד שמים. והנה הלויים, אלה הטובים והענוגים אשר לקחו לבבנו בנועם זמרתם בקדש בהתקדש חג, כאשר עלינו לראות בהדרת כבוד מקדש אל בירושלם לראות את פני האדון ד׳ אלהי ישראל. פניהם הצוהלים ועדינים מזכירים לנו את זמרתם קדש, ואנחנו מתעדנים בנחלי עדנים רוחניים ונותנים להם בלב מלא שמחה ואושר את חלקם, את המעשר. עוד נתראה בהר ד׳ במועד הקרוב, ומה ירהב לבבנו לראות אלה כהני ד׳ ולוייו בעבודת קדשם ובשירת עוזם. ״אשרי העם שככה לו אשרי העם שד׳ אלהיו״.

לקדמוניות ולשלמות הננו מתגעגעים, והגעגועים הם געגועים אלהיים, חפץ טמיר מלא חיים עזיזים מקוריים ממקור חיי עולמים: ממלכה ומקדש, כהונה ונבואה, המטביעים את חותמם על כל קניני חיים הכוללים, שאין אנו פחותים ביחושם מכל העמים. מדה גדולה של גבורה חמרית, של מוסר אנושי, של כבוד לאומי, של עושר עממי, ושל הרחבת החיים, דורשת היא לנו תכונת חיים כאלה, שמרגליות רוחניות מצוינות ומופלאות מכל האדם אשר על פני האדמה, המצויות בנשמתנו הלאומית יכולות להיות משובצות בקרבה לשכלל את יפיה ולהוסיף לה אומץ וגבורה בפנימיותה, והוד ותפארת בחיצוניותה. האידיאלוגיה שלנו של שלמות חיינו אשר היא כה רחוקה ומופלאת, היא גם כן קרובה ומוחשה במלוא נשמתנו, כל זמן שאין אנו עסוקים להשכיחה וכל זמן שאנו שומעים

saw their faces, when we went up on pilgrimage; when we saw them standing to serve within our Temple,[37] pride of our strength and delight of our eyes. How handsome and pleasant they are to us, and now here is our silo full of the blessing of the Lord from this Land of Delight that we inherited from our fathers, and the portions of these men, men of spirit, are with us. We are happy to give to them their tithes; we find within our midst an exalted feeling and rise together with the tithe to the spiritual niveau where these holy men ascend. Our soul is drenched with the bounty of heaven. And behold the Levites, these delicate ones who captivated our hearts with their harmonious music in the holy place during the festival, when we went up to see the glorious Temple of God in Jerusalem, to behold the face of the Master, the Lord, God of Israel.[38] Their joyous, delicate faces remind us of their holy music; we float in streams of spiritual joy and give them with a happy heart their portion, the tithe. Soon we will once again meet on the Mountain of the Lord at the next festival. How proud we will be to see these *kohanim* (priests) and Levites of the Lord at their holy work and music! *Happy the people who has this; happy the people whose God is the Lord.*[39]

We long for antiquity and wholeness. The longing is a divine longing, a hidden desire full of powerful, original life from the source of the Life of the Universe: Kingdom and Temple, Priesthood and Prophecy, which impress their seal on all the general assets of life, in which regard we are not inferior to all the nations. A great measure of material strength, of humane ethics, of national honor, of public wealth, of broad life, seeks for us a quality of life, that spiritual pearls more exquisite than all men on the face of the earth, which are found in our national spirit, can be set in its midst to enhance its beauty and add to it courage and strength in its interior, and majesty and glory on its exterior. Our ideology of whole life,[40] which is so distant and amazing, is also close and felt in the fullness of our soul, as long as we do not deliberately forget it and as long as we listen to our inner voice, which pulls us to provide a place for memories that enliven it [i.e., the nation] even in its days of lowliness, when *its voice is like a spirit from the earth.*[41]

בקולנו הפנימי, המושך אותנו לתן מקום לזכרונות המחיים אותה גם בימי שפלותה, בהיות כאוב מארץ קולה.

המקדש, זהו המכון של הקולטוס הדתי, העתיק אשר יהיה חדש לעד, אשר הכה חרם את האליליות עם תועבותיה ונתן לאנושיות בסיס טהור ונשגב לחיה הרוחניים, אשר ממנו יצאה אורה וחופשה ההולכות ומתפתחות בתולדה האנושית, ומתרשלות במהלכן כפי רחוקן ממקור מוצאן, והן אמנם עתידות להתגבר לפי חזרתן אל מקור מבוען. האנושיות הבריאה, כשהיא מכרת את הוד האלהות, תשאר נכחו כגמול עלי אמו, תשכח מפני גבהו, אורו ועזו, את כל התחכמויותיה, ותדע שיקר לה רגשה הטבעי המחכימה יותר מכל חכמה, כשהוא בנוי על יסוד האיתן של טבעה הפסיכי, ומעוטר בעטרת ההכרה, המתעלה עדי עד ולעד תשאר עלומה, ומשקקת אליה את כל נשמה, ולנצח תשלח קויה להעלות את כל אל מרום עזה. את היופי והתפארת האלהי תכניס אל נשמתה, הגעגועים של יחש ושל קירוב מעשי יתגברו, וכל פנות הדעת והמוסר ישפיעו על רגש נערץ זה את אוריהם. במקום אחד במלא התבל כדאי לה לאנושיות לראות את עצמה בתומת ילדותה, בחוסן גבורת הנער ובזיו עדן של עלית הנשמה הכללית, החתומה בחותם עם-פלאות זה העתיק, ישראל השב. אין קץ לעונג השירה אשר תתחולל בכל העולם הנעור לרגלי המחזה הנשגב הזה, של התחדשות העתיקות המקורית של מקור השירה האלהית אשר בישראל במרום עזו. רק סכל ואין לב, אשר לא יוכל קולו להיות נשמע בעת תחית האורה, יוכל לחפוץ לתן כחל ושרק של התרבות החדשה הלקויה בחסר ויתיר, באיבה ותחרות ובכל חלי וקצף, על גלי ים החיים הבריאים ועתיקים הללו, המתנשאים בגאונם למרומי שמים. הכל ישמח דוקא במחזה הנאור הטבעי כמו שהוא עם כל תמימות עתיקותו, שהוא מנהיר דוקא אז את כל שלל צבעי אורותיו ומפזם בישראל ועל אדם רב.

The Temple is the foundation of the ancient religious cultus, which will forever be new, which dealt a deathblow to idolatry and all its abominations,[42] and gave humanity a sublime, pure basis for its spiritual life, from which went out light and freedom that increasingly develop in human history, slackening their pace to the degree that they become distant from their source, but which will in the future grow stronger inasmuch as they will return to their source. Healthy humanity, which recognizes the majesty of godliness, will remain opposite it as a child to its mother. Humanity will forget as a result of its height, light and strength, all of its slick sophistication,[43] and esteem its natural feeling that wisens it more than any science, when it is built upon the solid foundation of its psychic nature and adorned with the crown of consciousness, which forever ascends and will forever remain hidden, attracting to it every soul and eternally sending its rays to uplift all to its mighty height. Mankind will bring into its soul the divine beauty and glory; the longing for relation and actual proximity will grow stronger, and all the foundations of knowledge and ethics will illumine this cherished feeling. In one place on all of earth it is worthwhile that humanity view itself in the innocence of its childhood, in the strength of adolescence, and in the radiance of the universal ascendance of the soul, stamped with the seal of this ancient wonder-people, old Israel. There is no end to the joy of the song that will break out in all the world as it awakens to this exalted sight: the renewal of the original antiquity of the source of divine song that is in Israel at its mightiest. Only an unfeeling fool, whose voice cannot be heard at the time of the enlightenment, would want to apply the makeup of modern civilization – which suffers both deficiencies and excesses, envy, competition, and every sickness and malady – on these living, healthy, ancient sea-waves, which reach up to the heights of heaven.[44] All will rejoice in this enlightened, natural spectacle, precisely as it is, with all the innocence of its antiquity. Only then does it reveal its full spectrum of colors, spreading them in Israel and to greater humanity.

ו

חיים אנו עם הציורים הרוחניים שבשאיפה של נשמת האומה. כל מקום שניצוצות אור הללו גנוזים שם הננו מקושרים אליו בקשר של נשמה, של חיים, של כל הויתנו, בין שיהיה מקום זה מקום ממשי, מדת ארץ, בין שיהיו מעשים שהציורים האלה כמוסים ביסודם, בין שיהיו מחשבות ורעיונות מאיזה מין שיהיו. מי שבא לקוץ סעיפים הללו, מי שממעט את חילם, את כבודם וחשיבותם אצלנו, הרי הוא ממעט את לשד חיינו ולנגדו אנו מתקוממים בכל מלא כחנו.

בכללותה של התורה הכתובה והמסורה ובהשתרגות כל ענפיה ספון הציור הרוחני היותר עליון ומקורי של חפץ האומה, מצד מגמת חייה היותר עליונים, בצורה מאירה בכלל הבנתה והרחבתה, בהגיונותיה, בסגנוני הרצאותיה, בתוצאות השקפותיה, על ההויה, על העולם, על האדם, על היחיד, על החברה, על הטוב ועל הרע, על החיים ועל המות. כל מה שההבנה וההכרה התורית מתגלה יותר באומה, מתבססת יותר ויותר נשמתה בקרבה וכח חייה מתעלה ומתאדר. והמעשים הם הבסיסים החמריים, הנושא הממשי, שהתיאוריה הגדולה הזאת מנחת בם את אוצרותיה, וכפי אותה המדה שתתגדל ההבנה התיאורית, בגדולת ערכה, כן יוסף להתנוצץ בקרב האומה כולה האור החבוי אשר במעשים כולם ותתגלה מדת התפארת שביהדות המעשית בכחה לאלהים.

יש אשר יכשלו החיים במהלכם ולא יעצרו כח ללכת עם הציורים הרוחניים, וייעף אז הרוח השואף להגשימם במעשה. אז תולד מבוכה והדעות מתפלגות. אמיצי הרוח יאמרו: החיים הם עלולי מחלה, אבל גם עלולים לשוב אל הבריאות השלמה. וכל

6
Ideals into Action

The inviolability of the aspirations of the nation's soul. Those aspirations are contained in the Torah. The arduous task of translating the ideals into action. Coming to terms with that responsibility. The price of devaluing the ideals. A ladder between thought and action, heaven and earth.

We live with the spiritual pictures contained in the aspiration of the nation's soul. In whatever place these sparks of light are hidden, we are connected to that place by a connection of soul, of life, of all our being, whether this place be a physical place, a measure of land, whether they be deeds in whose foundation these pictures are contained, whether they be thoughts or ideas of any type. Whoever would come to cut down these branches[45], whoever would diminish their strength, their honor, and importance to us, reduces the sap of our lives and we rise up against him with all our strength.

In the totality of the written and transmitted Torah and in the intertwining of her branches, is hidden the most sublimely spiritual and original conception of the desire of the nation, the direction of its highest life, in a way that illumines through its understanding, its thoughts, the styles of its lectures, the results of its outlooks – existence,[46] world, man, individual, society, good and evil, life and death. The more Torah understanding and realization that is revealed in the nation, the more established is its soul in its midst and its *élan vital* ascends and is fortified. The deeds are the material bases, the tangible subject, in which this great theory deposits its riches: To the extent that the theory is expanded, there will shine within the entire nation the hidden light that is in all actions and there will be revealed the glory of practical Judaism in its power for God.

Sometimes life stumbles on its way and lacks the strength to go with the spiritual conceptions. Then the spirit that aspires to realize the conceptions in action will tire. Then confusion arises and opinions differ. The strong of spirit will say: "Life is prone to illness but also

אשר יחובר אל החיים יש בטחון. האידיאלים היקרים, הגנוזים בחביוני המעשים, מחויבים הם לצאת אל האור דוקא על-ידי התגלמותם במעשים. הם צריכים להאיר את כל חשכת החיים, והחשך עדנה גדול הוא ורב מאד, לא נוכל לאמר עליהם שכבר גמרו את מלאכתם, נגמרו ובאו לתעודתם. לא נעזוב את הדגל, נשא ונסבל באהבה, נגלם בפעל במעשים את המחשבה הגדולה של הנשמה הישראלית, כאשר החלה האומה לעשות מאז התחילה לראות חיים כלליים שלה. ואם הסבל כבד יותר משכבר הימים, הלא כדאית היא המגמה לשאת בעבורה עול, הלא זה כבר יצאנו מהחוג של עמים-ילדים קלי-דעת הקצים בפעולות רציניות שאין הנאתן בצדן, הננו מבוכרים בדעת ורגש אישי מלא, יודעים איך לחיות ואיך לשא במנוחת לב וחפץ כביר את עול החיים לשם מטרה גדולה, אף על-פי שעודנה כמוסה סופה להגלות.

יחד עם שאיפתנו למגמה העליונה ולהחזיק לעומתה את היסוד המעשי, אם יכשל כחנו והמשא המעשי, המחכה למלוי כח בהגלות בו ועל-ידו האור האידיאלי הגדול, יהיה במשך הזמנים כבד יותר מדאי מפני כשלונה של האומה, נתור לנו עצות נכונות על-פי רוחה של נשמת האומה עצמה, על-פי דרכה של תורה במלואה, להקל את המעמסה בסגנון כזה, שלא יחדל הציור הרוחני מפעולות שאיפתו גם רגע בגלל ההקלה המוכרחת.

כשפוגמים את הרעיון, כשמתרחקים, על-ידי השקוע בקטנות החיים הרגילים, מרוממות המחשבות העליונות, שהן מחוללות את המעשים הגדולים ושהן גנוזות בתוכם בגניזה אלהית עצומה, ממילא הולכים המעשים ונפגמים. ערכם משתפל והדרם הולך ומועם, עד שהם מתגלים בצורה קצופה המעוררת קפידה ושממון,

capable of returning to complete health." Whatever is attached to life may rest assured. The precious ideals that are hidden within the deeds must come to light precisely through their embodiment in deeds. They must illumine all the darkness of life, and the darkness is still very great. We cannot say about them that they have already finished their work and reached their destiny. We will not abandon the flag; we will bear and carry with love,[47] we will embody in action, in deeds, the great thought of the Israelite soul, just as the nation began to do from the time it first saw collective life. And if the burden prove heavier than in the past, is not the goal worthy that we carry on its account a yoke? We have already left the orbit of light-headed, juvenile nations who detest serious activities that do not provide immediate gratification. We are mature of intellect and full human feeling; we know how to live and carry with tranquility and willpower the yoke of life for the sake of a great goal,[48] which though hidden, will eventually be revealed.

Together with our aspiring to the sublime goal while strengthening its corresponding practical foundation, if our ability will fail and the practical burden, which awaits energization by revealing in it and through it the great ideal light, will with the passage of time become too heavy because of the failure of the nation, we will seek correct counsel according to the spirit of the soul of the nation itself, according to the way of Torah in its fullness, to lighten the load in such a manner that the spiritual conception will not cease the activities of its ambition for even a moment because of the necessary lightening.[49]

When we damage the idea by distancing ourselves – through immersion in the pettiness of ordinary life – from the loftiness of great thoughts, which produce great deeds, in which they [i.e., the thoughts] are hidden by a mighty, divine hiding, automatically the deeds are increasingly damaged. Their value is lowered and their splendor dulled, until they appear in an angry way that arouses picking and boredom, whereas might and beauty are the actions' natural raiment. And when the actions are damaged, concomitantly the idea recedes,

תחת שהעז וההדר הוא לבושם הטבעי להם. וכשהמעשים נפגמים לעומת זה הולך הרעיון ומתרחק, עד שהוא נהפך למין מחשבה קלושה, המעוררת גם היא בוז מכל איש מעשה מצד מרחקה מן החיים ומצד רפיון כחה לפעול עליהם.

כדי למצא תרופה לעומת מצב איום זה, לעומת מחלה כזאת, האוכלת את שתי הקצוות אשר לחיים וממילא נחר תוכם, אנו צריכים להתאמץ בכל היכולת בשמירת המעשים, לחבבם ולאמצם, אבל לא לעמוד על תחום זה בלבדו. מאומה לא נשא בעמלנו, אם לא נצרף אל רוממות המעשים את ההשבה אל תעופת הרעיון האצור וגנוז בהם. אם ישארו המעשים מצות אנשים מלומדה, לא לבד שלא יועילו אלא גם ישפילו עוד את הרעיון, וסוף שפלות הרעיון להגמר בבטול המעשים. אבל לא נבהל כלל מהמפחידים אותנו מתעופת המחשבה, האומרים שאנו מתאמרים לעלות מרומי שחקים באין סולם. לא כן, יש לנו סולם מוצב ארצה וראשו מגיע השמימה: המאור שבנשמתנו, בנשמת הכלל ובנשמת הפרט, אשר יתעורר יפה על-ידי אור גנזי תורה.

ז

ממעמקי הגניזה של הנשמה נקח את האור אשר יחיה את העם כולו, להעמידו על רגליו. כח החיים הולך הוא ומתגבר, הוא פורץ לו את נתיבותיו, אבל אנו צריכים לחקר את תכנית רוחו. השאיפה לרוח הקודש עליון, רוח הקודש המתדמה לרוח גבורים אזורי כח אלהים שהיה לנו בימים מקדם, בעת אשר הכירה האומה את עצמה בגלוי, היא מתגברת והולכת. דרך הזרמתה היא פורצת גדרים, היא מוחקת צורות של תמימות רגילה ומאבדת על-ידי זה אוצרות חיים

until it becomes a sort of feeble thought, arousing the ridicule of any practical man because of its distance from, and inability to affect life.

In order to find a cure for this fearful condition, this illness, which consumes both the extremes of life, and thereby its middle, we must observe the actions as strenuously as possible, love them and fortify them,[50] but not be restricted to this domain. We will achieve nothing by our exertion if we do not combine with the loftiness of the deeds, the return to the flight of thought contained and hidden in them.[51] If the actions will remain *mitsvot* performed by rote, not only will they not abet but they will even lower the thought, and the end of lowliness of thought will be the cessation of the actions.[52] But we shall not be frightened by those who would scare us away from the flight of the thought, who say that we attempt to ascend to the heavens without a ladder. Not so. We have a ladder resting on the earth and extending to the heavens:[53] the light in our soul, in the soul of the collective and in the soul of the individual, which will be well aroused by the light of the mysteries of Torah.

7

Giving Direction to the Light

The ancient spirit of strength that blows in our midst breaks down fences of mediocrity, to arrive at new heights of spirituality. The great light calls for vessels: Temple, Prophecy, and Kingdom. Only a clear goal can energize the Nation.

From the hidden depths of the soul, we will take the light that will vivify the entire people, putting it on its feet. The life force grows stronger, it breaks its pathways, but we must examine the plan of its spirit. The longing for sublime divine inspiration, divine inspiration that resembles the spirit of strong men[54] girded with godly strength that was ours in the early days, when the nation clearly[55] recognized itself, grows stronger. By way of its gushing, it breaks down fences, erasing forms of usual simplicity,[56] thus losing treasures of high life.[57] It would seem the resulting state is terrible, neither here nor there. But

נשגבים, ולכאורה נשאר המצב איום, קרח מכאן ומכאן. אבל אין זה כי-אם מעבר, תיכף אנו צריכים לגשת אל ההזרחה העליונה, של אור החיים הנובע ממקורו הנשא מרום מראשון, שיטביע בכחו צורה איתנה, ממולאה בגבורת קודש יותר מכל מה שהתמימות הבינונית, שאינה מואר כל צרכה מאור הקודש הטהור, יכולה לתן.

האידיאלים שבמקור ישראל הולכים ומתגלים, מחיים הם את הרוח המוכן לקבלם בעצם רעם גבורתם, והם דורשים את תפקידם לכונן עבורם כלים, כלים רבים, נשמות בריאות של דור רענן, יושב על אדמתו ואזור בגבורת ישע ימינו. המקדש, הנבואה והמלכות וכל תכסיסיהם, שולחים אלינו את קום, את אורם הזורע בארץ חיים. קרנים מידם לנו, גלי אורותיהם מכים על עפעפינו, הסגורות בכל משך זמן הגלות הממסמסת את הכל. הננו נקראים להכון לקראת האור הגדול הזה, לדעת מה אנו ומה תפקידנו, מה נשמתנו בכל איתנותה דורשת מאתנו. הרוח הגדול והנעלה, השואף לגדולי גדולות, הוא רק הוא מחזיק את החיים ואת האנושיות בהודה וגבורתה. מתאימה עם גבורת החיים המלאים, שממלאים גויות מלאות דם בריא וחיל עצום, מרץ כביר וצהלת חיים אדירה, היא רק גבורת הרוח באיתן עליונותה, הזורחת ועולה על האנושיות בכח העז של ישראל, ההולך ומתבלט בחיינו בהתפרצם עתה בזרם של הנטיה להתקוממות האומה על אדמתה ההיסתורית.

באין מטרה לגבורת החיים תלך הלך ונמוג, חילה ימעט והיא תתנון ותצעד אל הבליה, הנכונה לפניה במורד, וגבורת החיים העליונה המעוטרת בכלל, בקהל עם, היא מופעת במטרתה הנכונה לפניה בחיינו אנו, בחיים התוכיים שלנו, שבשביל כך אנו חיים וקימים, נלחמים ומנצחים.

this is only a transition. Immediately we must approach the sublime shining, the light of life flowing from its lofty source, exalted from the first,[58] which, with its force, will imprint a solid form,[59] more replete with holy strength than what mediocre simplicity – insufficiently illumined by the pure, holy light[60] – could possibly provide.[61]

The ideals at the source of Israel continue to be revealed. They enliven the spirit ready to receive them in their thundering might. They ask that their role establish for them vessels, many vessels, healthy souls of a fresh generation, dwelling on its land and girded with the strength of its salvation. Temple, Prophecy, and Kingdom, and all their infrastructures, send us their rays, their light sown in the Land of Life. They radiate to us, their light waves beat on our eyelids, closed for the duration of the exile that dissolves all. We are called to ready ourselves for this great light, to know what we are and what our duty is, what our soul with all its might asks of us. Only the great exalted spirit that aspires to greatness upholds life and humanity in its [i.e., humanity's] splendor and strength. It is only the strength of the spirit that conforms to the strength of full life, filling bodies full of healthy blood and prodigious strength, powerful energy, and *joie de vivre* – the strength of the spirit, with its sublime might, shining over humanity with the force of Israel, which manifests in our lives as they [i.e., our lives] break forth now in the stream of the movement for the nation's independence upon its historic land.

Without a goal for life's strength, the nation will continue to dissipate, its strength will lessen,[62] and it will go to waste, lying ready at the bottom. Life's supernal strength, adorning the community of the people, appears with its goal prepared before it, in our lives, in our inner lives, for which we live and exist, fight and overcome.

ח

היהדות בגולה, לולא היניקה שהיא מקבלת מטל החיים של קדושת ארץ ישראל לא היה לה בסיס מעשי בעצם, כי-אם על-ידי חזון הלב, המיוסד על ציורים של תקוה ושל הגות יקר, מצד העתיד והעבר. אמנם יש קצבה כמה כח יש בחזיון לב זה לשא עליו את משא החיים ולסול בכחו נתיבה לחיי עם, והקצבה נראה שכבר מלאה צבאה. על כן יורדת היא היהדות בגולה פלאים, ואין לה תקוה כי-אם לנטע אותה במקור חיים של חיים ממשיים, של קדושה עצמית, שאינה מצויה כי-אם בארץ ישראל. אפילו ניצוץ אחד של החיים הממשיים הללו יחיה המון גדול ורב של חיים חזוניים. החיים הממשיים של קדושת היהדות אינם מתגלים כי-אם בשיבת האומה לארצה, שהיא המסלה הסלולה לשיבתה לתחיה, וכל העליונות שברוחה ובחזון לבה יקומו ויחיו כפי אותה המדה, שהיסוד המעשי יתפוס מקום להחיות את החזון המתעלף.

כל מה שהעולם מתבסס יותר, ורוח האדם מתפתח בקרבו, מתעוררת יותר התביעה לחיות על-פי הרוח הטבעי שבקרבו, בקול יותר חזק. תביעה זו יש בה הרבה מן האמת והצדק, ושלמי הדעת צריכים לזככה ולהעמידה על מכונה. האדם הולך ומוצא את אלהים בקרבו, בנטיותיו הנכונות; ואפילו באותן הנראות בראש שהן משגות מן הדרך הטובה המוסכמת מצד ההשקפה הרגילה, יוכל הוא לעלות למדה עליונה כזאת עד שידע לכונן את הכל לתכנית העז והאושר.

כשכנסת ישראל מתעוררת לתחיה מוצאה היא בקרבה פנימה את עזה וכבודה, וכל הטוהר והקודש הרגיל להמצא בהכנעה

8
Coming in from Exile

The inspiration of the Judaism of the Diaspora is drying up as the thrust of the People's energy returns to the land. Man's spiritual evolution requires that he become in touch with his natural inclinations. Knesset Yisrael *(Ecclesia Israel) will learn to achieve an interpenetration of holiness and power.*

Were it not for the nourishment that it receives from the dew-of-life of the sanctity of the Land of Israel,[63] Judaism in exile would essentially have no actual basis – only vision of the heart, founded on pictures of hope and rare reflection, of the future and the past. However, there is a limit to the power of this imaging to carry the burden of life and to pave a way for the life of the people, and it would seem that this quota has already been filled. Therefore, Judaism in exile goes down drastically, and there is no hope[64] for it other than planting it in the source of life, real life, of essential holiness, which may be found only in the Land of Israel.[65] Even one spark of this real life will vivify a great multitude of visionary life. The real life of sanctity of Judaism cannot be revealed other than by the People's return to its Land, which is the way paved for its renascence. All the sublimity in its soul and heart's vision will rise to life in proportion to the place the practical foundation will occupy to revive the fainting vision.

The more invigorated the world becomes, the more Man's spirit develops within him – the more vocal becomes the demand to live according to the natural spirit within him. This demand has a lot of truth and justice to it, and the intellectually whole must refine it and set it on a correct foundation. Man increasingly finds God within him, in his correct inclinations. Man may reach such a sublime level that he will know how to program for strength and happiness even those inclinations that at first blush appear to deviate from the good way accepted by the ordinary outlook.[66]

When *Knesset Yisrael* (Ecclesia Israel) is revived she finds within her strength and honor, and all the purity and holiness usually found

ומשמעת הולך הוא ומתנוצץ בעז הנשמתי של הופעת הגבורה של האומה, ובדעה טהורה מחברים את הרוחות וממתיקים את הגבורה המתעוררת על-ידי שלובם.

ט

הזוהמא הנשמתית כשם שהיא יכולה להתקבץ בתוך נפש יחידית, להסיר אותה מתכונתה הטובה, ולהפכה לתכונה שפלה, שתוריד אותה למדרגת שפלי החיים, כך היא יכולה להתקבץ בתוך הנפש הכללית של אומה שלמה, לעשות אותה לאומה שפלה ורשעה, בזויה ונגעלה, באופן שהיא ראויה לעבור מן העולם, כדי שלא לעכב על הנוי העולמי של יפיו של עולם מלהתפשט.

הטהרה האלהית כשהיא מוארה יפה היא מזככת את הלב. הנשמה היחידית של האדם היחיד נעשית מאירה, קדושה וגבורה על ידי אור האלהי המזריח עליה את קרני זהרו בתוקף ומילוי, והיא נטמאת ונעשית קדורה לפי אותה המדה שהאורה האלהית רחוקה ממנה או משובשת בקרבה. גם הנשמה של האומה כולה כשזורם בתוכה זרם חי של הופעת אלהים הרי היא בריאה, חזקה וטהורה, וכשהשכינה מסתלקת מקרבה, מיד היא מתנונת והולכת וטומאתה מתגלה בקרבה. הרוח הלאומי יוכל לקבל טומאה כמו רוח אדם פרטי, הוא יוכל לשאוף שאיפות שפלות ורעות, אשר כפי רוב כחו וגדלו יגדלו הרבה יותר לרוע משאיפות רעות של אנשים רעים יחידים. על כן טהרה צריך הוא הרוח, טהרה במקור הטוהר של המעין האלהי. כשהמעשים הם טובים, כשהמדות הן זכות, חולמת היא האומה חלומות של קדושה עליונה ושכלה מאיר באור אלהים, וכשהמעשים נפחתים והמדות מתעכרות אז השאיפות

in submission and discipline, shines in the soulful strength of the appearance of national power, and with pure opinion we combine the spirits and sweeten the rigor aroused by their interpenetration.[67]

9

An Indestructible Purity

The phenomenon of spiritual pollution. A covenant that Knesset Yisrael *(Ecclesia Israel) will never become totally impure. Jewish nationalists are connected to God willy-nilly. Individuals can deviate but not the nation as a whole. The land, language, history, and customs are all godly. It is up to "the righteous of the generation" to expose the godliness within the national spirit.*

Just as soul-pollution can collect in an individual soul, leading it away from its good character and turning it to evil, bringing it down to the level of low lives, so it can collect in the collective soul of an entire nation, making it an evil and lowly nation, despicable and disgusting, so that it best pass from the world, in order not to disrupt the expansion of the beauty of the world.

When divine purity is well illuminated, it cleanses the heart. The individual soul of a person becomes clear, holy, and mighty through the divine light shining on it its full, powerful rays of splendor. And the soul becomes impure and dark in direct proportion to the divine light's distance from it or confusion within it. So too the soul of the entire nation, when there streams within it the living stream of God's revelation, is healthy, strong, and pure. And when the divine presence departs from its midst, immediately the soul withers and its impurity manifests within it. The national spirit can be sullied just as the individual human spirit. It can aspire to evil, base aspirations. Due to the national spirit's great power, its aspirations can be much more evil than those of individual bad men. Therefore, the spirit requires purity, purity at the source of purity of the divine fount. When the deeds are good, the traits pure, the nation dreams visions of sublime holiness and its intellect shines with divine light; when the deeds are base and the traits muddied, then the national aspirations also become base

הלאומיות גם הן נעשות ירודות וכעורות, וממילא גם חלשות, כי אין גבורה של אמת רק גבורה של מעלה, גבורת אלהים.

ברית כרותה היא לכנסת ישראל כולה, שלא תטמא טומאה גמורה. גם עליה תוכל הטומאה לפעול, לעשות בה פגמים, אבל לא תוכל להכריתה כליל ממקור החיים האלהיים. רוח האומה שנתעורר עכשו, שאומרים רבים ממחזיקיו שאינם נזקקים לרוח אלהים, אם היו באמת יכולים לבסס רוח לאומי כזה בישראל היו יכולים להציג את האומה על מעמד הטומאה והכליון. אבל מה שהם רוצים אינם יודעים בעצמם, כל כך מחובר הוא רוח ישראל ברוח אלהים, עד אשר אפילו מי שאומר שאיננו נזקק כלל לרוח ד׳, כיון שהוא אומר שהוא חפץ ברוח ישראל הרי הרוח האלהי שורה בתוכיות נקודת שאיפתו גם בעל כרחו. היחיד הפרטי יכול לנתק את עצמו ממקור החיים, לא כן האומה כנסת ישראל כולה, על כן כל קניניה של האומה, שהם חביבים עליה מצד רוחה הלאומי, כולם רוח אלהים שורה בם: ארצה, שפתה, תולדתה, מנהגיה. ואם המצא תמצא בזמן מן הזמנים התעוררות רוח כזאת, שיאמרו כל אלה בשם רוח האומה לבדה, וישתדלו לשלול את רוח אלהים מעל כל הקנינים הללו וממקורם הגלוי שהוא רוח האומה, מה צריכים אז צדיקי הדור לעשות? למרוד ברוח האומה, אפילו בדבור, ולמאס את קניניה, זהו דבר שאי־אפשר: רוח ד׳ ורוח ישראל אחד הוא. אלא שהם צריכים לעבוד עבודה גדולה לגלות את האור והקדש שברוח האומה, את אור אלהים שבתוך כל אלה, עד שכל המחזיקים באותן המחשבות שברוח הכללי ובכל קניניו ימצאו את עצמם ממילא, שהם עומדים שקועים ומושרשים וחיים בחיי אלהים, מוזהרים בקדושה ובגבורה של מעלה.

and ugly and resultantly weak – for there is no true strength but the strength above, the strength of God.

A covenant was made with *Knesset Yisrael* (Ecclesia Israel) that it would never become totally impure.[68] Yes, impurity can affect it, causing imperfections to occur, but impurity can never sever it totally from the source of divine life. The national spirit that is awakened now, many of whose proponents say they have no need of the divine spirit – if they could truly found such a national spirit in Israel, they could present the nation on a basis of impurity and destruction. But what they want, they themselves do not know. So connected is the spirit of Israel to the spirit of God that even if one should say he has no need of the spirit of the Lord, as soon as he states a desire for the spirit of Israel, the spirit of God rests in the innermost point of his aspiration, though against his will.[69] The individual can sever himself from the source of life; not so the entire Jewish nation. Therefore all the national assets, which are beloved to the nation on account of its national spirit, are all invested with the spirit of God: her land, language, history, and customs. Now if at a certain time there should be found an arousal, whereby people speak only of the spirit of the nation and attempt to negate the spirit of God from all these assets and from their revealed source that is the national spirit – what should the righteous of the generation do? To rebel against the spirit of the nation, even verbally, and to reject its assets, this is something impossible: the spirit of the Lord and the spirit of Israel are one. Rather the righteous must work hard to reveal the light and the holiness in the national spirit, the light of God in all these, until all those who cling to those thoughts of the national spirit and to all its assets will find themselves automatically standing, sunk, rooted and living in divine life, resplendent with the holiness and strength on high.[70]

י

תכונת נפשה של כנסת ישראל היא נבדלת בעקרה מתכונת הנפש של כל עם ולשון. בכל עם ולשון הנקודה הפנימית של חפץ החיים הקבוציים מיוסדת היא על התוכן הכלכלי לכל צורותיו, ביסוד הדאגה הפנימית השרויה בקרב האדם לבצר את מעמד חייו הגשמיים, והרוח העליון המחיה ומאיר את הנקודה הזאת הוא רוח הסדר והיופי, שהוא חפץ העונג של החושים, על-פי משאלות לב האדם, וכשהם באיזה קיבוץ על-פי סגנון אחד, עושה השווי הזה את התוכן הלאומי. אמנם בישראל מונחת התכונה האלהית במעמקי טבע נשמת האומה. הצמאון לדעה והרגשה אלהית, בתכלית עליונותה וטהרתה, היא לו הנקודה שהחיים מורגשים בה, והעידונים הנובעים משלמות ציור זה בכל רחבי החיים ועמקיהם הן המגמות האסתתיות. הדעה הפנימית, המכרת שבמילוי תשוקה עליונה זו הכל מתמלא, שאין שום דבר מכל מגמות החיים ועדוני החיים, סדרי החיים ותכניהם, שלא יהיה כלול בתוך נקודת עולמי עולמים זאת, הכרה זו היא ענין מיוחד לישראל מונח בטבע נשמת האומה, מתגלה בהכרה פנימית אפילו להמוני המונים, והולכת ומתחוורת ומתבררת לסגולי הסגולות בכל דור ודור. הענין האלהי, בתוך כל ערך החיים בעומק טבע הנשמה, בהתאמה ללשד המחיה את ההיסתוריה הלאומית, המתגלה בכשרון של יצירת הנבואה בבחירי בניה, המביאה למדרגת עם עולם, שכל האנושיות תכיר את סגולת נשמתה, הוא העצם הישראלי שתאריו מתגלים בכל התנועות השונות, ורוחו של משיח הולך ופועל את השלמת צביון זה עד עת קץ השלמה.

10
Critiquing Marx

Economics are the essence of other national entities; God is the heart of Israel. Israel's spiritual evolution – "the spirit of Messiah."

The character of the soul of *Knesset Yisrael* (Ecclesia Israel) is distinguished at its root from the character of every people and tongue. In every people and tongue, the innermost point of the desire for collective life is founded on the economic content in all its forms, on the foundation of internal worrying within Man to fortify his material life's standing. The higher spirit that enlivens and illuminates this point is the spirit of order and beauty, which is the desire for sensual pleasure, according to the dictates of man's heart. When in a collective these are of a single style, this equation makes the national character.[71] However in Israel, the divine character is lodged in the depths of the nature of the nation's soul. The thirst for divine knowledge and feeling, in its utmost sublimity and purity, is for Israel the point wherein life is felt, and the pleasures that derive from the perfection of this picture in all the breadths and depths of life – these are the aesthetic directions. The inner opinion that recognizes that in the filling of this sublime longing, all is filled, that there are none of life's objectives, pleasures, orders and contents that are not contained within this eternal point – this recognition is something specific to Israel, embedded in the nature of the nation,[72] manifesting in the interior consciousness of even the masses, and progressively clarified and crystallized for the exceptionally gifted in every generation. The "divine phenomenon"[73] within life's every value, in the depth of the soul's nature, corresponding to the life-sap of the nation's history, manifesting[74] in the talent of prophetic creation in her chosen sons, elevating to the level of an eternal people, the gift of whose soul will be recognized by all humanity – this is the Israelite essence whose attributes are revealed in all the different movements. And the spirit of Messiah proceeds to complete this character until the time that it be perfected.

יא

השכל הישראלי, מצד מקור מחצבו הרוחני האלהי, הוא שכל אלהי, ורצונו רצון אלהי הוא. הגעגועים והאהבה של האומה כולה הם נוראים ועמוקים לאין קץ דוקא לשלמות האלהות העליונה. מובלטת אהבה זו בשיר השירים בהדר צבעיה, שאין העולם כדאי להם. מתגלה אור תכני זה בצדיקים עליונים של הדורות, שרצונם הוא יסוד העולם ודבריהם דברי אלהים חיים ודבר אחד מדבריהם לא ישוב ריקם. כי דבר ד׳ אלהי עולם בפיהם תמיד. רק החכמה העליונה וכל חירותה, עם כל הרגשת עידוניה, ההולכת ועולה על הספירות של ההכרות האלהיות, המתנשאות בכל הוד פארן עדי עד, היא היא הנותנת חיים לישראל. ובחגוי התורה כולה, בכללותה ובפרטיה, כשהיא מצטרפת עם הארת הדעה של יסודה ונשמתה, הכל הולך ומאיר, הולך ומתגלה, הולך וגואל, הולך ומשכלל, מביא ישועת עולמים לכל נוצר ומאיר עולמי עד מכבודו העליון הרוכב שמי שמי קדם ומחיה אפסי ארץ, מצמיח כל מיני ישועות, ומעודד כל ענוי ארץ, מאזר ישראל גבורת עולמים ומשיבם קוממיות לארצם, לחדש אותם כבראשונה. אור אחד, נשמת אחת, נשמת כל היקום, זרוע ד׳ הולך ומתגלה, הולך וקורא את ישראל לחיים, לשוב לבנות ולהבנות. בנשמתם העליונה של צדיקים יסודי עולם, שאור רזי אל מחיה אותם, רוח תחית המתים שרוי, ממקור חייו המפכים, הנקלטים מכל תמצית אוצרות החיים שבכל עולמים, הולכים פלגים, שריגים דקים ושונים, להכניס אור חיים, רוח תקוה ונטית אחדות, התעוררות תשובה והתעודדות גדולה בכל השדרות, ובאור עליון הזרוע לצדיק יופיע משיח, לרומם קרן לעם עולם.

11
A Cosmic Love Affair

The Song of Songs – an expression of Israel's love for God. The will of the righteous. Salvation for all. Treasures of the tsaddik's *spirit: Resurrection of the Dead, Return, Messiah.*

The Israelite intellect, since its source is spiritual, divine, is a divine intellect, and its will is a godly will. The longing and love of the entire nation for precisely supernal divine perfection, are awesome and infinitely deep. This love is pronounced in the Song of Songs in glorious colors, of which the world is not worthy.[75] This characteristic light is revealed in the exalted righteous *(tsaddikim)* of the generations, whose will is the foundation of the world,[76] whose words are those of the Living God – not one word of theirs will remain unfulfilled,[77] for the word of the Lord, God of the Universe, is in their mouth always. Only the supernal wisdom and all its freedom, with all the feeling of its delights, which rises beyond the spheres of divine realizations, which forever soar in all their majestic glory, is what gives life to Israel. And in the crevices of the entire Torah, as a whole and as specifics, when joined with the illuminated knowledge of its foundation and soul,[78] all proceeds to light up, to reveal, to redeem, to perfect, bringing eternal salvation to every creature, illuminating eternity with the effulgence of He who rides heavens-upon-heavens and vivifies the ends of the earth, producing all sorts of salvation and heartening the humble of the earth, binding Israel with eternal might and returning them upright to their land, to renew them as in the beginning. One light, one soul, the soul of all existence, the arm of the Lord is revealed, calling Israel to life, to return, to build and to be upbuilt. In the exalted soul of the righteous, foundations of the world, who are enlivened by the mysteries of God, the spirit of Resurrection of the Dead dwells.[79] From the flowing source of the *tsaddik*'s life, gathered from the essence of treasures of life of all worlds, flow streams, slight and diverse, to bring in a light of life, a spirit of hope and a unifying tendency, an arousal of return *(teshuvah)* and great encouragement in all the avenues, and with the supernal light sown for the righteous[80] will appear Messiah, to uplift the horn of an eternal people.

יב

הנטיה הלאומית בישראל היא שדה אשר ברכו ד׳, שאף על-פי שאין בה עדיין גדולים גמורים, מפני השממון הגדול של הגלות, ראויה היא, על-ידי עבודה רוחנית ומעשית, שיצמחו בה כל הגדולים הטובים שבעולם להוציא משפעה נשמות גדולות ועליונות המאירות את כל העולם כולו בכבודן. ויש לעומת זה נטיה לאומית של גוים, שהיא חורבה ומדבר, שבשום אופן אינה ראויה לגדל צמחים, והצמחים הרעים כגפן סדום, חמת תנינים ואשכלות מרורות, הלא העדרם טוב ממציאותם, ונמצא שהכל הוא בהם העדר גמור וחורבן מוחלט ואותם ״הגויים חרב יחרבו״. רק ההשפעה של הקדש המעורב בנטיה הלאומית הישראלית מרטבת את אלה הנטיות האנושיות בכלל ומחזירתן לטובה, עד בואן גם הן לידי עילוי להיות ראויות על-ידי תכיפת חבורם ויחסם אל ישראל, להצמחה רוחנית. ״ישושום מדבר וציה ותגל ערבה ותפרח כחבצלת״, אשר כל זה בא יבא על-ידי גאולתם השלמה של ישראל שתקדים לבא.

יג

הרצון הכללי, של הרוחניות הכללית שבאומה, יש לו מדתו. ולמעלה ממנה הוא הרצון של התוכן האלהי, לפי השגתה וחייה הפנימיים והחיצוניים. כל זמן שהתוכן הרוחני של האומה הוא מלא וגדול, מתגדל ממילא, במדה יותר עליונה, האור של התוכן האלהי שבהשגתה, והמבוקש של מציאותה מצויר בה בגונים בהירים; ולמעלה מזה מתגלה בגונים בהירים המבוקש של כל ההויה כולה, שזהו רז דעת עליון. כשירדה האומה בגלות המרה, נחשכה נשמתה,

12

The Coming of Age of Nationalism

Jewish versus Gentile nationalism. Gentile nationalism is redeemed through the Jewish national inclination.

The national inclination in Israel is a field blessed by God. Though it has not yet produced ripe crops because of the great wasteland of the Exile, it is worthy, through spiritual and practical work, of yielding all the good produce of the world, to bear great, high souls who illumine the entire world with their glory. Opposite this is the national inclination of the Gentiles, which is a desolate desert, in no way capable of producing vegetation. As for weeds, isn't their absence preferable to their existence? Effectively, in those nations all is total absence and absolute destruction, so those *nations will be destroyed.*[81] Only the influence of the holy, mixed into the Israelite national inclination, irrigates these general human tendencies and returns them to good, until even they are uplifted to the point of being worthy – through their constant connection and relation[82] to Israel – of spiritual fructification.[83] *The desert and the dry land shall be glad; and the wilderness shall rejoice and blossom as the lily.*[84] All this will come about through the complete redemption of Israel that hastens to arrive.

13

Setting God Free

The divine existential quest of the People. Its clouding over in exile. In exile, God shrinks the divine light of the cosmos to fit the People in their reduced state. Thus, the salvation becomes the salvation of God Himself, as it were.

The general will of the general spirituality of the people has its measure. Above it is the will of the divine content, according to its [i.e., the people's] understanding and inner and outer life. As long as the spiritual content of the people is full and great, automatically the light of the divine content in its grasp expands, and the quest of its existence is pictured in bright hues. Beyond that there is revealed in

והשגת מבוקשה הפנימי של מציאותה ומאויי חייה נתקטנה, עד שאינה מוצאה כלל את נתיבותיה, ומכל מקום יש בקרבה איזו השגה חלושה, של רשימת אורה, שממנה זורח אור כהה לפי הערך לצדיקים וחכמים דורשי ד׳ בכל לבבם גם במחשכים ו״כי אשב בחושך ד׳ אור לי״. אבל הענין האלהי והמגמה העולמית, אם היתה עומדת במקומה ומדרגתה הראשונה, לא יכלו להתחבר אז כלל עם מגמתה העצמית, ואז היו חייה בגלות נוטלים להם דרך חול, באין פנות להתקשר עם המגמה האלהית של צור כל העולמים, צדיק בכל הדורות. מה עשה הקב״ה? כשם שנתמעט האור הזורח בה לגבי תכונתה הפנימית, כן ירד האור האלהי הכללי בעולם, והשגוב של הענין האלהי שהוא אור חי העולמים איננו מבהיק כי־אם באור קלוש כזה, שהוא יכול להתאחד עם האור הזורח בנשמתן של ישראל, גם אחרי הירידה שגרמה הנפילה הגדולה שנפלה עטרת תפארת ישראל משמים ארץ. ובהיות הענין האלהי הכללי בתור אור העולם עומד במעמד כזה שוב הענינים הולכים ומתחברים, והמגמה של מציאות האומה ברוח קדשה הפנימי והמגמה הכללית האלהית הגדולה של ההויה כולה יכולות הן להתאחד כאחד, וממילא הן מתחברות ביחד בעצמן, ובנשמותיהן של ישראל בפרט ובנשמת כללות האומה בכלל, והן מוכנות יחד לעלות בישועת גוי ואלהיו, ״אני והו הושיעה נא״.

יד

שריד קטן מדבר גדול הוא יקר ומעולה מדבר קטן שלם. ניצוץ אחד מאור חיי האבות, מקדושתם וגבורת אלהים העליונה שבגדולתם, ההולך ואור באחרית הימים להשיב לתחית עולמים את ישראל,

bright hues the quest of all existence, which is the mystery of supernal knowledge.[85] When the people descended into the bitter exile, its soul was darkened, and the grasp of the inner quest of its existence, its life's desire, was reduced, so much so that it cannot find its way at all. Nevertheless, there is within its midst some faint[86] understanding of the trace of its light, from which there shines a somber light relatively for the saints and the wise who seek the Lord with all their heart[87] even in the darkness. *When I dwell in darkness the Lord is light for me.*[88] However, if the divine phenomenon[89] and the world agenda were to retain their original stature, they would not at all be able to join with the people's orientation. Then the people's life in exile would perforce adopt a secular direction, unable to connect to the divine plan of the Rock of all worlds, righteous in all His ways.[90] What did the Holy One, blessed be He, do? Just as the light of the people's inner disposition was diminished, so the general, divine light of the world descended, and the exaltedness of the divine phenomenon, which is the light of the life of worlds, shines but in a dull manner, so that it can unite with the light shining in the souls of Israel, even after the great fall when the glory of Israel fell from heaven to earth.[91] Once the general divine phenomenon, in its role of light of the world, assumes such a state, things can once again join up. The orientation of the people's existence with its inner holy inspiration and the great, general divine agenda of total existence can become as one, whereupon they bond together in themselves and in the individual souls of Israel and in the soul of the nation as a whole. And they are ready together to ascend with the salvation of the nation and its God. "He and I[92] – please save."[93]

14

Putting Together Pre-Torah and Torah

The "Light of Messiah" as the convergence of different periods of Jewish History – the period of the Patriarchs and the later chapter of Torah.

A small remnant of a great thing is more precious than an entire small thing. One spark of the light of the Patriarchs' life, their sanctity and their divine mightiness, which increasingly shines at the end of

ועמו יחד את העולם כולו, על-פי סדר והדרגה, הוא נעלה ונשגב מכל הקדושה הגלויה שבתוכן של אמונה ויראה, תורה ומצוה, של ההמשך המועתק מספיחי ספיחים של בנים, "יפה שיחתן של עבדי אבות יותר מתורתן של בנים". ושיחה זו היא מחיה דור אחרון באהבה מסותרת, בה מתגלה התוכן הכביר של "וזוכר חסדי אבות ומביא גואל לבני בניהם למען שמו באהבה". נדחים הם האורים הקלושים, "שרגא בטיהרא", החוצפא מגרשת אותם ובתוכה רוח ד' נוססת. גדולי קדושי עולם יכירו את הרז ויצדיקו קודש, הם, בתומתם העליונה, יחברו את תורת הבנים לשיחת האבות ועבדיהם, ותורה מעוטרת בכל הוד ובכל גבורה, בכל חן ובכל תפארה, תתגלה להיות לעטרת צבי ולצפירת תפארה לשאר עמו. חזקו אל תיראו! אור משיח מתנוצץ, גאולת עולמים מופיעה מכל החרכים, מחושך הרשעה והכפירה המנוולת, הבזויה וחדלת אישים, בא יבא אור עליון, אשר יעמיד במרחב רגלי ישראל וירומם בכבוד קרן עם יודעי אלהיו, יאיר אור על כל מחשכים ויעודד קדישי עליונים בישועת אמת, רק חסדי אבות ישארו, וכל ענוי לב, אשר ידעו איך להיות בעיניהם דכאים וגבורים יחד, אלה הם אשר יכירו אור התורה העליונה הנובעת משיחתם של עבדי אבות, שהיא גאולתם של בנים.

טו

כשכח ישראל גדול ונשמתו מאירה בקרבו בהופעה וענפיו המעשיים מתוקנים, בסדור מלא, בקדושה ביחוד ובברכה, במקדש וממשלה, בנבואה וחכמה, אז ההתרחבות לצד החול, לענוגי החושים הרוחניים והגשמיים, להצצה חדירית ופנימית לתוך חייהם

days to eternally revivify Israel, and together with it the entire world, in a gradual manner, is more exalted than all the revealed holiness, the faith and awe, Torah and Commandments, of the continuation, the aftergrowths-of-aftergrowths of the descendants. "More comely the conversation of the servants of the Patriarchs, than the Torah of the descendants."[94] This conversation vivifies the last generation with a hidden love, in which there is revealed the mighty content of (the prayer), "He remembers the love of the fathers and brings a redeemer to their children's children for His name's sake with love."[95] The feeble lights are dispelled – as "a torch in broad daylight"[96] – impudence *(ḥutspah)* drives them away and within it the spirit of God waves. The great saints will recognize the mystery and justify the holy. They, with their superb simplicity, will join the Torah of the sons to the conversation of the fathers and their servants, and a Torah adorned with all majesty and might, charm and glory, will be revealed as the crowning glory of the remnant people.[97] Be strong, do not be afraid! The Light of Messiah shines, eternal redemption appears from all the cracks. From the darkness of evil and from vulgar, despised, ineffectual atheism, there will come a supernal light that will redeem Israel and uplift with honor a nation that knows its God; a light will illuminate all the obscure places and encourage the most holy[98] with true salvation. Only the love of the fathers[99] will remain, and all the humble of heart, who knew how to be in their own eyes at once contrite and mighty – they will recognize the light of supernal Torah that flows from the conversation of Patriarchs' servants, which is the redemption of descendants.

15

The Relation of Periphery to Center

When Israel is whole – embracing Temple and State, prophecy and wisdom – it has the ability to encompass the secular and worldly. In exile, this is not possible. Sabbath limits: two thousand cubits versus twelve mil.

When the power of Israel is great, its soul shining splendidly in its midst and its practical branches fully in order – with holiness, unity and blessing, with Temple and State, with prophecy and wisdom

של המון עמים ולאומים שונים, למפעליהם וספריותיהם, התגברות עז החיים הטבעיים, כל אלה טובים הם ומסוגלים להרחיב את אור הטוב, והתחום ארוך הוא: י״ב מיל במחנה ישראל כולו, הכופל באמת את כל העולם באיכותו, ״יצב גבולות עמים למספר בני ישראל״. משחשך האור, משגלתה שכינה, משנעתקו רגלי האומה מבית חייה, החל הצמצום להיות נתבע. כל עז חילוני עלול להיות לרועץ, כל יופי טבעי וחשקו עלול להאפיל את אור הקדש ותם הטהרה והצניעות, כל מחשבה שלא נתגדלה כולה במחנה ישראל יכולה להרס את סדר האמונה והחיים הישראליים, כל שמינות קטנה מביאה לידי בעיטה. מכאן באו העוצב והסגוף, הקדרות והפחדנות, וביותר ממה שפעלו אלה על החיים הגשמיים פעלו על החיים הרוחניים, על רוחב המחשבה, על תעופת ההרגשה, עד אשר יקיץ הקץ, שקול קורא בכח: ״הרחיבי מקום אהלך, ויריעות משכנותיך יטו, אל תחשכי, האריכי מיתריך ויתדותיך חזקי, כי ימין ושמאל תפרוצי וזרעך גוים יירש, וערים נשמות יושיבו״. והתחום של אלפים אמה הקצר הולך הוא ומתרחב, כמדת ישועתן של ישראל, שהולכת ואורה קמעא קמעא.

טז

דבר פשוט הוא שהצדיק עושה כל מעשיו בקדושה, וכל פעולותיו הגשמיות עולות הן לתקונו של עולם, וזאת היא אהבת המלאכה, שכל כך שגבה מעלתה מצד עצמה ושנתנה בברית כמו שתורה נתנה בברית. ומעתה אין ספק שתקון עולם מלא והתרחבות אור הקדש נמצא באמת בכל מלאכה: כל תנועה שמצלת איזה חלק מן ההויה מן שליטת התוהו - דבר גדול וכללי יש כאן.

– then the expansion toward the secular side, toward indulging the spiritual and physical senses, toward penetrating, inner observation of the lives of sundry nations and different peoples, their deeds and literatures; the burgeoning of natural life – all these are beneficial and designed to expand the good light. Then the (Sabbath) limit is long:[100] twelve *mil*, or the entire camp of Israel (in the desert),[101] which really enfolds the entire world qualitatively, *He set the borders of nations to correspond to the number of the Children of Israel.*[102] With the waning of the light, the exile of the *Shekhinah* (divine presence), the removal of the people from its homeland, restriction became necessary. Any secular power could be destructive; any natural beauty or its affection could cloud the light of holiness and the innocence of purity and modesty. Any thought that did not develop wholly within the camp of Israel could subvert the edifice of Israelite faith and life; any fat could bring to "kicking."[103] Thence came the sadness and the asceticism, the depression and the fearfulness, and even more than these affected physical life, they impacted the spiritual life, the broadness of thought, the flight of emotion. Finally the end will arrive, calling with force: *Enlarge the space of your tent, and let them stretch forth the curtains of your habitation – spare not, lengthen your chords and strengthen your stakes. For to the right and to the left you shall spread forth, and your seed shall inherit nations, desolate cities they shall settle.*[104] And the short (Sabbath) limit of two thousand cubits[105] broadens, as the measure of Israel's salvation, which gradually brightens.[106]

16

Uplifting the Sparks within Labor, Languages, and Sciences

The righteous man's love of work. The union of the righteous of the generation with the common laborers. The conversion of the curse of work to blessing. The sanctification of all languages and wisdoms of the world. The influence of the Holy Tongue. Illuminating the embellishments of modern society.

It is a simple fact that the righteous man does all his deeds with holiness, and all his physical actions contribute to the perfection of the

אמנם הנעלה מכל היא ההצלה הכללית של הכשרת החיים הפנימיים של המציאות, להוציאם מידי גלמותם ולתקנם בתור כלים שלמים העושים את תפקידם יפה. אבל המחשבה של גדולי הדעת מתאחדת גם עם הנטיה ההמונית וקל-וחומר עם נטית אהבת המלאכה והעבודה הממשית, שהיא כבר נטיה של שאר רוח, ורוח אלהים חופף עליה. וכשישנם צדיקים בדור, שאור ד׳ מופיע עליהם תמיד, הם מאחדים נשמתם עם נשמת הכלל כולו, והגות לב הפנימי של המוני בני אדם עושי המלאכה מתאחדת עם הגות לבבם. וצד המארה שיש במלאכה, שהיא באה מצד קנאת איש מרעהו, ומצד שנאת הבריות היונקת הרבה ממלחמת החיים בצורתה הארורה בעולם הירוד, הרי היא הולכת ומתפכחת, ויוצאה היא מכלל ארור ובאה לכלל ברוך. לפעמים יש כח בצדיקים לתן אור קדושה בעצמות המלאכה עד שיהיה בה כח מעין של תורה, להביא לחיי עולם הבא ולתקן את הפגמים ולהשיב בתשובה גמורה את עוסקיה, ״גדול הנהנה מיגיע כפיו יותר מירא שמים״. וכשם שיש כח להמשיך את הקדושה והאור האלהי הפנימי בכל המלאכות ולהוציאם מכלל אתלטיא, כן יש כח להמציא אור קודש בכל הלשונות ובכל החכמות שבעולם, וצדיקים הגדולים צריכים להתפלל שיתמשך אור נועם ד׳ בכל החכמות ובכל הלשונות, באופן שמכל מקום יופיע כבוד ד׳ ומכל מקום יפוצו קרני אורה של תורה, ותפלתם של צדיקים והארת רצונם עושה רושם נמרץ עד אין קץ ותכלית. ביחוד צריכים להפנות לזה את התפלה בעת שרואים שהנטיה גדולה לשפות ומדעים, ואי אפשר להלחם עם כל הפונים אליהם, והזמן ואותותיו מראים את ההכרח, אז קמים צדיקים פנימיים לתשועה, בעבודה שבחשאי, ובגדולת נפש חיה יחידה, באים ופותחים את הצנורות הסתומים, לשום סוד ד׳

world. And this is the love of work, which is so exalted on its own, and which was given with a covenant as was the Torah.[107] Thus, there is no doubt that full world-perfection and expansion of the light of holiness is truly to be found in every labor: any movement that preserves some segment of existence from the rule of chaos is a great, general thing. Yet, most sublime of all is the general salvation – the preparation of the inner life of existence, its actualization and development into well-functioning, whole vessels. But the thought of the great of knowledge is able to unite with the common attitude, and all the more so with the attitude of love of work and physical labor,[108] which is already an inspired attitude, on which the spirit of God hovers. When there are in the generation *tsaddikim* (righteous) upon whom the light of God appears constantly, they unite their soul with the soul of the entire community, and the inner reflection of the heart of the common people, the laborers, joins with their heart's reflection. The aspect of the curse that is in work,[109] which arises from one man's envy of the next, and from misanthropy that is fed by the battle of life in its cursed form in a degenerate world, abates and is transformed from curse to blessing.[110] At times the righteous have the power to inject a light of holiness into the essence of labor so that it has a force reminiscent of Torah, to bring to life in the world-to-come, to correct flaws and to move those involved in it to complete return *(teshuvah)*: "Greater one who enjoys the toil of his palms than a fearer of Heaven."[111] Just as there is the capability of drawing holiness and inner, divine light into all categories of labor, bringing them out of their cursedness[112] – so there is the ability to discover a light of holiness in all the languages and wisdoms of the world. The great *tsaddikim* (righteous) must pray that the light of God's pleasantness come into all the wisdoms and languages, so that from every place will appear the glory of God, from every place will spread the light-rays of Torah. The prayer of the righteous and the illumination of their will produces an infinitely powerful effect. Espedally must prayer be directed to this at a time when there is seen a great attraction to languages and sciences, and it is not possible to battle all those who would turn to them, for the signs of the time show

בלמודיו, ולמודי ד׳ הם כל מה שבעולם, וביחוד כל מה שיש בו משום תקוני העולם, ומעוררים הם את הקדש שבכל לשון בכחו של יוסף, שכלל הכל באות ה׳ שבו נברא העולם הזה שנתוסף על שמו ובכחו של הדבור שבסיני שבא להרבות אור גדול יותר ויותר מזה, "ד׳ אלהים יתן אומר המבשרות צבא רב" שנחלק כל דבור לשבעים לשון, וכן באר משה את התורה היטב, והיטב זה היינו שמצא ערך הטוב האמתי שבכל לשון, הכח המאצילו בהוד קודש, ואז הולכת השפה ומתבררת, ושפה ברורה הולכה ומתהפכת אל כל העמים לקרא כולם בשם ד׳. וכל המלאכות יאירו באור החיים על-ידי מלאכת הקודש, וכל מה שמתוספות מלאכות ועבודות גשמיות בארץ ישראל, תצא על-ידי ישראל ביסודה המלאכה והעבודה משפלותה המאררה, וכל מה שתגדל השפעת לשון הקודש בעולם, וכל מה שיעלה כח התורה והתפלה הטהורה, המאמצת להרחיב את אור האצילות האלהית בעולם, לבררה ולהודיע לבני אדם הדר כבודה בכל דרכי הודעה ובכל דרכי ברור והסברה, כן יוסיף האור להגלות על כל שפה ולשון ועל כל חכמה ומדע, וקל-וחומר שיחול אור ד׳ על כל דברים שבטעם, ביופי ובשירה, בהליכות דרך ארץ ובארחות הנמוס, ואפילו בקשוטים והדורים ואפני ההנהגות והנמוסים היותר מודרנים, כמובן המובחרים והעדינים שבהם, ובכולם יחל אור ד׳ לפעם. והרעיון המקשר את הכל אל הטוב והיושר, אל העדן ואצילות הרות, אל אהבת העבודה בהדר הבטחון האלהי, והאהבה העליונה המשפיעה אור וחיים בכל נשמה, יגלה ויראה בכל הענפים הרחוקים הללו, וחיי עולם וחיי שעה יתקשרו בחוברת אמיצה, יקבלו דין מן דין, ויאירו כל הפרטים כולם באור הכלל, וכל ההופעות המעשיות והשכליות שבעולם - מאורה העליון של אור תורה אשר האיר אב המון גוים איתן האזרחי,

the necessity – then inner *tsaddikim* come to the rescue.[113] Through silent work,[114] through greatness of soul, they open shut conduits to put the mystery of God in His studies, and the "studies of God"[115] are all that is in the world, especially all that contributes to the perfection of the world *(tikkun ha-'olam)*. The righteous arouse the holiness that is in every language by the power of Joseph, who included all in the letter *hé* (through which this world was created)[116] that was added to his name,[117] and by the power of the speech at Sinai that came to add a light much, much greater. "*The Lord gave tidings, the messengers a numerous host*[118] – Every pronouncement was split into seventy languages."[119] So too Moses explained the Torah "well."[120] "Well" means that he found the true, positive value in each language,[121] the power that ennobles it with holy majesty. Then the language is clarified, and a clear language turns all nations to call by the name of God.[122] All labors will shine with the light of life through the labor of holiness. The more physical labor increases in the Land of Israel,[123] through Israel the work and labor will come out of its cursed baseness. The greater the influence of the Holy Tongue in the world, the stronger the power of Torah and pure prayer, which strives to broaden the light of the divine emanation in the world, to clarify it and to tell mankind its beautiful glory through all forms of communication and all means of clarification and explanation – the more the light will be revealed upon every tongue and language, upon every wisdom and science. All the more so will the light of God rest on the aesthetic realm, beauty and song, etiquette and manners, even the most modern frills, refinements, modes of behavior and manners – of course, the choicest and most delicate of them.[124] On all of these the light of God will begin to rest. The thought that binds all to the good and straight, to pleasure and loftiness of spirit, to the love of work with the beauty of divine confidence, and the supernal love that pours light and life on every soul, will be visible on all these distant branches. Eternal life and temporal life will be inseparably bound; they will receive from one another. All the details, and all the practical and intellectual manifestations of the world, will be illumined by the light of the whole – from the higher light of Torah that (Abraham) "the

שהעיר ממזרח צדק, יקראהו לרגלו, "והנה כבוד אלהי ישראל בא מדרך הקדים וקולו כקול מים רבים והארץ האירה מכבודו", ואפילו התכנים היותר נפולים יתרוממו ויתקדשו, "ומעין מבית ד' יצא והשקה את נחל השטים".

יז

האמונה והאהבה הן תמיד מחוברות זו עם זו כששתיהן זורחות בנשמה בשלמותן, וכשאור אחת מהן שלם לגמרי מתעוררת השניה בכחה, ויוצאת ממעמקי הנפש להאיר בכל מלואה. אין האדם מוכשר לשום כח רוחני שבעולם בשלמות גדולה כזאת שהוא מוכשר לאמונה ולאהבה, וזהו אות, שבכחות אלו מונחים כל יסודות הויות מהותיותו. כל מה שהיחיד והכלל עושה, בכל גלגולי הסבות וכל הכחות המתגלים בחיי התרבות, הכל הולך הוא להשלים במעלה העליונה את האמונה ואת האהבה. מתוך האמונה והאהבה מתאצלים כל האורות הרוחניים שבעולם, המאירים את כל דרכי החיים וההויה. האמונה והאהבה הן עצם החיים בעולם הזה ובעולם הבא; שום דבר איננו נשאר בחיים, כשעושקים מהם את שני המאורות הללו, את האמונה ואת האהבה.

התרבות הזמנית, כפי מה שהיא מתבססת עתה בעולם, בנויה היא כולה על הכפירה ועל השנאה, שהן שוללי החיים העצמיים, ואי אפשר להתגבר על מחלה זו, כי-אם לגלות את כל אוצרות הטוב המונחים בבית גנזיהן של האמונה והאהבה, וזאת היא מטרת גלוי סתרי תורה.

התורה היא האהבה, והמצות - האמונה, והן הנן גם כן הצנורות, שעל ידם שפע האמונה והאהבה שופע והולך תמיד, וכל התרבות

father of a multitude of nations"[125] illumined; "Ethan the Ezraḥite,"[126] who "waked from the east righteousness, called it in his steps."[127] *And behold the glory of the God of Israel came from the way of the east; and his voice was like a noise of many waters; and the earth was illumined from his glory.*[128] Even the most fallen contents will be exalted and sanctified. *And a spring shall come forth out of the house of the Lord, and shall water the valley of Shittim.*[129]

17

Two Great Luminaries: Faith and Love

Two luminaries of life: faith and love. Contemporary civilization is predicated on disbelief and hatred. Torah is love, and the commandments, faith. Hitkashrut *– connecting to the righteous. "The civilized wicked" are incapable of cleaving. Living spiritual life to its fullest in the Land of Israel.*

Faith and love are always interconnected when both shine in the soul with perfection, and when the light of one of them is complete, through it, the other is aroused and emerges from the depths of the spirit to illumine in all its fullness. In no spiritual domain is Man predisposed to achieve great perfection as in the domain of faith and love. This is a sign that in these faculties (of faith and love) rest the foundations of his essential being. Whatever the individual and the collective do – all the chains of events and all the powers revealed in civilization – all proceed to complete to the highest degree faith and love. Out of faith and love emanate all the spiritual lights of the world, which illumine the ways of life and existence. Faith and love are the essence of life in this world and the next. Nothing remains of life when robbed of these two luminaries, faith and love.

Contemporary culture,[130] as it is now constructed, is predicated on disbelief and hatred, the negaters of essential life. It is possible to overcome this illness only by revealing all the wealth of goodness stored in the treasury of faith and love. This is the purpose of revealing the secrets of Torah.

הרוחנית והחמרית של ישראל, בהתעוררות חיינו הלאומיים, צריך שתתרכז כולה סביב המרכז הכפול המאוחד הזה, שתים שהן ארבע: התורה והמצוה, האמונה והאהבה. שכלול האמונה והאהבה ואומץ קיומן מתחזק ביסוד דבקות נפשית בחכמים ותלמידיהם, או כפי המבטא של החסידות: התקשרות עם הצדיקים. יסוד זה, שהחסידות טפלה בו הרבה, צריכים אנו להקימו בשכלול גדול והדור מאד בתור אוצר חיים, והדום רגל לשכינה הכוללת את אור האמונה והאהבה, השרויה בחכמים צדיקים, שמהות חייהם כולה היא התגלות האמונה והאהבה, המחוזקה באיתנות התורה והמצוה, בכל מלוייהן המעשיים והרוחניים, עם סגולה נפשית מיוחדה, שיהא הסתגלות רוח הקודש, הראוי להולד דוקא בארץ ישראל. התרבותיים הרשעים, חסרי האמונה והאהבה, אינם עלולים לשום דבקות אפילו בינם לבין עצמם, והנם דומים לאפר שאינו בר גיבול, "ועסותם רשעים, כי יהיה אפר תחת כפות רגליכם", וממילא "אין חייהם חיים", והם נקראים בחייהם מתים. אמנם על-ידי אמונה גדולה ואהבה רבה נוריד טל של תחיה, להחיות בו גם כן את המתים, "יחיו מתיך נבלתי יקומון, הקיצו ורננו שוכני עפר כי טל אורות טליך וארץ רפאים תפיל".

אנחנו שואפים לתחית האומה ותחית הארץ, כדי להחיות את מעמד הנשמה שלנו, כדי להעמיד את ישראל חי, להחיות את האמונה והאהבה בחוסן של התורה והמצוה בכל מילוין. אנו מכירים את אור אלהי ישראל, אלהי עולם, והעונג שעל ד׳, על ד׳ דייקא, למעלה מכל מבטא ומכל מושג, לעילא מכל ברכתא ושירתא, תושבחתא ונחמתא, הגנוז וצפון, המתגלה באור האמונה והאהבה, המתראה בתכסיס התורה והמצוה כולה, אנו דורשים לציון, אנו משתוקקים לבנות את הארץ ולהבנות בה, כדי לקלוט את רוחה ואוירה, להתאחד עם כל החיים המקושרים בה. על כן

The Torah is the love, and the commandments, the faith. They are also the conduits through which faith and love constantly flow. When Israel's national life is aroused, its entire spiritual and material culture must pivot on this double (though unified) center, a twosome that in reality is a foursome: Torah and commandments, faith and love. Faith and love are strengthened by soulful clinging to sages and their disciples, or, to use the expression of Hasidism: *hitkashrut*, connection with the righteous. This foundation, which Hasidism greatly developed, we must erect as a treasure of life and a footstool for the *Shekhinah* (divine presence) – which includes the light of faith and love – that resides in righteous sages, the essence of whose lives is the revelation of faith and love, strengthened by the might of Torah and commandments, in all of their practical and spiritual applications, together with a special soul-gift, which is *ru'aḥ ha-kodesh* (divine spirit), worthy of being engendered only in the Land of Israel. The civilized wicked, devoid of faith and love, are incapable of any cleaving, even among themselves. They resemble ash that cannot be clumped together,[131] *and you will tread down the wicked, for they shall be ashes under the soles of your feet.*[132] Their lives are no lives; they are called dead while yet living.[133] However, through great faith and abundant love we will send down a resurrecting dew to bring the dead back to life. *Your dead shall live, my dead bodies shall arise. Awake and sing, that dwell in the dust, for a dew of lights is your dew and the earth shall cast out the departed.*[134]

We aspire to the renascence of the nation and the land, in order to resuscitate our state of soul,[135] in order to produce a living Israel, to vivify faith and love with the strength of Torah and commandments in full. We recognize the light of the God of Israel, Lord of the Universe, and the delight that is higher than "the Lord",[136] beyond all expression and conception, "beyond all blessing and song, hymn and comfort."[137] Though hidden, it is revealed in the light of faith and love, visible in the practice of Torah and commandments. We seek out Zion, we long to build the land and to be built through her, to absorb her spirit and her air, to unite with all the life connected to her. Therefore we need

תורה מרובה אנו דורשים, ולשם כך אנו שואפים לבריאות שלמה ולכח גופני חסון ואמיץ, מצות רבות אנו מבקשים, כדי שיהיו לנו די כלים להכיל בהם את האור הגדול של האמונה והאהבה, עם כל העונג והעדן וכל האור והטוהר העז והאמץ שלהם, שיתגלו לנו במלא מדתם, בשובנו לחיים עצמיים, לאומיים במלא ובמרום המובן. כל מה שיש לנו מזכרונות העתיקות וממצוה וחק, חביב עלינו חבת חיים, כי הם לנו כלים למקור חיים ועמם מקור חיים, האידיאלים הצפונים בהם חיים הם אתם ועם קיומם.

יח

שלשה כחות מתאבקים כעת במחנינו. המלחמה ביניהם נכרת היא ביותר בארץ ישראל, אבל פעולתם היא פעולה נמשכת מחיי האומה בכלל, ושרשיהם קבועים הם בתוך ההכרה החודרת במרחבי רוח האדם. אומללים נהיה אם את שלשת הכחות הללו - שהם מוכרחים להאחד אצלנו, לסייע כל אחד את חברו ולשכללו, שיבצר כל אחד מהם את הקצוניות שחברו יוכל להביא בצורה מקולקלת, כשלא יסויג דרכו - נניח בפזורם, במרידתם זה על זה, ובהחלקם כל אחד למחנה מיוחד, העומדת כצר למחנה השניה. הקודש, האומה, האנושיות - אלה הם שלשת התביעות העקריות, שהחיים כולם, שלנו ושל כל אדם, באיזו צורה שהיא, מורכבים מהם. איך שהן מניותיה של ההרכבה הזאת, אם חלק אחד מאלה תופס מקום פחות או יותר עקרי, אצל איזה יחיד או אצל איזה צבור, אבל לא נמצא ולא נוכל למצוא שום צורה קבועה של חיים אנושיים, שלא תהיה מורכבת משלשתם. ההתמזגות הדרושה של שלשת התביעות הגדולות הללו מוכרחת היא לבא בכל קבוצה, שיש לה תקוה של חיים עתידים, וכשאנו סוקרים בחיינו ורואים אנו, שהכחות הללו,

much Torah, and toward this end, we aspire to perfect health and physical prowess. We require many commandments so that we might have sufficient vessels to contain the great light of faith and love, with all their delight and pleasure, light, purity, and strength. These will be totally revealed to us when we return to a life of national independence, in the fullest and most sublime sense. All that we have in the way of ancient memories, commandment and law, we cherish as our lives, for they are the vessels for the source of life. The ideals contained therein come to life with their performance.

18

The Three Wrestlers – Orthodoxy, Nationalism, and Liberalism – and the Referee

Three forces wrestling in our camp: the Orthodox, the Nationalist, and the Humanist. Moving from divisiveness to unification. The positive aspect of the negation. Kemitsah *(the handful of flour in the Temple). Holiness as one of three camps; supernal holiness that transcends the three camps.*

Three forces are wrestling now in our camp. The battle between them is especially discernible in *Erets Yisrael*, but their effect draws from the life of the nation at large, and their roots are set within the consciousness penetrating the expanses of human spirit. We should be unfortunate if we allowed these three forces – which must necessarily unite among us, to aid one the other and perfect it, that each might check the extremism of the other – to remain scattered, mutually antagonistic, and schismatic. The Holy, the Nation, and Humanity – these are the three major demands of which all life, our own and every man's, is composed. However the distribution, whether one element occupies a major or minor portion, it is impossible to find a permanent form of human life that is not composed of these three elements. This goes for both the individual and the community. The desired mixture of these three great demands must arise in every group that aspires to future life. When we observe our lives and see that these forces, despite their potential for synthesis, are increasingly divided, we are

למרות תעודת התמזגותם, הולכים הם ונפרדים, הננו נקראים לבוא להצלה. יסודתו של הפירוד היא בצדדים השליליים שכל כח רואה בחברו, והצדדים השליליים מצד עצמם באמת אינם ראוים לשמם זה, כי בכל כח בודד, ביחוד נפשי, מוכרחים להיות צדדים שליליים, בפרט בהתפשטותו היתרה על חשבונם של כחות אחרים. בזה אין להפליא בין הקודש ובין החול: הכל נכנס תחת קו המדה והכל צריך משקל, "אפילו רוח הקודש ששורה על הנביאים במשקל הוא שורה". אבל הפירוד במקום שצריכים לאחד מביא לזה, שמעט מעט מתרוקן הרוח, ההכרה החיובית, במעמד הכח המיוחד, לפחות, לאותה האישיות או הקבוצה, הולכת ומתחסרת, מפני הצימוק ההולך ומתגבר באותו הכח המיוחד, הבודד בזרוע נגד טבע הרוח להיות מתאחד עם עוד יסודות המשלימים אותו, ותחתיה באה רק הכרה שלילית לפרנס את החיים, וכל בעל כח מיוחד מלא הוא רק מרץ של אש ביחש לשלילתו של הכח האחר או האחרים שאינו חפץ להכירם. ובאופן חיים כאלה המצב נורא, הרוח מתבוקק, עמדת האמת, הכרתה הפנימית יחד עם אהבתה, מתמוטטת והיא הולכת ונעדרת, על-ידי מה שנעשית עדרים עדרים.

שלשת הסיעות היותר רשמיות בחיי האומה אצלנו: האחת האורתודוכסית, כמו שרגילים לקראתה, הנושאת את דגל הקודש, טוענת באמץ, בקנאה ובמרירות, בעד התורה והמצוה, האמונה וכל קודש בישראל; השניה היא הלאומית החדשה, הלוחמת בעד כל דבר שהנטיה הלאומית שואפת אליו, שכוללת בקרבה הרבה מהטבעיות הטהורה של נטית אומה החפצה לחדש את חייה הלאומיים אחרי שהיו זמן רב עלומים בקרבה מתגרת ידה של הגלות המרה, והרבה ממה שהיא חפצה להכיר לטובה את אשר קלטה מרושם רוחם של עמים אחרים, באותה המדה שהיא מכרת שהיא טובה ונאותה גם לה; השלישית היא הליברלית, שהיתה

called to come to the rescue. The foundation of the schism consists of the negative aspects that each force views in its counterpart. The "negative aspects" in and of themselves are really not deserving of this title, for in every isolated faculty, especially the psychic, there are bound to be drawbacks, specifically when it expands at the expense of other faculties. In this, there is no discrimination between the holy and the secular: all must enter under the "line of measure"[138] and all require proportion. "Even the holy spirit which rests on the prophets, rests in proportion."[139] But divisiveness where there should have been unity brings about the gradual emptying of spirit. Positive awareness gradually dissipates in the individual or the collective, because of the progressive shrinking of that particular faculty, which stubbornly resists the nature of spirit to unite with additional complementary elements. Instead, a negative awareness comes to nurture life. Then each master of some specific faculty is filled with fiery energy vis-à-vis his negation of the other faculty or faculties that he refuses to recognize. In such a life-style, the situation is terrible, the spirit broken, the position of truth, its inner awareness together with its love, falters and disappears, by virtue of the fact that it [i.e., truth] has been parceled.

The three official parties in the life of our nation [are]: one, the Orthodox party, as we are accustomed to call it, which carries the banner of the holy, pitches stridently, jealously, bitterly for Torah and commandments, faith, and all that is holy in Israel; the second, the new Nationalist party, which campaigns for all the aspirations of the nationalist tendency, which comprises much of the pure naturalism of the nation, which desires to renew its national life, after it was so long hidden within due to the violence of the bitter exile, and much of that which it absorbed from other nations, which it desires to recognize as positive inasmuch as it deems it fitting for itself [i.e., the Jewish People] as well; the third is the Liberal party, which not so long ago carried the banner of Enlightenment and whose influence is still great in wide circles, does not fit into the nationalist scheme and seeks the universal human content of the Enlightenment, culture, ethics, and

נושאת את דגל ההשכלה בעבר לא רחוק ועדיין ידה תקיפה בחוגים רחבים, היא אינה מתכנסת בחטיבה הלאומית ודורשת את התוכן האנושי הכללי של ההשכלה, התרבות והמוסר ועוד. הדבר מובן, שבמצב בריא יש צורך בשלשת הכחות האלה גם יחד, ותמיד צריכים אנו לשאוף לבוא לידי המצב הבריא הזה, אשר שלשת הכחות הללו יחד יהיו שולטים בנו בכל מלואם וטובם, במצב הרמוני מתוקן שאין בו לא חסר ולא יתר, כי הקודש, האומה והאדם, יתדבקו יחד באהבה אצילית ומעשית, ויחד יתועדו היחידים וגם הסיעות שכל אחד מהם מוצא את כשרונותיו יותר מסוגלים לחלק אחד משלשת החלקים הללו, בידידות הראויה, להכיר בעין יפה כל אחד את התפקיד החיובי של חברו. אז תהיה ההכרה הזאת הולכת ומשתלמת, עד שלא די שיכיר כל אחד את הצד החיובי, שיש בכל כח, לדבר הגון ומקובל וראוי להשתמש בו, גם להטבה הכללית של מִזוג הרוח וגם להטבה הפרטית של בִסוסו של הכח המיוחד ההוא שהוא מוצא את עצמו שרוי תחת דגלו, אלא שעוד הלאה ילך, עד שאת התוכן החיובי אשר בצד השלילי של כל כח וכח, על-פי המדה הנכונה, גם כן יכיר לטוב, וידע שלטובתו של הכח המיוחד, שהוא יותר נוטה אליו, צריך הוא להיות מושפע באיזו מדה גם מהצד השולל, שהכח האחר שולל את הכח הזה החביב שלו. הוא מפני שבשלילתו הוא מעמידו על מדתו הראויה לו ומצילו מהגרעון המסוכן של התוספת וההפרזה, וזוהי העבודה המיוחדת מעבודות הקשות שבמקדש, הקמיצה, "שלא יחסר ושלא יותיר". וכן כשנסתכל בשכל טוב בתסיסות, שאנו סובלים מהן כל כך בדורנו, נדע שאך דרך אחד יש לפנינו: שכל אחד, בין יחיד ובין קבוץ, ישים אל לבו את המוסר הזה, ויחד עם ההגנה שכל אחד קרוא להגין על אותו הכח המיוחד שהוא מקושר אליו, על-פי טבע נפשו ועל-פי הרגלו וחנוכו, ידע איך להשתמש בכחות

so forth. It is understood that in a healthy state there is a need for these three forces together, and we must always aspire to come to this healthy state, in which these three forces together will reign in all of their plenitude and goodness, in a whole, harmonious state in which there is neither lack nor superfluity, for the Holy, the Nation and Man, will cleave together in a love lofty and practical. The individuals and also the parties, each of whom finds his talents best suited for one of these three elements, will congregate together in worthy friendship to recognize each the positive mission of his companion. Then this consciousness will be increasingly perfected, until not only will each recognize the positive aspect of each faculty as something worthy to be employed for the general welfare of the combined spirit and also for the individual benefit of the establishment[140] of that particular faculty under whose banner he finds himself – but beyond this, the positive content of the negative aspect[141] of each faculty, in proportion, he will recognize as good, and know that for the good of the particular faculty which he tends to, he must be influenced to a degree by the negating aspect, whereby the other faculty negates this force so dear to him. By negating, it puts into perspective and saves him from the dangerous liability of superfluity and exaggeration. This is that most difficult of rituals in the Temple, *kemitsah* (taking a precise handful of flour), "that he neither add nor detract."[142] Thus when we look intelligently at the eruptions from which we suffer so in our generation, we know that there is but one way before us: that everyone, whether individual or group, take to heart this lesson, and together with the defensiveness that everyone feels toward that particular strength to which he is attached, by natural temperament and by habit and training, he will know how to use faculties that reside in other persons and parties,[143] in order to round himself and his party, whether through the ratifying aspect of those other faculties or through the good portion of their negating qualities, which truly fortify his particular strength by preserving him from the ruination of exaggeration, which causes weakening and intellectual flabbiness. In this manner we can hope to arrive at a state of living worthy of one nation in the land.[144]

שהם מוצאים להם מקלטם באנשים אחרים ובסיעות אחרות, למען ישלים את עצמו ואת סיעתו, בין בצד החיובי של הכחות האחרים ובין בחלק הטוב של הצדדים השליליים שלהם, שהם יהיו מאמצים באמת את כחו המיוחד במה שישמרו אותו מקלקלת ההפרזה, הגורמת חלישות כח וטשטוש צורה. באופן זה נוכל לקוות להגיע למצב של חיים הראוים לגוי אחד בארץ.

מובן הדבר, כי מה שהכנסנו את הקודש בשדרת שלשת הכחות, שכל אחד צריך לצמצם את עצמו לפעמים כדי להניח מקום לחברו, איננו מובן כי אם בצד הטכני והמעשי של הקודש ובצדדים המחשביים וההרגשיים המתיחסים לזה. אמנם עצם הקודש העליון הרי הוא הנושא הכללי, שהצמצום הזה עצמו אף הוא מכלל עבודתו כמו כל העבודות הבאות לשכלול העולם והחיים בכל המובנים, שכולם הלא את ברכתם מקודש הם נושאים. על כן המחשבה האידיאלית הרוממה, המחשבה האלהית, היא בעצמה באמת חפשית היא מכל צמצומים, והקרבה האלהית היא ממולאה תמיד הרחבה עליונה למעלה מכל גבולים, "לכל תכלה ראיתי קץ רחבה מצותך מאד". ובהתהלך האדם והגוי בנתיבות הצדק המעשיים והמחשביים, הממודדים בגבולם, יבושר שלום לעלות גם כן אל האצילות הרחבה, "מן המצר קראתי יה ענני במרחב יה".

יט

סדר הגאולה ותחית האומה בארץ ישראל צריך ללכת על-פי סדרי הנבואה של "וזרעתי את בית ישראל ואת בית יהודה זרע אדם וזרע בהמה" - "זרע אדם לחוד וזרע בהמה לחוד". שלמות הצורה מוכרחת להברא. הנפשות הנוטות לבנין מעשי, לישוב ארצי ולשאיפה מדינית, מוכרחות להתיצר בכל הגונים החזקים הצריכים

It is understood that our lumping of the holy as one of three elements, each of which must sometimes restrain itself in order to leave space for the other, applies only to the technical and practical side of the holy and to the intellectual and emotional sides that relate thereto. However, the essence of supernal holiness[145] is the general subject; this very restraint is part of its task, just as all the tasks that come to perfect the world and life in all respects, carry their blessing from the Holy. Therefore the exalted ideal thought, the divine thought, is truly free of all restrictions. Closeness to God is filled always with an expansiveness beyond all borders.[146] *To all I have spied an end – Your commandment is very broad.*[147] When man and nation will stride in the practical and intellectual paths of righteousness, which are hemmed in, they will (eventually) rise to the expansive transcendence. *From the strait I called Yah; Yah answered me with an expanse.*[148]

19

"The Seed of Man and the Seed of Beast"

Heroes of transcendence, heroes of the material, and their interdependence. The Exile stunted psychic and physical growth; in the Land of Israel, there emerges a new, whole type.

The order of redemption and the national renascence in the Land of Israel must advance according to the order of the prophecy: "*I shall sow the House of Israel and the House of Judah, the seed of man and the seed of beast*[149] – the seed of man apart and the seed of beast apart."[150] The perfection of form must be created. The souls who incline to practical building, settling the Land, and national[151] aspiration, must be formed with all of the strident hues necessary for this characteristic; and men of transcendental souls, of the life of the spirit and the pleasures of the soul, who publicize and shine the supernal light of the Lord on the nation and the world, will also be realized in their fullness. It is precisely the full types who influence nicely one another,[152] and join together for the formation of a great organic national body, upon which shines the light of life of a powerful, holy soul. The higher,

למדה זו, והאנשים בעלי הנפשות האציליות, מחיי הרוח ומעדני הנשמה, המודיעים ומזריחים את אור ד׳ העליון על האומה והעולם, גם הם יצאו אל הפועל בכל מלואיהם. דוקא טפוסים מלאים משפיעים יפה אלו על אלו ומתחברים יחד ליצירת גויה לאומית אורגנית גדולה, שאור חיי נשמה קדושה כבירת כח זורח עליה. החיים האציליים העליונים, כשהם מלאים בכל יפעת גבורתם, הנם ממסד עד הטפחות שלהם נעלים מחיי ההמון, שעיקר מעינו הוא תקון המעמד הכלכלי, ואפילו החכם והסופר שבו סוף סוף המוני הוא, ארצי ומעשי, בכל מעינו לחיי הזמן והעולם, והקפה רוחנית, עולמית, לא תוצר ברוחו; אבל הטפוס השלם של גבורי האצילות מאציל על גבורי הגשמיות את הוד קדשם, על-ידי קרני זוהר המופיעים מהם. הגלות לא היתה יכולה להוציא אל הפועל טפוסים שלמים. לא המון גבור, כי הלא מקול עלה נדף מוכרח הוא להיות נרעד, ולא חכמים קדושים ברוח עוז, כיון שנסתלקה הנבואה וסר רוח הקודש, גם שרידי הקדושה שנשארו - צפונים ניצוצי גבורתם בקרבם פנימה כגחלים עוממות. כעת כבר הקיץ הקץ, ביאה שלישית הוחלה, הטפוס של זרע בהמה הולך ונוצר לעינינו, אבל לא יוכל לבא לשלמות גבורתו וקל-וחומר לספוג רוח עדינותו הפנימית ומגמת חבורו להעמיד גוי איתן, כי-אם על-ידי זרע אדם, שהם קרואים להוָצר על-ידי גדולת עז קודש, ״הנה אנכי והילדים אשר נתן לי ד׳ לאותות ולמופתים בישראל״.

כ

מחלוקת הדעות על דבר הדרכת הכלל, אם בזמן הזה, שרבו פריצים נושאי דגל ההפקרות ביד רמה, ראוי להפריד את האומה, שהכשרים נושאי דגל שם ד׳ לא יהי להם שום יחש עם פורקי-

transcendental life, when filled with beautiful strength, is thoroughly exalted beyond the life of the crowd, whose main concern is financial success[153] – even the sage and writer is, in the final analysis, [a man] of the crowd, earthy and practical, preoccupied with temporal and mundane life, while spiritual, global breadth is not formed in his spirit. However, the whole type of heroes of transcendence bestows on the heroes of the material their majestic holiness, through rays of splendor that radiate from them. The Exile was incapable of actualizing whole types, neither a courageous crowd, for it had to shudder at the sound of a falling leaf, nor holy sages at the pinnacle of their strength, for prophecy departed and divine inspiration left. Even in the remnants of holiness who survived, the sparks of their might were hidden inside them as dull coals. Now the End already approaches, a third entry[154] [into the Land] has begun, the type of "the seed of beast" is being formed before our eyes, but it will achieve its wholeness of strength (and absorb its inner sensitivity) and the purpose of its formation – to establish a solid nation – only through "the seed of man," who are called into creation by the might of holiness. *I and the children the Lord gave me are signs and wonders in Israel.*[155]

20

A Most Terrible Decree: "Cut!"

The question of religious secession from the community. The parable of the two mothers. Wicked: righteous :: dregs: wine. The deed of Amalek.

The difference of opinion concerning the communal direction – whether at this time, because of the proliferation of rebels who hold high the banner of anarchy, it is correct to divide the nation, so that the pious who raise the banner of the Lord will disassociate themselves from the rebellious sinners, or whether the power of overall peace outweighs all – this entire controversy comes about because of the overall lowliness, for purity has not been fully completed in the basic character of the nation as regards the exterior of its soul,[156] and it is being progressively purified. Both these parties are on the level of the

העול הפושעים, או שמא כח השלום הכללי מכריע את הכל - כל עקרה של פלוגתא זו באה מפני השפלות הכללית, שעדיין לא נגמרה הטהרה לגמרי ביסוד האופי של האומה, מצד חיצוניות נפשה, והיא מטהרת והולכת. אלה הכתות יחדו הנן בזה במדרגת שתים נשים זונות שבאו אל שלמה: הדבור "הביאו חרב" נסיון הוא מחכמת אלהים שבמלכות ישראל: אותה הראויה להדחות, היא הטוענת: "גזורו", ובהתמרמרה מבלטת היא את אמתת הטינא שבלב שהיא חשה בעצמה, שכל ענינה הוא רק "גם לי גם לך לא יהיה - גזורו!", והאם הרחמניה, אם האמת, אומרת: "תנו לה את הילוד החי, והמת אל תמיתוהו", ורוח הקודש צווחת: "תנו לה את הילוד החי, היא אמו!". אין קץ לרעות הגשמיות והרוחניות של התפרדות האומה לחלקים, אף על-פי שפרוד גמור כהעולה על לב המנתחים באכזריות אי-אפשר הוא והיה לא יהיה. זאת היא ממש מחשבה של עבודה זרה כללית, שהננו בטוחים עליה שלא תתקים, "אשר אתם אומרים: נהיה כגוים כמשפחות הארצות לשרת עץ ואבן, חי אני נאם ד' אלהים אם לא ביד חזקה ובזרוע נטויה ובחמה שפוכה אמלוך עליכם!", וככל מחשבה של עבודה זרה היא מחריבה ומדאיבה - אפילו כשלא באה ולא תבא לידי מעשה. יסוד צדקת הצדיקים בכל דור ודור נתמך הוא גם על-ידי הרשעים, שעם כל רשעתם כל זמן שהם דבוקים בחפץ לבם לכללות האומה, עליהם נאמר, "ועמך כולם צדיקים", וחיצוניות הרשעות שלהם מועילה היא לאמץ כחם של צדיקים "כדורדיא לחמרא", והפרוד המדומה חותר הוא תחת יסוד הקדושה כולה, כמעשה עמלק שזנב את הנחשלים, פליטי הענן, "שלח ידיו בשלומיו, חלל בריתו".

two harlots who came to Solomon.[157] The fiat, "Bring a sword,"[158] is a probing on the part of the divine wisdom of Israelite kingdom: The one who is to be spurned[159] is the one who says, "Cut!"[160] In her murmuring she pronounces the real gripe in her heart. Her only interest is, "It shall be to neither me nor you. Cut!"[161] And the merciful mother, the real mother, says: "Give her the living child, only do not slay it!"[162] And the divine spirit screams: "Give her the living child, she is its mother!"[163] There is no end to the physical and spiritual evils of dividing the nation into sectors, even though total separation as imagined by those who cruelly operate[164] is impossible and will never be. This is really a thought of general idolatry,[165] which we are promised will not be fulfilled. *That which you say, We shall be as the nations, as the families of the lands to serve wood and stone. As I live, says the Lord, if not by a strong hand and an outstretched arm and outpouring rage I shall rule over you.*[166] As every idolatrous thought, it destroys and worries, even though it has not, and will not, come to deed. The foundation of the righteousness of the just in every generation is supported by the wicked[167] as well, who with all their wickedness, as long as they cling with their heart's desire to the collectivity of the nation, are referred to (by the verse), *Your people are all righteous.*[168] Their outer wickedness serves to anneal the strength of the righteous, *"as dregs to wine."*[169] The imagined division undermines the foundation of all holiness, as the deed of Amalek,[170] who attacked the stragglers disgorged by the Cloud (of Glory).[171] *He stretched his hand against his peace, he profaned his covenant.*[172]

כא

כל חשק עבודה, שמחת מצוה, התמדת תורה, ברק חדושים והתנוצצות רוח הקודש בלב השרידים אשר ד׳ קורא, כונת התפלה ואור שלהבתה, כל אלה, ותולדות הנשמות בשלמותן, בכללותן ותמותן, מוכרחים הם להפגם על-ידי הכנסת יסוד פירוד בכללות כנסת ישראל, חלילה. אוהבי ד׳ ויראיו באמת וחושבי שמו הם הם העומדים בנסיון לסבול כל צער ועלבון מכל צד ועבר, ולעמד הכן נגד כל כחות עליונים ותחתונים החפצים לבלע נחלת ד׳ ולהפריד את האומה האחדיית, היחידה במלא עולמים, הם הם בנים דכנסת ישראל שהאם רובצת עליהם, ״מחצדי חקלא״ הבאים בסוד ד׳, תלמידי חכמים האמתיים המרבים שלום בעולם, ומשימים ומטילין שלום בין ישראל לאביהם שבשמים, בהוציאם מן הכח אל הפועל את אור הקודש הגנוז בכל אישי האומה, בכל אשר בשם ישראל יכנה, ובפרט בכל אשר ישא את דגל תקות האומה וחפץ תחיתה, את חותם אהבת ארץ אשר עיני ד׳ בה, וחבת ציון וירושלים על לבו חקוקה, באיזו צורה ואיזו הסברה שתהיה. כל המעקשים ייושרו, ואחדות האומה להכשרת גאולתה וגאולת העולם כולו תצא אל הפועל ביקר שגיא, ״כי רצו עבדיך את אבניה ואת עפרה יחוננו, וייראו גוים את שם ד׳ וכל מלכי הארץ את כבודך, כי בנה ד׳ ציון נראה בכבודו, פנה אל תפלת הערער ולא בזה את תפלתם, תכתב זאת לדור אחרון, ועם נברא יהלל יה, כי השקיף ממרום קדשו, ד׳ משמים אל ארץ הביט, לשמע אנקת אסיר לפתח בני תמותה, לספר בציון שם ד׳ ותהלתו בירושלים, בהקבץ עמים יחדו וממלכות לעבוד את ד׳״. ״וזרעתי את בית ישראל ואת בית יהודה זרע אדם וזרע בהמה – ״זרע אדם

21

The Indivisible Unity of the Nation

Against divisiveness. The sons of Knesset Yisrael *(Ecclesia Israel). Three types of souls: the seed of man, the seed of beast, and "people who are cunning in knowledge and place themselves as beasts." The essential unity of Israel.*

All the love of (divine) service, joy in commandments, diligent study of Torah, flashes of originality, divine inspiration in the heart of the remnant whom the Lord calls, intention of prayer and its illumination – all these, and the products of souls in their wholeness, totality, and perfection, must be spoiled by injecting an element of divisiveness in *Knesset Yisrael* (Ecclesia Israel), God forbid.[173] Those who love the Lord and fear Him truly, and respect His name, they are the ones who withstand the tribulation, to suffer pain and insult from every side, and to stand alert against all the forces above and below who desire to swallow the inheritance of the Lord and divide the one-and-only nation in all the worlds. They are the sons of *Knesset Yisrael*[174] (Ecclesia Israel) upon whom the mother bird[175] lays, mystical "harvesters of the field,"[176] the true scholars who increase peace in the world,[177] and make peace between Israel and their Father in heaven,[178] who release the light of holiness hidden in all members of the nation, in all who are called by the name *Israel*,[179] and particularly in whoever carries the banner of the nation's hope and desire for renascence, whoever carries the seal of the love of the Land on which are the eyes of the Lord, whoever has affection for Zion and Jerusalem engraved on his heart, in whatever form or expression. All perversities will be straightened, and the unification of the nation for the preparation of its redemption and the redemption of the entire world will come to fruition with great honor.

> *For your servants hold dear her stones and her dust they cherish. Then shall nations fear the name of the Lord, and all the kings of the earth Your glory. When the Lord shall have built Zion, he appears in His glory. He has regarded the prayer of the forsaken, and did not despise their prayer. This shall be written down for the last generation and the people created will praise*

לחוד וזרע בהמה לחוד", שמתאחדים יחד על-ידי אלה הנשמות שהן ממדרגת "אדם ובהמה תושיע ד'" - "אלו בני אדם הערומים בדעת ומשימים עצמם כבהמה", "ואני בער ולא אדע בהמות הייתי עמך, ואני תמיד עמך אחזת ביד ימיני, בעצתך תנחני ואחר כבוד תקחני, מי לי בשמים ועמך לא חפצתי בארץ, כלה שארי ולבבי צור לבבי וחלקי אלהים לעולם, כי הנה רחקיך יאבדו, הצמת כל זונה ממך, ואני קרבת אלהים לי טוב, שתי בד' אלהים מחסי לספר כל מלאכותיך". ומלאכות ד' היא היא כדבר ד' בידי מלאכי: "הלא אח עשו ליעקב - ואוהב את יעקב", שהיא תשובה נצחית מספקת לכל תאנתם של מתאוננים קטני-אמנה, האומרים בכל דור ודור, וביותר בדור התגלות אור ישועה: "במה אהבתנו?". ובאמת - "אהבת עולם ואהבה רבה אהבתנו ד' אלהינו חמלה גדולה ויתרה חמלת עלינו", "אבינו מלכנו, בעבור שמך הגדול ובעבור אבותינו שבטחו בך ותלמדם חקי חיים, כן תחננו ותלמדנו, והביאנו לשלום מארבע כנפות הארץ, ותוליכנו מהרה קוממיות לארצנו". ואומר: "מהר והבא עלינו ברכה ושלום, כי אל פועל ישועות אתה, ובנו בחרת מכל עם ולשון, להודות לך וליחדך באהבה", וחותם: הבוחר בעמו ישראל באהבה". להיות הקדמה ליחוד ד' ב"שמע ישראל" ו"ברוך שם כבוד מלכותו לעולם ועד", הנאמר בחשאי; ואף על-פי שהגלוי סותר זה לפעמים אין בכך כלום, כי האמת הברורה הוא מאמר השבטים כולם: "כשם שאין בלבך אלא אחד כך אין בלבנו אלא אחד", ו"יעקב אבינו לא מת", ד"מקיש הוא לזרעו: מה זרעו בחיים אף הוא בחיים", והרי זה בא ללמד ונמצא למד, מקיש זרעו לו: מה הוא כולו בחיים, "וישא יעקב רגליו, ויאסף רגליו אל המטה", אף זרעו כולו בחיים, "ואתם הדבקים בד' אלהיכם

> *Yah. For He has looked down from the height of His sanctuary, the Lord has glanced from heaven to earth. To hear the sighing of the prisoner, to release those doomed to death. To proclaim in Zion the name of the Lord and His praise in Jerusalem. When peoples are gathered together and kingdoms to serve the Lord.*[180]

"*I shall sow the House of Israel and the House of Judah, the seed of man and the seed of beast*[181] – the seed of man apart and the seed of beast apart,"[182] which are united by those souls who are of the level of "*Man and beast you shall save, Lord*[183] – these are people who are cunning in knowledge and place themselves as beasts."[184] *I was foolish and did not know; I was as a beast with You.*[185]

> *And I am always with You; You have held my right hand. With Your counsel You lead me, and after death will take me. Whom do I have in heaven? Beside You I desire nothing on earth. My flesh and heart are consumed; God is the rock of my heart and my portion forever. For, lo, those that are far from You will perish; You destroy everyone who strays from You. And as for me, the closeness of God is good for me; I have placed in the Lord God my trust, to relate all Your works.*[186]

And the works *(malakhot)* of the Lord are as the word of the Lord to Malakhi: *Is not Esau a brother to Jacob – but I loved Jacob!*,[187] which is an eternal answer sufficient for the grumblings of men of small faith, who say in every generation, especially in the generation of the revelation of the light of salvation: *With what have You loved us?*[188] In truth –

> *An eternal and great love You have loved us O Lord our God, a great and extra mercy You have had upon us. Our Father, our King, for the sake of Your great name and for the sake of our fathers who trusted in You, and whom You taught laws of life, so be kind to us and teach us ... And bring us to peace from the four corners of the earth, and lead us quickly upright to our land. Quickly bring upon us blessing and peace, for You are a God who works salvation, and You chose us from every people and tongue, to praise You and unify You with love.*[189]

חיים כולכם היום", "בימים ההם ובעת ההיא נאם ד' יבוקש את עון ישראל ואיננו ואת חטאת יהודה ולא תמצאינה, כי אסלח לאשר אשאיר".

כב

אש האהבה הטבעית לאומה ולתחיתה, ההולכת ומתגדלת בארץ ישראל ועל-ידי ארץ ישראל, תתלקח בגאון עוזה יחד עם אש ד', אש הקודש, של כל טוהר האמונה בעוצם חסנה וגבורתה. פזורי האמונה האלהית, וכל תנחומותיה והערותיה הרבות למוסר ולישור, לגבורה ולתקוה, לשלום ולנחמת עולמים, שכבר נתפשטו בין גוים רבים ועצומים על-ידי פזורנו בין הגוים, על-ידי התפשטות האמונות הנובעות ממקור כתבי הקודש, הולכים ושבים אלינו, מתכנסים לאוצרנו, מתקלטים עוד הפעם בכנסת ישראל ושבים לתחיה על-ידי המון נשמות חדשות של עם נברא. חלילה לנו לחסום את הדרך בפני אור החיים, לא נבהל אם הזרמים נראים שונים בחיצוניותם - אור ד' מאיר בהם, רוח ד' נוססה בהם. הלאומיות החולונית יכולה להזדהם בזוהמא רבה שתחתיה הרבה רוחות רעים גנוזים, אבל לא בהדוף אותה מתוך נשמת הדור נצליח, כי-אם בהשתדלות נמרצה להביאה אל מקורה העליון, לחברה עם הקודש המקורתי שממנו היא נובעת.

And (the blessing) concludes: *Who chooses His people Israel with love,*[190] as an introduction to the unification of the Lord in *Shema' Yisrael* (Hear O Israel) and *Barukh shem* (Blessed is the name [of His glorious kingdom forever unto eternity]) that is recited silently.[191] Even though the revealed [reality] sometimes contradicts this,[192] this is of no import, for the clear truth is the saying of all the tribes: "Just as in your heart there is but One, so in our heart there is but One."[193] "Jacob our father did not die,"[194] for "He is compared to his seed. Just as his seed are alive, so he is alive."[195] And the converse is to be inferred: His seed are compared to him; just as he is entirely alive (*Jacob lifted his feet;*[196] *he gathered his feet to the bed*[197]), so his seed are entirely alive. *You who cling to the Lord are all alive today.*[198] *In those days and at that time, says the Lord, the sin of Israel will be sought and it will not be, and the sin of Judah and it will not be found, for I shall forgive those I preserve.*[199]

22
Welcoming New Souls

The return of scattered lights through the multitude of new souls of a created people. The purification of secular nationalism.

The fire of natural love for the nation and its renascence, which is increasingly magnified in the Land of Israel and by the Land of Israel, will burn mightily together with the fire of the Lord, the fire of the holy, of all the purity of faith with its fortitude and courage. The scatterings of divine faith and all its many comfortings and arousals to ethics and rectitude, courage and hope, peace and eternal comfort, which have already spread among many mighty nations through our dispersion among the nations, through the spread of the beliefs that flow from the source of the Holy Writings, are returning to us, are gathering to our storehouse, are reinstated[200] in *Knesset Yisrael* (Ecclesia Israel), and return to life through a multitude of new souls of a created people.[201] Heaven forfend us from closing the door before the light of life. We shall not be upset if the streams appear strange on their surface – the light of the Lord shines through them, the spirit of the Lord inspires[202]

כג

כשהאהבה הלאומית מתגברת, מתלהבת היא על תורת ישראל, לאהבה אותה בין בלמוד בין במעשה, והחשק המתפתח מביא לידי אהבה מפעלת את הבליטה של הפרטים ופרטי הפרטים, בין בתלמוד בין בקיום המעשי. וצריך כל צדיק להגביר בעצמו ובעולם את אש האהבה הלאומית בישראל, ולהגבירה בכל מיני השפעות שבעולם, ובטוח יהיה שסוף כל סוף תבא אהבה כללית זו לבשול פריה הגמור עד כדי הולדת תולדותיה, שהם המעשים, המדות והדעות של כל התורה כולה בכל מלואה וטובה; וכל מה שאנו רואים שישנם אנשים מתאמרים באהבת ישראל, ולבם רחק מהתורה, מלמודה וקיומה, הוא מפני שעדיין אהבתם בוסרית היא, "וכרמנו סמדר".

כד

אשרי איש שחושב עצמו כשיריים לגבי כנסת ישראל כולה, שהיא נחלת ד', שכל מחשבות לבבו, הגיונותיו, חפצו ושאיפתו, אמונתו ורעיונו, אינם כי-אם חשק טמיר אחד לְהִכָּלֵל כולו באוצר חיים זה, "להתחסד עם קן דיליה - דא כנסת ישראל!" ההכרה הפנימית, שהננו שריגים מעץ חיים רב דליות ושגיא פרי, שכל מה שאנו יותר מעורים בגופו של אילן הננו חיים את החיים היותר שלמים ורעננים, בהוה ובנצח, היא תביא את תחית האומה למגמתה, היא ואך היא תקיץ את הקץ, שאליו אנו עורגים, ותתן לנו חוסן ישועות. והשרידים אשר ד' קורא, חסידי הדור, קדושי עליון, אין להם להסתכל בשום גרעון, בשום צד שלילי של כל

them. Secular nationalism may be infected with much poison,[203] under which lie hidden several evil spirits, but not by expelling it from the soul of the generation will we succeed, but rather by an earnest attempt to bring it to its supernal source, to fuse it to the source of holiness[204] from which it springs.

23

From Love of Israel to Love of Torah

Mature love of the nation perforce brings to love of Torah.

When the national love grows strong, it becomes enthused about the Torah of Israel, to love it whether in study or action, and the developing enthusiasm brings to a love that actualizes[205] attention to detail, both in study and actual practice. Every *tsaddik* (righteous person) must strengthen in himself and at large the fire of Jewish national love, through all the types of influence in the world. He can rest assured that eventually this general love will reach full maturation to the point of producing fruits, which are the deeds, characteristics and opinions of the entire Torah in all its fullness and goodness. If we see people who boast of love of Israel while their heart is far from Torah, its study and fulfillment, it is because their love is yet immature. *Our vineyard is immature.*[206]

24

The Ultimate Love: To Be the *Shirayim* (Leftovers) of the Jewish People

Connecting to the body of Knesset Yisrael *(Ecclesia Israel).*
Learning to love the nation.

Happy is the man who considers himself a remainder in relation to *Knesset Yisrael* (Ecclesia Israel),[207] the inheritance of the Lord; whose total thought, contemplation, desire and aspiration, belief and concept is not but a single hidden desire to be totally subsumed in this treasure of life. "To do kindness to His Nest – *Knesset Yisrael* (Ecclesia Israel)!"[208] The inner awareness, that we are branches of a luxurious,

נפש מישראל, הדבקה באיזה דבק בצור מחצבתה, כי-אם להעלות את הנקודה הכללית שבכל נשמה פרטית ברום גבהה ובעלוי קדושתה. האהבה הבלי-גבולית אל האומה, אֵם החיים שלנו, אינה יכולה לְהִפָּחֵת משום סבה וכשלון שבעולם, "לא הביט און ביעקב ולא ראה עמל בישראל, ד׳ אלהיו עמו ותרועת מלך בו". מתנשאים אנו מעל כל מחשבות השטנה של ההבנה השטחית, שתופסים בה מוסרים, מאמרים מיוחדים, שמעוררים על ידם כעס ושנאת אחים, ומלאי רצון ושקויי טל חסדים אדירים הננו שבים לחבק בזרועות אהבה את כל הנשמה לבית יעקב, החפצה לראות בשמחת גויינו ולהתהלל עם נחלתנו. דוקא מתוך האהבה הנאמנה, מתוך רחשי הכבוד היותר מסורים בכל חום רוח ונפש, הננו באים להכריז על התשובה אל התורה והמצוה, אל הקודש והאמונה, אל מורשת אבות ומסורת קדומים, אל אור ד׳ אלהי ישראל, המופיע על עמו ועל ארצו לעדי עד בגאון עזו. נתרחק נא מכל טינא, נתרומם מכל קטנות מח ולב, נתעלה מכל שנאה וקנטוריה, נספוג נא את האהבה הרעננה ממקור עדנה, נרכיב את ענפי החסד על שרשי הדעה, את הוד החופש על הדרת השיבה, של האֵמון של כבוד הורים ומורים, אשר לעם עתיק אציל ואיתן. לתחיה איתנה זו קרואים אנו ואליה נבא, ארץ אבות החמודה, ארץ חיים לנו, היא תכשירנו לעילוי-עילוים זה. "כי זה אלהים אלהינו עולם ועד, הוא ינהגנו על מות".

bountiful Tree of Life, that to the extent we are bound in the body of the Tree, we live life at its fullest and freshest, in the present and eternity – will bring the renascence of the people to its destination; only it will bring about the End for which we long and grant us the fortitude of salvation. The survivors to whom the Lord calls, the pious of the generation, the most holy, should not look at any shortcoming, any negative side of a Jewish soul, which clings by some attachment to its Source, but rather uplift the collective point in every individual soul to its loftiest height and holiness. The unbounded love of the nation, mother of our life,[209] cannot be diminished by any cause or failing in the world. *He saw no iniquity in Jacob, nor vexation in Israel; the Lord his God is with him, and the trumpeting of the King in his midst.*[210] We transcend all the hateful thoughts of superficial understanding, which seizes on isolated admonitions and sayings to arouse thereby anger and fraternal hatred.[211] Full of will and drenched with the dew of powerful loving-kindness, we return to embrace with arms of love any soul of the House of Jacob who desires to see the joy of our nation and take pride in our patrimony. Precisely out of faithful love, out of respect conveyed with all the passion of spirit and soul, we come to announce the return (*teshuvah*) to Torah and *mitsvah* (commandment), to holiness and faith, to the tradition of the fathers, to the light of the Lord, God of Israel, which is manifest on His people and land for all eternity. Let us distance ourselves from every grudge; transcend all smallness of mind and heart; rise above all hatred and baiting. Let us absorb fresh love from the source of delight, graft branches of love to roots of knowledge, the majesty of freedom to the beauty of age (the respect for parents and teachers that is characteristic of an ancient, noble, mighty nation). To this mighty renascence we are called and shall come. The delightful ancestral land, land of our life, will prepare us for this ascent-of-ascents. *For this is God, our God for eternity; He will conduct us through death.*[212]

כה

סמוך לעקבא דמשיחא מתרבה סגולת האחדות באומה, המעשים הטובים והדעות והאור האלהי הנמצאים בצדיקים פועלים על קדושת הכלל יותר מבשאר הזמנים. טמונה היא סגולה זו במטמון של קטיגוריא ומריבות, אבל תוכו רצוף אהבה ואחדות נפלאה, שמעוררת הרגשה כללית לצפיה לתשועת הגוי כולו.

כו

אחרי המגרעות הרבות, שאנו רואים בדרכי חיינו הכלליים בדורנו בכלל ובארץ ישראל בפרט, הננו מוכרחים להרגיש שאנו נולדים מחדש, מתחתית המדרגה הננו הולכים ונוצרים עוד הפעם כימים מקדם. כל הרכוש הרוחני של העבר הולך ונבלע לכאורה במקורו, ויוצא הוא בפנים חדשות, מקוטנות הרבה בכמותן, אבל רעננות מאד ועלולות לצמיחת גדולה, מלאה חיים עזיזים, באיכותן. הננו קרואים לעולם חדש מלא זוהר עליון, לתקופה חדשה שתעלה בחסנה על כל התקופות גדולות הערך שקדמו לה. מאמין הוא העם כולו, שאין גלות עוד אחרי הגאולה ההולכת ומתחלת שלפנינו, ואמונתו העמוקה הזאת היא בעצמה רז קיומו היא, סוד ד׳ נגלה במהלכו ההיסתורי, והמסורת העתיקה מעידה על אור נשמתו המכרת את עצמה ואת כל יחוסי מאורעותיה עד דור אחרון, דור צופה לישועה קרובה.

25

Getting It Together

Before Messiah, the nation becomes unified: negative and positive ramifications.

Before the epoch of the Messiah, the nation becomes more unified; the good deeds, the opinions and the divine light found in the righteous, exert a greater influence over the holiness of the collective than at other times. This quality is obscured in a hiding place of accusations and quarrels, but inwardly it is full of love and wonderful unity, which arouses a general feeling of anticipation of the entire nation's salvation.

26

The Very Last Exile

There will be no more exile after the present Redemption.

After all the shortcomings that we see in the general life-style of our generation as a whole, and in the Land of Israel in particular, we are forced to feel that we are born anew. From the lowliest level we are recreated as in days past. All the spiritual wealth of the past would seem to be absorbed in its source and emerges with a new face, much reduced in quantity, but in quality, exceedingly fresh and ready for great growth, full of surging life. We are invited to a new world[213] full of supernal splendor, to a new era that will surpass in strength all the great eras that preceded it. The entire People believes that there will be no more exile after the redemption[214] that is presently commencing, and this profound belief is itself the secret of its [i.e., the People's] existence, the mystery of the Lord revealed in its [i.e., the People's] historical process, and the ancient tradition attests to the light of its [i.e., the People's] soul that recognizes itself and the entire genealogy of events until the last generation, a generation looking for imminent salvation.[215]

כז

ההתגברות הרוחנית העליונה מחזקת את התכנים המעשיים ומגברת את ההתענינות בעולם ובחיים וכל אשר בם. רק בזמן החרבן, וקרוב לו, שהחיל הישראלי נעתק מאדמתו והוצרך להכיר את תעודתו רק במעמדו הרוחני המופשט, הושרשה ביחידים הדרכה לפרישות מחיי שעה בשביל חיי עולם, וגם על זה יצאה מחאה שמימית. אבל כאשר הגיע התור של בנין האומה בארצה, והצורך המעשי של הסדורים המדיניים והחברתיים נעשה חלק מתכנית פעלי הכלל, הרי הם הם גופי תורה, וכל מה שיתרחבו הגורמים המעשיים ויתבססו, יותר יפעל הרוח המלא קדושה וחיי אמת על העולם ועל החיים, ואור ישראל יאיר פני תבל בכליל יפעתו.

כח

הקדושה שבטבע היא קדושת ארץ ישראל, והשכינה שירדה בגלות עם ישראל הוא הכשרון להעמיד קדושה בנגוד לטבע. אבל הקדושה הלוחמת נגד הטבע אינה קדושה שלמה, צריכה היא להיות בלועה בתמציתה העליונה בקדושה העליונה, שהיא הקדושה שבטבע עצמה, שהוא יסוד תקון עולם כולו וביסומו הגמור, והקודש שבגולה, יחובר אל קודש הארץ, "ועתידין בתי כנסיות ובתי מדרשות שבבבל שיקבעו בארץ ישראל".

כשבאים להשכלה עליונה זו של הקדושה השלמה שבטבע, הכוללת בקרבה גם כן את הקדושה שלמעלה מן הטבע, והמתנגדת אל הטבע, אז המלחמה חודלת לגמרי, מדת הדין מתבסמת, והכל

27

Torah *Engagée*

Political and social organization become principles of Torah.

The higher spiritual resurgence strengthens the practical deeds and reinforces interest in the world and in life, and all contained therein. Only at and around the time of the destruction of the Temple, when the Israelite mass was uprooted from its land and forced to recognize its destiny only in its abstract spirituality, was there implanted in a few the direction[216] of seceding from temporal life for eternal life, and even then there issued a heavenly protest.[217] But with the arrival of the era of building the nation in its land, the practical requirement of political and social organization has become part of the agenda of the collective. These become principles of Torah,[218] and the more the practical factors expand and solidify, the more[219] the spirit of sanctity and true life will influence the world and life, and the light of Israel – with all its beauty – will illuminate the face of the earth.

28

Two Responses to Nature: *Erets Yisrael's* and the Diaspora's

The Shekhinah *(divine presence) in exile: sanctity in opposition to nature. The holiness of the land: sanctity in harmony with nature.*

The sanctity of nature is the sanctity of the Land of Israel, and the *Shekhinah* (divine presence) that was exiled with Israel[220] is the ability to preserve sanctity in opposition to nature.[221] But the sanctity that combats nature is not whole sanctity; it must be absorbed in the supernal essence of the higher sanctity, which is the sanctity of nature itself, the foundation of the entire world's perfection and complete invigoration. The holiness of exile will be joined to the holiness of the Land. "Eventually the synagogues and study-houses of Babylonia will be relocated to the Land of Israel."[222]

נוטה כלפי חסד. כל הכחות שבאדם הפרטי נראים בעדינותם המרוממה, כפי מה שהם בטבעם, והרי הם קדושים ומוכשרים לעלוי היותר עליון, והאור שלמעלה מן הטבע עומד אצור בהם לעת הצורך, והאדם חש בקרבו חופש של נועם קודש, ו״ימוד עצמו כאילו קדוש שרוי בתוך מעיו, שנאמר: בקרבך קדוש״.

כט

אין הטבע מתגלה למשורר הישראלי בכל הדרו ויפיו מפני שבר האומה והרחקתה מהחיים הטבעיים הבריאים. ואם ירצה משורר בעל כשרון להתמכר אל הטבע למרות כשלונה של האומה יוכל רק להטביע את עצמו בצד המוחש הגס שלה, אבל את יפיה השמימי לא יוכל לחוש בכל טובו והדר זיוו, כי כיון שירצה להתרומם אל הספירה הרוחנית ירגיש שבר האומה וידום רוחו, תחת אשר בשקיעה החושית יוכל לשכח לפעמים את המצב ההוה של האומה. ״מיום שחרב בית המקדש לא נראה רקיע בטהרתו, שנאמר: אלביש שמים קדרות ושק אשים כסותם״. התחיה הלאומית, הנכרת בבנין הארץ, כשהיא נלקחת עם מקורה החי, תוכל כבר להחזיר רשמים הגונים מזיו הרוחני של הדר הטבע, עד שתולד האפשרות להסתכל לא רק בארציותו כי־אם גם בזיוו השמימי בערך ידוע המכוון לפי ניצוצי האור שבתחיה המתפתחת.

When we attain this higher understanding of the whole sanctity that is in nature, which includes within it supernatural and[223] anti-natural holiness, then the battle stops, the attribute of judgment is sweetened, and all inclines to the attribute of love. All the forces of an individual human appear in the gentle state that they are by nature, holy and prepared for the highest upliftment. The light that is above nature is reserved within them for time of need, and a man feels in himself a freedom of pleasant holiness. "One should regard himself as if the holy rests within his stomach, as it says: *In your innards the holy*."[224]

29

The Israelite Poet

As Redemption beckons, the national poet of Israel becomes a poet of nature.

Nature is not revealed to the Israelite poet in all its splendor and beauty because of the destruction of the nation and its removal from natural, healthy life. Should a talented poet desire to be given over to nature despite the failure of the nation, he could only immerse himself in its gross, sensual aspect. However, he will not be able to sense its heavenly beauty with all of its goodness and brilliance, for as soon as he ascends to the spiritual sphere, he will be struck by the brokenness of the nation and his spirit will be silenced. This differs from self-immersion in the sensual side that sometimes allows forgetting the present state of the nation. "From the day the Temple was destroyed, the sky has not been seen in its purity, for it says: *I will dress the heavens in black, and I shall place sack as their clothing*."[225] The national rebirth, noticed in the building of the land, taken together with its living source, can already restore considerable traces of the spiritual brilliance of the beauty of nature, until the opportunity will arise to view not only its earthiness but also its heavenly brilliance – in direct proportion to the sparks of light in the developing rebirth.

ל

הנני רואה בעיני, אור חיי אליהו עולה, כחו לאלהיו הולך ומתגלה, הקודש שבטבע פורץ גדריו, הולך הוא בעצמו להתאחד עם הקודש שלמעלה מן הטבע הגס, עם הקודש הלוחם בטבע. לחמנו בטבע ויצאנו בנצחון, הטבע המגושם עשה אותנו לבעלי-מומים, נגע בכף ירכנו, אבל השמש הלא לנו זרחה לרפאותנו מצלעתנו. היהדות של העבר, ממצרים ועד הנה, מלחמה ארוכה היא נגד הטבע, בצדו הכעור של טבע העולם, טבע האנושי הכללי, אפילו טבע האומה וטבעו של כל יחיד. לחמנו בטבע כדי לנצחו, כיד לרדותו בתוך ביתו, הוא נכנע בפנינו, העולמות הולכים ומתבסמים, בעצם עומק הטבע תביעה גדולה מתגברת לקדושה ולטהרה, לעדינות נפש ולזכוך החיים, אליהו בא לבשר שלום, ובנשמתה הפנימית של האומה זרם חיים של טבע מתפרץ, והוא הולך ומתקרב אל הקודש. זכירת יציאת מצרים הולכת ונעשית לזכירת יציאת שעבוד מלכיות ההולכת ומתרקמת, והננו כולנו הולכים ומתקרבים אל הטבע והוא מתקרב אלינו, הולך הוא ונכבש לפנינו ודרישותיו הולכות ומתתאמות עם דרישותינו האציליות ממקור הקודש. הרוח הצעיר התובע את ארצו, שפתו, חרותו וכבודו, ספרותו וכחו, רכושו, רגשותיו, נזרמים הם על-ידי שטף של טבע, שבתוכיותו מלא הוא אש קודש.

לא

יתפתח הישוב בארץ ישראל, יבנה הבנין הלאומי, מתוכו יפוח רוח גדול, נשמת האומה תתעורר לתחיה, מעומק טבעה תכיר את כל מהותה, מעוצם כחה תכונן את סדרי חייה העצמיים: הרוח

30

"I See with My Eyes the Light of Elijah's Life Rising"

Elijah heralds the holiness of Nature.

I see with my eyes the light of Elijah's life rising,[226] his power for his God being revealed, the holiness in nature[227] breaking forth, uniting with the holiness that is above coarse nature,[228] with the holiness that combats nature.[229] We fought nature and emerged victorious.[230] Materialistic nature[231] crippled us, struck us in our thigh,[232] but the sun shone for us to cure us of our limping.[233] Judaism of the past, from Egypt until now, is a long battle against the ugly side of nature,[234] be it human nature in general, or even the nature of the nation and of every individual. We fought nature in order to subdue it. It succumbs before us; the worlds are increasingly refined. At the essential depth of nature a great demand wells up for holiness and purity, for delicacy of soul and refinement of life. Elijah comes to herald peace,[235] and in the inner soul of the nation a life stream of nature breaks forth and approaches holiness. The remembrance of the Exodus from Egypt becomes a remembrance of the delivery from the subjugation of nations,[236] which is taking shape. We are all approaching nature and it beckons to us. Nature is conquered before us and its demands are increasingly consonant[237] with our noble demands from the source of holiness. The youthful spirit[238] that demands its land, its language, its freedom and honor, its literature and strength, its wealth, its feelings, is flooded with a flow of nature, which within is full of holy fire.[239]

31

The Spiritual Forecast of the Emerging *Yishuv*

The People, once solidly rooted in the Land, will grow organically toward a life of observance of commandments. One needn't be overly alarmed by the outer husks of the nationalist movement that will naturally fall away.

The *Yishuv* (Settlement) in Israel will develop; the national home will be built. Out of it will blow a mighty spirit. The soul of the nation

המיוחד של האומה יכונן אמונת ד' אלהי ישראל בעולם, ואין צריך לומר בקרבה פנימה. המורך ודלדול הכח, השורר עכשיו, מונע הוא את גאון האמונה מהופיע בעולם, מעכב הוא את המהלך החי של המצות המעשיות וקשר האמונה האלהית אשר בתוכן מלהופיע בכל הדרו. אבל יתפרץ הכח הפנימי כהר פרצים, והחיים הישראליים, מתוך הכרח פנימי ומתוך הכרה חפשית גם יחד, יעשו באותו הצביון הראוי להם - והצביון הטבעי להם הוא אשר יביא את התשובה הגדולה, את התשובה מאהבה, בלא שום נפילה חמרנית, כי-אם תשובה פנימית נובעת מעומק האמת שבאור החיים של הנשמה. אין להצטער כלל מזרמי הרוח הלאומי הטבעי ההולך וסואן; גם הקלקולים, שהוא מקלקל במהלכו, סופם לבא לכלל בנין ותקון.

לב

אפיה של הגאולה הבאה לפנינו, שראשית צעדיה הננו חשים ומרגישים, הוא בתוכיותה של כנסת ישראל. מתפתחת היא האומה, בכל כחותיה, מגדלת היא את רוחה, את טבעה ואת עצמיותה, אינה מכרת עדיין את עומק הישות העליונה שהיא כל יסוד תקומתה. עינה לארץ, ולשמים עדנה לא תביט. היא אינה שבה עדיין אל אישה הראשון בפועל, היא מעבדת את חייה בכחותיה הנמצאים בשרשי נשמתה. אמנם בלא קריאת שם, בלא מגמה מבוררת, הכל הוא אור ד' וכבודו, אבל לא היא ולא העולם מכיר זה בבליטה, שם שמים לא שגור בפיה, אומץ וגבורה רודפת היא, אבל באמת הכל קודש ואלהי הוא. רק בהגמר התוכן, בהעלות האומה למרום מצבה, אז יוחל אור אלהי נקרא בשם

will be reawakened. From the depth of its nature, it will recognize its essence. With mighty strength, it will establish its life-patterns: the special spirit of the nation will establish the faith of the Lord, God of Israel in the world, and it goes without saying, within her own midst. The feebleness[240] and weakness that prevail now, prevent the genius of faith from appearing in the world, prevent the living process of *mitsvot ma'asiyot* (practical commandments) and the bond of divine faith within them, from gloriously manifesting. But the inner power will break forth as a volcano, and Israelite life, by both inner necessity and free consciousness, will assume its authentic form. That natural form will bring the Great Return; the return of love *(teshuvah me-ahavah)*, without materialist[241] faltering; an inner return flowing from the depth of truth that is in the luminous life of the soul. One need not be pained at all on account of the gushing streams of the natural national spirit; even the mistakes made along the way, in the end will contribute to building and *tikkun* (mending).

32

A Yet Anonymous Redemption

At present, the Redemption is an anonymous work – God's name is not called upon it. Eventually the divine nature of the Redemption will be revealed. The interim, painful period is referred to as ḥevlei mashiaḥ *(the Pangs of Messiah).*

The character of the redemption that is coming before us, whose first steps we sense and feel, is in the interiority of *Knesset Yisrael* (Ecclesia Israel). The nation develops with all its powers, expands its spirit, its nature and its essence. It does not recognize yet the depth of the higher existence that is the foundation of its uprising. Its eye is on the earth; to the heavens it does not yet look. She does not return yet in deed to her first husband;[242] she works out her life with powers found at the roots of her soul. However, without calling a name, without a clear objective,[243] all is the light of the Lord and His glory, but neither she [i.e., Israel] nor the world recognize this clearly.[244] The name of heaven is not constantly on her lips, she pursues brawn and strength, but truly all is holy and godly. Only when the content is complete, when the nation

המפורש להגלות, יגלה ויראה, שכל מה שהאיר וכל מה שיאיר, כל שחי וכל שיחיה בה, הכל אור אלהי עולם אלהי ישראל הוא, "וזה שמו אשר יקראו ד' צדקנו", "ושם העיר מיום ד' שמה". מצב גאולה זה הוא יסוד החזון של הרזים, שכנסת ישראל לא תשוב למקומה לעתיד כי-אם קודשא בריך הוא וכל חיליו יבאו אליה, ויקימו אותה מן עפרא ביקר סגי, אשרי עין ראתה כל אלה, ולמשמע אוזן ותקוה תשמח נפשנו. והמשך הזמן, העובר בין ההופעות המיוחדות המרוכזות בכנסת ישראל, עד שיופיע אור תפארת ישראל, לדעת כי שם ד' נקרא עליה, הוא זמן חבלי משיח, שרק אמיץ אונים כרב יוסף היה אומר עליו, בנגוד לכל האומרים, ייתי ולא אחמיניה: ייתי ואיתיב בטולא דכופתא דחמריה.

לג

גדולה היא תביעתנו הגופנית, גוף בריא אנו צריכים, התעסקנו הרבה בנפשיות, שכחנו את קדושת הגוף, זנחנו את הבריאות והגבורה הגופנית, שכחנו שיש לנו בשר קודש, לא פחות ממה שיש לנו רוח הקודש. עזבנו את החיים המעשיים, ואת התבררות החושים ואת הקשור עם המציאות הגופנית המוחשית, מפני יראה נפולה, מפני חוסר אמונה בקדושת הארץ, "אמונת זה סדר זרעים - שמאמין בחי העולמים וזורע". כל תשובתנו תעלה בידינו רק אם תהיה, עם כל הוד רוחניותה, גם תשובה גשמית יוצרת דם בריא, בשר בריא, גופים חטובים ואיתנים, רוח לוהט זורח על גבי שרירים חזקים, ובגבורת הבשר המקודש תאיר הנשמה שנתחלשה, זכר לתחית המתים הגופנית.

will ascend to its full height, [only] then will the light of the explicit name of God begin to be revealed.[245] It will be revealed and seen that all that illumined and will illumine, all that lived and will live in it – it is all the light of the God of the Universe, the God of Israel. *This is its name which they shall call, the Lord-is-our-righteousness.*[246] *The name of the city from today, the Lord-is-there.*[247] This state of redemption is the fundamental vision of the mystery that *Knesset Yisrael* (Ecclesia Israel) will not return to her place in the future, but rather the Holy One, blessed be He, and all His hosts will come to her, and raise her from the ground in great honor.[248] Happy is the eye that beholds all this,[249] and our soul is gladdened by the tidings and the hope. The duration of time that elapses between the singular manifestations concentrated in *Knesset Yisrael* (Ecclesia Israel) until the light of the glory of Israel appears, to know that the name of the Lord is called upon her – is the time of the "birth pangs of Messiah,"[250] concerning which, only a strong man such as Rav Yosef could say – in defiance of all who say, "May he [i.e., Messiah] come and may I not see him!"[251] – "May he [i.e., Messiah] come and may I merit to sit in the shadow of his donkey's dung!"[252]

33

Rediscovering the Holiness of the Flesh

Part and parcel of Teshuvah *is the return to the body, the rediscovery of the holiness of the flesh.*

Great is our physical demand. We need a healthy body. We dealt much in soulfulness; we forgot the holiness of the body.[253] We neglected physical health and strength; we forgot that we have holy flesh,[254] no less than holy spirit. We turned from active living, the clarification of the senses and the connection[255] with physical, sensate reality, due to a "fallen fear,"[256] due to lack of faith in the sanctity of the land. *"Faith,* this refers to the Order of *Zera'im* ("Seeds")"[257] – "for one believes in the 'Life of the Worlds' [i.e., God] and sows."[258] Our return *(teshuvah)* will succeed only if it will be – with all its splendid spirituality – also a physical return, which produces healthy blood, healthy flesh, mighty,

לד

ההתעמלות, שצעירי ישראל עוסקים בה בארץ ישראל לחזק את גופם בשביל המגמה להיות בנים אמיצי כח לאומה, היא משכללת את הכח הרוחני של הצדיקים העליונים, העוסקים ביחודים של שמות הקדושים, להרבות הבלטת האור האלהי בעולם, ואין גילוי אור אחד עומד בלא חבירו כלל. "ויעש דוד שם" - "ודוד עושה משפט וצדקה לכל עמו" - "ויואב בן צרויה על הצבא", "ולא נענש אבנר אלא מפני שעשה דמן של נערים שחוק". אבל שיצחקו הנערים לחזק כחם ורוחם, בשביל גבורת האומה בכללה, עבודת הקודש הזאת מעלה את השכינה מעלה מעלה, כעליתה על-ידי שירות ותשבחות שאמר דוד מלך ישראל בספר תהלים, אלא שעל-ידי הכונות העליונות עולה הנשמה הפנימית, ועל-ידי המעשים המאמצים את גוף היחידים לשם הכלל עולה הרוחניות החצונית. ושניהם כאחד משכללים את סדרי הקדושות כלם, בהבלטת אפיה של האומה בפרשה הקטנה שכל גופי תורה תלוים בה: בכל דרכיך דעהו.

ואל יפלא אם יש חסרונות במהלך החיים של העוסקים באמוץ הגופני ובכל החזוקים הארציים שבישראל, כי אפילו הופעת רוח הקודש צריכה ברור מתערובות צחצוחי טומאה שמתערבים בה, והיא הולכת ומטהרת, מתקדשת ומתבררת, פודה את עצמה מגלותה, עד שבאה לכלל דרך צדיקים, "ואורח צדיקים כאור נוגה הולך ואור עד נכון היום".

solid bodies, a fiery spirit shining[258*] upon powerful muscles. With the strength of the holy flesh,[259] the soul which was weakened will shine, reminiscent of the physical resurrection.[260]

34
On Physical Exercise

Just as King David combined his ability as warrior with his sacred liturgical activity, so nowadays physical exercise done to provide the Nation with strength and the spiritual exercises of the mystics are mutually reinforcing.

The exercise that Jewish youths in the Land of Israel engage in to strengthen their bodies in order [for the purpose[261]] to be powerful sons to the nation, enhances the spiritual prowess[262] of the exalted righteous, who engage in *yiḥudim* (mystical unifications) of the divine names,[263] to increase the accentuation of the divine light in the world. The one revelation of light cannot stand without the other. *David made a name.*[264] *David performed justice and righteousness for all his people.*[265] *Yo'av ben Zeruyah was over the army.*[266] "Avner was punished only because he made sport of the blood of youths."[267] However, if youths sport to strengthen their physical ability and spirit for the sake of the nation's strength at large, this holy work raises up the *Shekhinah* (divine presence), just as it rises through songs and praises uttered by David, King of Israel in the Book of Psalms. Through the supernal *kavvanot* (mystical intentions), the inner soul rises, and through actions to strengthen the body of individuals for the sake of the community, outer spirituality ascends. Both together round out all the orders of holiness by making more pronounced the character of the nation, by "the short passage upon which depends the entire corpus of Torah: *In all your ways know Him.*"[268]

Do not be astonished if there are shortcomings in the way of life of those engaged in physical and terrestrial strengthening in Israel, for even the manifestation of divine inspiration *(ru'aḥ ha-kodesh)* requires clarification from the admixtures of impurity that seep in,[269] yet it

לה

כל מה שמקיף את המציאות בכל הדרגותיה, בהשפעה רוחנית מוסרית וקדושה, צריך לטהרה יותר גדולה. המקדש וקדשיו כוללים את רוממות אצילות ההשכלה ואת תחתית טהרת הדם, הבשר, הדמיון והרגש, ובשביל אלה השלבים התחתיים, המקושרים לכללות הכל באגוד חי, נדרשת היא הטהרה המדויקת. ההשפעה העליונה לבדה, המכוונת אל הדעת, וממלאה בזה את תפקידה, בתקוה שממעין הרוחני יטהר הכל, היא אינה צריכה כל כך לפרטי טהרה מעשית, "הלא כה דברי כאש נאם ד' - מה אש אינו מקבל טומאה אף דברי תורה אינם מקבלים טומאה". החסידות האחרונה פנתה אל הרגש והדמיון יותר מאל השכל והמעשה, ובשביל כך העירה הרבה את תביעת הטהרה הבשרית. לכתחלה בימי עזרא היתה המגמה לקשר את ישראל אל הקודש, המקדש, גם בצד התחתיתי, שהוא אחד מדרכי החנוך הכלליים של האומה, והובלטה הטהרה. הגלות דלדלה את הכחות הרגשיים והציוריים, יחד עם גבורת החיים והמנוחה האסתתית ונשארה השפעת השכל, בדליגתה הרוחנית, מצורפת אל המעשה. מקום השלבים הרוחניים הממוצעים - הרגש והנטיה הבשרית - נשאר פנוי, "אין לנו שיור רק התורה הזאת". יצאה הדיקנות של הטהרה מכלל החובה, ונשארה קשורה בצפיה אידיאלית, במושג של קדושה וחסידות ליחידים, עד שבאה החסידות האחרונה וחפצה לשתלה בהמון. כמובן יש כאן גרעין בריא, שצריך הגבלה ופתוח, ביחוד ראוי הוא להתגדל ביחד עם תחיית האומה בארץ ישראל בחבור ההגדלה של השקוע ברוחניות, מצמאון בריא ומדעה קבועה ומסויימת להבראות את

becomes increasingly purified, sanctified, and refined, redeeming itself from its exile, until it becomes *the way of the righteous, a brilliant light growing increasingly brighter until morn.*[270]

35

Pitfalls and Purity of Flesh (and Imagination)

An historical survey of alternating periods of Intellect and Imagination: Ezra – Exile – Ḥasidism – National Renascence. Ritual purity as a demand of the in-body approach to spirituality.

Whatever encompasses existence in all of its levels, by exerting a spiritual, ethical, holy influence, requires utmost purity. The Temple and its sacrificial order include the most lofty, sublime intellect and the bottommost purity of blood and flesh, imagination and feeling.[271] For these lower rungs, connected to the overall totality by a living bond, a precise purity is required.[272] The higher influence alone, directed to knowledge (fulfilling in this way its duty, in the hope that from the spiritual fount all will be purified) does not require as much the details of practical purity. "*Is my word not as fire?, says the Lord*[273] – Just as fire does not become impure, so words of Torah cannot become impure."[274] Latter-day Hasidism[275] turned to feeling and imagination more than to reason and action, and for this reason, stepped up the demand for fleshly purity.[276] Originally in the days of Ezra, the objective was to connect Israel to the sacred [and[277]] the Temple, even on the lower side that is one of the general educational methods of the nation, so purity was stressed. Exile impoverished the emotive and imaginative abilities, together with life's strength and esthetic peace. There remained the influence of the intellect, with its spiritual sprint, combined with action. The place of the intermediate spiritual rungs – feeling and fleshly proclivity – remained empty. "Nothing remains but this Torah."[278] Precision purity no longer was obligatory and remained an idealistic longing, a concept of sanctity and piety reserved for individuals,[279] until modern Hasidism arrived and sought to implant it in the masses.[280] Understandably there is a healthy kernel here that requires definition[281]

כל האומה ואת שורש נשמתה בכל תכונת החיים שלה, שהטהרה הבשרית היא אחת מגבורותיה. "כי תצא מחנה על אויביך ונשמרת מכל דבר רע. כי יהיה בך איש אשר לא יהיה טהור מקרה לילה, ויצא אל מחוץ למחנה לא יבא אל תוך המחנה", ועל כולם אמור: "כי ד' אלהיך מתהלך בקרב מחנך להצילך ולתת איביך לפניך, והיה מחנך קדוש, ולא יראה בך ערות דבר ושב מאחריך!" בכל מקום שהגבורה העממית הישראלית מתגברת, מיד מוכרחת לבא תגבורת הטהרה הבשרית והרגשית, עם כל תכונתה, ולהזדוג עמה, וכל אלה הנם מכינים בסיס למעמד חי אורגני, הכולל את התחיה כולה, מראשית ההפשטה העליונה עד אחרית עליזת החיים ורעם גבורתם. "ונתתי צבי בארץ חיים".

לו

אי אפשר לספרות ישראלית שתצליח בלא התקדשות הנשמות של הסופרים. כל סופר שאינו עמל לטהר את מדותיו, לזכך את מעשיו ואת רעיונותיו, עד שיהיה עולמו הפנימי בעצמו מלא **אורה** והשלמות הפנימית מורגשת בתוכו, יחד עם הדאגה להשלים את החסר, ולהמלא ענוה ממוזגת בגבורה ושלות רוח עם התעוררות שכלית ורגשית חזקה להיטיב ולהשכיל את עצמו, וחפץ נשגב לעמוד ברום הטהרה והקדושה האצילית, כל זמן שאינו עומד במעמד כזה לא יוכל להקרא סופר באמת. רק "הראשונים היו נקראים סופרים, מפני שהיו סופרים אותיות שבתורה", וספירת האותיות שבתורה העלתם למדרגה עליונה של טוהר רוח וגבורת נשמה, עד ששם סופרים היה נאה להם. ואם את הספרות הישראלית אנו

and development. It is especially worthy of expansion at the time of the national renascence in the Land of Israel – in conjunction with the expanded immersion in spirituality, motivated by a healthy (spiritual) thirst and fixed notion to make healthy the whole nation and the root of its soul with all of its living quality, fleshly purity being one of its strengths. *When you go forth as a camp against your enemies, keep yourself from every evil thing. If there be among you a man that is not pure by reason of a nocturnal occurrence, he shall depart from the camp, he shall not enter within the camp.*[282] And above all, it states: *For the Lord your God goes about in the midst of your camp, to save you and to place your enemy before you, therefore your camp must be holy, that He see no unseemly thing in you and retreat from you.*[283] Wherever the folk strength of Israel burgeons, there must immediately join with it a reinforcement of fleshly and emotive purity. All these prepare a basis for a living, organic state of being, which encompasses the entire renascence, from the beginning of the highest abstraction to the end of the jubilation of life and its thunderous power. *I will bestow beauty in the Land of the Living.*[284]

36

On Modern Hebrew Literature

In attempting a renascence of Hebrew literature, writers must purify their souls to be worthy of the name soferim.

It is impossible for Israelite literature to succeed without the sanctification of the souls of the writers. Any writer who does not labor to purify his character, to crystallize his deeds and thoughts, until his internal world is itself full of light[285] and internal wholeness perceptible within him, together with concern to make up for lackings; to be filled with humility mixed with strength, and tranquility of spirit coupled with an intense intellectual and emotional arousal to improve and comprehend himself, and an exalted desire to reach the pinnacle of purity and holiness – as long as one does not stand on such a niveau, he cannot rightfully be called a writer. Only "the early ones were called

חפצים להחיות, צריכים אנו ללכת בדרך הקודש הזאת, לבא מן הקדושה אל הספרות, "והיה שם מסלול ודרך, ודרך הקודש יקרא לה והלכו גאלים".

לז

הספרות תתקדש, וגם הסופרים יתקדשו, יתרומם העולם להכיר את כחה הגדול והעדין של הספרות - הרמת היסוד הרוחני בעולם בכל עילויו. ילך האור ויפרוץ, התביעה האיתנה תתבע את שלה, התובעים הם נשמות רבות צמאות, נשמות מרגישות, מכירות בחכמת הפרצוף של המבטאים והסגנון את טומאת הרעיון שבסופרים רבים, שלא תכסה אותה כל מליצה מוסרית, כל הלבשה שירית, "עקוב הלב מכל ואנוש הוא". רוח טומאה זה ככל רוח הטומאה בכלל עבור יעבור, יבטל מן העולם וכליל יחלוף והספרות תתקדש, וכל סופר יחל לדעת את הרוממות ואת הקודש שבעבודתו, ולא יטבול עטו בלא טהרת נשמה וקדושת רעיון. לפחות תקדים המחשבה של תשובה, הרהורי תשובה עמוקים לפני כל יצירה. אז תצא היצירה בטהרתה, רוח ד׳ תחול עליה ונשמת הגוי כולו תגבל בה. אחרי אשר חכמת סופרים תסרח, יאמר לישראל עוד: "ואני זאת בריתי אותם אמר ד׳ רוחי אשר עליך ודברי אשר שמתי בפיך לא ימושו מפיך ומפי זרעך ומפי זרע זרעך, אמר ד׳ מעתה ועד עולם".

soferim (scribes), for they would count the letters of the Torah."[286] The counting of the letters in the Torah raised them to a niveau of purity of spirit and power of soul, so that the title "scribes" was fitting for them. If we desire to resurrect Israelite literature, we must follow this holy way, to come to writing from holiness. *There will be there a route, a way, and it shall be called the way of holiness.*[287] *And they shall go redeemed.*[288]

37

The Revolution in Hebrew Literature

The readers, who will be disgusted with the impurity of contemporary Hebrew literature, will force the writers to rewrite their souls.

Literature will be sanctified;[289] the writers too will become holy. The world will be elevated to realize the great and subtle power of literature – the uplifting of the spiritual foundation of the world with all its excellence. The light will continue to break forth, justice will demand its due. Those demanding are many thirsty souls, feeling souls, able to discern through the "physiognomy" of the expressions and the style, the impurity of thought of many writers, which no flowery moralizing can cover up. *Deceitful is the heart above all things, and sick.*[290] This spirit of impurity, as every spirit of impurity, will disappear totally from the world, and the writing will be sanctified. Every writer will begin to know the loftiness and holiness in his work, and will not dip his pen without purity of soul and sanctity of thought. At least, there will precede a thought of return, deep meditations of return, before each creation. Then the creation will come out pure, the spirit of the Lord will rest on it, and the spirit of the entire nation will reside in it.[291] After the wisdom of writers will have rotted,[292] it shall yet be said to Israel:[293] *And I, this is my covenant with them, said the Lord, My spirit which is upon you and My word which I have placed in your mouth, shall not depart from your mouth, nor the mouth of your seed, nor the mouth of your seed's seed, said the Lord, for now and forever.*[294]

לח

החכמה שמתרבה מתוך קנאת סופרים, כיון שבאה מתוך קנאה סופה להרקב, וכל רקבון יש בו סרחון, וזאת היא חכמת סופרים שתסרח בעקבתא דמשיחא. ועל-ידי סרחון זה תתבטל צורתה הקודמת, ויוחל להיות מאיר אור הנשמה של החכמה העליונה מכל קנאה, שהיא למעלה מחכמת סופרים, היא החכמה שתצא לאור על-ידי שיר חדש ושם חדש אשר פי ד׳ יקבנו, "ויהי כזית הודו וריח לו כלבנון".

לט

החוצפא של עקבתא דמשיחא היא מעוט אור לשם תקון הכלים, ואינה דומה כלל למאורעות של עברינות אחרים שהם היו לקותות גמורות, בדרך הריסה. אמנם ישנם בתוך המחנה הזה של בעלי החוצפא גם זיקין שהם מוכרחים להדעך לגמרי, ודעיכה זו תבא על-ידי הארה גדולה של אור תורה מגבורה של מעלה, על-ידי הופעת צדיקים גדולים מאד, "אור צדיקים ישמח, נר רשעים ידעך". בלא החוצפא דעקבא דמשיחא לא היה אפשר לבאר רזי תורה בגילוי גמור, רק על-ידי התעבות ההרגשות שעל-ידי החוצפא, יהיה אפשר לקבל הארות שכליות עליונות מאד, וסוף סוף שהכל ישוב לתקון גמור.

38

Wisdom Beyond *Kin'at Soferim* (Literary Envy)

Contemporary literature, a product of envy and competition between writers, will rot and a new, noncompetitive wisdom will be revealed.

Since the wisdom that increases as a result of the envy of writers,[295] results from envy, it will eventually rot,[296] and every rotting is accompanied by a stink, and this is the wisdom of writers that will stink in the "footsteps of Messiah."[297] Through this putrefaction, the original form will disappear, and the light of the soul of the wisdom[298] that is higher than envy, will begin to shine.[299] This is the wisdom beyond the wisdom of sages, which will appear through a new song[300] and a new name that the mouth of the Lord will pronounce.[301] *His beauty shall be as that of the olive tree and his fragrance as that of the Lebanon.*[302]

39

Ḥutspah and Kabbalah

One of the benefits of the ḥutspah *that arrives in the "Footsteps of Messiah," is the coarsening of feelings necessary to endure the mysteries of Torah.*

The insolence of the "footsteps of Messiah"[303] is a diminishing of the light for the sake of strengthening the vessels, and bears no resemblance to other cases of transgression that were totally destructive. However, there are within this camp of "masters of *ḥutspah*," flickers that must be completely extinguished. This extinguishing will come about through the great light of Torah from the might on high, through the appearance of very great *tsaddikim* (righteous persons). *The light of the righteous will expand, the flame of the wicked will sputter.*[304] Without the insolence of "the footsteps of Messiah," it would be impossible to explain mysteries of the Torah openly. Only through the coarsening of the emotions, the outcome of *ḥutspah*, will it be possible to receive very lofty intellectual illumination. Eventually all will result in perfect correction.

מ

הדור הראשון של עקבתא דמשיחא, בתחלת קץ המגולה של ישוב ארץ ישראל, הוא מכשיר את החומר של כנסת ישראל, והרוחניות צריכה לשמש בו שמוש של שמירת החיים הפנימיים, וכשיתחזק הכח החמרי של האומה, אז יגלו כל הסגולות הרוחניות הקדושות שבה, ותשוב התורה וכל מאורותיה לאיתנה, להיות לאור עולם, ל"עטרת תפארת ביד ד' ו(ל)צניף מלוכה בכף אלהיך".

מא

הרבה נשמות, נדחות בין האומות, שבות לכנסת ישראל בעקבתא דמשיחא, וכח העכול אינו מספיק בתחלה להפכם למזון מבריא. ומזה נצמחה המחלה של חוצפא, אבל היא רק מחלה עוברת, "זה חלי ואשאנו", ומהרה תעלה ארוכה לה, "וחיל גוים תאכלו ובכבודם תתימרו".

40

The First Generation of the Footsteps of Messiah

The first generation in the redemptive process prepares the material basis for the spirituality that will follow.

The first generation of the "footsteps of Messiah," at the beginning of "the revealed End,"[305] witnessed in the settlement of the Land of Israel, prepares the material of *Knesset Yisrael* (Ecclesia Israel), and the spirituality must serve then in a capacity[306] of preserving the inner life. When the material power of the nation will be strengthened, then there will be revealed all the holy spiritual treasures within her, and the Torah with all her lights will resume her might, to be an eternal light, *a glorious diadem in the hand of the Lord and a crown of kingdom in the palm of your God.*[307]

41

Souls Returning from the Nations

In the "Footsteps of Messiah," the influx of souls returning from the nations causes an outbreak of hutspah.

Many souls, cast among the nations, return to *Knesset Yisrael* (Ecclesia Israel) in "the footsteps of Messiah,"[308] and the digestive ability in the beginning is insufficient to convert them to healthy nutrition. From this arises the illness of *hutspah*, but it is only a passing ailment. [*This*[309] *is but illness, and I shall be able to bear it,*[310] and speedily it will be cured.[311]] *The bounty of nations you shall consume and you shall possess their honor.*[312]

מב

הלאומיות כשהיא רעננה תוכל להשביע מטל החיים הרוחניים שבה גם את היחיד, ומשרישה בקרבו די מוסר ודעת, כל אחד מבני העם, הדבקים בעמם בדבקות פנימית, מתמלא עז חיים כאלה לפי תכונת הדבקות והתעוררות הרוח שלו לקרבת האומה. אבל כשהאומה בכללה קודרת ונופלת צריך כל יחיד להרטיב את רוחו מהמקור המוסרי והמדעי הכללי ולבא ממולא טוב להדבק בעמו ולעורר רוחו לתחיתו ואז יהיה מכלל בוני האומה.

אוצר התורה לישראל הוא בשעת הירידה מכוון לקחת ממנו חיים לתן לאומה בכללה מאת כל יחיד להחיותה ולעוררה, ובעת התחיה הוא נמזג בכללות האומה ומשפיע ממנה האור והחיים על כל היחידים.

כשבאים להסתפק בדבקות הלאומיות בעת הירידה ושוכחים את אוצר החיים לא תוכל אז האומה לפרנס מרוחה את החיים הרוחניים, ומהדבקים רק ברעיונה הכללי, בלא חדירה לאור החיים של הקדש שבה, תשאר רק רשימת חיים, עד שיתעלו למקור חיים ומשם ישובו להחיות.

42

The Ethics of Nationalism and the Ethics of Torah

Only when the Nation is hale and healthy can ethics flow to the individual from nationalism; otherwise the individual must have recourse to Torah to remain ethical.

Nationalism, when it is fresh, can satisfy with the dew of spiritual life that is within it, the individual as well, and implant within him enough ethics and knowledge. Every member of the nation who clings to his nation with an inner attachment is filled with the vigor of life, to the degree that he cleaves and his spirit longs for the proximity of the nation. However, when the nation as a whole is obscured and falls, each individual must "moisten" his spirit from the general source of ethics and science, and come to his people already filled with goodness. Then he will be one of the builders of the nation.

The treasure trove of Torah is, at such times of descent, designed that each individual may take from it life to provide the nation as a whole, to renew and arouse it. At the time of the nation's renascence, the Torah is absorbed in the totality of the nation, and thus bestows light and life on all the individuals.

When we attempt to sustain ourselves at the time of descent by national enthusiasm and forget the treasure trove of life, the nation cannot provide then for spiritual life, and of those who cling only to the general nationalistic idea without penetrating to the living light of holiness within it, will remain only a shadow of life, until they ascend to the source of the nation's vitality and will thereby revivify it.[313]

מג

הנפש של פושעי ישראל שבעקבתא דמשיחא, אותם שהם מתחברים באהבה אל עניני כלל ישראל, לארץ ישראל ולתחית האומה, היא יותר מתוקנת מהנפש של שלמי אמוני ישראל, שאין להם זה היתרון של ההרגשה העצמית לטובת הכלל ובנין האומה והארץ. אבל הרוח הוא מתוקן הרבה יותר אצל יראי ד׳ ושומרי תורה ומצות, אף על-פי שההרגשה העצמית וההתעוררות של כח פעולה בעניני כלל ישראל אינן עדיין אמיצות אצלם, כמו ממה שהן אצל אלה שרוח עועים אשר בתוכם מעכר את לבם, עד כדי להתקשר בדעות זרות ובמעשים המטמאים את הגוף ומונעים אור הרוח מלהתקן, וממילא סובלת גם הנפש מפגמיהם. התקון שיבא על-ידי אורו של משיח, שיעזור לזה הרבה דבר ההתפשטות של תלמוד רזי תורה וגילוי אורות חכמת אלהים, בכל צורותיה הראויות להגלות, הוא, שיעשו ישראל אגודה אחת, ותתוקן הנפש של היראים שומרי תורה על-ידי שלמות הנפש שבפושעים, הטובים ביחש לעניני הכלל ותקות הגשמיות והרוחניות המושגות בהכרה והרגשה האנושית, והרוח של הפושעים האלה תתוקן על-ידי השפעתם של יראי ד׳ שומרי תורה וגדולי אמנה, וממילא יבא לאלה ולאלה אור גדול, והופעת תשובה שלמה תבא לעולם, ואז יהיו ישראל מוכנים לגאולה. והצדיקים העליונים, מארי דנשמתא, הם יהיו הצנורות המאחדים, שעל ידם יעבור שפע אור הנפש משמאל לימין ושפע אור רוח מימין לשמאל, ותהיה השמחה גדולה מאד, ״כהניך ילבשו צדק, וחסידיך ירננו״, וזה יהיה בכח אורו של משיח, שהוא דוד בעצמו, ש״הקים עולה של תשובה״, ״בעבור דוד עבדך אל תשב פני משיחך״.

43

Nefesh, Ru'aḥ and *Neshamah*: Three Types of Jews

The New Yishuv *excels in physicality; the Old* Yishuv *in spirituality. There will emerge a higher* tsaddik *who will know to combine both.*

The *nefesh* (the lower part of the soul in kabbalistic tradition[314]) of sinners of Israel in the "footsteps of Messiah" – those who join lovingly the causes of the Jewish People, *Erets Yisrael* and the national revival – is more corrected than the *nefesh* of the perfect believers of Israel who lack this advantage of the essential feeling for the good of the people and the building of nation and land. But the *ru'aḥ* (the higher part of the soul in kabbalistic tradition[315]) is much more corrected in the God-fearing and Torah observant, even though the essential feeling and arousal to Jewish activism are not yet[316] firm in them, as they are in those whose heart is polluted by a perverse spirit to the point of connecting to strange opinions and to deeds that sully the body and prevent the light of the *ru'aḥ* from being corrected, and concomitantly the *nefesh* too suffers from their flaws. The *tikkun* (correction) that will come about through the Light of Messiah – which will be greatly aided by the proliferation of the study of the mysteries of Torah and revelation of the lights of divine wisdom, in all forms fitting to be revealed – is that Israel should bond together, and the *nefesh* of the observant will be corrected by the perfection of the *nefesh* of the transgressors, who are good in regard to communal affairs, and material and spiritual ideals attained through human understanding and perception; whereas the *ru'aḥ* of these transgressors[317] will be corrected by the influence of the God-fearing, observant of Torah and great of faith, and thereby both groups will receive great light. Complete return *(teshuvah)* will appear in the world, and then Israel will be ready for redemption. The higher *tsaddikim* (righteous),[318] masters of *neshamah* (the third and highest part of the soul in kabbalistic tradition[319]), will be the uniting conduits, through which the light of the *nefesh* will flow from left to right, and the light of the *ru'aḥ*[320] from right to left, and the rejoicing will be very

מד

מקובלים אנו שמרידה רוחנית תהיה בארץ ישראל ובישראל, בפרק שהתחלת תחית האומה תתעורר לבא. השלוה הגשמית שתבא לחלק מהאומה, אשר ידמו שכבר באו למטרתם כולה, תקטין את הנשמה, ויבאו ימים אשר תאמר: אין בהם חפץ. השאיפה לאידיאלים נשאים וקדושים תחדל, וממילא ירד הרוח וישקע, עד אשר יבא סער ויהפך מהפכה, ויראה אז בעליל כי חוסן ישראל הוא בקודש עולמים, באור ד׳ ובתורתו, בחשק האורה הרוחנית, שהיא הגבורה הגמורה המנצחת את כל העולמים וכל כחותיהם. הצורך למרידה זו, היא הנטיה לצד החמריות, שמוכרחת להולד בכללות האומה בצורה תקיפה אחר אשר עברו פרקי שנים רבות, שנאפסו לגמרי מכלל האומה הצורך והאפשרות להתעסקות חמרית, וזאת הנטיה כשתולד תדרך בזעם ותחולל סופות, והם הם חבלי משיח אשר יבסמו את העולם כולו על-ידי מכאוביהם.

great. *Your priests will wear righteousness, and your pious will rejoice.*[321] This will be accomplished by the power of the Light of Messiah, who is David himself,[322] "who erected the yoke of return *(teshuvah)*."[323] *For the sake of David your servant, do not rebuff your Messiah.*[324]

44

The Spiritual Revolution

After having deserted the material realm for centuries, the Jewish People compensates by sinking into the material – at the expense of the spiritual. This spiritual torpor will terminate in a spiritual revolution.

We have received a tradition that a spiritual revolt[325] will occur in the Land of Israel and in the People of Israel at the time when the beginning of the national revival will be aroused.[326] The material prosperity that will come to a part of the nation, who will imagine that they have already achieved their complete goal, will shrink the soul, and there will come days regarding which you will say there is no desire.[327] The aspiration for lofty and holy goals will cease[328] and as a result, the spirit will sink, until there will come a storm and stir revolt. Then it will be seen clearly that the strength of Israel is the Eternal Holy, the light of the Lord and His Torah, the love for the spiritual light, which is the absolute might, victorious over all the worlds and their powers. The need for this revolt is the proclivity to materialism, which must be engendered in the nation in a pronounced manner, after so many chapters of Jewish history from which the need and opportunity for material pursuit were totally absent.[329] This material inclination, once born, will march in anger, stirring storms. These are the "birth pangs of Messiah" that will invigorate the entire world through their pains.

מה

כשם שאי אפשר ליין בלא שמרים, כך אי אפשר לעולם בלא רשעים. וכשם שהשמרים מעמידים את היין ומשמרים אותו, כך הרצון הגס של הרשעים גורם קיום ועמדה לשפעת החיים כולם, של כל הבינונים והצדיקים. כשהשמרים מתמעטים והיין עומד בלא שמריו, הרי הוא עלול לקלקול וחמוץ. הגלות דלדלה את כח החיים של האומה ושמרינו נתמעטו הרבה מאד, עד שיש סכנה לקיום החיים של האומה מחוסר תפיסת חיים מעובה, האחוזה בבהמיות ובאדמה ושקיעתה החמרית. הקיום בגולה הוא קיום רסוק, וזה הקיום המדולדל, שהוא חדלון יותר מהויה, היה אפשר לו להמשך איזה משך זמן גם בחוסר שמרים כפי ההכרח. אבל לכל זמן, וכבר כשל הכח, והקיום העצמי תובע את תפקידו, ושיבת ישראל לארצו בשביל קיומו העצמי הוא מאורע מוכרח, וקיומו זה יוצר את שמריו: נושאי הרשעה והחוצפא של עקבתא דמשיחא אשר ירגז כל לב לזכרן. אלה הם הצדדים העכורים שהקיום הצלול והמשמח מתהוה על ידם, וסוף המהלך הוא: שקוע השמרים בתחתית החבית, הנמכת הכחות הרשעיות בתהום החיים, ואז מתבטל מהם כל תכנם המכאיב ומזעזע. אבל בהמשך יצירתם שהנם הולכים ביחד עם היין, חיי האומה ורוחה המתעורר, הם מעכירים אותו והלבבות רועשים למראה התסיסה, וינוח הלב וישקוט במכונו רק למראה העתיד, ההולך ועושה את מסלתו, במפלאות תמים דעים, "מי יתן טהור מטמא לא אחד".

45

The Wine and the Dregs

Just as dregs are necessary for the production of wine, so the coarse, physical Jews, so far removed from the spirit, contribute to the total salubrity of the Jewish People.

Just as wine cannot be without dregs, so the world cannot be without wicked people.[330] And just as the dregs serve to preserve the wine, so the coarse will of the wicked strengthens the existence of the flow of life, of the spiritual middle class *(beinonim)* and the righteous *(tsaddikim)*. When the dregs are decreased, the wine tends to spoil and sour. The Exile weakened the life force of the nation and our dregs decreased greatly, to the point where the survival of the nation is endangered for lack of a thick grasp of life,[331] entrenched in animality, in the earth and its material plunge. Existence in exile is fragmented existence, and this impoverished existence, which is more impasse than existence, could exist for a time, if necessary, even without dregs. But there is a time for everything, the strength has already succumbed, and the essential existence demands its role. Israel's return to its land for the sake of its essential[332] existence is a necessary event, and its existence creates its dregs: the bearers of wickedness and the impunity *(ḥutspah)* of "the footsteps of Messiah," whose very mention troubles every heart. These are the murky sides through which the clear and gladdening existence occurs. The end of the process[333] will be the sinking of the lees to the bottom of the barrel, the lowering of the evil powers in the depth of life, whereby all their painful and alarming content is subdued. But for the duration of their formation, as long as the lees accompany the wine – the life of the nation and its awakening spirit – they oppress it and the hearts are disturbed at the sight of the fermentation. The heart will rest and be at peace only by beholding the future, which is continuing on its way, with wonders of the Perfect Intelligence.[334] *Who can make of the impure pure? Only One!*[335]

מו

כשם שנשמת האדם היא יותר עליונה ויותר פנימית מהמלאכים, דוקא מפני גדלותה ירדה עד לתחתית המדרגה, ומשם תעלה ברכוש גדול ועצום, ותכשיר את העולם כולו עמה לעליה עליונה מקורית, כן הקודש שבחול, שירד עד לידי החולין הגמורים, הוא יותר נשגב וקדוש מהקודש שבקודש, אלא שהוא מסתתר הרבה, ואין קץ ותכלית לתיקוני העולם שיבאו מכל הטוב הבא לעולם בדרך חול, שיגלה ויראה הודו והדרו לעת המאושרה, אשר "לא יהיה אור יקרות וקפאון" - "והיה לעת ערב יהיה אור". לפני אורו של משיח שיגלה במהרה בימינו, יתעורר כח הקודש שבחול, שיעורר בראשית התעוררותו את החול, והכל ידברו "בלישנא דבני נשא ולא בלישנא דקודשא בריך הוא" (זוהר), ועל זה נאמר: "גם לשוני כל היום תהגה צדקתך, כי בושו כי חפרו מבקשי רעתי".

מז

מפני שהציור של גדולת האור האלהי הוא גדול מאד בפנימיות הנשמות של דור האחרון של עקבא דמשיחא, במדה כזו שאין להן עדיין הסתגלות איך להנהיג את החיים הממשיים, על-פי גודל עליון כזה, מתוך כך באה הכפירה ואתה הדלדול הרוחני הדומה לחורבן, שאנו רואים אותו בדורנו. אבל דרך הרפואה הוא רק להרבות כלים, הסברות ותכניות, המועילים לסול דרכים בשביל הסתגלות מעשית על-פי האורות היותר עליונות, ומטעם זה באה גם כן הדרישה הגדולה לחרות הרוח ואמוץ הגוף, כי רק רוח חזק ואמיץ וגוף בריא ואיתן יוכלו להכיל בתוכם בלי זעזוע את ההארות

46

The Holy in the Secular

*Just as Man is higher than the angels,
so the holy found in the lowly is higher than the undescended holy.*

Just as the soul of Man is higher and more inward than the angels,[336] and precisely because of its greatness, it descended to the lowest level, and from there will arise with great and awesome (spiritual) wealth, to prepare thereby the entire world for ascent to the source – so the sacred that is within the mundane, which descended to the point of the utterly profane, is more lofty and holy than the sacred within the (proper realm of the) sacred, only that it is extremely hidden. There is no end to the corrections of the world *(tikkun 'olam)* that will accrue from all the good that comes to the world via the mundane, which will be manifestly revealed at the happy time when *there shall be no light, but fleeting light and thick darkness – but it shall come to pass, that at evening-time there shall be light.*[337] Before the Light of Messiah (may it be revealed speedily in our days), the power of holiness within the secular will be aroused, which initially will arouse the secular. All will speak "the language of Man, not the language of the Holy One, blessed be He" (*Zohar*).[338] In this regard it states, *My tongue will utter all the day Your righteousness, for those who seek to do me evil are ashamed.*[339]

47

Atheism and the Higher Belief

*Souls imprinted with a higher vision cannot be satisfied with mediocre religiosity
and end up in disbelief. The cure is to prepare "vessels" for the higher "lights."*

Because the picture of the greatness of the divine light is so immense inside the souls of the last generation of "the footsteps of Messiah," to the extent that they do not yet have the capability of conducting real[340] life according to this lofty greatness, there results the disbelief and spiritual impoverishment resembling destruction, which we witness in our generation. But the way of healing is to increase vessels,

היותר עליונות ולעמוד במעמד האיתניות הראוי לחיים פועלים מלאים עז של יצירה, ולהמשיך מתוכן המשכות של ארחות חיים, מתוך צרוף פנימי, שכל אלו ההכנות דרושות הן לתשובה השלמה, העומדת אחר כתלנו.

מח

"מִשחרב בית המקדש לא נראה רקיע בטהרתו, שנאמר: אלביש שמים קדרות ושק אשים כסותם". אם כן הארת התורה-מן-השמים של זמן הגלות מעולפת היא הקדרות והשק המכסה. בעת קרבת הקץ יבא רוח המטהר את השמים מקדרותם, המסיר את השק המכסה עליהם, ואז אלה אשר לא הסתגלו לתורה העולה למעלה, הבוקעת את הקדרות והשק, חושבים שאין להם תורה מן השמים, וצדיקים דורשי ד' ועזו מוסיפים אורה ושמחה ומבשרים צדק בקהל רב, שדוקא כעת יגלה אור חדש ושמים בטהרתם יראו, וידעו כל באי עולם, כי מן השמים דבר ד' לבית ישראל ולבית יעקב הגוי כולו.

explications, and plans, which will pave paths to actual implementation based on the loftiest illuminations.[341] For this reason, there is also a great demand for freedom of spirit and strength of body, for only a strong spirit and healthy body can contain without shock the highest illuminations,[342] can withstand active life full of vigorous creativity and extend from their very midst, from the midst of an inner catharsis – ways of life. All these preparations are necessary for the complete Return *(teshuvah)* that stands beyond our wall.[343]

48

Torah from Heaven

In Exile, the heavens were portrayed in a gross, corporeal manner. As the End approaches, the heavens are revealed in their ethereal light and the concept of "Torah from Heaven" is upgraded accordingly.

"Since the destruction of the Temple, the sky has not been seen in its purity,[344] as it says: *I shall dress the heavens in black and place sack as their garment.*"[345] If so, the illumination of Torah-from-Heaven in the time of Exile[346] is shrouded in the encompassing darkness and sack. At the time the End approaches, there will come a wind purifying the heavens of their obscurity, divesting them of the sack. Then, those who are unprepared for the Torah that transcends, that breaks the obscurity and sack, think that they have no Torah from Heaven.[347] And the righteous who seek the Lord and His might, add light and joy, and inform the public that just now there will be revealed a new light and the heavens will be seen in their purity, and all the inhabitants of the world will know that from the heavens the Lord spoke[348] to the House of Israel and to the House of Jacob, the entire nation.[349]

מט

אורו של משיח יבסס את הודאות של הטוב הגמור שבהויה בכלל, ותמלא הארץ אורה ושמחה, המרעיפות משמי שמים תמיד. ואז תבוא ההכרה שטוב להודות לד׳ על הרעה כמו על הטובה וגם ברוחניותו מיסוד החדוש של לאה, שאמרה בלדת יהודה: "הפעם אודה את ד׳", ו"כל הקרבנות בטלים חוץ מקרבן תודה", "באו שעריו בתודה".

נ

יניקת תורה שבעל-פה היא בגניזה מן השמים, ובגלוי מהארץ, וצריכה ארץ ישראל להיות בנויה, וכל ישראל יושבים עליה מסודרים בכל סדריהם: מקדש ומלכות, כהונה ונבואה, שופטים ושוטרים וכל תכסיסיהם, אז חיה היא תורה שבעל-פה בכל זיו תפארתה, פורחת ומעלה נצה, ומתחברת לתורה שבכתב בכל שעור קומתה. בגלות נפרדו התאומים, נתעלה תורה שבכתב למרומי קדשה, וירדה תורה שבעל-פה בעומק תחתית. ומכל מקום היא מקבלת יניקה חשאית מאור תורה שבכתב, מספיח העבר, המספיק להעמידה בחיים מצומצמים, והיא יורדת ונופלת בכל יום ויום, עד אשר מהרה יפוח היום ואור חיים יבא מאוצר גאולת עולמים, וישראל יעשה חיל, ינטע על ארצו וישגשג בכל הדר סדריו. אז תחל תורה שבעל-פה לצמח מעומק שרשיה, תעלה מעלה מעלה, ואור תורה שבכתב יזריח עליה קרני אורה מחדש, חדשים לבקרים, והדודים יתאחדו בנוה אפריונם, ואור נשמת אל חי העולמים המתגלה בתחית ישראל וברום קרנו יאיר באור שבעת הימים, על אור

49

Thank Offering for the Evil

The "Light of Messiah" will reveal that it is proper to thank the Lord for evil as well as good.

The Light of Messiah will establish[350] the certainty of the total good that is in existence in general, and the earth will be filled with light and happiness, which descend from the heavens always. Then will come the awareness[351] that it is good to praise the Lord[352] for the evil as for the good,[353] even in (the realm of) spirituality.[354] [This was] the innovation of Leah,[355] who said, at the time of Judah's birth: *This time I will praise the Lord.*[356] "All the sacrifices will be abolished except for the thanksgiving offering."[357] *Enter His gates with thanksgiving.*[358]

50

The Oral Torah: An Outcropping of Organic Jewish Life

In Exile, the Oral Torah receives ever-waning inspiration from the light of the past, from the Written Torah; with the Redemption, the Oral Torah will once again receive inspiration directly from the People of Israel.

The sustenance of the Oral Law is covertly[359] from heaven and overtly from earth.[360] The Land of Israel must be built, and all of Israel dwelling upon her, established in every way: temple and kingdom, priesthood and prophecy, judges and officers, and all their infrastructure. Then the Oral Law lives in all her glory, blossoms and flowers,[361] and joins with the Written Law in all of its stature. In Exile, the twins were sundered; the Written Law ascended to its heights of holiness, while the Oral Law descended to the depth of the abyss. Nevertheless, it [i.e., the Oral Law] receives secret sustenance[362] from the light of the Written Law, from the after-growth of the past, which is sufficient to preserve it in a reduced life. It [i.e., the Oral Law] descends and falls daily, until soon the day will arrive[363] when the light of life will come from the

החמה ואור הלבנה גם יחד. והיה אורם ישר, חודר ומושך, מזה לזו, ועונה את הארץ ואת העם בכל יפעת חיים, "והיה אור הלבנה כאור החמה, ואור החמה יהיה שבעתים כאור שבעת הימים ביום חבוש ד' את שבר עמו ומחץ מכתו ירפא".

נא

הסיגים שבהבנת האלהות, היראה, האמונה, וכל התלוי בהן, כל זמן שאין האומה צריכה לתקן את דרכי חייה המעשיים בכללותה, אין ההזק שלהם ניכר, אבל כיון שהגיע הזמן שהתחיה הלאומית מוכרחת לבא, וצמיחת קרן ישועה בפועל מוכרחת להגלות, מיד הסיגים מעכבים ואי אפשר לאומה שתתאגד ותשיג בעומק חייה את סוד גבורתה וציורי סדוריה כי-אם על-פי דעות מזוככות ומעשים היוצאים מטהרתה של דעת ד' אמת, בבהירות היותר עליונה. זאת היא הסבה שכח שלילי גדול מתעורר בעקבא דמשיחא, בחוצפה סגיאה, ושלילה זאת תבער את כל מה שהוא כהה בהמושגים האלהיים והתלוי בהם בכללות האומה. אף על-פי שנורא הדבר לראות שכמה עניני אמת, מדות טובות ומצות וחקים, הולכים ונשטפים ונעקרים לכאורה, על-ידי זרם השלילה, מכל מקום סוף סוף הכל יצמח בטהרה וגבורה, בקדושה עליונה, מגרעין האיתן, הטהור והמרומם, שכל שלילה לא תגיע אליו, ואורו יזרח בתור אור חדש על ציון בגדולה מופלאה למעלה מכל ציור שכחות דלים של נפשות עיפות, עיפות חמרית ורוחנית, של גלות ארוכה ודלדול, יכולים לצייר.

storehouse of eternal redemption, and Israel will wax mighty, will be planted on its soil and flourish in all the beauty of its orders. Then the Oral Law will begin to grow from the depth of its roots, will ascend higher and higher, and the light of the Written Law will shine on it anew its rays of light. In this new morning, the lovers will be reunited in their nuptial chamber, and the light of the soul of God, Life of Worlds, which is revealed in the renascence of Israel and its upliftment, will shine with the light of the seven days[364] (of creation), to include both the light of the sun and the light of the moon.[365] Their light shall be direct, penetrating and extending from one to the other and supplying the land and the people with resplendent life. *The light of the moon shall be as the light of the sun, and the light of the sun sevenfold, as the light of the seven days, on the day the Lord binds his people's break and heals the bruise of its wound.*[366]

51
Atheism: Cleanser of Belief

In Exile, the Nation could make do with foggy notions of God. With the national renascence, the concept of God must be purified. This is the raison d'être *of the passing phenomenon of atheism.*

As long as the nation has no need to correct in general its practical approach to life, the impurities in the understanding of divinity, awe, faith, and all that is dependent upon them, do no visible damage. However, when the time arrives in which national renascence is necessary, and the actual "horn of salvation" must be revealed, immediately these impurities impede, and it is impossible for the nation to bond together and achieve in the depth of its life the secret of its strength and the conceptions of its orders, with other than clear thinking and deeds that proceed from the purity of true knowledge of the Lord, with the utmost clarity. This is the reason that a great negative power is aroused in the "footsteps of Messiah" with great impudence,[367] and this negation will purge all that is indistinct[368] in theological ideas and matters of national concern that hinge upon them. Even

נב

ישנם דברים טובים וקדושים, שהסבות המחזיקות אותם בעולם הן כעורות, כמו חולשה, שקר, רשעות, שלפעמים הן תומכות את יסוד הטוב של בושה, צניעות, אמונה, וכיוצא בהם. אמנם כמו שטובתן של רשעים רעה היא אצל צדיקים, ככה היא הטובה שמקבל הטוב והקדוש מהרע והטמא, מחוללת היא רעות רבות, ואין אור גאולה יוצא אל הפועל כי-אם על-ידי מה שיהרסו כל היסודות הרעים, אפילו אותם שהם מחזיקים את הטוב והקודש ואף על-פי שעל-ידי זה סובל הטוב, הקודש והאמונה, והם יורדים ונראים כמתדלדלים, דלדול זה וירידה זו עליה והתעודדות הם באמת, שאחר הרקבון של היסודות הרעים הללו, יחל מיד לצמוח אור הזוהר והקודש על יסודות בריאים של דעה, חכמה, גבורה, תפארת, נצח והוד, ובזה תוסד מלכות עולמים לאור ד׳ וטובו באחרית הימים בחסדי דוד הנאמנים, שהם ברית עולם אשר לא יכזבו עדי עד. ״ויאמר אך עמי המה בנים לא ישקרו, ויהי להם למושיע, בכל צרתם לו צר, ומלאך פניו הושיעם, באהבתו ובחמלתו הוא גאלם, וינטלם וינשאם כל ימי עולם״.

though it is terrible to see so many truthful things, good qualities, commandments and laws, swept away and seemingly uprooted by the flood of negativity – despite this, eventually all will grow in purity and strength, in supernal holiness, from the firm, pure, exalted kernel, which no negativity can affect. Its light will shine as a new light upon Zion,[369] with a wondrous greatness that is above every conception that poor[370] powers of souls exhausted materially and spiritually by a long and debilitating[371] exile, could ever conceive.

52

Rejecting Questionable Means

The light of Redemption will reject all but the purest means, even though initially this will weaken the end.

There are things good and holy that are upheld by causes that are ugly, such as weakness, falsehood, wickedness, which occasionally support the good foundation of humility, modesty, faith, and the like. But just as the good performed by the wicked is abhorrent to the righteous,[372] so the benefit that the good and holy receive from the evil and impure produces many ills. The light of redemption will be actualized only by the destruction of all the evil foundations, even those that support the good and holy. Though goodness, holiness and faith will suffer, decline, and appear to be weakened thereby, in verity this weakening and descent are an ascent and an encouragement – for after the rotting of these bad elements, the light of splendor[373] and holiness will immediately begin to grow on the healthy foundations of knowledge[374] wisdom,[375] strength,[376] glory,[377] endurance[378] and splendor.[379] Thus will be founded[380] the kingdom[381] of eternity by the Lord's light and goodness at the end of days, through the faithful love of David, an eternal covenant[382] that is unceasing. *He said: Surely they are My people, children that will not lie, and He became to them a saviour. In all their affliction He was afflicted, and the angel of His presence saved them; in His love and in His pity He redeemed them, and He bore them and carried them forever.*[383]

נג

רוח הקודש מגלה בבהירות את האור האלהי הגדול המלא חיים הפרוש בכל העולם כולו הממלא את החיים כולם, ואת כל האדם בכללו ביחוד, איך הוא הולך ומתרכז, מוצא לו עמדתו בעולם, מקום מנוחה ופעולה בכנסת ישראל, שבקרבה קדוש שורה בהדר גאונו, מראש צורים של גזעה, מהליכות תולדתה, "אנכי ד' אלהיך - מארץ מצרים". מהופעת תורתה, מהארת נביאיה, עמדת מלכותה, בנין מקדשה, חורבנה ושבותה, פזורה וגלותה, נחמתה ותקותה, עד דור אחרון, פעולתה על המהלך הרוחני של העולם, התעוררותה לתחיה בזמננו, נפילותיה החמריות והרוחניות, עומק המחשבה האלהית המתגלה בעוצם הירידות, כונניותם לטובה לאישיה הפרטיים, לכללותה, למין האדם בכללו, להעלאת העולם בפועל ידה, דבר ד' אשר עמה בחיי שעה: החיים החברותיים והיחידיים, הלאומיים והעולמיים, חיי העולם: זכוך הנפשות, הגברת זיו החיים, התעלות הכשרונות, המשכת התרבות הכללית שבעולם אל האושר האמתי, התבססות חיי עולם על-ידי החיים הנצחיים הרוחניים, הסדרת הסיעות השונות שבבני אדם ושמירת עניניהם, רכושם וכבודם, הגדלת יפי החיים, כבוד החיים ועונג החיים, על-ידי הבעת דעת אלהים ד' אלהי ישראל, בשפה ברורה ורוח אדיר החי בנשמתה של אומת עולמים זו, התעוררות ספרות פרוזאית ושירית, בקרתית ופומבית, השבה אל אור הנבואה, בקשורה אל התורה, בתור הכרה בהירה שהכרח גמור הוא לרוח האדם המסובך, לשוב אל המקור העליון, שהדעות היותר נשגבות נשאבות ממנו - כל אלה וסעיפיהן מקשקשות כעת לפנינו בארץ ישראל כזוג.

53

Overviewing History

The divine inspiration that abounds in Erets Yisrael *today allows an overview of the "hand of God" manipulating the entire history of mankind.*

Divine inspiration *(ru'aḥ ha-kodesh)* reveals clearly[384] the great divine light, full of life, which is spread throughout the world, which permeates all life, and especially mankind – reveals how it concentrates, finding a base in the world, a place of respite and activity in *Knesset Yisrael* (Ecclesia Israel), in whom rests the Holy One in all His glory, from the beginning of her race, from her earliest history – *I am the Lord your God from the land of Egypt*[385] – from the appearance of her Torah, from the illumination of her prophets, the establishment of her kingdom, the erection of her Temple, her destruction and return, her dispersion and exile, her consolation and hope until the last generation, her influence on the spiritual advancement of the world, her renascence in our time, her material and spiritual falls, the depth of the divine thought that is revealed in the very descents, her readiness[386] for good, for her individual members,[387] for her totality, for the entire human race, for the upliftment of the world by her deeds;[388] the word of the Lord that is with her in temporal life: individual, social, national, global; (in) eternal life: the purification of souls; the strengthening of the radiance of life; the development of talents; the leading of general civilization to true happiness; the establishment of the world through eternal spiritual life; the arrangement of the various groups of people and preservation of their affairs, property, and respect; the enhancement of the beauty of life, the respect of life and the joy of life, through the expression of the consciousness of God, the Lord, God of Israel, in clear speech and mighty spirit that lives in the soul of this eternal people; the awakening of literature, prose and lyric, critical and public; return to the light of prophecy, as it connects to Torah, knowing that it is absolutely imperative that the complex spirit of Man return to its higher source, from which the most exalted opinions are drawn – all these and their ramifications now ring before us in the Land of Israel as a bell.[389]

נד

רק ישראל יכולים הם לקבל אמונת אלהי אמת ד׳ אחד במלואה וטובה, ואישיותם העצמית עוד תוסיף אומץ עם זה ותרבותם תשתגשג ותתגדל בפריחה מצוינת, "בד׳ יצדקו ויתהללו כל זרע ישראל". אבל הגויים לא באו עדיין לידי מדה זו, ומה שהוכנס מאורם של ישראל אמונה אלהית בסביבותם, שלא בדרך התפתחות הראויה להם לפי טבעם, נלחם הוא באישיותם הפרטית ומלקה את תרבותם, שהיא זרה, חיצונה, נכרית ומגושמת, בעצם תכונתה. אמנם יד ד׳ עשתה זאת שעל כל פנים תרוכך מעט הקליפה הקשה של הזוהמה האנושית, אבל סוף כל סוף מוכרחת הנכריות לנצח אצלם והמלכות תהפך למינות שתגעל את הניצוצות של רוח ישראל, הבאים מאור ד׳, שנמסך ברוחם, ותגבר בזה יותר שנאת ישראל, ואף על-פי שבתחלה יראו על-ידי זה הנגעים של עקבתא דמשיחא, וקטני נפש חושבים לחקות את הכפירה המתרחבת אצל הגוים, ומדמים אותה לתרבות אנושית כללית במקום שאינה כי-אם תרבות זרה ונכרית שישראל עומדים כבר למעלה ממנה, מכל מקום סוף כל סוף המחשבה הזאת בעצמה של החפץ להיות עומד על העצמיות הנקיה בלא עירוב השפעה חיצונה - שהיא מגדלת מעבר מזה את שנאת העמים לישראל ביותר, ומעבר השני את החקוי הרוחני מצד חלושי חיים מישראל, עד שהאנרכיה המחשבתית מהרסת את כל קושט וקודש - היא בעצמה הכרה זו, שיש לעמוד על הנקודה התוכית המסגלת להעצמיות, תקרא את ישראל לתשובה, לעשות חיל באלהים, ולשוב עוד הפעם לגבורה עליונה, "כי לא בחרבם ירשו ארץ, וזרועם לא הושיעה למו, כי ימינך וזרועך ואור פניך כי רציתם. אתה הוא מלכי אלהים צוה

54

The Mistake of Emulating European Nihilism

Europe rightly rejects Judaic morality, which is beyond its spiritual capacity. The rise of antisemitism. The folly of Jews aping this philosophic anarchy. Renewed nationalism will eventually bring Israel to teshuvah.

Only Israel can receive true monotheism in its fullness and goodness; their essential personality is invigorated thereby, and their civilization flourishes. *In the Lord all the seed of Israel shall be justified and glory themselves.*[390] However, the nations have not yet reached this level, and that divine belief that they have absorbed from the light of Israel in their surroundings, without the evolution suited to their nature, is at conflict with their individual personality and oppresses their civilization, which is essentially pagan and idolatrous.[391] However, the hand of the Lord did this,[392] so that to a degree the hard shell of human depravity should be softened,[393] but eventually the pagan in them will win out; "the kingdom will turn to heresy,"[394] which will resent the sparks of the spirit of Israel, that proceed from the light of the Lord that has infused their spirit, and hatred of Israel will increase. In the beginning there will appear thereby the plagues of the "footsteps of Messiah," when the small of soul think to imitate the atheism[395] that burgeons among the nations, considering it to be general human civilization, when in reality it is not but paganism, which Israel has already far surpassed. Nevertheless, this very thought [i.e., of the nations] to arrive at the pure essence[396] unmitigated by outside influence – which produces on the one hand an increase in antisemitism, and on the other, spiritual aping by devitalized Jews, until mental anarchy destroys all that is true and holy – this very thought, of arriving at the innermost point, the essence,[397] will call Israel to Return, to be strong in God, to return once again to the supernal strength. *Not by their sword did they obtain possession of the land, and their own arm brought them no victory; but Your right hand, and Your arm, and the light of Your countenance, because You favored them. You are my king, O God; ordain salvation for Jacob. Through You we will butt down our assailants; through Your name*

ישועות יעקב. בך צרינו ננגח בשמך נבוס קמינו". והכרה זו הבאה בהתפתחות אטית מאד, המתחילה מקנאת עם, חבת ארץ, שפה, תרבות גלמית, דעת התולדה, התלהבות עבודה גשמית ארצית בכח היד המגושמה, מוכרחת היא לעלות עד הראש, ולעורר את המחשבה וההרגשה היותר מיוחדה לישראל בלב כל האומה, הזקנים והצעירים יחדו, ובלב אחד, במחשבה וחשק אחד "ישובו בני ישראל ובקשו את ד' אלהיהם ואת דוד מלכם ופחדו אל ד' ואל טובו". כעת באחרית הימים, שכבר החלו להראות את נצניהם, כל החיל אשר נגע אלהים בלבם קרואים ועומדים הם, לעורר המון מחשבות והופעות מהספירות העליונות ממקור ישראל, ולעדור בלא לב ולב ביסודות התחתיות שהתחילה כבר ההרגשה לדפוק בהם בחזקה, והמחשבה והמעשה יפגשו יחדו לבנות עולם מלא, בשם מלא, "ימלוך ד' לעולם, אלהיך ציון לדור ודור, הללויה!"

נה

מהלך המחשבה הרחבה האידיאלית האלהית הולך ומתרחב בטבעו, מקפת היא חזיונות רבים ואופקים גדולים, ותכונת הציורים שלה הנה שונה מתכונת הציורים של דקדוקי הפרטיות שבתורת המעשה וניתוחי ההלכה, ומצב הנפש הדרוש לעומק של הלכה, על-פי סגנונה הקבוע המושגר אצלנו מאז נחתם התלמוד, הוא בטבעו אינו מתאים למצב הנפשי של ההתהלכות ברחבה במרומי האידיאלים האלהיים ורזיהם, שאיפותיהם והרחבת עידוניהם. לכן נפלגו האגדה וההלכה, הנגלה והנסתר, בהבדלה מקורתית. אמנם הונחה שאיפה פנימית במעמקי הנשמה לשלב את ההלכה והאגדה יחד. עשו נסיון זה מפלפלים בפלפולים שונים, שאנו רואים

we will defeat our opponents.[398] This awareness that develops gradually, which begins with patriotism, love of the land, language, raw culture, acquaintance with history, enthusiasm for physical labor with a brawny hand, must reach the head and arouse uniquely Jewish thought and feeling in the heart of the entire nation, young and old alike. Of one heart, a single thought and desire, *The Children of Israel will return and will seek the Lord their Lord and David their king and fear for the Lord and His goodness.*[399] Now, in the end of days, when these buds have already been seen, all whose hearts have been touched by God[400] are called[401] to arouse a multitude of thoughts and revelations from the higher spheres, from the source of Israel, and to sincerely cultivate the lower foundations in whom the sentiment has already commenced throbbing. The thought and the action will join together to construct a full world, with a full name. *The Lord will reign forever, your God, Zion, for generations. Halleluyah!*[402]

55

Halakha and Agadah

The revealed worlds and hidden worlds of Torah that were torn asunder by the Exile will be grasped as one in the "Light of Messiah."

The process of idealist divine thought is naturally expansive. The thought encompasses sundry visions and great horizons. Its imaging is different from the detail-oriented imaging of practical theory and halakhic analysis.[403] The state of mind required for the depth of Halakha, in the style we are accustomed to since the redaction of the Talmud, naturally does not comply with the state of mind of the expansive tour[404] of the heights of the divine ideals and their mysteries, their aspirations and their delights. Therefore Agadah and Halakha, the exoteric and esoteric, diverged at their source. However, in the depths of the soul was lodged an inner aspiration to interlace the Halakha and Agadah. This was attempted by various dialecticians (*mefalpelim*[405]), in whom we witness a holy spirit of experimental creativity, moistened by the dew of life, the desire for unity and total peace between the

בהם רוח קדוש של נסיון יצירה, משוקה מטל החיים של חפץ האחדות והשלום הגמור בין העלמין דאתגליין ובין העלמין דגניזין. אמנם לא יצא בצורה של גדלות וגמר פרי, כי־אם בצורה קטנותית ובסרית, ותכלית נטיה נפשית זו היא האחדות הרוחנית המחלטת של העולמות הללו הנראין כנפרדים, וכל מה שאורו של משיח הולך ומתקרב ושרשי הנשמות מתבסמים, הולכת ההארה של רזי תורה ומתגלה ומתבלטת יותר, ולפי גילוי זו הולכים הענינים הגלויים ומתאצלים יותר והם מתקרבים לצד הרזיות, "ואחד באחד יגשו ורוח לא יבא ביניהם". ההסברות המתחדשות בדרכה של התורה הנגלית מדור לדור יש בתוכן נקודה פנימית של התקרבות להרחבה הרזית של רחובות הנהר אשר לבינה העליונה, ותלמידי חכמים יקרי דעה הם עובדים בזה את השדה אשר ברכו ד׳ ומתקרבים בזה לאור "הגאולה" שהוא תלמוד הירושלמי, העומד לעומת "התמורה" שהוא תלמוד הבבלי, שהוא האור של ישיבת מחשכים שבארעא דמחשכא. באחרית הימים יגלה אור ד׳ ויתקרב הסגנון של ההלכות המאוששות עם האגדות דחקל תפוחין קדישין במועד קץ המגולה, שהוא שיבת ישראל לארץ ישראל ולהחיותה בבנין מעשי, "ואתם הרי ישראל, פריכם תתנו וענפכם תשאו לעמי ישראל כי קרבו לבא", שתכונתו היא קיבוץ החתום וסתום דליבא לפומא לא גליא, תוכן קץ החתום, עם הגלוי של עבודה גשמית מורגשת מכל המון עובד. בגאולה כפולה זו יוחל כח זרוע ד׳ לגאול את הגופים מכל שעבודם הקשה "מעצבך ומרגזך ומן העבודה הקשה אשר עובד בך", ואת הנשמות ממכאוביהן ומחשכיהן, מכל המדות הרעות, מכל השנאות והצמצומים, "ועשיתי אותם לגוי אחד בארץ בהרי ישראל". "אכן אתה אל מסתתר אלהי ישראל מושיע".

revealed and concealed worlds.[406] However, what resulted was not mature, full-grown fruit, but rather a stunted, unripe form. The goal of this soulful proclivity is the absolute spiritual unification of these seemingly disparate worlds. The closer the Light of Messiah comes and the more the roots of the souls are invigorated, the more the illumination of the mysteries of Torah is revealed and pronounced, and in proportion to this revelation, the revealed matters become transcendent and approach the mystical dimension. *They approach one another and no breath comes between them.*[407] The innovations in Talmudic methodology from generation to generation contain an inner point of approaching the mystical expanses, the "expanses of the River"[408] of the higher understanding. Exceptional Torah scholars toil in the field blessed by the Lord[409] and approach the light of "the redemption" that is the Jerusalem Talmud,[410] which stands opposite "the exchange" that is the Babylonian Talmud,[411] the light of dwelling in the darkness[412] of a somber land.[413] At the end of days, the light of the Lord will be revealed, and the style of the solid *halakhot*[414] will approach [that of] the *agadot* of the "holy apple orchard"[415] at the time of the "revealed end,"[416] which is the return of Israel to the Land of Israel to revivify it by practical upbuilding. *And you mountains of Israel, yield your fruits, bear your branches, for My people Israel who are approaching.*[417] It consists of the gathering, sealed and hidden, "which the heart does not reveal to the mouth,"[418] the content of the sealed end,[419] together with the revealed [end] of tangible physical labor of a working mass. In this double redemption, the power of the arm of the Lord will begin to redeem the bodies from their hard bondage – *from your trouble and your vexation, and from the hard bondage wherein you were made to serve*[420] – and the souls from their pains and obscurities, from all the evil traits, from all prejudices and narrows. *I shall make them one nation in the Land, in the mountains of Israel.*[421] *Verily, You are a hiding God, saving God of Israel.*[422]

נו

צריך לתן חופש גמור לנטיה הרוחנית שבנשמה שתתפשט ותתרחב בכל כחתיה. לפי רוב פעולותיה החפשיות יאומץ חילה ותגלה נפלאות הדרת גבורת קדשה על החיים ועל כל המעשים והמחשבות, בחופש הנשמה תעלה עמה את כל כחות החיים, המפוזרים והמשתלשלים ממנה, וכולם באגודה אחת יתרוממו למרום הקודש העליון. מדה זו הולכת ומאירה כל מה שאור התורה יותר חודר ויותר מאיר, כל מה שרזי תורה הפנימיים, בין מצד המדע, בין מצד הרגש, בין מצד הדמיון, יותר יתגלו ויתפשטו, יותר יוכשרו להיות העסק בהם קבוע ורגיל, כן תתעלה הנשמה בכלל, ונשמת העולם, אור החיים של השכינה האלהית, תוזהיר יותר, ותגלה אורה על כל הנפשות ועל כל מעשיהן. וישראל האחוזים מעומק טבע נשמתם באחיזת הקודש העליון, המגמה הרוחנית העליונה של אצילות החיים וההויה, יתרוממו על-ידי התגברותה של האורה הפנימית היוצאת מאור דעת עליון, יתעלו ויתפארו, והגבורה האלהית תעודדם בהדר תפארתה, ויתכשרו יותר ויותר לאור גאולה, לאורו של משיח, והדר השלום הכללי וחן האהבה לכללות האומה ולכל פרטיה, לפעולותיה ולהרחבת חייה, ילך ויתפשט בעולם, עד שמההדר הפנימי יפוצו קרנים גם כן על ההוד החיצוני, ויתחיל כל העולם מבחוץ גם כן להכיר את אור תפארת עוזנו, והכבוד הכמוס, המונח במעמקי הנשמה של כל העמים התרבותיים לאורן של ישראל, שנעצר על-ידי מעצורים רבים, יפרוץ את כל מעכביו וכנחל פרצים יזרם, לעטר ישראל בתפארה ולאזרו בגבורה.

56
Freedom of Spirit

The spirit must be given the freedom to expand and uplift all faculties. So too, the soul of the world and Israel, preparing for the "Light of Messiah," must be unfettered.

It is necessary to give full freedom to the spiritual inclination within the soul to develop and expand in all its abilities. According to the number of its free activities, its strength will wax and it will reveal its wondrous holy strength in life, in all actions and thoughts. In freedom, the soul will raise up with it all of life's scattered resources that derive from it [i.e., the soul], and in a single bond they will ascend to the height of supernal holiness. This proportion increases the more the light of Torah penetrates and illumines. The more the innermost mysteries of Torah – whether of intellect, emotion, or imagination – are revealed and disseminated; the more they [i.e., the secrets] are adapted to regular, steady study, the more the soul in general will ascend, and the soul of the world, the living light of the divine presence, will shine brightly, and its light will be manifest upon all the souls and their deeds. And Israel, linked from the depth of the nature of their soul to the supernal holiness – the higher spiritual destiny of transcendent life and existence – will be exalted by the strengthening of the inner light that emanates from the supernal intellect, will ascend and be glorious. The divine strength will encourage them with its splendid glory, and they will be increasingly prepared for the light of redemption, for the Light of Messiah. The beauty of the general peace and the charm of love for the entire nation and all its individuals, for its activities and its breadth of life, will spread in the world, until the inner beauty[423] will radiate[424] to the outer splendor,[425] and all the outside world will also begin to recognize the glory of our strength. The respect for the light of Israel contained within the depths of the soul of all the civilized nations, which had been blocked by many blockages, will break all its restraints and burst forth like floodwaters, to adorn Israel with glory and gird it with strength.[426]

נז

התוכן העליון של חכמת הרזים, מתוך שהיא מוכרחת להשתלם על-ידי הופעת רוח הקודש והתגלות נשמה בבינה עליונה, שלמעלה מכל חושי הבשר והחכמות המוגבלות, שהן תוצאותיהן, הוא בעצמו מכריח בהכרח פנימי את ההסתגלות הרוחנית להקשבה עליונה של רוח אלהים, ובני הנביאים היו מתרגלים בתכנים העליונים שאין מגיעים לציורם כי-אם בהקשבה נצחית פנימית הנובעת מאור חיי הקודש, עד שהציורים בעצמם, שדורשים את התפקיד של הבנתם, סדורם והפראתם, הם הם שהיו עוזרים להעלות את החיים הרוחניים של העוסקים בהם לידי המדה של הצפיה האלהית. כעת, בזמן היותר קרוב לקץ ישועה, קול התור נשמע בארצנו והנצנים נראו בארץ, והתביעה של דרישת אור ד׳, של דרישת גאולה רוחנית עליונה, של נהירה אל ד׳ ואל טובו, הולכת היא וגדלה. כעת הזמן מחיב להרבות קנין בתורה הפנימית, בחזיונות הקודש שאין להם מבא של הקשבה כי-אם בהתעלותה של הנשמה ורוממות גבורתה באור חייה היותר זכים ועליונים, וחיל אשר נגע ד׳ בלבם ממחנה אלהים זה, זה יהיה לנו הכח המיסד את יסוד הישועה, הכח הנותן חן ואור חיים וגאון של גדולה בכל תעופת החיים אשר לתחית האומה בארץ ישראל. ספר הזוהר, הפורץ נתיבות חדשות, משים במדבר דרך, מסלה בערבה, הוא וכל תבואתו מוכן הוא לפתח פתחי גאולה, ״ובגין דעתידין ישראל למטעם מאילנא דחיי דאיהו האי ספר הזהר, יפקון מן גלותא ברחמי״.

57
The Book of *Zohar* Beckons

The mysteries of Torah themselves, whose time has come, will force the Jewish People into a state of attunement.

Since the high content of the secret wisdom must be perfected by the manifestation of divine inspiration and the revelation of the soul with supernal understanding, beyond the fleshly senses and the finite wisdoms that are their results – this itself inwardly forces spiritual adaptation to higher attunement to the spirit of God. The disciples of the prophets became accustomed to higher contents whose imaging can be reached only by an internal, eternal listening that flows from the light of the holy life. Thus the images (*tsiyyurim*) themselves, which demand the function of their comprehension, arrangement, and fructification – they themselves helped to raise the spiritual life of those engaged in them to the level of divine vision. Now, when the final salvation is imminent, *the voice of the turtledove is heard in our land and the buds are seen in the land,*[427] and the demand of seeking the light of the Lord, of seeking exalted spiritual redemption, of streaming to the Lord and His goodness,[428] increases and burgeons. Now the time requires acquiring the inner Torah, with holy visions that cannot begin to be heard but by the ascent of the soul and the exaltation of its strength in the light of its highest, purest life. A mass whose hearts have been touched by the Lord,[429] of this divine camp,[430] will be the power that establishes the foundation of the salvation, the power that gives grace, the light of life and the pride of greatness to the entire *élan vital* of the national renascence in the Land of Israel. The Book of Splendor (*Zohar*) that breaks new pathways, making a way in the desert, a road in the wilderness,[431] it and all its crop are ready to open doors of redemption. "Since Israel are destined to taste of the Tree of Life which is the Book of Splendor (*Zohar*), they will emerge from exile with mercy."[432]

נח

הסיבוכים שבמחשבות וחלוקי הדעות שאינם מתאחדים, בחיים וברעיון, באים ממקום אחד: מהמחשבה הרישומית, שאיננה מבוררת. צללי המחשבה, העוטפים את אורותיה, הם יותר רחבים, יותר אידיאליים, מהאורה המחשבתית, מהצד הברור שלה, אבל הרבה פחות ידועים ומבוררים, ומתוך כך כל זמן שהחושב מתחמם מרחוק לאור נגהם, הרי דעתו מתרחבת, רצונו מתעדן והרגשתו מתאצלת, וחיי שלוה מלאי הוד קודש ובטחון של גודל וענוה מתמזגים בכל רוחו, והצבור המרווה מהשפעות רבות חן וערך כאלה הולך הוא על המסילה של חיי עולם, וברכת השלום, הסבלנות הטהורה, הערות הרוחנית, חפץ החיים ותפארת הטהרה, הולכים הם ומתגדלים. אבל הרבה פעמים יזדמן, שאיזו נטיה זרה מתגנבת בתוך הרוח, ואותה ההקשבה הרחוקה, שהאדם מקשיב את צליל הקול האידיאלי מתוך אלה המרחקים הנשגבים של צללי האורות הרחבים והאידיאליים, אינה דיה לו, הוא חפץ להזין מהם את אזניו בשמיעה סואנת, את עיניו בראיה מובלטת, את דמיונו בצבעים, את שכלו והרגשתו במושגים מוצקים תפושים בחוקה. אז יהפך לו הטוב העליון לרועץ, מאותו הצמצום שבאור הבהיר המצומצם, שנכנס במדעו ובהכרותיו, יקח גדרים וצבתים, שהם מתהפכים לגדרים לוחצים ולצבתים מעיקים על הצללים הגדולים, נגוהות האור הרחוקים והרחבים, ומתוך אותו הלחץ יולד חום עשני של אש זרה מלאה ממרורות, חמה גדולה וסוערת, קנאה כעסנית לאין גבול, לאין נחת ואין שלום, ובמקומה של האמונה הגדולה, הבטחון השלו, הצפיה המעונגה, יכנס רוח עועים של חפץ שררה ושלטון, מלא אכזריות ומחוסר בושה, צניעות ויושר, ותגרות תדיריות יתלקחו, ומלחמות דמים יולדו, ורצח ותועבה

58
Big Faith and Little Faith

The illegitimate attempt to reduce and corporealize divinity produces fanaticism. Israel's spiritual evolution is yet incomplete. With the return to the Land, it will soar to the heights of pure idealism.

The mental complications and irreconcilable[433] differences of opinion, in life and theory, come from one source: from superficial thought that is not crystallized. The shadows of thought that envelop its lights, are broader, more ideal than the thoughtful light, than its clarity, though much less known and precise. Therefore, whenever a thinker warms himself by their bright light, his knowledge broadens, his will becomes tender, and his feeling becomes noble. Tranquil life full of holy majesty and the assurance of greatness and humility mix throughout his spirit. The community satiated by such gracious and valuable influences travels the way of eternal life, and the blessing of peace, pure patience, spiritual alertness, the will for life, and the glory of purity are increased. However, many times it happens that some strange tendency creeps into the spirit, and the distant listening,[434] whereby a man listens to the sound of the ideal voice through these lofty distances of the broad, ideal light-shadows, is insufficient for him. He wants his ears to be nourished by them with raucous hearing, his eyes with magnified seeing, his imagination with colors, his mind and feeling with concrete, tangible concepts.[435] Then the highest good turns destructive. From the constriction of the bright light that has entered his knowledge and consciousness, he will take definitions and "tongs,"[436] which become fences crunching[437] and pincers squeezing the great shadows, the broad, distant splendors. From that pressure will result a smoky heat of foreign fire, full of bitterness, stormy fuming, angry vengeance without limit, pleasure or peace. Instead of great faith, tranquil trust and delicate longing will enter a perverse will-to-power, cruel and lacking shame, pudency and rectitude. Constant fights will erupt, bloody wars will ensue, and murder and horror will creep as serpents from lairs. All majesty[438] will turn to affliction,[439] as impure as the menstruant[440]

יזחלו כנחשים ממחבואים וכל הוד לדוה יהפך, וכטומאת הנדה יטמא כל המתימר בשם קודש, וחושך יכסה ארץ וערפל לאומים. ומתוך מעוף צרה זו, מתרוממת לה המשפחה הגאיונה בגאות קודש, המשפחה שהפדות והפאר היא מנת גורלה מאז, המשפחה שנחלתה עמוקה וגדולה היא עד שהיא בעצמה לא גמרה עדיין את כל ההסתגלות הדרושה לגדולת נשמתה, המשפחה אשר יצאה מבית עבדים ממצרים ומצפה לאור שעה ולאור העולם, לחרות הנשמה וחרות הגוף - ושבה היא אל מקורה, שבה אל הארץ, שהיא כולה מרגשת בה את סגולה חייה, מסתגלת היא להקשבה עדינה, לצלילים עליונים, באים וטסים מעולמים גבוהים ונאצלים, אשר כל חד וחד מקבל מהם כפום שיעורא דיליה, "נודע בשערים בעלה", ומכל השיעורים יחד יגלה הוד השלום וזיו האמת, יסוד העונג ומילוי החיים, המלאים עבודה וחפץ אידיאלי טהור קבוע, בלא נדידה, "ולא יכנף עוד מוריך והיו עיניך רואות את מוריך", "ירעה מקניך ביום ההוא כר נרחב". והולכת היא העדינות וסובבת היא את כל שדרה, את כל כח עובד, יורדת היא עד כדי דעת נפש הבהמה כראוי לגוי צדיק, "והאלפים והעירים עובדי האדמה בליל חמיץ יאכלו, אשר זרה ברחת ובמזרה".

נט

הנסתר ינצח את העולם בחפשיותו אשר לא תדע גבול של מועקה, ודוקא הוא יודע דוקא בדיוק נמרץ את הגבול של כבוד ושל חכמה ויושר לבב. רק הסגול אל הצפיה הנסתרת מודיע אל האנושיות את ערכה ואת ערך התבל. הרציונליות מתפתחת רק מפני שמעבר לסף ההכרה שלה עושה הנסתר את פעולתו המדעית והמוסרית. מזויפת היא ההנחה ההמונית שהנסתר מעכר את המדע הבהיר

will be all who pretend to the title "holy," and *darkness will cover the earth and fog, nations.*[441] Out of this dimness of oppression[442] the proud family is exalted[443] with holy pride, the family whose lot has always been redemption and glory,[444] the family whose portion is so deep and great that it has yet to complete the adaptation necessary for the greatness of its soul, the family who departed from the house of bondage, from Egypt, and waits for temporal and eternal light,[445] for freedom of soul and body. It [i.e., the family] returns to its source, to the Land, in which it feels the treasure of its life. It adapts to a delicate listening, to high notes, flying from transcendental worlds. "Each receives according to his measure."[446] *Her husband is known in the gates.*[447] And from all these measures[448] together will appear the majesty of peace and the brilliance of truth, the foundation of joy and the fullness of life, brimming with work and permanent, pure, ideal will. *No longer will your teacher hide; your eyes will behold your teacher.*[449] *On that day your flock will graze in a wide pasture.*[450] The gentleness continues and encompasses every avenue,[451] every work force. It descends to the level of knowing the soul of the beast, as is proper for a righteous nation.[452] *The oxen and the young asses that till the ground shall eat salted provender which has been winnowed with the shovel and with the fan.*[453]

59

Mysticism and Rationalism

Mysticism and rationalism are, contrary to common belief, not antithetical. The science of mysticism places the rational on firm footing.

The esoteric will conquer the world with its freedom that knows no constricting limit; paradoxically it is the esoteric that knows with exquisite precision the limit of honor and wisdom and straightness of heart. Only adaptation to hidden vision informs mankind of its worth and the value of the earth. Rationalism develops only because beyond the fore of consciousness, the esoteric carries on its scientific and ethical activity. False is the assumption of the masses that the esoteric muddies clear science and exact critique. Precisely through the esoteric, through

ואת הבקורת המדוייקת. דוקא על-ידי הנסתר, ובעוזו שירתו ועומק הגיונו, יוסד על יסוד איתן המעמד של המדע ההולך ומתחדש והבקורת המדויקה המנתחת וחודרת. מצרופם של שני אלה השפעים בעשרם הגדול, הנסתר והבקורת, יבנה יסוד האיתן אשר לאור האלהי העליון, העומד למעלה מכל הגה והכרה. דופק רוח גדול זה על דלתותינו, והולך ומנשב הוא במחנינו, ויוצר הוא בחביונו אורו של משיח, לכל ערכיו, מובניו והופעותיו, והוא יתן כח חדש, וחדוש נשמה חדשה לישראל, לשוב להצמיח קרן ישועה ולהנטע עוד על אדמת הקודש כימי עולם, ברוחב דעת ובתכונה חפשית מקורית הראויה להיות מוכרת מכל אפסי תבל לכבוד ותפארת, לגאול רצוצי גליות, עשוקי משפט, ולפדות נשמות נעשקות וקודרות מיסורי מחשכיהם, ולחדש עוד את זיו האדם הקדמוני בטוהר טבעו, עם כל תוספת הברכה של התרבות החדשה וטובה.

ס

הסתירה שבין הנסתר והנגלה באה תמיד מחסרון השלמה של שני היסודות. הנגלה המצומצם בגבוליו, שאינו הומה אחרי מקורו ושרשו, יחוש איזה שנאה אל הנסתר, שאינו חפץ לדעת צמצום וגבול. מעוט ההכשר אל הנסתר, בקפיצה לתוכו רק משום חולשה של תאבון פנימי המצורפת עם רשלנות ובטלנות, הוא גורם שתטושטש הצורה של הנסתר, שרק שלילת הממשיות, רק רפיון החיים וחוסר הכשרון לתפוס את העולם החי, את מעשיו, תנועותיו, עלילותיו ורמיו המקסימים, מלאי ההוד והגבורה, הוא הגורם לשיקוע בעומק הנסתר למרות חסרון ההכנה. אבל לא זה וזה יתכן, לא בצד אחד של המטבע העולמית והתורנית יבוססו החיים. הנסתר גרעינו מוכן,

its strident song and deep utterance, will be firmly established the state of progressive science and exact, analytic, penetrating critique. From the synthesis of these two rich influences, the esoteric and the critical, will be erected the firm foundation of the supernal divine light, which stands beyond every utterance and consciousness. This mighty wind knocks on our doors, it blows through our camp, and in its hiddenness, it forms the Light of Messiah, in all of its values, connotations and manifestations. It will provide Israel a new force and a renewed soul[454] to return to produce a "horn of salvation" and to once again be planted on the holy soil, with expanded consciousness and with an original, free character, worthy to be recognized throughout the earth, honored and glorified, to redeem those broken by exile and deprived of justice, to redeem souls deprived and suffering darkness, and to restore once again the splendor of primordial Man in his pure nature, with all the additional blessings of beneficial modern civilization.

60

Legitimate and Illegitimate Mysticism

Mysticism should never be a form of escapism from the solid reality of this world. One must prepare for mystical study by mastering the revealed knowledge of this world.

The schism between the esoteric and exoteric comes about always due to the lack of wholeness of both elements. The exoteric that is restricted to its borders, which does not long for its source and root, will feel a certain antipathy to the esoteric, which cares to know no restriction or limitation. Lack of preparation for the hidden, jumping into it only because of a weakness of inner appetite, coupled with sloppiness and impracticality, causes the form of the esoteric to be distorted. Only unrealism, weak vitality, and lack of ability to grasp the living world, its deeds, movements, events, and charming currents, full of majesty and strength, cause immersion in the depth of the esoteric despite lack of preparation. But neither can exist exclusive of the other; life cannot be based on only one side of the global and Torah coin. The germ of the esoteric is ready, but it will be successfully actualized

אבל אל הפועל יצא בהצלחה רק אחרי ההכשר המלא של הנגלה. מילוי הכרס ב״לחם, בשר ויין״ מוכרח להיות קודם ל״טיול בפרדס״, ומילוי כרס זה במובנו המלא כולל בקרבו גם כן את מדע העולם והחיים ואת ההסתגלות המוסרית, המדתית, את גבורת הרצון ואת הכרת ערך האדם, ואת כל הטוב הנאה והמסודר שבמציאות הבא מתוך חנוך טוב והגון לכל צדדיו, המצטרף אל כל המתעורר לחיים ולרעננות מכל צד ופנים, באדם ובאומה, בספרות ובחיים, בחול ובקודש ובקודש הקדשים. תביעת הנסתר, שהיא מתמלאת בבא עתה, היא תביעה איתנה, שהיא מביאה את המלה הגואלת, שהיא משחררת את האמרה הישראלית הגדולה ממאסר אלמותה, היא מחדשת החיים האיתנים, היא מעוררת את רוח הגבורה שבקודש המוחלט, שהוא הרבה יותר פשוט ויותר טבעי מכל חול ורגיל, ועם זה עומד הוא בשגובו ובתפארתו.

סא

חמדת התורה משתלהבת בהכרה פנימית, מתחיל האדם לחוש את הארג הגדול של כל אות ונקודה, שכל רעיון ותוכן, שכל ידיעה וסברה, של כל ניד רוחני, של כל זעזוע, שכלי והרגשי, מקרוב וכללי, עד רחוק ופרטי, מדברים אציליים, רוחניים ומוסריים על-פי הפרצופיות הגלויה שלהם, עד דברים מעשיים, חמריים, חוביים, נראים כמטילי אימה ומכריחים, ועם זה מסובבים ומלאי ענין והטרחה שכלית גדולה - כולם יחד מוכרים הם בהכרת קודש עליונה, שתמימות האמונה, שבחבת התורה היא מוצאה את רוממות אמתה וגדולת שירתה, לדברים חיים וקימים, ששטפי חיים עזוזים, מלאי חמדה ששון ויפעה, עוברים בהם וממלאים אותם, ומתק אין

only after the full preparation of the exoteric. Filling the belly with "bread, meat and wine" must precede the "stroll in paradise."[455] "Filling the belly" in its full sense[456] includes within it also knowledge of the world and life, ethical and character development, strength of will and recognition of human value, and all the good, esthetic and orderly in existence that comes from an education good and proper in all its facets, which joins together with all that is aroused to life and freshness, in all areas:[457] man and nation, literature and life, secular and holy and holy-of-holies. The demand of the esoteric, which is filled when its time comes, is a firm demand, which brings the liberating word, which frees the great Israelite saying from the prison of its muteness. It renews firm life, it arouses the spirit of strength in the absolute holiness, which is much simpler and more natural than anything secular and mundane, and yet retains its loftiness and glory.

61

The Torah of *Erets Yisrael*

Delight in Torah reveals the spirituality of Torah – in all its minutiae. The inner light of Torah becomes apparent in the Land of Israel.

The delight of the Torah is ignited by an inner awareness. A man begins to sense the great tapestry of each letter and point. Every concept and content, every notion and idea, of every spiritual movement, of every vibration, intellectual and emotional, from the immediate and general to the distant and detailed, from matters lofty, spiritual, and ethical according to their outward profile, to matters practical, material, obligatory, seemingly frightening, and forceful, and at the same time complex and full of content and great mental exertion – all together become known by a supernal holy awareness. The simplicity of faith that is inherent in love of Torah finds its lofty truth and great song, for living, enduring things, that powerful currents of life, full of delight, joy and beauty, pass through and fill, and an infinite sweetness is felt in the palate of the thinker. *Your palate is like the best wine, that glides down for my friend gently, exciting the lips of those that are asleep.*[458] *How beautiful and how pleasant are you, delightful love.*[459]

קץ מורגש בחיך ההוגה, "וחכך כיין הטוב הולך לדודי למשרים דובב שפתי ישנים", "מה יפית ומה נעמת אהבה בתענוגים!"

מפעמת היא החבה, ומתחדשת היא, גלי גלים הומים, המון כנורות ונבלים, מנעימים נועם שיח סודם, מעומק נשמת האומה, מרוממות נשמת האדם המרכזה בקרבה, מרוחב נשמת כל היקום, כל היש שבנקודת ציון הפנימית, מקור התענוג, משולל כל תוכן ותואר מוגדר, משם, מן הכל, הומה וסוער המון גלגלי חיים רועשים ממתיקים סוד שיח קודש. התורה מתגלה בהדר יפעתה, נשמת האומה החיה והמקורית, הרעננה והעשירה, הנשמה רוממת הרוח, רווית העדן, הנה היא מוצגה לפנינו בשלל צבעי יפעת כליל חמדתה, ערגה לה נפשי, לבי ובשרי ירננו אל אל חי, כמו חלב ודשן תשבע נפשי, ושפתי רננות יהלל פי. מתגלה היא התורה בכליל הודה אל הדור הרענן מלא כח עלומים, והצפיה הולכת היא ומפעמת על דלתי נשמתו הגאיונה, עוד לא הסירה מעליה את צעיף סתרה, מעולפת היא בת שמים חמודה זו, אבל קרני הודה כבר חודרים מבעד הצעיף, ממלאים הם את פינות חיינו נוגה ואור חיים, מזלת היא כבר טללי חיים אל תוכיות הנשמות המקיצות לתחיה, תורת ארץ ישראל הולכת ונעורה, יחד עם תחית הבנין, העבודה הפרודוקטיבית וההכרה העצמית.

סב

הגלות מעטה את צביוננו, דכאה אותנו, אבל לא השמידה אפילו גרגר אחד מכל סגלותינו. כל מה שהוא מוכן לנו הרי הוא נמצא אתנו, כל מה שצריך להיות גדול ופורח הוא קטן, קמוץ, וכמוש, אבל הכל יתגדל, הכל ישוב לפרח, "יציץ ופרח ישראל".

The love wells up and is renewed. Waves upon waves roar, the sound of harps and lyres providing harmony for their secret conversation. From the depth of the nation's soul, from the height of the soul of man concentrated in its midst, from the breadth of all existence that is within the inner point of Zion,[460] source of delight, lacking any definable content or description, from there, from all, roars and storms the noise of life's loud wheels, speaking in holy secret. The Torah is revealed in its charming beauty. The living, original soul of the nation, fresh and rich; the soul lofty of spirit, satiated with delight, is presented before us in its versicolor beauty. My soul longs for it. *My heart and my flesh shout with joy unto the Living God.*[461] *As with fat and marrow will my soul be satisfied; and with tuneful lips shall my mouth praise.*[462] The Torah is revealed in its crowning majesty to the fresh generation full of the vigor of youth. The vision[463] continues to pound at the doors of its [i.e., the generation's] proud soul. It [i.e., the Torah] has not yet removed its veil of mystery;[464] this comely "daughter of heaven" is concealed, but her rays of glory already penetrate through the veil, they fill our lives with brightness and the light of life. She already pours life-giving dew into the interior of the souls that are roused to renascence. The Torah of the Land of Israel is increasingly aroused, together with physical building, productive[465] labor and self-awareness.

62

Israel Contains All the Ingredients of Its Redemption

Exile did not destroy but only shrunk Israel. All the ingredients necessary for rebirth are already found – in shrunken form.

Exile diminished our character, oppressed us, but did not obliterate even one grain of our singularity. All that is prepared for us is found in our midst; all that must be large and flourishing, is small, bunched, wrinkled. But all will expand, all will once again flourish. *Israel shall blossom and flower.*[466]

סג

הגוים טמאו את היהדות הגלויה במגעם, נגעו בשמנים הקדושים ושקצו אותם, אבני מזבח הקודש נתפגלו. אבל בקדושתם נשארו פנימיות הסודות שהם עלומים וחתומים ממגע זר - ודוקא הפנימיות היותר נשמתית, כי המבטאים אשר לסודות כבר באו פריצים וחללום. ופנימיות זו, שהיא נשמת הנשמה העליונה, קבועה היא בנשמה הסגולית אשר לישראל, ואינה זזה ממנה, כל זמן שהקשור לכללות האומה ולצביונה חי בקרבו, כל זמן שהוא חפץ בכלל באושר והצלחת האומה הישראלית, אף על-פי שאינו יודע לקרא בשם ולפרש את צפונותיו; ואפילו אם הוא טועה במעשיו ודעותיו, תוכו קודש קדשים הוא.

סד

סתרי תורה מביאים את הגאולה, משיבים את ישראל לארצו, מפני שתורת אמת בעז הגיונה הפנימי, דורשת בהרחבתה את הנשמה השלמה של האומה, והאומה מתחילה על ידה להרגיש את הכאב של הגלות, ואיך שאי אפשר כלל שצביונה יצא אל הפועל כל זמן שהיא דחופה וסחופה על אדמת נכר. אבל כל זמן שאור התורה העליונה הוא חתום ועזוק, אין התביעה הפנימית של שיבת ציון מתעוררת בעומק אמונה. ההתעוררות שבאה מצד הצרות והרדיפות של האומות אינה כי-אם התעוררות מקרית, של צרוף. היא ראויה להלהיב על ידה כחות נחשלים, אבל יסוד החיים מוכרח לבא מצד עצמיותה של התביעה הצורתית של האומה, וזה יתגדל ויתאמץ כל מה שאור תורתה הפנימית, עומק

63

The Hidden Cruse of Oil

The Nations defiled only the outer trappings of Judaism; within, the soul of Israel – and each individual Jew – burns brightly.

The Gentiles defiled revealed Judaism by their touch; they touched the holy oils and rendered them impure.[467] The stones of the holy altar were made unfit.[468] However, the inner mysteries [i.e., of Judaism] that are hidden and sealed from foreign touch retained their sanctity – but only the most soulful inwardness, for the [outer] expressions of the mysteries were already desecrated by intruders. This inwardness, which is the soul of the supernal soul, is fixed in the characteristic soul of Israel, and never moves thence, as long as the connection to the totality of the nation and its character lives in its midst, as long as it desires at all the well-being and success of the Israelite nation. Though it does not know to call by the Name and enunciate its mysteries, and even if it errs in its deeds and opinions – its inside is holy of holies.

64

The Mysteries of Torah Bring Redemption

The true arousal to return to the Land comes not through outer persecution but rather through the unleashing of the mysteries of Torah, which demand the Land of Israel.

The secrets of Torah bring the redemption[469] and return Israel to its land, for the Torah of Truth, with the strength of its inner logic, demands with its broadening the whole soul of the nation, and through it, the nation begins to feel the pain of the Exile and how it is utterly impossible for its character to be actualized, as long as it is oppressed[470] upon foreign soil. Yet as long as the light of the higher Torah is sealed, the inner demand of return to Zion is not aroused with the depth of faith. The arousal that comes as a result of the troubles and persecutions of the nations is but an accidental arousal, of purification. It is capable of firing up weak forces, but the foundation of life must

דעותיה וחביוני חביוניה, ילכו ויחיו בקרבה בגאון גדלם. לזאת סובב סובב הולך הרוח, עוקר הוא הרים, פורץ הוא פרצות, מסבב הוא חבלים וצירים, אבל מגמתם היא פריצת דרך בפני האורה העליונה הנובעת מנשמתה העזיזה של כנסת ישראל, סתרי תורתה, קבלתה, מורשת אבות, ואדירות נשמה, באופי המיוחד לה, בהשקפת עולמה, ורוממות מוסרה ההולך ומתרחב עד אין קץ, ההולך ומתעטר בכל תרבות עליונה והולך ומתעלה לגבהי שמים, מציץ את סגולת עם סגולה, עם יודעי אלהיו, ונותן שלטון לקדישי עליונין.

סה

דכשהאורה מתגברת בנשמה, בראשי האומה, בבחירי הבנים, בגדולי הכשרון, הולך הזרם ומשפיע, החיים הגדולים מתחילים שוטפים, מתגלים בחוגים הרוחניים והחמריים, בספרות, בחברה, בתולדה ובמזג, בנעימות הנפשות וברחבת הלבב. זוהר עליון מתחיל פורש זיו עננו והוד כבודו, ושם ד׳ הגדול הולך ומתראה עוד על עמו. הסגולה הגנוזה מתבצבצת ועולה נגד כל שוטניה וכופריה, ״וראו כל עמי הארץ כי שם ד׳ נקרא עליך״, ״וכל רואיהם יכירום כי הם זרע ברך ד׳״.

come from the essence of the formal demand of the nation. And this will be magnified and strengthened in proportion to the light of the inner Torah – the depth of its opinions and mysteries of mysteries – coming alive in its midst with great genius. Toward this end, the wind churns about, uprooting mountains, making breaches, inducing labor and birth pangs, but the end is the breaking of a way before the supernal light that wells up from the powerful soul of *Knesset Yisrael* (Ecclesia Israel) – the secrets of its Torah, its *Kabbalah* (tradition), the inheritance of fathers and mightiness of soul – with its particular character, its *Weltanschauung* and its exalted ethic, which broadens infinitely, which is adorned with every higher culture and reaches to the heights of heaven, which distinguishes the particularity of a peculiar people,[471] a people that knows its God,[472] and gives rule to the high holy ones.[473]

65

The Light Grows Strong

The spiritual light begins to radiate out from the souls of the elite to encompass all aspects of life.

And when the light grows strong in the soul, in the heads of the nation, in the chosen children, in the great of talent, the current proceeds to radiate, the great Life starts flowing, manifesting in the spiritual and material circles, in literature, society, heredity, and temperament, in the pleasantness of the souls and in the expanse of the heart. A lofty splendor begins to spread its radiant cloud and glorious honor, and the great Name of the Lord is seen once again on His people. The hidden quality surfaces and overcomes all its adversaries and scoffers. *All the peoples of the earth will see that the name of the Lord is called upon you.*[474]*All who behold them will recognize them as seed blessed by the Lord.*[475]

סו

אל מעין הנבואה הננו נקראים, צחיי צמא אנחנו, אבל מעין גנים, מקור מים חיים לפנינו הוא. החפצים הטובים שכל הסולת האנושית מתפארת בהם, ושוקקת אליהם, תמיד בכל דור ודור ובכל עת, מתחדשת בהמון חידושיה, במעשה ובהכרה, בשאיפה ובנטיה, כולם הנם גם חפצינו, אבל עוד עליון מכל, הוא מה שאנו חפצים, ומה שאנו מגשמים בחיים, מה שלא יגרע כחו גם אם תקופות עוברות ואין יודע ואין מבין. סתר רז קדוש שוכן בנו, נשמה חיה מיוחדה שרויה בקרבנו, מרוחו של משיח זורמים ונושבים רוחות, והנם באים עדינו, הננו מתקוממים, מתנערים ומבקשים חיים חדשים, חידוש ימים כקדם, על יסודנו אנו, על יסוד אבן פנתנו, על יסוד איתן רשום זה, שהננו יודעים שאין לו דוגמא ומשל, גם אם אין אנו יכולים לפרש את תכנו גם להגות רוחנו הפנימי. התעלומה אינה ממיטה אסון של ספקנות על הודאיות הנמצאה בגדולת חיה.

סז

החכמה העליונה השרויה בישראל, חכמת אלהים, שהגויה המקבלת אורה היא האומה כולה לכל דורותיה, העוברים ההוים והעתידים, יש לה השקפת עולמה הבהירה, דעותיה הקבועות, מדותיה, תכונותיה, רגשותיה, חזיונותיה, אמונותיה, תקותיה ואדירות חפצה ושאיפתה, שכולם הם מצויים ממשיים, פועלים ועושים תפקידם, מעבדים את הטבע הישראלי, קשורים קשר אמיץ בכל התכנים ההיסתוריים של האומה ובכל המהלכים

66

To the Wellspring of Prophecy

We aspire to what all nations aspire to, but more: prophecy. The fact that we have not yet reached it, does not cast us into skepticism.

To the spring of prophecy we are called; we are parched with thirst, but an oasis, a source of living waters, is before us. The good desires that the cream of humanity takes pride in, and longs for, in every generation and epoch – with its numerous new inventions, whether in action or in consciousness, ambition and attitude – they are our desires as well, but even higher than all this is what we desire and accomplish in life, something whose power will not diminish even though aeons go by and no one knows or understands.[476] A holy mystery resides in us, a special living soul rests in our midst. From the Spirit of Messiah stream and blow winds; they reach us, and we arise and seek new life, rejuvenation,[477] based on our foundation, our cornerstone, on this mighty fundament that we know has no equal or comparison, even if we are unable to explicate its content to our very own thought. The mystery does not bring down the tragedy of skepticism upon the certainty that exists in its great life.

67

The Laws of the Universe and the Laws of the Torah

The interconnection of the laws of the universe and the laws of Torah. The national renascence, by which the People returns to the Land and to Torah, rebounds throughout the cosmos.

The body that receives the light of the higher wisdom[478] that rests in Israel – the divine wisdom – is the entire nation of all generations: past, present, and future. It has its sparkling world-outlook, its *idées fixes*, its qualities, traits, feelings, visions, beliefs, hopes, and mighty desire and ambition – all of them are tangibly real, perform their function, shape the Israelite nature, are integrally bound[479] to all the historical contents of the nation and to all the specific and general processes of life. This wisdom is concentrated in the greater divine wisdom of the

הפרטיים והכלליים של החיים. מרכזה היא חכמה זו בחכמת אלהים הגדולה אשר לעולם הגדול, אשר לצבאי צבאות כולם, ותנאי השלמתה והשפעותיה הרעננות הם הם חקי החיים אשר לתורת ישראל, שבה היא מתבלטת. התשובה אל הטבע הישראלי, ההולכת ומפעמת בהתעוררות התחיה הלאומית ותקותיה, אך היא תביא את התשובה השלמה, האחוזה בחכמת ישראל המצומצמת וקשורה גם יחד בחכמת אלהים חיים העליונה, שורש העליון אשר לתורה בכל מלואיה, שבכתב ושבעל-פה, של החק הכתוב והמסור ושל כל תכונה יקרה, כל מדה הגונה וכל רעיון נאה, וכל יצירה טובה וחיה, היוצאת ממקור ישראל ונובעת מצלם אלהים אשר נתן באדם, ומנשמת חיים אשר נפח באפיו מרוחו העליון, "ומאן דנפח מתוכיה נפח". על כן מי הוא זה אשר יוכל לתאר כמה גדול הוא אוצר החיים, תיקון העולם, הצלת הנשמות, כל האושר הגדול וכל הדר התשובה, הגנוז בתחית האומה, ההולכת ומתגלמת בארץ ישראל.

סח

התשובה הנובעת מאור סתרי תורה, המתעוררת מתוך הגיון פנימי, המתפתח ממעין החי במעמקי הנשמה, הכולל כל יושר וכל הגיון, כל מוסר וכל חק ומצוה, גדולה ונשגבה היא באין ערוך מכל תשובה פרטית, היוצאת מתוך חשבונות הנפש הקטנים הפרטיים, שאין בהם אלא מקומם, שעתם ופרטם, "ולא חזיין לחפאה על כל עובדין". ים התשובה הגדול בהמון גליו, הוא רק אותו השטף, הבא מתוך בינת הלב של חירות עולם, ההולכת ומאירה מתוך חרכי רזי עולם, אשר בסודות התורה וחכמת הרזים, וכל ההופעה הרוחנית

entire world, of hosts upon hosts; the conditions for its perfection and its fresh influences are the living laws of the Torah of Israel, in which it [i.e., the wisdom] is most visible.

The return (*teshuvah*) to Israelite nature, which throbs in the arousal to national renascence and its hopes – only it will bring the complete Return (*teshuvah*), tied to the particular wisdom of Israel and also bound to the higher wisdom of the Living God, the supernal root of the Torah in all its plenitude, written and oral, of the law transcribed and transmitted and of every precious trait, every decent quality, every aesthetic thought, every good and vital creation, which comes out of the source of Israel[480] and flows from the image of God[481] placed in Man, from the breath of life blown into his nostrils[482] by the higher spirit. "One who blows, blows from within him."[483] Therefore, who can describe how great is the treasure of life, the correction of the world, the saving of souls, all the great fortune and all the beauty of the Return (*teshuvah*), hidden in the renascence of the nation, which is increasingly embodied in the Land of Israel?

68

Major *Teshuvah* and Minor *Teshuvah*

Two species of Return: fear of punishment/freedom born of the mysteries of Torah. Israel aspires to the latter.

The return (*teshuvah*) that flows from the light of the mysteries of Torah, which is aroused by inner logic, which evolves from the living fount in the depths of the soul, which includes all rectitude and all reasoning, all ethics, laws and commandments – is incomparably greater than any private return (*teshuvah*) that stems from private stocktaking, which is localized in time and place. "It [i.e., the private *teshuvah*] is incapable of atoning for all misdeeds."[484] The great Sea[485] of Return (*teshuvah*) with its multitude of waves is but the flow from the understanding of the heart of eternal freedom,[486] which shines from between the cracks of eternal mysteries, that are in the secrets of Torah and the mystical wisdom,[487] and all the spiritual manifestation[488] and the entire treasury of song and

וכל אוצר השירה וההגיון אשר במאור התורה. אל אורה זו מיחל ישראל, ובאור גדול זה יראה אור גאולה, ופדות עולמים, "שובו אלי - ואשובה אליכם".

סט

התשובה הגדולה, שתחיה את האומה ותביא גאולה לה ולעולם, תהיה תשובה שנובעת מרוח הקודש שיתרבה בה. כשרון הנבואה במקורו, קודם שהוא מתפתח במלואו, הרי הוא רוח הקודש, אשר נזדוג לישראל בתחלת מטעם, "ורוחך הטוב נתת להשכילם". רוח קודש זה אינו סר מבחירי האומה, מפעם הוא בכל ישרי לב, לפי שעור וערך מיוחד, לכל אחד לפי מדתו. מרומם ומעדן הוא את רוח גדולי דעה, חכמי לב העוסקים בתורה לשמה; גדולי הנדיבים, שכל המשכת חייהם הרוחניים, הוא נחל גדול של טוב וחסד; משוררים מלאי רוח מוסר וקודש; חושבי מחשבות טובות על ישראל ועל העולם כולו. ורוח הקודש ביסודו הכללי גנוז הוא באוצר החיים הגדול של הנשמות העליונות, החשות את הוד רזי תורה, ואת שפעת יקרת פנימיותה של העבודה האלהית בהדרת גדולתה, המקשיבים קול קדושת החיים, וזמירות פרקי שירה מן השמים והארץ וכל אשר בהם, מימים ותהומות וכל מלואם, ונשמת כל יצור, ומרגשי כל מרגיש, המתעלים ומתרוממים ברוממות האחדות העליונה, בעשרה הגדול, הנערץ והמבהיק. גנוז הוא רוח הקודש, בנקודה הפנימית העזיזה של נשמת ישראל, חתום וטמיר הוא באוצר המהותיות הישראלית, שהקודש האנושי כלו הוא סגולת סגולתה. בגבור כח ישראל הקדושה מתגברת, בכל מקום שפעולת ישראל חיה, אור אלהי אמת מתלהב, מאיר ומגיה. עומק חסד

meditation that is in the light source of Torah. For this light,[489] longs Israel, and through this great light will behold the light of redemption and the emancipation of worlds. *Return to Me – and I will return to you.*[490]

69

The Great Return

Before full-fledged Prophecy, ru'aḥ ha-kodesh *(divine inspiration). The Great Return that flows from* ru'ah ha-kodesh.

The Great Return (*teshuvah*) that will revive the nation and bring redemption to it and to the world, will be a return that flows from the divine spirit that will increase in it [i.e., the nation]. The prophetic ability at its source, before it has fully developed, is *ru'aḥ ha-kodesh* (divine inspiration), which was coupled to Israel from their inception. *Your good spirit You gave to enlighten them.*[491] This divine inspiration does not depart from the chosen of the nation,[492] it throbs in all the straight of heart, according to a specific measure[493] and value, to each according to his capacity.[494] It uplifts and sensitizes the spirit of the great savants, the wise of heart who study Torah for its own sake; the great philanthropists, whose entire spiritual lives are one great stream of goodness and kindness; poets imbued with a spirit of ethics and holiness;[495] thinkers of good thoughts concerning Israel and the entire world. *Ru'aḥ ha-kodesh* (divine spirit) in its general fundament is stored in the great treasury of life of the lofty souls, who sense the majesty of the mysteries of Torah, and the precious inner flow of the divine service in the beauty of its greatness; who listen to the sound of the sanctity of life and the tunes of the Song of Nature (*Pirkei Shirah*) from the heavens and the earth and all contained therein, from seas and depths and all their plenitude, the soul of every creation, the feelings of every sentient being,[496] who ascend to the heights of the higher unity, with its great, esteemed, brilliant richness. The divine spirit (*ru'aḥ ha-kodesh*) is hidden in the inner, mighty point of the soul of Israel; it is sealed and hidden in the treasury of the Israelite essence, whose dearest treasure is the holiness of all mankind. When Israel grows mighty, holiness grows stronger. Wherever the activity of Israel is alive, the light of the True God

עליון זה, זיו ברק מתנוצץ בצחצחות עליונות, בכל אופן שהוא מתגלה, אפילו בדרך טבעית פשוטה, אפילו במשאלי החיים היותר רגילים, ואפילו בשעת קלקלה וחטא, אור האלהי איננו כבה, "נצח ישראל לא ישקר ולא ינחם".

ע

התשובה הנועדה לישראל, לרומם את קרנם בגאולה שלמה, תבא על-ידי השבת עז רוח הקודש, שהוא הסגולה הנבואית בהתחלתה, המתפשטת על כל האומה כולה. מתוך שרוח עליון זה מתאמץ להופיע, מתגרשים ונדחים רוחות קטנים ממנו. התוכן המיוחד לישראל בתור עם לבדד ישכון, לא יתברר על-ידי המעשים החצוניים והקצובים והדברים הלמודיים בלבדם, כי-אם על-ידי הרמת החיים בסגולתם הפנימית. תוצאת הדבר תבא על-ידי רצון כביר פנימי, שיבררוהו גדולי הנשמה, המכירים את הליכות דפק החיים של כללות האומה כולה, והם הם בעלי היסוד העליונים, אשר יעלו את כל הירידות, בין שלהם, בין של כלל ישראל, בין של כל הנפילים, אשר עמדו להיות משיחים ונפלו ונוקשו ונשברו, הנה נתפזרו ניצוציהם ומבקשים תקון חי וקיים, ביסוד דוד מלך ישראל, רוח אפנו משיח ד'. ורוחא דמשיחא הולך הוא באור תורה הפנימית, וכל מה שיתאמצו גדולי טהורי לב, ללחום נגד שכחתה של התורה העליונה והעלמתה, יתעורר כח התחיה הלאומית יותר ויותר, יסיר מעליו בגדיו הצואים וילבש בגדי הקודש, ויזכר לכל ישראל ולכל העולם, שפעמי דלים אלו, עקבות גאולת עולם הם, לישראל ולעולם כולו, לכל אשר יחובר אל החיים ולנשמות ישני עפר, המצפים גם הם ליום גאולה, לאור חדש על ציון.

bursts into flame and shines bright. However the depth of this exalted kindness, this bright bolt flashing with supernal splendors be revealed – even in a simple, natural way; even in the most mundane pursuits of life; and even at times of undoing and sin – the divine light will not be extinguished. *The Eternal of Israel will neither lie nor retract.*[497]

70

Fallen Giants and the Flames of Inner Torah

Great masters effect the return of the fallen souls of Israel, not through externals but by putting people in touch with the inner Torah. In this way, the fallen messianic potential of the national revivalist movement will be repaired.

The return *(teshuvah)* destined for Israel, to uplift their "horn" with complete redemption, will come about through the return of the might of divine inspiration *(ru'aḥ ha-kodesh),* which is the beginning of the prophetic ability, which envelops the entire nation. Since this supernal spirit struggles to manifest, lesser spirits are banished and dispelled. The special content of Israel as *a people that dwells alone,*[498] will not crystallize solely through external, measured actions and academic pursuits[499] but by the uplifting of life[500] with its inner quality. The result will be produced by an inner, mighty will, to be crystallized by the great of soul, who recognize the pulse beat of the entire nation as a whole. They are the exalted masters of the foundation,[501] who will raise up all the descents, whether their own, those of the Jewish People,[502] or those of the fallen giants,[503] who stood to be Messiahs but fell,[504] were trapped and broken. Their [i.e., the fallen giants'] sparks were scattered and seek a living and enduring[505] correction in the foundation of David, King of Israel. *The breath of our nostrils – the anointed (*meshi'aḥ*) of the Lord.*[506] The spirit of Messiah proceeds by the light of the inner Torah, and the more the great and pure of heart combat the forgetting of the higher Torah and its suppression, the more the power of national renascence will be aroused, will remove its soiled clothes[507] and don holy raiment. It will become apparent to Israel and to the whole world that the footsteps of these poor,[508] are (in fact) the footsteps of eternal redemption, for Israel and for the entire world, for all who are connected to life, and for the souls of those who slumber in dust, who also await the day of redemption, a new light upon Zion.[509]

עא

על הגוף, בתור מרכז חיים מצומצם ומוגבל, פועלת היא נשמת החיים הרחבה והמתפשטת במעופה למרחקים עולמיים. אידיאליים הם מאד טהרת הגוף, חסנו, בריאותו, חילוץ עצמותיו, עֵרות חייו, אור וחום רגשותיו. העולמים כולם הנם הגוף של הנשמה האלהית, אצילות השכינה, מלכות שמים, העשירה, המתפשטת. בעולמנו מרגישים אנו את רכוזה על-פי מדותינו. על כל יציר נברא היא מתפשטת, על כללות היצירה היא מתרכזת, מאירה היא באור חייה, מגלה היא את עשרה וכבודה. בעולם החי היא מתגלה בצביונה המיוחד, באנושיות כולה ברב חוסן ובליטה הדורה, בעוזז קודש הרי היא מתגלה בכנסת ישראל, זאת היא מנוחתה, טרקלינה הכלול בהדר תפארתו. מי שחודר בנשמה הישראלית, מסתכל באופיה המצוין והמיוחד, בהודה ההיסתורי, בגורלה, בנצח קיומה, והופעת חייה, במחשבות הגיונותיה, בשאיפותיה, תקותיה, חלומותיה ויעודיה, בטחונה ואמתה, הרי הוא מוצא כמה נאה הוא המרכז אשר לבחירה האלהית, אשר לאצילות השכינה. מתוך דיוקן של מטה עולה הוא ומסתכל בדיוקן של מעלה, ונותן כבוד ופאר למלכות, מלכות כל עולמים, אשר על ישראל הדרתו. והגויה הלאומית וכל מכשיריה, ארצה, שפתה, רוחה, מוסרה, מנהגיה, נטיותיה, והנשמה שלה, תורתה, נבואתה, תפלתה, אמונתה וכל הפלגים הרבים, יבלי מים נאמנים, מים עליונים ומים תחתונים, יחד מתרוממים גלי גלים, מתנשאים בהוד עדים, מתחבבים ומתאהבים חבת ידידות שאין על עפר משלה. והאהבה הלוהטת מתהוה לקנאת עם מחוללת גבורים אזורי עז, רוח מלא אש לוהט, ומתמזגת הגבורה הלוהטת עם השכל והיושר, וספרות גדולה מלאה עצה, שירה ויושר מתיצרת, לתחית גוי על ארץ ירושתו לעולמים. [ושופרו של משיח מתחיל לתקע.]

71

Soul: Body :: God: World

The soul, which is not bounded by space, works through the body. So the divine soul works through the universe, and in more concentrated form, through Israel.

The soul of life, which is expansive and whose trajectory extends to galactic distances, acts upon the body as a restricted, concentrated life-center. The purity of the body, its strength, health, vigor, alertness, sensuality – are very ideal. All the worlds are the body of the divine soul,[510] the emanation of the *Shekhinah* (divine presence), the rich, expansive kingdom of heaven. In our world, we[511] feel her [i.e., the *Shekhinah's*] concentration according to our measure. She extends over every creation, she is concentrated in the totality of creation, she illuminates with her living light, she reveals her richness and glory. In the organic world, she is revealed in her particular character; in humanity as a whole, with great strength and splendid visibility; with mighty holiness she is manifested in *Knesset Yisrael* (Ecclesia Israel), her repose, her beautiful banquet hall. He who penetrates the Israelite soul, who observes its special, distinctive character, its historical majesty, its destiny, its eternal existence, its life manifested in its thoughts, ambitions, hopes, dreams, promise, trust, and sincerity – discovers how comely is the center of divine choice, of the *Shekhinah*'s emanation. From the image below he may glimpse the image above, and give honor and glory to the kingdom,[512] the kingdom of all worlds, whose loveliness is upon Israel.[513] The national body and all its appurtenances, its land, its language, its spirit, ethics, customs, proclivities, its soul, Torah, prophecy, prayer, faith, and all the many tributaries, waters above and waters below, together soar, wave upon wave, are lifted in their majesty, and are loved and cherished – an affectionate friendship such as none other upon earth. This burning love becomes a patriotism, producing powerful heroes, a spirit full of intense fire. The intense courage mixes with intellect and straight thinking, and a great literature, full of counsel, song and straightness is being formed, for the renascence of a nation upon its eternal inheritance. And the *shofar* (ram's horn) of Messiah begins to sound.[514]

עב

הדבקות, הרצונית והמדעית, הדמיונית והמעשית, כשהן מתארגנות ביחד הן פותחות את צנורות החיים של טללי הרצון אשר לחיים העדינים, חיי האמת, שאין קצה לעושר כבודם ולזיו מתקם, אשר צדיקים הרואים עולמם בחייהם יודעים ומרגישים קצת ערכם. ומה מאד קרואים אנו להיטיב לעצמנו ולכל העולם, לישר דרך ד׳, לפנות כל מכשול מאור התענוג העליון, מחיים האמיתיים של הדבקות האלהית האמיתית, שהיא רק היא מקור ההצלחה ומגמת החיים וההויה כולה. מה אומללים הם הולכי חשכים! מה עלובים הם אותם שאין להם אלהי אמת, במדעם וברצונם, בדמיונם ובמעשיהם! ומה מאושרים הם המתהלכים לפני ד׳, השמחים באור זיוו, ״בשמו יגילון כל היום ובצדקתו ירומו״! הלב מתכווץ מרוב צער על האפלה האיומה, שבני אדם יושבי חושך נתונים בה. היושר הפנימי דוחק את הנשמה להאיר את אבוקת חיי האמת, להרים נס לרבים. ישראל אוצר החיים הוא בעולם, בהויתו ממוזגת היא הדעת את ד׳ אלהי אמת, בתחיתו יחיה את העולם, יסיר את המסכה הנסוכה על כל הגוים, את האפלה של הכפירה, שהיא המות המכוער לעולם כולו, המתהלך כקטב. יקום ישראל על רגליו, יתרומם בגבורה בארץ חמדתו, יביע את אמרת נבואתו ממקור חיי נשמתו, יקיץ לתחיה את גרעיני החיים האלהיים הנרדמים בלב כל אדם וכל חי, ״כל הנשמה תהלל יה, הללויה!״

72

Devekut (Divine Communion)

The joys of devekut*, communing with God. The darkness of unspiritual life. Israel will reawaken the entire world to the thrill of God.*

When (the various forms of) *devekut* (communion) – volitional, intellectual, imaginative and practical – are organized as one, they open the life-conduits of the dew of desire, of sensitive living, of true life. There is no end to the richness of their glory, nor to the splendor of their sweetness. The *tsaddikim* (righteous) who behold eternity in their lifetime,[515] know and feel a bit of their worth. How much we are invited to benefit ourselves and the entire world, to pave the way of the Lord, to remove every obstacle from the light of the supernal delight, from the true life of divine communion (*devekut*), which is the only source of success, and the purpose of life and all of existence! How unfortunate are those who walk in darkness! How poor those who have no true God in their intellect and will, in their imagination and deeds! And how fortunate those who walk before the Lord, who rejoice in the light of His splendor, *in His name they rejoice all the day and by His righteousness are uplifted!*[516] The heart contracts from pain at (beholding) the terrible obscurity in which men who dwell in darkness are placed. Inner rectitude pushes the soul to light the torch of true life, to raise a banner for the masses. Israel is the treasury of life in the world; in its existence is assimilated knowledge of the Lord, the true God; with its renascence it will enliven the world, will remove the mask spread over all the nations, the darkness of disbelief,[517] which is a cruel death for the entire world, which goes about as a demoniac. Israel will rise up on its legs, will stand mightily in the land of its love, will express its prophetic word from the source of life of its soul, will awaken the seeds of divine life slumbering in the heart of every human and every life-form. *Every soul will praise the Lord, Halleluyah!*[518]

קריאה גדולה

נדפס בלוח "ארץ הצבי" שנת תרס"ח
הוצאת המוסד "שערי תורה" בעיר הקודש יפו

"ההכרח" הוא עכשיו הפתגם היותר שגור בעולם, ודוקא קול המון זה יהפך לקול שדי בידי חכמי לב וקדושי רעיון, דוקא הנחש יהפך למטה האלהים, אשר בו יעשו אותות ומופתים למען דעת כי לד' הארץ.

ההכרח, הכרח החיים ומרירות סבלם, יביא את האורה האלהית לעולם, ההכרח יסגל את הלבבות להפתח לקבל את האור הגדול של זוהר האמונה בכל הדר גאונה.

נדמה הדבר כאילו העולם מתמוטט הוא וכושל, מתמומז ומתמסמס, תחת ענות יד הכפירה הגסה - המפלצת הבלה היבשה והאכוריה הרובצת עליו. השלהבת האלהית מתלקחת בקרב הלב פנימה, בקרב כל רוח ונפש, היא מכה גלים גדולים סוערים מגלי כל ים, היא עולה שמים ויורדת תהומות בחדרי כל רוח ונפש, והכפירה האיומה, השפחה הבלה, בת העבדות הבזויה, סוגרת בעדה את בריחיה לבלי תראה החוצה, היא יראה מאד מאורה הבהיר, היא -

A Great Call

PRINTED IN THE CALENDAR "ERETS HA-TSEVI"
FOR THE YEAR 5668 [1908], A PUBLICATION OF THE
INSTITUTION "SHA'AREI TORAH," JAFFA

"Necessity" is now the most frequently used cliche. Just this *vox populi* will be transformed into the voice of God by the wise of heart and holy of thought. The very serpent will be turned into the staff of God, with which signs will be performed that it may be known that the earth is the Lord's.

Necessity, the necessity of life and its bitter burden, will bring the divine light to the world. Necessity will condition the hearts to open to receive the great light of faith's splendor in all its beautiful pride.

It would appear as if the world is tottering and falling, dissolving under the cruel hand of coarse disbelief – the wasted, dry, cruel monster that crouches over it. The godly flame ignites inside, within the heart, within every spirit and soul, making great waves, stormier than the waves of any sea. She [i.e., Faith] rises to the heavens and descends to the depths within the chambers of every spirit and soul. And terrible Disbelief, the wasted maidservant, the despicable daughter of slavery,

האחרונה - יודעת שבניצוץ זק אחד מרשפיה של שלהבת האלהית תכלה כליל. אבל כל אשר תוסיף לשום מחנק לה, כל אשר תוסיף לעצור בעד נשמת אלהים חיים הגדולה והחזקה אשר בנשמת כל חי, כה תוסיף זאת הנשמה לאגור את חילה פנימה, ובמלאות ספקה הנה תצא ברעם ורעש, בקול נפץ וזרם "ביום הרג רב בנפול מגדלים".

הנה יום בא ולא ירחק חק, והאנושיות תתעורר כדוב שכול וכארי על טרפו להנקם מהכפירה הבזויה בעד כל רעתה אשר עוללה לה, בפתע תבקש להשליך ממנה את עבותיה, בחמה גדולה ובקצף גדול תבקש ממנה את נקמת החיים הטובים, את השלוה והעדן של הדעות הטהורות, של החיים הטהורים והזכים אשר שללה ממנה, שללה ותאבד, שמה למרמס, מבלי אשר יש לה כח, לאותה הרשעה, להשיב תמורתם אף חלק אחד מני רבבה. הבהלה הזעומה, שעל ידה ערבבה הכפירה את העולם, להמם את הכוחות ואת הלבבות, להעביר את האדם על דעתו ועל דעת קונו, תעבור ותשקוט, והדעה הצלולה והמתונה היודעת גם כן איך לחיות ואיך להתבונן, איך להשקט איך להתלהב; והגבורה האלהית, היודעת לכונן גוי איתן, ועם אדיר בקודש, תקח את מקומה בחיים, ושבט בקורת של מוסר אכזרי תניף על השפחה אשר העיזה לרשת את גבירתה, על העבד אשר התנשא למלך, וחותם העבדות חקוק לעד על מצח נשמתו.

"החפש" זאת התרועה ההולכת עם התקיעה של ההכרח, הוא יצא כארי נורא ממסגרתו, אשר ירמס בזעפו את הכפירה, כרמס תולעת ארסית, בזויה ומגואלה. תשוקת החופש תבא למרום פסגתה, והאדם יכיר שהוא יש לו רשות לחיות ברוחו פנימה כאשר הוא, כפי חפץ הטבע האביר של נשמתו החיה, והנשמה הזאת חיה רק באלהים. באין אמונה עמוקה וזוהרת, אין לה חיים ואורה, היא מתנודדת כצל ומתדכאת ביסורים נוראים וצחיית צמא אכזרי,

shutters her in so that she may not be seen by the outside world. The maidservant is very afraid of her clear light; she knows that with one pure spark of the billows of godly flame, she would be consumed. But the more she suffocates her, the more she stops the great and powerful soul of the Living God that is within the soul of every living creature – the more this soul will inwardly consolidate its strength, and when it has had its fill, it will explode: "On the day of the great slaughter when towers tumble down."[1]

A day, not very distant, is coming, when mankind will wake up as a bereaved bear and as a preying lion to exact revenge of despicable Disbelief for all the evil that she perpetrated against mankind. Suddenly it will desire to throw off its shackles; outraged, it will take vengeance for the good life, the tranquility and bliss of pure opinions, of pure life, of which this wicked woman deprived it – deprived and despoiled, trampled, without having the power to recompense by even one ten-thousandth. The confusion by which Disbelief mixed up the world, to dull minds[2] and hearts, to move man to act against his better judgment and that of his Creator – will subside and pass. Its place in life will be taken by placid intellect – which knows also how to live and consider, how to be still, how to be enthused – and by godly strength that knows to establish a solid nation, a mighty holy people. And the rod of cruel criticism, she will raise against the maidservant who dared usurp her mistress, against the servant who pretended to be king when the seal of servitude is engraved eternally on his brow.

"Freedom" – this is the counterpoint to "Necessity." It will break out of its cage as a ferocious lion, which in its rage will trample Disbelief as a lethal, despicable, disgusting worm. The longing for freedom will reach its peak, and Man will realize that he is entitled to live in his spirit (inside) as he actually is, according to the desire of the mighty nature of his living soul – and this soul lives only in God. Without deep, vibrant faith, this soul has no life or light. It is fleeting as a shadow, oppressed by terrible suffering, and parched with cruel thirst. Who would prevent her? Who would not allow her to live in

ומי מעכב על ידה, מי לא יתן לה לחיות באלהים, מי מפריח צפור שמים זאת מקנה, מי ישים אותה בסוגר, מי יעצרנה מלשוט מלא רחבי שמים, מקום הזוהר והאויר הרענן, המלא אור וחיים? הנשמה, נשמת האדם בעצמה תכיר מיד את אויבתה, במבט בוז ושאט נפש תשקיף על פני השפחה הנחרפת, אשר תתגלה בכל נבלותה, אחרי אשר יקרע ממנה המסוה של הדמיון החשוך והלוהט, שהספיקה איזה זמן לשים על פניה הסכלים והמגועלים. "הדשאים עומדים על פתח קרקע", ההכרה האמתית הזאת הולכת היא וקרובה. אסיה, ואמריקא, ואירופא הנאורה, וכל העולם הממודן בכלל כבר נלאו נשא את סבל עול הכפירה הקשה, המכבדת על האדם ועל רוחו, יותר מכל תכסיס של אמונה היותר טרחנית - ונתון לא תתן מאומה.

במצב של צחיית צמא כזאת יתנפל האדם אל מעין האמונה, בכל לב ונפש ישתה יגמא מכוס נחל העדנים של אור אלהים עליון, אבל האדם הוא כבר מנוסה במסה, הוא כבר יודע היטיב מה היה אחריתו עת אשר שתה לרויה את מי האמונה עם כל הרפש והטיט אשר גרש הים הגדול הזה במשך הימים, אחרי אשר המו חמרו מימיו. על כן יאבה לשאוב בכל לב ונפש מים טהורים מפלג אלהים.

הרוח התוקף את כל האנושיות תקף גם כן את איזה חלק מבנינו, אמנם יותר קרובים אנחנו למקום האורה, יותר קרובים למעין החיים, יותר מלאים בחיי הנשמה האלהית, אשר הרבינו לינק ממנה מימי עלומנו עד ימי זקנה ושיבה. מוצל הוא ישראל ממארת אלהים זאת באמת, ואם נדמה לנו שעול הכפירה השתרג ועלה על צואר רבבות מבנינו, וישם בסד רגלם ועתה הם כמפרפרים בין החיים והמות, לא ידעו חיים ומנוחה, לא ידעו עדן שלות תם, והם צמאים להרטיב את חכם היבש, הנה קרובות הן העינים להיות מתפקחות, קצרה רוחם בעול הברזל של הכפירה שנתהפכה בתקופה קצרה למין אמונה קנאית וחצופה, והנם דופקים על דלתי תשובה, שאך

God? Who would drive this skybird from her nest? Who would put her in prison? Who would stop her from cruising the full expanses of heaven, the place of splendor and fresh air, full of light and life? The soul, the soul of Man, will itself immediately recognize its enemy. With a disdainful look she will observe the face of the shameful servant, who will be revealed in all her ugliness, after there will be torn from her the mask of dark, febrile imagination, which she had for some time placed over her foolish, obnoxious face. "The grass is ready to burst through the ground."[3] This true consciousness comes closer. Asia, America, enlightened Europe, and the entire civilized world have tired already of bearing the burdensome yoke of disbelief, which is more demanding of Man and his spirit than the trappings of even the most bothersome faith – while giving nothing in return.

In such a state of immense thirst, Man will plunge into the spring of faith. With all his heart and soul he will gulp from the cup the soothing stream of sublime divine light. But Man is experienced. He already knows what the end was when he drank to content the waters of faith with all the silt that this great sea sent up after its waters had foamed. Therefore he will want with all his heart and soul to draw pure waters from the Divine Flow.

The spirit that besets all humanity has also taken possession of a certain portion of our children. However, we are closer to the place of light, closer to the fount of life, more full of divine soul-life – we have been nourished by it from youth through old age. Israel is truly spared this curse of God. If it appears to us that the yoke of disbelief has wound around the neck of tens of thousands of our children, has fettered their feet, and now they are dangling between life and death, not knowing life or rest, not knowing the bliss of simple tranquility, thirsting to wet their palate – soon those eyes will be opened. Their spirit grows impatient with the iron yoke of disbelief, which, within a short period of time, has turned into a sort of intolerant, impudent faith. These youth knock on the doors of Return, which seem closed before them, when in reality but a single push would suffice to open

נדמים להם כאילו הם סגורים לפניהם, בשעה שאך דחיפה אחת מספקת היא לפתח את השערים לרוחה, "פתחו שערים ויבא גוי צדיק שומר אמונים", בזקניו ובצעיריו, מחנה גדול כמחנה אלהים.

אחינו היקרים, חכמי תורה, וסופרים משפיעים. גם אנו נואלנו וחטאנו. למדנו וחקרנו, פלפלנו וחדשנו, כתבנו וציירנו, אבל שכחנו את האלהים ועזו, לא שמענו לקול נביאי האמת, לקול מעולי חכמי דורות עולמים, לקול הצדיקים והחסידים, חכמי המוסר וחכמי העיון והרזים, שצוחו והכריזו בקולי קולות כי סוף הנהר של התלמוד המעשי לבדו להיות יבש וחרב, אם לא נמשוך לתוכו תמיד מים מני ים, מימא דחוכמתא וקבלה, מים דעת האלהים, מים טוהר האמונה הטהורה הנובעת מנשמתנו פנימה, משרשה, ממקור החיים.

עתה בא הקץ, הננו קרואים בתחיתנו הלאומית לתבע את עלבון האדם כלו, עלבון הנשמה האלהית, שבידינו הופקדה לרוממה ולשגבה, נשמת אלהים חיים, הצריכה להתפשט על כל העולם כלו, להאירו ולהחיותו, האורה, היוצאת מתוך אור התורה ואור הנבואה, השוה לכל נפש ומחיה כל חי, בחזקה הוא נתבע ממנו, עתה לעת קץ.

ובתוך הארת התחיה, יבא לנו הגורם הכללי, ההכרח, וישיב אותנו אל אור החיים, יפתח את אור האמונה ממסגרותיה, לחכמת ישראל המקורית, החפשית מכל עול נכר, לחכמת אלהים חיים הקבועה באוצר החיים שלנו, הוא יביא אותנו לידי תלמוד קבוע, לחכמת האמונה האידיאלית, לכל צדדיה, לנגלותיה ולנסתרותיה, למען נחיה באורה, וברוח אמיץ נקרא בקול מארץ חיים, ממקום אשר שם אלהים הופיע ועדי-עד אוה למושב לו:

"בית יעקב לכו ונלכה באור ד'!"

the gates wide. "Open gates that there may enter a righteous nation which keeps faith,"[4] old and young, a great camp of God.

Dear brothers, Torah sages, influential writers! We too have committed folly and sinned. We learned and researched, debated and developed, wrote and illustrated – but we forgot God and His might. We did not hearken to the voice of the truthful prophets, to the voice of the finest sages throughout the ages, to the voice of the saintly and pious, masters of ethics, masters of contemplation and of mysteries, who screamed at the top of their lungs that eventually the river of the practical Talmud, on its own, would dry up, if unfed by waters of the sea, the Sea of Wisdom and Kabbalah,[5] the sea of God-knowledge, the sea of pure faith that flows from within our soul, from its root, from the source of life.

Now the time has come. In our national renascence, we are called upon to redress the insult of all mankind, the insult of the divine soul, which has been entrusted to our hands, that we may uplift and ennoble it – the soul of the Living God, which must spread over the entire globe, enlightening and enlivening. Now at the appointed time, there is demanded of us the radiance that is emitted from the light of Torah and the light of Prophecy, which is of equal concern to all and enlivens all.

In the midst of the illumination of the renascence, will come the general motivation – Necessity – and return us to the light of life; will expose the imprisoned light of faith to the original wisdom of Israel, which is free of foreign yoke; to the wisdom of the Living God, which is planted in our treasury of life. Necessity will bring us to permanent study, to the ideal wisdom of faith,[6] to all its facets, exoteric and esoteric, so that we might live by its light and courageously call out from the Land of Life, from the place where God appeared and that He chose as His eternal dwelling place:[7]

House of Jacob, Come, let us walk in the light of the Lord![8]

Notes

Translator's Preface

1. See S.K. Mirsky, *Ha-Zofeh* (3 Ellul, 5720), cited in M.Z. Neriyah, *Ḥayyei ha-RAYaH* (Tel Aviv: Moriah, 5743), p. 252. See also Shmuel Avidor, *Ha-Ish Neged ha-Zerem* (Jerusalem: Orot, 1962), p. 159.

2. See Yosef Ḥayyim Brenner's positive review of the style of *Ha-Tarbut ha-Yisraelit* in *Ha-Aḥdut*, 5674, no. 9, and *Kol Kitvei Y. H. Brenner* VIII, pp. 300-301, cited in Ya'akov Hadani, *Ha-Rav Kook ve-ha-Hityashvut ha-Ḥilonit* (Jerusalem, 5740), pp. 56-58.

3. See remark of Rabbi Yitsḥak Hutner, quoted in Langsam's avant-propos to *Orot ha-Emunah* (Jerusalem, 1985).

4. Robert Pring-Mill touched on some of the difficulties of translating poetry in his preface to Nathaniel Tarn's translation of Pablo Neruda's *The Heights of Macchu Picchu* (New York: Farrar, Strauss and Giroux, 1967). See especially pp. xii-xiii.

5. See his method in *Orot ha-Kodesh* I, Introduction, bottom p. 22, and beginning vol. III.

6. See Dov Schwarz, *"Ha-ḥiddushim ha-ra'ayoniyim she-be-Zikhronot Ha-Rav Ha-Nazir,"* in *Yonati be-Ḥagvei ha-Sela'*/Sarah Cohen Memorial Volume (Jerusalem: Nezer David, 5747), pp. 203 and 207; Dov Schwarz, *"'Arikhah mul yetsirah"* ("Editorship versus Authorship") in *Da'at* 24 (Winter 1990): 87-92; Yoninah Dison, *"Arba'ah motivim be-'Orot ha-Kodesh' ke-basis la-'arikhah ḥadashah"* (*"Orot ha-Kodesh* Reedited and Organized According to Four Motifs"), ibid., pp. 41-86.

7. See Rabbi Y. Isser Klonsky's article, *"Bi-Netivei ha-Orot,"* *Ha-Zofeh* (10 Adar I, 5752/14.2.92), p. 9.

8. See *Orot ha-Kodesh* (Jerusalem, 5723), beginning vol. I (unpaginated), and Introduction, pp. 22-24; end vol. II (unpaginated). Much thought went into choosing the exact wording for these headings. See Rabbi M.Z. Neriyah, *Bisdeh ha-RAYaH* (Jerusalem, 5747), pp. 385-386. From the note Rabbi Neriyah quotes, one could get the impression that Rav Kook often participated in the process of naming chapter headings. However, another passage in the Nazirite's archives reveals that this was not so: "When I would turn to him [=Rav Kook] several times for advice and instruction, regarding the names of the chapter headings ... he would hold back, saying, he does not know about order" (*Nezir Ehav* I [Jerusalem, 5738], p. 302, cited in Schwarz, *Da'at* 24, p. 88).

9. *Orot ha-Teshuvah* first appeared in Jerusalem, 1925; the subheadings in the Or Ezion 1970 edition were penned by two students of Yeshivat Merkaz Harav, Y. Elstein and M.Z. Littman.

10. One notes that in *Nitsnutsei Orot* by Rabbi Moshe Ushpizai (vol. I, Ramat Gan, 5739; vol. II [also titled *Nitsnutsei ha-Teḥiyah*], Ramat Gan, 5744), companion volumes to *Orot*, the chapters of *Orot* have been given titles. The book was endorsed by Rav Zevi Yehudah Kook (approbation dated 3 Iyyar, 5737).

11. According to Rabbi Yitsḥak Shilat (Greenspan) in his preface to the Jerusalem 5743/1983 edition, the eruption of World War I prevented completion of publication. Others speculate that there was a conscious decision to suppress the edition.

12. Cf. Rabbi Zadok Hakohen Rabinowitz of Lublin, *Tsidkat ha-Tsaddik*, chap. 100. See too B. Naor, *"Zedonot na'asot ke-zakhuyot be-mishnato shel ha-rav kook,"* *Sinai* 97 (Nissan-Iyyar 5743): 86-87.

13. See pp. 193-213, *Yisrael u-Teḥiyato*.

14. See Ushpizai, vol. I, memorial in front of book (unpaginated); Rabbi S.Z. Sonnenfeld, *Ha-Ish 'al ha-Ḥomah* (Jerusalem, 5731), p. 243, n. 19; Rabbi M.M. Porush, *Be-Tokh ha-Ḥomot* (Jerusalem: Mosad Ha-Rav Kook, 5708), p. 240; Rabbi M.M. Frankel-Thomim, *B'air ha-Aboth* (New York: Moinester Photo-Offset, 1944), pp. 86, 117 n. 1.

Introduction

1. Rabbi. Shim'on Starelitz, a disciple of Rav Kook during the Jerusalem period, had the impression that Rav Kook's home was the center of the entire renascence movement, that his master was the source of inspiration for all. See Rabbi S. Starelitz, *Me-ha-Makor*, pp. 119-126; cited in Rabbi M.Z. Neriyah, *Bisdeh ha-RAYaH* (Kfar Ha-Ro'eh, 5747), p. 505.

2. The question to what degree there was orchestration on a London-Jerusalem axis versus *hashgaḥa peratit*, serendipity or telepathy, makes for an interesting study. Rabbi Y.D. Ḥarlap claimed that his father, Rav Y.M. Ḥarlap's call for spiritual renascence in Jerusalem at the very time Rav Kook launched his *Degel Yerushalayim* campaign in London, was one of many instances when the two, unbeknown to each other, would come out with similar concepts. See Ḥayyim Lifshitz, *Shivḥei Ha-RAYaH* (Jerusalem: Makhon Harry Fischel, 5739), p. 141. See also Rabbi M.M. Porush, *Be-Tokh ha-Ḥomot* (Jerusalem: Mosad Ha-Rav Kook, 5708), p. 230.

3. The three Jerusalemites, Rabbis Harlap, Frank, and Porath, as young, budding scholars had studied informally under Rav Kook in Jaffa, so attracted were they to the rising light of Torah that beckoned to them from the Mediterranean port city. See *Iggerot la-RAYaH* (Jerusalem: Makhon RZYH, 5750), Letter 43, pp. 80-81; RZYH Kook, *Li-Netivot Yisrael* II (Jerusalem: Kiryat No'ar, 5739), pp. 14-15; Lifshitz, *Shivḥei ha-RAYaH*, p. 82; Rabbi M. Z. Neriyah, *Hayyei ha-RAYaH* (Tel Aviv-Jaffa: Moriah, 5743), pp. 275-276. It was Rabbi Frank who introduced Rabbi Ḥarlap to the Rav of Jaffa. See Rabbi M.Z. Neriyah, *Siḥot ha-RAYaH* (Tel Aviv: Moreshet, 5739), pp. 333-334.

Rabbi Israel Porath later emigrated to the United States, where he served for many years as the much beloved Rabbi of Cleveland, Ohio.

4. Rabbi Mendel Porush was instrumental in assisting Rav Kook in the work of *Degel Yerushalayim*. See *Iggerot ha-RAYaH* IV, Letter 1076, p. 87. Note 3 at the bottom of the page incorrectly identifies R. M. P. as "R. Moshe (!) Porush." As Rav Kook indicates in his letter, Rabbi Porush left Israel at the beginning of 5681. His destination was America. See Porush, p. 303.

5. Porush, pp. 248-249; Neriyah, *Bisdeh ha-RAYaH*, pp. 427-428.

6. Shmuel Avidor, *Ha-Ish Neged ha-Zerem* (Jerusalem, 1962), p. 170; Lifshitz, p. 210.

7. See *Ma'amrei ha-RAYaH* I (Jerusalem, 5740), pp. 189-194; Porush, pp. 269-274, 280-286. Cf. letter of Rabbi A.D. Kahana-Shapiro, Rav of Kovno (Kaunas) to Rav Z.Y. Kook, in *Iggerot la-RAYaH*, Addenda, Letter 22, p. 557.

8. See Porush, p. 210; Jacob Klatzkin, quoting his father, the Gaon Rabbi Eliyahu Klatzkin (Lublin-Jerusalem), in Leo Jung, *Jewish Leaders* (New York: Bloch

Publishing Co., 1953), p. 330. For a letter of Rav Kook to Dr. Klatzkin regarding the latter's father, see *Iggerot ha-RAYaH* IV, Letter 1079, p. 89. On another, unrelated point, Rav Z. Y. Kook dismisses Dr. Klatzkin's testimony as heresay. See *LNY* II (Jerusalem, 5739), p. 202.

9. Porush, p. 203; Rav Z.Y. Kook, *LNY* II, p. 247, par. 3.

10. Porush, p. 201.

11. Porush, pp. 201-202. For a picture of the intimate relationship that existed between Rabbis Y.Y. Diskin and Ya'akov Moshe Ḥarlap, see the latter's *Mikhtevei Marom* (Jerusalem, 5748), Letter 4, p. 14. In his introduction to his halakhic work, *Beit Zevul* I (Jerusalem, 5747), p. 7a, Rabbi Ḥarlap explains that his interest in the son was aimed at being allowed to study the deep writings of his great father, Rabbi Yehoshua Leib Diskin of Brisk. From Porush, one gets the distinct impression that Rabbi Ḥarlap considered himself a *talmid* (disciple) of Rabbi Y.Y. Diskin. See pp. 201-202, 241-242, 251. See also *Beit Zevul* I, 67b; II, 37a.

In a telephone interview (7.13.92), Rabbi Zevulun Charlop rectified that his paternal grandfather Rabbi Ya'akov Moshe Ḥarlap considered himself a *talmid* (disciple) of Rabbi Zevi (Hirsch) Mikhel Shapiro and Rav Kook. The interviewee's father, Rabbi Yeḥiel Mikhel Charlop, considered himself a *talmid* of both Rabbis Y.Y. Diskin and A.Y. Kook. Cordial relations between Rabbis Yitsḥak Yeruḥam Diskin and Yeḥiel Mikhel Charlop continued even after the falling out between Rabbis Yitsḥak Yeruḥam Diskin and Ya'akov Moshe Ḥarlap. Interestingly, after the passing of the Brisker Rav Yehoshua Leib Diskin, his writings were in the possession of the very young Ya'akov Moshe Ḥarlap, until members of the Blau family took away the *kesten* (chest) of papers. They subsequently published them in the form of a book, *She'elot u-Teshuvot Maharil Diskin*. When later, Rabbi Yehoshua Leib's son, Rabbi Yitshak Yeruḥam, arrived in Jerusalem from Europe, he was outraged. (See also Porush, p. 201, n. 9.) Rabbi Ya'akov Moshe Ḥarlap was ordained by Rabbi Ya'akov David Wilovsky (RIDBaZ) and Rav Kook; see Neriyah, *Bisdeh ha-RAYaH*, pp. 328-329.

12. Published in Rabbi Ḥayyim Hirschensohn, *Malki ba-Kodesh* IV (St. Louis: Moinester Printing Co., 5679-5682), Letter 10 (dated 18 Adar Sheni, 5681/1921), pp. 43-44. (See also Porush, pp. 236-237.)

Because of the tremendous halakhic stature of the Gaon Rabbi Zevi Pesaḥ Frank (later Rav of Jerusalem), it would be worthwhile to cite the passage in its entirety, to serve as a corrective to much of the revisionist history concerning the Kook-Sonnenfeld dispute, which unfortunately passes in Orthodox circles today as authoritative:

> As I wind up my letter, I should let His Honor know a bit of the affairs of the town [i.e., Jerusalem], though it is not my way to write such things, for we could not write enough. However ... directed us to inform His Honor. According to ... His Honor has the ability to correct things. Having heard

that it will be of benefit, I find myself obligated to uncover the mystery enveloping the conduct of our city.

The Gaon, our Master R. A.Y. Hakohen Kook (may he live) was accepted here as Rav by the majority of the Holy Community here. It is well known that the members of Kollel Ungarin are envious of our Russian and Polish brethren. Especially, so that the proceeds earmarked to the Hungarians should increase, it is not good for them that the Chief Rabbi of the Holy City be other than Hungarian. So what did the members of Kollel Ungarin do? A few of them gathered together .... At their head the old lad ... He propagandized to found *Va'ad Ashkenazi* (Ashkenazic Council). Now this old lad is a great expert in arranging elections hidden from all, revealed only to him. The entire electoral process is invisible. It is difficult to describe in writing his diligence in this matter. He puts together a list of a large committee, also a steering committee. On the surface, all is lovely. On the inside, all is rotten, for from the ranks of the Hungarians and Galicians he picks ... youngsters, and from the other *kollelim*, when he sees an old man or imbecile who won't understand his tricks, he brings him into the Va'ad. So the result of the invisible election is that he is the Secretary and a young fellow ... the Chairman. They write and sign tens of thousands of letters to America and the entire world in the name of all the Ashkenazim in Jerusalem ... that Rabbi Ḥayyim Sonnenfeld is the Rav here, when all see and know that Rabbi Ḥayyim Sonnenfeld was never, and will not be, the Rav, for he is an old, frail man, for whom it is not possible to get involved in the affairs of the town. But this old lad uses him and his name as a pawn to destroy an entire city. He and his gang of empty fellows publicly, brazenly insult the Gaon Kook (may he live). The old lad got together with young writers who frequent the home of the ancient Rabbi Yitsḥak Yeruḥam Diskin (may his light shine), for this old man is under the influence of young secretaries.... They manipulate him whichever way they please and obtain his signature for all their antics. In my estimation, he is not guilty at all for he cannot see writing, and signing is also difficult for him. The secretaries made for him a stamp of his signature which is an exact replica and they write and sign whatever they please. Woe to a generation whose leaders are such lads, little foxes.

About six weeks ago, I spoke with Rabbi Ḥayyim Sonnenfeld, and at one point, I asked him if it is right that he signs himself as the Rav of the Ashkenazim in our Holy City? ... He answered me that the truth is, he himself does not sign so, but they made for him a stamp and wrote this on the stamp.

The Gaon, our Master R. A.Y. Kook (may he live) is the Rav here. All the largest institutions are under his presidency. He is the Rav of the city and carries the burden of the community. They placed new, inexperienced

> people to carry the load of the community.... These sycophants and insolent fellows stroke these old men to their advantage.
>
> I wrote these things hurriedly, without order, as it does not fit my temperament to take care of such things. The upshot is, if His Honor can publicize the truth that the aforementioned elder sages – without disparaging them – are not communal leaders and one cannot pay attention to their signature. The affairs of the Jerusalem community, general and specific, temporal and spiritual, are neither the domain of the elder sages nor their followers who, as a rule, are simple folks who have put on a cloak of hypocrisy, announcing that they are zealots of the Lord. They use the names of the elder sages to blind people's eyes, while anyone discerning sees that their aim is not truth. They employ smut sheets to stir up controversy in Israel.
>
> His honor should let me know if any benefit may come of my words, which are but a drop of the sea of what should be let known ...

The most puzzling thing about Rabbi Frank's letter is the statement that Rabbi Sonnenfeld will not be *Rav*, when at the time of its writing, Rabbi Sonnenfeld had already accepted the position. However, see Porush, p. 320 (translation of article, *"Rekht far gerekhtikeit," Dos Vort*, Vilna, 17 Menaḥem Av, 5692/1932), who writes, "Even the rabbinate which they forced on the Gaon, the Tsaddik, Rav Yosef Ḥayyim Sonnenfeld *zt"l* did not carry – as the local inhabitants know – any serious or official form."

13. See Rav Z.Y. Hakohen Kook, *LNY* II, p. 209, par. 5.

14. Porush, pp. 203, 218; Avidor, pp. 156-157.

15. Rabbi Ḥayyim Hirschensohn, *MBK* IV, pp. 258-260.

16. Rav A. Y. Hakohen Kook, *IHR* IV, Letter 1074, p. 86.

17. See Rav Z.Y. Hakohen Kook, *Li-Shelosha be-Ellul* I (Jerusalem, 5738), p. 26, par. 55.

18. Avidor, p. 184.

19. Porush, pp. 246, 266.

20. Unofficially, since his entry to Jerusalem on 3 Ellul, 5679, and officially since receiving the traditional *ketav rabbanut* or rabbi's contract in Tevet, 5680. See Porush, pp. 266-268 and Rav Z.Y. Kook, *LNY* II, pp. 209-210.

21. See Porush, p. 252, and the many letters contained in the beginning of *IHR* IV.

22. See *IHR* (Jerusalem: Mosad Ha-Rav Kook, 1965), III, pp. 143-151, 178-180, 182-200, 315-316.

23. *IHR* IV, Letter 1014, p. 44.

24. Ibid., Letter 1049, p. 68.

25. It is an open secret that the author of *Kol ha-Shofar* was Rabbi Akiva Porush. *Porush* by metathesis becomes *Shofar*. The anonymous author dropped another hint to his identity by prefacing the diatribe with a quote from Rabbi Akiva: "Said Rabbi Akiva, 'Israel are compared to a bird. Just a bird cannot fly without wings, so Israel cannot make a move without their elders'" (*Leviticus Rabbah* 11:8). See Rivkah Schatz, *"Reshit ha-massa' neged ha-rav kuk,"* *Molad*, Vol. VI (XXX), No. 32 (242), *Tevet* 5734/December 1974, p. 257; Menaḥem Friedman, *Ḥevrah ve-dat: Ha-Ortodoksia ha-lo tsiyonit be-Erets Yisrael 5678-5696* (Jerusalem: Yad Yizḥak Ben-Zvi, 5748/1988), p. 107, n. 67; Yosef Moshe Sofer and Menaḥem Mendel Gerlitz, *Mara de-Ar'a Yisrael: Rabbi Yosef Ḥayyim Sonnenfeld* II (Jerusalem, 5763/2003), p. 301, n. 41; *Mishnato shel Rabbi Amram* (Jerusalem, 5772/2012), bottom p. 99.

Rabbi Akiva Porush edited a florilegium of *Hekhalot* literature from manuscripts found in the Shelomo Mousaieff collection, Jerusalem, which he titled *Merkavah Shelemah* (Jerusalem: Salomon, 1921). The book was issued posthumously, the editor Rabbi Akiva Porush having passed at midnight of 27 Marḥeshvan, 5682 [1921]. (See Mousaieff's epitaph for the editor who had wished to remain anonymous.) A posthumous collection of Porush's halakhic novellae was issued under the title *Mishnat Rabbi Akiva* (Jerusalem, 5715/1955).

Ironically enough, Rabbis Akiva Porush and Ya'akov Moshe Ḥarlap had once been close companions, both having studied under the ascetic Jerusalem saint Rabbi [Yehoshua] Zevi Mikhel Shapiro (1840-1906), author Responsa *Tsits ha-Kodesh* (edited by Rabbi Ḥarlap). (Rabbi Ḥarlap published a hagiography of his first teacher, entitled *Tsevi la-Tsaddik* [1907]. The work was adorned by the lengthy approbation of Rabbi Ḥarlap's second teacher, Rav Kook.) By the time of the *Orot* controversy, "a mountain had gone up between" Rabbis Porush and Harlap. (The falling out between Rabbis Porush and Ḥarlap was pointed out to me by the Gaon Rabbi Shelomo Fisher *shelit"a*.) Rabbi Amram Blau recalled that yet a third disciple of "Rabbi Hirsch Mikhel" was Rabbi Meir Heller Semnitzer. See *Mishnato shel Rabbi Amram* (Jerusalem, 5772/2012), p. 51. See also Sofer and Gerlitz, *Mara de-Ara' Yisrael* (Jerusalem, 5763/2003), p. 346 where the unnamed author (*"Ba'al ha-Keruz"*) recounts that he is a disciple of Rabbi Yehoshua Zevi Mikhel. For some reason, the authors Sofer and Gerlitz wished to preserve the anonymity of the author of the notorious placard lumping together the two "Abrahams" (Gerrer Rebbe and Rav Kook). Rabbi Amram Blau had no such compunction, revealing that the author was Rabbi Meir Heller Semnitzer (*Mishnato shel Rabbi Amram*, p. 51).

All twelve pages of *Kol ha-Shofar* are reproduced in the recently published memoir of Rabbi Amram Blau, founder of the Neturei Karta, *Mishnato shel Rabbi Amram* (Jerusalem, 5772/2012), pp. 133-144.

26. An allusion to 2 Kings 4:40, where the word *orot*, rather than "lights," has the meaning of "poisonous herbs." See B. Naor, "Death in the Pot" (A Poem about A Poem), in *Orot Newsletter* 2:4 (Nissan-Sivan 5752/April-June 1992).

27. See below letters of R. Ya'akov Moshe Ḥarlap to the Bendiner Rav, and Rabbi Avraham Mordechai Alter (Gerrer Rebbe) from aboard ship. See also Rabbi Zevi Pesaḥ Frank's letter cited above, note 12.

28. Copies of *KS* were sent to rabbis throughout the world. See the letter of R. Asher L. Zarḥi of Louisville, Kentucky (dated 15 Tevet, 5681), in Hirschensohn, *MBK* IV, Letter 31, p. 196. See also David Solomon Sassoon, *Ohel Dawid: Descriptive Catalogue of the Hebrew and Samaritan Manuscripts in the Sassoon Library, London*, Vol. II (Oxford University Press, 1932), p. 1054, K: "*Igeret.* A letter denouncing a newly-published book with the title *Orot*, addressed to R. Jacob b. Joseph Ḥayyeem and to the ecclesiastical court of Baghdad, signed by Isaac Jeruḥam b. Moses Joshua Judah Löb Diskin, Joseph Ḥayyeem Sonnenfeld, Moses Nahum Wallenstein, Mordecai Löb Rubin, Isaac Frank[el], Moses Joseph Hoffman, and endorsed by Jacob Ḥayyeem Sofer. The letter is dated 8 Elul, 5680 (=1920) at Jerusalem. Typewritten." Cf. Y.M. Sofer and M.M. Gerlitz, *Mara de-Ara' Yisrael*, Vol. II (Jerusalem, 5763/2003), pp. 303-305.

It would appear that in some instances, Rav Kook's opponents sent the entire book *Orot* to select rabbis in the Diaspora. Thus Rabbi Philip I. Israelite of Chelsea, Mass. in a four-page response to Rav Kook dated "2nd day of Rosh Ḥodesh Marḥeshvan 5681" [i.e., 1920] acknowledges receipt of his book *Orot*. It was apparent to Rabbi Israelite that Rav Kook's opponents were responsible for having sent it "for they indicated in the book those chapters that are objectionable in their opinion." After pretty much concurring with Rav Kook's critics that those passages in *Orot* are potentially hazardous to the youth who may take them out of context, Rabbi Israelite sums up by saying: "I am grateful to those who sent me his dear book, for from it, I merited to recognize the spiritual picture of His Honor, the holiness of his thoughts and spirit, and his pure aspiration. From his book, I saw that his love for his people is overflowing and gives him the strength of *mesirut nefesh* (self-sacrifice) to withstand the fierce battle being waged front and rear" (ms.). A halakhic responsum of Rav Kook to Rabbi Yehudah Yehoshua Falk Israelite of Chelsea, Mass. (dated 21 Iyyar 5686/1926) concerning *ḥalitsah* performed by a *yavam* (levir) whose foot was amputated, was published in Rav Kook's *'Ezrat Kohen*, no. 109 (pp. 394-396).

29. First letter of Rav Y.M. Ḥarlap to Bendiner Rav.

30. Though I would not go so far as to attribute Rav Kook's theology to the *Sefat Emet*, it is a fact that Rav Kook was extremely enamoured with that work, having discovered it during his sojourn in London during the First World War. The Gerrer Rebbe and his brother-in-law the Bendiner Rav were duly impressed when at their first meeting with Rav Kook, the latter quoted from memory entire passages

of *Sefat Emet* verbatim. *Sefat Emet* was one of the few books that Rav Kook took with him on board the ship when he travelled to America in 1924. This fondness for the *Sefat Emet* continued with Rav Zevi Yehudah Hakohen Kook, and to this day, the book remains a staple of the intellectual diet of RZYH Kook's spiritual heirs. See Shmuel Avidor Hakohen, *Ha-Ish Neged ha-Zerem* (Tel-Aviv: Yedi'ot Aḥaronot, 2002), p. 209; Rabbi M.Z. Neriyah, *Likkutei ha-RAYaH* II, pp. 143-144, cited in Rabbi Eliezer Melamed, *Revivim* (Har Berakha, 5770/2010). Eliezer Meir Lifshits saw an affinity between Rav Kook's style of writing, whereby kabbalistic notions are presented stripped of their technical terminology, and the style of the *Sefat Emet*. E.M. Lifshits, *Ketavim* II (Jerusalem: Mosad Harav Kook, 5709/1949), p. 231; cited in M.Z. Neriyah, *Likkutei ha-Rayah* I (Tel-Aviv, 5750/1990), p. 64.

31. Porush, pp. 282, 295, has his name as "Hirshbom." In RZYH Kook, *LNY* II, p. 44 and also Avidor, p. 187, it is "Hirschbein."

I recently learned that the elderly *ḥasid* Rabbi Hirsch David was one of the Jews evacuated from the old walled city of Jerusalem at the time of the Jordanian conquest in 1948. See Shimon Yosef Meller, *'Uvdot ve-Hanhagot le-Beit Brisk* IV (Jerusalem, 5760/2000), p. 236 (quoting Rabbi Ḥanina Schiff, *gabbai* of the Gerrer Rebbe).

32. RZYH Kook, *LNY* II, p. 45. According to Porush, p. 282, n. 47, the two were companions, having studied together under the *Sefat Emet*.

33. *LNY* II, p. 45. See also Porush, p. 282, n. 47 and Avidor, p. 187.

34. Rav Kook and Rav Ḥarlap address him in their letters as "R. Zevi Ḥanokh."

35. *Iggerot la-RAYaH*, Addenda, Letter 21, pp. 556-557.

36. *IHR* IV, Letter 1073, pp. 84-85.

37. In Porush, pp. 295-298; in Avidor, pp. 187-190.

38. See *Iggerot la-RAYaH*, Letter 59, pp. 101-103; *IHR* II (Jerusalem: Mosad Ha-Rav Kook, 1961), Letter 671, pp. 280-281; *LNY* II, pp. 208, 247 (see there p. 246 concerning R. Yosef Ḥayyim Sonnenfeld's attitude toward Rav Kook's pending voyage to *Erets Yisrael* to accept the rabbinate of Jerusalem; also in Porush, pp. 239-240); R. M.Z. Neriyah, *Siḥot ha-RAYaH* (Tel-Aviv, 5739), p. 67; idem, *Ḥayyei ha-RAYaH* (Tel-Aviv, 5743), pp. 293-294; idem, *Tal ha-RAYaH* (Kefar Ha-Ro'eh, 5745), pp. 18-19; idem, *Bisdeh ha-RAYaH* (Kefar Ha-Ro'eh, 5747), p. 332; Lifshitz, p. 99.

39. Porush, pp. 299-302; Avidor (but a few lines), p. 191. According to Sofer and Gerlitz, Rav Ḥarlap was responding to the Gerrer Rebbe's postscript to the letter of his brother-in-law, the Bendiner Rav. See Y.M. Sofer and M.M. Gerlitz, *Mara de-Ar'a Yisrael* II, p. 327, n. 54.

40. Objectively, this was the case. See, e.g., *Ha-Derekh* (Agudah organ, published in Zurich) 2:8 (Iyyar, 5680), p. 1 concerning R. Avraham Yitsḥak and R. Zevi Yehudah Kook's efforts to prevent Sabbath desecration by youths in Jerusalem.

41. *KS*, p. 6.

42. *Ha-Derekh* (Vienna) 8-9 (Nissan-Iyyar, 5681): 41; *Der Jud* (Warsaw) (24 Nissan 5681/2 May, 1921), p. 2.

43. *Der Jud* (20 Nissan 5681/28 April, 1921), p. 2.

Rabbi Israel Porath (a close disciple of Rav Kook), recalled the events surrounding the Gerrer Rebbe's first visit to *Erets Yisrael.* According to Rabbi Porath, the Rebbe was very desirous of convincing Rav Kook to join Agudat Israel. Before actually encountering Rav Kook, the Rebbe invited several persons to a secret meeting in the home of Rabbi Ḥarlap, one of whom being Rabbi Porath. Rabbi Porath had the audacity to tell the Rebbe that he would have to promise Rav Kook that the Agudah, rather than contenting itself with critiquing the Zionists and the Mizrachi, would encourage its members to immigrate (*'aliyah*) to the Land and make a concrete contribution to its settlement. Afterward, the Gerrer Rebbe visited Rav Kook and was duly impressed with his greatness. See Rabbi Israel Porath, "*Torato shel Rabbenu,*" *'Or ha-Mizraḥ* (New York), Year 8, Nos. 1-2 (29-30), *Tevet* 5721 [1961], p. 39.

44. *Der Jud* (20 and 24 Nissan), p. 2.

45. See above notes 35, 36.

46. This becomes apparent from the Rebbe's letter written aboard ship and published serially in three successive issues of *Der Jud*, the Agudah's Warsaw paper: 19 Iyyar 5681/27 May, 1921; 26 Iyyar/3 June; and 4 Sivan/June 10. The original Hebrew of the letter was preserved. Yiddish translation was provided for the 19 Iyyar portion.

47. *Ha-Derekh* (Nissan-Iyyar 5681), p. 41.

48. Ibid.

49. The Gerrer Rebbe, by all accounts a most able statesman, recognized both Rabbis Kook and Sonnenfeld as being legitimate Rav of Jerusalem, each within his own circle. See the definitive letter to the *ḥasidim* in Jerusalem, published in *Iggerot la-RAYaH* (Jerusalem, 5750), Addenda, Letter 21, pp. 556-557.

50. Neriyah, *Ḥayyei ha-RAYaH*, p. 117.

51. *Ha-Derekh*, Nissan-Iyyar 5681, p. 41, article signed "Assaf Ha-Mazkir, Jerusalem, 9 Nissan"; article in *Der Jud, "Di Sholem-Oiszikhten Tsvishen di Ortodoksishe Yuden in Yerushalayim,"* signed "Y. Yosifun" (Jerusalem correspondent); and Porush, p. 304.

52. "Assaf Ha-Mazkir" and "Y. Yosifun," cited in previous note.

53. See R. A.M. Alter, *Mikhtevei Torah me-Admor Zatsal mi-Gur* (Tel Aviv, 5747), Letter 50 (Monday, *Metsora*', 5681/1921, to his family), p. 67; R. Zevi Yehudah Kook in *Oraḥ Mishpat* (Jerusalem: Mosad Ha-Rav Kook, 5745), pp. 268a-269a; and R. M.Z. Neriyah, *Ḥayyei ha-RAYaH*, pp. 117-119. See also *Mikhtevei Torah*,

Letter 49 (Monday, Va'era, 5687/1927, to his brother R. M. of Pabianice), p. 66. Finally, the Gerrer Rebbe's biographer recorded details of the halakhic exchange between the Rebbe and Rav Kook. See Rabbi A.I. Bromberg, *Ha-Rabbi mi-Gur* (Vol. IV of the series *Gedolei ha-Torah ve-ha-Ḥasidut*).

Rabbi Amiḥai Kinarti speculates that the ruling of Rabbi Zevi Ḥanokh Hakohen Levin of Bendin (son-in-law of *"Sefat Emet"* and brother-in-law of the Gerrer Rebbe) that a *kohen* (priest) before going up to bless the people, first remove his right shoe and then his left, was received from Rav Kook. See the monograph concerning RAYH Kook and RSZ Auerbach, *'Or Shelomo*, ed. Kinarti (5765/2005), p. 40, n. 73.

54. R. Moshe Blau, *'Al Ḥomotayikh Yerushalayim* (Tel Aviv, 5706), p. 112; RZYH Kook, *LNY* II, p. 210, par. 6.

55. *Bava Kamma* 92b.

56. Blau, p. 112. Also cited in Porush, p. 306. The incident of the outrageous poster "Abraham—Abraham" occurred during the visit of the Gerrer Rebbe to *Erets Yisrael* on the 29th of Sivan, 5687 (1927). See Menaḥem Friedman, *Hevrah ve-Dat* (5748/1988), pp. 277-282. Concerning the "fallout" from the incident which provoked a stern response from the Polish rabbinate including Rabbis Ḥayyim Ya'akov Naftali Silberberg and Meir Dan Plotski, see Sofer and Gerlitz, *Mara de-Ar'a Yisrael* II (5763/2003), pp. 341-348. The author of the "Abraham—Abraham" placard was Rabbi Meir Heller Semnitzer. See now *Mishnato shel Rabbi Amram* (Jerusalem, 5772/2012), p. 51.

The Polish Rabbinate were of the opinion that Rabbi Meir Heller Semnitzer insulted the Gerrer Rebbe due to the resentment he harbored against Rav Kook for having been the cause of his imprisonment, although they were stumped by the illogic of Semnitzer's behavior. It was public knowledge in Jerusalem that Rabbi Sonnenfeld many times officiated together with Rav Kook at celebrations such as circumcisions and weddings. Yet Semnitzer lashed out at the Gerrer Rebbe for his "state visit" to Rav Kook, while sparing Rabbi Sonnenfeld indignity. See a complete record of the Polish Rabbinate's reaction to Semnitzer's disrespect to the Gerrer Rebbe and the unsuccessful attempt to convince Rabbi Sonnenfeld to declare a ban (*niduy ve-ḥerem*) on "Meir Heller Semnitzer," in *Kuntress 'Itona'i* (Warsaw: Agudath ha-Rabbanim be-Polin, Kislev 5688/1928). 8pp. Bound in *Kovets Derushim*, No. 7 (Warsaw: Agudath ha-Rabbanim be-Polin, 5688). Available at www.hebrewbooks.org. (For "Piotrkow" read "Warsaw.")

57. *Mikhtevei Marom*/Letters of R. Ya'akov Moshe Ḥarlap to his son R. Yeḥiel Mikhel Charlop (Jerusalem, 1988), Letter 10, p. 20.

58. *IHR* IV, Letter 1099, pp. 102-103.

59. *IHR* IV, Letter 1103, p. 105.

60. See above note 46.

61. See, e.g., *Algemeiner Journal* (June 5, 1992), p. 13, where only the positive statements regarding Rav Kook's personality are given coverage, irrespective of the Gerrer Rebbe's honest opposition to his ideology.

62. The Gerrer position was consistently one of accommodating *both* Jerusalem rabbinates. See the letter from Rabbi Ḥanokh Zevi Hakohen Levin placating Rav Kook that he and his brother-in-law the Rebbe of Gur intended no slight to Rav Kook when they wrote a letter of congratulations to Rabbi Sonnenfeld upon his investiture as Rav of the Ashkenazim. See appendices to *Igrot la-Rayah*, Letter 21 (pp. 556-557).

63. See R. Zadok Hakohen Rabinowitz of Lublin, *Dover Tsedek*, 4b-5a; *Takkanat ha-Shavin* (Beit-El, 5748), p. 222. See also Rabbi Yitsḥak Dov Baer Schneerson, *Siddur Tefillah 'im Peirush MaHaRID* II (Berdichev, 1913), *Sha'ar ha-Ḥanukkah*, 175b.

64. *Der Jud* (25 Nissan, 5681/3 May, 1921), p. 2.

65. Published in S.Z. Shragai, "*Ḥasidut ha-Ba'al Shem Tov bi-tefisat Izbica-Radzyn*," *Sefer ha-Besht* (Jerusalem: Mosad Ha-Rav Kook, 5720), pp. 200-201; reprinted in S.Z. Shragai, *Bi-Netivei Ḥasidut Izbica-Radzyn* (Jerusalem, 5732/1972), pp. 66-67.

Shragai, a Radzyner Ḥasid who drew close to Rav Kook in *Erets Yisrael* (and who would one day serve as Israel's first elected Mayor of Jerusalem), recounted that during a trip to Poland he paid a visit to his Rebbe (the "*Tif'eret Yosef*") and spent practically the entire evening, from 11:00 p.m. until dawn, discussing the published works of Rav Kook which lay before the Rebbe. The Rebbe was thoroughly familiar with their contents. Specifically in regard to *Resh Millin*, the Rebbe said: "*Dos iz a heilig sefer'l, full mit hoikhe kedusha. Die velt veist nisht vie a heilig sefer'l dos iz.*" ("This is a holy little book, full of lofty holiness. The world does not know how holy a book this is.") Shragai, *Bi-Netivei Ḥasidut Izbica-Radzyn*, p. 137.

Resh Millin is a diminutive kabbalistic tract on the letters of the Hebrew alphabet, published by Rav Kook in London in 1917.

Further confirmation of the Radzyner Rebbe's high regard for Rav Kook comes from the recent biography of Rav Zevi Yehudah Hakohen Kook. There we learn that during his visit to Warsaw in 1921, Rav Zevi Yehudah developed an intimate friendship with the Radzyner Rebbe, who became actively involved in the nascent "Yerushalayim" (or "Degel Yerushalayim") movement founded by Rav Kook. (Let there be no mistake though. Politically, the Radzyner Rebbe was subordinate to the Gerrer Rebbe.) In addition, the Radzyner Rebbe was instrumental in introducing the yet unmarried Zevi Yehudah to the daughter of a wealthy Warsaw Jew. See Rabbi Shelomo Aviner, *Zevi Kodesh* I (5765/2005), pp. 145, 148, 155.

Shragai recorded that because they encouraged Jews to leave Poland for *Erets Yisrael*, the Rebbes of Gur and Radzyn (President and Vice-President of the

Agudah in Poland, respectively) received blistering letters from the Rebbe of Lubavitch, Rabbi Joseph Isaac Schneersohn—both private and public—castigating them in this regard. Shragai, op. cit., p. 179 (Appendix 5).

See now *Igrot Kodesh ADMO"R MOHaRYaTs*, Vol. 14 (*Milu'im*) (Brooklyn: Kehot, 1998), Letter 5,106 (pp. 111-113) to Rabbi Abraham Mordechai Alter (Gerrer Rebbe); and Letter 5,107 (pp. 114-115) to Rabbi Moshe Bezalel Alter and Rabbi Menaḥem Mendel Alter of Pabianice (brothers of the Gerrer Rebbe). See also Letter 5,108 (p. 116). All three letters are dated "beginning Kislev 5682," i.e. end 1921. In the letter to the Gerrer Rebbe, the Lubavitcher Rebbe states his opposition to the use of the sacred tongue for mundane matters, and to human attempts to build the land before the ordained divine redemption. According to the footnote to an earlier volume of *Igrot Kodesh ADMO"R MOHaRYaTs* (Vol. 1 [Brooklyn: Kehot, 1982], Letter 198 [p. 399]), an editorial decision was made not to publish Rabbi Joseph Isaac Schneersohn's letters of opposition to the Agudat Israel movement (headed in Poland by the Rebbe of Gur). Some of this material was published (with Rabbi J.I. Schneersohn's approval) by Rabbi David Shifrin in his book *Ḥakhmei Yisrael BEShT* (New York, 1924). See ibid., f.56, the letter of Rabbi J.I. Schneersohn to Rabbi Shifrin, dated "Sunday, 8 Tevet 5684" (i.e. 1924). A censored version of that letter appears in *Igrot Kodesh ADMO"R MOHaRYaTs*, Vol. 1, Letter 165 (p. 352). Noteworthy in Rabbi Shifrin's collection are Letter 8 to him from Rabbi Schneersohn, datelined "Sunday, 5 Adar Rishon 5684, Rostov-on-Don" concerning his historic opposition to Agudat Yisrael from its very inception (35a); and Letter 9, again to him from Rabbi Schneersohn, datelined "25 Marḥeshvan 5684," discussing his interfacing with the Rebbe of Munkacs and the latter's vehement opposition to the Rebbe of Gur who stood at the helm of the Agudah (37b-38a).

66. See B. Naor, *Ba-Yam Derekh* (Jerusalem: Zur Ot, 5744), pp. 143-144, 146-150.

67. See *Orot Newsletter* 2:1 (Tammuz-Ellul 5751/July-September 1991), pp. 5-7.

68. See *Takkanat ha-Shavin*, p. 223.

69. R. Shelomo Ḥayyim Hakohen Aviner, *Siḥot ha-Rav Zevi Yehudah*, no. 34, p. 8; see also RZYH Kook, *LNY* II, pp. 159, 223. The version in *LNY*, p. 159 (=*Ha-Zofeh*, 15 Sivan, 5727/1967), is less reliable than that in Rav Aviner, which was transcribed from a tape recording of the actual address.

70. *Genesis Rabbah* 20:12. See the fascinating portrayals of Rabbi Meir in *IHR* (Jerusalem: Mosad HaRav Kook, 5722) I, p. 142; III, p. 87; and Zuriel, *Otserot ha-RAYaH* (Tel Aviv, 5748) I, p. 146.

71. Porush, pp. 304-306.

72. Rav Zevi Yehudah Kook told of once having met the "*Beit Yisrael*" (R. Yisrael Alter, son of R. Avraham Mordechai ["*Imrei Emet*"]) in the street accompanied by a retinue. The Rebbe, who was openly friendly to Rav Zevi Yehudah, expressed

surprise that someone of Rav Zevi Yehudah's stature would walk alone unescorted. Shvarts, *Mi-Tokh ha-Torah ha-Go'elet* (Jerusalem: Zur Ot, 5751) IV, p. 206. In a phone interview (June 19, 1992), Rabbi Zevulun Charlop told the writer that after having concluded the *shiv'ah* (mourning period) for his father, the *"Imrei Emet,"* in 1948, the first place that the *"Beit Yisrael"* went was to the home of the interviewee's grandfather, R. Ya'akov Moshe Ḥarlap. When the "Beit Yisrael" told his mentor Rav Ḥarlap that he did not want to become Rebbe, Rav Ḥarlap responded by saying he would not let him out of the room until he accepted the hereditary position. The interviewee, Rabbi Zevulun Charlop, is also in possession of letters of Torah from the *"Beit Yisrael"* to himself.

73. *Mishnah, Sotah* 9:9. In a letter to R. Fishel Bernstein, the Gerrer Rebbe justified his use of the title in Rav Kook's regard based on Tosafot, *Bava Metsi'a* 29b. See Porush, p. 305, and Lifshitz, p. 187, for a different justification based on Rashi, *Sotah* 47b.

74. It seems that in Rav Kook's circle it was believed that the Rebbe in his letter had purposely toned down his immense respect and admiration for Rav Kook, so as not to play into the hands of the zealots. See Lifshitz, p. 187, citing R. Fishel Rosner.

75. Rav Y.M. Ḥarlap, *Mikhtevei Marom*, Letter 14, p. 25.

76. R. M.Z. Neriyah, *Tal ha-RAYaH* (Kefar Ha-Roeh, 5745), p. 122.

77. R. M.Z. Neriyah, *Ḥayyei ha-RAYaH* (Tel Aviv, 5743), pp. 171-172; B. Naor, "Rav Kook's Role in the Rebirth of Agadah," in *Orot/A Multidisciplinary Journal of Judaism* I (5751/1991): 108-110.

78. Concerning R. M.H. Luzzatto, see the evaluation of the Maggid of Mezhirech, cited by his disciple, R. Ya'akov Yosef of Ostrog (Ostroh) in the latter's approbation to Luzzatto's *KaLaḤ Pitḥei Ḥokhmah* (Korets, 5545).

79. R. H. Hirschensohn, *Malki ba-Kodesh* (St. Louis, 5679-5682), pp. 259-260.

80. R. Aryeh Levin, quoted in Neriyah, *Bisdeh ha-RAYaH* (Kefar Ha-Ro'eh, 5747), p. 407. Again, see R. Aryeh Levin quoted in Lifshitz, p. 255.

81. *IHR* IV, Letter 1184, p. 164.

82. Elyashev Cohen (pseudonym of Eliyahu Cohen Steinberger), *Likht Shtrallen* (London: Mesorah, 5747) V, pp. 85-86.

Mutatis mutandis, Salman Rushdie's apology to the Muslim faithful concerning his novel *The Satanic Verses*, was likewise rejected by the Iranian leadership who had issued a *fatwa* on the book. Rushdie wrote: "As author of *The Satanic Verses* I recognize that Muslims in many parts of the world are genuinely distressed by the publication of my novel. I profoundly regret the distress that publication has occasioned to the sincere followers of Islam. Living as we do in a world of many faiths this experience has served to remind us that we must all be conscious of the sensibilities of others." Like Rav Kook, Rushdie apologized for the distress but not for the book itself. His subtext was that while we should be conscious of others' sensibilities, we needn't surrender to them. Of course, nothing but a straightforward apology could remove Imam Khomeini's *fatwa*. See Rushdie's autobiographical account, *Joseph Anton: A Memoir* (New York: Random House, 2012), p. 145.

83. A substantial portion of the *Kol Gadol* was reprinted in R. Zevi Hirsch Friedman, *Zevi Ḥemed* III (New York, 5686), pp. 23-31.

84. Semnitzer also went by the name "Heller."

85. Author of *Mei Be'er Mayyim Ḥayyim* on Tractate *Berakhot*; referred to in Jerusalem as the *"Pupaner Dayyan."*

86. *Ha-Aretz*, 5 Av 5682 (July 30,1922), p. 4; *Kol Yisrael* (official organ of Agudat Yisrael, Jerusalem) no. 19, 6 Menaḥem Av, 5682. According to Blau, p. 91, the two were later released from jail upon payment of bail by Mr. Yosef Levi Ḥagiz, a member of the directorship of Va'ad Ha-'Ir Ha-Ashkenazi. See also *Ha-Aretz*, 7 Av, 5622 = 8.1.22, p. 4.

87. Porush (p. 265) sums up by saying: "If they tried once to touch (God forbid) or punish one of their brazen number for attacking and belittling the honor of the Rav, they let out a holler, 'The Inquisition is upon you, *Ḥaredim*!'"

For further details concerning this chapter in history, see Rivkah Schatz, *"Reshit ha-massa' neged ha-rav kuk,"* *Molad*, Vol. VI (XXX), No. 32 (242), *Tevet* 5734/ December 1974, pp. 258-261; Menaḥem Friedman, *Ḥevrah ve-Dat*, pp. 229-230; Sofer and Gerlitz, *Mara de-Ar'a Yisrael* II, pp. 306-310.

88. See *Kol Yisrael* 1:20, 10 Menaḥem Av, 5682/8.4.22, letters of R. Moshe Semnitzer and "As. F."; *Kol Yisrael*, 17 Menaḥem Av/8.11, letter of Y. Malakhov, Jaffa, and excerpt from *Der Jud* (Warsaw).

89. *Kol Yisrael*1:20, 10 Menaḥem Av 5682/Aug. 4, 1922.

90. *Do'ar Ha-Yom*, no. 238. Quoted in *Kol Yisrael*, 8.4.22, *"Teshuvah ka-Halakha."* Unfortunately, the New York Public Library's copy of *Do'ar ha-Yom* for that year could not be consulted due to its horrendous state. I am told by the librarians that it has been rendered literally "untouchable." Fortunately, it appears that the identical notice of the Chief Rabbinate was placed in the Aug. 1 (= 7 Av) issue of *Ha-Aretz*, which was accessible to me.

Rivkah Schatz was shown a manuscript of Rabbi Meir Heller by the Heller family of Jerusalem which casts Rabbi Zevi (or "Hirsch") Pesaḥ Frank in a very negative light. In Heller's retelling of events, the Sephardic Ḥakham Shelomo Alfandari ("*Sabba Kadisha*") of Safed had suggested to Rabbi Zevi Pesaḥ Frank that the way to defuse this potentially explosive situation was to have Rav Kook issue a statement in which he would back away from his more inflammatory statements in *Orot*. Rabbi Frank responded that such a note in Rav Kook's hand had already been passed to the Rebbe of Gur. But more to the point, when confronted by

Rabbi Alfandari with the fact that the *Beit-Din* (of which Rabbi Frank was a member) had turned someone over to the non-Jewish British authorities, Rabbi Frank replied by saying that they had merely requested from the Government that it intervene by preventing publication of the incendiary pamphlets maligning Rav Kook. Allegedly, Rabbi Alfandari felt that Rabbi Frank had misrepresented the facts. See Rivkah Schatz, *"Reshit ha-massa' neged ha-rav kuk,"* p. 261. The reported conversation between Rabbis Alfandari and Frank, contained in a letter of Rabbi Alfandari to Rabbi Joseph Ḥayyim Sonnenfeld, has since been published in the latter's biography *Mara de-Ara' Israel.* See Yosef Moshe Sofer and Menaḥem Mendel Gerlitz, *Mara de-Ara' Yisrael* (Jerusalem, 2003), pp. 307-309. **(See continuation of note on page 541.)**

One cautions against this partisan portrayal of Rabbi Alfandari. (See below note 93.) The Gaon Rabbi Shelomo Fisher told the writer (BN) in private conversation that Rabbi Asher Zelig Margoliot, author of *Mas'ot Yerushalayim* (a highly romanticized account of the meeting of the Rebbe of Munkacs, Rabbi Ḥayyim El'azar Spira, and Rabbi Alfandari in Jerusalem in 1930) greatly distorted the image of Rabbi Alfandari, portraying him as a *"kana'i"* (zealot) when that was not the case. The Gaon's father, Rabbi Aaron Fisher, was a close disciple of Rabbi Alfandari (as well as a confidant of Rabbi Sonnenfeld).

91. *Kol Yisrael,* letter of "As. F., Jerusalem," entitled, *"Teshuvah ka-Halakha."*

92. See *Shulḥan 'Arukh, Ḥoshen Mishpat* 26:2.

93. Maimonides, MT, *Hilkhot Sanhedrin* 25:8; *Shulḥan 'Arukh, Ḥoshen Mishpat* 11:1. In Halakha, the ban *(shamta)* is considered more severe than corporal punishment. See *Pesaḥim* 52a, *Mo'ed Katan* 17a, *Kiddushin* 70b; Maimonides, MT, *Hilkhot Talmud Torah* 7:1; *Shulḥan 'Arukh, Yoreh De'ah* 334:42. Based on this principle, "As. F." argues in his letter, par. 5, that pronouncing a ban and confiscating the copies of *KG* would have been more than sufficient without imprisonment that may affect physical well-being.

The Sephardic Gaon Rabbi Shelomo Alfandari of Tsefat (and later of Jerusalem) in his letter of Shevat, 5684/1924, to Rav Ḥarlap, remonstrates that those who denigrate Rav Kook be subjected to economic sanctions. A facsimile of the letter appeared in *Yom ha-Shishi*, 26 Tishri, 5782 (4.10.91). (Publication of the facsimile set straight one of the most blatant distortions of this chapter in Jewish history, that Rav Alfandari *zt"l* was a die-hard leader of the zealots who persecuted Rav Kook!) It is well known that Rav Kook opposed economic or other discrimination against his enemies. See *Li-Shelosha be-Ellul* I, p. 46.

For Rav Kook's thoughts concerning upholding the honor of the *beit din* as opposed to forgiving slights, see his conclusion to *Be'er Eliyahu* (Jerusalem: Mosad Ha-Rav Kook, 5745), *Ḥoshen Mishpat* 27:2 (pp. 241-242).

94. See the recently discovered letter of Rav Kook to Rabbi Joseph Messas of Tlemcen, Algeria, in Zuriel, *Otserot ha-RAYaH* IV (5753/1993), p. 189.

95. Cf. RAYH Kook, *"Kirvat Elohim,"* chap. 2, in *Ma'amrei ha-RAYaH* I, pp. 34-37.

96. Cf. *'Arfilei Tohar* (Jerusalem: Makhon RZYH, 5743), bottom p. 48.

97. Cf. *Ma'amrei ha-RAYaH* I, p. 59, citing MaHaRaL of Prague, *Netsaḥ Yisrael* (London: L. Honig and Sons, 1960), chap. 11, pp. 68-69. See also MaHaRaL, *Derekh Ḥayyim* (London: L. Honig and Sons, 1960), *Avot* 5:17 (p. 262).

98. Cf. quote in Neriyah, *Bisdeh ha-RAYaH*, p. 349. Rav Kook would always come back to Rabbi Akiva. See RAYH Kook, *Resh Millin* (Jerusalem: Mosad Ha-Rav Kook, 5745), p. 47; Introduction to *Shir ha-Shirim*, in *Siddur 'Olat Re'iyah* II (Jerusalem, 5749), pp. 3-4; *Orot ha-Emunah*, pp. 14-15; *Ma'amrei ha-RAYaH* I, pp. 202-203; II, p. 501, *Iyyar*; R. M.Z. Neriyah, *Mo'adei ha-RAYaH* (Tel Aviv, 1981), pp. 73; 420-421. See further RZYH Kook in H. A. Shvarts, *Mi-Tokh ha-Torah ha-Go'elet* III, pp. 247-248; B. Naor, *Ba-Yam Derekh* (Jerusalem, 5744), pp. 169-171; Rabbi Zevulun Charlop in B. Naor, *Hartsa'at ha-Teshuvah* (Jerusalem, 5750), pp. 8-9; Rav Ya'akov Moshe Ḥarlap, *Beit Zevul* II, Introduction, par. 2; idem, *Mei Marom* III [*Leḥem Abirim*] (Jerusalem: Beth Zevul, 5713), p. 22; R. Yitsḥak Arieli, *'Eynayim la-Mishpat*, end Tractate *Makkot*.

99. *Pesikta, Ha-Ḥodesh* (15:15); *Yalkut Shim'oni*, Amos, chap. 549.

100. *Tovim Me'orot*, p. 6.

101. *KS*, pp. 7-8. The founder of the Neturei Karta, Rabbi Amram Blau recalled that it was said in the Ḥaredi world of Jerusalem that there was contained more *"apikorsut"* (heresy) in Rabbi Ḥarlap's *Tovim Me'orot* than in Rabbi Kook's *Orot me-Ofel*! See *Mishnato shel Rabbi Amram* (Jerusalem, 5772/2012), p. 131.

102. *KS*, p. 12.

103. *Ha-Derekh*, 5680, no. 11-12, pp. 126-127.

104. Presumably Ḥayyim Yisrael Eis, the *Erets Yisrael* correspondent for *Ha-Derekh*.

105. See Zevi Kaplan, *Be-Shipulei Gelimato* (Jerusalem, 1984), pp. 17-23; R. Moshe Yeḥiel Zuriel, *Otserot ha-RAYaH* I (Tel Aviv; 5748), pp. 53-56.

106. Moses Maimonides, *The Guide of the Perplexed*, trans. Shlomo Pines (Chicago: The University of Chicago Press, 1964), III, 25 (p. 503). This passage from the *Guide* was quoted by Rabbi Naḥman Shelomo Greenspan of Leeds, England, in his glowing review of *Orot* in the Jerusalem Torah journal *Sha'arei Zion*. See Rabbi N.S. Greenspan, *"'Or zaru'a la-tsaddik,"* *Sha'arei Zion* 3-4 (*Shevat-Adar Rishon* 5681/1921), 16b.

107. Ḥayyim Lifshitz, *Shivḥei ha-RAYaH* (Jerusalem; 5739), p. 186; Zuriel, pp. 53-56.

108. *Ha-Zofeh* (5 Iyyar, 5752/8.5.92), p. 6.

109. *Ha-Zofeh* (26 Iyyar, 5752/29.5.92), pp. 6, 10.

110. *IHR* IV, Letter 1078, p. 89.

111. See *Zohar* I, 6a, 7b.

112. *Yated Ne'eman* (11 Sivan, 5752/June 12, 1992), p. 6.

113. Reprinted in Elyashiv Cohen (pseudonym of Eliyahu Cohen Steinberger), *Likht Shtrallen* V (2nd ed., London: Mesorah, 5747), pp. 39-41.

114. Unfortunately, this ghastly error has crept into the very popular biography of Rabbi Yosef Ḥayyim Sonnenfeld, *Guardian of Jerusalem*, by Rabbi S.Z. Sonnenfeld (Brooklyn: Mesorah Publications, 1983). On page 428 we read: "Suddenly members of Rav Kook's party ... showed Rav Kook *Kol ha-Shofar*, a pamphlet published by right-wing extremists, which made some particularly nasty statements against him in regard to his puzzling statements about *soccer players*" (italics – BN). The ridiculous assertion is backed up by a note citing *Orot*, chapter 34, which of course, makes absolutely no mention of "soccer players."

See Zuriel, *Otserot ha-RAYaH* II, citing *Ḥazon ha-Ge'ulah*: "The Maccabi insists on publicly profaning the Sabbath; their holy *futbol* takes precedence over the Sabbath. What a disgrace!" Also the placard photocopied in *Otserot ha-RAYaH* IV, p. 131: "The game of soccer is absolutely forbidden on Sabbath and festivals."

115. Published in *Peri Ha-Arets*, no. 4 (Tishri 5742), pp. 6-7; reprinted in Zuriel, *Otserot ha-RAYaH* II; pp. 1060-1061.

116. Cf. *Eder ha-Yekar* (Jerusalem: Mosad Ha-Rav Kook, 5745), pp. 56-57.

117. Rabbi Yitsḥak Hutner once remarked: "Rav Kook knew the root of the soul (*shoresh ha-neshamah*) of the secularists, but he did not know where their body stood." Quoted in R. M.Z. Neriyah, *Bisdeh ha-RAYaH*, p. 433. See Rabbi Neriyah's rebuttal there, pp. 433-434, and Rabbi Hutner's letter to Rabbi Neriyah, pp. 434-436.

118. To an intimate group of disciples, Rav Kook confided his intention in *Orot*: "There is value even to a spark of holiness. If there is but the minutest spark of holiness, even within the very midst of impurity, when this spark is revealed, automatically the impurity must evacuate. Therefore the *Sitra Aḥera* (Other Side) does not allow the revelation of the spark of holiness. Physical exercise contains a spark of holiness. However, some of our youth surround it with impurity. So we must reveal the holy spark in exercise – then all of the accompanying impurity will disappear, for holiness and impurity are mutually exclusive and cannot dwell together ..." (Lifshitz, p. 163).

119. See *'Arfilei Tohar*, p. 17: "*The children of the impudent fence-breakers* will in the future be prophets of the first rung..." In *Orot ha-Kodesh* II, p. 298, the italicized words were censored to: "Their children." According to Maimonides, *Shemonah Perakim* (Introduction to Commentary on *Avot*), end chap. V, the ability to perform even mundane activities "for the sake of heaven," is a level slightly lower than that of the prophets.

120. I have taken the term from a poem of Shin Shalom (pseudonym of Shalom Shapiro) by this title. See *Shin Shalom/Yalkut Shirim*, ed. Yitsḥak 'Akavyahu (Tel Aviv: Yavneh, 1973), p. 89.

121. See R. Avraham Yehoshua Heschel of Apt, *Ohev Yisrael, Tetsaveh*, s.v. *ve-atah tesaveh* (II).

The celebrated Israeli *rosh yeshivah* and novelist Rabbi Ḥaim Sabato was told by his grandfather Rabbi Aaron Shweke, an Aleppine rabbinic authority in Cairo, that when Rav Kook's book arrived in Egypt, a Cairene rabbi of the Ashkenazic community pointed out the puzzling passage, "The exercise that Jewish youths in the Land of Israel engage in....raises up the *Shekhinah* (divine presence), just as it rises through songs and praises uttered by David, King of Israel in the Book of Psalms." Everyone came to Rabbi Shweke with this book (i.e., *Orot*) to solicit his opinion. Rabbi Shweke's response to all was: "Do you know who Rav Kook is? Do you know what greatness of vision he has? How dare you?"

According to Rabbi Sabato, it was Rav Kook's writings (and his own grandfather's endorsement thereof) that finally convinced him that he could combine the two worlds of Torah learning and creative writing. (From an interview with Rabbi Sabato by Ze'ev Galili. See Ze'ev Galili's blog *"Higayon be-shiga'on"* ["Method to Madness"],

http://www.zeevgalili.com/2009/01/1045.

Thanks to Prof. Rachel Elior for bringing this anecdote to my awareness.

122. *"Zedonot na'asot ke-zakhuyot be-mishnato shel ha-Rav Kook,"* subsequently published in *Sinai* (Nissan-Iyyar, 5743/1983), and with slight revisions in B. Naor, *Ba-Yam Derekh* (Jerusalem, 5744), pp. 140-152. (The article was reprinted a third time with further revisions by the author in *'Ofer ha-'Ayyalim*, ed. Dani Kochav [Koch] [Jerusalem, 5754/1994], pp. 299-312.) The section that dealt with Nietzsche, among other non-Jewish philosophers, was deleted out of deference to Rav Zevi Yehudah Hakohen Kook *zt"l*.

123. See RZYH Kook, *Li-Shelosha be-Ellul* I (Jerusalem, 5738), pp. 46-47; also cited in Shvarts, *Mi-Tokh ha-Torah ha-Go'elet* (Jerusalem: Zur Ot, 5747) III, 243-244; RAYH Kook, *AT* (Jerusalem, 5743), bottom p. 88; *OHK* III, p. 340; R. M.Z. Neriyah, *Siḥot ha-RAYaH* (Tel Aviv, 5739), p. 178.

During Rav Kook's year of study at the famed Volozhin Yeshivah, his daylong wearing of *tefillin* was regarded with consternation by certain fellows and even by the *Rosh Yeshivah* (Dean), Rabbi Ḥayyim Soloveitchik (later to be known as Rabbi Ḥayyim "Brisker"). However, the senior Rosh Yeshivah, Rabbi Naftali Zevi Yehudah Berlin, defended him, saying. "He is a *ga'on* (genius) and a *tsaddik* (saint)." When some of Rav Kook's classmates countered that there were other *ge'onim-tsaddikim* in the yeshivah who did not wear *tefillin* all day, Rabbi Berlin retorted: "He is a *ga'on* and a *tsaddik* and a *yashar* (straight, upright individual)."

This anecdote was told to the writer (BN) by Rabbi Aharon Soloveichik of Chicago *zt"l*. (Cf. Rabbi N.Z.Y. Berlin, *Ha'amek Davar*, Introduction to *Bereshit*.]

124. *Orot ha-Teḥiyah*, chap. 3: "Europe rightly gave up on God, whom she never knew ... when in our day nationalism grew strong and penetrated the system of philosophy, the latter was forced to place a big question mark over all the content of absolute ethics, which truly, came to Europe only on loan from Judaism, and as any foreign implant, still cannot be absorbed in its spirit."

Orot ha-Teḥiyah, chap. 54: "... that divine belief that they [= the Nations] have absorbed from the light of Israel in their surroundings, without the evolution suited to their nature, is at conflict with their individual personality and oppresses their civilization, which is essentially pagan and idolatrous. However the hand of the Lord did this, so that to a degree, the hard shell of human depravity should be softened, but eventually the pagan in them will win out; 'the kingdom will turn to heresy,' which will resent the sparks of the spirit of Israel, that proceed from the light of the Lord that has infused their spirit, and hatred of Israel will increase ..."

125. Friedrich Nietzsche, *Genealogy of Morals*, trans. Francis Golffing (Garden City, NY, 1956), pp. 167-170, 185-186.

126. Eldad's musing was not idle. Nikos Kazantzakis, in his youth a Nietzschean, and even after the discovery of Zorḅa, still half a Nietzschean, was much enamored of Rabbi Naḥman of Braslav. See Kazantzakis, *Journeying* (Boston: Little, Brown and Company, 1975), p. 147, and *Report to Greco* (New York: Simon and Schuster, 1965), pp. 474-475.

127. Cf. the remarks by the Nazirite, R. David Cohen, eminent disciple of Rav Kook, concerning Nietzsche, cited in Dov Schwarz, "*Ha-Ḥiddushim ha-ra'ayoniyim she-be-Zikhronot ha-Rav ha-Nazir*," *Yonati be-Ḥagvei ha-Sela'*/Sarah Cohen Memorial Volume (Jerusalem, 5747), p. 211, par. 4.

128. *Zemah Zevi: Letters of Rav Zevi Yehudah Hakohen Kook*, Vol. I: 5667-5679/1907-1919; ed. Landau, Neuman, Rahmani (Jerusalem, 5751). Cf. RZYH Kook, *LNY* II, p. 120, and H. A. Shvarts, *Mi-Tokh ha-Torah ha-Go'elet* III, pp. 226-227. For Nietzsche's attitude toward Jews, see Walter Kaufmann's edition of *The Gay Science* (New York: Random House, 1974), pp. 21-24.

129. RAYH Kook, cited in RZYH Kook, *Li-Shelosha be-Ellul* II (Jerusalem, 5738), p. 18.

130. *Berakhot* 6a; RAYH Kook, *Ḥevesh Pe'er* (Jerusalem: Mosad Ha-Rav Kook, 5745/1985), pp. 6, 7, 9, 54, 55, 58, 59, 60, 74, 75; *Siddur 'Olat Re'iyah* (Jerusalem: Mosad Ha-Rav Kook, 5749/1989), p. 22; Zuriel, *Otserot ha-RAYaH* IV, pp. 41-42.

131. *KS*, p. 2.

132. Distortions of Rav Kook's words became so rampant, that at one point Rav Zevi Yehudah issued at his father's behest a general disclaimer entitled, "*Le-hassir mikhshol*," adjuring the public to be vigilant, not to trust *ḥaredi* partisan

reportage of Rav Kook's sayings and doings (especially the Jerusalem newspaper, *Kol Yisrael*), but rather consult the source, i.e., Rav Kook's own printed word. The advertisement was displayed in the newspapers. See e.g., the American *Degel Yisrael* (September 1927), p. 19. (The American article was brought to the writer's attention by Rabbi Joshua Hoffman.)

133. *Orot* (1950 edition), p. 179.

134. Zeitlin, *Sifran shel Yeḥidim* (Jerusalem: Mosad Ha-Rav Kook, 1979), pp. 235-237.

135. Rav Kook held Rabbi Hirsch in the highest esteem, referring to him as "the great of intellect, the exalted prince of God, the Ga'on Rabbi Samson Raphael Hirsch, of blessed memory" (*IHR* I, Letter 144, p. 182).

136. Mordechai Lipson, *Di Velt Dertsehlt* (New York: Doros, 1928), pp. 47-48. Conceming Lipson, see G. Kressel, *Leksikon ha-Sifrut ha-Ivrit ba-Dorot ha-Aḥaronim* (Sifriyat Po'alim, Ha-Kibbutz Ha-Artzi Ha-Shomer Ha-Tza'ir). Courtesy Rabbi Aaron B. Shurin.

137. N.Z.Y. Berlin, *Meshiv Davar* I, responsum 44. See RZYH Kook, *LNY* II, pp. 210, 241.

138. Rav Kook never tempered his opposition to separatism. On his deathbed he declared: "Separation is the foundation of disbelief. There is no permission for separate communities in Israel" (RZYH Kook, *Li-Sheloshah Be-Ellul* I, p. 48). In fact, his last signature was affixed to a document designed to prevent separate communities. See Lifshitz, pp. 301-302. See also Rav Kook's open letter in defense of Rabbi Glasner of Cluj (Klausenberg) Romania, reprinted in *Ma'amrei ha-RAYaH I*, pp. 55-61, especially pp. 58-60. On page 58, Rav Kook considers separatism heresy, based on Rashi, *Megillah* 25a, s.v. *yevarekhukha tovim*. (In that connection, see also *Iggerot La-RAYaH*, pp. 215-216, and *IHR* IV, Letter 1139, p. 132.)

139. *IHR* I (Jerusalem: Mosad Ha-Rav Kook, 5722), Letter 111, p. 139; Letter 118, p. 148; Letter 137, pp. 169-170; *IHR* II, Letter 647, p. 265; Letter 648, pp. 265-266; Letters 649, 650, 652.

140. *IHR* II (Jerusalem, 1961), Letter 635, pp. 254-255; Letter 639, p. 257; Letter 644, pp. 260-262; Letter 654, pp. 269-271. As early as 1908, Rav Kook had to reassure his Jerusalem friends who were alarmed by his endorsement of the Mizraḥi school. See *IHR* I, Letter 151, p. 197. Also, Porush, p. 234, and J.H. Lewis, *Vision of Redemption* (New Haven, 1979), pp. 82-93. More recently, see N.R. Auerbach, *Me-Halberstadt 'ad Petaḥ Tikvah: Zikhronot Ha-Rav Moshe Auerbach Zt"l* (Jerusalem, 5747), pp. 88-90 (n. 125), 104-106, and Shnayer Z. Leiman, "R. David Friedman of Karlin: The Ban on Secular Study in Jerusalem," *Tradition* 26:4 (Summer 1992): 102-105.

See also the letter of RZYH Kook to Rav Ya'akov Moshe Ḥarlap, dated 5674 (1914), in *Zemah Zevi* I, pp. 47-51; and the letter of Rav Kook to Rav Sonnenfeld and Dr. Wallach asking their support of Taḥkemoni, in Zuriel, *Otserot ha-RAYaH* IV, pp. 163-164.

141. *IHR* II, Letter 671, pp. 280-281.

142. Porush, pp. 243, 210, n. 16.

One observes with interest that the two pillars of the Ḥaredi world in the 1940s and 1950s both expressed qualifications concerning the *ḥerem* of Maharil Diskin against the study of foreign languages. Rabbi Isaac Ze'ev Halevi Soloveitchik ("Brisker Rav") held the opinion that the ban was binding only in Jerusalem but not in the rest of *Erets Yisrael*; Rabbi Abraham Isaiah Karelitz ("*Ḥazon Ish*") opined that the ban was binding only upon the descendants of those Jews who inhabited *Erets Yisrael* in the days of Maharil Diskin. See Shimon Yosef Meller, *'Uvdot ve-Hanhagot le-Beit Brisk* IV (Jerusalem, 5760/2000), p. 231.

143. Reprinted in *Ma'amrei ha-RAYaH* I, pp. 1-9. The passage on Christianity is found on pp. 5-6.

144. Reprinted in R. Zevi Hirsch Friedman, *Zevi Ḥemed* (New York, 5686). See p. 28.

145. *IHR* II, Letter 375, p. 34. This letter, dated 19 Menaḥem-Av, 5671/1911, is a lengthy, well-reasoned defense of the article in *Ha-Nir*. See also *IHR* IV, pp. 217.

146. *AT* (Jerusalem, 5743), p. 23.

147. See chapters 3, 4, 5, 6, 7, 9, 10, 15 of "Israel and Its Renascence." See further Zuriel, pp. 147-148, and R. Zevi Yehudah Kook, in Shvarts, *Mi-Tokh* III, pp. 38-41.

148. See *Orot, Yisrael u-Teḥiyato* ("Israel and Its Renascence"), chaps. 3, 5, 9, 15; *Orot ha-Teshuvah* 12:10; *Orot ha-Emunah*, ed. R. Moshe Gurevitz (Jerusalem, 5745), p. 6, and chapter entitled *"Minut,"* pp. 8-17; *OHK* II, p. 315; *Ma'amrei ha-RAYaH* I, p. 59; and RZYH Kook, *LNY* II, p. 206.

149. See *Berakhot* 28b and *Halakhot Gedolot* (Aspamia edition), p. 27. See also B. Naor, *Hassagot ha-RABaD le-Mishneh Torah* (Jerusalem: Zur Ot, 5745), *Hilkhot Teshuvah* 3:9.

150. MT, *Hilkhot 'Avodah Zarah* 9:4 in uncensored editions. Rav Zevi Yehudah Hakohen Kook showed this writer that in his father's printed (censored) copy of Rambam, the original wording concerning "the Christians" had been restored in his father's handwriting.

151. See RAYH Kook, *Mishpat Kohen* (Jerusalem: Mosad Ha-Rav Kook, 5745), chaps. 58, 63.

152. See B. Naor, "Rav Kook and Emmanuel Levinas on the 'Non-Existence' of God," in *Orot: A Multidisciplinary Journal of Judaism* I (New York, 1991), pp.1-11.

153. This essay was included by Rav Z.Y. Hakohen Kook in the 5710 [i.e., 1950] edition of *Orot*. The passages seized upon by the zealots are to be found there in chapter 5, "*Yissurim Memarekim*" ("Cathartic Suffering"), pp. 126-128.

154. *Orot* (Jerusalem: Mosad Ha-Rav Kook, 5710), p. 126.

155. Ibid.

156. Ibid., p. 127.

157. Ibid.

158. Ibid., p. 128.

159. *KS*, p. 10. *'Orot ha-Teḥiyah* ("Lights of Renascence") with an *'aleph* is deliberately misspelled *'Orot ha-Teḥiyah* ("Skins of Renascence") with an *'ayin*.

160. *Likkutei MOHaRaN* I, 64. See B. Naor, "Rav Kook and Emmanuel Levinas on the 'Non-Existence' of God," in *Orot: A Multidisciplinary Journal of Judaism* I (New York, 1991), pp. 6-7.

161. Rabbi G.H. Leiner, *'Eyn ha-Tekhelet* (Jerusalem: Va'ad Ḥasidei Radzyn, 5723), pp. 181-182. See *Orot Newsletter* 2:1 (Tammuz-Ellul, 5751/July-September 1991), pp. 5-7.

162. H. Zeitlin, *Sifran shel Yeḥidim* (Jerusalem, 1979), pp. 235-237.

163. Yonina Dison, *Da'at* 24 (Winter 1990):81 is convinced that Rav Kook's method of thinking "is not similar to the way of thinking Hegel presents, which is based on a process of thesis-antithesis-synthesis." I beg to differ. It is clear that Rav Kook's thought abounds in instances of just such thinking. For example, in terms of character typology, oftentimes Rav Kook will posit a higher type of *tsaddik* who is in effect the synthesis of the two antithetical elements of *tsaddik* (righteous) and *rasha'* (wicked). See *Orot, Orot ha-Teḥiyah*, chaps. 21 and 43, and *Orot ha-Teshuvah* 16:12. (Some years ago, Rabbi Alter B.Z. Metzger, translator of *Orot ha-Teshuvah*, brought this typology to my awareness.) Or take Rav Kook's notion of the *kodesh ha-kodashim* being the reconciliation of the two opposites *kodesh* and *ḥol* (*Orot ha-Kodesh* II, p. 311).

164. Cf. *Orot, Orot ha-Teḥiyah*, chap. 18.

165. Cf. Rav Kook's dialectical interpretation of history in his commentary to the *Hagadah*, *'Olat Re'iyah* II (Jerusalem: Mosad Ha-Rav Kook, 5749), pp. 262-264, s.v. *ha laḥma 'anya*.

166. *KS*, p. 11.

167. Reprinted in Elyashiv Cohen (pseudonym of Eliyahu Cohen Steinberger), *Likht Shtrallen* V (2nd. ed., London, 5747), pp. 39-41.

168. In old Jaffa edition (5674/1914); in new Jerusalem edition (5743/1983), p.15.

169. The new Jerusalem edition engages in censorship: "long-lasting" (*arukat zeman*) is omitted; "essence" (*'atsmah*) is substituted for "externals" (*hitsoniyutah*); and "purpose" (*takhlitah*) for "inner content" (*penimiyutah*).

170. Rabbi Aharon Halevi Horowitz, *Sha'arei 'Avodah* 4:10.

171. Rabbi Zadok Hakohen Rabinowitz, *Yisra'el Kedoshim* (B'nei Berak, 5727), 16a.

172. The late Rabbi Aaron Israel Bornstein, son of Rabbi Samuel Bornstein of Sokhatchov (author *Shem mi-Shemuel*) transmitted to the present Rebbe of Sokhatchov that there was an ideological element to the famous Kotsk-Izbica schism. According to this version of the rift between the two men, Rabbi Mordechai Joseph of Izbica parted ways from Rabbi Mendel of Kotsk over the issue of whether God ever subjects man to a *nisayon* (test) that he is incapable of withstanding. The Kotsker, so it is alleged, would not endorse the Izhbitser's radical theology (whose most notorious example is the Izhbitser reading of the confrontation between Zimri and Pinḥas, see *Mei ha-Shilo'aḥ*, *Pinḥas*; Rabbi Zadok Hakohen of Lublin, *Zidkat ha-Zaddik*, chap. 43).

Rabbi Aaron Israel Bornstein, of blessed memory, was considered the authoritative historian of Sokhatchov. His father, the *Shem mi-Shemuel*, was the grandson of the Kotsker Rebbe.

(Courtesy Rabbi Eli DiPoce, MD, who was told this by the present Rebbe of Sokhatchov, Rabbi Samuel Bornstein *shelit"a* of Bayit ve-Gan, Jerusalem)

We should clear up a miscomprehension here. Many think the enemies of Rav Kook were necessarily *Ḥasidim*. Actually, Rav Kook enjoyed excellent relations with many of the Russian and Polish *Ḥasidim*—Braslav, Gur, Lelov, Lubavitch, Rachmastrivka (a branch of Chernobyl), Rizhin, Sokhatchov, Zhevil—to mention a few schools. By and large, the opponents of Rav Kook were from the ranks of the *Perushim* (old Lithuanian families of Jerusalem) and the Hungarians. See Porush, p. 214, n. 18.

173. *IHR* IV, Letter 1049, p. 68.

174. Rav Kook's point is certainly well borne out by the historical facts. Rabbi Moshe Blau, p. 50, writes:

> In general, his [= Rav Kook's] approach, which was publicized in his booklet *'Ikvei ha-Tson*, was not accepted by the rabbis and zealots of Jerusalem. My father-in-law [= R. Ya'akov Orenstein] *zt"l* was one of his staunchest opponents. Also my grandfather [= R. Yeshayah Orenstein] *zt"l* opposed him, and when Rav Kook began to deliver in Yaffo a class on *Kuzari* (by Rabbi Yehudah Halevi) of a philosophical nature according to his bent, my grandfather wrote Rav Kook a gentle reproof. My grandfather showed me his [= Rav Kook's] reply to him, in which he stated he was lecturing to his students "the words of the Living God."

Cf. *IHR* I (Jerusalem, 5722), Letters 40, 43; p. 37, n. 3, and pp. 41-42. The first letter counsels R. Zevi Yehudah not to be upset over R. Yeshayah Orenstein's campaign against *'Ikvei ha-Tson*, especially considering the fact that other rabbis responded positively to the work. The second letter is a lengthy response to R. Yeshayah's letter criticizing the booklet. The letters are dated 13 Marḥeshvan and 12 Kislev, 5667, respectively.

Sixty years before the events described here, the Jerusalemite Rabbi Ḥazan was persecuted for his study of *Kuzari*. See José Faur, *Rabbi Yisrael Moshe Ḥazan: The Man and His Works* (Hebrew) (Haifa: Raphael Arbel Academic Publishers, 5737), pp. 16-18.

175. In times of personal hardship and tragedy, Rav Kook's first thought was of his parents' welfare. See *IHR* I, Letter 314, pp. 352-354, regarding the blows of the Shemitah controversy, and Lifshitz, p. 148, regarding the death of his daughter.

176. *KS*, p. 9.

177. See Harold Bloom, The Anxiety of Influence (New York: Oxford University Press, 1973); idem, *Kabbalah and Criticism* (New York: Seabury Press, 1975), pp. 64-71; Jacques Derrida, *Of Grammatology* (Baltimore: Johns Hopkins University Press, 1976) ("trace"); Paul Valery, "Letter About Mallarme," in *The Collected Works of Paul Valery*, vol. 8 (Princeton: Princeton University Press, 1972), pp. 241-242. On the blurred distinction between tradition and originality, see T.S. Eliot, "Tradition and the Individual Talent," in his *Selected Essays* (New York: Harcourt, Brace, 1950), pp. 3-11.

178. Bloom, *Kabbalah and Criticism*, pp. 86-92.

179. *IHR* IV, Letter 1063, pp. 76-77.

180. Ibid., Letter 1074, p. 86.

181. Even in the so-called heat of battle, Rav Kook's higher, transpersonal self was able to appreciate his opponents' antithetical contribution to the distillation of Jewish history: "Even all those who stand apart, or oppose all the actions which bring the visible redemption, are also included with the meritorious, because through their demands, the content of the redemptive activity becomes clearer and more distinct; it becomes purer, more luminous, more vital, more truly Israelite, more convective of the pure life flowing from the Source of Israel, from the wellspring that issues from the House of the Lord" (Ms., in *Eretz Tzvi: Tzvi M. Glatt Memorial Volume* [Jerusalem, 1989], p. 183, par. 1).

182. *IHR* IV, Letter 1076, p. 87.

183. Rabbi Nathan Horowitz of Monsey, NY, remembered Rabbi Zevi Yehudah Hakohen Kook as a young man, praying in the Viennese synagogue of his (Rabbi Horowitz's) grandfather, the Galician Ga'on Rabbi Ḥayyim Yitsḥak Jeruchem, the Rav of Altstadt. In private conversation, Rabbi Jeruchem told Rabbi Zevi Yehudah Kook that he should burn his father's book. Interestingly, about the time that Rabbi Zevi Yehudah Kook would have written to his father, we find him in Vienna. See *Iggerot la-RAYaH* (Jerusalem, 5750), Addenda, Letter 22, p. 557. Of course, all this is supposition on our part. Undoubtedly, there were many "respected rabbis" who would have fit the description. Confirmation of Rabbi Zevi Yehudah's meeting with the Rav of Altstadt in Vienna comes now from the biography by Rabbi Shlomo Aviner, *Zevi Kodesh* I (5765), p. 134.

184. *IHR* IV, Letter 1225, p. 186.

185. R. Ḥayyim Hirschensohn, *MBK* (St. Louis, 5679-5682), pp. 258-260.

186. *Mishnah, Yadayim* 3:5.

187. See the first line of Rav Zevi Yehudah Hakohen Kook's introduction to the 1950 edition of *Orot;* Ḥayyim A. Shvarts, *Mi-Tokh ha-Torah ha-Go'elet* III, pp. 193-194; IV, p. 87.

188. Rav Zevi Yehudah Hakohen Kook, in Shvarts, *Mi-Tokh ha-Torah ha-Go'elet* III, pp. 193-194; IV, p. 87.

189. *Orot ha-Kodesh* II, p. 311.

190. *Yoma* 54a-b.

191. *Yoma* 54b.

192. I now see that Rav Zevi Yehudah's own explanation for dubbing *Orot* "holy of holies," is that *Orot*, as opposed to the other works, is devoted exclusively to the People of Israel. See Shvarts, *Mi-Tokh ha-Torah ha-Go'elet* III, pp. 16-17, 193-194; IV, p. 87.

Degel Yerushalayim (The Banner of "Jerusalem")

1. Isaiah 51:16.

Orot Me-Ofel (Lights from Darkness)

ERETS YISRAEL (THE LAND OF ISRAEL)

1. The title derives from the phrase inserted in *Birkat Yotser* (Morning Service) according to the Ashkenazic *Maḥzor* for festivals. For Rav Kook's interpretation of this *piyyut*, citing his grandfather, see Ḥayyim A. Shvarts, *Mi-Tokh ha-Torah ha-Go'elet* (Jerusalem: Zur Ot, 5747) III, p. 140.

2. In Halakha, we do find the concept that the Land of Israel bonds individual Jews into a collective, something that cannot occur outside the Land. See *Berakhot* 58a; Maimonides, *MT, Hilkhot Berakhot* 10:11, *Kessef Mishneh* and *Tsafnat Pa'ane'aḥ* ad locum; *Minḥat Ḥinukh, Komets ha-Minḥah, mitsvah* 284; Rabbi R. Weinberg, *Teshuvot Rav Sar Shalom Gaon* (Jerusalem: Mosad Ha-Rav Kook, 5736), pp. 75-76, n. 8; Rabbi M.N. Brizel in *Kovets Bet Aharon ve-Yisrael* (Av-Ellul 5749), p. 109; *Horayot* 3a; Maimonides, *Peirush ha-Mishnah, Bekhorot* 4:3; *Avnei Nezer, Oraḥ Ḥayyim*, responsum 314, citing Maharal of Prague, *Netivot 'Olam, Netiv ha-Tsedakah*, chap. 6.

Rabbi Aharon Lichtenstein, *"Be-'inyan semikhah be-Erets Yisrael u-be-ḥutsah la-arets," Beit Yitzhak,* 5719, has pointed out that the converse—that in exile, the Jewish People do not constitute a unified entity—is inconceivable. We must differentiate between juridic formalities and doctrinal subleties. See there pp. 95-96, also quoting Rabbi Yitsḥak Hutner. (Rabbi Hutner's remarks are reminiscent of Rav Kook's in *Mishpat Kohen*, chap. 124, pp. 273-274 and *Shemu'ot ha-RAYaH* [ms.], *Ki Tissa*, 5689.) Cf. Maharal, *Netsaḥ Yisrael,* chap. 1, and Tosafot, *Sotah* 34a, s.v. *'odam*, citing Yerushalmi *Sotah* 7:5.

Rav Kook, of course, subscribes to the halakhic notion. (See e.g., H. Shvarts, *Mi-Tokh ha-Torah ha-Go'elet* IV, p. 192.) His objection is leveled at reductionists who would say that the Land is merely a cohesive factor to bond Jews together, analogous to a basket that bonds many small rolls into *ḥallah*, an halakhic mechanism known as *tseiruf sal* (see Mishnah, *Ḥallah* 2:4). (This analogy of *tseiruf sal* was actually pointed out to the writer many years ago by one anti-Kookian Torah scholar in Jerusalem!) Rav Kook is emphatic that the Land of Israel must not be viewed as a means to an end but rather as an end in itself.

3. In general, *kedushah* (sanctity) is by definition something that cannot be understood rationally. (The non-Jew Rudolf Otto understood this truth in his book, *Das Heilige.*) The root *kdš* means "removed" or "transcendent." We refer to God as *Ha-Kadosh Barukh Hu* because He is totally transcendent and remote from our grasp. Concerning specifically *Kedushat Erets Yisrael*, the sanctity of the Land of Israel, Rav Kook observed that the name of the second patriarch Yitsḥak (Isaac) forms the initials of four different appellations for the Land: *Erets Yisrael* (The Land of Israel), Erets ha-*TS*evi (The Land of Beauty), Erets ha-*Ḥ*ayyim (The Land of Life), Erets ha-*K*edoshah (The Holy Land). (See Rav Kook's *Siddur 'Olat Re'iyah* I, *Berit Milah*, pp. 398-399.) Isaac was the first "sabra." He is symbolic of the Land. Abraham was born outside the Land. Jacob died elsewhere. But Isaac was born in the Land and never left it (see Rashi, Genesis 26:2). Is there any biblical figure as inscrutable as Isaac? Rav Zevi Yehudah Hakohen Kook referred to Isaac's behavior as *nif'alut* (passivity). (See *Siḥot Harav Tsevi Yehudah*, *Bereshit*, ed. Shelomo Aviner [Jerusalem, 5753], pp. 191-194, 204-206, 218-219, 228-230, 247.) On the passivity of Isaac, see also Robert Alter, *The Art of Biblical Narrative* (New York: Basic Books, 1981), p. 53. Isaac's passivity is a mystery to us. What motivates this man? What lies below that passive exterior? Why was he so fond of the wicked Esau, apotheosis of physicality? Thus it is fitting that Isaac, most mysterious of men, symbolizes a land that defies rational definition.

4. "Shaky compared to the holy might of the Land of Israel" (*ra'u'a be-'erekh eitan ha-kodesh shel erets yisra'el*). For this circumlocution, we find in *SK* 7:13: "shaky and rotten" (*ra'u'a ve-rakuv*).

5. Cf. below *Orot ha-Teḥiyah*/"Lights of Renascence," beginning chap. 8.

6. "The Judaism of the Land of Israel is salvation itself" (*ve-ha-yahadut shel erets yisra'el hi ha-yeshu'ah 'atsmah*). This concluding sentence is not found in *SK* 7:13.

7. Rav Kook viewed the Jewish mystic tradition, Kabbalah, as a force agitating for Return to the Land. Cf. below *Orot ha-Teḥiyah*, chaps. 57, 60, 64, and *Iggerot ha-RAYaH* II, p. 91. See B. Naor, "Mashiaḥ Watch 5753," *Orot Newsletter* (Tishri 5753).

8. "Mighty" (*'adir*). In *SK* 6:23: *eitan*. The meaning remains unchanged.

9. Cf. *Sotah* 47a: "the charm of a place upon its inhabitants." See Rashi s.v. *ḥen makom 'al yoshvav*.

10. *Shabbat* 31a. Rav Zevi Yehudah Hakohen Kook used to close his letters with the formula "*Bi-tsefiyat ha-yeshu'ah ha-shelemah*" ("With expectation of the complete salvation"), an indication of how much a part of everyday awareness this longing must be.

11. "Side" (*tsedadi*). In *SK* 6:23: *epizodi* (episodic).

12. "Of any form" (*be-'eizo tsurah she-hi*). In *SK* 6:23 these words do not occur.

13. In the 1920 edition of *Orot*: *mitbaletet* (protrudes). Corrected in the 1950 edition to *mitbatelet* (is subsumed). In *SK* 5:18: *mitbatelet*.

14. "The essential spring" (*ha-ma'ayan ha-'atsmi*). In *SK* 5:18: "the essential Israelite spring" (*ha-ma'ayan ha-'atsmi ha-Yisra'eli*).

15. Numbers 19:13.

16. Zechariah 2:10; *Ta'anit* 3a.

17. "Flowing" (*nova'at*). In *SK* 5:18: "pounding" (*dofeket latset*).

18. Jeremiah 31:15-16. See Maharal, *Netsaḥ Yisrael*, end chap. 1.

19. Joshua 14:15; *Genesis Rabbah* 14:6.

20. "Through precisely this return" (*davka 'al-yedei shivah zo lehitgalot*). These words are not found in *SK* 5:18.

21. Genesis 12:2; *Pesaḥim* 117a.

We are presented with a Hegelian progression of thesis-antithesis-synthesis. Rav Kook is grappling with the dialectic of nationalism (particularism) versus universalism. In Phase One, Israel is a landed nation. In Phase Two, Israel stops functioning as a nation and assumes the form of religion. Phase three, entered into with the return to Zion, is the perfect synthesis of the nationalist-particularist phenomenon and the religious-universalist conception. (Cf. *Le-mahalakh ha-ide'ot be-yisrael* ["To the Procession of Ideas in Israel"] in *Orot* [1950 ed.], pp. 102-118.) When this occurs, authentic universalism is expressed through the medium of Israel's nationhood. Certain German-Jewish thinkers viewed the Exile as Israel's evolution from a primitive tribal state to a more advanced cosmopolitan form and therefore regarded the return to Zion as a step backward. (A prime example is Hermann Cohen; see his *Religion of Reason, Out of the Sources of Judaism* [New York: Frederick Ungar, 1972], chap. XIII, "The Idea of the Messiah and Mankind," and the anecdotes concerning him in N. Glatzer, *Franz Rosenzweig: His Life and*

Thought [New York: Schocken, 1961], pp. 53-54, 351.) To this, Rav Kook retorts: It is only through this Return, that Israel will achieve global influence and impact. The nation that was founded by Abraham, a universalist, "Father of a Multitude of Nations," will come full circle and conclude its history on a universalist note.

22. Cf. Rabbi Nathan of Nemirov, *Likkutei Tefillot*, beginning chap. 20.

23. *Bava Batra* 158a.

24. *Ketubot* 75a. The notion that spiritual attachment to the Land supersedes spatial barriers may be implicit in *Berakhot* 28b, 30a, and is certainly explicit in *Likkutei MOHaRaN*, I, 44; *Iggerot ha-RAYaH* II, p. 154; letter of Rav Y.M. Ḥarlap to RZYH Kook, published in *Hed Harim* and as the frontispiece to *Resh Millin* (Jerusalem: Attiyah, 5732); and letter of Rav Ḥarlap to his son, *Mikhtevei Marom,* p. 9. See B. Naor, *"Mikhtevei Marom"* ("Letters of Rabbi Ya'akov Moshe Ḥarlap"), *Jewish Action* (Summer 5749), p. 82.

25. Isaiah 66:10; *Ta'anit* 30.

26. R. Menaḥem Mendel of Shklov, *Mayim Adirim* (Jerusalem, 5747), p. 172; R. Zadok ha-Kohen of Lublin, *Siḥat Mal'akhei ha-Sharet* (Lublin, 5687), 4d.

27. It is an ancient rabbinic tradition that prophecy rests only in the Land of Israel. (See following Chap. 6.) See beginning *Mekhilta*. The question arises why this should be so. Rav Kook takes a psychological approach. Maimonides (*Guide of the Perplexed* II, 36, 37) had written that prophecy is the product of the imaginative faculty. (See B. Naor, *Lights of Prophecy* [New York: Orthodox Union, 1990], p. 11, and below, *Israel and Its Renascence*, chaps. 17-18.) Rav Kook couples this assumption to the mystic belief that imagination must suffer in the impure atmosphere outside the Land. It must be stressed that this is Rav Kook's takeoff on Maimonides. There is absolutely no indication in the writings of Maimonides that he subscribed to the belief that prophecy is limited to the geographical borders of *Erets Yisrael.* Quite the contrary, the entire tenor of Maimonides' theory of prophecy is universalistic. See B. Naor, *Ba-Yam Derekh* (Jerusalem: Zur Ot, 5744), p. 94, notes 8-9.

28. See Maimonides, *Guide* II, 36, 37; B. Naor, *Lights of Prophecy*, pp. 11-13, 44-47. Also RAYH Kook, *Orot Yisrael* (in 1950 edition of *Orot*), p. 165, par. 16.

29. *Bava Batra* 158b.

30. Ezekiel 1:3.

31. *Mo'ed Katan* 25a. Rav Kook follows the second interpretation in Rashi there.

32. Rav Kook found himself stranded for the duration of World War I in Europe, far from his beloved *Erets Yisrael.* He believed that heaven must have a mission for him to accomplish outside the Land; there must be some souls lying there waiting for him to uplift them. One such extraordinary soul was the Nazirite, Rabbi David Cohen (at the time, a student of philosophy at the University of Basel), who after their initial mystical encounter in St. Gallen, Switzerland on

the Eve of Rosh Hodesh Ellul, 5675 (1915) followed Rav Kook to the end of his days, geographically – to Jerusalem and Yeshivat Merkaz Harav – and spiritually: through the editing of *Orot ha-Kodesh* (*Lights of Holiness*), perhaps Rav Kook's *magnum opus*. (Three volumes were published during the Nazirite's lifetime and a fourth posthumously by Rabbi Yoḥanan Fried.) The day of their meeting became the most significant in the life of the Nazirite. Twenty years later to the day, he would present his dying master with the finished galleys of their joint venture, *Orot ha-Kodesh* (see *OHK* I, Intro., pp. 17, 24):

> On Rosh Ḥodesh Ellul, 5695 [1935], twenty years after receiving the face of the Rav, I visited him for the last time, with the frontispiece of *Orot ha-Kodesh*. He lay on his deathbed, rejoiced and cried, commanding [me] not to write about him any titles. Two days later, on the third day of Ellul, 5695, the light of lights was extinguished. The world became dark for us. But the light of his holy Torah will appear and light up the world.

Rabbi M.Z. Neriyah (*Bisdeh ha-RAYaH*, pp. 388, 399) wrote that the day of the Nazirite's passing—28 Av, 5732 [i.e., 1972]—was the exact date of the initial, fateful encounter with Rav Kook, but that is not possible, as the Nazirite himself attests that he met Rav Kook on Erev Rosh Ḥodesh Ellul, which would have been the 29th of Av. (See further, Preface to *Shivḥei Kol ha-Nevuah*, appended to *Kol ha-Nevu'ah* [5739 edition].)

In *Ha-Zofeh* of 29 Av, 5752/28.8.92, p. 9, the Nazirite's son, Rabbi She'ar-Yashuv Cohen of Haifa, clarified that his father traveled from Basel to St. Gallen on the 28th of Av in order to spend Erev Rosh Ḥodesh and Rosh Ḥodesh Ellul with Rav Kook.

33. Deuteronomy 11:12.

34. In his farewell letter to his family, the Vilna Gaon writes that he is journeying to the Holy Land, which is "the delight of all Israel and the delight of the Lord, and all those above and those below desire her (*ḥemdat kol Yisrael ve-ḥemdat Hashem yitbarakh, kol ha-'elyonim ve-ha-taḥtonim teshukatam elehah*).

35. "A spirit of vision" (*ru'aḥ habatah*). In *SK* 5:76: "the height of vision" (*rum habatah*).

36. According to the kabbalistically inspired intention (*Yehi Ratson*) recited at the time of performing specific *mitsvot*, each individual *mitsvah* taps the universal root of all the *mitsvot* and thereby interconnects with all 613 *mitsvot*. See Rav Kook's *Siddur 'Olat Re'iyah* I, pp. 10-11, 18-19 (*tsitsit*) and 29 *(tefillin)*, and comments by Rav Zevi Yehudah Hakohen Kook, *Siddur 'Olat Re'iyah* II, p. 398, par. 2. See also *Zemaḥ Zevi: Letters of Rav Zevi Yehudah Hakohen Kook* (Jerusalem, 5751), Letter 39, p. 97. The letter discusses at great length the difference between "the organic conception of Judaism" and the rationalistic variety.

37. "And grow stronger" (*u-mitgabrim*). In *SK* 5:76: *mit'adrim*. The meaning remains unchanged.

38. "They expose the light" (*maḥsifot hen neharah*). In *SK* 5:76: "they add light" (*mosifim hem neharah*).

39. "Produces" (*mamtsi*). In *SK* 5:76: *motsi* (brings forth).

40. Isaiah 4:3.

41. *Ketubot* 75a.

42. Psalm 87:5, 6

43. Introduction to *Tikkunei Zohar, Pataḥ Eliyahu.*

44. *Exodus Rabbah*, beginning *Mishpatim* (30:3): "*And these are the laws.* What is written above? *They shall judge the people at all times* [Exodus 18:22]. While it says here, *And these are the laws.* And the Ten Commandments are intervening. This may be compared to a noblewoman *(matrona)* who was walking, an escort on this side and on that, and she in the middle. So the Torah: laws before her and laws after her, and she in the middle." (Cf. RZYH Kook's introduction to *Da'at Kohen, "Reshit Da'at."*) Rav Kook understands this to mean that civil laws are an essential, indispensable aspect of Torah. Cf. below *Israel and its Renascence,* chap. 3.

45. Exodus 28:30.

46. Lamentations 4:20.

47. Jeremiah 23:6.

48. Exodus 28:30.

49. *Yoma* 73b. The very suggestion that the letters on the breastplate of the High Priest, the *Urim ve-Tummim,* might somehow relate to the process of halakhic decision, raises problems. See Rashi and Rabbi Zevi Hirsch (MaHaRaTs) Ḥayyot, *'Eruvin* 45a and Rashi *'Eruvin* 63a. In general, it is important to know that Rav Kook—in opposition to Maimonides—advocates the interpenetration of the rational and the preterrational in terms of Halakha. Rav Kook would follow in the tradition of the Tosafists (*'Eruvin* 6b, *Pesaḥim* 114a, *Yevamot* 14a, s.v. *Rabbi*). See also Rabbenu Nissim Ga'on, *Berakhot* 19b; Yehudah Halevi, *Kuzari* III, 39, 41 (cited in *IHR* II, p. 101); Rabbenu Menaḥem ha-Me'iri, introduction to *Avot*; and *Mishnat Rabbi Eliezer* (32 *Middot*) ed. Enelow (New York, 5693), p. 117. For Rav Kook's formal position, see *IHR* I, p. 123; *'Ets Hadar,* chap. 34; *Mishpat Kohen* (Jerusalem, 1985) 92:7 (p. 208a), and notes of RZYH Kook, pp. 380-381; *Ginzei RAYaH* III, p. 10 (reprinted in Zuriel, *Otserot ha-RAYaH* II, p. 1251). See further Zevi Kaplan, *Be-Shipulei Gelimato* (Jerusalem, 1984), pp. 30-34, and Menaḥem Klein, "'*Ekronot tefisato ha-ra'ayonit shel ha-RAYaH et ha-halakha,*" *Be-'Oro,* ed. Ḥamiel (Jerusalem, 5746), pp. 153-166. For general discussions of the problematic, see Rabbi Ḥayyim Yosef David Azulai, *Shem ha-Gedolim*, entry *Rabbenu Ya'akov He-Ḥasid; Encyclopedia Talmudit,* s.v. *Urim ve-Tummim*, *Eliyahu* and *Bat-Kol;* Aron Maged, *Beth Aharon* (Encyclopedia of Talmudic Principles), vol. XI (Brooklyn, 1978), s.v. *Bat-Kol;* Rabbi Judah Leib Graubart, *Ḥavalim ba-Ne'imim*, vol. I (Jerusalem: Feldheim, 1975), chap. 32, "*Lo ba-shamayim,*" pp. 48a-49d; Rabbi

J.B. Soloveitchik, *Reshimot Shi'urim—Sukkah,* ed. Rabbi H. Reichman (New York, 5750), p. 229; R. Mordechai Fogelman, *Beit Mordechai* (Jerusalem, 5731), *Meḥ karim ba-halakha,* chap. 39; and B. Naor, *Hassagot ha-Rabad le-Mishneh Torah* (Jerusalem: Zur Ot, 5745), Introduction. pp. 15-16. See now Avinoam Rosenak, *Ha-Halakha ha-Nevu'it (The Prophetic Halakha: Rabbi A.I.H. Kook's Philosophy of Halakha)* (Jerusalem: Magnes, 2007), pp. 209-211.

50. Leviticus 6:6.

51. Psalm 119:127.

52. Rav Kook posits that some Zionists, though outwardly devoid of faith in God, are inwardly attracted to the Land of Israel because that is the only place on earth where a Jew can fully actualize his spiritual potential. If that sounds absurd, Rav Kook assures us that there are hidden recesses of a Jewish soul that are revealed only to the adept. Other great rabbis called into question Rav Kook's claim that he was able to see into the souls of the generation. See Rav Kook's reply to Rav Y.D. Wilovsky ("RIDBaZ"), *Iggerot ha-RAYaH* II, pp. 186-189. Rav Kook invoked the saying of the *Tikkunei Zohar* (*tikkun* 60) that the generation(s) before Messiah will be "good on the inside and bad on the outside." So too in conversation with Hillel Zeitlin, see H. Zeitlin, *Sifran shel Yeḥidim* (Jerusalem: Mosad Ha-Rav Kook, 5740), p. 240.

53. Leviticus 18:5.

54. A conflation of two verses, Psalm 56:14 and 116:9.

55. *Midrash Tehillim*, ed. Buber (Vilna, 1891), end chap. 56. See Buber's note there. The concluding sentence "To walk before the Lord in the Land of life. This is the Land of Israel " is not found in *SK* 5:242.

ḤA-MILḤAMAH (THE WAR)

56. Song of Songs 2:12.

57. Isaiah 25:5. Cf. Zuriel, *Otserot ha-RAYaH* II, p. 938, par. 3.

58. Song of Songs 2:12.

59. *Mo'ed Katan* 28a.

60. *Genesis Rabbah* 42:4 (to Genesis 14:1): "If you see nations warring with one another, expect the feet of Messiah, for so it was in the days of Abraham. Through the warring of kingdoms, greatness came to Abraham." One might inquire what "greatness" came to Abraham out of the War of the Four Kings and the Five Kings? One must remember that Abraham's interest in involvement was to save Lot, progenitor of "Ruth [the Moabitess] and Na'amah [the Amonitess], from whom will come the light of Messiah, strength of Israel, destined to be a light to the Nations" (*Ginzei RAYaH* II [*Ḥodesh ha-Aviv*], p. 20). Cf. *'Arfilei Tohar* (Jerusalem, 5743), p. 21. See *Yevamot* 77a; *Bava Kamma* 38b.

61. *Sanhedrin* 98a.

62. Rav Kook interprets the juxtaposition to mean that God has preordained wars in order to produce through them salvation. The seeds of righteousness, ironically, are planted in the soil of the battlefield; after the war the harvest of salvation will be reaped. Cf. *Resh Millin*, *Tagin* (Crownlets), end *"Ha-Zayin"*; *Ma'amrei RAYaH* I, bottom p. 153, and Rabbi M.Y. Zuriel, *Otserot ha-RAYaH* II, p. 937, par. 4 (reprinted from *Sinai* 12 [5703/1943]: 326-334). Though Rav Kook did spend a good portion of the First World War in London, I do not think that we should dismiss Rav Kook's thoughts on the subject as being merely a reflection of the English optimism of the period whereby the "Great War," as it was called, was to be the "war to end all wars." In the case of Jewish nationalist aspirations, the war did result in the defeat of the Turks by the British and the latter's formal endorsement of the Jews' right to self-determination in Palestine ("the establishment in Palestine of a national home for the Jewish people"), as expressed in the Balfour Declaration of 1917. Rav Kook writes, "As Europe and Asia revolutionize their lifestyles, with the passing of the storm of war, a flow of new life, holy and fresh, will come to the elder of peoples – and its eyes and heart will be on the foundation of its life, the source of its flourishing, its native land, its homeland" (Zuriel, p. 942, par. 6).

Parenthetically, the selection in *Sinai*, originally entitled by Rav Zevi Yehudah Hakohen Kook *"Devarim Niḥumim"* ("Words of Comfort"), besides the material found in our section, *Ha-Milḥamah* ("The War"), includes many other pieces from the period of the First World War that may be read as a supplement to the discussion before us. See Zuriel, pp. 936-943. The fact that Rav Zevi Yehudah Kook felt his father's reflections written during the agony of the First World War could be meaningful to a Jewish Nation in the throes of World War II—"Holocaust"—is highly instructive. There are historians who would argue that World War II was the continuation of World War I. Jewishly speaking, this has enormous implications. We should not view our section, "The War," as restricted parochially to the First World War, when it was composed. Rav Kook is prophesying *The* War, the pre-Messianic war, referred to in the tradition as the War of Gog and Magog. (See *Megillah* 17b, "War is the beginning of the Redemption [*atḥalta di-ge'ulah*]"; *Midrash Tanḥuma*, end *Koraḥ*, "*Gog u-Magog* has the numerical value of seventy—they are the seventy nations.") Rav Kook has raised war to the level of a philosophic and existential category: "War as an absolute—fundamental, seminal—applied to the war of that generation, called 'the First World War'" (Rav Zevi Yehudah Hakohen Kook, in H. A. Shvarts, *Mi-Tokh ha-Torah ha-Go'elet* III, p. 195). Thus, Rav Zevi Yehudah Kook was perfectly justified in publicizing his father's vision of The War in 1943. Though Rav Kook, who passed away in 1935, did not witness World War II (he did refer to Hitler by name in his sermon on Rosh ha-Shanah 5694/1933, as a "*shofar* [horn] of an impure beast, turned into the *shofar* of Messiah, arousing the Redemption" – *Ma'amrei ha-RAYaH* I, p. 269), his interpretation of history, whereby world conflagration is designed to set in motion Jewish independence, certainly applies to this more recent chapter of Jewish history as well. Though for some the very idea is morally repugnant, there is no denying that the establishment of the State of Israel was the direct outcome of World War II.

Rav Ya'akov Moshe Ḥarlap, Rav Kook's eminent disciple, did live through World War II. At its conclusion, he charged the inhabitants of the D.P. camps: "Know and see that your gatherer is the Lord, God of Israel. Rally to His name. Throw off from yourselves the yoke of Exile, both exile of the soul and exile of the body. Distance yourselves from the air and soil of the Land of the Nations, from their impurity, their abominations. Settle in the holy and sanctifying air of our Holy Land, oxygen for souls" (*Imrei No'am* [Jerusalem: Beit Zevul, 5707/1947], pp. 6-7). I believe that essentially this would have been Rav Kook's response as well to the Holocaust.

In recent Halakhic literature there has been discussion whether martyrs of the Holocaust who were other than observant are to be considered as having died *'al kiddush hashem* (for the sanctification of the Name). See *'Or ha-Mizraḥ* 36:3-4 (April-July 1988):311-314. Rav Ḥarlap's answer is a most emphatic "yes," quoting *Sanhedrin* 47a. See Rav Y.M. Ḥarlap, *Imrei No'am*, p. 16.

63. *Siddur*, Morning Prayer, *Birkat Yotser*.

64. Psalm 23:4. In *SK* 6:103 the quote continues "for You are with me."

65. This may be an inversion of *Mo'ed Katan* 16b: "*'Adino ha-'Etsni* [refers to King David because] when he would sit and study Torah, he would soften himself as a worm, and when he would go out to war, he would harden himself as wood."

66. Cf. below, *Lights of Renascence*, beginning chap. 7.

67. "We left" (*'azavnu*). In *SK* 6:101: *hinaḥnu*. The meaning remains unchanged.

68. *Genesis Rabbah* 75:4; *Deuteronomy Rabbah* 1:20. The royal purple is symbolic of dominion. Jacob's sending it to Esau is an expression of Judaism temporarily relinquishing political power to the Nations for the duration of the Exile.

69. Genesis 33:14.

70. Song of Songs 2:12.

71. *Exodus Rabbah* 32:1; Rabbi Aaron Moses Friedensohn, *Nishmat Shelomo Mordekhai* (Johannisberg, 1853), 32a. Cf. Rabbi Obadiah Seforno, Numbers 1:2.

72. Isaiah 61:9.

73. This was also the observation of the prophet of atheism, Friedrich Nietzsche (who was *not*, let it be stressed, an antisemite) in his *Genealogy of Morals*. See our lengthy introduction above. Cf. below *Lights of Renascence*, chaps. 3 and 54.

74. In *Orot Yisrael* (in 1950 ed. *Orot*, p. 178, par. 1), Rav Kook calls Jewish History the *tamtsit* ("essence") of general history. Judah Halevi, *Kuzari* II, 36, wrote: "Israel among the nations is as the heart among the organs." Cf. *Orot ha-Kodesh* III, p. 117, where Rav Kook speaks of *Knesset Yisrael* in kabbalistic terms as being

"*Malkhut,* which has nothing of its own." (See Rabbi Moses Codovero, *Pardess Rimonim* 23:1, s.v. *Aspaklaryah.*) See Rabbi Mordechai Joseph Leiner of Izbica, *Mei ha-Shilo'ah* Pt. II (Lublin, 1922), *Tetse, 37d-38a*; B. Naor, *Avirin* (Jerusalem: Zur-Ot, 1980), pp. 26-27.

75. *Genesis Rabbah* 42:4.

76. In *SK* 6:152 the sentence concludes "Amen."

77. Written in St. Gallen, Switzerland in 1915-16, this would seem to be a reference to the formation in 1915 of the Zion Mule Corps (under the command of Trumpledor and Jabotinsky) attached to the British Army, which in 1917 morphed into the Jewish Legion. For Rav Kook's later involvement with the Legion during his days in London, see *Iggerot ha-RAYaH* III, pp. 134-8, 141-2, 282, and RZYH Kook, *Li-Sheloshah be-Ellul* I, chap. 65.

78. "And through all of this together" (*ve-'al-yedei kol zeh yaḥad*). The words are not found in *SK* 6:165.

79. "Of all the foundations of contemporary civilization" (*le-khol mekhonot ha-tarbut shel akhshav*). In *SK* 5:267 instead of this circumlocution we find simply: "Of all the contemporary civilized peoples" (*le-khol ha-'amim ha-tarbutiyim shel 'akhshav*).

80. In the original, the phrase is *malkhut 'elyonin kaddishin.* This is a rearrangement (and also slight Hebraization) of the Aramaic phrase in Daniel 7:18: *malkhuta kaddishei 'elyonin.*

81. "With peoples imbued with a new spirit" (*be-'amim ba'alei ru'aḥ ḥadasha*). In *SK* 5:267 simply: "with new peoples" (*be-'amim ḥadashim*).

82. "The new idolaters" (*ha-mit'halelim be-elilim ha-ḥadashim*). In *SK* 5:267: "the peoples of Europe who secretly profess idolatry" (*'amei Eropa ha-mit'halelim be-elilim be-seter levavam*).

83. The exact phrase *kos ha-tar'elah* ("the cup of poison") occurs in Isaiah 51:17, 22, but there it is used in reference to Israel. In reference to the Nations, we find the prophecy in Jeremiah 25:15-31 where the term used is *kos ha-ḥemah* ("the cup of wrath"). (In Isaiah ibid., *ḥemah* and *tar'elah* are used as synonyms.)

84. Jeremiah 50:25.

85. "This situation is but a moment in history" (*matsav zeh hu rig'i be-rig'ei ha-toladah*). This phrase does not occur in *SK* 5:267.

86. "Perforce" (*be-hekhraḥ*). The word is not found in *SK* 5:267.

87. Isaiah 2:20.

88. Isaiah 2:17.

89. Psalm 58:4.

90. "Nations" (*ha-le'umim*). In *SK* 5:267: "civilized nations" (*ha-le'umim ha-tarbutiyim*).

91. Isaiah 2:2.

92. Deuteronomy 4:7.

93. *Yalkut, Va-Etḥanan*, chap. 825.

94. Isaiah 60:2.

95. Ḥaggai 2:4-5.

96. Genesis 18:18.

97. "Forcefully and visibly *(be-tokef u-be-galuy)*. The words are not found in *SK* 5:64.

98. Exodus 3:14.

99. Deuteronomy 32:3.

100. See below, n. 103.

101. "In its clarity" *(bi-behiruto)*. So too in *Shemonah Kevatsim* 7:12. In the 1950 version, *bi-beḥirato*—"at its choicest."

102. Numbers 23:21.

103. In the Hebrew, *"Razei Torah la-ḥitsonim nimseru."* This theme is a *leitmotif* of the Lurianic rite of the midnight vigil, *Tikkun Ḥatsot*. Verily, the entire piece in *Orot* seems to have been written under the spell of *Tikkun Ḥatsot*. See Rabbi Ḥayyim Vital, *Sha'ar ha-Kavvanot* (5663), 58a; Rabbi Joseph Ḥayyim of Baghdad, *Ben Ish Ḥai*, Year One, sec. *Vayyishlaḥ*. Cf. *Otserot RaMḤaL* IV (B'nei Berak, 5746), *Iggerot*, pp. 330-331.

It is possible that this piece is one of many rejoinders in *Orot* to Christianity. Christianity is "some mystical enlightenment or faith" that would undermine the election of Israel (cf. below, *Israel and Its Renascence,* beginning chap. 9). In *Orot ha-Emunah,* p. 12, Rav Kook speaks at length of how Christianity appropriated the mystic, agadic elements of Judaism, while holding in total contempt the Halakha, or legal portion of Torah.

104. A metathesis. See Isaiah 61:3 and *Bava Batra* 60b.

105. See *Megillah* 29a: "Wherever Israel are exiled to, the *Shekhinah* is with them." See also *Berakhot* 3a: "Every day a heavenly voice coos as a dove, saying, 'Woe to children for whose sins I destroyed my House, burnt my Temple and exiled them among the nations!'" ... "The Holy One, blessed be He, shakes His head, saying, 'What good is it to a father who exiled his children, and woe to the children who were exiled from their father's table!'" Cf. *AT* (Jerusalem, 5743), p. 46.

Rav Y.M. Ḥarlap, eminent disciple of Rav Kook, in a letter addressed to Holocaust survivors in D.P. camps in Italy, entitled "*Naḥamu, Naḥamu 'Ami*" ("Comfort My People") holds up the ideal of empathizing with the pain of the *Shekhinah*.

(Published in pamphlet *Imrei No'am* [Jerusalem: Beit Zevul, 5707/1947], p. 10. See also *Imrei No'am*, pp. 20-21.)

106. "From the source of its joy" (*mi-mekor ta'anugeha*). In *SK* 7:12 there occurs here the additional word *mi-shelemutah* ("from its wholeness").

107. "The volitional spirit" (*ha-ru'aḥ ha-retsini*). In *SK* 7:12: *ha-ru'aḥ ha-retsoni*. It is doubtful whether the meaning is at all affected.

108. *Mishnah, Sukkah* 5:4. The initials of the Hebrew words *anu le-Yah ve-'eyneinu le-Yah* ("We are to the Lord and our eyes are [turned] to the Lord") form the word *Ellul*, the month of preparation before the *Yamim Nora'im* (Days of Awe, or High Holy Days, as they are known in English), which is reserved for return, *teshuvah*. See Rabbi Abraham Twersky, Maggid of Trisk (Turisk), *Magen Avraham* (Lublin, 1887) *Re'eh*, 80c.

YISRAEL U-TEḤIYATO (ISRAEL AND ITS RENASCENCE)

109. Isaiah 43:21: "This people which I have formed for myself shall relate my praise." This first piece in *Israel and Its Renascence* is a takeoff on this verse, which makes Israel's *raison d'être* its ability to recount the greatness of God.

110. Psalm 111:6.

111. Isaiah 43:12.

112. "Israel is full of" (*male hu yisra'el me-*). The words are not found in *SK* 5:66.

113. "Israel reflects this light in its spirit" (*yisra'el 'omed hu be-keren orah zo be-ruḥo*). In *SK* 5:66: "Israel stand in their spirit, in their lives" (*yisra'el 'omedim be-ruḥam, be-ḥayeihem*).

114. Psalm 144:12.

115. Psalm 144:13-15.

116. Psalm 20:9.

117. "By a rebellious picture" (*temunah sorerah*). In *SK* 5:66: "by a rebellious desire" (*ta'avah sorerah*).

118. "The beat of redemption" (*et halmut ge'ulato*). The words are not found in *SK* 5:66.

119. Psalm 111:6-9.

120. Job 26:7.

121. Psalm 95:4.

122. Deuteronomy 33:27.

123. Psalm 90:1-2.

124. *Siddur, Taḥanun, Ve-Hu Raḥum* (Penitential Prayer for Monday and Thursday mornings).

125. Psalm 80:3; *Talmud Yerushalmi, Sukkah* 4:3.

126. 2 Samuel 7:23; *Talmud Yerushalmi,* loc. cit.

127. Jeremiah 10:7.

128. Jeremiah 10:6.

129. Psalm 89:9-13.

130. Psalm 89:19.

131. Psalm 96:5.

132. A reversal of the order in *SK* 7:1: "the *causal* approach and the *ethical* approach."

In Lurianic Kabbalah (see R. Ḥayyim Vital, *'Ets Ḥayyim* 1:1:1, *Derush 'Iggulim ve-Yosher*), the two modalities of existence are termed *'Iggulim* (Circles) and *Yosher* (Line). The first mode of concentric circles is the "causality" of which Rav Kook speaks. The linear model symbolizes Ethics, again to use Rav Kook's terminology. (The Hebrew word, *yosher*, besides having geometric significance, also has the meaning of "rectitude," "righteousness," etc. Cf. the two meanings of the English word *straightness.*) Or so the Lithuanian Kabbalist, Rabbi Yitsḥak Eizik Ḥaver, explained the two alternate Lurianic models in his work, *Pitḥei She'arim, Netiv 'Iggulim ve-Yosher de-A"K,* chap. 3. Rav Kook follows this interpretation. See *Orot ha-Kodesh* III, pp. 24-25; IV (Jerusalem: Mosad Ha-Rav Kook, 1990), pp. 543-544. (Cf. R. David Cohen, *Kol ha-Nevu'ah* [Jerusalem: Mosad Ha-Rav Kook, 5739], pp. 287-288, quoting Rabbi M.H. Luzzatto, *KaLaḤ Pitḥei Ḥokhmah, Petaḥ* 9, 10, 12, 13, 17. It makes sense that Rabbi Y.E. Ḥaver's interpretation is an expansion of Rabbi M.H. Luzzato's earlier exegesis.)

Regarding Rav Kook's understanding of *'Iggulim ve-Yosher*, see now *Me'orot ha-RAYaH: Yeraḥ ha-Eitanim* (Jerusalem, 5755), p. 49.

Mordechai Pachter ("*'Iggulim ve-Yosher – le-toldotehah shel idea,*" *Da'at* [Winter 5747], pp. 69-83) has traced the stages of development of this symbolic approach to *'Iggulim* and *Yosher*, from RaMḤaL through the Gaon of Vilna (selections published at the end of the Commentary to *Sifra di-Tseni'uta*) and Rabbi Yitsḥak Eizik Ḥaver until Rav Kook. (The "missing link" between the Gaon and Rabbi Yitsḥak Eizik Ḥaver is not Rabbi Ḥayyim of Volozhin [cited by Pachter, pp. 73-74] but rather Rabbi Menaḥem Mendel of Shklov! See the latter's *Bei'urim ve-Likkutim*, printed in *Mayyim Adirim* [Jerusalem, 5747], p. 14.)

Pachter (p. 79) is correct that Rav Kook has adopted the Mitnagdic rather than Ḥasidic interpretation of *'Iggulim* and *Yosher*. However, his assertion that in this instance, Ḥabad remained with the literalist understanding of *'Iggulim ve-Yosher*, is not something I can subscribe to. According to Ḥabad as well, there is a valuational dimension to *'Iggulim ve-Yosher*. Though in Ḥasidism the focus is on *hassagah* rather than *hashgaḥah*, divine consciousness rather than divine historiosophy (*historiosofia di-mehemnuta,* to use R. Shim'on Starelitz's term, quoted in Neriyah, *Bisdeh ha-RAYaH,* p. 505), as in RaMḤaL and the Vilna Gaon's school, nevertheless *'Iggulim* and *Yosher* definitely are not without moral connotations. See e.g., R. Shelomo Zalman of Kopyst, *Magen Avot, Ḥukkat,* 47d-48a, where it is explained that Torah and *mitsvot* are a function of the *Kav;* the *ba'al teshuvah* or penitent, having so to speak "burned his bridges," must reach to the higher, pre-Torah level of the *'Iggul ha-Gadol* (the Great Circle). And see Rabbi Menaḥem Mendel of Lubavitch *(Zemaḥ Zedek), Derekh Mitsvotekha* (Brooklyn, 5733), *Mitsvat Korban Pesaḥ,* 77a, who based on *'Ets Ḥayyim,* writes: "The source of the *'Iggulim* is the *'Iggul ha-Gadol* ... and the source of *Yosher* is the *Kav.*" (Cf. Rabbi Shneur Zalman of Liadi, *Likkutei Torah, Koraḥ,* 52c and Rabbi Menaḥem Mendel of Shklov, ibid.) For other interpretations of *'Iggulim ve-Yosher,* see Rabbi Zadok Hakohen Rabinowitz of Lublin, *Resisei Laylah,* chap. 15; idem, *Likkutei Ma'amarim* (in *Divrei Soferim*), 98b-l00d; and B. Naor, *Avirin* (Jerusalem: Zur Ot, 5740), pp. 13-15.

In this piece, Rav Kook means to convey that beyond the outer shell of existence, the external physical laws of the universe, which appear to be totally oblivious to the deeds and misdeeds of Man, there is an internal, ethical apparatus at work which relates directly to human morality, and in which Israel plays a central role. Rabbi Yitsḥak Eizik Ḥaver points out that Israel is also referred to as "*Yeshurun,*" from the word *yosher. Pitḥei She'arim,* Pt. I (Warsaw, 1888), *Netiv 'Iggulim ve-Yosher de-A"K,* chap. 3, foonote on f.11r. (Cf. RAYH Kook, *Orot Yisrael* 1:7, reprinted in 1950 edition of *Orot,* p. 140.)

Earlier, MaHaRaL of Prague connected *Yeshurun* to *yosher,* see *Tif'eret Yisrael,* chap. 11. In that chapter, MaHaRaL deals with the question why ultimately it is more beneficial to study the laws of God's Torah than astrophysics. MaHaRaL's answer, which we won't delve into here, is that Torah is referred to as *yosher* ("straightness"). (Cf. MaHaRaL, *'Or Ḥadash* [B'nei Berak: Yahadut, 5732], pp. 218-220.)

Rabbi J.B. Soloveitchik of Boston once pointed out the difference between the first two blessings of *Shema', Yotser 'Or* and *Ahavah Rabbah.* The first blessing focuses on the Cosmos. Dissatisfied with the "silent" panorama, the worshiper breaks through in the second blessing to Torah, where he finds himself addressed by a world of meaning. Cf. R. Meir Leibush Malbim's commentary to Psalm 19, where the first, cosmic half of the psalm is contrasted to the second half which speaks of Torah. Regarding the collapse of the two "tracks" – causal and ethical (Rav Kook's terminology) – into one, see Malbim, Psalm 36:6. (It seems that Rabbi J.B. Soloveitchik has been preceded by Rabbi Abraham Bornstein of Sokhatchov, author *Avnei Nezer.* See *Ne'ot ha-Deshe,* ed. Aaron Israel Bornstein, Vol. I [Tel-Aviv, 5743], p. 39.)

133. "Freedom" (*ḥofesh*). In *SK* 7:1: "freedom and full light" (*ḥofesh ve-'or maleh*).

134. "Is weakened" (*mitḥaleshet*). In *SK* 7:2: "all is weakened" (*ha-kol mitḥalesh*).

135. This same thought was expressed by the late Rabbi Joseph David Epstein: "If they tell you there is in the world a sentiment of justice, ethical nobility, ethical wisdom – believe; if they tell you there is in the world a Torah of ethical justice – do not believe. Perhaps somewhere the world did merit a strain of ethical justice, but it never merited Torah – a judicial system of ethical justice. An iron curtain divides between the world's Law and Ethics; they are two separate domains" (*Mitsvot ha-Mussar* [New York: Torat HaAdam, 1973], p. 37). Rabbi Epstein devoted a lifetime to producing a veritable encyclopedia of what he termed *Mussar ha-Halakha* (the Ethics of Halakha). The volumes cover the Home *(Mitsvot ha-Bayit),* Peace *(Mitsvot ha-Shalom),* and Counseling *(Mitsvot ha-'Etsah).* The mandate for his approach he found in the legacy of Rabbi Israel Salanter, founder of the Mussar movement in Eastern Europe; Rabbi Israel Meir Kagan *(Ḥafets Ḥayyim);* and Rabbi Abraham Isaiah Karelitz *(Ḥazon Ish),* the sage of B'nei Berak. See *Mitsvot ha-Mussar* (premier volume in the set), pp. 11, 53-56, 72-73. See also Rabbi Elie Benamozegh, *Morale juive et morale chretienne* (Neuchatel, 1946); Rabbi Moshe Avigdor Amiel, *Ethics and Legality in Jewish Law* (*Ha-zedek ha-soziali ve-ha-zedek ha-mishpati ve-ha-mussari shelanu*) trans. Menaḥem and Bracha Slae (Jerusalem: Rabbi Amiel Library, 5752/1992); Alan L. Mittleman, *Between Kant and Kabbalah: An Introduction to Isaac Breuer's Philosophy of Judaism* (Albany: State University of New York Press, 1990), pp. 146-149.

136. "On us internally" (*be-kirbenu penimah*). In *SK* 6:290: "on our innermost desires" (*be-ma'avayenu penimah*).

137. Proverbs 3:6.

138. *Berakhot* 63a.

139. Sages who have been ritually ordained to rule in matters of law *(semukhim)* are referred to in the Torah as *elohim*. See Exodus 22:8; *Bava Kamma* 84b, Rashi s.v. *elohim be'inan*. In context, the word *elohim* means "judges" (see Onkelos, Exodus, ibid.; also Rashi, *Sanhedrin* 2b, s.v. *i kasavar 'eruv parshiyot*), but Rav Kook interprets it as relating to *Elohim*, God. According to Ibn Ezra, Exodus 21:6, the judges are referred to as *elohim* because they "enact the laws of God on earth." (Cf. Ibn Ezra, Exodus 4:14: "the holy ones below who execute God's laws on earth.") Naḥmanides (Exodus 21:6) differs, saying that *Elohim* should be taken in a literal sense as meaning God, for He is present in the Court of Law. (Cf. Naḥmanides, Exodus 22:27.) Consult further Ibn Ezra, Genesis 1:1, Exodus 3:4, and R. Avraham Lifshitz, *Hadorom* 59 (Ellul 5750): 139-140, who cites R. Shmuel Zarza, *Mekor Ḥayyim* (Mantua, 5319/1559), 4a: "*Elo'ah* is the term for God .... Mortal judges and leaders are called *elohim* because they behave in a godly manner and functionally resemble God." See also Rabbi Ḥayyim of Volozhin, *Nefesh ha-Ḥayyim* I, 2. According to Maimonides (*Guide* I, 2; II, 6), the case is just the opposite: the primary meaning of *elohim* is "judge" or "leader"; its use for God is derivative. Yehudah Halevi (*Kuzari* IV, 1) assumes *elohim* to be an equivocal term

for both the heavenly and earthly judge. See R. Yehudah Moscato, *Kol Yehudah* ad locum. See Abravanel's refutation of Maimonides in his commentary to Genesis 1:1. I have dealt with the significance of the term *elohim* for judges in my study, "*Beit-Din be-Erets Yisrael u-be-Bavel*" in B. Naor, *Ben Shanah Sha'ul* (Jerusalem: Zur-Ot, 5755/1995), pp. 257-258.

140. *Sanhedrin* 14a.

141. "When it was first instituted in the nation." These words are not found in *SK* 6:290.

142. One of Rav Kook's abiding concerns is the divine character of halakhic jurisprudence. See RAYH Kook, *Orot Yisrael* 8:2 (reprinted in 1950 edition of *Orot*, p. 168); *Orot ha-Torah* 4:4; idem, *Be'er Eliyahu* (Rav Kook's commentary to *Bei'ur ha-GRA, Ḥoshen Mishpat*) ḤM 26:1 (p. 228); idem, *AT* (Jerusalem, 5743), pp. 93-94; Zuriel, *Otserot ha-RAYaH* II, pp. 870-873; *Ginzei RAYaH* II, pp. 19-20; *Shemu'ot ha-RAYaH* (ms.), *Yitro*, 5689/1929; *Mishpatim*, 5690/1930. See further *Sikkumei Siḥot ha-Rav Zevi Yehudah: "'Ezrat Kohen,"* ed. Ilan Tor and Shelomo Ḥayyim Aviner, pp. 25-26; Rabbi S.H. Aviner, *Tal Ḥermon* (Jerusalem, 5745), pp. 115-116; 387-388 (quoting Rabbi Eliezer Waldman). Cf. Rabbi Ya'akov Leiner of Izbica, *Beit Ya'akov* II (Lublin, 1903), *Mishpatim* 138c-140d; Isaac Breuer, *Naḥliel* (Jerusalem: Mosad Ha-Rav Kook, 1982), p. 313.

143. "And the search for God came together with Israelite jurisprudence." These words are not found in *SK* 6:290.

144. Exodus 18:15-16.

145. True *semikhah*, which entitles a sage to serve in the Sanhedrin or High Court, applies only in the Land of Israel. See Maimonides, *Hilkhot Sanhedrin* 4:4, 6, 11.

146. The Hebrew reads, *Minut* (Heresy). This is the rabbinic term for Christianity. See Rashi, *Berakhot* 12b, s.v. *minut; Berakhot* 28b; Maimonides, MT, *Hilkhot Tefillah* 2:1; and RZYH Kook, *LNY* II (Jerusalem, 5739), p. 230. See also our Introduction.

147. Rav Kook has some choice words for Christianity, the "religion of love" that gave precedence to the "forty-eight prophets" (see *Megillah* 14a) over the Torah of Moses. Quoted by RZYH Kook in *Sikkumei Siḥot ha-Rav Zevi Yehudah*, ed. Tor and Aviner, p. 29, and Shvarts, *Mi-Tokh ha-Torah ha-Go'elet* III, p. 225. See too RZYH Kook, *LNY* II, pp. 60-61. The kernel of the idea is a *remez* or pun on Exodus 22:1: *maḥteret* = *maḥ-teret*. See now *Kevatsim mi-Khetav Yad Kodsho*, ed. Boaz Ofen (Jerusalem, 5766/2006), *Pinkas Rishon le-Yaffo*, par. 43 (p. 98). Regarding Christianity as *geneivah*, spiritual theft, see below, chap. 6.

148. In *SK* 5:98 the words "the light of the Lord" (*'or Adonai*) are not found.

149. 2 Samuel 23:1.

150. Psalm 9:9.

151. The reference is to Christianity, which with Paul's Epistle to the Galatians, removed the barrier to Christianity becoming a world religion suited to non-Jews, by neutralizing the specifically Judaic content of the original "Heresy," i.e., Christianity. Cf. the uncensored text of Maimonides, MT, *Hilkhot Melakhim* 11:4.

Concerning Paul (Saul of Tarsus), see *IHR* I, p. 103: "The idea conceived by the one who went out to teach statutes prematurely to those of whom it is said, "laws they did not know" – resulted in their carrying the banner of statutes of faith without relation to the overall order of life, especially the communal. It was inevitable that they would be confused. They were confounded in belief (approaching idolatry), and in deed, not reaching the characteriological refinement worthy of those who profess to carry the banner of love and kindness."

"Paul had his problems and a good psychiatrist reading Paul's Epistles would find him mixed up in his thinking. Jesus was preaching the Old Testament. It was Paul that made the changes" (*Grauel/Rev. John Stanley Grauel: An Autobiography As Told To Eleanor Elfenbein* [Freehold; NJ: Ivory House; 1983], p. 155).

152. Cf. Isaiah 24:12.

153. Christianity makes the claim that it is *Verus Israel*, "True Israel." See Edward H. Flannery, *The Anguish of the Jews* (New York: Macmillan, 1979), p. 35: "The people the Church claimed to have supplanted, continued to co-exist and, more important, laid claim to the same sources of faith, asserting its anteriority and its title to the Old Testament ... the Church had to prove to the gentiles – and to the Jews – that it was the true Israel, that Judaism was a pretender that refused to abdicate a lost kingdom – and all this from Judaic sources." See Flannery's accompanying note 34.

154. In *SK* 5:32 "of the Lord" (*Adonai*) is not found.

155. Isaiah 43:21.

156. Genesis 14:19.

157. Numbers 23:9.

158. Deuteronomy 32:12.

159. *Shabbat* 88a.

160. *Avot* 3:14.

161. *Genesis Rabbah* 1:1.

162. Isaiah 30:26.

163. In *Orot*, *minut* (heresy). In *SK* 5:32 stated explicitly: *notsriyut* (Christianity).

Cf. *Ma'amrei ha-RAYaH* II, p. 421. Paul's Letter to the Galatians, which abolished circumcision, spelled a significant turning point in Church doctrine. See above n. 151.

164. "From our religion" (*mi-datenu*). In *SK* 5:32: "from us" (*me-'itanu*).

165. Cf. *Bava Batra* 74a: "Come, I will show you where earth and heaven kiss." See RZYH Kook quoted in Shvarts, *Mi-Tokh ha-Torah ha-Go'elet* IV, p. 107. Parenthetically, Abraham Abulafia wrote: "The heavens will be earth, and the earth will be heavenly" (*Sefer ha-Ot,* ed. Jellinek, III).

166. "And all their hosts" (*ve-khol tseva'am*). In *SK* 5:32: "and all existence" (*ve-khol ha-yekum*).

167. Isaiah 14:22.

168. Psalm 112:4.

169. Rav Kook holds up the holism of Judaism versus the dualism of Christianity. See further B. Naor, *Emunat 'Itekha* (Jerusalem: Zur Ot, 5747), pp. 125-126. Many authors have interpreted the *halakha* that a non-Jew may only bring an *'olah* (burnt-offering) while an Israelite may also sacrifice a *shelamim* (peace-offering), as symbolic of the non-Jewish world's inability to harmonize spiritual and material realms. The non-Jewish approach to spirituality is extreme: total consumption on the divine altar. The Jewish approach is holistic: part of the sacrifice is burnt while the rest is reserved for human consumption. See *Zevaḥim* 116a; *Menaḥot* 73b; Maimonides, MT, *Hilkhot Ma'aseh ha-Korbanot* 3:3; Rashi, Leviticus 3:1 quoting *Sifra*; Naḥmanides, Leviticus 19:5; Rav Kook, quoted in *Be-Shemen Ra'anan: Rabbi Shalom Nathan Ra'anan-Kook Memorial Volume* (Jerusalem, 5750), p. 203; Rabbi Zadok Hakohen Rabinowitz of Lublin, *Peri Zaddik, Vayyigash,* 101a; *Bo,* 27a; Rabbi Samuel Aaron Rubin, *Zera' Yishai,* commentary to *Pesikta* (B'nei Berak, 5729), *Va-yehi be-yom kelot* (5:4), p. 374, s.v. *'olot hikrivu b'nei no'aḥ;* Rabbi Samuel Bornstein of Sokhatchov, *Shem mi-Shemuel* (Jerusalem, 5734), *Yitro*, Year 5675 (p. 268); Rabbi Samuel Wolk, *Sha'arei Tohar,* vol. VI, Introduction; B. Naor, *Ba-Yam Derekh* (Jerusalem: Zur Ot, 5744), p. 174.

170. The Hebrew term is *shituf* (syncretism), a term that has a very troubled *halakhic* history. There are Ashkenazic *poskim* (decisors) who have ruled that *shituf,* combining belief in God with some other entity, is halakhically permissible for non-Jews. However, the entire basis for this in the sources is extremely shaky. See B. Naor, *Ger toshav be-hagut Rabbi Eliyahu Benamozegh, Sinai* 88 (Shevat-Adarim 5741): 260-261; reprinted in B. Naor, *Ba-Yam Derekh* (Jerusalem: Zur Ot, 5744), pp. 74-76; B. Naor, "*Ve-Zaraḥ mi-se'ir lamo: Ha-Notsrut bi-re'i ha-yahadut*" (unpublished paper). See the recent discussion by Rabbi Yitsḥak Hutner, *Sefer ha-Zikaron le-Maran Ba'al "Paḥad Yitsḥak,"* pp. 269-272, demolishing the theory.

It is my understanding that Rabbi Eliyahu Zini of Ḥaifa is readying for publication a superior edition of Rabbi Benamozegh's *Israel et l'Humanite.* I am told that it will shed new light on the latter's view of Christianity. The previous edition of *Israel et l'Humanite* (Paris: Albin Michel, 1961) and its Hebrew version *Yisrael ve-ha-Enoshut* (Jerusalem: Mosad Ha-Rav Kook, 5727/1967), scandalized the Orthodox world. Rav Zevi Yehudah Hakohen Kook had the last-mentioned volume removed from the library of Yeshivat Merkaz Ha-Rav. To date, see *Oeuvres completes du rabbin Elie Benamozegh*, ed. Eliyahu Zini, Vol. I: *Morale juive et morale chretienne* (Jerusalem: Erez, 2002).

See in support of the *shituf* theory, Mordechai Dov Friedenthal, *Yesod ha-Dat* I (subtitled *Migdol 'Oz*) (Breslau, 5582/1822), 46a; and Hermann Cohen, *Religion of Reason* (New York: Frederick Ungar, 1972), p. 239.

Objectively, the only inkling I ever gleaned from a *rishon* (early halakhic authority) that there may be a different standard for non-Jewish belief is the statement by Rabbi Abba Mari Moshe ben Yosef Ha-Yarḥi (Don Astruc) in his *Minḥat Kena'ot* (Pressburg, 1838), chap. 14 (p. 15), that a non-Jew is not required by the "Seven Noahide Commandments" to believe in the creation of the world but may subscribe, as did Aristotle, to the belief that the world is pre-eternal. Cf. Rabbi Ya'akov Kamenecki, *Emet le-Ya'akov, Nashim-Nezikin* II (New York, 5749), pp. 9b-10a.

We have already seen (viz. Introduction) that Rav Kook inveighs with the ruling of Maimonides that Christianity is considered classic *'avodah zarah* (idolatry) and forbidden to non-Jews as well. (See RZYH Kook, quoted in Ḥayyim A. Shvarts, *Mi-Tokh ha-Torah ha-Go'elet* III [Jerusalem: Zur Ot, 5747], pp. 39-40; IV [Jerusalem: Zur Ot, 5751], pp. 312-313.) The way to square Rav Kook's present statement with that halakhic posture is by saying that Rav Kook – as Yehudah Halevi, Maimonides himself, and Naḥmanides – viewed Christianity, despite its pagan elements, as playing a part in paving the way for Messiah, by familiarizing billions of the earth's inhabitants with the words of Scripture and some basic (albeit highly distorted) conception of Torah and *mitsvot*. See Yehudah Halevi, *Kuzari* 4:23; Maimonides, MT, *Hilkhot Melakhim* 11:4 (in uncensored editions); Naḥmanides, *Torat Hashem Temimah*, in *Kitvei Ramban*, ed. C.D. Chavel (Jerusalem: Mosad Ha-Rav Kook, 5728), I, 143-144. This very possibly was the talmudic sage Rav Yitsḥak's intention when he uttered this statement: "The Son of David will not come until the entire kingdom will be converted to Heresy (Christianity)" (*Sanhedrin* 97a in uncensored editions). Cf. too Rav's statement (*Sanhedrin* 98b): "The Son of David will not come until the evil kingdom will expand over the entire world nine months" (censored editions delete the word "evil"). Rav Kook, *Orot ha-Emunah*, p. 11, reads for "evil kingdom" – "Heresy," i.e., Christianity. See also Mishnah, *Sotah* 9:15: "The kingdom will be converted to heresy." When in 329 C.E. Emperor Constantine converted to Christianity, the Roman Empire became the vehicle for Christianity's domination of the world.

171. *Leviticus Rabbah* 13:5: "Just as a swine, when it crouches, kicks out its feet, and says, See that I am pure! – so the Kingdom of Edom," etc.; *Midrash Tehillim*, chap. 80; MaHaRaL of Prague, *Ner Mitsvah* (B'nei Berak: Yahadut, 5732), p. 18. The swine based on external appearances alone is a pure species, for its hooves are split; what makes it non-kosher is the fact that internally, it does not chew its cud. This image of the swine extending its feet as if to boast of its purity, has carried over into Yiddish, where "*ḥazir feess*" ("swine feet") is an expression for a hypocrite.

172. "To whose height" (*le-rumo*). In *SK* 5:33: "to whose glory" (*li-khevodo*).

173. "Lowered and debased" (*makh ve-nishpal*). In *SK* 5:33: "corporealized and lowered" (*mugsham ve-nishpal*).

174. Psalm 74:18.

175. Psalm 10:17.

176. *Shabbat* 104a; *Tikkunei Zohar, tikkun* 22.

177. Rabbi Ḥayyim Vital, *Likkutei Torah* (Vilna, 1880), 1 Kings 3:16 (113a); Rabbi M.H. Luzzatto, *Otserot Ramḥal* IV (B'nei Berak, 5746), *Pinḥas*, p. 106; idem, *Adir ba-Marom* II (Jerusalem, 5748), p. 115. Cf. above note 147. See *Orot ha-Teshuvah* 12:10 and Shvarts, *Mi-Tokh ha-Torah ha-Go'elet* III, p. 199. "Europe acquired the word of God through the muddy channel of Christianity which had been sullied by paganism, and lost the relic of treasure she stole from the Eternal People. Darkness covers these people who boasted that they had taken the light of Israel and placed it in their vessels. Our essential culture, in which no nation of the world is our partner…" (*IHR* I, p. 214).

178. *Berakhot* 9a; *Pesaḥim* 119a. I believe the correct interpretation of what Rav Kook is saying here, is as follows: The nations of the world through the vehicle of Christianity have ingested certain moral and ethical elements of Judaism that are really foreign to their nature. These elements Rav Kook refers to as "*orot genuvim*" ("stolen lights"). At a certain point, the Nations' natural instincts will reject the entire sham of the so-called "Judeo-Christian tradition." This will spell an unparalleled spasm of antisemitism, whereby the alien Jewish entity will be spewed out. Thereby Judaism will take back that which was plundered from it, in terms of bodies, souls, and spiritual baggage. Hence, the purging of the Nations will result in the spiritual enrichment of Israel. This is the opposite side of the Nietzschean scenario. Nietzsche thought only of the benefit to European civilization that would result from breaking the yoke of Judeo-Christian morality; he was not equipped to consider how that disentanglement would eventuate a purer, stronger Judaism.

Writing to the survivors of the Holocaust, Rav Ya'akov Moshe Ḥarlap, companion and closest disciple to Rav Kook, touched on the enormous historical processes that were taking place:

> Woe to these oppressors who are blind, oblivious to what is happening to them and what motivates them to do all this. If they were wise, they would understand the outcome, they would appreciate the curse waiting for them. More than they do to us, they do to themselves. They think to ascend, and they descend. They think to build and they are destroyed; to live, and they are undone by their sins.
>
> However, that which is hidden from the oppressing nations and from the indifferent who laugh at our misfortune, is revealed to Israel, His holy

nation. From the beginning, we have known that at the End of Days, at the time the Lord will hasten to redeem those waiting for His salvation, to gather His sheep and settle them in His Land of Delight, there will arise Hamans and Amaleks, who – through the Lord's mercy to his devout – have been scattered over several generations.... Truly their entire uprising and hatred are but death-throes before they perish totally from the world. Our suffering is the result of the kicking out of their feet that comes from their final twitches ...

At that time they will be nauseated by every glimmer of light and will choose to live in darkness and the shadow of death. They will vomit that which was bestowed upon them of Israel's influence and discerning light. The beginning of their way of folly will be shaking off all contact they had with Israel – blow after blow, in order to be separated from Israel and all its qualities. This itself will be their curse, for every disengagement from Israel is a disengagement from life. For us, Israel, His holy people, it will be a blessing. Thereby will be fulfilled the prophecy, "I shall separate you from the peoples to be Mine." To be separated from them and their multitudes, and also to salvage all the good, the pleasant fields of Israel, which were damaged and spiritually lessened by entering into the territory of strangers; to purify them and return them to the source of their holiness (Rav Y.M. Ḥarlap, *Imrei No'am* [Jerusalem: Beit Zevul, 5707/1947], pp. 14-16).

179. Proverbs 7:5.

180. Proverbs 7:27.

181. Proverbs 5:5.

182. Proverbs 7:22; *'Avodah Zarah* 17.

183. In *IHR* I, p. 226, Rav Kook refers to Christianity as "the daughter who bites her mother's [= Judaism's] breasts." So much for the "daughter religion"!

184. Perhaps reminiscent of Psalm 62:8, 9, 12.

185. Psalm 111:6.

186. *Makkot* 24a.

187. Exodus 20:2; Deuteronomy 5:6.

188. Exodus 20:3; Deuteronomy 5:7.

189. As opposed to Christian dualism's distrust of the body, holistic Judaism has a healthy outlook on physicality. The power of Torah is not antithetical to the power of Creation and Nature; rather it is the identical power.

190. *Sifré* to Numbers 15:7 and 28:8; Rashi, *Zevaḥim* 46b, s.v. *ha-naḥat ru'aḥ*.

191. "A power of destruction and obliteration" (*gevurat ḥurban ve-kilayon*). In *SK* 5:35: "to the point of destruction" (*'ad lekhaleh*). Cf. 2 Chronicles 31:1.

192. "Full" (*mele'ah*). In *SK* 5:35: "made" (*'asuyah)*.

193. *Sefer Yetsirah* 6:2: "Good accentuates evil and evil accentuates good." Cf. *OHK* II, p. 475; *Orot ha-Teshuvah* 9:9.

194. "Which will never end—that keeps us alive" (*she-lo tipasek la-'ad, hi mekayyemet u-meḥayyah otanu*). In *SK* 5:35: "which will not end, and forever keeps us alive" (*she-lo tipasek, ve-la'ad hi mekayyemet u-meḥayyah otanu*).

195. Psalm 20:8, 9.

196. In *SK* 5:35 the words "and all glows with the appearance of redemption" (*ve-ha-kol noher hofa'at ge'ulah*) are not found.

197. "The critique" (*havrakat ha-bikoret*). In *SK* 5:35: "the sharp critique" (*ḥarifut ha-bikoret*).

198. "Truthful recognition" (*hakarat ha-emet*). In *SK* 5:35: "holy recognition" (*hakarat ha-kodesh*).

199. Ezekiel 38:23.

200. Isaiah 54:3-5.

201. Psalm 73:25; *Yalkut Shim'oni, Ḥukkat,* chap. 759.

202. "Divine oaths" (*shevu'ot 'elyon*). In *SK* 5:36: "eternal oaths" (*shevu'ot 'olamim*).

203. According to Christian doctrine, as a result of the Jewish Nation's manifold sins, it is no longer God's Chosen People! See *Ma'amrei ha-RAYaH* II, pp. 421-422.

204. Christianity did away with circumcision. See note 163 above.

205. Probably based on the narrative in *Ketubot* 112a wherein "that heretic" (in uncensored editions of the Talmud) tells Rav Zeira that the Jews are being hasty about entering the Land.

206. Isaiah 45:7. In *Ma'amrei ha-RAYaH* II, pp. 421-422, Rav Kook gives two reasons God ordained the Exile: (1) to make known His supervision over His people in exile as well; (2) that *kedushah* (holiness) impact the most mundane plane of existence and uplift it to the level of spirit. This touches on the *sod ha-yiḥud,* the Secret of Unity, whereby it is revealed that all the different and seemingly irreconcilable dimensions of reality – Law/Love; Flesh/Spirit – are brought into existence by God and subsumed in His unity. Furthermore, says Rav Kook, this demonstrates His omnipotence, for all the possible powers of opposition, of Evil, have been unleashed on the world and have been revealed to be nothing more than divine lackeys. This *sod ha-yiḥud,* evidently, was acquired from Rabbi Moses Ḥayyim Luzzatto's work, *Da'at Tevunot*. (See *Da'at Tevunot*, ed. Rabbi Ḥayyim Friedlander [B'nai Berak, 5735], pp. 26-31, 185-187.) In his essay, *Le-mahalakh ha-ide'ot be-yisrael* (reprinted in 1950 edition of *Orot,* p. 115), Rav Kook reasons that God ordained the Exile to demonstrate the nonrestriction of God to geopolitical boundaries. He bases himself on the verse in Malachi 1:5. Cf. Hermann Cohen, *Religion of Reason*, trans. Simon Kaplan (New York: Frederick Ungar, 1972), pp. 242-244, 251-253. See too B. Nyer (Naor), *In tiefkeit fun golus*

(poem), in *Reshit Oni* I (New York, 5735), pp. 92-94. In one of his earliest works, *'Eyn Ayah,* Rav Kook reasons that the Exile was designed to bring to Israel's awareness that the essence of its national identity is divine, not geopolitical. See *Eretz Tzvi: Tzvi Glatt Memorial Volume*, pp. 169-170.

Before Rav Kook, R. Judah Löw (MaHaRaL of Prague) responded to the Christian attempt to impugn the divine election of Israel by advancing the notion that the Jewish People have not been chosen for any specific reason. Israel's election is essential and thus irrevocable. God's love for Israel is an unconditional love (*"ahavah she-einah teluyah be-davar").* See MaHaRaL, *Netsaḥ Yisrael,* chap. 11, and *Derekh Ḥayyim* to *Avot* 5:17. Regarding this fundamental belief of MaHaRaL, see *Ma'amrei ha-RAYaH* I (Jerusalem, 5740/1980), p. 59 (reprinted from *Yashuv Mishpat* [Klusz/Klausenberg, 5682/1922]). Rabbi M.H. Luzzatto also took up the Christian challenge in *Da'at Tevunot,* pp. 15-17.

207. Jeremiah 10:16.

208. *Genesis Rabbah* 11:5; *Tikkunei Zohar,* beginning *tikkun* 24; *Tikkunei Zohar Ḥadash* (Vilna, 5627), 25c; Rabbi Ḥayyim Vital, *'Ets Ḥayyim, Sha'ar ha-Melakhim,* end chap. 7.

209. Deuteronomy 4:35.

210. *Sanhedrin* 67b; *Hullin* 7b.

211. "Force, external or spiritual, internal" (*hagbarah ḥitsonit o ruḥanit penimit*). In *SK* 5:36: "spiritual, internal force" (*hagbarah ruḥanit penimit*). The words "external or" (*ḥitsonit o*) are not found.

212. Zechariah 9:9. A description of Messiah's arrival.

213. Daniel 7:13. A very different description of Messiah's arrival. See *Sanhedrin* 98a.

214. *Pesaḥim* 54a; *Genesis Rabbah* 1:4.

215. *Mo'ed Katan* 28a; *Genesis Rabbah* 49:11.

"The red heifer atones." In the 1920 edition of *Orot*, as in *SK* 5:51: "The red heifer, atonement is written in regard to it" (*parah adumah, kaparah ketiv bah*). Changed in the 1950 edition of *Orot* to *"parah adumah mekhaperet,"* to conform to the text of *Mo'ed Katan* 28a.

216. We are given here a brief glimpse of Rav Kook's theory of immortality that comes to full view in *Orot ha-Kodesh,* in the section entitled (with Rav Kook's approval – see *OHK* I, Intro., p. 19) "*Ḥayyim 'ad ha-'olam*" (Eternal Life). See also *Orot ha-Teshuvah* 11:3. This theory has intrigued such a professional philosopher as Shmuel Hugo Bergman. (See Dov Schwarz, *"Ha-zikah shel Shmuel Hugo Bergman le-mishnat ha-Rav,"* *Zikhron RAYaH* [Jerusalem: Mosad Ha-Rav Kook, 1986], pp. 229-230.) See *OHK* II, pp. 371-386, and *Be-Shemen Ra'anan: R. Shalom Nathan Ra'anan-Kook Memorial Volume* (Jerusalem, 5750), p. 205. This is the

sharpest, most startling statement of Rav Kook's position: "Death is an illusion, its impurity is its lie; what people refer to as death, is but the overpowering of life" (*OHK* II, p. 380). (See also RAYH Kook, *Resh Millin, "Azla Geresh."*)

Cf. Anonymous, *Ma'arekhet ha-Elohut* (Mantua, 5318/1558), chap. 10 (141b); Rabbi Shneur Zalman of Liadi, *Likkutei Torah, Ḥukkat*, 61c-d, s.v. *ve-hizah*; Rabbi Zadok Hakohen Rabinowitz of Lublin, *Peri Zaddik* II (Lublin, 5667/1907), *Parashat Parah*, f.105; Rabbi Gershon Ḥanokh Leiner of Radzyn, *Sod Yesharim* (Warsaw, 5662), *Erev Yom Kippur*, 63d.

See too the later Jewish thinkers, Isaac Breuer, *Naḥliel* (Jerusalem: Mosad Ha-Rav Kook, 1982), pp. 78-79, 114-116, and Eric Gutkind, *Choose Life* (New York: Schuman, 1952), pp. 280-286.

In terms of the textual basis for Rav Kook's perception of the Red Heifer as removing not only the stigma of death but death itself, I believe Rav Kook arrived at this conclusion in the following manner. According to the Midrash, the Red Heifer atones for the sin of the Golden Calf:

> A maid's son soiled the palace of the King.
> Said the King: Let his mother come and clean the mess.
> So said the Holy One: Let the Heifer come and atone for the Calf.
> (*Pesikta, Parah,* 14:14).

But in the entire ritual of *Parah Adumah,* there is not the slightest indication of this atonement. (However, see R. Moshe Hadarshan cited in Rashi, Numbers 19:22 and the expanded version in the *Siluk* for *Parashat Parah*, beginning *Ein le-soḥe'aḥ.*) The connection between the Cow and the Calf must lie on a deeper level. Were it not for the sin of the Golden Calf, after the theophany on Mount Sinai the Hebrews were slated for eternal life as in Eden of old (*'Avodah Zarah* 5a). (See Rabbi Moshe Alsheikh, *Torat Moshe,* beginning *Ḥukkat.*) The true rectification of the flaw of the Golden Calf must subsist in the elimination of the very phenomenon of death. Ergo, concludes Rav Kook, the Red Heifer not only "cleanses from the impurity of death," it "is linked to the removal of death from its very foundation."

217. Rashi, Genesis 1:11; *Talmud Yerushalmi, Kil'ayim* 1:7; *Genesis Rabbah* 5:9. The earth was commanded to produce trees whose wood would have the same taste as their fruits. Having disobeyed, the earth was cursed along with Adam and Eve (Genesis 3:17). Rav Kook (*Orot ha-Teshuvah* 6:7; 14:7; *OHK* III, pp. 140, 244) interprets "fruits" as symbolic of ends, while "wood" represents means. The *tikkun* of this particular flaw will consist in raising the means to the spiritual level of the end.

218. *Ḥullin* 60b; *Genesis Rabbah* 6:3; *Pirkei de-Rabbi Eliezer*, chap. 6. Originally sun and moon were the same size, "the two great luminaries" (Genesis 1:16). As a result of the moon's accusation ("It is impossible for two kings to wear the same crown!"), the Holy One shrunk the moon's size. Rav Kook (*OHK* I, pp.

253-254) understands sun and moon to be metaphors for intellect and emotion. At present, the stature of feeling is diminished. See Shlomo Katz, "Raḥav and Yehoshua: Imagination and Intellect," *Orot: A Multidisciplinary Journal of Judaism* I (5751/1991):55-58, and Editor's Apercu, p. 66.

219. Regarding the Nazarene, see *Sotah* 47a; *Sanhedrin* 107b (in uncensored editions). On brick-worship in general, see *'Avodah Zarah* 46a. The Talmud relates that Jesus uprighted a brick and worshiped it. Rav Kook takes this symbolically to mean that Christianity is satisfied with some sort of partial rectification of the world, while Judaism will not rest until it has achieved a total *tikkun* and overhauling of the entire structure of reality. Cf. *Orot ha-Emunah*, p. 11, where the trope of *zekifat leveinah* (uprighting a brick) is interpreted differently to mean that after an initial act of sundering, there follows from the new vertical placement of the brick a grotesque restructuring.

Several *Rishonim* or medieval Jewish authorities called into question whether the Jesus of which the Talmudic narrative speaks is truly the object of devotion of Christianity. The Jesus of the Talmud is the disciple of Rabbi Yehoshua ben Peraḥyah, who lived some generations before the man known as "Jesus of Nazareth." See *Viku'aḥ Rabbenu Yeḥiel mi-Paris* in J.D. Eisenstein, *Otsar Vikuḥim* (New York, 5688/1928), p. 84; *Tosfot ha-Rosh, Sotah*, ed. Lifshits (1968), p. 90 [47a], s.v. *Yeshu*; Rabbi Menaḥem ha-Me'iri of Perpignan, *Beit ha-Beḥirah*, Introduction to Tractate *Avot*; in the recent edition of S.Z. Havlin and A. Shoshana, *Seder Ha-Kabbalah le-Rabbeinu Menaḥem ha-Me'iri* (Jerusalem: Ofeq, 5755/1995), p. 69.

220. Isaiah 66:22.

221. At the time of the Second Temple, the Jewish People were divided between *Perushim* (Pharisees) and *Zadokim* (Sadducees). Historically speaking, there remain many basic questions concerning this schism. Whence the names *Perushim* and *Zadokim*? What beliefs did the Sadducees hold? Finally, what was the essential difference between the Pharisaic and Sadducean *Weltanschauungen*? Rav Kook's historiosophy prods this controversy from many different angles. See *Ma'amrei ha-RAYaH* I, pp. 177-181; *Mishpat Kohen*, pp. 273-274. In the piece before us, Rav Kook develops one differential: the fact that the Sadducees denied immortality. Perforce, this means that their brand of nationalism was exclusively this-worldly and thus circumscribed. It was the Pharisees who saved the day. Because they held to the belief in an afterlife, they were able to infuse their nationalism with eternal life. The lesson Rav Kook would like to derive from this model is transparent. Secular Zionism, with its restrictive temporal vision, cannot last any longer than did Sadduceanism. It is a passing phenomenon. It is religious Zionism, the spiritual heir to the Pharisaic tradition, which will persist into the future.

It is interesting that Rav Kook, in drawing up a blueprint for the Third Temple, talks as if we are still living in the Second Temple period. In previous pieces he did intellectual battle with Christianity; now he takes on the Sadducees. (See

Ma'amrei Ha-RAYaH I, pp. 176-177, where Rav Kook portrays Sadduceanism and Christianity as two poles of distorting Torah: literalism and allegorism.) As Maimonides writes, "In the days of the Second Temple, heresy cropped up in Israel, and there emerged the Sadducees (may they soon perish) who do not believe in the Oral Law" (MT, *Hilkhot 'Avodat Yom ha-Kippurim* 1:7). Why is Rav Kook expending so much energy in this direction? Shouldn't these sorties be left in the past?

Rav Zevi Yehudah Hakohen Kook said the precise order of *Orot* was devised with his father's consent. He further revealed that the order of the book – *Erets Yisrael*, the War, Israel and Its Renascence – is the chronology of events in our generations. First the People will come back to the Land. Then there will be wars. This will be followed by a period of national soul-searching, when the Jewish People as a whole will engage in a collective search for spiritual identity. *Israel and Its Renascence* – the title itself is most instructive. Not "Israel's Renascence" but two elements: Israel *and* Its Renascence. In order for there to be renascence, first there must be a thorough examination of who Israel is. Israel must first recognize itself. The way to learn its true identity is by contrast to all its false identities. Once all the masks are pulled down, the true face of Israel will be revealed.

> This is the idea of all these chapters .... Our struggle with the heretics. Examination of our faith in all its wholeness, as opposed to heresy. In every chapter, different aspects for analysis: What is Heresy? ... Israel, in their hour of renascence, are obliged to conduct this huge analysis, just as it was more than two thousand years ago at the time of Ezra and the Second Temple. Israel in its renascence, its eternity, its revival, opposite the Heresy founded by crumbling souls.
>
> (RZYH Kook, quoted in Ḥayyim Avihu Shvarts, *Mi-Tokh ha-Torah ha-Go'elet* IV [Jerusalem, 5747], pp. 195-200)

Rav Zevi Yehudah Kook's statement is reflective of what his father wrote concerning Sadduceanism:

> In our great epoch of national awakening ... we are doubly obligated to rummage through our archives to know what were the currents in our national life of old. Only through this knowledge will we be able to achieve equilibrium, to know which current is essentially and originally our own ... and which current is accidental, foreign...
>
> During the time the national life ... could not be manifest in deed, these currents were also dormant ... therefore they were not known to us, in both their positive and negative aspects. But now, at the time of the national renascence ... suddenly there are revealed in our midst the various undercurrents which had lain comatose because of the profundity of the exile. It is an obligation and an opportunity to learn the theory of collective life from the ancient golden days...

> In the period of the Second Temple too, when we returned to the ancestral land, after the great crisis of Babylonian captivity, it was necessary to dig deep the living well of renascence. Then too obstacles presented themselves ... there arose briars in the form of Sadduceanism.
>
> (*Ma'amrei ha-RAYaH* I, pp. 177-179)

Granted that the modern State of Israel must engage in some soul-searching, and that reflections are necessary for one to develop a sense of self. But who is to say that the counterfeit brands of Judaism today are essentially those that ran rampant in the Second Temple? Does this kind of thinking stem from a deep-seated belief on Rav Kook's part that history does indeed repeat itself, that the same kinds of problems that plagued us in the Second Temple will reincarnate as we ready for the Third Temple? Or is it something even more basic than that – the belief that essentially the Third Temple is the continuation of the Second, and that those selfsame heresies, never having been totally expurgated, continue to plague us to the present day? In my book *Avirin* (Jerusalem: Zur Ot, 57540), pp. 85-87, I argued in the latter vein, based on the opinion of Ḥasdai Crescas. See R. Nissim b. Reuben Gerondi, *Derashot ha-Ran*, ed. Leon A. Feldman (Jerusalem, 1973), *ha-Derush ha-Shevi'i* (p. 123); R. Ḥasdai Crescas, *'Or Adonai*, ed. R. Shelomo Fisher (Jerusalem, 5750), 3:1:8:2 (pp. 368-369); Rabbi Solomon ben Abraham ibn Adret, *Peirush Agadot*, *Megillah* 12a (published by L. Feldman in *Rabbi Joseph H. Lookstein Memorial Volume* [New York, 5740/1980]); Rabbi Moshe Ḥayyim Luzzato, *Mishkenei 'Elyon*, in *Ginzei RaMḤaL*, ed. H. Friedlander (B'nei Berak, 5740), pp. 155-157. This approach would appear to be supported by Rav Kook's contention:

> The days of the Second Temple were just days of recuperation in order to gird for the long, arduous burden to come – the burden of Exile.... In the first days of the Second Temple the leaders of our people knew that this redemption was to be followed by exile... Ezra from the beginning prepared a defense for the Torah to last into the days of the long Exile.
>
> (*Ma'amrei ha-RAYaH* I, pp. 209-211)

222. A conflation of Psalm 41:14 and Nehemiah 9:5. *Mishnah Berakhot* 9:5; *Ta'anit* 16b.

223. Job 37:16.

224. *Pesaḥim* 54a.

225. Judges 5:13.

226. Cf. 2 Chronicles 35:3.

227. Isaiah 11:2.

228. "There sprouts and blossoms the light of the strong Messianic renascence" (*tsats u-fore'aḥ hu 'or ha-teḥiyah ha-meshiḥit ha-'azizah*). In *SK* 7:27 "sprouts and blossoms" is the conclusion of the previous sentence. There then begins a new sentence not found in *Orot*: "The personal renascence which precedes the collective; the strong spiritual [renascence] which precedes the physical..." (*ha-*

teḥiyah ha-'ishit ha-makdemet et ha-kelalit, ha-ruḥanit ha-'azizah ha-makdemet et ha-gufanit...)

229. Isaiah 11:3-4.

230. See above note 216.

231. Psalms 90:2-3.

232. *Tsur yisrael ve-go'alo*. From the morning prayer in the version of the Talmud Yerushalmi, *Berakhot* 1:6. Cf. Psalm 19:15. (Our own custom is to conclude with *ga'al yisrael*.) This phrase was incorporated in the *Tefillah li-Shelom ha-Medinah* (Prayer for the Peace of the State) prescribed by the Chief Rabbinate of Israel to be recited in synagogues. After much acrimonious debate, the phrase *Tsur Yisrael* (Rock of Israel) was included in the State of Israel's 1948 *Megillat 'Atsma'ut* (Declaration of Independence). Rav Kook's disciple, Rabbi David Cohen (the "Nazirite") writes of the theological implications of this term that has become symbolic of our time, in *Kol ha-Nevu'ah* (Jerusalem: Mosad Ha-Rav Kook, 5730), p. 132. He juxtaposes it to the "Source of Israel" in 2 Samuel 23:3, a verse central to understanding the phenomenon of prophecy.

233. In Isaiah 47:4: "Our redeemer – the Lord of Hosts is His name." Also recited in the morning prayer immediately preceding *'Amidah*.

234. Jeremiah 32:27.

235. 2 Kings 19:15; Isaiah 37:16.

236. From the blessing after the *Haftarah*.

237. Naḥmanides (Genesis 12:6) and later Rabbenu Nissim Gerondi (*Derashot ha-RaN*, ed. Feldman [Jerusalem: Shalem, 1973], pp. 27-28) enunciated the principle that prophecies must be concretized by some *po'al dimyoni* (sympathetic action). Naḥmanides' paradigms are Jeremiah 51:63-64 (Jeremiah is commanded by God to tie a rock to the book prophesying Babylon's doom and sink it in the river in order to precipitate the downfall of the Babylonian Empire) and 2 Kings 13:17-19 (Joash is commanded by Elisha to shoot an arrow in Aram's direction and afterward beat the arrows on the ground in order to precipitate Aram's defeat). However, see RaN's objections to Naḥmanides' theory. Also, see the problem raised by Rabbi Yitsḥak Hutner concerning Hosea and the solution he offers, in his letter to RZYH Kook, published in *Iggerot la-RAYaH* (Jerusalem, 5750), p. 567. Cf. A.J. Heschel, *The Prophets* (Philadelphia: Jewish Publication Society, 1962), pp. 56, 117-118. Also Rabbi Samson Raphael Hirsch, *The Collected Writings*, Vol. III, *Jewish Symbolism* (New York: Feldheim, 1984), pp. 19-46.

Cf. to our piece, the passage in *OHK* I, p. 272, entitled by the Nazirite, "*Ha-Nevu'ah ha-Po'elet*" ("Active Prophecy"). There Rav Kook contrasts the *vita activa* of the *navi*, the prophet, to the *vita contemplativa* of the *ḥakham* or sage. A prophet is a social activist; this is *art engagé*. The sage is a theoretician; he lives in a world of abstractions. Rabbi Zadok Hakohen of Lublin states this succinctly: The *ḥakham's* world is one of thought; the *navi* inhabits a world of speech. See *Resisei Laylah*, chap. 16 (9c-10a).

238. Psalm 34:2.

239. A kabbalistic meditative practice. In many prayer books of Sephardic and also Ḥasidic communities, the name of God is written out this way: YAHDVNHY. This is the *shiluv* or interpenetration of two names of God, YHVH and ADNY. (See *Tikkunei Zohar*, Introduction, and *tikkun* 10.) Rav Kook dwells here on the symbolic significance of this practice, which is the coming together of the transcendental and immanental aspects of existence.

240. Deuteronomy 33:2.

241. Isaiah 40:10.

242. Psalm 94:11.

243. Isaiah 40:8.

244. Psalm 25:14.

245. The view of the world as a *macroanthropus* goes back a long way in Jewish Thought. See e.g., *Berakhot* 10a; Baḥya ibn Pakuda, *Ḥovot ha-Levavot*, Part II (*Sha'ar ha-Beḥinah*), chap. 4, and at length chap. 5; Yehudah Halevi, *Kuzari* IV, 3, 25 (commenting on *Sefer Yetsirah*); Maimonides, *Guide of the Perplexed* I, 72 – not to mention the Jewish mystical doctrine of the *Shi'ur Komah*. Rav Kook is about to extrapolate his psychology of the individual to the macro level. Just as the individual does best to uplift all of his life's energies – even those considered primitive and animalistic – to a higher level, so on the macro level, none of the Earth's natural tendencies are to be left out of the cosmic scheme. As Rabbi Alter Ben-Zion Metzger has already observed in the introduction to his English translation of *Orot ha-Teshuvah* (*Lights of Repentance*), Rav Kook's liberating psychology is heavily indebted to that of the *Tanya*, by Rabbi Shneur Zalman of Liadi, founder of Ḥabad Ḥasidism, and happens to coincide with trends in modern psychology. Rav Kook would advocate *it-hafkha* (sublimation) rather than *itkafya* (repression). See *Lights of Repentance*, trans. Metzger (New York, 1968), pp. 20-21; *Tanya*, Part I (*Likkutei Amarim*), chap. 27; R. Zadok Hakohen Rabinowitz, *Zidkat ha-Zaddik*, chap. 242; B. Naor, "'*Zedonot na'asot ki-zekhuyot*' *be-mishnato shel ha-Rav Kook*," *Sinai* 97 (Nissan-Iyar 5743/1983): 78; reprinted in B. Naor, *Ba-Yam Derekh* (Jerusalem, 5744), p.140.

A significant omission from Rav Kook's published works, which scan the entire *Zeitgeist* of the twentieth century, is the name of Sigmund Freud. One may wish to juxtapose Rav Kook's bold statement in *OHK* I, p. 17 [*SK* 5:275], to the famous "Freudian slip":

> All thoughts are logical, systematically connected. Even those in which we recognize only a surfacing of a thought, if we were to investigate thoroughly

> their root, we would discover that they proceed chainlike from the source of logic. For so is the nature of thought.

See also the piece in *OHK* I, p. 189, entitled *"Ha-Zeramim mi-ma'al u-mi-taḥat la-hakarah"* ("The Streams Above and Below Consciousness").

I found a veiled reference (apparently negative) to Freud's theory of the unconscious in RZYH Kook, *"Ha-Ḥiyyut ha-Yisraelit,"* in *Li-Netivot Yisrael* II, p. 119: "…all the follies of mechanization and egocentrization, in relation to the process of human life, until the subterrain of the 'Unconscious.'"

There are two more lights that must be trained on the discussion at hand. First, we must mention the Nietzschean critique of what he termed *Sklavenmoral* (slave morality). At times, this became a derision of Judaic ethics, but in other instances actually upheld the "affirmative religion" of the "Old Testament" against what he viewed as the "negative religion" of the "New Testament." (See *The Will to Power*, in *Complete Works of Friedrich Nietzsche*, ed. Oscar Levy, vol. 14, trans. Anthony M. Ludovici [New York: Russell and Russell, 1964], p. 126.) See the aforementioned essay by RZYH Kook, *LNY* II, p. 120, and the expansion on it in Shvarts, *Mi-Tokh ha-Torah ha-Go'elet* III, pp. 226-227, both of which cite Nietzsche directly. The sources of Rav Zevi Yehudah Hakohen Kook's citations are: *The Dawn of Day*, end aphorism 205, in *Complete Works*, vol. 9, trans. J. M. Kennedy, pp. 213-214; and *Beyond Good and Evil*, aphorism 52, in *Complete Works*, vol. 12, trans. Helen Zimmern, p. 71. See further Walter Kaufmann's article on Nietzsche in *The Encyclopedia of Philosophy* V (New York, 1967), p. 512, and Nathan Rotenstreich, *Jews and German Philosophy* (New York: Schocken Books, 1984), pp. 208-213.

The other angle is Rav Kook's ambivalence toward the "praxis" of Rabbi Israel Salanter's modern Mussar movement. Rabbi Israel Lipkin (popularly referred to as Rabbi Israel Salanter after his place of residence) is credited with having preempted the findings of modern psychology, when he wrote in 1849 of "light powers" (or "translucent powers"; in Hebrew *koḥot me'irim,* in Yiddish *klare*) versus "dark powers" (or "opaque powers"; in Hebrew *koḥot kehim;* in Yiddish *dunkele*). (See *'Or Yisrael* [Vilna, 5660/1900], 25b-c; Rabbi Dov Katz, *Tenu'at ha-Mussar* I [Jerusalem, 5742], pp. 250-251.) However, Yitsḥak Ahren has found the source for the Salanterian terminology in Kant; see Hillel Goldberg, *Israel Salanter: Text, Structure, Idea* (New York: Ktav, 1982), pp. 170-176, and Immanuel Etkes, *Rabbi Israel Salanter and the Beginning of the Musar Movement* (Hebrew) (Jerusalem: Magnes, 1982), pp. 326-335. Rabbi Salanter advocated the emotive study of Mussar literature (with a mournful tune) and *yir'at ha-'onesh* (fear of punishment) as the corrective to those "dark powers." In this respect, in the interesting dialogue between the schools of Ḥabad Ḥasidism and Mussar, Rav Kook very much sided with the former. Rather than striving for *yirat ha-'onesh* (fear of punishment) by appealing to one's emotion, Rav Kook felt that the spiritually sensitive should be reaching for *yir'at ha-romemut* (awe) by cultivating the intellect. Rav Kook thought that raw fear should be reserved for coarse souls; in the truly spiritual it would breed only depression and morbidity. See *Ginzei ha-RAYaH* IV, pp. 22-23, and *'Al Penimiyut ha-Torah* (alternative title: *Hosafot le-Orot ha-Torah*), ed. RZYH Kook and Rabbi Shelomo Aviner, pp. 17-18 (par. 19) (reprinted in Rabbi Moshe Zuriel, *Otserot ha-RAYaH* [5762/2002] Vol. 2, pp. 329-330). See also Rabbi David Cohen's Preface to the third volume of *OHK*, *"Mussar ve-Yir'at Elohim."*

246. Psalm 26:12.

247. "Revelation of all being" (*hitgalut kol ha-yesh*). In *SK* 7:31: *hitgalut ha-yeshut*. This may translate as "revelation of the egoism," assuming that Rav Kook was drawing on Ḥabad Ḥasidic terminology.

248. See *OHK*, beg. vol. II, where the editor, the Nazirite, has affixed the motto (from *Zohar* III, 94b), "The Holy – is a thing unto itself." For Rav Kook, this phrase is loaded with meaning. (See introduction to *OHK* I, pp. 18-19.) There is a realm of the Holy that is beyond all the bifurcations and antinomies of this world. On that level, there are no conflicts between divergent life tendencies. In another passage, he refers to this world of unity that is beyond the division of holy and secular as "Holy of Holies" (*OHK* II, p. 311). Cf. *OHK* II, pp. 317-318.

249. Psalm 46:3.

250. Isaiah 40:31; *Sanhedrin* 92b.

251. "The cosmic vision" (*ḥazon ha-'olamim*). In *SK* 7:31 simply "the vision" (*he-ḥazon*).

252. Rashi, *Sanhedrin* 92b explains that during those thousand years that God will be in the process of renewing His world and the present world will be desolate, the *tsaddikim* (righteous) must have a place to be. Cf. *Sanhedrin* 97a: "Said Rav Ketina, The world exists for six millennia, and for one (millennium) it is destroyed."

253. Psalm 46:4-6.

254. The Vilna Gaon in his commentary to *Tikkunei Zohar* (Vilna, 1867), *Tikkun* 70 (147b), s.v. *afrish bein tarvayhu*, speaks of *kadruta de-shaḥra*, the blackness of predawn. See *Zohar* I, 170a: *kadruta de-tsafra*.

255. "The strength of life" (*'oz ha-ḥayyim*). In *SK* 7:31: "the mystery of life" (*raz ha-ḥayyim*).

256. Isaiah 37:16.

257. "In the territorialism" (*be-hitgadrut*). In *SK* 7:31: "in the aggression" (*be-hitgabrut*).

258. "Cunning" (*'ormat*). In *SK* 7:31: "wisdom" (*ḥokhmat*).

259. Psalm 119:91.

260. Proverbs 8:26-28.

261. Psalm 50:2.

262. In *SK* 7:31 there occurs here the phrase "which draws the water from all the deep wells" (*ha-doleh et ha-mayim mi-kol ha-be'erot ha-'amukim*).

263. The word *real* appears in the original as a loanword: *bisus re'ali*. In *SK* 7:31: *basis re'ali*.

264. Numbers 12:8.

265. *Da'at*.

266. *Yesod*.

267. "And rises with all of them" (*ve-'olah 'im kulam*). In *SK* 7:31: "and raises all of them" (*ve-ha-ma'alah et kulam*).

268. *Netsaḥ*.

269. *Shalom*, code for *Hod* (see R. Ya'akov Yolles, *Kehillat Ya'akov*, s.v. *Shalom*). *Shalom* is the numerical equivalent of Samlah, the king who represents *Hod*. Cf. below *Lights of Renascence*, chap. 58: *hod ha-shalom*. Aaron the Priest is the Lover of Peace (*Avot* 1:12) and also corresponds to the *sefirah* of *hod*.

270. *Tif'eret*.

271. Rav Kook is alluding here to one of the most profound doctrines of the Kabbalah, the *sod mitat ha-melakhim*, the Mystery of the Death of the Kings, based on the passage in Genesis 36:31-39, and elaborated on in the portion of the *Zohar* known as the *Idra* (section *Nasso*). The seven kings who die are symbolic of seven *sefirot*: Bela' = *Da'at*, Yovav = *Ḥesed*, Ḥusham = *Gevurah*, Hadad = *Tif'eret*, Samlah = *Hod*, Sha'ul = *Yesod*, Ba'al Ḥanan = *Netsaḥ*. See Rabbi Hayyim Vital, *'Ets Ḥayyim* 8:4 (*Derushei Nekudot*, chap. 4). (This is according to ARI; GRA has a different reckoning. See Rabbi Shelomo Elyashiv, *Sefer ha-De'ah* II [Piotrkow, 5672] 1:5:1 [6c].) The eighth king in the series, who does not die, is Hadar = *Malkhut*. The key to undying versus dying is the *sefirah* of *Ḥokhmah*: "They die, and this without wisdom" ("*yamutu ve-lo be-ḥokhmah*") (Job 4:21); "The wisdom will enliven its masters" ("*ha-ḥokhmah teḥayyeh be'alehah*") (Ecclesiastes 7:12). Cf. RAYH Kook, *'Al Penimiyut ha-Torah* (alternative title, *Hosafot le-Orot ha-Torah*) (pamphlet), dictated by RZYH Kook to Rabbi Shelomo Aviner, p. 9, par. 12 (reprinted in Rabbi Moshe Zuriel, *Otserot ha-RAYaH* [5762/2002], Vol. 2, p. 323): "Anything whose wisdom (*ḥokhmato*) is not studied in the kingdom (*mamlekhet*) of the spirit, is doomed to fall (*lipol*)." (Cf. *Zohar* III, 135b: "Whoever descends from his original rung is referred to as having died." Also *Orot ha-Teshuvah* 11:4.) See Rabbi Moses Cordovero, *Elimah* (Lvov, 1881) 57c-58b, Rabbi Ḥayyim Vital, *'Ets Ḥayyim, Sha'ar ha-Melakhim*; Rabbi M.H. Luzzatto, *Adir ba-Marom* II, Spinner ed. (Jerusalem, 5748), pp. 93-131 (*Ma'amar Be'ur Zayin Melakhin*); Elijah Gaon of Vilna, *Commentary to Sifra di-Tseni'uta*, Luria ed. (Vilna, 1882), chap. 1 (9c-10a); Rabbi Eizik Ḥaver, *Pitḥei She'arim, Netiv Shevirat ha-Kelim*, chap. 15 (55b-57a); Rabbi Solomon Elyashev, *Hakdamot u-She'arim, Sha'ar ha-Poneh Kadim*, chap. 39 (85c-87a); Rabbi Shneur Zalman of Liadi, *Torah 'Or, Hosafot, Tetsaveh*, 110d; Rabbi

Ya'akov Yolles, *Kehillat Ya'akov*, s.v. *Samlah mi-Masrekah*; RAYH Kook, *Orot Ha-Kodesh* IV (Jerusalem: Mosad Ha-Rav Kook, 1990), pp. 400-401 [=*SK* 1:164]; Rabbi David Cohen, *Kol ha-Nevu'ah* (Jerusalem, 5730), pp. 225-226, 239-240, 294-296.

272. *Hadrot* (plural of *Hadar*, the king who represents *tikkun*).

273. *Gevurah*.

274. *Ḥassadim* (plural of *Ḥessed*).

275. Cf. B. Nyer (Naor), *'Alma de-Yiḥuda* (Muse), in *Reshit Oni* I (New York, 5735), pp. 91-92.

276. "The pupil of man's eye" (*ishon ha-adam*). In *SK* 7:31: "the pupil of the eye" (*ishon ha-'ayin*).

277. Zechariah 9:1.

278. "Sublimity" (*rom*). In *SK* 7:31: "simplicity" (*tom*).

279. The words "are its stratagems" (*hem takhsisav*) are not found in *SK* 7:31.

280. Song of Songs 2:9.

281. In *SK* 7:31 there occurs here an entire sentence missing in *Orot*: "Heaven and earth will rejoice at His name, rivers will clap hands in refrain" (*shamayim va-arets yeranenu li-shemo, neharot yimḥa'u khaf le-han'imo*).

282. Proverbs 18:10.

283. Isaiah 2:11,17.

284. The idea that nature itself is miraculous ("*nissim nistarim*" or "hidden miracles") runs throughout Naḥmanides' writings. See Naḥmanides' commentary to Genesis 17:1; 46:15; Exodus 6:2; 13:16; Leviticus 26:11; Introduction to Job; *Torat Hashem Temimah* in *Kitvei RaMBaN*, ed. Chavel (Jerusalem: Mosad Ha-Rav Kook, 5723) I, pp. 152-155. In *OHK* I, p. 232, Rav Kook writes that only illusion prevents us from seeing that nature is indeed a miracle. (*Nes* [Miracle] and *Dimyon* [Illusion] are antithetical; they are numerical equals: 110.)

285. Isaiah 52:13.

286. *Zohar* II, 8b; III, 196b.

287. Cf. *Resh Millin* (Jerusalem: Mosad Ha-Rav Kook, 1985), *Ḥet*, p. 10:

> The crisis which arises out of conceptions locking horns, ideals contradicting one another, this breakdown comes at the onset of perfection, as a preface to an eternal structure, whole and lovely. Two forces pitched opposite one another, one camp facing the other, the force of the destructive army, and directly opposite the force of the constructive camp. They unite in the process of confronting each other. The bombardment begins, the breakdown is revealed, and the lofty ideal bonds these forces together. At the pinnacle of the world, One Who dwells in secrecy, by an awful logic thinks thoughts and far-reaching plans. There is the Living One, there is

> vitality, there is the relation of Life to all that lives ... The power of war, and the war against the war, brings into being Life in all its values and respects, in all its branches and ramifications.

Cf. MaHaRal, *Netsaḥ Yisrael*, end chap. 26 and our Introduction.

288. *Zohar* I, 6a.

289. Aramaic, *mila di-shtuta*. This is the *Zohar's* term for the element of folly that enhances overall wisdom, "there is an advantage to the wisdom *from* the folly" (as it understands the verse in Ecclesiastes 2:13). The *Zohar* also cites Ecclesiastes 2:3: "My heart conducting itself with wisdom and holding on to folly." See next note.

290. "When the colleagues would learn from Rav Hamnuna Saba mysteries of wisdom, he would read to them some matter of folly *(milei di-shtuta)*, so that the wisdom would be enhanced thereby" (*Zohar* III, 47b). Also *Tikkunei Zohar, tikkun* 21. See Rabbi Ḥayyim Hirschensohn's article *"Rav Hamnuna Saba"* in *Ozar Yisrael*, ed. J.D. Eisenstein. Cf. *AT* (Jerusalem, 5743), p. 100; *OHK* I,78. See *Shabbat* 30b; *Pesaḥim* 117a; *Ketubot* 17a; *Leviticus Rabbah* 2:1; *Orot: A Multidisciplinary Journal of Judaism*, vol. 1(5751/1991), pp. 65-67. One famous Ḥasidic Rebbe, Barukh of Mezhbizh, grandson of the Ba'al Shem Tov, maintained a *badḥana de-malka* (court jester), by the name of Hershel Ostropolier. See also R. Shalom Dov Baer Shneurson, *Kuntress u-Ma'ayan mi-Beit Hashem* (Brooklyn: Kehot, 1958), on *shtut di-kedushah*, "holy folly."

291. Job 37:16.

292. *Zohar* II, 212; R. Elijah of Vilna's commentary to *Tikkunim mi-Zohar Ḥadash*, appended to *Tikkunei Zohar* (Vilna, 5627/1867), 30d-31b; *Pesikta Rabbati*, chap. 32:10; R. Judah Löw of Prague, *Netsaḥ Yisrael*, chap. 34; Rabbi M.H. Luzzatto, *Kin'at Adonai Zeva'ot* (B'nei Berak, 5740), p. 132. Messiah symbolically undergoes the four forms of capital punishment (*arba' mitot beit-din*), from most severe to most mild: *sekilah* (lapidation), *sereifah* (burning), *hereg* (the sword), and *ḥenek* (strangulation). See *Mishnah, Sanhedrin* 7:1.

293. Psalm 89:52-53.

294. Jeremiah 5:17.

295. "Distances" (*merḥakim*). In *SK* 7:32: "coincidences" (*mikrim*).

296. Rav Kook commiserates with Messiah, of whom he has a "Kafkaesque" vision: In the final phase of Exile, *Mashi'aḥ* is asphyxiated by the constricted consciousness of the apparatchiks and bureaucrats through whom the agenda of Redemption must pass for implementation.

297. *Genesis Rabbah* 2:4; *Tosafot*, *'Avodah Zarah* 5a, s.v. *ki ru'aḥ mi-lefanai ya'atof*; *Tikkunei Zohar, tikkun* 30 (81b); *tikkun* 25 in commentary of GRA.

298. "Comes" (*ba*). In *SK* 7:45: "is based" (*mevusas*).

299. "Existential extravagances" (*motarot ha-metsi'utiyot*). In *SK* 7:45: "extravagances of the existential tendencies" (*motarot ha-netiyot ha-metsi'utiyot*).

300. Proverbs 30:28.

301. Genesis 4:5.

302. Genesis 4:7.

303. "Cainite man" (*ha-adam ha-Kayini*). So too in *SK* 7:45. In the 1950 edition of *Orot*: "Cainite blood" (*ha-dam ha-Kayini*).

304. Gittin 57a.

305. "This is not its objective." The words are not found in *SK* 7:45.

306. Rabbi Isaiah Halevi Horowitz writes in *Shnei Luḥot ha-Berit* (*Parashat Koraḥ*) that Koraḥ was a reincarnation of Cain. (Moses was the reincarnation of Abel. This time around Abel triumphed over Cain. Instead of Abel [or his blood] crying out of the ground, it was the other way around: Koraḥ calling from the earth that had swallowed him up. See *Buvu Batra* 74a.)

307. Numbers 16:3.

308. In *Orot*, the word "descend" is in the singular, *yered*, which would refer to Koraḥ alone. In *SK* 7:45 "descend" is in the plural (*yerdu*), a reference to the entire congregation of Koraḥ.

309. Numbers 16:33.

310. Numbers 17:5.

311. Rav Kook decries the spiritual egalitarianism of Christianity, which having erased the "Chosen People" doctrinally (if not physically), then goes on to tell all peoples that they have the identical aptitude for godliness. Cf. *OHK* II, pp. 139-141.

312. Isaiah 24:20.

313. Song of Songs 2:17; 4:6.

314. Isaiah 24:21.

315. Hebrew *minut*. See Introduction.

316. *Shabbat* 155b and Rashi there.

317. *Ta'anit* 21b. In the 1920 edition, *le-me'ei de-insha*. Corrected in the 1950 edition to *li-b'nei inshei* to conform to the exact wording of the Talmud. Cf. *Orot ha-Emunah*, p. 4.

318. Job 28:3.

319. Isaiah 49:7.

320. In the 1920 edition the words, "for the sake of the Lord" until "will run to you" were inadvertendy omitted due to the dittography *for the sake of the Lord – for the sake of the Lord*.

321. Isaiah 55:4-5.

322. "Hidden" (*sefunah*). In *SK* 7:45: *tsefunah*. The meaning remains unchanged.

323. "With all might" (*be-khol 'oz*). In *SK 7:45: masaḥ*. See II Kings 11:6. The meaning of the Hebrew word is uncertain. It might be translated as "vigilantly."

324. Isaiah 25:7 (the quotation is inexact).

325. Jeremiah 16:19.

326. Isaiah 2:17-18.

327. Isaiah 11:9.

328. Deuteronomy 6:5.

329. *Berakhot* 9:5. See Rabbi Shneur Zalman of Liadi, *Tanya* I, chap. 9.

330. Psalm 25:14.

331. Joshua 15:19.

332. Ecclesiastes 1:5.

333. "Culture" (*tarbut*). In *SK* 5:189 we find the loanword *kultura*.

334. "The pagan legacy of the civilized nations" (*moreshet goralam ha-elili shel 'amei ha-tarbut*). For this circumlocution, we find in *SK* 5:189: "the lot of the pagan nations" (*goralam shel ha-'amim ha-eliliyim*).

335. The Talmud (*Megillah* 6a) predicts that one day the princes of Judah will teach Torah publicly in the theaters and circuses of Edom. The Ga'on Rabbi Ovadyah Yosef *shelit"a* (*zt"l*) interpreted this to mean that the scholars of Israel will be teaching Torah over the radio and television.

336. Mishnah, *Sotah* 9:15.

337. Ecclesiastes 10:16.

338. As Rabbi Akiva of old, who laughed when he saw a fox darting out of the ruins of the former Holy of Holies (*Makkot* 24b), so Rav Kook, rather than becoming disheartened by the materialism of our age, saw it as part of a divine plan. The priority modern society places on imagination over intellect, will predispose the eventual return of prophecy to Israel.

I have devoted a study, entitled *Lights of Prophecy* (New York: Orthodox Union, 1990), to elucidating Rav Kook's theory of prophecy, which has its source in Maimonides' *Guide* II, 36-37. See *Orot Yisrael* 7:16; in 1950 ed. *Orot*, p. 165.

Rav Kook is indebted to Maimonides for making the imaginative faculty (*ko'aḥ ha-medameh*) an (and perhaps *the*) essential component of prophecy. See Moses Maimonides, *Guide of the Perplexed* II, 36. Another latter-day visionary who pursued this line (while downplaying the indebtedness to Maimonides, of course) was Rabbi Naḥman of Breslov. Rabbi Naḥman, as Rav Kook (who was very attached to and inspired by the writings of Breslov), is intent on the rectification and clarification of imagination as a means to reviving prophecy. See e.g. *Likkutei*

Moharan II, 8 (*Tik'u Tokhaḥa*), pars. 7-8. See now Zvi Mark, *Mistikah ve-Shiga'on bi-Yetsirat R. Naḥman mi-Breslov* (*Mysticism and Madness in the Work of R. Naḥman of Bratslav*) (Tel Aviv, 2003), chap. 5 (*"Dimyon, Nevu'ah ve-Emunah"*), especially pp. 86-95.

339. Cf. *Siddur 'Olat Re'iyah* (*Hagadah*) II, 261.

340. Isaiah 11:2.

341. The opposition here is between imagination and intellect, the latter being the realm of Torah law. See Shlomo Katz, "Raḥav and Yehoshua: Imagination and Intellect," in *Orot: A Multidisciplinary Journal of Judaism* I (5751/1991): 49-64.

342. See Psalms 105:8; Rashi, *Ḥagigah* 14a.

343. Hosea 12:11.

344. *Yevamot* 49b. According to Maimonides, a basic difference between the prophecy of Moses and that of the lesser prophets was that unlike those inferior to him in stature, the prophecy of Moses the Lawgiver was not predicated on the imaginative faculty but rather was purely intellectual in character. See Maimonides, Thirteen Articles of Faith (*Commentary to the Mishnah*, Introduction to *Sanhedrin* chap. 10 [*Perek Ḥelek*]), seventh article; *Shemonah Perakim* (*Commentary to the Mishnah*, Introduction to Tractate *Avot*), chap. 7; *MT*, *Hil. Yesodei ha-Torah* 7:6; *Guide of the Perplexed* II, beginning chap. 35 and end chap. 45. See also Rabbenu Nissim ben Reuben Gerondi, *Derashot ha-Ran*, ed. Feldman (Jerusalem, 1973), end *Derush ha-Shemini* (p. 143).

345. *Ḥokhmah tata'ah* is synonymous with the *sefirah* of *Malkhut* (Kingdom).

The kabbalistic term signifies human as opposed to divine wisdom. See Rabbi Zadok Hakohen of Lublin, *Likkutei Ma'amarim* (in *Divrei Soferim*), pp. 41d-42a, 118b-d; *Orot: A Multidisciplinary Journal of Judaism*, Vol. I (5751/1991), pp. 65-67.

346. The nationalistic connection to the Land is strengthened by the power of imagination. This is reminiscent of Rav Kook's characterization of the First Temple period as a world of prophecy and nationalism, as opposed to the Second Temple period, which he regards as a universe of Torah and individualism, even to the point of atomization. See "*Le-mahalakh ha-ide'ot be-yisrael*" ("To the Process of Ideas in Israel"), reprinted in the 1950 edition of *Orot*, pp. 102-118.

347. In a play on the halakhic ruling, *"Dina de-malkhuta dina"* ("The law of the kingdom is law"), the Kabbalists envisioned the *sefirah* of *Malkhut* (Kingdom) as being a conduit for the divine attribute of judgment (Hebrew, *middat ha-din*). See Rabbi Ḥayyim Vital, *Sefer ha-Likkutim*, I Kings, chap. 3 (*"dinei ha-malkhut"*). The Kabbalists also transposed the letters of *"dina"* to form *Adonai*, the divine name synonymous with the *sefirah* of *Malkhut*. See above note 345.

348. "When the time had as yet not arrived for all the purity to appear at the final heights." In *SK* 5:190 this is approximately the conclusion of the previous

sentence. It reads there: "...without yet arriving in all purity at the final heights" (*be-lo haga'ah 'adayin be-khol ha-tohar el ha-meromim ha-megamatiyim).*

349. Joshua 2:2; *Zohar* II, 178b-179a (*Sifra di-Tseni'uta*, chaps. 4-5); Rabbi Ḥayyim Vital, *'Ets Ḥayyim, Sha'ar ha-Kelipot*, chaps. 2, 4. See *Orot: A Multidisciplinary Journal of Judaism*, Vol. I (1991), pp. 65-67. Raḥav represents the epitome of imagination. See now Rabbi Yitsḥak Eizik Ḥaver, *Pitḥei She'arim, Netiv Binyan ha-Kelipot u-Merkavah Teme'ah* (ms.) in *Mi-Ginzei ha-GRA u-Beit Midrasho*, ed. Kalman Redish (Lakewood, 5759/1999), pp. 226-228.

350. "True" (*amitit*). Not found in *SK* 5:190.

351. 1 Kings 3:16; *Zohar* II, 178b; Rabbi Ḥayyim Vital, *'Ets Ḥayyim, Sha'ar ha-Kelipot*, chap. 4; *Sha'ar Kelipat Nogah*, chap. 9; idem, *Sefer ha-Likkutim* and *Likkutei Torah*, Joshua, chap. 2; I Kings, chap. 3; *Be'ur ha-GRA le-Sifra di-Tseni'uta* (Vilna, 5580/1820), 49b, 50a-52c, 55d-56c; Luria ed. (Vilna, 5642/1882), 30c, 31a-32c, 34c-35a; Naor ed. (Jerusalem, 5758/1998), 110a, 111b-117a, 125a-126b.

See *Song of Songs Rabbah* 1:10: "'Then two harlots came'—Rav said: They were spirits."

352. The divine judgment was informed by Solomon's own subjective judgment. See *Rosh ha-Shanah* 21b; *Makkot* 23b; *Zohar* II, 78a and note 367 below. Thus there was an interplay of the rational and preterrational.

353. 1 Kings 11:1, 8.

354. *Shabbat* 56b; *Sanhedrin* 21b: "At the moment Solomon married the daughter of Pharaoh, Gabriel went down and stuck a reed in the sea; the alluvium mounted there, upon which was built the great city of Rome." The forces of imagination and human, subjective wisdom which King Solomon attempted unsuccessfully to integrate within Jewish life, were sidetracked to Rome, i.e., Western civilization with its arts: plastic, performing, and literary. See above, chap. 17.

355. *Yoma* 69b; *Sanhedrin* 64a. According to the Agadah, at the beginning of the Second Temple Period, the Men of the Great Assembly (*anshei knesset ha-gedolah*) abolished the hankering for idolatry (which had been responsible for the destruction of the First Temple) by capturing this "fiery lion" in a lead pot. See B. Naor, *Lights of Prophecy/Orot ha-Nevu'ah* (1990), pp. 21-29.

356. *'Avodah Zarah* 17.

357. Psalm 74:9. According to the *Sefer Ḥasidim*, Vilna Gaon and Rabbi Zadok Hakohen of Lublin, the cessation of prophecy is linked to the eradication of idolatry. See Bezalel Naor, *Lights of Prophecy*.

358. "Pain" *(tsa'ar*). In *SK* 5:190: "state" (*ma'amad*).

359. Rav Kook has traced the historic process of "*birur ko'aḥ ha-medameh*," "the clarification of the power of imagination" (to use Rabbi Naḥman of Breslov's term): Joshua's encounter (through the intermediacy of his spies and directly, according

to rabbinic tradition) with Raḥav; Solomon's Judgment and his involvement with foreign ladies; the hamstringing of Imagination by the Men of the Great Assembly at the beginning of the Second Temple Period; and finally, the reemergence of the imaginative spirit in the rebuilt homeland. The relation of Judaism to imagination has not been easygoing, to say the least. But imagination, or rather prophecy, is an integral part of the Messianic agenda, the "Light of Messiah." See Maimonides, *Sefer ha-Mitsvot*, end *shoresh* 14.

360. Isaiah 60:22. In *SK* 5:190 the conclusion reads: "The smallest will become a thousand," "the thousand for you, Solomon" [Song of Songs 8:12]. This is actually the more logical conlusion. Logic would dictate that Solomon reappear in the conclusion to the *pensée*.

361. A hint to Christianity. Cf. *Orot ha-Emunah*, p. 11. This is confirmed by Rav Zevi Yehudah Kook's commentary, in Shvarts, *Mi-Tokh ha-Torah ha-Go'elet* III, p. 205. See above note 219.

362. Heb. *zohamat ha-naḥash*. According to rabbinic tradition, the serpent injected into Eve a certain spiritual pollution which she passed on to her descendants. On Mount Sinai, the pollution abated. Non-Jews (converts to Judaism excepted) retain this "snake venom." See *Shabbat* 146a; *'Avodah Zarah* 22b.

363. "Be absorbed" (*lehikalet*). In *SK* 5:216: "be invasive" (*lehitpalesh*).

364. Proverbs 12:4; 31:10.

365. *Sanhedrin* 107b (in uncensored editions): "Jesus bewitched, enticed and deceived Israel."

366. Psalm 56:1 and *Targum* there.

367. It is possible that Rav Kook is suggesting a synthesis of the objective, divine dimension and the subjective, human dimension in Law. See *Zohar* II, 78a and B. Naor, *Orot: A Multidisciplinary Journal of Judaism*, vol. I (5751/1991), p. 67.

368. Zechariah 14:9.

369. Hebrew, *ha-tsefiyah ha-ide'alit*. This might also be translated, "the longing for the ideal."

370. Cf. *OHK* III, p. 353: "The longing for salvation purifies life, expands the mind and refines the spirit."

371. "Weak" (*refuyah*). In *SK* 5:235: "murky" (*'akhurah*).

372. Ezekiel 23:20.

373. Genesis 25:29-30, 34.

374. *Berakhot* 6a.

375. 1 Chronicles 17:21.

376. Israel, the Woman of Valor, is the crown of her Husband, the crown atop the *Sefer Torah*. *Zohar* II, 158a; *Tikkunei Zohar*, *tikkun* 21.

377. A description of Zionism.

378. *Mishnah*, *Sukkah* 4:5.

379. In 2 Samuel 7:23 instead of *goy* (singular), "a nation," it states *goyim* (plural), "nations." See *Talmud Yerushalmi*, *Sukkah* 4:3.

380. Isaiah 24:20.

381. Habakkuk 2:13.

382. *Le-me-raḥok she'ot de'ah*. Cf. Job 36:3: *essa de'i le-me-raḥok*.

383. Cf. *Sefer Yetsirah* 1:3; Rabbi Moses Cordovero, *Pardess Rimonim*, *Sha'ar 'Erkei ha-Kinnuyim*, s.v. *berit*. See too Rashi, Genesis 45:12, quoting *Genesis Rabbah*.

384. See above note 216.

385. "Human hands" (*yedei adam*). In *SK* 5:235: "human beings" (*b'nei adam*).

386. Hebrew *'omek rom*, "the depth of the height," from *Sefer Yetsirah* 1:5. The expression *'omek tov*, "the depth of good," also occurs there.

387. Zechariah 13:2.

388. Isaiah 25:8.

389. "Majesty" (*hodo*). In *SK* 5:235: "pleasantness" (*no'amo*).

390. Psalm 83:5.

391. In this chapter, Rav Kook works with a linear model, literally.

(Yonina Dison has advocated a new schematic edition of *Orot ha-Kodesh* to organize the material according to four geometric motifs, which she purports are the underground of Rav Kook's *oeuvre*. Our own chapter would evidently fall into the pattern of Dison's "*Motiv Bet*." See Y. Dison, "*'Arba'ah motivim be-'Orot ha-Kodesh*," *Da'at* 24 [Winter 1990]: 78.)

Our entire chapter is based on the theme of the line, *kav*. The line is both vertical, connecting the real with the ideal, and horizontal, linking present to future. The Hebrew word for hope, *tikvah*, comes from *kav*, a line. In fact, the primary meaning of *tikvah* is a line, a rope. Rabbi Yitsḥak Hutner once said, commenting on the phrase "*asirei ha-tikvah*" in Zechariah 9:12: "We Jews are prisoners of hope." (Though Rabbi Hutner spoke in Yiddish, the phrase "prisoners of hope" was distinctly offered in English. The writer heard this public discourse from the "Rosh Yeshivah" in the *sukkah* of Yeshivah Rabbi Chaim Berlin, Brooklyn on *Ḥol ha-Mo'ed Sukkot* 5737. See now Rabbi Leibel Rutta, *Reshimot Lev* [5760/2000], Vol. II, bottom p. 171.) We are all bound by this ray of hope. It is ineluctable.

392. Micah 2:13.

393. *Pesaḥim* 66b: "Let Israel be. If they are not prophets, they are sons of prophets."

394. *Zohar* III, 136a, 289b, 296a.

395. *Zohar* II, 27b.

396. The different factions of the Jewish polity flow from the divine source of inspiration. "The great and pure of intellect" try to reach to the source itself, before it subdivides into the 499½ right chambers and 499½ left chambers.

397. Leviticus 26:6.

398. "Wonderful" (*mafli'ah*). In *SK* 5:264: "sublime" (*'elyonah*).

399. On the unification of the esoteric and exoteric dimensions of Judaism, see below *Lights of Renascence*, chaps. 55, 59, 60 and *OHK* I, pp. 19-38 (*"Iḥud ha-Nistar ve-ha-Nigleh"*).

400. "Contemplative" (*'iyyuniyim*). In *SK* 5:264: "theoretical" (*te'oriyim*).

401. "Branching" (*mista'afot*). In *SK* 5:264: "multiplying" (*ravot*).

402. Isaiah 54:13.

403. Psalm 134:1. Rav Kook appeals for a new type of Torah scholar who will personify all these elements: halakhic acumen, *ru'aḥ ha-kodesh* (divine inspiration), *ahavat yisrael* (love of the Jewish People), physical bravery, meticulous observance of *mitsvot*, and worldliness.

404. *'Avodah Zarah* 19a: "A person should learn only that area which his heart desires." Rashi: "His rabbi should teach him only that tractate which he requests from him, for if he were to teach him another, it would not remain with him, for his heart is set on his desire."

405. Zechariah 8:10; *Ḥagigah* 10a.

406. Isaiah 24:20, 21.

407. The new universalism of the Age of Messiah is ushered in by the spiritual dislocations of the premessianic era.

The sentence "The 'command' is not oppression and destruction but rather switching states and features" does not occur in *SK* 6:176.

408. "Said R. Aleksandri: Whoever studies Torah for its sake, makes peace among the host above and the host below, as it says, *If he will hold on to My strength, he will make peace with Me, he will make peace with Me* [Isaiah 27:5]" (Sanhedrin 99b).

409. *Sanhedrin* 97a.

410. Isaiah 30:15.

411. "Basis for the sublime spirit" (*basis le-ruaḥ 'elyon*). So in the 1920 edition of *Orot* and *SK* 5:129. Emended in the 1950 edition of *Orot* to *basis 'elyon*, "sublime basis."

412. See *Soferim* 16:3: "Said R. Yitsḥak: In the past, when the economy was sound, a person's soul would hunger for a word of Halakha; now that the economy

is troubled, a person's soul hungers for a word of Agadah." Cf. the recension in *Yalkut Shim'oni, Yitro*, chap. 271.

413. In *Ginzei RAYaH* III, 13; IV, 14-15 (reprinted in Zuriel, *Otserot ha-RAYaH* II, 1250-1252), Rav Kook expresses some reservations regarding Beshtian Ḥasidism. He feels that it was something of a stopgap measure, which having served its purpose of restoring spiritual balance, is then reabsorbed in mainstream Judaism. It is possible that our piece, though camouflaged, is also intended in this vein. This reminds me of a parable attributed to the inimitable Kotzker Rebbe, Rabbi Menaḥem Mendel Morgenstern, of blessed memory:

> There once was a poor man whose coat was filthied.
> What did he do? He turned his coat inside out.
> But eventually that new exterior as well became grimy.
> He reasoned: Since now both sides are equally shabby,
> I might as well wear the coat right side up.

So as regards the Baal Shem Tov's teaching, said the Kotzker. Once Rabbinic Judaism was lacking in vitality, so Ḥasidism came along to invigorate it. But now that even Ḥasidism has lost its spirit, we might as well go back to straight Talmudic Judaism.

Cf. Aaron Marcus, *Ha-Ḥasidut* (B'nei Berak: Nezah, 5740), p. 134 in the name of Rabbi Abraham Joshua Heschel of Apta.

414. Isaiah 8:6.

415. "It attains perfection when strengthened and rooted in..." (*ve-hi ba'ah le-tikkunah ha-shalem ke-she-hi mitḥazeket u-mishtareshet ba-...*) These words do not occur in *SK* 5:129.

416. Proverbs 1:8; 6:20. An expression for the Oral Torah.

417. "Disposed to whole renascence" (*mesugalim li-teḥiyah shelemah*). In *SK* 5:129: "scrolls [?] of renascence" (*megillot li-teḥiyah*).

418. Isaiah 30:15.

419. Proverbs 8:30, 31.

420. The ultimate *Teshuvah* (Return) is the realization that one has truly never left the divine embrace. This is reminiscent of the Ḥasidic twist Rabbi Zadok Hakohen of Lublin gave to the saying of the talmudic sage R. Yitsḥak:

> *If your sins be as* shanim (scarlet), *they will become white as snow* [Isaiah 1:18].
>
> It should state *shani* (singular for "scarlet"). What is the significance of *shanim* (plural)?
>
> The Holy One said to Israel: If your sins be as the years (*shanim*) arranged from the Six Days of Creation until now, they will become white as snow.
>
> (*Shabbat* 89b)

Explained Rabbi Zadok Hakohen: The Talmud did not use years as a mere expression of quantity, i.e., if your sins be as numerous as the years from Creation until now, but rather intended it qualitatively. Just as the years from the Six Days of Creation are orderly arranged (*sedurot u-ba'ot*), so your sins were all divinely preordained (*Zidkat ha-Zaddik*, chap. 242). See B. Naor, "'*Zedonot na'asot ke-zekhuyot' be-mishnato shel ha-Rav Kook*," *Sinai* 93 (Nissan-Iyyar, 5743); reprinted in B. Naor, *Ba-Yam Derekh* (Jerusalem, 5744), p. 149.

Before Rabbi Zadok Hakohen of Lublin, this thought was portrayed so beautifully by King Solomon. In the Song of Songs (5:2-6), the Lovely Maiden awaking heartbroken at the loss of her Beloved, beseeches the hostile watchmen to help her find her Man (vs. 7-8). After a lengthy, soul-pouring monologue (vs. 10-16) in which she describes His distinguishing features, the watchmen, who were initially skeptical, are sufficiently motivated to help with the search: "Where did your Beloved go, lovely lady? Which way did He turn? We will seek Him with you" (6:1). She answers: "My Beloved went down to His garden ..." (v. 2). To His garden? But that is exactly where she led Him before she went to sleep! (4:16; 5:1). So He never left her! The Beloved has been patiently waiting in the Garden all along.

421. *Zohar* II, 240a; III, 6b; Introduction to *Tikkunei Zohar*.

422. See note 232 above.

423. Amos 9:11.

424. Isaiah 33:20-22.

425. Genesis 49:24.

426. Cf. Esther 2:7, where it says of Mordechai, "And he had brought up (*omen*) Hadassah, that is Esther." The root *amn*, besides denoting raising a family, is also the root of the word *emunah* (faith). Thus, Rav Kook arrives at the idea that there is some intricate connection between the way in which we relate to our families and the way in which we relate to God, and vice versa.

427. "Rabbi 'Akiva preached: If a man and woman merit, the *Shekhinah* (Divine Presence) is between them; if they do not merit – fire consumes them" (*Sotah* 17b). Rashi explains that the difference (*vive la difference!*) between *ish* (man) and *ishah* (woman) is the letters *yod* and *hé*. Together, those letters *yod-hé* form the divine name: *Yah*. If those divine letters are subtracted, there remains of *ish* (man) and *ishah* (woman) naught but *esh-esh* (fire-fire). The name *YaH*, to use Rav Kook's phrase, does "subsume all the life of the worlds." "*For in YaH the Lord is the source of worlds* [Isaiah 26:4]. Preached Rabbi Yehudah bar Ila'i: These are two worlds which the Holy One created, one with the *yod* and one with the *hé*" (*Menaḥot* 29b).

428. See Numbers 5:11-31; *Mishnah, Sotah* 2:3-4; 3:3; *Nedarim* 66b; Maimonides, MT, *Hilkhot Sotah*, chap. 4; *Hilkhot Ḥanukkah* 4:14. The suspected adulteress underwent trial by ordeal in the Temple. She was given to drink water

into which had been scraped the Name of God from a scroll written especially for the occasion (*megillat sotah*). Rav Kook wishes to convey that the Divine Name acts as the barometer to gauge whether this home in Israel is intact. This bears out the interconnectedness of the two planes, divine and familial. If there had been irreparable damage to family life, it would have registered with the Name. Cf. Rashi, Numbers 5:12; *Numbers Rabbah* 9:2; *Sotah* 3b; 17b; *Zohar* I, 49b-50a; B. Nyer (Naor), *Reshit Oni* (New York, 5735), pp. 43-44.

429. "The content of familial structure" (*ha-tokhen be-binyan mishpaḥti*). In *SK* 5:266: "The faithful content of familial structure" (*ha-tokhen ha-emuni be-binyan mishpaḥti*).

430. Hosea 2:21, 22.

431. "Built and perfected" (*be-hibanoto be-shikhlulo*). In the 1920 edition of *Orot* and in *SK* 5:266 the conjunctive *vav* is missing. It was added in the 1950 edition of *Orot*.

432. "Conducted" (*derukhim*). In *SK* 5:266: "arranged" (*'arukhim*).

433. Isaiah 62:3.

434. Proverbs 12:4.

435. According to Rabbi Isaac Luria (ARI), there are twelve "gates" in heaven, each reserved for the prayers of one of the twelve tribes of Israel. Beyond the twelve gates, he taught, there is the *sha'ar ha-kollel* (universal gate) wherein are accepted all prayers, regardless of tribal origin. The ARI's rite (*Nussaḥ ARI*) is directed to that universal gate. Thus the ARI remedied the problem that in Exile, tribal origins have been lost. See the introduction to *Sha'ar ha-Kollel* by Rabbi Abraham David Lavoot in *Siddur Torah 'Or* (Vilna: Romm, 5695).

436. The Talmud (*Pesaḥim* 4a) says that one who is very litigious must be from the tribe of Dan; one who is madly in love with the sea must be from Zebulun. See B. Naor, *Avirin* (Jerusalem, 5740), p. 103.

437. Song of Songs 1:13; *Shabbat* 88b.

438. The future vision of the twelve (or rather thirteen!) tribes is contained in Ezekiel chap. 48. See also *Bava Batra* 122a; B. Naor, *Avirin*, p. 168.

439. Jeremiah 33:13.

440. 1 Kings 18:31.

441. 1 Kings 18:39.

442. Malachi 3:24.

443. Jeremiah 29:11.

444. Jeremiah 23:20.

445. Deuteronomy 4:34; 5:15; 26:8; Ezekiel 20:33, 34; Psalms 136:12. For Rav Kook, the "strong hand" is symbolic of the actual; the "outstretched arm" – the

potential. See *Siddur 'Olat Re'iyah* II, *Hagadah shel Pessaḥ*, pp. 279-280, 282-283, and *Ginzei RAYaH* II, pp. 16-21. Thus, the "strong hand" refers to the one-time, immediate redemption from Egypt; the "outstretched arm" evokes the ongoing redemptive process culminating in the Final Redemption. The idea that the future redemption proceeds from the original redemption from Egypt, and that they are conceptually one unit, may be found in MaHaRaL, Introduction to *Netsaḥ Yisrael.* See also Rabbi Nathan Sternhartz, *Likkutei Halakhot, Hilkhot Netilat Yadayim Shaḥarit* 2:4.

446. *Zohar* I, 26, 27; III, 260; *Tikkunei Zohar, tikkun* 21 and commentary of GRA *ad locum*; Rabbi Ḥayyim Vital, *Likkutei Torah, Vayyeḥi*, s.v. *'ad ki yavo shiloh;* idem, *Sha'ar ha-Gilgulim, hakdamah* 36.

447. MaHaRaL, *Netsaḥ Yisrael*, chap. 1.

448. Zechariah 9:11.

449. Malachi 3:1 and commentaries of Rabbi David Kimḥi (RaDaK) and Rabbi David Altschuler (*Metsudat David*) there. RaDaK writes: "*Mal'akh ha-berit*, the Angel of the Covenant, refers to Elijah the Prophet. So says the Agadah that Elijah avenged the covenant of circumcision which the Kingdom of Ephraim halted. As it says, *I have been very zealous for the Lord, the God of Hosts, for the Children of Israel have forsaken Your covenant* [1 Kings 19:10]. Said God to him: You were zealous on behalf of circumcision. By your life, Israel will not perform a circumcision ceremony unless you see it with your eyes! From this derives the custom of placing a seat of honor [at the *Berit Milah*] for Elijah who is called the Angel of the Covenant." See further B. Naor, *Ba-Yam Derekh* (Jerusalem, 5744), pp. 175-176.

450. Cf. *Ginzei RAYaH* II, pp. 26-28, where Rav Kook employs the figures of Moses and Messiah to symbolize the Light of Torah and Light of Israel, respectively. In that essay, the fleshly, physical holiness of Israel is also the source of prophetic inspiration, as opposed to Mosaic Torah inspiration. Elijah, champion of the holy Israelite body, is also the daimon of preterrational illumination, the famous *Giluy Eliyahu* (Revelation of Elijah). If we take together the many rays of light spread throughout *Orot*, we begin to picture the long-awaited Light of Messiah as being the lost, alternative side of Judaism, consisting of Body, Imagination, and Prophecy. Cf. below *Lights of Renascence*, chapter 34, and our lengthy Introduction. No doubt, this is hinted at in Rav Kook's epigram for the month of Iyyar (5674):

> The supernal strength of Rabbi Akiva's disciples and the hidden [strength] of the martyrs of the communities combine in the treasury of mysteries of Rabbi Shim'on bar Yoḥai.
>
> (*Ma'amrei ha-RAYaH II*, p. 501)

Rabbi Shim'on bar Yoḥai is credited with the *Zohar*.

451. Malachi 3:24.

452. "In the nation" (*ba-'ummah*)/"of Israel" (*mi-Yisrael*). These words, not found in *SK* 5:110, were added in *Orot*.

453. Hebrew *Abir Ya'akov*. The great kabbalist Rabbi Ḥayyim Vital points out that these two Hebrew words may be transposed to read "Rabbi Akiva." See Rabbi Ḥayyim Vital, *Likkutei Torah*, *Vayyeḥi*, s.v. *ben porat yosef*. In *Ginzei RAYaH* II, p. 27, Rav Kook discusses how Rabbi Akiva is the *meḥabber* (synthesizer) of Moses and Messiah (who is equivalent to Elijah in our piece), the one who bonds together the two lights, of Torah and of Israel's innate holiness. Rabbi Akiva combined the height of Torah learning (see *Sanhedrin* 86a) with the national spirit of bravery during the period of Bar Kokhba's revolt against Rome. See *Meged Yeraḥim* (Iyyar 5674) in *Ma'amrei ha-RAYaH* II, p. 501, where Rav Kook speaks of the supernal bravery of Rabbi Akiva's students (who it is assumed were recruits in Bar Kokhba's army of liberation).

454. Genesis 49:24.

455. *"Av u-venin de-beit Yisrael."* Targum Onkelos *ad locum*. But in our version: *"avahan u-venin zar'a de-Yisrael."*

456. Psalm 50:2.

457. "Each and every individual of Israel" (*kol eḥad v-eḥad mi-yisrael*). In *SK* 5:194 the sentence begins with the conjunctive *vav* (*ve-khol*): "And each..."

458. See *Ketubot* 75a: *"But of Zion it will be said, this and that man were born in her*, etc. [Psalm 87:5]. Said Rabbi Maisha, grandson of Rabbi Yehoshu'a ben Levi: One born there and one who longs to see her."

459. In *SK* 5:194 there appear here two additional words: *lah ve-la-'olam*, "for her and for the world" or "hers and the world's."

460. "In their uplifting" (*be-romemutam*). In *SK* 5:194: "in our uplifting" (*be-romemutenu*).

461. "Encompassed" (*mukaf*). In *SK* 5:194: "awakened" (*mukats*).

462. See below *Lights of Renascence*, chap. 10, n. 73.

463. "Would-be separatism" (*hafradatam ha-mahabelet*). *Mahabelet* from *hevel* (vanity). So in *Orot*. However in *SK* 7:181: "destructive separatism" (*hafradatam ha-meḥabelet*).

464. Rav Kook says the Orthodox who battle Zionism as if it were a separate, self-contained entity and not part of the total phenomenon of Judaism, err as much as the anti-religious Zionists who have adopted this posture. The solution, says Rav Kook, is not to "buy into" the illusion to begin with. Those who are true to the Torah perspective must not give credence to the lie that there is such a creature as a *ḥiloni*, "a secular Jew." This is a contradiction in terms. A Jew by his very nature is *elohi*, godly. (I don't say *dati* [religious] because the term *dat* is a Persian loanword that gains currency only in the Second Temple Period [see

Daniel, Esther, Ezra] and is itself part of the problem, being indicative of "split brain" consciousness.) See *"Le-Mahalakh ha-Ide'ot be-Yisrael"* ("To the Process of Ideas in Israel"), chap. 5 (*"Ha-Idea ha-Datit"*), in the 1950 edition of *Orot*, pp. 109-115, and RZYH Kook's commentary in Shvarts, *Mi-Tokh ha-Torah ha-Go'elet* III, p. 225. Cf. Samson Raphael Hirsch, *The Collected Writings* (New York: Feldheim, 1984), III, 89: "Judaism is not a religion."

465. "Intended" (*meyuḥedet*). In *SK* 7:181: "Founded" (*meyusedet*).

466. In *SK* 7:181 there appears here an additional word: *keivan* (since). Thus the sentence reads: "...only to reveal to them their error and clarify for them, *since* all their bold attempts...will not succeed."

467. "Fantasts" (*ba'alei ha-ru'aḥ*). In *SK* 7:181: "the retainers of the portion" (*ba'alei ha-ḥelek*).

468. Cf. Psalms 34:6; Jeremiah 31:11; Hosea 3:5.

469. *Genesis Rabbah* 5:4; Rashi, Leviticus 2:13. The "lower waters" are symbolic of the base instincts of man, which desire to play an active role in the service of God. "The lower waters cry: We want to appear before the King!" (*Tikkunei Zohar, tikkun* 5.) See B. Naor, *Be-Mayim 'Azim Netivah* (New York, 5748), p. 134. When these nether waters are able to praise their Creator, they are automatically "sweetened." See *Talmud Yerushalmi, 'Avodah Zarah* 2:8.

470. "Prisons of pain" (*kil'ei ha-yissurim*). In *SK* 7:187 "prison" in the singular (*kil'at*). Cf. the noun *mikhla'ah*. See Isaiah 53:4-5, Messiah described as a "suffering servant," and *Sanhedrin* 98a, Messiah sitting at the portals of Rome among the lepers.

471. Jeremiah 31:14.

472. Jeremiah 31:15, 16.

Orot Ha-Teḥiyah (Lights of Renascence)

1. Hebrew, *sympatia elohit.*

2. Hebrew, *moreshet p'leitah.* Cf. Judges 21: 17, *yerushat p'leitah.* The sense is: "the key to survival."

3. Psalm 145:9.

4. Hosea 2:19.

5. Isaiah 41:8.

6. Hebrew *erets ha-yerushah, erets ḥemdah, erets kodesh, erets tsevi ve-erets ḥayyim.* Rav Kook is hinting to the name of the second patriarch Isaac. The initials of the words *yerushah, ḥemdah/ḥayyim, kodesh, tsevi,* when transposed, form YiTsḤaK. See Rav Kook's Siddur *'Olat Re'iyah* I, pp. 398-399 (*Berit Milah*). The

question is why Ray Kook should suddenly introduce Yitsḥak to our discussion. I believe the answer lies in the fact that our piece grapples with the problem of fear (*yir'ah*). Rav Kook has declared war on the negative variety of fear of the Lord. Rav Kook's conception of *yir'at shamayim* (fear of heaven) is one of awe (*yir'at ha-romemut*) rather than fear of punishment (*yir'at ha-'onesh*). The patriarch who symbolizes the attribute of fear is Isaac: *paḥad yitsḥak* (Genesis 31:42). Yitsḥak is also synonymous with *Erets Yisrael.* (See above our commentary to *The Land of Israel,* chap. 1.) This means that authentic fear of the Lord is to be gleaned from the Land of Israel. It is an awe of Delight, Holiness, Beauty and Life. Cf. *'Ikvei ha-Tson, "Ha-Paḥad"* ("Fear"), pp. 119-121 and 150; *AT*, p. 46; 1950 edition of *Orot*, p. 126; *IHR* I, pp. 42, 46-47, 214, 347; II, pp. 38, 187; *Middot ha-RAYaH* (Jerusalem: Mosad Harav Kook, 1985), pp. 75-80 ("*Yir'ah*"), pp. 87-88 ("*Paḥdanut*"); *Otserot ha-RAYaH* I, p. 919. Also, Rabbi M.H. Luzzatto, *Mesillat Yesharim* (*Path of the Just*), chap. 24.

7. Isaiah 47:4.

8. For further thoughts of Rav Kook on mass psychology, see *'Eyn Ayah* to *Shabbat* 63a, s.v. *'atsei yerushalayim shel kinamon hayu.*

9. See above *Israel and Its Renascence*, chaps. 4-5.

10. Cf. Proverbs 24:6.

11. Job 2:4.

12. While he certainly understands the position of the Old Guard who, seeing the antireligious stance of some of the enlightened modernists, advocate that the Torah camp close ranks against the attack, Rav Kook believes the best defense is an offense, i.e., the ultimate solution to the problem is the revelation that not only are Torah and Science not incompatible but on the contrary, Torah provides the optimal climate for objective scientific inquiry. In another instance, Rav Kook quotes the saying attributed to the Vilna Ga'on: "However much one lacks in worldly wisdom, correspondingly he will lack tenfold in Torah wisdom" (*'Ikvei ha-Tson*, "*Derishat Hashem*," p. 129, n. 19). See further Tzvi Feldman, *Rav A. Y. Kook: Selected Letters* (Ma'aleh Adumim: Ma'aliyot Publications, 1986), chap. 1, "Torah and Science."

13. The description fits Friedrich Nietzsche's philosophy. Cf. below chap. 54. See the section of our Introduction entitled, "The Man Who Wore *Tefillin* All Day and—Nietzsche?"

14. "Force ourselves (*nitgabber*) to be cloaked in foreign clothing." The word *nitgabber* seems out of place in this context. Perhaps it should read *nitnakker* (be alienated).

15. "The branching (*hista'afut*) of our visions" may be intended as a *double entendre*. The word *se'if*, besides meaning a branch, can also mean a thought.

Cf. I Kings 18:21. This other definition would yield something like: "the thought process of our visions."

16. Psalm 84:8.

17. Isaiah 42:16.

18. *Midrash Tanḥuma, Ḥukkat* 8; *Numbers Rabbah* 19:6; *Yalkut Shim'oni*, chap. 452, to Isaiah 42:16: "It is not written 'these things I will do,' but rather 'I did them,' I already did them for Rabbi 'Akiva and his colleagues ... Things that were not revealed to Moses, were revealed to Rabbi 'Akiva and his colleagues."

19. Baḥya ibn Pakuda, *Ḥovot ha-Levavot* (*Duties of the Heart*), *Sha'ar ha-Perishut*, chaps. 2, 7.

20. One might juxtapose Rav Kook's theory of the complementarity of the material and spiritual elements of the nation with that of R. Ya'akov Yosef of Polenoye's doctrine of *anshei ḥomer* and *anshei tsurah*. See C. Nigal, *K'tonet Passim* (Jerusalem, 1985), pp. 172-173, 303, 311, and B. Naor, "Two Types of Prayer," *Tradition* 25:3 (Spring 1991): 32, n. 15.

21. For example, in the Second Temple Period, the priesthood was rife with corruption; the office of high priest could be bought for the right price. See *Yoma* 9a, 18a.

22. The word occurs in the Hebrew: *ḥasidut ha-elohit ha-radikalit*.

23. Cf. above *The War*, chap. 6: "Israel is the universal speculum of the entire world, etc." It is this sort of statement that gives balance and proper perspective to Rav Kook's conception of *Atah Veḥartanu* ("You have chosen us"). The chosenness is not a form of self-aggrandizement, but rather consists in the awesome responsibility of acting as the soul, the conscience, or to use Yehudah Halevi's image, the "heart" of the nations. *Atah Veḥartanu* is not a nationalistic jingo but a spiritual indenture. See Dov Schwarz, "*Ha-Zikah shel Shmuel Hugo Bergman le-mishnat ha-Rav*," *Zikhron RAYaH*, ed. Yitsḥak Rafael (Jerusalem: Mosad Harav Kook, 1986), pp. 271-272. See too Even Shmuel's (Kaufman) defense of Halevi against the charge of racism, *The Kosari of R. Yehuda Halevi* (Tel Aviv: Dvir, 1972), Introduction, pp. 30-31, n. 21. And finally, Abraham Maimonides, Commentary to Pentateuch, Exodus 19:6, s.v. *mamlekhet kohanim*, citing his father Moses Maimonides (in Jerusalem, 5744/1984 ed., bottom p. 35).

24. "The unity of the world" (*yiḥudo shel olam*). A rabbinic expression for the divinity is "*yeḥido shel 'olam*" ("the Only One of the world"). Rav Kook may have had in mind the passage in *Berakhot* 6a: "Said the Holy One, blessed be He, to Israel: You made Me unique (*ḥativah aḥat*) in the world, and I shall make you unique (*ḥativah aḥat*) in the world..."

25. This is probably one of the most important statements in the entire book. The same Judaism that hitherto was renowned for its ethical contribution to human civilization will now be noted for contributing a new ethic that is pleasurable and

vivacious as well. The rabbinical source for this idea is undoubtedly the Midrash (quoted by Rav Kook in *OHK* III, pp. 106, 138): "Now I gave you Torah; in the future I will you give life!" From within, redeemed Judaism will redefine itself. The impact of this new self-definition will then be felt abroad by all the nations of the world. With apologies to Nietzsche, the salvation of mankind will come about not through the destruction of the Judaic ethic, but rather through that very Judaic ethic that will have undergone radical transformation, making peace between the so-called Reality and Pleasure Principles. See further *Eder ha-Yekar* (Jerusalem, 5745), pp. 31-33. There, Rav Kook gives an historical explanation of Christianity's warped development—the fact that it is a spin-off of the vitiated Judaism of the Second Temple, never having been exposed to the vitality of First Temple Judaism.

26. The word occurs in the Hebrew: *re'ali.*

27. Cf. *OHK* III, p. 353: "The longing for salvation purifies life, expands the mind and refines the spirit."

28. Many, if not most, of the *mitsvot ha-teluyot ba-arets*, commandments dependent on the Land, such as *terumot* and *ma'aserot* (tithes), and *shemitah* (the sabbatical year), do not apply today biblically (*de-'oraita*), in the opinion of many halakhists. Their full biblical obligation awaits the return of the entire Jewish nation to the Land. For the time being, the exact status of the observance is a difference of opinion. In the case of *shemitah*, there are those who judge it a rabbinic obligation, while for a minority, it is not even a rabbinic obligation, but only a *middat ḥasidut*, an act of piety (Rabbi Abraham ben David [RABaD] of Posquières, Glosses to Alfasi, *Gittin* 19a, et al). See *IHR* II, p. 185; RAYH Kook, *Shabbat ha-Arets*, Introduction. See too the newly discovered Me'iri; cited in Rabbi S.J. Zevin, *Le-'Or ha-Halakha* (Jerusalem, n.d.), p. 111.

29. The sanctity of the fruits of *ma'aser sheni* is transferred to a coin specially reserved for this purpose. The biblical source for this practice is Deuteronomy 14:25.

30. Hosea 14:3.

31. Hebrew *menayot*, portions or shares (of the Kohanim and Levites). See Nehemiah 12:44, 47; 13:10. Rav Kook makes a strong philosophic case for adherence to the commemorative observances of the Land-related statutes. Though no longer biblically binding, that does not mean the observances are meaningless, mechanical actions. We are not merely "going through the motions" of agricultural halakha. These observances bind our consciousness to a future far grander than the present situation in *Erets Yisrael.* They remind us how far we must go to reach the goal of true national fulfillment. Cf. the segment from the manuscript work on *Hilkhot Kil'ayim* published in Rabbi Moshe Zuriel, *Otserot ha-RAYaH* III, 1327-1330.

32. See *Sifré*, *'Ekev* (Deuteronomy 11:18) based on Jeremiah 31:20, and *'Emek ha-Netsiv* there.

33. "Majesty and beauty" (*ha-hod ve-he-hadar*). The word *ve-he-hadar* (beauty), missing in the 1920 edition of *Orot*, was supplied in the 1950 edition.

34. Malachi 3:4.

35. In the 1920 edition of *Orot* the conjunctive *vav* ("and") did not occur. It was added in the 1950 edition: "and aged" (*u-mezukan*).

36. *Siddur*, Morning Service, section of *Korbanot* (Sacrifices).

37. See Tosafot, *Bava Batra* 21a, s.v. *ki mi-tsiyon tetse torah*. In the 1920 edition, the wording was "*le-sharet ba-kodesh*," "to serve in the Holy Place" (cf. Exodus 28:43; 29:30). This was changed in the 1950 edition to "*le-sharet be-tokh mikdashenu*," "to serve within our Temple." See also Deuteronomy 18:5.

38. Exodus 34:23.

39. Psalm 144:15.

40. I.e., our holistic ideology.

41. Isaiah 29:4.

42. Cf. Maimonides, *Guide of the Perplexed* III, 32, 45-46.

43. Rav Kook contrasts to the phony sophistication of European civilization the naturalness and naivete of ancient Israelite culture.

44. See *Sukkah* 51b. The Talmud relates that King Herod wished to cover over the blue and white marble of the Temple's exterior with gold. He was told by the Sages to leave the exterior as it was, for it resembled the undulation of the waves of the sea.

45. "Branches." Also, "thoughts." See above note 15.

46. In *SK* 1:3 there occurs here an additional word: "divinity" (*Elohut*).

47. "With love" (*be-ahavah*). In *SK* 1:5 the word is not found.

48. "Great goal" (*matarah gedolah*). In *SK* 1:5: "respected goal" (*matarah nikhbadah*).

49. I doubt whether these words were written in a vacuum devoid of historical context. The concrete example that comes to mind is Rav Kook's handling of the *Shemitah* controversy, which arose in 5670 (1910). In light of the economic realities of the time, the hardships that would be incurred by an overly stringent attitude and the potential havoc it would wreak on the developing Yishuv in *Erets Yisrael*, Rav Kook defended the earlier (5649/1899) ruling of Rabbi Isaac Elḥanan Spektor of Kovno that the prohibition of working the land on the Sabbatical year may be circumvented by selling the land to a non-Jew. Rav Kook's *heter mekhirah* ("dispensation by sale"), as it is known, placed him in a most unenviable position. On the one hand, many of his rabbinical colleagues were outraged by his permissive attitude and called for literal observance of the law. On the other, antireligious elements among the *ḥalutsim* (pioneers) mocked the entire concept

of *Shemitah*—including, or especially, the "legal fiction" of selling the lands to a non-Jew for the duration (actually two years). Rav Kook defends the *ha'aramah* or circumvention as a necessary *hora'at sha'ah* (emergency measure), which preserves intact the aspiration to complete fulfillment of the commandment in the future, though taking into account the vicissitudes of the present. See above chapter 5. (A historical aside: Rav Kook's father-in-law, Rabbi Elijah David Rabinowitz-Te'omim [Aderet] while attempting to persuade him to accept the rabbinate of Jaffa, added reluctantly that perhaps Rav Kook would not want to accept the position as it entailed endorsing the wines produced during the sabbatical year in accordance with the *heter ha-mekhirah*. See *Iggerot ha-Aderet* in *Eder Ha-Yekar* [Jerusalem: Mosad Harav Kook, 1985], Letter 12, p. 91.)

50. In *SK* 1:8 there occurs here the additional phrase: "to the best of our ability" (*ke-fi otah ha-middah she-nukhal*).

51. This would be the other side to the coin we discussed above: *Shemitah*, as a prime example. In the same work (*Shabbat ha-Arets*) in which Rav Kook explicates his permissive attitude to the practical implementation of *Shemitah* in his day, he reveals (in the lengthy introduction) the philosophic richness and kabbalistic depth of the commandment. The conceptual underpinning that Rav Kook gives to the *halakhot* of *Shemitah* and *Yovel* (the Jubilee year), must be seen as a contribution to Rav Kook's extensive oeuvre of *ta'amei ha-mitsvot*, the rationales of commandments. See "*Afikim ba-Negev*," *Ha-Peless*, 5663-5664, reprinted in Zuriel, *Otserot ha-RAYaH* II, pp. 733-761; "*Talelei Orot*," *Taḥkemoni*, Bern, 5670, reprinted in *Ma'amrei ha-RAYaH* I, pp. 18-28; Rabbi David Cohen, "*Ḥazon ha-Tsimḥonut ve-ha-Shalom*," *La-Ḥai Ro'i: Avraham Yitsḥak Ra'anan-Kook Memorial Volume* (Jerusalem: Merkaz Harav, 5721), pp. 205-254; "*He'arah Kolelet*," *Ma'amrei ha-RAYaH II*, pp. 538-544; B. Nyer (Naor), *Kuntress Kol Dodi Dofek* (Brooklyn, 1976), pp. 3-16.

52. In *SK* 1:8 the sentence concludes with the words "with impunity" (*be-sh'at nefesh*).

53. Genesis 28:12.

54. On the relation of *ru'aḥ ha-gevurah* (strength, courage, bravery, heroism) to *ru'aḥ ha-kodesh* (divine inspiration), see Targum, Judges 13:25; 14:6, 19; 1 Samuel 16:13 (in Rabbenu Yeshayah, cf. RaShI and RaDaK) and verse 14. "This spirit of strength (*ru'aḥ ha-gevurah*) inspired David to slay the lion, the bear and the Philistine. So divine inspiration (*ru'aḥ ha-kodesh*) was born in him from that day on and he said the songs and psalms with the divine inspiration engendered in him. For within the Spirit of God (*ru'aḥ Hashem*) is divine inspiration and a spirit of strength" (Rabbi David Kimḥi, 1 Samuel 16:13). Cf. Maimonides, *Guide of the Perplexed* II, 45; *Orot ha-Teshuvah* 11:2 and *OHK* I, p. 271.

55. "Clearly" (*be-galuy*). Not found in *SK* 1:14.

56. "Simplicity" (*temimut*). In *SK* 1:14 there occurs here an additional word: "and religiosity" (*va-ḥaredut*).

57. "Thus losing treasures of high life." The phrase does not occur in *SK* 1:14.

58. Jeremiah 17:12.

59. "A solid form" (*tsurah eitanah*). In *SK* 1:14: "A new and solid form" (*tsurah ḥadasha ve-eitanah*).

60. "More replete with holy strength than what mediocre simplicity—insufficiently illumined by the pure, holy light—could possibly provide." The language of *SK* 1:14 is much sharper: "Much better, more replete with holy strength than what mediocre simplicity *and failed religiosity* (*ve-ha-ḥaredut ha-koshelet*) could possibly provide."

61. Rav Kook believes that the emphasis on physical strength and bravery, so much a part of the renascence movement, i.e., Zionism, is the outcropping of a much larger phenomenon that is the incursion of classic prophetic consciousness into the modern State of Israel. (Though Rav Kook died in 1935 before the establishment of the State, he already spoke in terms of *Medinat Yisrael.*) The "primitive" thirst for God inherent in this spirit of prophecy is unquenched by the intellectual, ratiocinated, "modern" form of Judaism it encounters, which it is quick to dismiss. What results is a horrendous situation where the Judaism of the Exile is torn down and the Judaism of the Redemption has not yet arrived. Rav Kook comforts us with the thought that this is but a transition period, a "changing of the guard."

62. "Will lessen" (*yim'at*). In *SK* 1:18: "will lessen and be stooped" (*yim'at ve-yishaḥ*).

63. "Were it not for the nourishment it receives from the dew-of-life of the sanctity of the Land of Israel." This phrase which tempers the severe judgment passed on the Judaism of the Diaspora, does not occur in *SK* 1:38. There the paragraph begins simply: "Judaism in exile essentially has no actual basis; it is but a vision of [the] heart..."

64. "Hope" (*tikvah*). In *SK* 1:38: "remedy" (*takkanah*).

65. "Essential holiness, which may be found only in the Land of Israel." This phrase is not found in *SK* 1:38.

Rav Kook sees the vitality of the Jewish People seeping out of the *Golah*, the Exile, returning to its source, the Land of Israel. But Rav Kook does not negate Diaspora Judaism. The tone is not that of *shelilat ha-golah* ("negation of the Exile"). Rav Kook is not a *nevi ha-za'am*, a "prophet of rage." His vision is also not the two centers of Simon Rawidowicz: Jerusalem and Babylonia. Rather, lovingly, as a father speaks to his wayward children, Rav Kook tries to coax his people back to their one and only spiritual center, *Erets Yisrael*. Par contre, in *'Eyn Ayah* to

Shabbat 108a, Rav Kook uses this very term – *"shelilat ha-galut"* – to describe the Talmud Bavli's self-image.

Cf. Rabbi Nathan Sternhartz (disciple of Rabbi Naḥman of Braslav), *Likkutei Tefillot*, beginning chap. 20: "Help me to come quickly to the Holy Land, which is the source of our holiness, for you know God that all our holiness and purity and all our Judaism depends on *Erets Yisrael*, and it is impossible to truly be an Israelite, and to ascend from level to level, except by coming to *Erets Yisrael*."

66. Cf. above *Israel and its Renascence*, chap. 16. Rav Kook's philosophy may differ with that of Ḥabad Ḥasidism. According to the *Tanya*, *'avodat it-hapkha* (the service of sublimation) is reserved for the *tsaddikim* (wholly righteous). The *beinonim* (middle of the road) are adjured to stick to *'avodat itkafya* (the service of repression). See *Tanya* I, chap. 27. It is possible that the "Alter Rebbe," Rabbi Shneur Zalman of Liadi, would not approve of Rav Kook's democratization of the ideal.

67. "We combine the spirits and sweeten the rigor aroused by their interpenetration." In *SK* 1:40 the sentence concludes: "We combine the spirits, *the new and the old together* (*he-ḥadash ve-ha-yashan yaḥdav*)."

Hamtakat ha-gevurah (sweetening the rigor) is a kabbalistic phrase. It is possible that Rav Kook is merely "co-opting" the language of the *Zohar* for his own purposes. The idea he wishes to convey is that Judaism, after two thousand years of life in the Exile, wrongly equates piety with physical weakness. Jewish spirituality must now come to terms with the phenomenon of physical strength characteristic of a sovereign nation. Rather than canceling out *gevurah* (strength), a refinement or "sweetening" is necessary. However, it is also possible that Rav Kook is actually invoking the *terminus technicus* of the Kabbalah. See his letter to Rabbi Zrihen of Tiberias, quoted in our Introduction.

68. Cf. RAYH Kook, *'Eyn Ayah* III (Tractate *Shabbat*), ed. Filber (Jerusalem, 5754), chap. 2, par. 12 (p. 65), s.v. *paḥ eḥad shel shemen she-hayah munaḥ be-ḥotamo shel kohen gadol.*

69. God is referred to by the Midrash as the "Heart of Israel." See *Shir ha-Shirim Rabbah*, Song of Songs 5:2, based on Psalms 73:26. (This Midrash is cited innumerable times by Rabbi Zadok Hakohen of Lublin. See e.g. *Resisei Laylah* [Lublin, 5663/1903], 42d, par. 44.) Ḥasidism taught the existence of "*dos pintele Yid*," the point or spark (*nitsots*) of Jewishness which lies buried deep within. In the more learned language of the *Tanya*, this is the *ahavah mesuteret*, the "hidden love" that a Jew feels for God, though it may be expressed on only rare occasions. See *Tanya* I, chaps. 15, 16, 18, 19, and *Sefer ha-'Arakhim – Ḥabad*, vol. I (Brooklyn: Kehot, 1970), s.v. *Ahavat Hashem – Ahavah Mesuteret*, pp. 348-402. Thus the Theory of the Jewish Unconscious!

70. Rav Kook does not believe it realistic to oppose the innovations of Zionism: the renewed attachment to the soil of Israel, the renascence of the Hebrew

language, the focus on physical brawn and military might, etc. Rather the *tsaddikei ha-dor*, the righteous of the generation, must reveal the divine light in all these national assets. More than that, they must make the Zionists conscious of their true spiritual identity; must bring them to the realization that their aspiration for all these outer manifestations stems from a deep longing for holiness—so deep that they are not even aware of it!

71. Until now Rav Kook has no differences with the materialist, capitalist reading of society. His objection is to subjecting *Israelite* society, which he believes radically dissimilar, to this form of reductionism. Cf. RZYH Kook in Shvarts, *Mi-Tokh ha-Torah ha-Go'elet* III, p. 217. See also *'Eyn Ayah* to *Shabbat* 41a, s.v. *kol ha-'oleh mi-bavel le-Erets Yisrael 'over ba-'asseh*. Cf. R. Meir Simḥa Hakohen of Dvinsk, *Meshekh Ḥokhmah*, Leviticus 23:21.

72. In the 1950 edition of *Orot*: *be-teva' ha-'ummah*. The 1920 version reads: *be-teva'* nishmat *ha-'ummah*, "in the nature *of the soul* of the nation." So too in *SK* 1:774.

73. This is Yehudah Halevi's term in the *Kuzari*, translated from the Arabic *al-'amr al-ilahi* into Tibbonide Hebrew as *ha-'inyan ha-elohi*. See *Kuzari* I, 42 passim and note in Even Shmuel's edition (Tel-Aviv: Dvir, 1972). *Ha-'inyan ha-elohi* would subsume the essence of the Jewish Nation, namely, its spiritual, prophetic, godly nature. See RZYH Kook's commentary to *Kuzari* in Shvarts, *Mi-Tokh ha-Torah ha-Go'elet* III, pp. 50-53. Cf. Hillel Zeitlin, *'Al Gevul Shnei 'Olamot* (Tel Aviv: Yavneh, 1965), pp. 284-285. I would translate the phrase into contemporary English as "the God-thing." For Rav Kook, *Kuzari* was the primer of Jewish existence, which he commenced teaching from the inception of Yeshivat Merkaz HaRav in Jerusalem. See Shvarts, p. 24. Some notes of those lectures have survived; see *Ma'amrei ha-RAYaH* II, pp. 485-495. Concerning Rav Kook's *Kuzari* classes in his first Jaffa yeshivah, see *IHR* II, pp. 4, 139, 297, and our Introduction.

74. "Manifesting" (*ha-mitgaleh*). In *SK* 1:774: "gifting" (*ha-mesaglah*). And so in the 1920 text of *Orot*. In the Corrigenda to that edition and in the text of the 1950 edition of *Orot*, we read: *ha-mitgaleh*.

75. *Mishnah*, *Yadayim* 3:5.

76. Proverbs 10:25; *Ḥagigah* 12b.

77. Based on the blessing after the reading of the *Haftarah*, which in turn is based on Isaiah 55:11.

78. "The illuminated knowledge of its foundation and soul" (*he'arat ha-de'ah shel yesodah ve-nishmatah*). In *SK* 1:775: "The illuminated knowledge *which is* its foundation and soul (*he'arat ha-de'ah, she-hi yesodah ve-nishmatah*).

79. *'Avodah Zarah* 10b: "The least among you revives the dead."

80. Psalm 97:11.

81. Isaiah 60:12.

82. "And relation" (*ve-yaḥasam*). Not found in *SK* 1:744.

83. Rav Kook feels that nationalism *per se* is decadent but will be uplifted through the phenomenon of Jewish nationalism. However, this piece should be contrasted to another in *Orot Yisrael* (in the 1950 edition of *Orot*, p. 160), where Rav Kook seems to be saying that even specifically Jewish nationalism, symbolized by Messiah Son of Joseph, is basically flawed.

84. Isaiah 35:1.

85. Hebrew, *da'at 'elyon* (Numbers 24:16). In Kabbalah, *da'at 'elyon* (the higher knowledge) is contrasted to *da'at taḥton* (the lower knowledge). (The notion of multiple levels of *da'at* is based on the verse in 1 Samuel 2:3.) See Rabbi Ḥayyim Vital, *'Ets Ḥayyim, Sha'ar ha-Kelalim*, chap. 11; Rabbi Shneur Zalman of Liadi, *Torah 'Or, Vayyera*, 15a-b; *Mishpatim*, 76a-b; *Shemu'ot ha-RAYaH* (ms.), *Mishpatim* 5690. For Rav Kook, the "higher knowledge" is, to use Bucke's term, "cosmic consciousness," which transcends normal rationality to encompass all of existence in a unitive outlook. See Richard Bucke, *Cosmic Consciousness: A Study in the Evolution of the Human Mind* (New York: E. P. Dutton, 1956).

86. "Faint" (*ḥalushah*). In *SK* 1:670: *kelushah*. The meaning is essentially unchanged.

87. Deuteronomy 4:29.

88. Micah 7:8.

89. See note 73.

90. From the blessing recited after reading the *Haftarah*.

91. Lamentations 2:1.

92. Hebrew *Ani ve-hu*. (Vocalization of *Talmud Yerushalmi, Sukkah* 4:3; Rabbi Shneur Zalman of Liadi, *Siddur* [see R. Abraham David Lavut, *Sha'ar ha-Kollel*, chap. 45]; and Rabbi Y.M. Halevi Epstein, *'Arukh ha-Shulḥan*, OḤ 660:2. In *'Olat Re'iyah* II, pp. 371-373, 378, vocalized *va-ho*. So too Rabbi Moshe Feinstein in *Beit Yitzchak* [New York: Yeshiva University, 5752/1992], pp. 27-28.)

There are various explanations as to what this cryptic phrase signifies. Rav Kook follows the explanation of several medieval commentators whereby the implicit idea is that God participates in the suffering of Israel and is as much in need of salvation as Israel itself! See *Tosafot, Sukkah* 45a; Maimonides, *Peirush ha-Mishnah, Sukkah* 4:5; and Rabbenu Menaḥem ha-Me'iri, ibid.

93. Mishnah, *Sukkah* 4:5.

94. *Genesis Rabbah* 60:8. The Rabbis observed that the Torah gives extensive "coverage" to the everyday conversation of Eliezer, servant of Abraham (see Genesis 24), while whole laws must be derived from a single letter! Rav Kook's point is that with the return to the Land, we are once again in a situation where the mundane activities of settling and peopling the land are on a par with Torah

study. His plan is the combination of both Torah study and mundane activities in a spirit of mutual respect and harmony.

95. *Shemoneh 'Esreh* prayer.

96. *Ḥullin* 60b.

97. Isaiah 28:5.

98. *Kaddishei 'elyonim*. Hebraized form of Daniel 7:18.

99. *Shemoneh 'Esreh* prayer.

100. "Long" (*arokh*). In *SK* 1:615: "wide" (*raḥav*).

101. *Talmud Yerushalmi, 'Eruvin* 3:4; Alfasi, *'Eruvin*, end chap. 1; Maimonides, *Hilkhot Shabbat* 27:1. According to the opinion of Rabbi Isaac Alfasi (RIF) and Maimonides, biblically speaking, the Sabbath limit is twelve *mil* corresponding to the size of the Israelites' camp in the desert. The more confining limit of two thousand cubits is of rabbinic origin. Rav Kook uses the two spatial limits as metaphors of spiritual limits. When Israel is living a wholesome spiritual life which goes with Temple, Kingdom, Prophecy, etc., it has the capability of broadening its intellectual horizons, of taking in the world around and integrating it within a context of *kedushah*. When Israel's internal resources are depleted, it is more threatened by outside influences and must set narrower limits to the degree of interaction with surrounding cultures. Cf. J.H. Lewis, *Vision of Redemption* (New Haven: Four Ouarters, 1979), pp. 59-60.

102. Deuteronomy 32:8.

103. Deuteronomy 32:15.

104. Isaiah 54:2-3.

105. *Sotah* 27b. See note 101 above.

106. *Talmud Yerushalmi, Berakhot* 1:1.

107. *Avot* 1:10; *Avot de-Rabbi Nathan*, chap. 11.

108. "And physical labor" (*ve-ha-'avodah ha-mamashit*). The words are not found in *SK* 1:887.

109. Genesis 3:17-19.

110. Literally, "leaves the category of *cursed* and enters the category of *blessed*." Cf. *Genesis Rabbah* 60:7, commenting on Genesis 24:31 and Rabbi M.M. Kasher, *Torah Shelemah* there. Eliezer, the servant of Abraham, who was originally cursed (see Rashi, Genesis 24:39), as are all slaves (Genesis 9:25), emerges as the "blessed of the Lord." Thereupon the rabbis comment that Eliezer "had gone out of the category of *cursed* and entered the category of *blessed*."

111. *Berakhot* 8a.

Compare Rav Kook's outlook on work to that of the Ḥabad school of Ḥasidism. See B. Naor, "The Curtains of the Tabernacle: Rabbi Shelomo Zalman of Kopyst,"

Orot: A Multidisciplinary Journal of Judaism, vol. 1(5751/1991), pp. 33-41, especially p. 35.

According to legend, the antediluvian figure Enoch worked as a cobbler, performing mystical unifications (*yiḥudim)* with every stitch. Enoch is first mentioned as a shoemaker in Rabbi Isaac of Acre, *Me'irat 'Eynayim*, citing one of the Ḥasidei Ashkenaz. Subsequently, the legend became popular among the kabbalists of Safed. The legend is often cited in Ḥasidic literature as a paradigm of "working holiness." See *Me'irat 'Eynayim*, ed. Goldreich (Jerusalem, 1981), p. 398; Rabbi Joseph Karo, *Maggid Meisharim* (Jerusalem, 1970), p. 42; Rabbi Menaḥem 'Azariah da Fano cited in *Yalkut Re'uveni* (Warsaw, 1892), *Bereshit*, p. 120; Rabbi Elijah Cohen of Izmir, *Midrash Talpiyot*, s.v. *Ḥanokh*, quoting Rabbi Menaḥem 'Azariah da Fano, *'Assarah Ma'amarot*; Rabbi Naphtali Bachrach, *'Emek ha-Melekh, Sha'ar Kiryat Arba'*, chap. 94, citing anonymous Midrash; Rabbi Ḥayyim of Volozhin, *Nefesh ha-Ḥayyim*, chaps. between Gates III and IV, chap. 7, citing Rabbi Joseph Karo, *Maggid Meisharim*, sec. *Mikets.*

See also *Midrash Tanḥuma, Vayyetse*, chap. 13, "The merit of labor is beyond the merit of the fathers"; and Rabbi Nathan Sternhartz (disciple of R. Naḥman of Braslav), *Likkutei Tefillot*, chap. 13, "... even when engaged in commerce, I should merit that my thought be connected to You and to Your Holy Torah which is garbed and hidden in all the business, commerce and labor of the world."

112. Aramaic *itlatya*. Rav Kook alludes to one of the profound mysteries of the Kabbalah, whereby the thirty-nine (*LaT*) categories of labor may be transformed into the "dew (*tal*) of lights" (Isaiah 26:19). See *Zohar* III, 243b; R. Moses Cordovero, *Pardess Rimonim, Sha'ar 'Erkei ha-Kinuyyim*, s.v. *tal* and *lat*; R. Menaḥem Mendel of Shklov, *Mayim Adirim* (Jerusalem, 5747), pp. 28-29; R. Naḥman of Breslov, *Likkutei Moharan* I, 11:4, R. Nathan Sternhartz, *Likkutei Halakhot, Hil. Tsitsit* 3:21; *Hil. Netilat Yadayim* 4:2. In the proper mind-set and ambience, the bane of work is transformed into a life-giving blessing, a truly ennobling experience. RZYH Kook in his notes to *Orot*, quotes R. Ḥayyim Vital, *Likkutei Torah*, (Vilna, 5640/1880), *Behar* (79d): "*Melakhah* (labor) is numerically equivalent to *El Adonai* [= 96]."

113. This chapter is reflective of social currents of the period. First, the *ḥalutsim*, the pioneers, influenced by socialist and Marxist thinking, advanced the concept of the holiness of work. To them, physical labor was sacred. Second, there was the desire for worldliness, to which the key was language, the ability to communicate with the outside world in its idiom. Third, was the drive to study secular knowledge. All of this struck the Old Yishuv (as it was referred to) as being wrong. The original settlement of pietists, by and large, had come to the Land to study Torah, not to work the Land. They were supported by the *ḥalukkah*, a welfare system funded by their coreligionists in the Diaspora. As far as non-Jewish languages and sciences were concerned, the great rabbis of Jerusalem had declared a ban forbidding their study. Rav Kook's approach was to realize that the purpose of the original ban was

to defend the souls of the young growing up in *Erets Yisrael*. When it was declared, it was possible to win out over the forces of secularism by repression. Since then, the tide had turned. Those forces had grown much stronger and threatened to overwhelm the youth. Given the times, the only realistic tactic would be to point out from the deepest sources of Judaism precisely the holiness of work, the Torah within work; the *leshon ha-kodesh* or "sacred tongue" within all languages; and the godliness in all disciplines.

114. *Zevaḥim* 88b.

115. Isaiah 54:13.

116. *Menaḥot* 29b.

117. Instead of Yosef—Yehosef. See Psalm 81:6. According to *Sotah* 36b, at the time of Joseph's appointment as viceroy, some of Pharaoh's officers attempted to veto the appointment, bringing up his past as a slave and his unworldliness. "The angel Gabriel came and taught him the seventy languages [of the ancient world]. Joseph had difficulty absorbing it all. Gabriel added to his name one letter of God's name and he was able to learn, as it says, *As a testimony in Jehoseph he placed it, when he went out over the land of Egypt. A language I did not know, I understood* [Psalm 81:6]." Cf. *AT* (Jerusalem, 5743), p. 100.

"Through which this world was created, that was added to his name." These explanatory words are not found in *SK* 1:887.

118. Psalm 68:12.

119. *Shabbat* 88b.

120. Deuteronomy 27:8.

121. *Sotah* 32a, 35b.

122. Zefaniah 3:9.

123. It is interesting to read in this regard the approbation Rav Kook wrote to *Merḥavei Yitsḥak* (Merḥaviah, 5689) by Rabbi Yitsḥak Ravid (father of Prof. Simon Rawidowicz of Brandeis), who worked the soil of Merḥaviah and at the same time composed a supercommentary to Rashi on the Talmud. Rav Kook observes that through Rabbi Ravid, the Land is bearing both its physical and spiritual fruits. Reprinted in *Haskamot ha-RAYaH* (Jerusalem: Makhon RZYH, 5748), p. 55.

124. "Even the most modern frills, refinements, modes of behavior and manners—of course, the choicest and most delicate of them" (*va-afilu be-kishutim ve-hiddurim ve-ofanei ha-hanhagot ve-ha-nimusim ha-yoter modernim, ka-muvan ha-muvḥarim ve-ha-'adinim she-bahem*). In *SK* 1:887 the passage reads: "Even the adornments of the women and the most modern methods of minding the house" (*va-afilu be-kishutei ha-nashim ve-ofanei hanhagot ha-bayit ha-yoter modernim*). The version of *Orot* has been pronouncedly de-feminized.

125. Genesis 17:4-5.

126. Psalm 89:1.

127. Isaiah 41:2. The Talmud (*Bava Batra* 15a) explains that Ethan the *Ezraḥite* refers to Abraham who had come from the East (*Mizraḥ*).

128. Ezekiel 43:2.

129. Joel 4:18.

130. In *SK* 1:225: *kultura*.

131. *Shabbat* 18a.

132. Malachi 3:21.

133. *Berakhot* 18b.

134. Isaiah 26:19; *Ketubot* 111b.

135. "Our state of soul" (*ma'amad ha-neshamah shelanu*). In *SK* 1:229, simply "our soul" (*ha-neshamah shelanu*).

136. Isaiah 58:14; *Zohar* I, 219a; II, 83a. Cf. *OHK* I, pp. 175, 194. See also Rabbi M.H. Luzzatto, *Mesillat Yesharim*, chap. 1.

137. From the *Kaddish*.

138. There is a section of *Zohar Ḥadash* (*Va-Etḥanan*) known as *Ma'amar Kav ha-Middah*. See also *Zohar* II, 233a, 258a; *Tikkunei Zohar* (Vilna, 5623), beginning *tikkun* 5; *tikkun* 19 (37a); Rabbi Ḥayyim Vital, *'Ets Ḥayyim*, Gate 10 (*Sha'ar ha-Tikkun*), chap. 1.

139. *Leviticus Rabbah* 15:2.

140. "Establishment" (*bisuso*). In *SK* 3:2: "perfection" (*bisumo*).

141. See above *Israel and Its Renascence*, chap. 14.

142. *Yoma* 49.

143. In *SK* 3:2 there are additional words here: "which are foreign to his spirit" (*she-hem zarim le-ruḥo*).

144. 2 Samuel 7:23; 1 Chronicles 17:21.

145. Hebrew *ha-kodesh ha-'elyon*. In *OHK* II, p. 311, Rav Kook differentiates between *kodesh* (holy) and *kodesh ha-kodashim* (holy-of-holies). In English, it might be stated as the difference between lowercase "holy" and uppercase "Holy." The point is, there is a level of holiness that is one of the combatants in the arena; there is a higher level of Holiness which subsumes all that is transpiring in the arena.

146. In *SK* 3:2 there occurs here an additional sentence: "And in her [i.e., the divine thought's] expansiveness, she, from the depth of her wisdom, brings out the plan of the 'line of measure' (*kav ha-middah*), and she measures every border, and thus it is self-understood that she herself is broad beyond border" (*ve-hi*

be-harḥavatah harei hi me-'omek ḥokhmatah motsi'ah et ha-tokhnit shel kav ha-middah, ve-hi modedet et kol gevul, u-me-meila muvan she-hi be-'atsmah reḥavah mi-kol gevul).

147. Psalm 119:96.

148. Psalm 118:5.

149. Jeremiah 31:26.

150. *Ḥullin* 5b. See Rabbi Shneur Zalman of Liadi, *Torah 'Or, Mishpatim*, 74c-76b; idem, *Likkutei Torah*, *'Ekev*, 13c.

151. "National" (*medinit*). In *SK* 1:793, *mamlakhtit*. The meaning remains virtually unchanged.

152. Cf. above chap. 4.

153. "Whose main concern is financial success." The phrase is not present in *SK* 1:793.

154. *Bi'ah shelishit*, a halakhic term. See e.g., Maimonides, *Hilkhot Shemitah ve-Yovel* 12:16.

155. Isaiah 8:18.

156. In other words, the purity has not reached to the present rebels, who represent the *ḥitsoniyut*, the exterior of the collective soul of the Jewish People.

157. 1 Kings 3:16.

158. 1 Kings 3:24.

159. "The one who is to be spurned" (*otah ha-re'uyah lehidaḥot*). The version in *AT* (Jaffa, 5674), p. 71, reads: "The harlot who is to be spurned, who trumps up false accusations" (*ha-zonah ha-re'uyah lehidaḥot, ha-ma'alilah 'alilot sheker*). See now *SK* 2:283.

160. 1 Kings 3:26.

161. 1 Kings 3:26.

162. 1 Kings 3:26.

163. 1 Kings 3:27; *Makkot* 23b.

164. "Those who cruelly operate" (*ha-menatḥim be-'akhzariyut*). In *AT* (Jaffa, 5674), p. 71: "the cruel surgeons" (*ha-menatḥim ha-'akhzarim*). See now *SK* 2:283.

165. See Rabbi Naphtali Zevi Judah Berlin, *She'elot u-Teshuvot Meshiv Davar* I, no. 44.

166. Ezekiel 20:32, 33.

167. "The foundation of the righteousness of the just in every generation is supported by the wicked as well, who with all their wickedness, as long as they cling with their heart's desire to the collectivity of the nation, are referred to (by the verse), *Your people are all righteous.*" The more provocative version of *AT*

(Jerusalem, 5743), pp. 101-102, reads: "The foundation of the righteousness of the just in every generation is supported by the wickedness of the wicked, who in truth are not wicked at all, as long as they cling with their heart's desire to the collectivity of the nation, *Your people are all righteous*." See now *SK* 2:283.

168. Isaiah 60:21; *Sanhedrin* 90a.

169. *Megillah* 12b; *Zohar* III, 128b. Cf. below chap. 45.

170. *AT*, p. 102, reads: "By the imagined division they undermine the foundation of all holiness, doing the deed of Amalek ..." See now *SK* 2:283.

171. Deuteronomy 25:18; *Midrash Tanḥuma* (cited in Rashi) ibid.; *Pesikta, Zakhor*, chap. 13.

172. Psalm 55:21; *Midrash Tanḥuma, Lekh Lekha* 20; *Genesis Rabbah* 48:8; *Exodus Rabbah* 19:4; Buber ed. *Midrash Tehillim* 6:1.

173. This chapter, as the previous one, comes to decry the suggestion that the Orthodox separate themselves from the rest of the community. Not only would this be tantamount to sentencing the non-Orthodox to spiritual death; it would also impair the spirituality of the righteous themselves. Their prayers and study of Torah could never be the same after such a terrible division.

174. *Zohar* II, 85b; beginning Introduction to *Tikkunei Zohar*.

175. I.e., the *Shekhinah* (Divine Presence).

176. *Zohar* II, 79b, 85b; III, 127b. *Meḥatsdei ḥakla*, a Zoharic term for spiritual adepts. Rabbi Reuben Margaliyot (*Nitsutsei Zohar*, ibid.) puts forth the novel suggestion that the term arose in opposition to the Talmudic term for scholars held in low esteem, *katlei kanei be-agma* (*Sanhedrin* 33a), "gatherers of reeds in a swamp." See also Rabbi Ḥayyim Vital, *Sefer ha-Likkutim, Behar*, chap. 25; idem, *Likkutei Torah* (Vilna, 1880), *Behar* (80b); Rabbi Naḥman of Braslav, *Likkutei MOHaRaN* I, 65.

177. *Berakhot* 64a.

178. *Shabbat* 116a.

179. Isaiah 44:5.

180. Psalm 102:15-23.

181. Jeremiah 31:26.

182. *Ḥullin* 5b.

183. Psalm 36:7.

184. *Ḥullin* 5b. Rav Kook has set up a third type who synthesize both elements of man and beast. As in Ḥabad Ḥasidism (see above note 150), Rav Kook uses the "seed of man" and the "seed of beast" as metaphors for two types of Jews, one materially oriented and the other spiritually oriented. Cf. above chap. 19. See also the Introduction to *'Ets Hadar* (Jerusalem, 5745) entitled *Rosh Amir*, pp.

7-8. The third type, the man-beast, would incorporate the most salient features of the previous types. Very often Rav Kook sets up an ideal *tsaddik* who provides salvation through synthesis in some deadlocked dialectic. Cf. below chap. 43 and *Orot ha-Teshuvah* 16:12.

185. Psalm 73:22. Cf. Rabbi Shneur Zalman of Liadi, *Tanya* I, 18, 46.

186. Psalm 73:23-28.

187. Malachi 1:2.

188. Malachi 1:2.

189. Blessing before *Shema*ʻ recited in the Morning Prayer. The quoted phrases represent an amalgam of Ashkenazi and Sephardi rites, definitely not the Ashkenazi *nussaḥ* of *Siddur 'Olat Re'iyah*. Was Rav Kook moving in the direction of a *nussaḥ aḥid* (unified rite) that would incorporate elements of both Ashkenazic and Sephardic prayer books? See his letter of 14 Kislev, 5680, to Rabbi Ḥayyim Hirschensohn:

> We should attempt to purchase the buildings adjoining the Holy *Kotel* (Wall). On that site we should erect a great stately synagogue.... It should be conducted according to a consensus of the majority of rabbis of Israel in a way accepted by the totality of the nation, above all division of *nussaḥ* (rite) and partisan custom.... This will complete the vision of Herzl in *Altneuland* concerning the temple that will arise not exactly on the Temple site. He prophesied and knew not what he prophesied.
>
> (Rabbi Ḥayyim Hirschensohn, *Malki ba-Kodesh* IV [St. Louis, 5679-5682], 3a)

The version of the letter published in *IHR* IV, p. 24, omits the reference to Herzl's *Altneuland*.

190. Blessing before *Shema'* in the Morning Prayer.

191. *Pesaḥim* 56a.

192. One who looks on the surface, oftentimes will not see the righteousness hidden within the Jewish People. The Talmud (see previous note) attributes the saying of *Barukh shem*, etc., to the following episode. At the end of his days, Jacob suspected his twelve sons of dereliction or heresy. The sons responded in unison: "Hear O Israel, the Lord our God, the Lord is One! Just as in your heart there is but One, so in our heart there is but One." Thereupon Jacob our Father answered, "Blessed is the name of His glorious kingdom forever unto eternity." The fact that *Barukh shem* is to be uttered silently (except for Yom Kippur in the Ashkenazic rite), Rav Kook interprets as being symbolic of the fact that by and large (again, with the exception of Yom Kippur), the righteousness of the tribes of Israel is hidden from the beholder. "The source for saying *Barukh shem* on Yom Kippur in a loud voice is *Pirkei de-Rabbi Eliezer*: 'On Yom Kippur when they are pure as angels, they say it openly'" (*Hagahot Maimoniyot, Hilkhot Keri'at Shema*ʻ 1:4).

193. *Pesaḥim* 56a.

194. *Ta'anit* 5b.

195. *Ta'anit* 5b.

196. Genesis 29:1.

197. Genesis 49:33. Rabbi Yitsḥak Shilat, in his notes to *AT* (p. 161), points out that the feet are symbolic of the lowest type of Jew, who is nevertheless included within the mainstream of Israel by Jacob's gesture of gathering in his feet. See *AT*, p. 51. (See now *SK* 2:140.) Cf. *Tanya* I, chap 2.

198. Deuteronomy 4:4.

199. Jeremiah 50:20.

200. "Reinstated" (*mitkaltim*). In *SK* 2:285: "gathered" (*mitlaktot*).

201. Psalm 102:19. Cf. Rabbi Naḥman of Braslav, *Likkutei MOHaRaN* I, 17:4-6.

202. Isaiah 59:19; *Sanhedrin* 98a.

203. "Secular nationalism may be infected with much poison" (*ha-le'umiyut ha-ḥolonit yekholah lehizdahem be-zohama rabbah*). In *AT* (Jerusalem, 5743), p. 104 and *SK* 2:285: "Secular nationalism is infected with the poison of misanthropy" (*ha-le'umiyut ha-ḥolonit mizdahemet hi ba-zohama shel sin'at ha-beriyot*).

204. "The source of holiness" *(ha-kodesh ha-mekorati*). Literally, "the original holiness." *Mekorati* should probably read *mekori.*

205. "A love that actualizes" (*ahavah maf'elet*). In *SK* 3:171: "a love pushing" (*ahavah doḥeket*). Cf. *Bava Metsi'a* 84a.

206. Song of Songs 2:15. In *SK* 3:171 there occurs here an additional sentence: "But the maturation will finally come. *On that day sing a song of the vineyard of fine wine* [Isaiah 27:2]." (*Aval sof ha-bishul lavo'. Ba-yom ha-hu kerem ḥemer 'anu lah.*)

207. *Rosh ha-Shanah* 17.

208. Introduction to *Tikkunei Zohar*.

209. Genesis 3:20; *Berakhot* 35b; *Zohar* II, 124a.

210. Numbers 23:21.

211. In *AT* (Jerusalem, 5743), p. 96: "We transcend all the hateful thoughts, all the superficiality of admonitions and sayings which arouse anger and fraternal hatred." See now *SK* 2:274.

212. Psalm 48:15. *AT* (Jerusalem, 5743), p. 97, includes the earlier words of the verse: "This is God." See now *SK* 2:274.

213. Hebrew *'olam ḥadash*. In *AT*, p. 95, *'atid ḥadash*, "a new future." See now *SK* 2:272.

214. *Pesikta*, end *Sos Asis* (38:3).

215. *Shabbat* 31a.

216. "Was there implanted in a few the direction" (*hushreshah ba-yeḥidim hadrakhah*). In *SK* 3:366: "did Rabbi Shim'on ben Yoḥai implant his way" (*hishrish Rabbi Shim'on ben Yoḥai et darko*).

217. *Shabbat* 33b. Rabbi Shim'on bar Yohai and his son El'azar had pursued a monastic life in the cave where they hid from the Roman authorities. Emerging from the cave, they were disdainful of the ordinary mundane activities of the world.

> They saw people plowing and sowing. They said: "They desert eternal life and busy themselves with temporal life."
>
> Every place their eyes rested was immediately consumed by fire.
>
> A heavenly voice went out: "Did you emerge to destroy My world? Back to your cave!"

See Rav Kook's commentary to this narrative in *'Eyn Ayah* III, ed. Filber (Jerusalem, 5754), pp. 201-213. An English translation of this portion of *'Eyn Ayah* is available in *Of Societies Perfect and Imperfect: Selected Readings from 'Eyn Ayah, Rav Kook's Commentary to 'Eyn Ya'akov Legends of the Talmud*, ed. Naor (New York: Sefer-Hermon, 1995), pp. 55-125.

218. See Rabbi Moses Sofer (Schreiber), *ḤaTaM Sofer* VI, *Ḥiddushei Lulav ha-Gazul, Sukkah* 36a, s.v. *ha-domeh le-kushi.*

219. "The more" (*yoter*). So in the 1950 edition of *Orot*. In the 1920 edition: "and the more" (*ve-yoter*).

220. *Megillah* 29a.

221. Cf. *OHK* II, p. 317.

222. *Megillah* 29a.

223. In *AT* (Jerusalem, 5743), p. 125, the word *and* does not occur. See *SK* 2:327.

224. Hosea 11:9; *Ta'anit* 11. In the 1920 edition of *Orot* the quote from *Ta'anit* 11 was imprecise. For "*yamod*," *Orot* had "*yir'eh*" (so too in *SK* 2:327) and for "*be-tokh me'av*," simply "*be-me'av*." These slight deviations were corrected in the 1950 edition of *Orot*.

225. Isaiah 50:3; *Berakhot* 59a.

226. Cf. *Eder ha-Yekar*, p. 19: "... the great deed which will eventuate returning the heart of the fathers to the sons, and the heart of the sons to their fathers, to be completed by Elijah of blessed memory, *whose spirit lives in our midst*."

227. Elijah represents the holiness of Israelite nature and physicality. See above, *Israel and Its Renascence*, chap. 29.

228. "Coarse nature" (*ha-teva' ha-gas*). In *SK* 3:223 the word "coarse" (*ha-gas*) is not found.

229. See above chap. 28, concerning the two types of holiness, one that is harmonious with nature, and the other, exilic variety, which views nature as a threat.

230. Jacob's new name of Israel signifies: "You strove with God (*Elohim*) and men, and were able" (Genesis 32:29). *Elohim* may signify Nature (see Rabbi Shneur Zalman of Liadi, *Tanya* II, 6).

231. "Materialistic nature" (*ha-teva' ha-megusham*). In *SK* 3:223 the word "materialistic" (*ha-megusham*) is not found.

232. "Struck us in our thigh" (*naga' be-khaf yerekhenu*). In *SK* 3:223: "dislocated our thigh" (*nikka' kaf yerekhenu*). Cf. Genesis 32:26.

See MaHaRaL of Prague, *Netsaḥ Yisrael*, chap. 16; idem, *Gevurot Hashem*, chap. 68. MaHaRaL explains that the thigh represents corporeality. Ya'akov had inherited the spiritual dimension (*tselem*) of Adam; Esau was heir to the material grandeur (*levush*) of Adam. In the "short run," the guardian angel of Esau bested Jacob on the level of corporeality, but in the "long run," Jacob emerged victorious over Nature.

233. An allusion to Jacob's wrestling match in Genesis 32:24-32. The idea that Elijah makes Jacob whole may be found in Rashi, Leviticus 26:42. See also Rabbi Jacob ben Asher, *Ba'al ha-Turim*, Genesis 33:14, who points out that the final letters of the words avo el adoni se'irah ("I will come to my master to Se'ir") form the acrostic "Elijah." This may be interpreted to mean that at the end of days Jacob will come to inherit the physical world of Esau, in the spirit of Elijah.

234. "The ugly side of nature" (*ha-teva' be-tsido ha-ka'ur*). In *SK* 3:223 the words "the ugly side" (*be-tsido ha-ka'ur*) are not found.

235. *'Eduyyot* 8:7; *Birkat ha-Mazon* (Grace after Meals).

236. *Berakhot* 12b-13a; MaHaRaL, *Netsaḥ Yisrael*, Introduction. Rabbi Moshe Ushpizai in his commentary to *'Orot ha-Teḥiyah*, entitled *Nitsnutsei ha-Teḥiyah* (pp. 249-250) points out that according to the Talmud (*Berakhot* 13a), the exodus from Egypt corresponds to the name *Jacob*, while the final exodus from the Diaspora would correspond to the new name of *Israel*, symbolic of victory over the forces of nature.

237. "Are increasingly consonant" (*holkhot u-mit'atemot*). So too in *SK* 3:223 with two *tavin*. However in the Corrigenda at the conclusion of the 1920 edition of *Orot*, this was emended to a single *tav*: *u-mita'emot*. In the 1950 edition of *Orot*, the word was printed with a single *tav*. The meaning is unchanged. The double *tav* version is the more archaic, the single *tav* version the more modern usage.

238. "The youthful spirit" (*ha-ru'aḥ ha-tsa'ir*). In *SK* 3:223: "the younger generation" (*ha-dor ha-tsa'ir*).

239. Rav Kook does not view the legitimate aspirations of the Zionist youth as being essentially opposed to the deepest spiritual aspirations of the Jewish People.

240. "The feebleness" (*ha-morakh*). In *SK* 3:224: "only the feebleness" (*rak ha-morakh*).

241. "Materialist" (*ḥomranit*). In *SK* 3:224: *materialistit.*

242. Hosea 2:9.

243. "Clear objective" (*megamah mevureret*). In *SK* 3:225: "discernible turning" (*peniyah yedu'ah*).

244. To use Rabbi Shelomo Aviner's expression, God is "incognito." See S. Aviner, *Tal Ḥermon* (Jerusalem, 5745), p. 474. Rabbi Aviner attributes the expression to his teacher, RZYH Kook. See *Siḥot Harav Zevi Yehudah*, ed. Aviner (Jerusalem, 5753/1993), p. 44. Cf. *Ma'amrei ha-RAYaH* I, p. 171: "They are called by name but know not Who it is that calls them." I believe that an allusion to such a state of affairs may be found in the *Talmud Yerushalmi, Rosh Hashanah* 3:1: "In the days of Rabbi Abahu [the witnesses] came. They were supposed to say *'Go'alenu'* ('Our Redeemer'). Instead they said, *'Ge'ulatenu'* ('Our redemption'). Yet they accepted them."

245. Genesis 4:26; *Pesaḥim* 50a. See Rav Kook's autobiographical revelation in Shvarts, *Mi-Tokh ha-Torah ha-Go'elet* IV, p. 196: "Is this an empty thing, my great pain that I am unable to pronounce the Great Name with its letters?! *I am dumb in deep silence, stilled from speaking good, my hurt is oppressive* (Psalms 39:3)."

See now *Ḥadarav*, ed. Ran Sarid (5762), pp. 25-26. Cf. *Kevatsim mi-Khetav Yad Kodsho* II, ed. Boaz Ofen (Jerusalem, 5768), *Pinkas ha-Dapim* 4:47 (p. 128).

246. Jeremiah 23:6.

247. Ezekiel 48:35.

248. *Zohar* II, 240a; III, 6a.

249. Meshullam ben Kalonymos, Ashkenazic rite for *Mussaf* (Additional Service), Yom Kippur.

250. Hebrew, *ḥevlei mashiaḥ*. See *Shabbat* 118a, *Sanhedrin* 98b.

251. 'Ulla and Raba, *Sanhedrin* 98b.

252. Rav Yosef, *Sanhedrin* 98b; see MaHaRaL, *Netsaḥ Yisrael*, chap. 36.

253. Rabbi Isaiah Halevi Horowitz, *Shnei Luḥot ha-Berit, Toledot Adam, Beit Yisrael; Torah she-bi-Khetav, Bereshit:* "the body holy, and the soul holy of holies."

For further thoughts of Rav Kook concerning the holiness of the body, see *Orot Yisrael*, chap. 9 (*"Kedushat Yisrael"*), reprinted at the conclusion of the 1950 edition of *Orot.*

254. *Tikkunei Zohar, tikkun* 19 (Vilna, 1867), 41a. See *Be'ur ha-GRA* there.

255. "The connection" (*ha-kishur*). In *SK* 3:273: "the direct connection" (*ha-kishur ha-yashar*).

256. "Fallen fear" (*yir'ah nefulah*). In *SK* 3:273: "Some fuzzy fear" (*eizeh yir'ah metushteshet*).

Yir'ah nefulah ("fallen fear") is a Ḥasidic term. See Rabbi Nathan Sternhartz (disciple of Rabbi Naḥman of Braslav), *Likkutei Tefillot*, chaps. 5, 15. In Exile, the *Shekhinah* (Divine Presence), synonymous with *yir'at hashem* (fear of the Lord), has fallen into the domain of the *kelipot* (literally "shells" or "husks," i.e., Evil) and in the process, been warped. See Rabbi Yitsḥak Eizik of Komarno, *Otsar ha-Ḥayyim* (in *Heikhal Berakha*), *Ki Tissa*, 272d and 62a; Rabbi Hillel of Paritch (one of the major exponents of Ḥabad philosophy), *Hakdamat Derekh Ḥayyim* (reprint Jerusalem, 5740), 10b-c. The import of the term is a fear that is counterproductive or even destructive, as it paralyzes and haunts, while true awe of the Lord ennobles, invigorates, and breeds creativity.
257. Isaiah 33:6; *Shabbat* 31a.

258. *Numbers Rabbah* 13:16; Buber ed. *Midrash Tehillim* 19:4; *Tosafot, Shabbat* 31a, s.v. *emunat zeh*.

258* "Shining" (*zore'aḥ*). In *SK* 3:273: "resting" (*shoreh*).

259. "The holy flesh" (*ha-basar ha-mekudash*). In *SK* 3:273 simply "the flesh" (*ha-basar*).

260. "Reminiscent of the physical resurrection" (*zekher li-teḥiyat ha-metim ha-gufanit*). In *SK* 3:273: "resurrection of the dead in bodies" (*teḥiyat ha-metim ba-geviyot*).

Cf. Rabbi Nathan Sternhartz, *Likkutei Tefillot*, chap. 22: "I should merit that the soul have compassion on the flesh of my body, that the soul come close to the body, and reveal to it, and enlighten it with all the illumination and attainment the soul constantly enjoys, so that the body might also benefit thereby. Then the soul will be able to constantly revert to its level through the imprints of the illuminations it shone in the flesh of the body."

261. Hebrew *ha-megamah*. The word, which occurred in the 1920 edition of *Orot* (and *SK* 1:716), was omitted from the 1950 edition, presumably because it is redundant.

262. RZYH Kook in his endnote here refers to Maimonides, *Guide of the Perplexed* III, chap. 25. See at length in our Introduction.

263. For Rav Kook's understanding of the unification of the transcendental and immanental aspects of divinity (*yiḥud Kudsha-berikh-hu u-Shekhinteh*), see *Orot Yisrael* 1:9-10, reprinted in the 1950 edition of *Orot*. (See now *SK* 1:314.) See also *SK* 2:249; *Siddur 'Olat Re'iyah* I, pp. 13-15, 23-24, 193.

264. 2 Samuel 8:13; *Zohar* III, 113.

265. 2 Samuel 8:15.

266. 2 Samuel 8:16. The point of these citations is that David was equally involved in praising God through singing psalms and reciting divine names as in pursuing the enemies of Israel. "Said Rabbi Abba bar Kahana: Were it not for David, Yo'av could not have waged war; were it not for Yo'av, David could not have studied Torah, as it is written, *David was performing justice and righteousness for all his people – And Yo'av ben Zeruyah was over the army* [2 Samuel 8:15,16]" (*Sanhedrin* 49a).

267. *Talmud Yerushalmi, Sotah* 1:8; *Leviticus Rabbah* 26:2.

268. Proverbs 3:6; *Berakhot* 63a. See above *Israel and its Renascence*, beginning chap. 3.

"By making more pronounced the character of the nation, by the short passage upon which depends the entire corpus of Torah: *In all your ways know Him*." This conclusion is missing in *SK* 1:716.

269. Rabbi Ḥayyim Vital, *Sha'arei Kedushah* 3:7; idem, *Sha'ar ha-Pesukim*, Isaiah chap. 1, s.v. *va-omar oy li ki nidmeiti*; idem, *Sefer ha-Likkutim*, Isaiah 6:5; Rabbi Isaiah Halevi Horowitz, *Koraḥ*, note s.v. *ve-yesh lefaresh*.

270. Proverbs 4:18.

271. Cf. *AT* (Jerusalem, 5743), p. 10. See now *SK* 2:20.

272. According to the editors of *SK*, the words "a precise purity is required" (*nidreshet hi ha-toharah ha-meduyyeket*) did not occur in *SK* 2:234 and were supplied by Rav Kook at the time of the printing of *AT* in 1914.

273. Jeremiah 23:29.

274. *Berakhot* 22a.

275. Rav Kook's term for the Ḥasidic movement founded by Rabbi Israel Ba'al Shem Tov (1698 or 1700-1760) in Eastern Europe, to distinguish it from the earlier Ḥasidic movement of the medieval Rhineland pietists (most notably Rabbi Judah he-Ḥasid of Regensburg), referred to as *Ḥasidei Ashkenaz*.

276. "Fleshly purity" (*ha-toharah ha-besarit*). In *SK* 2:234 simply "purity" (*ha-toharah*).

277. The conjunctive *vav* (and) is supplied in *AT* (Jerusalem, 5743), p. 82. See now *SK* 2:234.

278. *Seliḥot, Zekhor Berit*.

279. See Maimonides, *Hilkhot Keri'at Shema'* 4:8; *Hilkhot Tefillah* 4:4-6.

280. The modern Ḥasidic movement encourages its male followers to perform daily ablutions in the *mikveh* or ritual bath. (By the way, we have reports – see Introduction – that this was Rav Kook's custom as well.) Rav Kook understands that this phenomenon is conceptually concomitant with the fact that Ḥasidism placed renewed emphasis on music and imagination, a return to the Judaism

of the Prophets. See 2 Kings 3:15. See at length Bezalel Naor, *Lights of Prophecy* (New York: Orthodox Union, 5750/1990), pp. 13-14, 48. Cf. *Eretz Tzvi/Tzvi Glatt Memorial Volume* (Jerusalem, 5749), p. 183, par. 3, and R. Zadok Hakohen Rabinowitz of Lublin, *Poked 'Akarim* (Piotrkow, 1922), 14d.

281. "Definition" (*hagbalah*). This should probably read "expansion" (*hagdalah*).

282. Deuteronomy 23:10, 11. In *AT* (Jerusalem, 5743, p. 83) verse 12 is included as well: "But it shall be that toward evening he shall bathe himself in water, and when the sun goes down, he may enter within the camp." Its exclusion from our version is no doubt a copyist's error due to the dittography: *enter within the camp – enter within the camp.*

283. Deuteronomy 23:15.

284. Ezekiel 26:20.

285. The stress placed in the Hebrew text on the word *'orah* (light) reminds this writer (BN) of an anecdote told him by Rav Zevi Yehudah Kook *zt"l.* The elder sage recalled that Yosef Ḥayyim Brenner, a legendary figure in the creation of modern Hebrew literature, was one of "*unzer shalosh se'udos yiden*" ("one of our *Shalosh Se'udot* Jews"), meaning one of those who attended the third Sabbath meal in the home of Rav Avraham Yitsḥak Hakohen Kook during his tenure as Rav of Jaffa. One time Brenner cornered the young Zevi Yehudah in the kitchen and told him: "I don't understand how your father can constantly speak of *'or, 'or, 'or* (light, light, light) when in my soul there is only darkness!"

This is the first of three chapters in which Rav Kook calls to the writers of the reborn Hebrew literature to rise to the spiritual occasion. For an analysis of the depth of Rav Kook's struggle with, and attempt to uplift, modern Jewish literature, see B. Naor, *Hartsa'at ha-Teshuvah* (Jerusalem, 5750), pp. 43-47. Rav Kook's influence on the writers of his generation—Alexander Ziskind Rabinowitz (AZaR); Ḥayyim Naḥman Bialik, the national poet; Shmuel Yosef Agnon, novelist and later Nobel laureate; Yosef Zevi Rimon, tortured poet of the divine – was considerable. See *Zemaḥ Zevi*: Letters of RZYH Kook I, pp. 1-2, 51-52; *IHR* I, pp. 247-248, 338; *Haskamot ha-RAYaH* (Jerusalem, 5748), pp. 88-89.

286. *Ḥagigah* 15b; *Kiddushin* 30a. Cf. *Eder ha-Yekar*, p. 56.

287. Isaiah 35:8.

288. Isaiah 35:9.

289. Cf. *AT* (Jerusalem, 5743), p. 67. See now *SK* 2:188.

290. Jeremiah 17:9.

291. "Will reside in it" (*tigbal bah*). In *SK* 4:64 the sentence concludes: "and be revealed in its midst and through it" (*ve-tigaleh be-tokhah ve-'al-yadah*). Then, there follows an entire sentence: "This is the destiny of the new creation about to be revealed in the rebirth of Israel." (*Zot hi te'udatah shel ha-yetsirah ha-ḥadasha ha-'atidah lehigalot bi-teḥiyatam shel yisra'el.*)

292. *Mishnah, Sotah* 9:15.

"After the wisdom of writers will have rotted." In *SK* 4:64: "After the great rotting of the wisdom of writers" (*aḥarei ha-siraḥon ha-gadol shel ḥokhmat soferim*).

293. "It shall yet be said to Israel." The words do not occur in *SK* 4:64.

294. Isaiah 59:21.

295. *Bava Batra* 21a: "The envy of scribes will increase wisdom." Rabbi Samuel Edels (MaHaRShA) points out that it does not say "the envy of wise men" but only "the envy of *scribes*," a lower level of intellect, e.g., schoolteachers, who have not yet attained to the degree of wisdom. The truly wise are not envious of their peers.

296. Proverbs 14:30: "Jealousy is the rotting of the bones."

297. *Mishnah, Sotah* 9:15.

298. In *AT* (Jerusalem, 5743), p. 59: "the higher wisdom, that is higher than envy." See now *SK* 2:166.

299. Cf. *Tosefot Rabbi Akiva Eiger, Avot* 5:20. The import is that in the messianic future, wisdom will no longer be in need of aggressive behavior.

300. Isaiah 42:10.

301. Isaiah 62:2.

302. Hosea 14:7.

303. *Mishnah, Sotah* 9:15. Simply, the *Mishnah* in its doomsday scenario is decrying this negative phenomenon of *ḥutspah*. Rav Kook, on the other hand, views it as a blessing in disguise. The truth is that he was preceded in this positive attitude to *ḥutspah* by the Ḥasidic masters. See Rabbi Uri Feivel of Krystnopol, *'Or ha-Ḥokhmah* (Jerusalem, 5730), *'Ekev*, 29a, and Rabbi Zadok Hakohen of Lublin, *Zidkat ha-Zaddik*, chaps. 46, 47. Neither should we omit the Ḥasidic concept of *'azut di-kedushah* – "holy arrogance." See Rabbi Naḥman of Braslav, *Likkutei MOHaRaN* I, 22, 30, 147, 271. Cf. below chap. 45; *'Ikvei ha-Tson*, pp. 119-121; *Orot* (1950 ed.), pp. 122-123; *Orot ha-Teshuvah* 9:8; 12:1. See further B. Naor, *Ba-Yam Derekh* (Jerusalem, 5744), pp. 142-144.

304. Proverbs 13:9.

305. *Sanhedrin* 98a.

306. "In a capacity" (*shimush*). In *SK* 2:88 "strictly in a capacity" (*rak shimush*).

307. Isaiah 62:3 (with minor variations).

308. Cf. above chap. 22.

309. The words in brackets appeared in the 1920 edition of *Orot* and were also referenced in RZYH Kook's notes in the back of the 1950 edition. (They also appear in *AT* [Jerusalem, 5743], p. 99. See now *SK* 2:279.) Their omission from the text of the 1950 edition must be due to a printer's oversight. In Hebrew the deleted text reads: *"Zeh ḥoli ve-essa'enu, u-meherah ta'aleh arukhah lah."*

310. Jeremiah 10:19.

311. Isaiah 58:8; Jeremiah 33:6.

312. Isaiah 61:6.

313. "To the source of the *nation's vitality* and will thereby revivify *it*." The translation is based on the text of the 1950 edition of *Orot*: "*li-mekor ḥayyehah u-mi-sham yashuvu le-haḥayotah*." In the 1920 edition, the text read simply: "*li-mekor ḥayyim u-mi-sham yashuvu le-haḥayot*" ("to the source of vitality and will thereby revivify").

314. *Zohar* I, 81; III, 25. Rabbi Zadok Hakohen characterizes the level of *nefesh* as *ahavat yisrael* (*love of Israel*) and the level of *ru'aḥ* as *ahavat torah* (love of Torah). See *Zidkat ha-Zaddik*, chap. 196.

315. See previous note.

In a letter of clarification to Rabbi David Tevel Deinovski (1865-1943), a spiritual giant of the Lithuanian world of Mussar, Rav Kook cited Rabbi Ḥayyim Vital's *Sha'ar ha-Gilgulim* (end *hakdamah* 7) as his source for the notion (found curious by many readers) that there exist sinners of Israel whose *nefesh*, despite their sins, is more perfected than that of some righteous men. The reference is to King Aḥab, who according to the Rabbis (TB, *Sanhedrin* 102b) was "*shakul*" (50-50). Rabbi Ḥayyim Vital explains Aḥab's balance or "equipoise" based on his theory of personality which subdivides into *nefesh-ru'aḥ-neshamah*. The letter (tentatively dated by the editors 5694? / 1934?) appeared in the journal of Merkaz Harav, *Nitsanei Arets* 11 (*Iyyar* 5755 / 1995), pp. 48-49. The editors of the journal cross-reference to the parallel work by Rabbi Ḥayyim Vital, *Sefer ha-Gilgulim* (Frankfurt, 5444/1684), end chap. 9 (f.9c).

316. "Yet" (*'adayin*). The word does not occur in *AT* (Jerusalem, 5743), p. 11. See now *SK* 2:21.

317. Hebrew *ha-posh'im ha-eleh*. The word *these* does not occur in *AT* (Jerusalem, 5743), p. 12. There the text reads simply, *ha-posh'im*. See now *SK* 2:21.

318. Hebrew *ha-tsaddikim ha-'elyonim*. Cf. *Orot ha-Teshuvah* 16:12.

319. See above note 314.

320. "The *ru'aḥ*" (*ha-ru'aḥ*). The definite article "the" (*ha*) was missing in the 1920 edition of *Orot*. It was supplied in the 1950 edition.

321. Psalms 132:9; *Zohar* III, 244a (*Ra'aya Mehemna*) and 242a.

322. From *Kol Mevaser* recited Hoshana Rabba; *Talmud Yerushalmi, Berakhot* 2:4; *Sanhedrin* 98b; *Zohar* I, 82b; II, 232b. Rav Ya'akov Moshe Ḥarlap, eminent disciple of Rav Kook, writes that the soul of our generation is that of King David. See *Mi-Ma'ayenei ha-Yeshu'ah*, chap. 63, p. 214.

323. *Mo'ed Katan* 16b; *'Avodah Zarah* 5a.

324. Psalm 132:10.

325. Hebrew *meridah ruḥanit*. The wording is a bit misleading. The intention is not a spiritually motivated revolt but rather an overturning of time-hallowed spiritual values. In brief, an upsurge of unprecedented materialism.

326. *Sifré, Ha'azinu*: "*You grew fat, thick, fleshy* [Deuteronomy 32:15] – these are three generations before the days of Messiah."

327. Ecclesiastes 12:1; *Shabbat* 151b.

328. "Will cease" *(teḥdal)*. In *AT* (Jerusalem, 5743), p. 86, the outlook is even gloomier: "will totally cease" (*kalil teḥdal*). See now *SK* 2:247.

329. Cf. above chap. 40.

330. *Zohar* III, 128b; *Zohar Ḥadash* (Margaliyot edition, Jerusalem, 5754, 64b; Ashlag edition, London, 5730, p. 51) s.v. *yishakeni* (III); Rabbi M.Ḥ. Luzzatto, *Adir ba-Marom*, Spinner ed. (Jerusalem, 5750), pp. 139-140; Rabbi Elijah of Vilna, Commentary to Isaiah 5:6; Talmidei Rabbenu Yonah, *Berakhot*, chap. 5, *Mishnah*, s.v. *ha-omer yevarekhukha tovim* (23b). Cf. *OHK* II, pp. 315-316. The Ba'al Shem Tov taught that Evil is a *kisei* (seat) for Good. See *Keter Shem Tov* (Brooklyn: Kehot, 1987) I, 5a, par. 26, 27.

331. "For lack of a thick grasp of life" (*me-ḥoser tefisat ḥayyim me'ubah*). In *SK* 4:25: "*From the dwindling of the wicked and* for lack of a *coarse and* thick grasp of life" (*mi-mi'ut ha-resha'im u-me-ḥoser tefisat ḥayyim gasah u-me'ubah*).

332. Rabbi Eliezer Waldman pointed out that Rav Kook's use of the word *'atsmi*, here translated as "essential," contains the sense of the more modern Hebrew term *'atsma'i* (independent).

333. "The process" (*ha-mahalakh*). In *SK* 4:25: "the breach" (*ha-pirtsah*).

334. Job 37:16.

335. Job 14:4; *Numbers Rabbah* 19:1, Rabbi Judah Löw (MaHaRaL of Prague), *Gevurot Hashem*, chap. 5 (quoted in our Introduction).

336. Actually, this is a point of debate between the Philosophers and the Kabbalists. See Rabbi Meir Ibn Gabbai, *'Avodat ha-Kodesh* III, 3-7. Rav Kook has inveighed with the latter.

337. Zechariah 14:6, 7.

338. *Zohar* I, 216a. (See however the note of the Mantua editors, 211b; and Daniel Matt's note to the Pritzker Edition of *The Zohar*, Vol. III [Stanford, CA, 2006], p. 302.) The quote is imprecise.

339. Psalm 71:24; *Zohar* I, 216a.

340. "Real" *(mamashiyim)*. In *AT* (Jerusalem, 5743), p. 131, *ma'asiyim* (practical). See now *SK* 2:348.

341. Hebrew *ha-'orot ha-yoter 'elyonot*. The version of *AT* (p. 132) reads: *he'arot ha-yoter 'elyonot*. See now *SK* 2:348.

342. Cf. above chap. 39. See also B. Naor, *Avirin* (Jerusalem: Zur Ot, 5740), p. 229.

343. Song of Songs 2:9.

344. In the 1920 edition: *lo nir'ah raki'a be-toharato*. Emended in the 1950 edition to: *lo nir'ah raki'a be-toharatah*.

345. Isaiah 50:3; *Berakhot* 59a.

346. "In the time of Exile" *(shel zeman ha-galut)*. In the earlier work *AT* (Jerusalem, 5743), p. 130, simply *she-ba-galut*, "in the Exile." The emendation was designed to clarify that the difference is temporal, not spatial. See now *SK* 2:343.

347. "These have no portion in the World to Come: ... One who says Torah is not from Heaven" (*Mishnah, Sanhedrin* 10:1). Cf. *Orot ha-Emunah* (Jerusalem, 5745), p. 25:

> There is disbelief which is accounted belief, and belief which is accounted disbelief. How so? A man admits that Torah is from Heaven, but the "heavens" he pictures are so strange that nothing of true belief remains. And how might disbelief be considered admission? A man denies that Torah is from heaven, but his disbelief is based only on the conception of "heaven" which is to be found in minds filled with rubbishy, nonsensical thoughts, while he maintains that Torah must be from a higher source ... This denial is considered as admission.

See B. Naor, "Rav Kook and Emmanuel Levinas on the 'Non-Existence' of God," *Orot: A Multidisciplinary Journal of Judaism* I (5751/1991).

348. Exodus 20:19.

349. Malachi 3:9.

350. "Establish" (*yevases*). In *AT* (Jerusalem, 5743), p. 130: *yevarer* (clarify). See now *SK* 2:344.

351. "The awareness" (*ha-hakarah)*. In *AT*: *ha-hakarah 'al buryah* (the clear awareness).

352. Psalm 92:2.

353. *Mishnah, Berakhot* 9:5; *Pesaḥim* 50a.

354. In the 1920 edition: *be-ruḥaniyuto* (in its spirituality). Emended in the 1950 edition to *be-ruḥaniyut* (in spirituality). In *AT*, p. 130, the entire phrase "for the evil as for the good, even in spirituality" is missing. (See now *SK* 2:344.) See B. Naor, *Hartsa'at ha-Teshuvah* (Jerusalem, 5750), Fifth Lecture (pp. 36-47).

355. *Berakhot* 7b.

356. Genesis 29:35.

357. *Leviticus Rabbah* 9:7.

358. Psalm 100:4.

359. Hebrew *bi-genizah*. In *AT* (Jerusalem, 5743), p. 25 (as in *SK* 2:61), the Aramaic (Zoharic) form of the word is used: *bi-genizu*. (See e.g., *Zohar* III, 111b.) So too in *Orot ha-Torah* 1:3. In *Orot ha-Torah* (1:1, 2) Rav Kook elaborates on this theme. He views the Oral Torah as an organic outgrowth of the Jewish People ("*Torah she-be-'al peh* is lodged in the very character of the Nation"). This view is very much the kabbalistic one that equates the Oral Law with the final *sefirah* of *Malkhut* and thus with *Knesset Yisrael*. Cf. Rabbi Joseph Dov Baer Soloveitchik of Brisk, *She'elot u-Teshuvot Beit ha-Levi* III, *Derush* 18: "Israel are as the parchment of the Oral Torah, as it says, 'Write them on the tablet of your heart'.... The Torah and Israel are one." Also idem, *Beit ha-Levi* (Warsaw, 5644/1884), *Yitro*, s.v. *Yishakeni* (23b-d); Rabbi Mordechai Joseph Leiner of Izbica, *Mei ha-Shilo'aḥ* II (Lublin, 5682/1922), 72b, *Massekhet 'Eruvin*; Rabbi Zadok Hakohen Rabinowitz of Lublin, *Likkutei Ma'amarim* in *Divrei Soferim* (Lublin, 5673/1913), 40b-44d, especially 40c: "They said in *Tikkunim* [=*Tikkunei Zohar*], '*Your father* – this is the Written Torah; *Your mother* – this is the Oral Torah.' This is exactly what the *Zohar* writes several times (II, 90b), also the *Gemara* (*Berakhot* 35b), '*Your father* – this is the Holy One; *Your mother* – this is *Knesset Yisrael*'."

Despite the Oral Torah's overtly human, earthly overtones, there is nevertheless a subtle divine, heavenly influence on it, which is expressed either in the fact that all that future sages would innovate was already revealed to Moses on Sinai, or in the fact that there was a heavenly need for Israel to accept the Torah. (See *Orot ha-Torah*, ibid.)

360. See Rabbi Elijah Gaon of Vilna, *Aderet Eliyahu*, beginning *Ha'azinu*.

361. Since the Oral Torah is synonymous with the Jewish People, understandably it cannot shine forth when there is a slump or decline in creativity. And in order for the Nation to be fully creative, it must enjoy its full spiritual infrastructure.

362. Hebrew *yenikah*, literally "sucking." Cf. MaHaRaL of Prague, *Derush 'al ha-Torah* (in *Be'er ha-Golah* [London: L. Honig and Sons, 1960], 49a): "At this time, Israel have no wisdom and knowledge of their own, only that which they suck from those referred to as the 'mother' of Israel, their predecessors, who compiled the books which they search as an infant searches the breasts of his mother in order to nurse, but that they should have knowledge of their own – this is not possible." MaHaRaL too is bemoaning the lack of creativity which is the fate of Israel during Exile.

363. Literally, "the day will shine" (Song of Songs 2:17). See A. Even-Shoshan, *Ha-Milon he-Ḥadash* (Jerusalem: Kiryat-Sepher, 1977), entry *fu'ah*.

364. Isaiah 30:26.

365. Sun (*Tif'eret*) and Moon (*Malkhut*) are symbolic of Written Torah and Oral Torah, respectively.

366. Isaiah 30:26.

367. *Mishnah, Sotah* 9:15.

368. "Indistinct" (*keheh*). In *AT* (Jerusalem, 5743), p. 28 (as in *SK* 2:68), *ḥalush u-mekhoʻar*, "weak and ugly." As *AT* preceded *Orot* in time, we must conclude that the version before us is an attempt to subdue the more derogatory tone of the original.

Rav Kook was of the opinion that Judaism as it emerged from the long Exile into the light of Day (Redemption), would have to outgrow certain misconceptions which had crept into theology and colored Jewish life with somber hues. Consider the following passages:

> With the general moratorium on spiritual study of divine matters, the concept of divinity becomes increasingly obscure, lacking pure intellectual and emotional labor. At the same time, the external fear, the natural faith and the contrite subjugation remain in many hearts as an inheritance from the ages when the knowledge and the emotion of God shone so intensely that commensurate with its enormity was its grip over all souls. Since the inner point of God-consciousness is dull, the divine essence continues in the masses – and even in individuals who are supposed to be luminaries to those masses – as merely a dominating force from which there is no escape and to which subjugation is necessary. When a person comes to be subjugated to divine service according to such a vacuous situation, of a somber conception full of confusion which comes to mind when we think of God without intellect and without Torah – lower fear (*yir'ah tata'ah*) sundered from its source, which is higher fear (*yir'ah 'ila'ah*) – the person progressively loses the splendor of his world, by the fact that he attaches himself to small-mindedness (*katnut ha-moḥin*). Then what is revealed within the soul is not the glory of God, but rather the lowliness of wild fantasies, which paint a picture of some fictitious, hazy being, impoverished and raging, which frightens whoever believes in it, and depresses his spirit, stopping up the heart and preventing human gentleness from asserting itself, while uprooting the divine splendor which is within his soul. And even if such a person were to say all the day that this belief is in the One God – it is an empty cliché of which the soul has no knowledge. Any sensitive soul would have to ignore such a cliché, and this is the disbelief of the "footsteps of Messiah," when the waters have emptied from the sea of God-consciousness, in *Knesset Yisrael* (Ecclesia Israel) –and the entire world. (*Zer'onim*, chap. 5, "Cathartic Suffering," reprinted in the 1950 edition of *Orot*, p. 126)
>
> When prayer is corporealized, it becomes a fake, an idolatry. One calls to a god who is conceived as being tough, dictatorial and seeking servile bondage of those impressed into his service. He is gratified when they grovelingly ask of him favors. Then his stern nature is mollified and he

grants the request, which is nothing lofty but just a base wish. Such a prayer is unfit, drunken and pagan; it lacks the inner essence of prayer and is considered sinful. (*Otserot ha-RAYaH* II, p. 919)

369. From Morning Prayer. In the Ashkenazic rite, the conclusion to the first blessing of *Shema'*.

370. In the 1920 edition, *dal* (singular), corrected in the 1950 edition to *dalim* (plural) to conform to grammar. In *SK* 2:68: *dalim*.

371. Hebrew *dildul*, literally "impoverishment." In *AT* (Jerusalem, 5743), p. 28, *delulah* (impoverished). See now *SK* 2:68.

372. *Nazir* 23b; *Yevamot* 103.

373. "Splendor" (*zohar*). In *AT* (Jerusalem, 5743), p. 109, *tohar*, "purity." See now *SK* 2:296.

374. Hebrew *da'at*.

375. Hebrew *ḥokhmah*.

376. Hebrew *gevurah*.

377. Hebrew *tif'eret*.

378. Hebrew *netsaḥ*.

379. Hebrew *hod*.

380. Hebrew *tussad*, from *yesod*.

381. Hebrew *malkhut*. It seems that Rav Kook, once again (see above *Israel and Its Renascence*, chap. 13) is alluding to the "Mystery of the Death of the Kings" or "Mystery of the Breaking of the Vessels." On the ruins of the evil kingdoms will arise *malkhut 'olamim*, "the kingdom of eternity."

382. Isaiah 55:3; *Zohar* III, 262b; Rabbi Shneur Zalman of Liadi, *Siddur 'im D[ivrei] E[lohim] Ḥ[ayyim]* (Brooklyn, 1965), *Sha'ar ha-Tefillin*, s.v. *Amar R' Yehudah (*13d-14a).

383. Isaiah 63:8, 9.

384. "Clearly" (*bi-behirut)*. In *AT*, p. 111 (as in *SK* 2:301), *be-veirur*. I am not sure what the difference (if any) between the two is.

385. Hosea 13:4.

386. Hebrew *koneniyut*. This might be an allusion to Rabbi M.H. Luzzatto's image of history as the gears or interlocking wheels (*koneniyot*) of a timepiece (*orlogin*). See Rabbi David Cohen's Introduction to *OHK* I, pp. 31-32, 36. Cf. *OHK* II, p. 555.

387. "For good, for her individual members" (*le-tovah le-ishehah ha-peratiyim)*. So in the 1920 edition of *Orot*; in *AT*, p. 111 and *SK* 2:301. Changed in the 1950 edition of *Orot* to *le-tovat ishehah ha-peratiyim* (for the good of her individual members).

388. "By her deeds" (*be-fo'al yadah*). In *AT*, p. 111 and *SK* 2:301, *bah ve-'al yadah*, "through her."

389. *Sotah* 9b.

390. Isaiah 45:25.

391. An apt description of Nietzschean philosophy that attempts to free European civilization from the shackles of the so-called Judeo-Christian tradition. See our Introduction. Cf. above chapter 3.

392. Isaiah 41:20; Job 12:9.

393. Cf. *Eder ha-Yekar* (Jerusalem, 5745), p. 31. It was the consensus of the *Rishonim* – Judah Halevi, Maimonides, Naḥmanides – that the spread of Christianity in the world was part of some divine plan whereby the nations of the world would be exposed indirectly (albeit perversely!) to Judaic influence. See above *Israel and Its Renascence*, chap. 5, n. 170.

394. *Sanhedrin* 97a.

395. Agus, in his biography of Rav Kook, *High Priest of Rebirth* (New York: Bloch, 1972), pp. 49-50, points out that Micha Yosef Berdichevsky, a figure influential in evolving Hebrew literature had in fact adopted the Nietzschean stance in his call for a "transvaluation" and repudiation of Judaic morality. Rav Kook's response should be compared with the earlier response to the Jewish Nietzschean by Aḥad Ha'am, "*Shinui ha-'Arakhin*," in *Kol Kitvei Aḥad Ha'am* (Jerusalem: Jewish Publishing House, 1956), pp. 154-159.

Ironically enough, in his youth, Berdichevsky had studied in the Volozhin Yeshiva, where Rav Kook made his acquaintance. Rav Zevi Yehudah Kook told this writer (BN) of his father's experience with Berdichevsky. One day, a fellow student approached Abraham Isaac Kook asking his help with "the RoN (= Rabbenu Nissim) on Tractate *Yevamot*." Rav Kook knew immediately that his questioner could not be much of a scholar, for the commentary to the RIF on *Yevamot* is not that of "RoN" at all but rather *Nimmukei Yosef*! The second thing that struck Rav Kook about his questioner was his distinctive accent. He came from a region of Russia where *a* was pronounced *o*, e.g., *Tote* for *Tate* (Yiddish for Daddy). Thus RaN had become RoN! (See Ḥayyim Lifshitz, *Shivḥei ha-RAYaH*, pp. 46-47, where the story of the "RoN" has been mangled.)

396. Or "independence." See note 332 above.

397. See note above.

398. Psalm 44:4-6.

399. Hosea 3:5.

400. 1 Samuel 10:26.

401. Hebrew *keru'im ve'omdim*. Cf. in the Sabbath song, *Menuḥah ve-Simḥah*, "*beru'im ve-'omdim*."

402. Psalm 146:10.

403. Cf. *Zer'onim*, chap. 2; reprinted in the 1950 edition of *Orot*, pp. 120-121.

404. Psalm 119:45.

405. Those who engage in casuistry, *pilpul*.

406. *Zohar* I, 158; *Tikkunei Zohar*, Second Introduction, *Pataḥ Eliyahu*.

407. Job 41:8.

408. Genesis 36:37. A trope for the *sefirah* of *Binah* (Understanding). See Rabbi Joseph Gikatilia, *Sha'arei Orah*, *Sha'ar Shemini*; *Zohar* III, 142a; RAYH Kook, *Shabbat ha-Arets* (Jerusalem, 1985), Introduction, p. 10.

409. Genesis 27:27; *Zohar* I, 122a, 224b; II, 127b, 218a.

410. Ruth 4:7; *Zohar Ḥadash, Ruth*. Cf. *IHR* I, p. 112; *Orot ha-Torah*, chap. 13.

411. See note above.

412. Lamentations 3:6; *Sanhedrin* 24a.

413. *Pesaḥim* 34b. Rav Kook juxtaposes the Jerusalem Talmud to the Babylonian Talmud. In *IHR* I, pp. 112-113, 123-126, Rav Kook goes to great length to demonstrate that in the Halakha of Talmud Yerushalmi there exists an interplay of intuitive (agadic or quasi-prophetic) and rational abilities, whereas the Halakha of Talmud Bavli is bereft of inspiration and must rely on plodding reason. But the Halakha need not remain in the uninspired state. When studied in the enlightening atmosphere of *Erets Yisrael*, Talmud Bavli will ascend to the level of inspiration of Talmud Yerushalmi. See Rabbi Moses Sofer (Schreiber), *Ḥatam Sofer*, *Yoreh De'ah*, end responsum 233; *IHR* I, p. 237; *Haskamot ha-RAYaH*, p. 25; *Da'at Kohen*, chap. 178; *OHK* I, p. 134; Rav Y.M. Ḥarlap, *Beit Zevul* II (Jerusalem, 5747), chap. 1 of Introduction. On the difference between the two Talmudim, see further Rabbi Dov Baer Shneuri of Lubavitch, *Sha'arei Orah*, *Sha'ar ha-Hanukkah*, 22b-24a; Rabbi Naphtali Zevi Judah Berlin, Introduction to *Ha'amek She'elah* on *She'iltot de-Rav Aḥai Gaon*, *"Kidmat ha-'Emek,"* pars. 9, 11; B. Naor, *Ba-Yam Derekh* (Jerusalem, 5744), p. 133; idem, "Rav Kook's Role in the Rebirth of Agadah," *Orot: A Multidisciplinary Journal of Judaism I* (5751/1991):100-111.

414. *Song of Songs Rabbah*, chap. 2.

415. *Song of Songs Rabbah*, chap. 2; *Zohar* I, 224b; II, 60b, 88a.

416. *Sanhedrin* 98a.

417. Ezekiel 36:8.

418. *Ecclesiastes Rabbah*, 12:10; *Sanhedrin* 99a.

419. "The sealed end" (*kets he-ḥatum*). In *SK* 2:313 the word *"he-ḥatum"* ("the sealed") is not found.

420. Isaiah 14:3.

421. Ezekiel 37:22.

422. Isaiah 45:15.

423. Hebrew *hadar penimi.*

424. Hebrew *karnayim.* Cf. the rabbinic expression *"karnei hod" (Midrash Tanḥuma,* end *Ki Tissa).* See Rabbi Zadok Hakohen, *Peri Zaddik* V (Lublin, 5694), *Ki Tetse,* 63d-64c (par. 16).

425. Hebrew *hod ḥitsoni.* Rav Kook here overturns the accepted notion that *hod* is inner beauty and *hadar* outer beauty. See Rabbi Meir Leibush Malbim's commentary to Leviticus 19:15, 32; Numbers 27:2; Psalms 104:1; 1 Chronicles 29:11, 25; Rabbi Gershon Ḥanokh Leiner of Radzyn, *Tif'eret ha-Ḥanokhi* (Warsaw, 5660/1900), *Shemot,* 27a; idem, *Sod Yesharim* (*Tinyana*) (Brooklyn, 5743/1983), *Ḥanukkah,* 117a; RAYH Kook, *Siddur 'Olat Re'iyah* I, 207; Rabbi Yitsḥak Hutner, *Paḥad Yitsḥak, Ḥanukkah, ma'amar* 7. Rav Kook here derives from the expression *karnei hod* ("rays of *hod*") (e.g., *Exodus Rabbah* 47:6) that *hod* is something radiated outward, therefore an external phenomenon.

426. Based on the two Morning Blessings, *'oter yisra'el be-tif'arah* and *'ozer yisra'el bi-gevurah.*

427. Song of Songs 2:12; *Zohar* I, 215b.

428. A conflation of Jeremiah 31:11 and Hosea 3:5.

429. 1 Samuel 10:26.

430. Genesis 32:3.

431. Isaiah 40:3.

432. *Zohar* III, 124b.

433. "Irreconcilable" (*she-einam mit'aḥdim*). In *SK* 4:112: *she-einam mit'aḥim.* The meaning is unchanged.

434. Cf. Isaiah 30:21; *Megillah* 32a; *Talmud Yerushalmi, Shabbat* 6:9.

435. "With concrete, tangible concepts" (*be-musagim mutsakim tefusim be-ḥozkah*). In *SK* 4:112: "with tangible concepts and presentations" (*be-musagim u-mutsagim tefusim be-ḥozkah*).

436. In the 1920 edition of *Orot* and *SK* 4:112: *tseva'im* (colors). This was corrected in the 1950 edition to *tsevatim* (tongs).

437. Cf. Numbers 22:24, 25.

438. Hebrew *hod.*

439. Hebrew *daveh.* The word also relates to menstruation; see Leviticus 12:2. *Dvh* is the metathesis of *hvd.* See *Zohar* III, 243a. Cf. above, *The War,* chap. 10, regarding the metathesis of *pe'er* and *efer.*

440. Isaiah 30:22 and commentaries.

441. Isaiah 60:2.

442. Hebrew *me'uf tsarah*. Cf. Isaiah 8:22: *me'uf tsukah*.

443. "Is exalted" (*mitromemet*). In *SK* 4:112: "Is seated" (*yoshevet*).

444. "Redemption and glory" (*ha-pedut ve-ha-pe'er*). This phrase is taken from the hymn *"Ha-Aderet ve-ha-Emunah,"* which in turn, comes out of the *Hekhalot* literature. (The hymn is sung in Ḥasidic congregations Sabbath morning before *Barukh she-Amar*.)

445. "For temporal and eternal light" (*le-'or sha'ah u-le-'or ha-'olam*). In *SK* 4:112: "For the light of her salvation and for the light of the world" (*le-'or yish'ah u-le'or ha-'olam*).

446. *Zohar* I, 103.

447. Proverbs 31:23.

448. Rav Kook, following the *Zohar*, puns on the word *ba-she'arim* (in the gates) – *ba-shi'urim* (in measures).

449. Isaiah 30:20.

450. Isaiah 30:23.

451. "And encompasses every avenue" (*ve-sovevet hi et kol sderah*). In *SK* 4:112: "And encompasses all, encompasses every avenue" (*ve-sovevet hi et kol, sovevet hi et kol sderah*). It is conceivable that the first phrase was lost in transcription due to the dittography *"sovevet hi et kol."*

452. Proverbs 12:10: "A righteous man knows the soul of his beast." See Gersonides there: "It wishes [to convey] by *nefesh behemto* (the soul of his beast), the material soul which a man has in his capacity as animal, not in his human capacity." (Cf. Rabbi Shneur Zalman of Liadi, *Tanya* I, beginning chap. 9.) Rav Kook extrapolates to the level of the collective: A "righteous nation" (Isaiah 26:2) knows the soul of *its* beast. Cf. above chaps. 19, 21.

453. Isaiah 30:24. Rav Kook's use of verses from the Bible is disturbing to many. The best explanation I have been able to find for Rav Kook's enigmatic interspersing of Biblical material in his visions, is that of the martyred Hillel Zeitlin:

> This is the special need to conclude practically every piece with whole verses from the Bible as [a means of] tying and binding together the latest concepts in Kabbalah and the deepest studies in Philosophy with the source of all truths – Prophecy and books of divine inspiration.
>
> Our Master, RAYaH does not come in *Orot* to interpret verses or sayings of the Rabbis, passages of the *Zohar* and parables of the greatest kabbalists, but all the material quoted in the book in passing or at the conclusion of entries, is interpreted automatically through the concepts and symbols which he, our Master, RAYaH, expresses, and the reader begins to see those verses or passages themselves through a brilliant speculum, such as he had not seen before.

> Our Master, RAYaH does not interpret the verses homiletically, neither does he employ *remez*, hints (with few exceptions), and virtually never removes them from their simple meaning, and despite this, they are revealed before the eyes of the reader as fresh novellae. The *ḥiddush* (novelty) here essentially consists not in the exegesis of the verses, but rather in the light shed on them. (H. Zeitlin, *Sifran shel Yeḥidim* [Jerusalem: Mosad Harav Kook, 1979], p. 237)

I believe in this instance – our own chapter 58 – we can come up with a reasonable reconstruction of the underlying "story line" in Isaiah 30. In verse 20, the prophet predicts that the nation will be privileged to divine revelation: *No longer will your teacher hide; your eyes will behold your teacher.* In the following verse (21), the people are told that they must accustom themselves to a "distant listening" or "refined listening," to use Rav Kook's phrases: *Your ears shall hear a word behind you.* At that point, having been exposed to a "higher frequency," the people will repudiate all forms of idolatry, even idolatry posing as religion ("all who pretend to the title *Holy*"), regarding them as impure as a menstruant: *You will regard as impure the covering of your graven idols of silver, and the ornament of your molten images of gold; you will cast them away as an impurity* (or *menstruant*); *"Get out!" you will say to it* (verse 22). This higher frequency will impact all levels of society, even the masses with their bovine tendencies: *On that day your flock will graze in a wide pasture* (verse 23); *The oxen and young asses that till the ground shall eat salted provender,* etc. (verse 24).

454. "And a renewed soul" (*ve-ḥiddush neshamah ḥadashah*). The Corrigenda (*Lu'aḥ ha-Tikkun*) printed at the end of the 1920 edition, calls for the word "*ḥ adashah*" to be deleted from the text. In the 1950 edition of *Orot*, the word does not occur. However in *SK* 4:1 the text reads: *u-neshamah ḥadashah le-Yisrael* (*sans "hiddush"*). The meaning is virtually unchanged.

455. See Maimonides, *Hilkhot Yesodei ha-Torah* 4:13; gloss of Rabbi Moses Isserles to *Shulḥan 'Arukh, Yoreh De'ah* 246:5. Rav Kook conflated Maimonides' "bread and meat" and Isserles' "meat and wine," resulting in "bread, meat and wine." Cf. *Orot ha-Torah* 9:12.

456. "In its full sense" (*be-muvano ha-male*). The phrase is not found in *SK* 4:3.

457. "In all areas" (*mi-kol tsad u-panim*). In *SK* 4:3: *mi-kol tsad u-pinah*. The translation remains unaffected.

458. Song of Songs 7:10.

459. Song of Songs 7:7.

460. *Yoma* 54b; *Tikkunei Zohar*, end *tikkun* 37; Rabbi Ḥayyim Vital, *'Ets Ḥayyim 32:5 (Sha'ar He'arat ha-Moḥin*, chap. 5).

461. Psalm 84:3.

462. Psalm 63:6.

463. "The fresh generation full of the vigor of youth. The vision continues to pound" (*ha-dor ha-ra'anan male ko'aḥ alumim, ve-ha-tsefiyah holekhet hi u-mefa'emet*). In *SK* 4:5 the text reads: "The fresh generation full of the vigor of youth and vision. It [i.e., the Torah] continues to pound" (*ha-dor ha-ra'anan male ko'aḥ ha-'alumim ve-ha-tsefiyah, holekhet hi u-mefa'emet*).

464. "Its veil of mystery" (*tse'if sitrah*). In *SK* 4:5: "its veil of glory" (*tse'if pe'erah*).

465. The word *produktivit* appears in the Hebrew.

466. Isaiah 27:6.

467. *Shabbat* 21b.

468. *'Avodah Zarah* 52b; *Mishnah, Middot* 1:6.

469. See *Zohar* (*Ra'aya Mehemna*) III, 124b.

470. Hebrew *deḥufah u-seḥufah. Yevamot* 47a.

471. Exodus 19:5.

472. Daniel 11:32.

473. Daniel 7:18, 22, 27; *Zohar* I, 170a; II, 215b.

474. Deuteronomy 28:10.

475. Isaiah 61:9.

476. "And no one knows or understands" (*ve-ein yode'a ve-ein mevin)*. So in the 1920 edition of *Orot* and *SK* 4:21. Shortened in the 1950 edition to *ve-ein mevin* (and no one understands). See Daniel 8:27.

477. "Rejuvenation" *(ḥiddush yamim ke-kedem)*. Cf. Lamentations 5:21.

478. The theme of the next four chapters (67-70) is that the authentic Return of the Jewish People will come about only through the dawn of a new, higher divine consciousness.

479. "Integrally bound" (*keshurim kesher 'amits*). In *SK* 4:59: "*keshurim kesher mesabev* (*mesubav*)." This would translate as "bound [by] a knot surrounding."

480. Psalm 68:27.

481. Genesis 1:27.

482. Genesis 2:7.

483. Rabbi Shneur Zalman of Liadi (*Tanya* I, 2) cites *Zohar* as the source of the statement. So too RZYH Kook in his notes to *Orot*. Rabbi C.B. Chavel writes in his notes to Naḥmanides, Genesis 2:7, that he was told by Rabbi Yeruḥam Leiner that the source of this idea is *Sefer ha-Kanah*.

See now Moshe Ḥallamish, "*Li-Mekoro shel pitgam be-sifrut ha-kabbalah*," *BarIlan* 13 (5736):211-223. According to Ḥallamish, the origin of the saying is Rabbi Isaac the Blind, from whom it was transmitted to Naḥmanides. See *Kitvei Ramban*, ed. Chavel (Jerusalem: Mosad Harav Kook, 5728), vol. I, p. 159 ("*Torat Hashem*

Temimah"); vol. 2, p. 285 ("*Torat ha-Adam*"). The saying is not found in the *Zohar*. It is found in *Sefer ha-Peli'ah*.

484. *Zohar* II, 214b.

485. The sea (*yam*) is a trope for *Binah*. The word *yam* has the numerical value of 50, thus the "Fifty Gates of Understanding." (See e.g., Vilna Gaon's commentary to *Tikkunei Zohar* [Vilna, 5627], *tikkun* 19 [37a], s.v. *bein yam*.) *Teshuvah* (return) too is synonymous with *Binah* (Understanding). See Isaiah 6:10; *Megillah* 17b; Rabbi Joseph Gikatilia, *Sha'arei Orah, sha'ar shemini*.

486. "Of eternal freedom" (*shel ḥerut 'olam*). In *SK* 4:48: *he-ḥofshit*, "the free (understanding of the heart)."

In Kabbalah, the eternal freedom of the Jubilee is equated with the *sefirah* of *Binah* (Understanding). See Rabbi Joseph Gikatilia, ibid., and *Zohar* III, 108b. See further *Orot ha-Teshuvah* 12:9 and *Zohar* III, 122-123.

487. "And the mystical wisdom" (*ve-ḥokhmat ha-razim*). In *SK* 4:48: "and the wisdom of Kabbalah" (*ve-ḥokhmat ha-kabbalah*).

488. "And all the spiritual manifestation" (*ve-khol ha-hofa'ah ha-ruḥanit*). In *SK* 4:48: "and all the spiritual wisdom" (*ve-khol ha-ḥokhmah ha-ruḥanit*).

489. "For this light" (*el orah zo*). In *SK* 4:48: "and only for this light" (*ve-rak el orah zo*).

490. Malachi 3:7.

491. Neḥemiah 9:20.

492. Rabbi Pinḥas Elijah Hurwitz of Vilna, *Sefer ha-Berit* (Brünn, 1797), writes that the inferior level of *ru'aḥ ha-kodesh* (divine inspiration)—as opposed to outright *nevu'ah* (prophecy)—is available even today and is also not restricted to *Erets Yisrael*. See *Sefer ha-Berit*, beginning first Introduction; beginning Part I; II, 9, 11.

493. Cf. above note 446.

494. *Leviticus Rabbah* 15:2.

495. "And holiness." In *SK* 3:45: *ve-kodesh*. In *Orot*: *ve-kadosh*. (The latter is ungrammatical).

496. "The soul of every creation, the feelings of every sentient being" (*ve-nishmat kol yetsur, u-me-rigshei kol margish*). (There is a remote possibility that rather than *u-me-rigshei*, the word should be vocalized *u-margashei*, but the latter is a colloquial form, seemingly out of place in our context.) In *SK* 3:45 the word is spelled *u-margishei* ("and those who feel every sentient being").

497. 1 Samuel 15:29.

498. Numbers 23:9.

499. "Will not crystallize solely through external, measured actions and academic pursuits." In *AT* (Jerusalem, 5743), p. 14 and *SK* 2:29: "will not crystallize through external actions, nor by academic pursuits."

500. In *AT*, p. 14 and *SK* 2:29: "their life."

501. "Masters of the foundation" *(ba'alei ha-yesod).* RZYH Kook adduces the Vilna Gaon's commentary to *Tikkunei Zohar* (Vilna, 5627), beginning *tikkun* 21 (42a), s.v. *de-nuna ḥada.* In *AT*, p. 14 (*SK* 2:29): *ba'alei ha-sod* (masters of the secret doctrine).

502. In *AT*, p. 14 (*SK* 2:29): "those of all Israel."

503. "Fallen giants" *(nefilim).* See Genesis 6:4. In *AT*, p. 15 (*SK* 2:29): *nefalim* (aborted fetuses).

504. *Sanhedrin* 96b; Commentary of Vilna Gaon to *Tikkunei Zohar Ḥadash* (Vilna, 5627), 7b, s.v. *le-me'ebad*; B. Naor, *Hartsa'at ha-Teshuvah* (Jerusalem, 5750), pp. 41-42. *Mashi'aḥ* (Messiah) is referred to by the *Gemara* as *bar niflei*, i.e., a child born after several miscarriages. The Vilna Gaon explains that several times the Messiah was already being "gestated" but was spontaneously aborted because of the unworthiness of the generation. On the term *bar niflei*, see further Rabbi Moses Ḥayyim Luzzatto's letter to Rabbi Isaiah Bassani, published in *Otserot RaMḤaL* (B'nei Berak, 5746), pp. 341-343; Rabbi Yitsḥak Eizik Ḥaver, *Pitḥei She'arim* II, *Netiv Partsufei Leah ve-Raḥel*, 107b; and Rabbi Gershon Ḥanokh Leiner of Radzyn, *Sod Yesharim* (*Tinyana*) (Brooklyn, 5743), *Devarim*, 340; *Va-Etḥanan*, 343b, 345b.

505. "Living and enduring" *(ḥai ve-kayyam)*, an illusion to King David. See *Rosh ha-Shanah* 25a.

506. Lamentations 4:20.

507. Zechariah 3:4.

508. Isaiah 26:6.

509. In the Ashkenazic rite for the Morning Prayer, the conclusion to the first blessing of *Shema'*.

510. *Berakhot* 10a; Rabbi Ḥayyim of Volozhin, *Nefesh ha-Ḥayyim* I, 5.

511. "We" (*anu*). The word is not found in *SK* 3:177.

512. "To the kingdom" (*la-malkhut*). In *SK* 3:177: "to His kingdom" (*le-malkhuto*).

513. Hebrew *'al yisra'el hadrato*. From the *piyyut* (religious poetry) that begins *'Al yisra'el emunato*, recited in the Ashkenazic rite during the repetition of *Shemoneh 'Esreh*, *Shaḥarit*, the morning of Yom Kippur.

514. "And the *shofar* of Messiah begins to sound." This concluding sentence, found in *SK* 3:177, was omitted in the 1920 edition of *Orot*, and restored in the 1950 edition.

515. *Berakhot* 17a.

516. Psalm 89:17.

517. "The darkness of disbelief" (*et ha-afelah shel ha-kefirah*). In *SK* 3:330 there occurs a verb: "*will drive out* the darkness of disbelief" (*yegaresh et ha-afelah shel ha-kefirah*).

518. Psalm 150:6.

A Great Call

1. Isaiah 30:25.

2. "To dull minds" (*lehamem et ha-moḥot*). So in the 1950 edition of *Orot*. In the 1920 edition: "to dull strengths" (*lehamem et ha-koḥot*).

3. *Ḥullin* 60b.

4. Isaiah 26:2.

5. "Woe to those who make the Torah dry, not wanting to strive for the wisdom of the Kabbalah" (*Tikkunei* Zohar, *tikkun* 30). Cf. *IHR* I, p. 110.

6. "The ideal wisdom of faith" (*ḥokhmat ha-emunah ha-ide'alit*). The word *ide'alit* (ideal) was omitted from the 1950 edition. Perhaps the phrase should be translated, "the wisdom of ideal faith." Cf. *Zer'onim*, chap. 5, reprinted in the 1950 edition of *Orot*, p. 128.

7. "From the place where God appeared and that He chose as His eternal dwelling place." This concluding sentence, not found in the 1920 edition, was included in the 1950 edition of *Orot*.

8. Isaiah 2:5.

Continuation of Page 446, note 90:

The manuscript of Rabbi Meir Heller (Semnitzer) that Rivkah Schatz described in *Molad* is housed in the National Library of Israel (Scholem MS RS 14).

The Library also possesses a sarcastic personal letter from Rabbi Meir Heller (Semnitzer) to Rabbi Ya'akov Moshe Ḥarlap, informing him that as long as he does not repent and yet clings to "the Rav of Jaffa," he will not be allowed to eulogize in public. Scholem MS RS 40. (According to the catalogue description, the letter was written between the years 1904-1914. The cataloguer was probably unaware that the circle of Rabbi Ḥayyim Sonnenfeld continued to refer to Rav Kook as "the Rav of Jaffa" even after he assumed the role of Rav of Jerusalem.)

Recently, Rabbi Meir Heller of Beit Shemesh published correspondence between his grandfather (and namesake) Rabbi Meir Heller (Semnitzer) and Rabbi

Joseph Rosen of Dvinsk ("Rogatchover Gaon") seeking halakhic permission from the Gaon to terrorize a Sabbath desecrator into observing the Sabbath. The correspondence is from the year 5691/1930. See Rabbi Meir Heller, *"Be-'inyan 'im mutar lehazik te-tsorekh kevod shamayim,"* *Tif'eret* (Jerusalem-Beit Shemesh), No. 13, Adar 5770/2010, pp. 61-71. Available at hebrewbooks.org

Indexes

Index of Sources

Bible

Genesis

Deuteronomy

Joshua

Judges

1 Samuel

2 Samuel

1 Kings

Rabbinic Literature

Mishnah

Talmud Yerushalmi

Midrash

Zohar

Zohar I

Zohar II

Zohar III

Ra'aya Mehemna and Tikkunei Zohar

Ra'aya Mehemna

Tikkunei Zohar

Maimonides

Commentary to the Mishnah (Peirush ha-Mishnah)

Sukkah

Sanhedrin

Avot

Bekhorot

Book of Commandments (Sefer ha-Mitsvot)

Shoresh 14

Mishneh Torah

Guide of the Perplexed

Index of Names

A

B

C

D

K

L

Y

Z

Index of Subjects

Maggid Books
The best of contemporary Jewish thought from
Koren Publishers Jerusalem Ltd.